SwiftUI
for Masterminds

How to take advantage of SwiftUI and AI Agents to develop insanely great apps for iPhones, iPads, and Macs

J.D Gauchat
www.jdgauchat.com

The source code for this book is available at **www.formasterminds.com**

Copyright Registration Number: 1165896

ISBN: 978-1-0699942-4-0

1st Edition 2020 John D Gauchat
2nd Edition 2022 John D Gauchat
3rd Edition 2022 John D Gauchat
4th Edition 2023 John D Gauchat
5th Edition 2024 John D Gauchat
6th Edition 2026 John D Gauchat
7th Edition 2026 John D Gauchat

Table of Contents

Chapter 1

App Development

Chapter 2

SwiftUI Framework

Chapter 3

Declarative User Interface

Chapter 4

Lists

Chapter 5

Navigation

Chapter 8

Graphics & Animations

Chapter 13

Framework Integration

Chapter 14

Media

Chapter 15

iCloud

Chapter 16

Internationalization

Chapter 17

App Store

About this Book

This book covers the essential concepts and advanced techniques needed to develop applications for Apple devices with the SwiftUI framework. To help you navigate the content and focus on the topics that best match your goals, each section is identified with one of the following labels:

BASIC

The topics presented in the BASIC sections provide the fundamental knowledge required to develop applications for Apple devices and understand the code generated by AI agents. Study these sections first if your goal is to learn how applications are built, understand how SwiftUI works, and collaborate effectively with an AI agent to finish your first applications.

PRO

The topics presented in the PRO sections introduce advanced concepts and techniques that become important as your skills grow. These sections are intended for readers who want to become proficient in app development or fully understand every piece of code generated by an AI agent.

Every topic introduced in this book is explained through fully functional examples that you can try on your own. We recommend opening Xcode and experimenting with the code as you learn, but you can also download the projects from our website to work through the material at your own pace (**www.formasterminds.com**).

IMPORTANT

In this book, we assume the reader has a basic understanding of the Swift programming language. All the examples are fully functional, so this background is not strictly required to follow along. However, we recommend becoming familiar with Swift to fully leverage the potential of SwiftUI. For more information on Swift, read our book *Swift for Masterminds*. Apple's official documentation is available at **developer.apple.com**. The official Swift documentation is available at **www.swift.org**.

COUPON AVAILABLE

Readers of *SwiftUI for Masterminds* can download a free copy of *Swift for Masterminds*. Visit **www.formasterminds.com/redeem** and enter the following code to get your copy:

GENKA

Chapter 1

App Development

BASIC

1.1 - Overview

SwiftUI is a modern abstraction layer that builds on earlier technologies to simplify development and redefine how applications are created. With SwiftUI, developers can create applications that adapt naturally to different devices and screen sizes, making it possible to deliver a consistent and cohesive experience across the entire Apple ecosystem.

BASIC

1.2 - Requirements

Apple provides the tools and resources needed to get started at no cost. However, to use these tools and develop applications efficiently, we need a relatively modern Mac and a mobile device for testing. The following are the requirements to develop applications with the latest technologies.

Mac Computer
We need a Mac capable of running the latest operating system (currently macOS 27 Golden Gate). In practice, this means a relatively recent Mac equipped with an Apple Silicon chip such as M1, M2, M3, M4, or M5.

Xcode
Xcode is the development software provided by Apple. The latest version is 27, available for free from the App Store.

Apple Developer Account
The Apple Developer account is a free account we can open at **developer.apple.com**. From this account, we can manage our membership and get the certificates and identifiers needed to prepare our apps for distribution.

Mobile Device
Apple recommends we test our apps on a real device before distribution. The device can be any model that supports the latest versions of Apple's mobile operating systems, such as iOS 27 or iPadOS 27.

Apple Membership
We can run our applications on our own devices, but sharing them with the public requires an Apple Developer membership. As of this writing, the cost of this membership is 99 US dollars per year.

Do It Yourself

Go to **developer.apple.com**, click the Account option at the top of the page, and sign in with your Apple account or create a new one if needed. Apple will request personal information and then grant you access to your developer account. Note that a membership is not required until you are ready to distribute your app.

BASIC

1.3 - Xcode

Once we have our Mac running the latest operating system, the next step is to install Xcode 27. Xcode is available for free in the Mac App Store. To install it, open the App Store from the Applications folder in Finder and search for "Xcode" (Figure 1-1, number 1). The window displays the Xcode icon along with a Get button to install it (Figure 1-1, number 2).

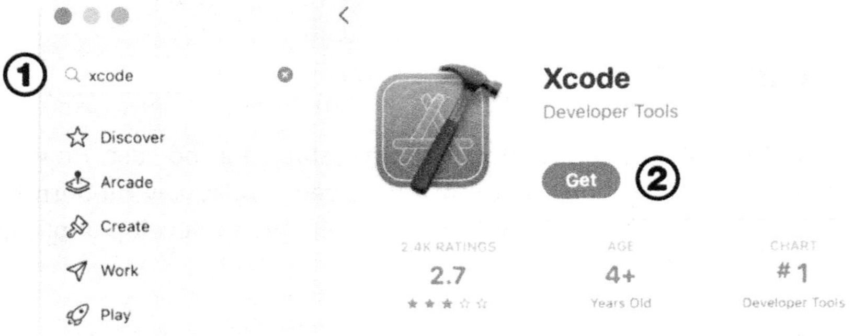

Figure 1-1: *Xcode in the App Store*

IMPORTANT

At the time of writing, Xcode 27 is available in Beta mode. To download this version of Xcode, go to Apple's developer website at **developer.apple.com**, sign in with your Apple account, click on Downloads/Applications, and select the latest beta version available.

After downloading Xcode, we can run the application from the Applications folder in Finder. The following is Xcode's welcome screen.

Figure 1-2: *Xcode's welcome screen*

The welcome screen provides buttons to open an existing project, clone a project from a repository, or create a new project. Clicking the button to create a new project opens a popup menu with options to select the project's type, as shown below.

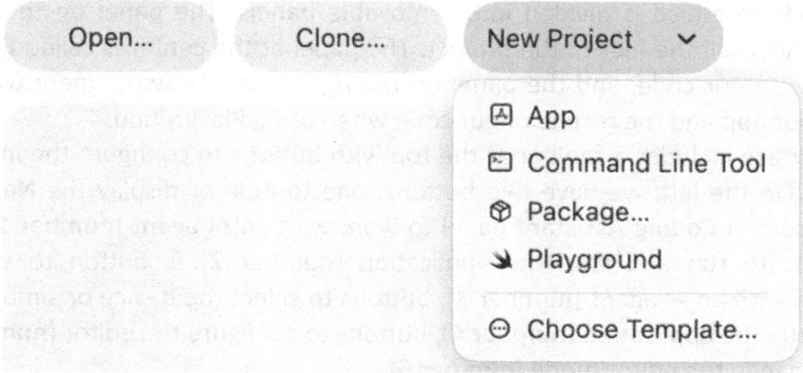

Figure 1-3: *Project options*

The **App** option is used to create a new application, the **Command Line Tool** option is used to create an application without a user interface, the **Package** option is used to create a package with code we can share with other developers, and the **Playground** option is used to create a single Swift file for testing. Of all the available options, the **App** option is the one we are going to use the most because it creates a project that allows us to test our code, learn how to program, and create fully functional applications.

BASIC

Project

When we select the **App** option, Xcode creates a new project. An Xcode project includes all the information and resources we need to create an application. After the project is created, Xcode opens an interface with all the tools necessary to manage it, as shown below.

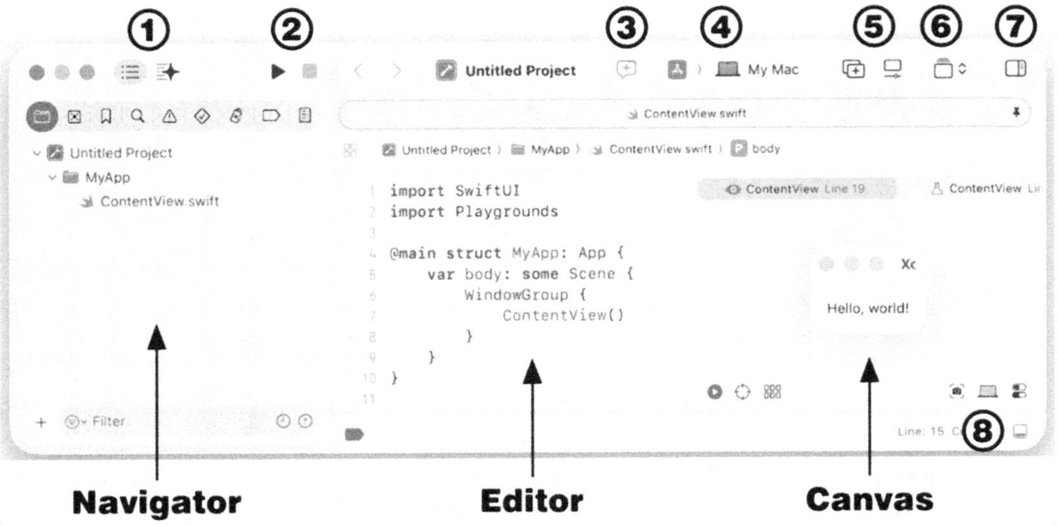

Figure 1-4: *Xcode's interface*

The Xcode interface is divided into removable panels. The panel on the left, called **Navigator**, shows all the files in the project. The panel at the center is called **Editor** and is where we write our code, and the panel on the right is the **Canvas**, where we can see a preview of our app and the results of our code when using Playground.

The interface includes a toolbar at the top with buttons to configure the interface and the project. On the left, we have two buttons, one to hide or display the **Navigator** and another to open a **Coding Assistant** panel to work with an AI agent (**number 1**). Next, we have buttons to run and stop the application (**number 2**), a button to start a new conversation with an AI agent (**number 3**), buttons to select the device or simulator where we want to run the application (**number 4**), buttons to configure the editor (**number 5**), and buttons to change the editor mode (**number 6**).

The interface also includes additional panels that can be useful for configuration and testing. There is a button at the top right corner to open the inspector panel with information about files and targets (**number 7**), and a button at the bottom right corner to open a console where we can see errors and print our own messages when debugging our code (**number 8**).

Do It Yourself

Install Xcode 27 on your Mac as explained in Figure 1-1, or download the latest beta version from **developer.apple.com**. Once installed, open Xcode, click the **New Project** button, and select the **App** option to create a new project (Figure 1-3). You should see an interface similar to Figure 1-4. Click the buttons in the toolbar to get familiar with the interface. Buttons also perform the opposite action, so if you change something and do not know how to go back, try pressing the same button again, or simply close the project and create a new one from the File menu at the top of the screen (**File -> New -> Project**).

BASIC

Project Settings

When we create a new project, Xcode generates a template and all the files required for the application to run, but does not save the project to disk. To save it, we must press **Command + S** or select **Save** from the **File** menu, type a name, select a folder, and click the **Save** button. After the project is saved, the interface resets and the new name appears at the top of the Navigator, as shown below.

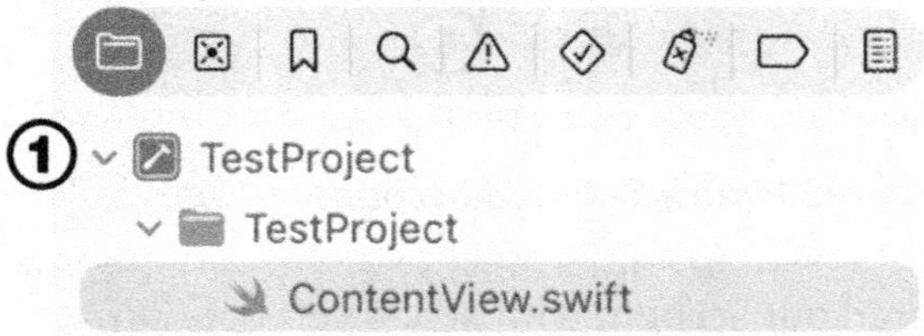

Figure 1-5: *Project saved*

> **IMPORTANT**
>
> The name you assign to the project becomes the name of your app, so pick something appropriate, though you can change it later if needed. Once the project is saved, any further changes are saved automatically.

After the project is saved, we need to assign our developer account to it from settings to be able to test our app on a real device. To access the project's settings, click the project's name in the **Navigator** (Figure 1-5, number 1). This opens a panel with multiple tabs for configuration, as shown below.

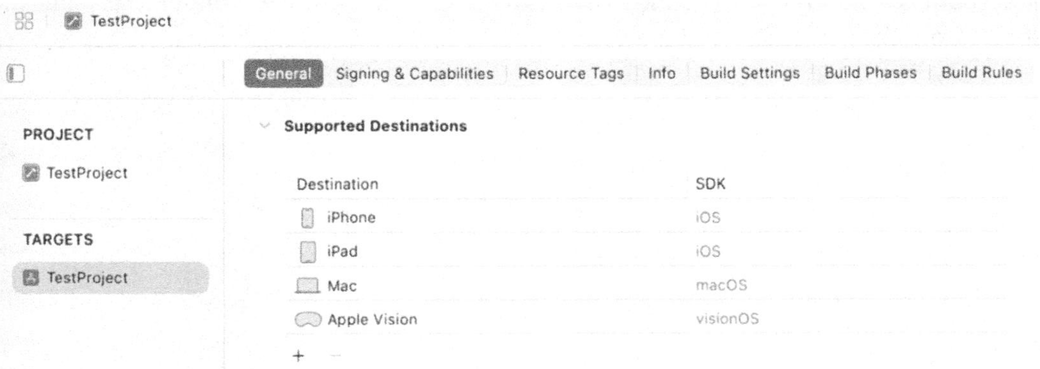

Figure 1-6: *Project settings*

The panel opens in the **General** tab, where we can select the platforms and operating systems our app supports. Another useful tab is the **Info** tab, where we can manually define configuration values including supported orientations, launch screens, and custom fonts (we will see some practical examples later). The option to associate the project with our developer account is available from the **Signing & Capabilities** tab, as shown below.

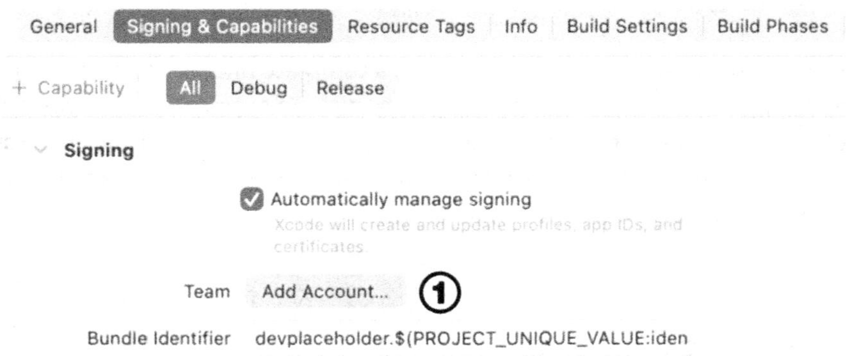

Figure 1-7: *Add account button*

If we haven't registered our account with Xcode yet, the Add Account button appears at the top of the Signing section (Figure 1-7, number 1). Pressing this button opens Xcode's settings panel to sign in.

Figure 1-8: *Xcode sign in*

The settings window opens with the **Apple Accounts** option selected and a Sign in button that we must press to sign in with our Apple account (Figure 1-8, number 1). After our account is registered with Xcode, we can go back to the **Signing & Capabilities** panel and select it from the list, as shown below.

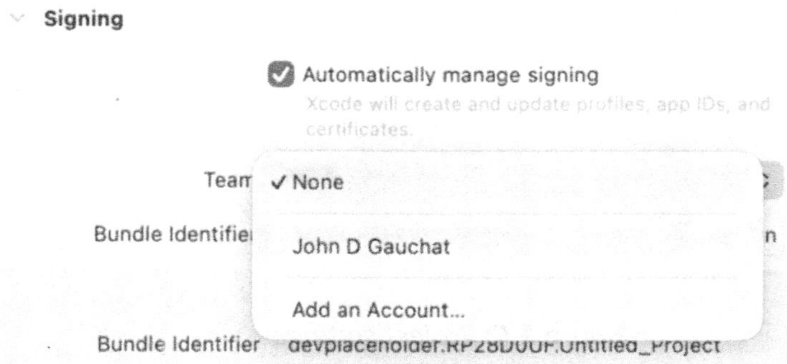

Figure 1-9: *Selecting developer Team*

Do It Yourself

If you haven't done it yet, create a new **App** project (**File -> New -> Project**). Press **Command + S** to save it. Once the project is saved and the new name appears in the **Navigator** (Figure 1-5, number 1), click the project's name to open the settings panel, open the **Signing & Capabilities** tab, and select your account from the **Team** option or press the **Add Account** button to add a new one, as explained before. After this, you are ready to develop and test your app on the simulator or a real device, as we will see later.

IMPORTANT

The settings panel also includes tabs with options to determine how the app is built, including the Swift version and how Xcode processes Swift concurrency. To learn more about Swift concurrency and how to enable Swift 6, read our book *Swift for Masterminds*.

BASIC

SwiftUI Views

An application needs a window and views to show the content. Figure 1-10 below shows how a basic user interface is structured.

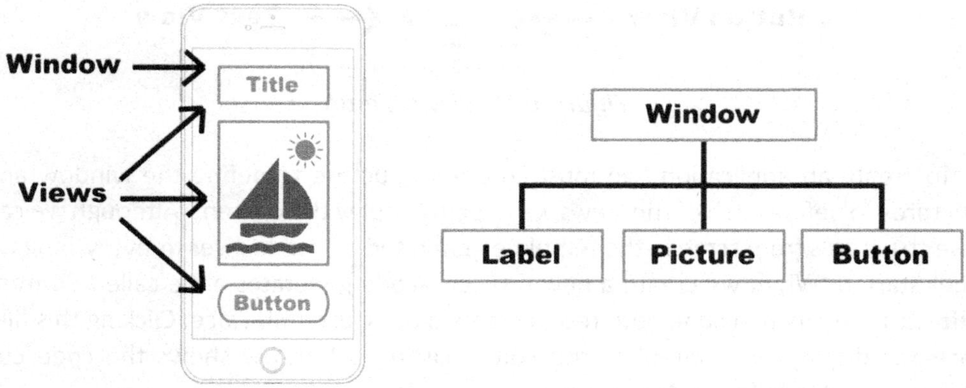

Figure 1-10: *App interface*

A window defines the area occupied by the current instance of the application, and views generate the window's content. Since we can have multiple windows per application, each is represented by a scene. A scene is defined by a structure that conforms to the **`Scene`** protocol. Although we can create our own scenes, SwiftUI provides several built-in structures to create standard scenes, including **`WindowGroup`**, **`Window`**, **`DocumentGroup`**,

Settings, and **MenuBarExtra**. Some of these structures are specific to Mac, while others are more generic. For example, the **WindowGroup** structure can manage multiple windows on iPhones, iPads, and Macs, making it the recommended choice for most projects. The following is the structure's initializer.

```
WindowGroup(Text, id: String, content: Closure)
```

This initializer creates a scene to manage all the windows of an instance of the application. The first argument defines the window's title, the **id** argument specifies the window's identifier, and the **content** argument is a closure that defines what the windows are going to display.

Windows created from the **WindowGroup** structure define the space where content is displayed, but the content itself is built from views. Views are created from structures that conform to the **View** protocol, which defines all the functionality necessary to display and interact with them. We can create empty views that work as containers, views that present controls such as buttons and switches, or views that display content such as images and text. Because views can contain other views, they can be nested to build the user interface, as shown below.

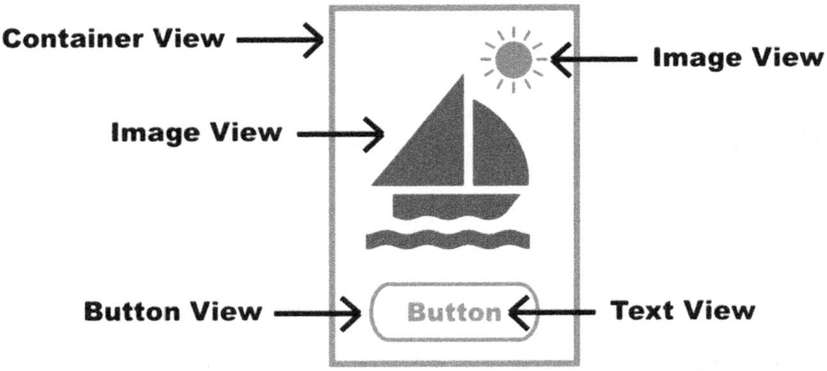

Figure 1-11: *Views hierarchy*

To create an application, we must create a structure to define the window and then structures to define each of the views we need to display the content. Although we can build these structures from scratch, the template generated by Xcode gives us everything we need to get started. When we create a new project, Xcode generates a file called **ContentView.swift** with the minimal code required to create a basic user interface. Clicking this file in the **Navigator** displays its content in the Editor. Listing 1-1 below shows the code currently generated by Xcode for an **App** project.

Listing 1-1: Xcode template

```
import SwiftUI
import Playgrounds

@main struct MyApp: App {
```

```
    var body: some Scene {
        WindowGroup {
            ContentView()
        }
    }
}
struct ContentView: View {
    var body: some View {
        Text("Hello, world!")
            .padding()
    }
}
#Preview {
    ContentView()
}
#Playground {
    _ = 1 + 2
}
```

The **import SwiftUI** statement at the top imports the **SwiftUI** framework, giving the code access to all the tools needed to design the user interface and develop the app. The **MyApp** structure creates an instance of the **WindowGroup** structure to define a scene, and the **ContentView** structure produces the views that define the window's content. When the app is launched, the system creates an instance of **MyApp**, which creates an instance of **WindowGroup**, which creates an instance of **ContentView**, which creates an instance of the **Text** structure, and therefore the message "Hello World!" is displayed on the screen.

> **IMPORTANT**
>
> The **Playground** framework imported at the beginning of the file and the **#Playground** macro at the end are only used for testing. To learn more about Playground and how to use it, read our book *Swift for Masterminds*.

BASIC

SwiftUI Files

The **ContentView** structure included in Xcode's template represents the initial screen of our app, but we can generate more. Although we can define the structures that represent new views within a single file, it is recommended to create a separate file for each view that represents an entire screen in our interface. The option to create new files is available in the File menu. We must open the **Navigator**, click the folder where we want to place the file (in this case, **MyApp**) and then select the option from the **File -> New** menu (Figure 1-12, number 1).

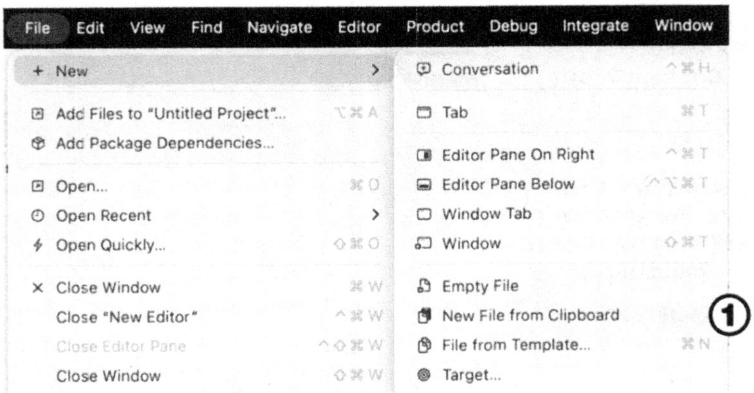

Figure 1-12: *New file options*

There are three options available: we can create an empty Swift file to store new classes, structures, or functions (**Empty File**), create a Swift file with the contents of the clipboard (**New File from Clipboard**), or create a file from an Xcode template (**Create from Template**). This last option is the best for SwiftUI files because it generates a template with all the code needed to create the view. The template we need to choose is called **SwiftUI View**, as shown below.

Figure 1-13: *Files templates*

After we select the **SwiftUI View** template, Xcode asks for the name of the file and then uses that name to define the structure for the view. For example, if we name the file **MyNewView.swift**, Xcode creates a structure named `MyNewView`, as shown below.

Listing 1-2: Playground file

```
import SwiftUI

struct MyNewView: View {
    var body: some View {
        Text("Hello World!")
    }
}
#Preview {
    MyNewView()
}
```

Do It Yourself

Open your project, click on the project's folder in the **Navigator** (Figure 1-5, number 1), open the **File** menu (**File -> New**), and select **New from Template** (Figure 1-12, number 1). Select the **SwiftUI View** template and press **Next**. Give the file the name you want to assign to the new view and press **Create**. After this, Xcode adds a file to the **Navigator** containing a structure with the same name, as shown in Listing 1-2. We will learn how to define the content for these views and how to add them to the interface in later chapters.

BASIC

Canvas

Once we create the views that make up our interface, we need a way to preview them and make further changes if necessary. Although we can run the app on a physical device or a simulator, Xcode provides a **Canvas** panel that displays our views in real time, allowing us to inspect the interface and immediately see the results of any changes we make. When we create a new project, Xcode opens the source code in the **Editor** and the **Canvas** on the right, displaying a preview of the content generated by the project template. By default, the preview shows a Mac window, but we can change the device using the destination controls on the toolbar, as shown below.

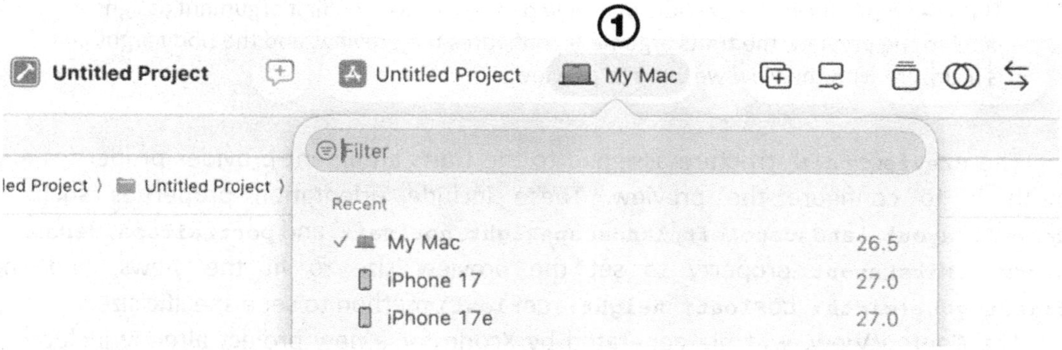

***Figure 1-14:** Device button*

The device button (Figure 1-14, number 1) determines the destination when we run the app, either a real device or a simulator, but this setting is also used by the **Canvas** to determine which device to simulate. For example, if we select an iPhone simulator, the **Canvas** reproduces the screen of that device and renders the view, as shown below.

```swift
import SwiftUI
import Playgrounds

@main struct MyApp: App {
    var body: some Scene {
        WindowGroup {
            ContentView()
        }
    }
}

struct ContentView: View {
    var body: some View {
        VStack {
            Text("Hello World!")
                .padding()
        }
    }
}
```

Figure 1-15: *iPhone on the Canvas*

Previews are not generated automatically; we must tell Xcode to do it. For this purpose, SwiftUI provides the **`#Preview`** macro. When included in our code, this macro generates all the code necessary to create a preview of a view on the **Canvas**. The macro has different options for configuration. The following are the most frequently used.

`#Preview(``String?`**`, traits:`**` PreviewTrait`**`, body:`**` Closure`**`)`**

This macro produces the preview of a view on the canvas. The first argument assigns a label to the preview, the **traits** argument configures the preview, and the **body** argument is a closure with the view we want to preview.

The **`PreviewTrait`** structure assigned to the **traits** argument provides properties and methods to configure the preview. These include orientation properties such as **`defaultLayout`**, **`landscapeLeft`**, **`landscapeRight`**, **`portrait`**, and **`portraitUpsideDown`**, a **`sizeThatFitsLayout`** property to set the preview size to fit the views, and the **`fixedLayout(width: CGFloat, height: CGFloat)`** method to set a specific size.

The **ContentView.swift** file generated by Xcode for a new project already includes a **`#Preview`** macro to create a basic preview, but we can specify a different configuration or add more. The following example shows how to generate two previews, one with the device in landscape mode and another in the default mode.

Listing 1-3: Generating multiple previews

```swift
#Preview("My iPhone", traits: .landscapeLeft) {
   ContentView()
}
#Preview("My Second iPhone") {
   ContentView()
}
```

This example generates two previews. The **Canvas** can only display one at a time, but if more are available, it includes buttons at the top to switch between them.

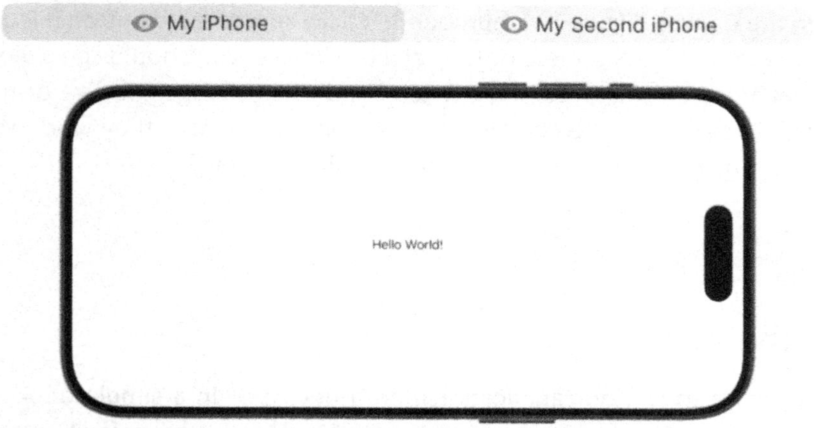

Figure 1-16: *Preview buttons*

Do It Yourself

Click the **ContentView.swift** file. In the Editor, update the **`#Preview`** macro with the code in Listing 1-3. Select an iPhone simulator from the destination button (Figure 1-14, number 1). If the **Canvas** is not visible, click the Show Canvas button on the toolbar (Figure 1-4, number 6). Press the Refresh button on the **Canvas** if necessary. You should see two buttons at the top (Figure 1-16). Click these buttons to switch between previews.

The configuration options provided by the **`#Preview`** macro are limited to orientation and size, but we can also adjust other aspects of the preview from the buttons at the bottom of the **Canvas**, as shown below.

Figure 1-17: *Preview configuration*

The buttons are split into three groups. The buttons on the left configure the preview and the **Canvas**. The first button (**number 1**) enables a live preview, so we can interact with the views on the screen. The second button (**number 2**) generates a resizable view, so we can change the view's size to see how it looks in different screen configurations. The third button (**number 3**) enables selection, so we can click on a view to select it and highlight the code that generates it. The fourth button (**number 4**) displays the interface in different appearance modes (Light or Dark), orientations, and font sizes. The button at the center (**number 5**) zooms the **Canvas** in and out. And the buttons on the right configure the device. The first button (**number 6**) takes a snapshot of the current device, the second button (**number 7**) provides another way to select the device we want to simulate, and the third button (**number 8**) sets the device's appearance, orientation, and font size.

Do It Yourself

Open the **Canvas** (Figure 1-4, number 6). Click the Resizable button (Figure 1-17, number 2). Regardless of the selected device, you should see a view with handles on the sides. Drag these handles to change the size of the view. Try the rest of the configuration buttons to see how they work. We will learn how to create resizable interfaces in Chapter 6.

BASIC

Running the App

There are two ways to run our applications: on a device or in a simulator. As mentioned earlier, when we create a new project, Xcode sets **My Mac** as the default run destination, but we can control the destination and run or stop the app from the buttons on the toolbar, as shown below.

Figure 1-18: *Running the app on a device or the simulator*

As we have seen before, we can change the destination from the device button (Figure 1-18, number 3), but the toolbar also includes a button to select a scheme (Figure 1-18, number 2). By default, the app runs with the configuration set by the user on the device, but, as we will see later, we can set a new scheme to determine how Xcode builds, runs, and tests our app, including settings like the language or region used to simulate different locales.

Once the destination and scheme are set, we can press the Play button to run the app (Figure 1-18, number 1). If we selected a simulator, Xcode opens an application called **Device Hub** that works like the **Canvas** but allows us to test the entire app as if we were using a real device, navigate through the views, and try different configurations, as shown below.

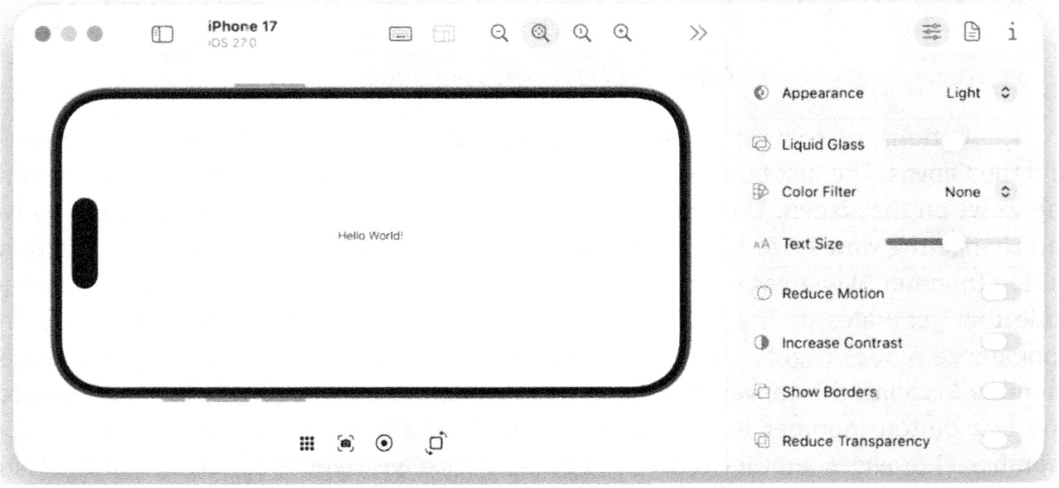

Figure 1-19: *App running in the Device Hub*

Do It Yourself

Select an iPhone simulator from the device button (Figure 1-18, number 3). Press the Play button (Figure 1-18, number 1). The Device Hub should open with a simple interface. Click the Expand button in the top right corner to expand the interface. You should see something similar to Figure 1-19.

IMPORTANT

The option used to select the simulator or device (Figure 1-18, number 3) also tells Xcode which development tools are available for the application. Some tools are available only on specific platforms. For this reason, you should always select the system you are targeting. For example, when developing an iOS application, select an iPhone or iPad simulator. When developing a Mac application, select the My Mac option. We will learn how to design applications for different devices in Chapter 6.

The **Device Hub** works out of the box, but to run the application on a physical device, we must first enable it for development. This option is available in the **Settings** app. We must open the **Settings** app on our device, select **Privacy & Security** (Figure 1-20, number 1), scroll to the bottom, select the **Developer Mode** option (Figure 1-20, number 2), and turn it on (Figure 1-20, number 3).

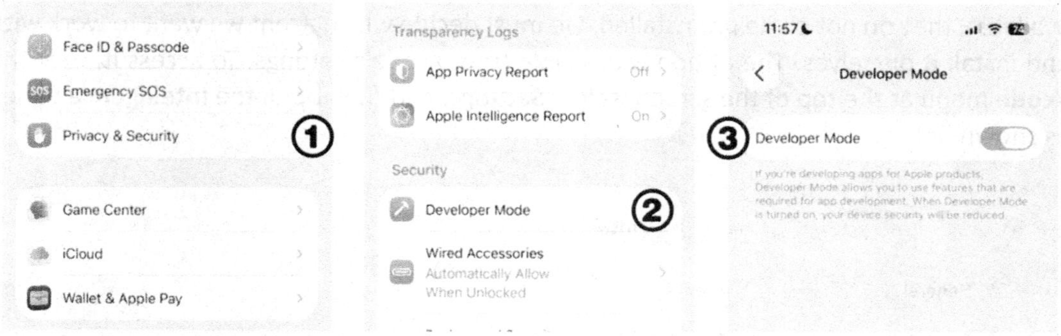

Figure 1-20: *Enabling developer mode*

After we enable Developer Mode, we must connect the device to the computer using a USB cable. Xcode will then attempt to pair the device with the computer. Once the pairing process is complete, the device will appear in the list of available destinations, allowing us to select it and run the application. This step is required only once. After the device and the computer are paired, we no longer need to connect them with a USB cable to run our applications.

BASIC

1.4 - AI Agents

As we mentioned in our book Swift for Masterminds, artificial intelligence has transformed app development, but contrary to early concerns, AI models and agents have not replaced programmers. Instead, they have become powerful tools that help developers work more efficiently. Today, building an application requires a solid understanding of how code works, along with the ability to use AI agents to solve problems and accelerate development. As AI becomes an increasingly important part of the software development process, the ability to program applications and collaborate effectively with AI agents is becoming an essential skill for developers who want to remain competitive.

> **IMPORTANT**
>
> You do not need to use AI agents to develop applications for Apple devices, but it is highly recommended to get used to these tools as soon as possible. Learning how to use AI agents today will give you an advantage when they become essential for any project in the future.

BASIC

Coding Assistants

Xcode comes integrated with the most popular agents, but because there are many options available, they do not come preinstalled; we must decide which agent we want to work with and install it ourselves. The option is available from Xcode's settings. To access it, click the **Xcode** menu at the top of the screen, select **Settings**, and then open the **Intelligence** panel, as shown below.

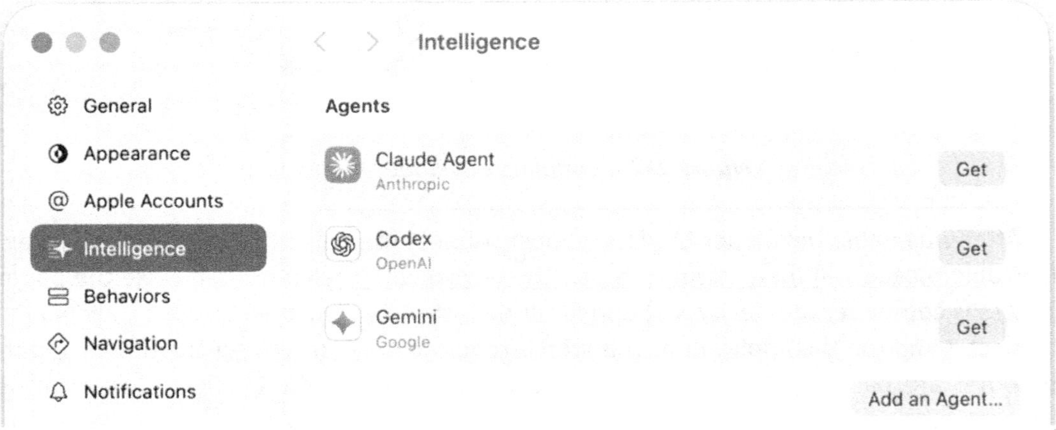

Figure 1-21: *Installing AI Agents*

At the time of this writing, there are three options available: **Claude** from Anthropic, **Codex** from OpenAI, and **Gemini** from Google. **Claude** is only available to paid customers. Currently, a Claude Pro account costs $20 USD per month (check **claude.ai/pricing** for up-to-date information). **Codex** and **Gemini**, on the other hand, are offered for free with limitations; we are limited in the number of requests per minute or per hour, depending on the model, but we can use them for free as long as we want and get a Pro account only when necessary.

To make these agents available, we must install them and sign in with the corresponding account. The first step is to press the **Get** button for the agent we want to install. When we press this button, Xcode downloads all the data and information it needs to run the agent on our computer. After that, we must select the agent and sign in with our account. If we do not have an account, we must create one from each provider's website. In the case of **Claude**, we need to visit **claude.ai/login**, sign up, and then subscribe to the Pro plan. After the account is ready, we must press the Sign In button in Xcode to enter our credentials (Figure 1-22, number 1).

Figure 1-22: *Signing in with Claude*

For **Codex**, the process is similar. We must press the **Get** button to download the agent, and then visit **chatgpt.com/codex/** and click Log In to create our account. Once we have an account with OpenAI, we must select the agent in Xcode and press the Sign In button (Figure 1-23, number 1).

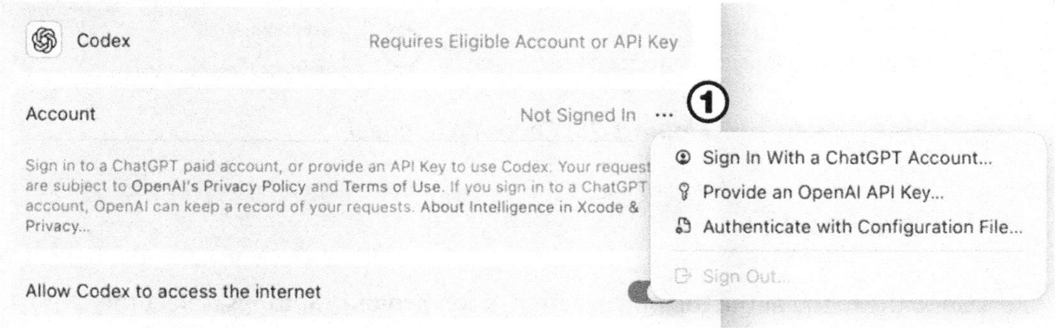

Figure 1-23: *Signing in with OpenAI*

If we prefer to use Google's **Gemini** instead, the process is similar, we must press the **Get** button to download the agent, but rather than signing in with a Google account directly, we must obtain an API key from Google's website. To obtain this key, we need to visit **aistudio.google.com**, press Get Started, and sign in with our Google account. Once inside our account, we must click on **Dashboard -> API Keys** and press the **Create API Key** button. A window opens asking for a name and a project. We must create a new project with any name we want, assign a name to the key, and then press the Create Key button. This generates a new key that we can copy and paste into Xcode. The option to paste the key is also available from the Sign In button (Figure 1-24, number 1).

***Figure 1-24:** Providing an API key to enable Gemini*

Agents use different artificial intelligence models to perform their tasks. If we use **Claude** or **Codex**, the model is set automatically, but if we use a free account with **Gemini**, we must select the free model ourselves. The option is available when we select the agent. For **Gemini**, the free models are called Flash (Figure 1-25, number 1).

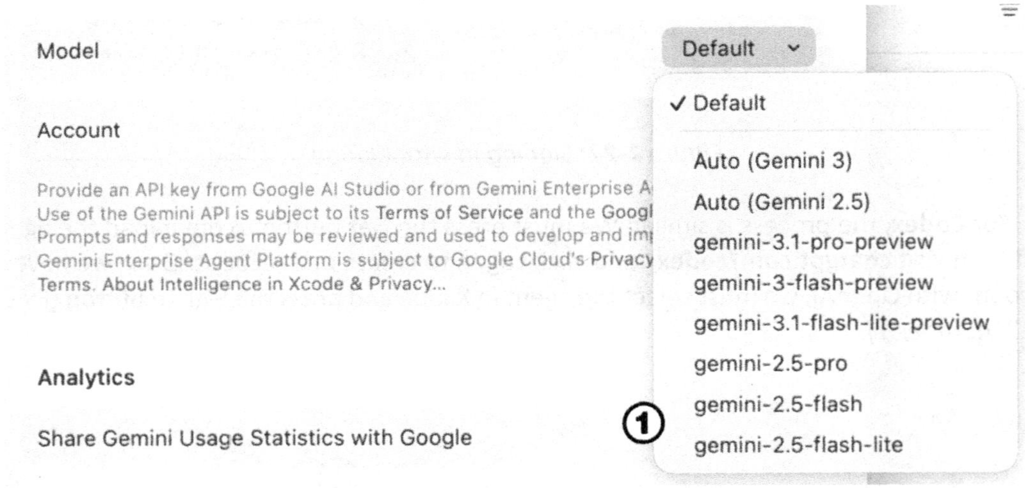

***Figure 1-25:** Choosing a model*

Do It Yourself

Go to the menu at the top of the screen, open **Xcode -> Settings**, select the **Intelligence** panel, and press the **Get** buttons to download the agents you want to install (Figure 1-21). Once Xcode finishes downloading the agent, select it and press the Sign In button (Figures 1-20, 1-21 and 1-22). If you do not have an account with the agent provider, visit the corresponding websites. For **Claude**, visit **claude.ai/login** and follow the instructions to sign up and subscribe to their Pro plan. For **Codex**, visit **chatgpt.com/**

codex/, click Log In, and follow the instructions to create your account. For **Gemini**, visit **aistudio.google.com**, sign in with your Google account, click on **Dashboard -> API Keys**, and press the **Create API Key** button to get the key you need to provide to Xcode, as explained before. If you do not find the API Keys option, there is a button with a key icon at the bottom of the main panel to create your keys. After you enable the **Gemini** agent with the API key, you must select the agent again, and pick a **Flash** model from the list, as shown in Figure 1-25, number 1.

IMPORTANT

Choosing the right agent is not always straightforward and may change over time. At the moment, we recommend starting with the free **Codex** account and, when possible, upgrading to a Pro account with **Claude**. The models used by **Codex** are quite good, but for programming Apple applications, the **Sonnet** model offered by **Claude** has proven to be more efficient and useful. Try different options, and if you subscribe to a model, always choose monthly billing so you can easily switch to a different model if the current one does not perform as expected.

Once the required data has been downloaded and we have signed in to our account, the agents are ready to use. To start a new conversation with an agent, we can press the New Conversation button on the toolbar (Figure 1-4, number 3), but when multiple agents are available, we must first select the one we want to use from the **Coding Assistant** panel, as shown below.

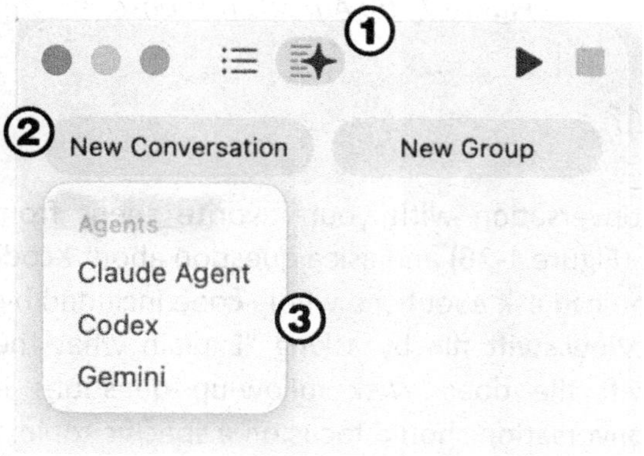

Figure 1-26: *Selecting an agent*

The **Coding Assistant** panel shows a list of previous conversations and buttons to start a new one. To open it, we press the **Coding Assistant** button on the toolbar (Figure 1-26, number 1), and to start a new conversation, we click the New Conversation button (Figure 1-26, number 2). This opens a menu to select the agent (Figure 1-26, number 3). After the agent is selected, a new panel opens in the **Editor** to start the conversation, as shown below.

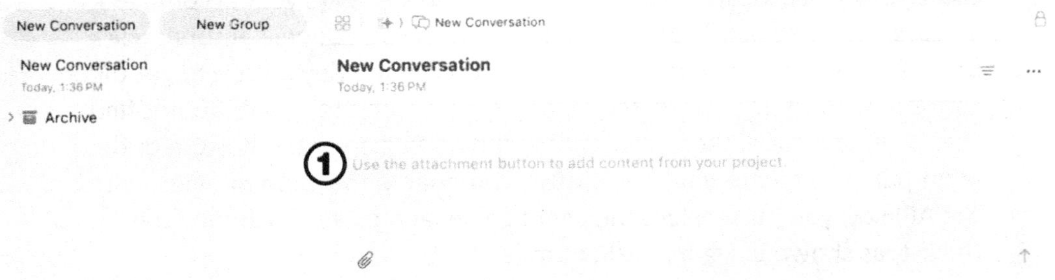

Figure 1-27: *Talking with an agent*

Now it is simply a matter of asking what we need. For example, we can get information about the code generated by Xcode by asking, "What is the code in the ContentView structure doing?" The answer will vary depending on the agent, but they will all offer some kind of description of the code's functionality, as shown below.

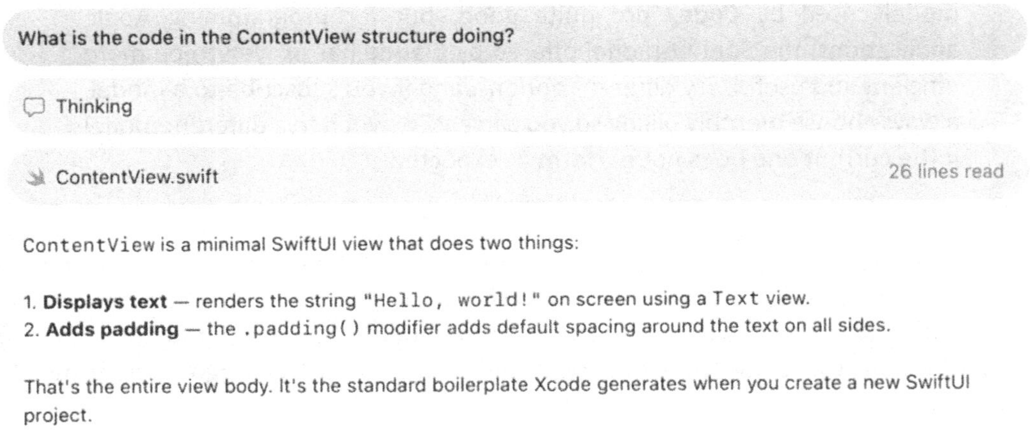

Figure 1-28: *Agent's response*

Do It Yourself

Start a new conversation with your favorite agent from the **Coding Assistant** panel (Figure 1-26) and ask a question about Xcode or the code. For example, you can ask about the whole code included by the template in the **ContentView.swift** file by asking "Explain what the code in the ContentView.swift file does." Ask follow-up questions if anything is unclear. Each conversation should focus on a specific topic; if you want to ask about something unrelated or request the agent to write code for you, start a new conversation. This keeps the context focused, helps the agent better understand your requests, and reduces the amount of information it has to process, lowering the risk of exceeding your usage limit.

In the previous example, we used a single panel to talk to the agent, but most of the time we need to ask the agent questions about the code or request changes to a specific file. To work with the code alongside the agent, we must open a second panel. The option is available from the Add Editor Tab button on the toolbar (Figure 1-29, number 1).

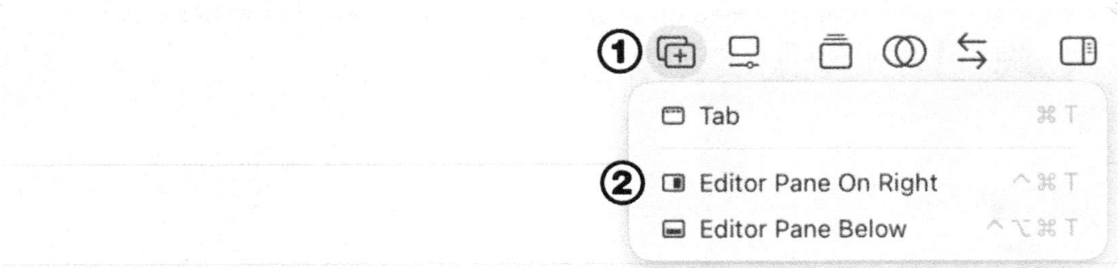

Figure 1-29: *Opening new panels in the Editor*

The Add Editor Tab button opens a menu with options to create a new tab inside the current panel or open a new panel (Figure 1-29, number 2). When we open a new panel, Xcode loads it with a tab containing the currently selected content, but we can use the **Navigator** to load any file we want. For example, we can have a conversation in the left panel and the code of our **ContentView.swift** file in the right panel, as shown below.

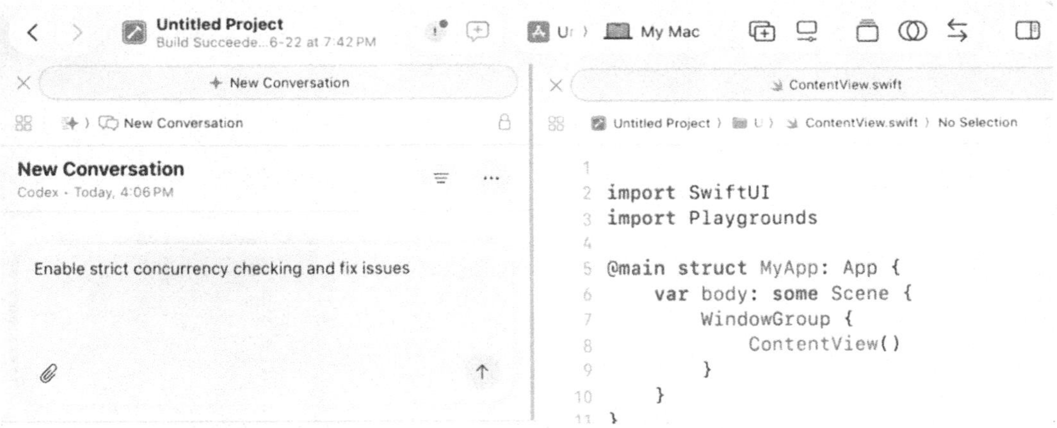

Figure 1-30: *Working with code alongside the agent*

Do It Yourself

If you have already selected the agent you want to work with from the **Coding Assistant** panel, you can start a new conversation with the same agent by clicking the New Conversation button in the toolbar (Figure 1-4, number 3). The conversation opens in the selected panel, but if you want to open it in a new panel, you can hold the **Shift** and **Option** keys while clicking the button. Xcode creates a new panel and starts the conversation there.

IMPORTANT

In addition to the built-in agents, Xcode allows you to add external agents and AI models, such as GitHub Copilot or Cursor, and connect to online models or models installed on your computer. For more information, visit our website and follow the links for this chapter.

Chapter 2
SwiftUI Framework

BASIC

2.1 - Declarative Interface

As explained in Chapter 1, in SwiftUI the user interface is declared by defining structures that conform to the **View** protocol. The only requirement of this protocol is for the structure to implement a computed property called **body** that returns a view. We can see an example of this implementation in the **ContentView** structure defined by Xcode's template, as shown below.

Listing 2-1: Initial view

```
struct ContentView: View {
    var body: some View {
        Text("Hello, world!")
            .padding()
    }
}
```

The **ContentView** structure conforms to the **View** protocol, implements the **body** property, and returns another view (structure) called **Text**. This is a view defined by the **SwiftUI** framework to display text on the screen. When the system creates an instance of the **ContentView** structure, it reads the **body** property, the property returns an instance of the **Text** view, this view is added to the interface, and the message "Hello World!" is displayed on the screen.

The **Text** view used by the **ContentView** structure is one of the views provided by SwiftUI to define the content of the interface, but there are more. The framework provides a wide range of built-in structures that represent standard views, each designed to serve a specific purpose. As we will see next, we have views that contain and arrange other views, views to display text and images, views that create controls to get user feedback, and also specialized views for drawing and rendering graphics.

IMPORTANT

The examples in this chapter are fully functional and ready to use in your own projects. However, we recommend you become familiar with the Swift programming language to fully understand how these examples work. For more information on Swift, read our book *Swift for Masterminds*. You can find a coupon to download a free copy from our website in the **About This Book** section at the beginning of this book.

BASIC

Text View

Of all the structures defined by SwiftUI to create views, the **Text** structure is probably the most useful. This structure takes a string and returns a view that displays the text on the screen. The structure defines multiple initializers. The following are the most frequently used.

Text(String)

This initializer creates a **Text** view with the text defined by the argument.

Text(Date, **style:** DateStyle)

This initializer creates a **Text** view to present a date. The first argument defines the date, and the **style** argument is a structure that determines the format. The structure includes the type properties **date**, **offset**, **relative**, **time**, and **timer** to define this value.

Since text is the primary means of communication, **Text** views are used extensively in SwiftUI applications. The **Text** view included by default in the **ContentView.swift** file is created with a **String** value to display the text "Hello World!", but a **Text** view can also include values through string interpolation, as shown below.

Listing 2-2: Displaying values with a `Text` view

```
struct ContentView: View {
   let number: Float = 30.87512

   var body: some View {
      Text("My Number: \(number)")
   }
}
```

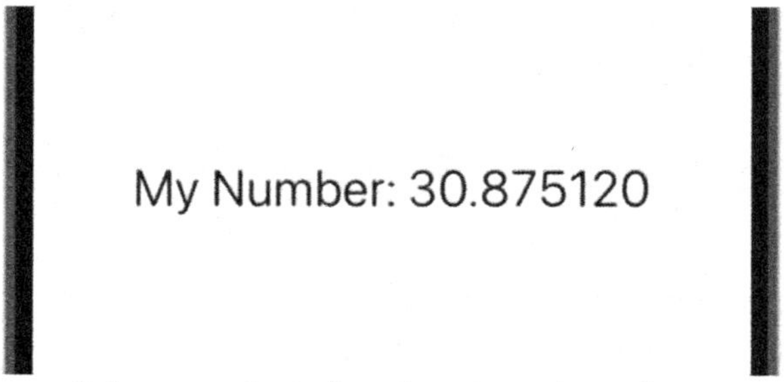

Figure 2-1: *`Text` view showing the value of a property*

Do It Yourself

Create a new **App** project and save it to your computer. Update the `ContentView` structure in the **ContentView.swift** file with the code in Listing 2-2, select an iPhone simulator from the device button on the toolbar, and open the Canvas. You should see something similar to Figure 2-1. Use this project to test the rest of the examples in this chapter.

The last example displays the value as it is, but we can use the `formatted()` method to format the number. For instance, we can turn it into currency to represent US Dollars.

Listing 2-3: Formatting a value for a `Text` view

```
struct ContentView: View {
   let number: Float = 30.87512

   var body: some View {
      Text("My Number: \(number.formatted(.currency(code: "USD")))")
   }
}
```

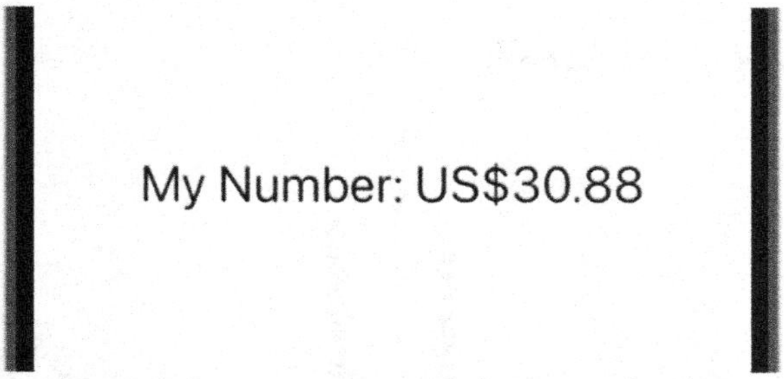

Figure 2-2: `Text` *view with formatted values*

Of course, we can include and format other types of values. For instance, we can use the `formatted()` method on a `Date` value to show a date.

Listing 2-4: Displaying a date with a `Text` view

```
struct ContentView: View {
   let today = Date()

   var body: some View {
      Text(today.formatted(date: .abbreviated, time: .omitted))
   }
}
```

Figure 2-3: *Date displayed with a* `Text` *view*

Although this works fine, the **`Text`** structure defines a specific initializer to show dates. The initializer includes an argument that takes a **`DateStyle`** structure to format the date. The formats available are not as comprehensive as those provided by the **`formatted()`** method, but the advantage of using this formatter is that some of the styles available can update the values as they change. For instance, one of the type properties included by the **`DateStyle`** structure is called **`timer`**. This formatter displays the date as a counter that starts counting from the current date.

Listing 2-5: Displaying a timer with a `Text` view

```
struct ContentView: View {
   let today = Date()

   var body: some View {
      Text(today, style: .timer)
   }
}
```

Figure 2-4: `Text` *view displaying a timer*

BASIC

Modifiers

Views are created with default attributes, such as a standard font and color, but the **`View`** protocol defines methods to customize their appearance. These methods are called *modifiers*. SwiftUI offers a wide range of modifiers, many of which are designed for specific views. For example, the following modifier is used to define the font of a **`Text`** view.

`font``(Font)`

This modifier assigns a font to the text. The argument is a **`Font`** structure that provides type properties and methods to select the font we want.

Fonts in SwiftUI are defined using the **Font** structure provided by the framework. This structure offers multiple ways to define and configure fonts. Apple recommends using dynamic fonts, which automatically adjust their size based on the text size selected by the user in Settings. The **Font** structure defines many properties to specify dynamic fonts. The currently available are **largeTitle**, **title**, **title2**, **title3**, **headline**, **subheadline**, **body**, **callout**, **caption**, **caption2**, and **footnote**. Figure 2-5, below, shows how some of the fonts produced by these properties compare to the system standard font.

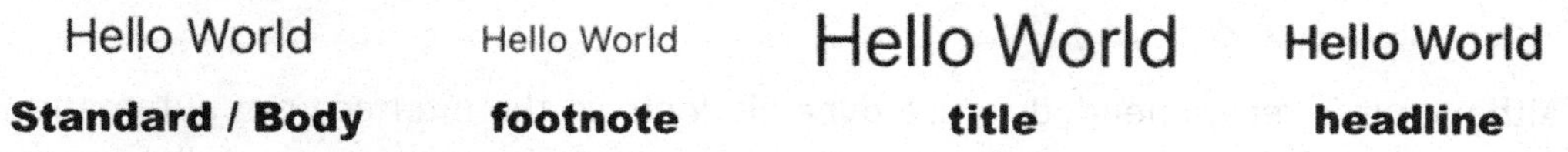

Figure 2-5: Dynamic font types

Modifiers are declared right after the view is initialized. The following example illustrates how to apply the **font()** modifier to assign a **largeTitle** font to a **Text** view.

Listing 2-6: Applying modifiers to a view

```
struct ContentView: View {
   var body: some View {
      Text("Hello World")
         .font(.largeTitle)
   }
}
```

Modifiers do not change an existing view. Instead, they create a new view with the updated attributes and return it. When the system reads the **body** property of the example in Listing 2-6 to build the interface, it creates an instance of the **Text** structure with the string "Hello World", and then calls the **font** method on this structure. This method creates a new view with the **largeTitle** attribute applied to the text and returns that view. As a result, the **body** property produces a view with a large title.

Figure 2-6: `Text` *view before and after the modifier is applied to it*

Do It Yourself

Update the **ContentView** structure with the code in Listing 2-6. Try adding and removing the modifier. You should see the text changing size on the canvas, as shown in Figure 2-6.

IMPORTANT

Dynamic fonts have a predefine size, but they change according to the size set by the user from Settings. If you want to see how your text looks like in different sizes, press the Device Settings button at the bottom of the Canvas (Chapter 1, Figure 1-17, number 8), activate the Dynamic Type option, and select the size you want to apply.

Although it is recommended to use dynamic fonts so the interface can automatically adapt to the size selected by the user, the **`Font`** structure also includes the following type method to assign a system font of any size we need.

`system(size:` `CGFloat)`

This type method returns the system font with the size defined by the **size** argument.

With the **`system()`** method, we can get the standard font provided by the system but of any size we want. The font and size defined by this method are not affected by the choices the user makes from Settings. In the following example, we assign a system font of a size of 50 points to a **`Text`** view.

Listing 2-7: Using the system font

```
struct ContentView: View {
   var body: some View {
      Text("Hello World")
         .font(Font.system(size: 50))
   }
}
```

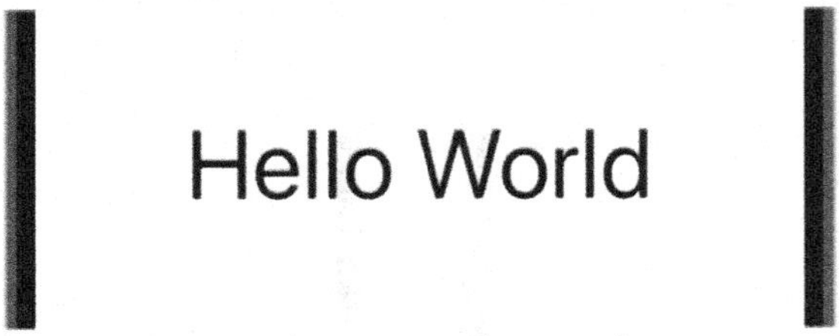

Figure 2-7: *Using the system font with a custom size*

The **`font()`** modifier can define both the font and its size, but the **`View`** protocol also provides modifiers to apply additional styling to text.

`bold``(Bool)`

This modifier applies a bold style to the text. The argument is a Boolean value that allows us to dynamically enable or disable the modifier.

`italic``(Bool)`

This modifier applies an italic style to the text. The argument is a Boolean value that allows us to dynamically enable or disable the modifier.

fontWeight(Weight)

This modifier applies a weight to the text. The argument is a structure with the type properties **black**, **bold**, **heavy**, **light**, **medium**, **regular**, **semibold**, **thin**, and **ultraLight**.

textCase(Case)

This modifier transforms the text to lowercase or uppercase letters. The argument is an enumeration with the values **lowercase** and **uppercase**.

dynamicTypeSize(DynamicTypeSize)

This modifier sets the dynamic type size to apply to the text. The argument is an enumeration with the values **large**, **medium**, **small**, **xLarge**, **xSmall**, **xxLarge**, and **xxxLarge**. It can be declared as a range of values to determine the minimum and maximum size allowed.

underline(Bool, **color:** Color)

This modifier underlines the text. The first argument is a Boolean value that indicates if the style is applied to the text or not, and the second argument defines the color of the line.

strikethrough(Bool, **color:** Color)

This modifier draws a line through the text. The first argument is a Boolean value that indicates if the style is applied to the text or not, and the second argument defines the color of the line.

shadow(**color:** Color, **radius:** CGFloat, **x:** CGFloat, **y:** CGFloat)

This modifier assigns a shadow to the text. The arguments define the color of the shadow, its size, and the horizontal and vertical offsets.

These modifiers can be used with any type of font, including dynamic or custom fonts, and they can be applied sequentially to achieve the desired result, as shown below.

Listing 2-8: Applying multiple styles to a text

```
struct ContentView: View {
   var body: some View {
      Text("Hello World")
         .font(.largeTitle)
         .underline()
         .fontWeight(.heavy)
         .shadow(radius: 1, x: 1, y: 1)
   }
}
```

In this example, a **Text** view is defined with a **largeTitle** font, and modifiers are then applied to underline the text, assign a heavy font weight, and add a shadow. In the **shadow()** modifier, we set the **radius**, **x**, and **y** arguments to **1**, creating a subtle shadow that extends to the right and bottom of the text.

Figure 2-8: Multiple styles applied to a text

`Text` views can be provided as the content of other `Text` views, which allows us to assign different styles to each portion of the text, as shown below.

Listing 2-9: Nesting `Text` views

```
struct ContentView: View {
   var body: some View {
      Text("Hello \(Text("World").underline())")
         .font(.largeTitle)
   }
}
```

In this example, we applied the `largeTitle` and `underline()` modifier, but because the `underline()` modifier was applied to the second `Text` view, only the text in this view is underlined.

Figure 2-9: Nested `Text` views with different styles

The `Font` structure also includes similar modifiers that apply styles directly to the font. The following are the most commonly used.

`bold()`

This modifier applies a bold style to the font.

`italic()`

This modifier applies an italic style to the font.

`weight(Weight)`

This modifier assigns a weight to the font. The argument is a structure of type `Weight` with the properties `black`, `bold`, `heavy`, `light`, `medium`, `regular`, `semibold`, `thin`, and `ultraLight`.

Because these modifiers are defined by the `Font` structure, they are applied to the font, not the view. For instance, we can apply the `weight()` modifier to the `Font` structure returned by the `largeTitle` property to get a bold text.

Listing 2-10: Styling the font

```
struct ContentView: View {
   var body: some View {
      Text("Hello World")
         .font(.largeTitle.weight(.semibold))
   }
}
```

***Figure 2-10:** Semibold text*

By default, **Text** views can display multiple lines of text, but the **View** protocol includes the following modifiers to format the text and limit the number of lines allowed.

lineLimit(Int)

This modifier determines how many lines the text can contain. The argument is an optional that indicates the number of lines we want. By default, the value is set to **nil**, which means the view will extend to include the number of lines necessary to show the whole text.

multilineTextAlignment(TextAlignment)

This modifier defines the alignment of multiline text. The argument is an enumeration with the values **center**, **leading** (default), and **trailing**.

lineSpacing(CGFloat)

This modifier determines the space between lines.

truncationMode(TruncationMode)

This modifier determines how the text is truncated when it doesn't fit inside the view's frame. The argument is an enumeration with the values **head**, **middle**, and **tail** (default).

textSelection(TextSelectability)

This modifier determines if the text is selectable by the user. The argument is a structure with the type properties **enabled** and **disabled**.

privacySensitive()

This modifier indicates that the view contains sensitive information. It is used to prevent the system from exposing private data.

The following example displays a text aligned to the center and with a space of 5 points between lines.

Listing 2-11: Formatting text

```
struct ContentView: View {
   var body: some View {
      Text("Monsters are real, and ghosts are real too. They live inside
us, and sometimes, they win. Stephen King.")
         .padding()
         .multilineTextAlignment(.center)
         .lineSpacing(5)
         .textSelection(.enabled)
   }
}
```

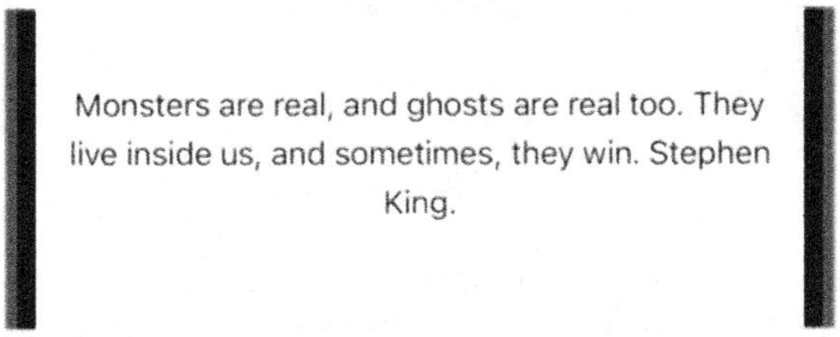

Figure 2-11: *Multiline text*

IMPORTANT

By default, the text displayed in a **`Text`** view is not selectable, which means users cannot select or copy it. To allow text selection, the **`textSelection()`** modifier must be applied with the value **`enabled`** to each view where this behavior is required, as shown in the example in Listing 2-11.

If we limit the number of lines, we must consider how the text is going to be displayed to the user when it is too long or does not fit within the view. By default, the system truncates the text and adds ellipsis at the end to indicate that part of the text is missing, but we can move the ellipsis to the beginning or the middle with the **`truncationMode()`** modifier, as shown below.

Listing 2-12: Truncating text

```
struct ContentView: View {
   var body: some View {
      Text("Monsters are real, and ghosts are real too. They live inside
us, and sometimes, they win. Stephen King.")
         .padding()
         .lineLimit(1)
         .truncationMode(.middle)
   }
}
```

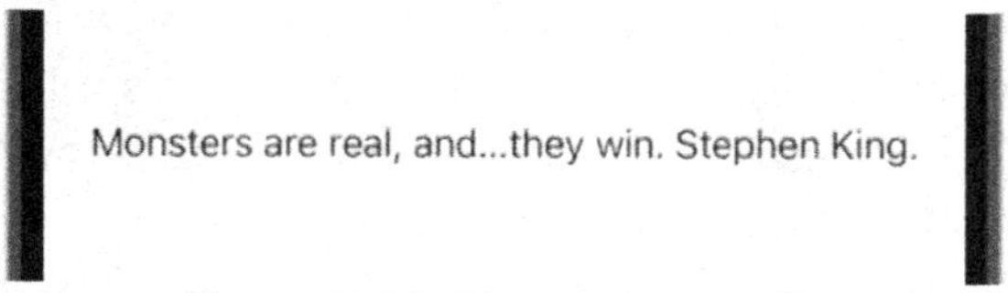

Figure 2-12: *Truncation mode*

So far, we have used dynamic fonts or the system font, but we can also specify custom fonts. For this purpose, the **`Font`** structure includes the following method.

```
custom(String, size: CGFloat)
```

This type method returns a font of the type specified by the first argument and with the size specified by the **size** argument.

Operating systems come with a set of standard fonts. If the font we want to use is already included in the system, we just need to specify its name and size, as in the following example.

Listing 2-13: Using standard fonts

```
struct ContentView: View {
   var body: some View {
      Text("Hello World")
         .font(Font.custom("Georgia", size: 50))
   }
}
```

Figure 2-13: *Text with the Georgia font*

On the other hand, if the font we want to include is not provided by the system, we must copy the file into the project and configure the app to use it. Including the file in our project is easy; we just need to drag it from **Finder** to the **Navigator** area, as shown below.

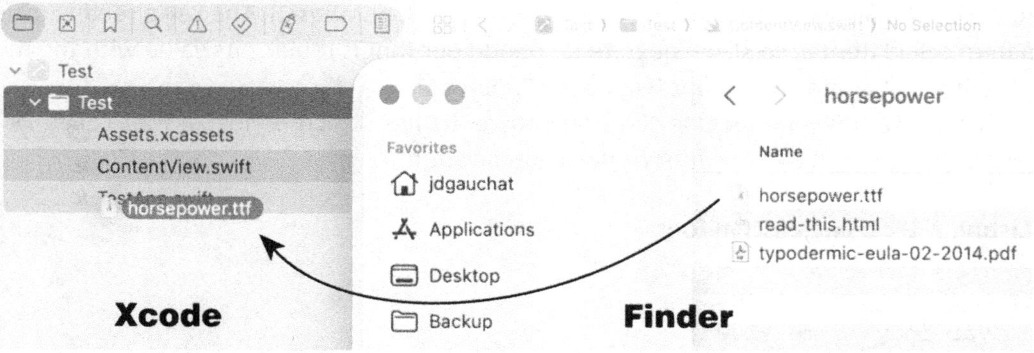

Figure 2-14: *Dragging files from Finder to our Xcode's project*

When files are added to an Xcode project, a window prompts for information about the destination and the target. To copy the files into the project's folder (recommended), we must select the *Copy files to destination* option from the drop-down menu and make sure the project is selected under Targets, as shown below.

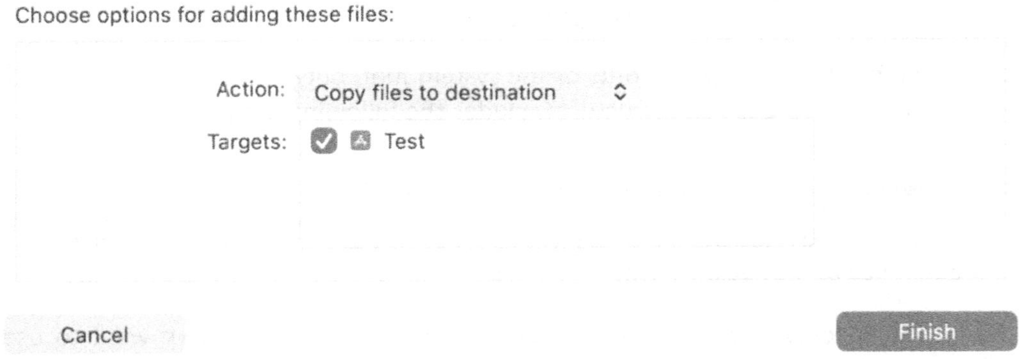

Figure 2-15: *Options to add files to the project*

After the file is added to the project, we need to configure the app to use it. This is done from the **Info** tab in the project's settings. To access this tab, we must click on the project in the **Navigator** area and select it from the **Editor** area (see Chapter 1, Figures 1-5 and 1-6). The tab shows a list of keys and values we can edit, as shown below.

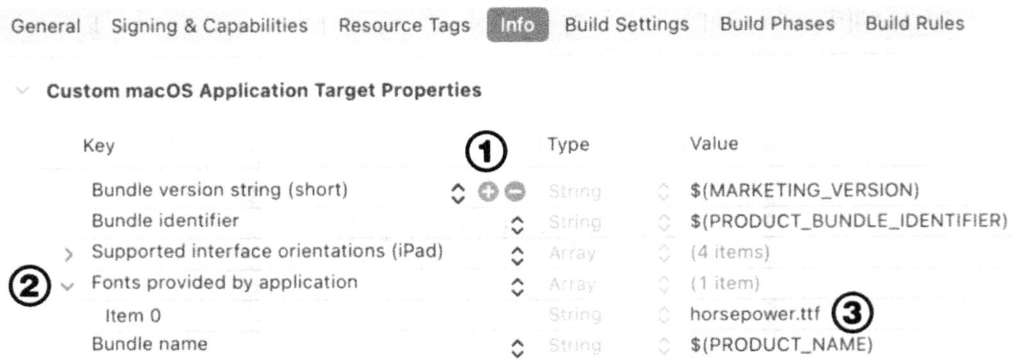

Figure 2-16: *Adding fonts to the project*

To include a custom font for our app, we must add a key called "Fonts provided by application" to this list. For this purpose, we must click the plus button on one of the existent options (Figure 2-16, number 1) and select the key from the list. After the key is added, we must click the arrow on the left to open it (Figure 2-16, number 2). The key already includes an item called Item 0, so all we need to do to add our font is replace its value with the name of the file that contains the font (Figure 2-16, number 3).

In this example, we include the **horsepower.ttf** file, which defines a font called *Horse Power*. Now, we can use this font from our application.

Listing 2-14: Using custom fonts

```
struct ContentView: View {
   var body: some View {
      Text("Hello World")
```

```
        .font(Font.custom("Horsepower-Regular", size: 50))
    }
}
```

Figure 2-17: *Text with a custom font*

Do It Yourself

Download the **horsepower.ttf** file from our website or provide your own. Drag the file from **Finder** to the project's **Navigator** area (Figure 2-14). Make sure to check the option "Copy files to destination" and the target, as shown in Figure 2-15). Go to the app's settings, open the **Info** panel, click on the + button in any of the rows, and select the key "Fonts provided by the application" (Figure 2-16, number 1). Click on the arrow on the left hand side to reveal the items (Figure 2-16, number 2). You should see the item 0 with no value. Click on the value field to change it (Figure 2-16, number 3). Copy and paste the name of your font file, including the extension. Modify the `ContentView` structure with the code in Listing 2-14. You should see the text styled with the new font in the canvas.

IMPORTANT

The names we have to provide to the `custom()` method are the PostScript names. To find the PostScript name of the font you want to add to your project, open the Font Book application from the Applications folder, open the View menu, and select the option Show Font Info. Click on the font. The PostScript name is shown in the panel on the right.

BASIC

View Frame

The screen of a device is composed of a grid of hundreds of dots called pixels, arranged in rows and columns. The number of pixels varies from one device to another. To address these differences, Apple introduced the concept of points (sometimes called *logical pixels*). A point corresponds to a square made up of one or more pixels, depending on the device. For example, the screen of an iPhone 17 uses three pixels per point. This device has a grid of 1206 by 2622 pixels, but views are positioned and sized using a grid of 402 by 874 points, with the origin located at the top-left corner, as shown below.

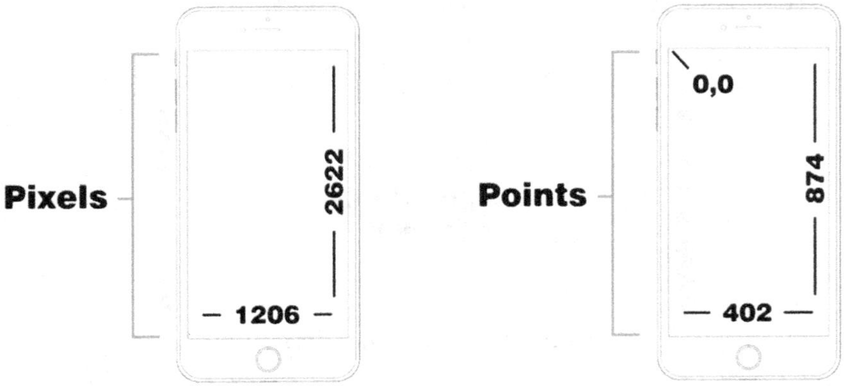

Figure 2-18: Coordinate system of an iPhone

This means that when positioning and sizing views on the screen, we must work with coordinates expressed in points rather than pixels. For this purpose, the **View** protocol defines the following modifiers.

```
frame(width: CGFloat?, height: CGFloat?, alignment: Alignment)
```

This modifier assigns a new size and alignment to the view. The **alignment** argument determines the alignment of the view's content. It is a structure of type **Alignment** with the type properties **bottom**, **bottomLeading**, **bottomTrailing**, **center**, **leading**, **top**, **topLeading**, **topTrailing**, and **trailing**.

```
frame(minWidth: CGFloat?, idealWidth: CGFloat?, maxWidth:
CGFloat?, minHeight: CGFloat?, idealHeight: CGFloat?, maxHeight:
CGFloat?, alignment: Alignment)
```

This modifier assigns a minimum and a maximum size to the view. We can also define an ideal width and height that will be taken into consideration when the space must be distributed among the views. The **alignment** argument determines the alignment of the view's content. It is a structure of type **Alignment** with the type properties **bottom**, **bottomLeading**, **bottomTrailing**, **center**, **leading**, **top**, **topLeading**, **topTrailing** and **trailing**.

```
padding(CGFloat)
```

This modifier adds padding between a view's content and its frame. The argument determines the amount of padding applied. We can provide a single **CGFloat** value to apply padding to all sides, specify padding for each side using an **EdgeInsets** value, or supply a set of **Edge** values along with a **CGFloat** value to define which sides are modified and by how much.

IMPORTANT

Because human languages can have different writing directions, SwiftUI uses the terms **leading** and **trailing** to represent each horizontal edge. When an app runs in a left-to-right language, like English, **leading** refers to the left side and **trailing** to the right. In a right-to-left language, like Hebrew, **leading** refers to the right side and **trailing** to the left.

Since these methods define the size in points, we don't need to consider the screen resolution of each device. For example, if we want a view to occupy half the width of the screen on an iPhone, we can assign it a width of 200 points, and it will always appear the same regardless of the device's model.

Listing 2-15: Assigning a fixed size to a view

```
struct ContentView: View {
    var body: some View {
        Text("Hello World!")
            .frame(width: 200, height: 100, alignment: .leading)
    }
}
```

In this example, we use the **alignment** argument to align the text to the leading edge (**leading**). If we click the Selectable button on the canvas (Chapter 1, Figure 1-17, number 3) and then click on the view, a blue rectangle appears, indicating the frame that was created by the **frame()** modifier, as shown below.

Figure 2-19: *View with a fixed size and the content aligned to the left (leading)*

Do It Yourself

Update the **ContentView** structure with the code in Listing 2-15. Press the Selectable button to activate the Selectable mode on the canvas (Chapter 1, Figure 1-17, number 3). Click on the **Text** view in the canvas to select it. You should see a blue rectangle indicating the area occupied by the view, as illustrated in Figure 2-19.

The arguments in the **frame()** modifier are optional. We can declare only the width or the height, and the rest of the arguments will be defined by the view and its content. This is particularly useful when we want to turn one side of the view flexible. Flexible views are defined with the **maxWidth** and **maxHeight** arguments. For instance, we can apply the **maxWidth** argument to extend the view to the left and right side of the window, and let the content determine the height.

Listing 2-16: Creating flexible containers

```
struct ContentView: View {
```

```
    var body: some View {
        Text("Hello World!")
            .frame(minWidth: 0, maxWidth: .infinity)
    }
}
```

The value **`infinity`** is a type property defined in the **`CGFloat`** structure that asks the system to expand the view to occupy all the space available in its container. In our example, we applied this value to the **maxWidth** argument, so the **`Text`** view extends to the edges of the screen.

Figure 2-20: *Flexible view*

IMPORTANT

Note that for a flexible view to work properly it is recommended to always declare the minimum size, as we do in our example. If you are declaring a flexible width, you should set the **minWidth** argument, and if you are declaring a flexible height, you should also include the **minHeight** argument.

Another way to affect the size of a view is with the **`padding()`** modifier. This modifier inserts padding between the content and the edges of the view. There are different ways to determine the padding's thickness. For instance, if we don't specify any value, the system assigns one by default, but we can also provide a **`CGFloat`** value to declare a specific thickness in points.

Listing 2-17: Adding padding to a view

```
struct ContentView: View {
    var body: some View {
        Text("Hello World")
            .padding(25)
    }
}
```

The code in Listing 2-17 assigns a padding of 25 points to the **`Text`** view. The padding is applied between the text and the view's frame, as shown below.

Figure 2-21: *View with padding*

The **View** protocol defines a structure called **EdgeInsets** that we can use to specify a width for each side of the view.

```
EdgeInsets(top: CGFloat, leading: CGFloat, bottom: CGFloat,
trailing: CGFloat)
```

This initializer returns an **EdgeInsets** structure with the values specified by the arguments.

The following example implements this structure to assign a padding of 40 points only to the left and right sides of the view.

Listing 2-18: Assigning a specific padding for each side

```
struct ContentView: View {
   var body: some View {
      Text("Hello World")
         .padding(EdgeInsets(top: 0.0, leading: 40.0, bottom: 0.0,
            trailing: 40.0))
   }
}
```

Figure 2-22: *Padding only on the sides*

The code in Listing 2-18 assigns padding to specific sides of the view. Another way to achieve the same is with the values of an enumeration provided by SwiftUI called **Edge**. This enumeration includes the values **all, top, bottom, leading, trailing, horizontal** and **vertical** to represent each side. We must declare a set with the values that represent the sides we want to modify and a second argument with the thickness we want to assign to the padding. The following example adds a padding of 50 points at the view's top and bottom. (The same can be achieved by using the value **vertical**.)

Listing 2-19: Assigning padding with Edge values

```
struct ContentView: View {
   var body: some View {
      Text("Hello World")
         .padding([.top, .bottom], 50)
   }
}
```

Figure 2-23: *Padding at the top and bottom*

BASIC

Color View

Some of the modifiers introduced in the previous section can change the colors of the view and the content. Colors in SwiftUI are defined by the **Color** view. The following are some of the structure's initializers.

Color(RGBColorSpace, **red:** Double, **green:** Double, **blue:** Double, **opacity:** Double)

This initializer returns a **Color** view with the color and opacity defined by the arguments. The first argument defines the color system used to interpret the values. It is an enumeration with the values **sRGB**, **sRGBLinear**, and **displayP3**. If ignored, the application will use the default color system set on the device. The **red**, **green**, and **blue** arguments determine the levels of red, green, and blue with values from 0.0 (no color) to 1.0 (full color). And the **opacity** argument determines the level of opacity with a value from 0.0 (transparent) to 1.0 (opaque).

Color(RGBColorSpace, **white:** Double, **opacity:** Double)

This initializer returns a **Color** view with the color defined by the arguments. The first argument defines the color system used to interpret the values. It is an enumeration with the values **sRGB**, **sRGBLinear**, and **displayP3**. If ignored, the application will use the default color system set on the device. The **white** argument determines the level of white with a value from 0.0 to 1.0 (black to white), and the **opacity** argument determines the level of opacity with a value from 0.0 (transparent) to 1.0 (opaque).

Color(hue: Double, **saturation:** Double, **brightness:** Double)

This initializer returns a **Color** view with the color defined by the arguments. The arguments determine the level of hue, saturation, and brightness of the color with values from 0.0 to 1.0.

The **Color** structure also offers an extensive list of type properties that return a **Color** view with a predefined color that adapts to the interface mode (Light or Dark). The properties available are **black**, **blue**, **brown**, **cyan**, **gray**, **green**, **indigo**, **mint**, **orange**, **pink**, **purple**, **red**, **teal**, **white**, and **yellow**. There is also a property to make the element transparent called **clear**, a property to get the color by default called **accentColor**, and two properties called **primary** and **secondary** that return predefined colors that also change depending on the interface mode.

Most of the time, **Color** views are used to define a color for the content of other views, but they can also be included in the interface as standalone views, as shown below.

Listing 2-20: Implementing Color views

```
struct ContentView: View {
   var body: some View {
      Color(red: 0.9, green: 0.5, blue: 0.2)
         .frame(width: 250, height: 100)
   }
}
```

Figure 2-24: `Color` *view*

The code in Listing 2-20 creates an orange **`Color`** view with a size of 250 by 100 points. In this case, the **`Color`** initializer specifies values from 0.0 to 1.0 to determine the levels of red, green and blue, but RGB colors (Red, Green, Blue) are usually defined with integer values from 0 to 255. If we want to work with these values, we can divide the number by 255. For instance, the following initializer assigns an RGB color with the values 100, 228, 255 (cyan).

Listing 2-21: Defining the color with RGB values

```
struct ContentView: View {
   var body: some View {
      Color(red: 100/255, green: 228/255, blue: 255/255)
         .frame(width: 250, height: 100)
   }
}
```

The colors defined by the initializers are static, that is, they are always the same regardless of the appearance of the interface (Light or Dark), but we can assign dynamic colors with the properties of the structure. Dynamic colors adapt to the appearance. The following example creates a **`Color`** view with the **`red`** property. In Dark mode, this color will look slightly different than in Light mode.

Listing 2-22: Assigning a dynamic color

```
struct ContentView: View {
   var body: some View {
      Color.red
         .frame(width: 250, height: 100)
   }
}
```

In addition to the adaptable colors defined by the **`Color`** view, we can also define our own. This option is provided by the **Asset Catalog**. This is a container provided by Xcode to help us organize and access the app's resources, including images, colors, symbols, and more. To create an Asset Catalog, we must open the **File** menu, select **New**, and click on **New from Template** (see Chapter 1, Figure 1-12). The template for the Asset Catalog is under the Resource section, as shown below.

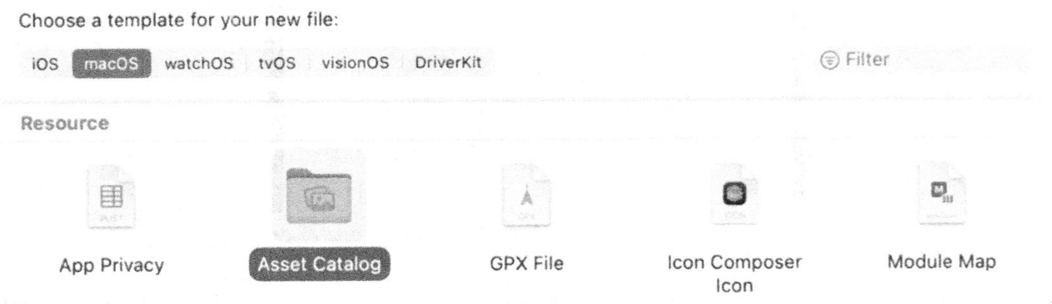

Figure 2-25: Asset Catalog template

After selecting the template and giving the file a name, Xcode adds it to the **Navigator**. Selecting the file opens an interface in the **Editor** for managing and configuring the app's resources. The interface is divided into two columns: the left column lists the available resources, and the right column displays the contents of the selected resource, as shown below.

Figure 2-26: Empty Asset Catalog

The resources are organized into sets, so if we want to define a custom adaptive color, we must create a new Color set. The option is available from the button in the lower-left corner (circled in Figure 2-26). Once we select the **Color Set** option, Xcode creates a new set with two color placeholders: one for the Any appearance and another for Dark mode.

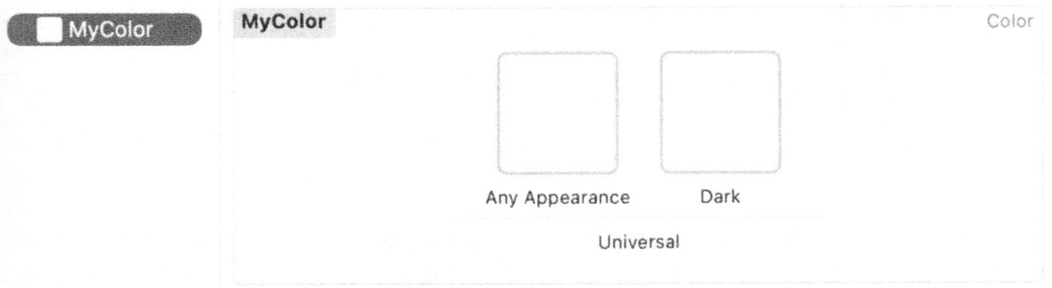

Figure 2-27: Colors for Light and Dark appearances

To define the colors, we click on the placeholder we want to change and select it from the Attributes Inspector panel on the right. For instance, in the following example, we change the color for the dark appearance to orange, resulting in a color set that switches from white to orange depending on the mode.

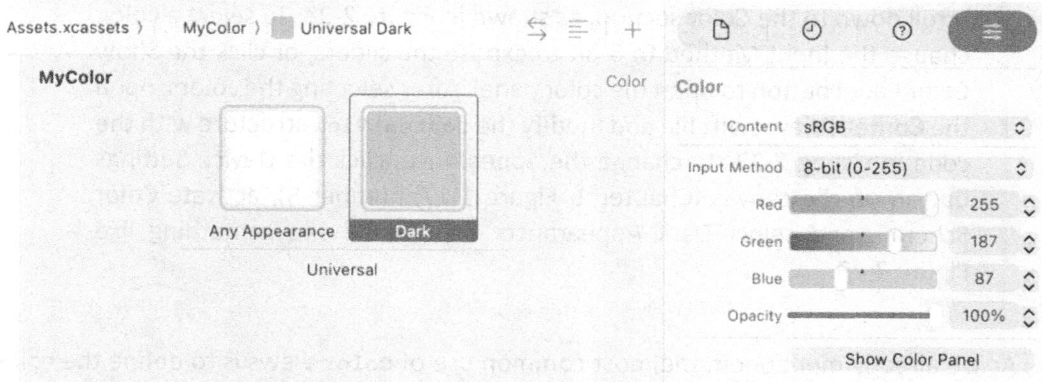

Figure 2-28: *New color for Dark appearance*

The name of the set is the identifier we use to reference the color from code. For instance, in the previous example, we called the set **MyColor**, so to assign this color to a view, all we need to do is specify that name, as shown below.

Listing 2-23: Assigning a custom color

```
struct ContentView: View {
   var body: some View {
      Color("MyColor")
         .frame(width: 250, height: 100)
   }
}
```

In this example, the `Color` view will be white in Light appearance, but orange when the appearance is changed to Dark.

Figure 2-29: *Custom color in Dark appearance*

Do It Yourself

Open the **File** menu, select **New**, and click on **New from Template**. On the template window, scroll down to the **Resource** section and select the **Asset Catalog** icon. Click **Next** and assign the file a name. You should see the new file in the Navigator. Click on the file to open the interface in the Editor. Click the plus button (circled in Figure 2-26), select the **Color Set** option, and change the name of the set to MyColor (Figure 2-27). Click on the squares that represent the colors in the Editor, open the Attributes Inspector panel on the right (see Chapter 1, Figure 1-4, number 7), and scroll down to the Color section, as shown in Figure 2-28. To select a color, change the Input Method to 8-bit to expose the sliders, or click the Show Color Panel button to open the color panel. After selecting the colors, open the **ContentView.swift** file and modify the **`ContentView`** structure with the code in Listing 2-23. To change the appearance, click the Device Settings button on the canvas (Chapter 1, Figure 1-17, number 8), activate Color Scheme, and select Dark Appearance. You should see something like Figure 2-29.

As we already mentioned, the most common use of **`Color`** views is to define the colors of other views. The following are some modifiers that apply **`Color`** views to set view colors or that are particularly useful when working with colors.

`foregroundStyle``(ShapeStyle)`

This modifier assigns a style to the view's content. The argument is a value that conforms to the **`ShapeStyle`** protocol, such as the **`Color`** structure for colors, the **`AngularGradient`** and **`LinearGradient`** structures for gradients, and the **`Material`** structure for materials.

`border``(Color, `**`width:`**` CGFloat)`

This modifier assigns a border to the view. The first argument determines the border's color and the **width** argument determines its width.

`background``(View, `**`alignment:`**` Alignment)`

This modifier assigns a view as the view's background. The first argument is a SwiftUI view, including **`Color`** views, and the **alignment** argument determines how the view is going to be aligned within the bounds of the parent view.

`overlay``(View, `**`alignment:`**` Alignment)`

This modifier displays a view in front of the view that is being modified. The first argument is a SwiftUI view, including **`Color`** views, and the **alignment** argument determines how the view is going to be aligned within the bounds of the view we are modifying.

Using these modifiers, we can apply colors to different parts of the view. For instance, the **`foregroundStyle()`** modifier assigns a color to the view's content. In the following example, we use it to change the color of the text in a **`Text`** view.

Listing 2-24: Assigning a color to the text of a `Text` view

```
struct ContentView: View {
   var body: some View {
      Text("Hello World")
         .font(.largeTitle)
         .foregroundStyle(Color.red)
   }
}
```

Figure 2-30: *Text in different color*

Besides changing the color of the text, we can assign a color to the view's background. The `background()` modifier can take any view, but it is usually applied with a `Color` view.

Listing 2-25: Assigning a background color to a Text view

```
struct ContentView: View {
   var body: some View {
      Text("Hello World")
         .font(.largeTitle)
         .background(Color.gray)
   }
}
```

Figure 2-31: *View with a background*

The area occupied by the view is determined by a rectangular frame. In `Text` views, the size of this rectangle is determined by the size of the text. If we want to extend the background, we can set the frame's size with the `frame()` modifier or add a padding with the `padding()` modifier, as we do in the following example.

Listing 2-26: Assigning a background color to a view with a padding

```
struct ContentView: View {
   var body: some View {
      Text("Hello World")
         .font(.largeTitle)
         .padding(20)
         .background(Color.gray)
   }
}
```

Note that the padding was applied before the background. This is important because the order of the modifiers matters. Every time a modifier is executed, a new view is created with the characteristics of the previous view plus the changes requested by the modifier. For example, the code in Listing 2-26 creates a `Text` view with the text "Hello World", then the `font()` modifier creates a new view with a larger font, after that the `padding()` modifier creates another view with the characteristics of the previous one but with a padding of 20 points, and finally the `background()` modifier creates another view with a background that covers the whole area occupied by the previous view, which includes the padding. If we had declared the background before the padding, the background color would have been applied to the view generated by the **font()** modifier, which didn't include the padding. Figure 2-32, below, shows what we see when we apply the **background()** modifier before the padding and after.

Figure 2-32: *Background applied before and after the padding*

In addition to the background, we can assign a border to the view with the **border()** modifier. This modifier takes a view that represents the style of the border (usually a **Color** view) and the width, and adds a border with those characteristics.

Listing 2-27: Assigning a border to the view

```
struct ContentView: View {
    var body: some View {
        Text("Hello World")
            .font(.largeTitle)
            .padding(20)
            .background(Color.gray)
            .border(Color.yellow, width: 10)
    }
}
```

Figure 2-33: *Background and border applied to a view*

IMPORTANT

The border is applied to the frame occupied by the view. If we want to add a border to a view with a different shape, like a circle, we must create an overlay with a shape view. We will learn more about overlays next and how to create shape views in Chapter 8.

The **overlay()** modifier works like the **background()** modifier, but instead of displaying the view in the background, it displays it in the foreground. For example, the following code adds a translucent yellow view in front of the view created in the previous example.

Listing 2-28: Displaying a view in front of another view

```
struct ContentView: View {
    var body: some View {
        Text("Hello World")
            .font(.largeTitle)
            .padding(20)
            .background(Color.gray)
            .overlay(
                Color(red: 1, green: 1, blue: 0.3, opacity: 0.2)
            )
    }
}
```

Figure 2-34: *Overlay*

The **`Color`** view also includes the following property and method to apply simple effects to the views.

`gradient`

This property applies a gentle gradient to the color.

`opacity``(Double)`

This method defines the color's opacity. The argument takes values from 0.0 (fully transparent) to 1.0 (fully opaque).

The **`gradient`** property returns a gentle gradient generated from the original color. It can be applied anywhere a **`Color`** view is implemented. For instance, in the following example, we apply it to the background of our **`Text`** view.

Listing 2-29: Applying a predefined gradient to a view

```
struct ContentView: View {
    var body: some View {
        Text("Hello World")
            .font(.largeTitle)
            .padding(20)
            .background(Color.gray.gradient)
    }
}
```

Figure 2-35: *Gradient*

The **Color** structure also includes a type method to blend two colors.

mix(with: Color, **by:** Double, **in:** Gradient.ColorSpace)

This type method mixes the original color with the color specified by the **with** argument and returns a **Color** view with the result. The **by** argument specifies the amount of blending (0.0 to 1.0), and the **in** argument determines the color space used to blend the colors (**.perpetual** by default)

In the following example, we define the background color of the text view with a 50% blend between red and blue.

Listing 2-30: Blending colors

```
struct ContentView: View {
    var body: some View {
        Text("Hello World")
            .font(.largeTitle)
            .padding(20)
            .background(Color.blue.mix(with: Color.red, by: 0.5))
    }
}
```

BASIC

Materials

Modern interfaces make extensive use of blur effects and transparency. With the introduction of the Liquid Glass interface, these effects have become essential for making our apps look up to date. To recreate these effects, the **SwiftUI** framework provides the **Material** structure. A **Material** structure behaves like a color, but it applies a visual effect that resembles frosted glass. To apply this effect, the structure includes several properties that return instances with different levels of blur and transparency. The currently available properties are **ultraThin**, **thin**, **regular**, **thick**, **ultraThick**, and **bar**.

Materials are applied to the view with the **background()** modifier. The translucent effect they produce is useful when the view appears on top of other views, but we can test it with a single view, as shown below.

Listing 2-31: Applying a material

```
struct ContentView: View {
    var body: some View {
        Text("Hello World")
            .font(.largeTitle)
            .background(.thickMaterial)
    }
}
```

Because we only have one view and the window's background is white, the effect is barely visible, but materials become useful when working with multiple views and images, as we will see later.

Figure 2-36: *Material applied to a view*

Materials can also be applied to the view's content with the **`foregroundStyle()`** modifier, as in the following example.

Listing 2-32: Applying a material to the view's content

```
struct ContentView: View {
   var body: some View {
      Text("Hello World")
         .font(.largeTitle)
         .background(.red)
         .foregroundStyle(.thickMaterial)
   }
}
```

Figure 2-37: *Material applied to the text*

BASIC

Images

As we already mentioned, Apple devices have screens with different resolutions and scale factors. Currently, there are three scales: 1x, 2x, and 3x. The 1x scale defines one point as one pixel, the 2x scale defines one point as a square of two pixels, and the 3x scale defines one point as a square of three pixels. As a result, an area measured in points maps to a different number of pixels depending on the device. This means that small images may need to be enlarged to fill the required area, losing quality in the process, while larger images may need to be reduced. To address these issues, Apple requires developers to include three versions of each image, one for each scale factor.

There are two ways to incorporate these images into our project. We can drag the files into the **Navigator**, as we did earlier for the font file (see Figure 2-14), or add the images to an Asset Catalog, as we did for colors (see Figure 2-26). Adding images to an Asset Catalog is the recommended approach because it keeps images organized and easy to manage. In this case, we must create an **Image Set**, as shown below.

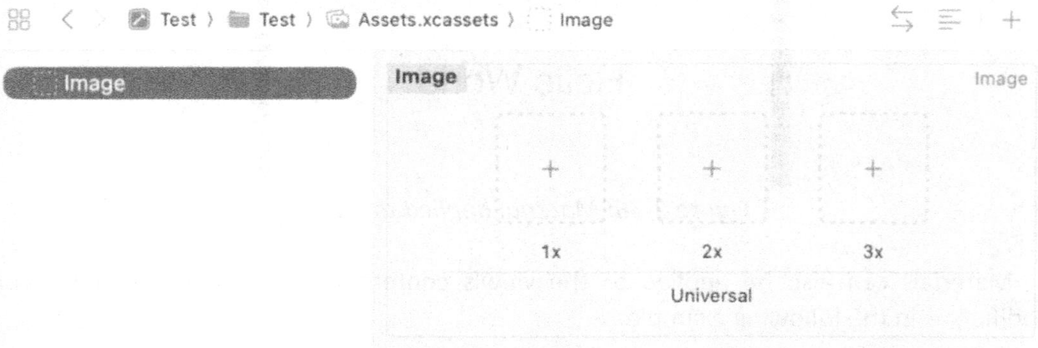

Figure 2-38: *New set of images*

The name of the set is the name we use to reference the image from code. Xcode names the new set *Image* by default, but we can give it any name we want. Once the set is created, we can drag the image files from **Finder** into the corresponding squares. Figure 2-39, below, shows the Editor Area after the husky images are dragged from Finder into the Asset Catalog and the name of the set is changed to husky.

Figure 2-39: *The husky set is ready*

In addition to the image for every scale, we can also add versions for different devices and appearances. By default, the set of images is assigned to a Universal device, which means that the images of the set are going to be displayed on all devices, but we can add to the set images for a specific device by selecting the options in the Attributes Inspector panel.

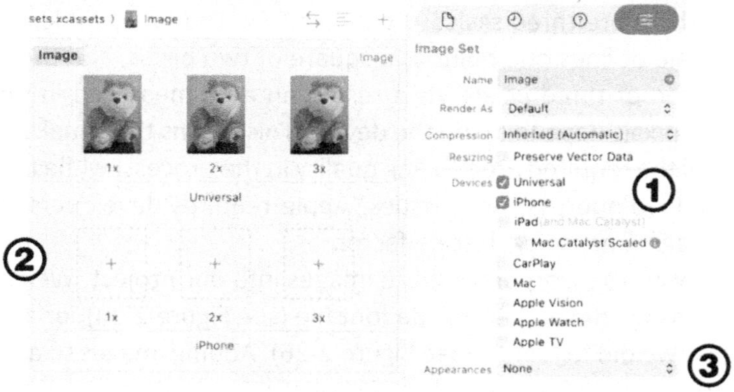

Figure 2-40: *Images for iPhones*

When a set is selected, the Attributes Inspector panel shows the list of properties assigned to the set, including Devices and Appearance (Figure 2-40, numbers 1 and 3). If we check the box for a device or select a different appearance value (Dark or Light), the interface adds placeholders where we can drag and drop the images for that specific attribute. For instance, in Figure 2-40, we checked the box for iPhones, and now we have three placeholders to add images for that specific device (number 2).

IMPORTANT

To identify the files for each scale factor, Apple recommends using a naming convention that appends a suffix to the file name. The image for the 1x scale uses only the base name and extension, as in **husky.png**, the file for the 2x scale includes the **@2x** suffix, as in **husky@2x.png**, and the file for the 3x scale includes the **@3x** suffix, as in **husky@3x.png**. Once you name the files using this convention, you can drag them to the Asset Catalog and Xcode automatically creates a set and assigns the images to it.

After the images are incorporated into the Asset Catalog, we can load them from our code using their name, and the system automatically selects the correct version based on the characteristics of the device on which the app is running. To display images, SwiftUI provides the **Image** view. The following are some of the initializers.

Image(ImageResource)

This initializer creates an **Image** view with the image indicated by the argument. The argument is a reference to the **ImageResource** structure that represents the image in the Asset Catalog or a string with the name of the set.

Image(systemName: String, **variableValue:** Double**)**

This initializer creates an **Image** view with an SF symbol. The **systemName** argument is the name of the symbol, and the **variableValue** argument is a value between 0.0 and 1.0 that determines the symbol's appearance.

Image(uiImage: UIImage**)**

This initializer creates an **Image** view from a **UIImage** object.

An **Image** view can load and display any image in the Asset Catalog. All we need is to specify its name. For instance, the following example creates an **Image** view with an image we added to the Asset Catalog called "Toronto".

Listing 2-33: Displaying an image

```
struct ContentView: View {
   var body: some View {
      Image("Toronto")
   }
}
```

When an image is added to the Asset Catalog, Xcode creates an **ImageResource** structure to represent it, and this structure is assigned to a static property that we can reference to load the image. Note that the name of the property is defined after the name of the set, but in lowercase letters, as shown below.

Listing 2-34: Loading an image from the `ImageResource` structure

```
struct ContentView: View {
   var body: some View {
      Image(.toronto)
   }
}
```

Whether we use a string with the image name or the **ImageResource** property, the result is the same: the image is loaded from the Asset Catalog and displayed on the screen.

Figure 2-41: *Image view*

Do It Yourself

Download the **Toronto.jpg** image from our website or provide your own. If you haven't done it yet, create an Asset Catalog file, as explain in Figure 2-25. Drag the image files to the Asset Catalog in your project. Xcode will automatically create an Image set. Modify the **ContentView** structure with the code in Listing 2-34. You should see a picture of Toronto on the canvas.

By default, **Image** views size themselves to their content. If an image is larger than the window, as in this case, the view extends beyond the screen boundaries (see Figure 2-41). To fit the image within the space provided by the view, we must apply the following modifiers.

clipped()

This modifier clips the image to the view's frame.

```
resizable(capInsets: EdgeInsets, resizingMode: Image.
ResizingMode)
```

This modifier resizes the image to fit the view frame. The **capInsets** argument specifies the portion of the image that shouldn't be resized, and the **resizingMode** argument specifies how the image is resized to fit the available space. It is an enumeration with the values **stretch** (default) and **tile**.

```
aspectRatio(CGSize, contentMode: ContentMode)
```

This modifier changes the image's aspect ratio to the values specified by the first argument and resizes the image according to the mode specified by the **contentMode** argument. This argument is an enumeration of type **ContentMode** with the values **fill** and **fit**. If we want to use the original aspect ratio, we can declare the first argument as **nil** or just ignore it.

```
scaledToFit()
```

This modifier scales the image to fit within the view. It works like the **aspectRatio()** modifier with the aspect ratio set to **nil** and the mode to **fit**.

```
scaledToFill()
```

This modifier scales the image to fill the view. It works like the **aspectRatio()** modifier with the aspect ratio set to **nil** and the mode to **fill**.

```
interpolation(Interpolation)
```

This modifier controls how an image is resampled when it is scaled. Low interpolation produces a pixelated result, while higher interpolation creates a smoother image. The argument is an enumeration with the values **high**, **medium**, **low**, and **none**.

There are several types of transformations we can perform on an image using these modifiers. An alternative is to clip the image to the frame of the view with the **clipped()** modifier.

Listing 2-35: Clipping the image

```
struct ContentView: View {
   var body: some View {
      Image("Toronto")
         .frame(width: 250, height: 100)
         .clipped()
   }
}
```

The **clipped()** modifier creates a new view that displays only the portion of the image that falls within the view frame. In this case, we assign the **Image** view a size of 250 by 100 points, so only the part of the image that fits within that area is visible.

Figure 2-42: *Image clipped*

This reduces the size of the visible image, but the image is still presented in its original size, independent of the size of the view. To adapt the size of the image to the size of the view, we have to make the image flexible with the **`resizable()`** modifier.

Listing 2-36: Resizing the image

```
struct ContentView: View {
   var body: some View {
      Image("Toronto")
         .resizable()
         .frame(width: 250, height: 100)
   }
}
```

The **`resizable()`** modifier creates a view that scales the image to fit the available space, making the entire image visible, as shown below.

Figure 2-43: *Image resized*

IMPORTANT

As we already mentioned, modifiers return a new view and therefore the order in which they are applied matters. The **`resizable()`** modifier applied in Listing 2-36 is implemented by the **`Image`** structure and therefore it must be applied first. If we try to declared this modifier after the **`frame()`** modifier, we will get an error because the **`frame()`** modifier does not return an **`Image`** view, it returns a view of type **`some View`**.

In the previous example, we didn't need to clip the image because the **`resizable()`** modifier scales the image to fit the view, but this introduces a different problem. The image becomes distorted. If we want to resize the image while preserving its original aspect ratio, we must specify the content mode using the **`aspectRatio()`** modifier. The available values are **`fit`** (Aspect Fit) and **`fill`** (Aspect Fill).

Listing 2-37: Resizing an image to fit the view

```
struct ContentView: View {
    var body: some View {
        Image("Toronto")
            .resizable()
            .aspectRatio(contentMode: .fit)
            .frame(width: 250, height: 100)
    }
}
```

The **`aspectRatio()`** modifier supports two modes: **`fit`** and **`fill`**. The **`fit`** mode resizes the image to fit within the view, which may leave some empty space in the frame, while the **`fill`** mode resizes the image to fill the view, which may cause part of the image to extend beyond the view's frame. (This is the same as applying the modifiers **`scaledToFit()`** and **`scaledToFill()`**.) The result is shown below.

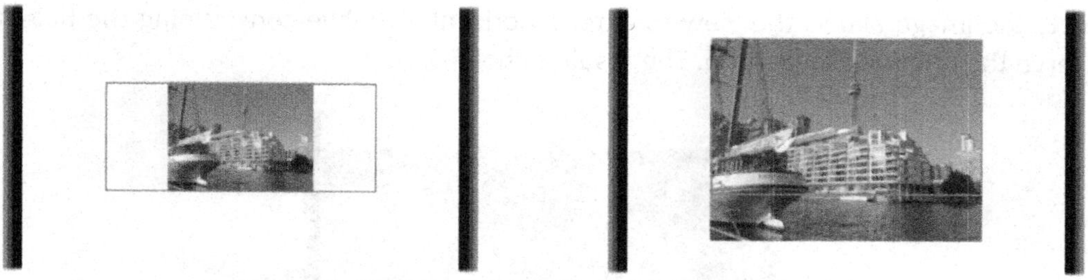

Figure 2-44: *Aspect fit (left) and aspect fill (right)*

When using the **`fill`** mode, parts of the image may extend beyond the boundaries of the view (see Figure 2-44, right). In cases like this, we can use the **`clipped()`** modifier to remove the excess.

Listing 2-38: Resizing and clipping the image to fill the view

```
struct ContentView: View {
    var body: some View {
        Image("Toronto")
            .resizable()
            .scaledToFill()
            .frame(width: 250, height: 100)
            .clipped()
    }
}
```

Figure 2-45: *Clipping resized image*

If we need the image to adapt to the available space, we can set the mode to **fit** and let the **Image** view determine the size, as shown below.

Listing 2-39: Resizing image to fill the container

```
struct ContentView: View {
    var body: some View {
        Image("Toronto")
            .resizable()
            .scaledToFit()
    }
}
```

When the frame size is not explicitly defined, the view and its content work together to determine the final size. Initially, the view expands to occupy the available space in its container, and then it queries the image for its preferred size. Because the image mode is set to **fit**, the image allows the view to extend horizontally while constraining the height to preserve the original aspect ratio. The result is shown below.

Figure 2-46: *Flexible* Image *view*

Of course, we can also apply common modifiers to an **Image** view. Some modifiers affect the view itself, while others affect the image. In the following example, we use a few of these modifiers to add padding and a shadow to our image.

Listing 2-40: Applying style modifiers to an Image view

```
struct ContentView: View {
    var body: some View {
        Image("Toronto")
            .resizable()
            .scaledToFit()
            .shadow(color: Color.black, radius: 10, x: 10, y: 10)
            .padding(30)
    }
}
```

Figure 2-47: *Image view with common modifiers*

The **View** protocol also defines modifiers that are particularly useful with **Image** views. The following are some of the most frequently used.

blur(radius: CGFloat, **opaque:** Bool)

This modifier applies a blur effect to the view. The **radius** argument determines how diffuse the blur effect is, and the **opaque** argument determines whether the blur effect is going to be opaque or transparent.

colorMultiply(Color)

This modifier multiplies the colors of the view by a specific color. The result is that the original colors of the view tend to the color defined by the argument.

grayscale(Double)

This modifier adds a grayscale effect to the view. The argument is a value between 0.0 (colorful) to 1.0 (grayscale).

contrast(Double)

This modifier applies contrast to the view.

opacity(Double)

This modifier defines the view's opacity. The argument takes values from 0.0 (fully transparent) to 1.0 (fully opaque).

scaleEffect(CGSize)

This modifier changes the horizontal and vertical scales of the view to the values specified by the argument. The modifier only affects the view's content.

The implementation of these modifiers is straightforward. The following example scales the image to half its size and makes it blurry.

Listing 2-41: Applying visual effects to an `Image` view

```
struct ContentView: View {
   var body: some View {
```

```
        Image("Toronto")
            .resizable()
            .scaledToFit()
            .padding()
            .scaleEffect(CGSize(width: 0.5, height: 0.5))
            .blur(radius: 5)
    }
}
```

The size of the view remains the same, but the size of the image is reduced by half with the **`scaleEffect()`** modifier. The result is shown below.

Figure 2-48: *Visual effects applied to an image*

> **IMPORTANT**
>
> The image effects introduced in this section are those provided by SwiftUI. However, Apple offers additional frameworks, such as **Core Image**, that enable low-level image transformations capable of producing virtually any effect. We will explore images and graphics in depth in Chapter 8. For more information on **Core Image**, read our book *Apple Intelligence for Masterminds.*

BASIC

SF Symbols

Apple systems provide predefined images that we can use in our applications, such as emojis. Emojis can be included in strings like any other character by pressing Control + Command + Space. Their purpose is to convey information or mood, so they do not scale well and should be used primarily alongside text to establish an emotional connection with the user or between users. To incorporate icons that represent functionality, Apple recommends using SF Symbols, which are designed specifically for this purpose. These symbols are scalable, available in multiple variants, and adapt to the current font, allowing them to integrate seamlessly with the rest of the interface.

There are a variety of symbols for any need our application might have. To help us find the symbols we want, Apple offers a free application called SF Symbols, which we can download from **developer.apple.com** (Downloads > Applications). The application includes options to search for symbols by name or category.

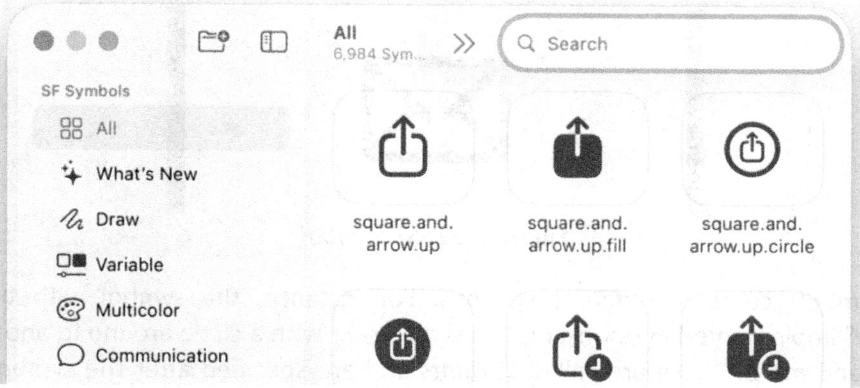

Figure 2-49: *SF Symbols app*

Symbols are displayed with an **`Image`** view using the initializer **`Image(systemName:)`**, as in the following example.

Listing 2-42: Displaying SF symbols

```
struct ContentView: View {
    var body: some View {
        Image(systemName: "envelope")
    }
}
```

Figure 2-50: *SF Symbol*

SF symbols were designed to work with text and therefore their size and style can be determined by a **`Font`** structure, as shown below.

Listing 2-43: Styling a symbol

```
struct ContentView: View {
    var body: some View {
        Image(systemName: "envelope")
            .font(Font.system(size: 100).weight(.semibold))
    }
}
```

In this example, we define a **`Font`** structure using the system font with a size of 100 and a semibold weight. The symbol now has a new size and style without losing quality.

Figure 2-51: SF Symbol

SF Symbols come in different versions. For instance, the symbol with the name "envelope" implemented in our example has a version with a circle around it, another with a badge, and more. These are called *Variants* and are specified after the symbol's name using dot notation, as in **envelope.circle**, or **envelope.fill**. All the variants of a symbol can be found in the SF Symbol application, but the framework also includes the following modifier to specify a variant.

symbolVariant(SymbolVariants)

This modifier assigns a variant to a symbol. The argument is a structure with the type properties **none**, **circle**, **square**, **rectangle**, **fill**, and **slash**.

The image is created as before, but now the modifier determines the symbol's variant, as shown below.

Listing 2-44: Assigning a variant to a symbol

```
struct ContentView: View {
   var body: some View {
      Image(systemName: "envelope")
         .font(Font.system(size: 100))
         .symbolVariant(.fill)
   }
}
```

Figure 2-52: A variant of an SF Symbol

IMPORTANT

What we did in the last example is the same as creating the **Image** view with the name "envelope.fill", but selecting the variant from a modifier allows us to modify the symbol and animate the changes according to changes in the state of the view, as we will see later.

SF Symbols are rendered using the color and size of the font, but some symbols can include up to three additional colors, and all of them can be scaled up or down. SwiftUI provides the following modifiers for this purpose.

symbolRenderingMode(SymbolRenderingMode**)**

This modifier sets the symbol's rendering mode. The argument is a structure with the type properties **hierarchical**, **monochrome** (default), **multicolor**, and **palette**.

symbolColorRenderingMode(SymbolColorRenderingMode**)**

This modifier sets the symbol's color rendering mode. The argument is a structure with the properties **flat** (default) and **gradient**.

symbolVariableValueMode(SymbolVariableValueMode**)**

This modifier determines the rendering mode of a symbol with variable values. The argument is a structure with the properties **color** (default) and **draw**.

imageScale(Scale**)**

This modifier sets the symbol's scale. The size is determined from the size of the font and the scale specified by the argument. The argument is an enumeration with the values **small**, **medium**, and **large**.

The **symbolRenderingMode()** modifier can set up to four different color modes. By default, the **monochrome** mode is selected, which means that the symbol is displayed in a single color (the color of the font or the view), but we can change this behavior by selecting a different mode. The **hierarchical** mode defines a set of colors derived from a base color, the **multicolor** mode shows the symbol with its original colors, and the **palette** mode shows the symbol with custom colors.

Not all the symbols are multicolor. We can find multicolor symbols by selecting the Multicolor category in the SF Symbol app. For instance, in the following example we show the **mic.badge.plus** symbol, which has two colors.

Listing 2-45: Displaying multicolor symbols

```
struct ContentView: View {
   var body: some View {
      Image(systemName: "mic.badge.plus")
         .font(Font.system(size: 100))
         .symbolRenderingMode(.multicolor)
   }
}
```

Figure 2-53: *Multicolor symbol*

The microphone is displayed with the color by default (the font color or the foreground color assigned to the view), and the badge is green. These are the symbol's original colors, but we can change them by specifying the **hierarchical** or **palette** modes. The colors for these modes are specified by the **foregroundStyle()** modifier, as in the following example.

Listing 2-46: Displaying a multicolor symbol with custom colors

```
struct ContentView: View {
    var body: some View {
        Image(systemName: "mic.badge.plus")
            .font(Font.system(size: 100))
            .symbolRenderingMode(.palette)
            .foregroundStyle(.red, .blue)
            .symbolColorRenderingMode(.gradient)
    }
}
```

The colors are declared using the **foregroundStyle()** modifier, separated by commas. In this example, the symbol requires two colors, one for the microphone and another for the badge, although some symbols may use more. In this example, we also apply the **symbolColorRenderingMode()** modifier with the **gradient** value to add a gentle gradient to both colors. The result is shown below.

Figure 2-54: *Multicolor symbol with custom colors*

Some SF Symbols support variable colors to represent different states. For example, certain symbols include graphics that resemble radio waves and change color to indicate different signal levels. To use these symbols, we must initialize the **Image** view with the **variableValue** argument. The value of this argument determines which variant of the symbol is displayed. The value required to move from one state to another depends on the number of states supported by the symbol. In the following example, we display a symbol with five states.

Listing 2-47: Displaying a variable SF Symbol

```
struct ContentView: View {
    var body: some View {
        Image(systemName: "dot.radiowaves.forward", variableValue: 0.8)
            .font(Font.system(size: 100))
    }
}
```

Depending on the value of the **variableValue** argument, the view displays different symbol variants. Below are the possible values for this symbol and the states it can represent.

Figure 2-55: *Variable SF Symbol*

The previous example works out of the box because we use a symbol that supports the default rendering mode (`color`), but some symbols rely on a new rendering mode for variable values called `draw`. Depending on the symbol we want to use, we may need to set one mode or another. For example, the **thermometer.high** symbol is a multicolor symbol and uses the `draw` mode to adapt to variable values, so we must set this mode for the symbol to respond correctly, as shown in the following example.

Listing 2-48: Displaying a variable multicolor SF Symbol

```
struct ContentView: View {
   var body: some View {
      Image(systemName: "thermometer.high", variableValue: 0.6)
         .font(Font.system(size: 100))
         .symbolRenderingMode(.multicolor)
         .symbolVariableValueMode(.draw)
   }
}
```

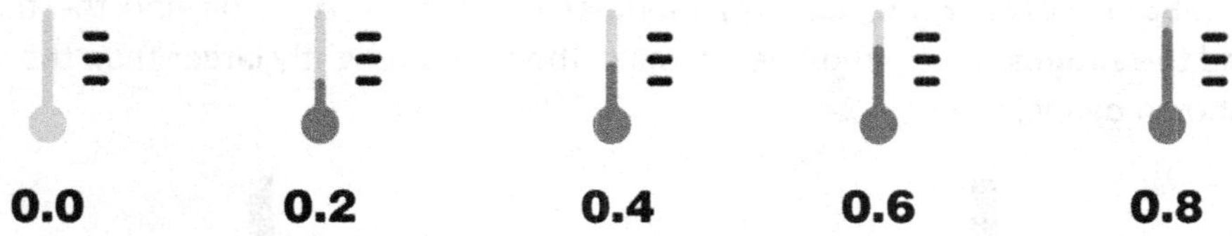

Figure 2-56: *Variable multicolor SF Symbol*

As we will see later, we can combine `Text` views with symbols to build the interface, but SwiftUI also includes a view called `Label` that was specifically designed to show a text along with an image. The structure includes the following initializers and modifiers to create these views.

`Label(String, systemImage: String)`

This initializer creates a label with the text specified by the first argument and the SF Symbol specified by the **systemImage** argument.

`Label(String, image: String)`

This initializer creates a label with the text specified by the first argument and the image specified by the **image** argument.

labelStyle(LabelStyle)

This modifier configures the label. The argument is a structure that conforms to the **LabelStyle** protocol, which defines type properties to tell the label what to include. The properties available are **automatic** (default), **iconOnly**, **titleAndIcon**, and **titleOnly**.

labelReservedIconWidth(CGFloat)

This modifier determines the width in points occupied by the icon.

labelIconToTitleSpacing(CGFloat)

This modifier determines the space in points between the icon and the label.

A **Label** view determines the text and the image to be shown, but we can use modifiers to specify the font and configure the label, as shown below.

Listing 2-49: Displaying a text with an SF Symbol

```
struct ContentView: View {
    var body: some View {
        Label("Hello", systemImage: "envelope.circle")
            .font(.largeTitle)
            .labelIconToTitleSpacing(20)
            .imageScale(.large)
    }
}
```

In this example, we implement the **font()** modifier to assign the label a **largeTitle** font, the **labelIconToTitleSpacing()** modifier to separate the icon and the text by 20 points, and the **imageScale()** modifier to make the symbol slightly larger than the text. The result is shown below.

Figure 2-57: *Label with an SF Symbol*

IMPORTANT

SF Symbols can be used to create controls, such as buttons and sliders, and they can also be animated. We will learn how to create and use controls in Chapter 3 and how to animate graphics in Chapter 8.

BASIC

Event Modifiers

In addition to the modifiers used to style and format views, SwiftUI also includes modifiers to respond to events. These events can be triggered by the user, such as when the user touches the screen, or by the system, such as when information is received from a network. For example, the following modifiers are used to perform tasks when a view appears or disappears from the screen.

onAppear(perform: Closure)

This modifier executes the closure specified by the **perform** argument when the view appears on the screen.

onDisappear(perform: Closure)

This modifier executes the closure specified by the **perform** argument when the view disappears from the screen.

These modifiers are applied like any other, but they are executed when the system detects the event to which they respond. For instance, in the following example we print a message on the console with the **onAppear()** modifier, but the text is not printed until the view appears on the screen.

Listing 2-50: Performing a task when the view appears

```
struct ContentView: View {
   let fontSize: CGFloat = 100

   var body: some View {
      Image(systemName: "envelope.circle")
         .font(Font.system(size: fontSize))
         .onAppear(perform: {
            print("Current font size: \(self.fontSize)")
         })
   }
}
```

IMPORTANT

In addition to the **onAppear()** and **onDisappear()** modifiers, SwiftUI includes other event modifiers, such as gesture modifiers to perform a task when a gesture is detected. We will see some practical examples of these modifiers in later chapters and study gesture modifiers in Chapter 9.

PRO

Custom Modifiers

Interfaces with single views, like those we have created so far, are the exception. User interfaces are created from the combination of multiple views. This means that more often than not we will find ourselves applying the same modifiers over and over again. In cases like this, we can avoid repetition by implementing custom modifiers. Custom modifiers encapsulate multiple modifiers in a single structure that we can apply later to the views with the **modifier()** modifier.

The structure that defines the list of modifiers to apply must conform to the **ViewModifier** protocol and implement a method called **body** that receives a parameter of type **Content**. The parameter represents the view we want to modify and, therefore, it is to this parameter that we apply the actual modifiers, as shown below.

Listing 2-51: Applying custom modifiers

```
struct MyModifiers: ViewModifier {
   func body(content: Content) -> some View {
      content
         .font(Font.system(size: 100).weight(.semibold))
         .foregroundStyle(Color.blue)
   }
}
struct ContentView: View {
   var body: some View {
      Image(systemName: "envelope.circle")
         .modifier(MyModifiers())
   }
}
```

In this example, we define a structure that conforms to the **ViewModifier** protocol and apply the **font()** and **foregroundStyle()** modifiers to the **content** parameter of the **body()** method. This defines a custom modifier called **MyModifiers** that we can then apply to the views in our interface. The result is the same as applying the modifiers directly to the views, but it allows us to apply the same modifiers to multiple views, making our code less repetitive.

Figure 2-58: *Custom modifiers applied to a view*

As any other structure, the **ViewModifier** structure can include properties, and those properties may get different values every time the modifier is applied. For example, we can include a property to store a **CGFloat** value, so every time the custom modifier is applied, we can select the size to be assigned to the font.

Listing 2-52: Customizing a custom modifier

```
struct MyModifiers: ViewModifier {
   var size: CGFloat

   func body(content: Content) -> some View {
      content
         .font(Font.system(size: size).weight(.semibold))
         .foregroundStyle(Color.blue)
   }
}
struct ContentView: View {
   var body: some View {
      Image(systemName: "envelope.circle")
         .modifier(MyModifiers(size: 50))
   }
}
```

BASIC

2.2 - Layout

The closure assigned to the **body** property must return only one view. This means that if we want our interface to include multiple views, we must be able to group them into a single view. The solution proposed by SwiftUI is to work with stacks.

BASIC

Stacks

Views can be arranged in three different ways: horizontally, vertically, or overlapping. SwiftUI defines the following views to create these stacks.

VStack(alignment: HorizontalAlignment, **spacing:** CGFloat?, **content:** Closure)

This view creates a vertical stack to arrange a group of views vertically. The **alignment** argument determines the horizontal alignment of the views. It is a structure with the type properties **center**, **leading**, and **trailing**. The **spacing** argument determines the space between the views, and the **content** argument is a closure that defines the list of views we want to show in the stack.

HStack(alignment: VerticalAlignment, **spacing:** CGFloat?, **content:** Closure)

This view creates a horizontal stack to arrange a group of views horizontally. The **alignment** argument determines the vertical alignment of the views. It is a structure with the type properties **bottom**, **center**, **firstTextBaseline**, **lastTextBaseline**, and **top**. The **spacing** argument determines the space between the views, and the **content** argument is a closure that defines the list of views we want to show in the stack.

ZStack(alignment: Alignment, **content:** Closure)

This view creates a stack that overlays a group of views. The **alignment** argument determines the horizontal and vertical alignment of the views. It is a structure with the type properties **bottom**, **bottomLeading**, **bottomTrailing**, **center**, **leading**, **top**, **topLeading**, **topTrailing**, and **trailing**. The **content** argument is a closure that defines the list of views we want to show in the stack.

Stacks are created with values by default. For instance, a **VStack** aligns its views to the center and with a standard space in between. If that's all we need, we just have to declare its content.

Listing 2-53: Creating a vertical stack of views

```
struct ContentView: View {
   var body: some View {
      VStack {
         Text("City")
         Text("New York")
      }
   }
}
```

The closure assigned to the **content** argument is a **Content** closure. **Content** closures are processed by a property wrapper called **@ContentBuilder** which job is to construct views from closures. This means that all we need to do to create the content of a stack is to list the views one after another, and the compiler takes care of creating the code to present them on the screen in that same order.

In Listing 2-53, we include two **Text** views inside a **VStack** view. The **Text** views take the size of their content and are displayed one on top of the other, and the **VStack** view takes the width of its largest child and the height from the sum of the heights of its children, as shown below.

Figure 2-59: *Vertical stack*

By default, the views inside a **VStack** are aligned to the center and separated by a standard spacing, but we can change this behavior using the **alignment** and **spacing** arguments. In the following example, we align the views to the left (**leading**) and set the spacing between them to 20 points.

Listing 2-54: Adding a space between the views

```
struct ContentView: View {
    var body: some View {
        VStack(alignment: .leading, spacing: 20) {
            Text("City")
            Text("New York")
        }
    }
}
```

The space is added only between the views, not on the sides, as shown below.

Figure 2-60: *Vertical stack aligned to the left with a space of 20 points in between*

The **HStack** view works in a similar way. The views are declared as before, one after another, and the compiler takes care of creating the code to display them side by side.

Listing 2-55: Creating a horizontal stack of views

```
struct ContentView: View {
    var body: some View {
        HStack {
            Image(systemName: "cloud")
                .font(.system(size: 80))
            Text("New York")
        }
    }
}
```

By default, the views in a horizontal stack are aligned to the center and positioned with a standard space in between.

Figure 2-61: *Horizontal stack*

An **HStack** view includes the same alignment and spacing arguments as a **VStack**, but the **alignment** argument specifies the vertical alignment. This is useful when the stack is composed of views with different heights, as in our example. By default, the views are aligned to the center, but we can change this by specifying a different alignment value, as shown below.

Listing 2-56: Aligning a horizontal stack of views

```
struct ContentView: View {
    var body: some View {
        HStack(alignment: .top) {
            Image(systemName: "cloud")
                .font(.system(size: 80))
            Text("New York")
        }
    }
}
```

Figure 2-62: *Horizontal stack aligned to the top*

Stacks can be combined and nested as required by the interface. For instance, we can incorporate a **VStack** inside the previous **HStack** to include more text next to the image.

Listing 2-57: Nesting stacks

```
struct ContentView: View {
    var body: some View {
        HStack {
            Image(systemName: "cloud")
                .font(.system(size: 80))
            VStack(alignment: .leading) {
                Text("City")
                    .foregroundStyle(.gray)
                Text("New York")
                    .font(.title)
            }
        }
    }
}
```

In this example, we define a **Vstack** view inside an **HStack** view. The **VStack** includes two **Text** views aligned to the left and with different styles. The result is shown below.

Figure 2-63: *Nested stacks*

The alignment options available for **VStack** and **HStack** views align the views in the perpendicular axis. A vertical stack can align the views horizontally, and a horizontal stack can align the views vertically. To align the views on the same axis, we must add a flexible space. SwiftUI includes the **Spacer** view for this purpose.

Spacer(minLength: CGFloat)

This initializer creates a **Spacer** view that generates a flexible space. The **minLength** argument determines the minimum size in points the space can take. If the argument is not declared, the minimum length is 0.

A **Spacer** view can be implemented any time we need to add a flexible space. It provides a more customizable way to align the views or extend them to the sides of its container. For instance, in the following example we add a flexible space between the image and the **VStack** of our view to move the views to the left and right side of their container.

Listing 2-58: Aligning the views with a flexible space

```
struct ContentView: View {
   var body: some View {
      HStack {
         Image(systemName: "cloud")
            .font(.system(size: 80))
         Spacer()
         VStack(alignment: .leading) {
            Text("City")
               .foregroundStyle(.gray)
            Text("New York")
               .font(.title)
         }
      }
   }
}
```

The system calculates the widths of the image and the stack, and then assigns the rest of the space available to the **Spacer** view in the middle.

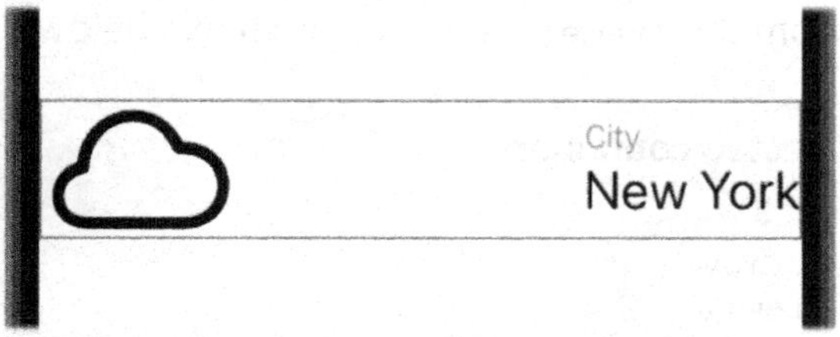

Figure 2-64: *Flexible space between views*

A **Spacer** view can be positioned anywhere on the list, not only between views. This is useful when we want the views to be at the top or the bottom of the screen. For instance, we can embed the **HStack** of previous examples in a **VStack** and add a **Spacer** at the bottom to move our views to the top of the screen.

Listing 2-59: Aligning the views to the left and the top

```
struct ContentView: View {
    var body: some View {
        VStack {
            HStack {
                Image(systemName: "cloud")
                    .font(.system(size: 80))
                VStack(alignment: .leading) {
                    Text("City")
                        .foregroundStyle(.gray)
                    Text("New York")
                        .font(.title)
                }
                Spacer()
            }
            Spacer()
        }
    }
}
```

In this example, we use two **Spacer** views, one at the end of the **HStack** to move the views to the left, and another at the end of the main **VStack** to move the **HStack** to the top. This **Spacer** view takes all the space available at the bottom, moving the rest of the views up.

Figure 2-65: *Views at the top of the screen*

Another way to align views inside a stack is by using the **alignment** argument of the **frame()** modifier. This is useful to align views inside other views. For example, if we have an **HStack** inside a **VStack**, by default, the **HStack** will be aligned to the center, but we can change this alignment from the **frame()** modifier, as shown below.

Listing 2-60: Aligning nested containers

```
struct ContentView: View {
    var body: some View {
        VStack {
            HStack {
                Image(systemName: "cloud")
                    .font(.system(size: 80))
                Text("New York")
            }
            .background(.gray)
        }
```

```
            .frame(minWidth: 0, maxWidth: .infinity, alignment: .leading)
    }
}
```

In this example, we give the **VStack** an infinite width to occupy all the space available and assign the **leading** value to the **alignment** argument to align the **HStack** view to the left. The result is shown below.

Figure 2-66: *Views aligned to the left*

In addition to vertical and horizontal stacks, SwiftUI also provides the **ZStack** view for overlaying views. The views appear on the screen on top of one another in the same order in which they are declared in the stack.

Listing 2-61: Creating a `ZStack`

```
struct ContentView: View {
    var body: some View {
        ZStack(alignment: .center) {
            Image(systemName: "cloud")
                .font(.system(size: 80))
            Text("New York")
                .font(.body.bold())
                .foregroundStyle(.gray)
        }
    }
}
```

Figure 2-67: *Views in a* ZStack

When views overlap, like those included in a **ZStack** view, the system determines the order in which they appear on the screen from the order in the code. The first view is drawn first, then the second view is drawn in front of it, and so on. The **View** protocol defines the following modifier to change this order.

zIndex(Double)

This modifier sets the order of the view in the Z axis (the axis perpendicular to the screen).

By default, all the views are assigned the index 0, which means they are all at the same level, but we can move a view to the back by assigning a negative Z index or to the front with a value greater than 0. When views have different indexes, they are drawn in the order determined by those values, starting from the view with the smallest index. In the following example, we include the same **Image** view and **Text** view used before, but because we set an index of -1 for the **Text** view, it is drawn in the back.

Listing 2-62: Setting the Z index of a view

```
struct ContentView: View {
   var body: some View {
      ZStack {
         Image(systemName: "cloud")
            .font(.system(size: 80))
         Text("New York")
            .padding(8)
            .background(Color.yellow)
            .zIndex(-1)
      }
   }
}
```

The **Image** view should be drawn first, and then the **Text** view should cover most of the image, but because we set an index of **-1** for the **Text** view, it is drawn in the back.

***Figure 2-68:** Custom Z index*

When we group views with a stack, we can apply style modifiers to all the views at the same time by assigning them to the stack instead of the individual views. For instance, if we want to assign the same color to the **Text** view and the **Image** view of the previous example, we can apply the **foregroundStyle()** modifier to the **ZStack** view.

Listing 2-63: Assigning modifiers to the stack and its content

```
struct ContentView: View {
   var body: some View {
      ZStack(alignment: .center) {
         Image(systemName: "cloud")
            .font(.system(size: 80))
         Text("New York")
            .font(.body.bold())
      }.foregroundStyle(Color.red)
   }
}
```

Figure 2-69: *Styles for the views applied to the container*

BASIC

Safe Area

The system defines a layout guide called *Safe Area* where we can place the content of our interface. This area is determined by the space remaining in the window after all the toolbars and special views are displayed by the system, including the island at the top of modern iPhones. Although it is recommended to build the interface inside this area, the **View** protocol provides the following modifier to ignore it.

ignoresSafeArea(SafeAreaRegions, **edges:** Edge**)**

This modifier expands the view outside the safe area. The first argument determines the parts of the safe area that are ignored. It is a structure with the type properties **all**, **container**, and **keyboard**. The **edges** argument is a value or a set of values that indicates the sides to be ignored. This is an enumeration with the values **all**, **bottom**, **leading**, **top**, and **trailing**.

In practice, there are two safe areas, one called **container** that determines the space available inside the window after all the navigation bars and toolbars are displayed, and another called **keyboard** that determines the remaining space after the virtual keyboard becomes visible.

Figure 2-70: *Safe areas*

For instance, if we want our interface to always extend to the edges of the screen, we can apply the **ignoresSafeArea()** modifier to the main view with the value **all**.

Listing 2-64: Ignoring the safe area

```
struct ContentView: View {
   var body: some View {
      VStack {
         HStack {
            Image(systemName: "cloud")
               .font(.system(size: 80))
            Text("New York")
            Spacer()
         }
         .background(.orange)
         Spacer()
      }.ignoresSafeArea(.all)
   }
}
```

In this example, we assign an orange background to the **HStack** view to clearly identify the area occupied by the view. The result is shown below.

Figure 2-71: *Views ignoring the safe area*

SwiftUI includes a modifier to expand the safe area. The modifier changes the safe area inset to include additional space.

> **safeAreaInset(edge:** Axis, **alignment:** Alignment, **spacing:** CGFloat?, **content:** Closure)

This modifier expands the safe area with a custom view. The **edge** argument determines the side we want to modify. It is specified with the values **leading** and **trailing**, provided by the **HorizontalEdge** enumeration, or the values **bottom** and **top**, provided by the **VerticalEdge** enumeration. The **alignment** argument determines the alignment of the views inside the area. It is specified with the type properties **center**, **leading**, and **trailing**, provided by the **HorizontalAlignment** structure, or the type properties **bottom**, **center**, **firstTextBaseline**, **lastTextBaseline**, and **top**, provided by the **VerticalAlignment** structure. The **spacing** argument determines the space between the views inside the area. And finally, the **content** argument is a closure that returns the views to show inside the area.

This modifier may be used to make sure that important views at the edge of the screen are always visible, or to create our own navigation bars, as shown below.

Listing 2-65: Expanding the safe area

```
struct ContentView: View {
    var body: some View {
        VStack {
            Spacer()
            HStack {
                Image(systemName: "cloud")
                    .font(.system(size: 80))
                VStack(alignment: .leading) {
                    Text("City")
                        .foregroundStyle(.gray)
                    Text("New York")
                        .font(.title)
                }
                Spacer()
            }
        }
        .safeAreaInset(edge: .bottom, content: {
            HStack {
                Spacer()
                Text("Important")
                    .padding()
                Spacer()
            }.background(.yellow)
        })
    }
}
```

In this example, we add an **HStack** view at the bottom of the safe area. This creates a yellow bar at the bottom of the screen with the text "Important", but because this view is part of the safe area, the rest of the content is shown on top.

Figure 2-72: *Views expanding the safe area*

PRO

Priorities

Stacks divide the space equally among the views, but we must decide what to do when there is not enough room to show them all. By default, the system assigns a fixed size to images and reduces the size of **Text** views to make them fit, as shown below.

Listing 2-66: Arranging the views with priorities by default

```
struct ContentView: View {
    var body: some View {
        HStack {
            Text("Manchester")
                .font(.title)
                .lineLimit(1)
            Image(systemName: "cloud")
                .font(.system(size: 80))
            Text("New York City")
                .font(.title)
                .lineLimit(1)
        }
    }
}
```

This example creates an **HStack** with three views: a text, an image, and another text. In a small iPhone in portrait mode, where there is no room to display them all, the system preserves the image's original size but compresses the **Text** views to make them fit in the remaining space.

Figure 2-73: *Priorities by default*

Because in our example we limited the **Text** views to a single line, the system truncates the text. If we want to display one of the texts in full, we must assign a higher priority to it. The **View** protocol defines the following modifiers for this purpose.

layoutPriority(Double**)**

This modifier sets the view's priority. A higher priority determines that the view will get as much space as possible. The value by default is 0.

fixedSize(horizontal: Bool, **vertical:** Bool**)**

This modifier fixes the view to its ideal horizontal or vertical size. If no arguments are specified, the size is fixed on both dimensions.

All the views have a priority of 0 by default. If we want the system to reserve more space for a view, we must declare its priority higher than 0, as in the following example.

Listing 2-67: Assigning a higher priority to a view

```
struct ContentView: View {
   var body: some View {
      HStack {
         Text("Manchester")
            .font(.title)
            .lineLimit(1)
         Image(systemName: "cloud")
            .font(.system(size: 80))
         Text("New York City")
            .font(.title)
            .lineLimit(1)
            .layoutPriority(1)
      }
   }
}
```

In this example, we assign a priority of 1 to the second **Text** view. Now the system calculates the space required by this view first and therefore the "New York City" text is shown in full.

Figure 2-74: *Custom priorities*

When we assign a higher priority to a view and there is no space to show them all, the system lays out the views with lower priority first, gives them the minimum possible size, and then assigns the remaining space to the view with the higher priority. So, if there is still no room to show the entire view, its content is clipped. If what we want is to force the view to take the size of its content no matter what, we must apply the **fixedSize()** modifier.

Listing 2-68: Defining a view with a fixed size

```
struct ContentView: View {
   var body: some View {
      HStack {
         Text("Manchester")
            .font(.title)
            .lineLimit(1)
            .fixedSize()
         Image(systemName: "cloud")
            .font(.system(size: 80))
         Text("New York City")
            .font(.title)
            .lineLimit(1)
            .layoutPriority(1)
      }
   }
}
```

This is the same code as before, but now we assign the **fixedSize()** modifier to the first **Text** view. In consequence, this view is going to adopt the size of its content and the "Manchester" text will always be shown in full, regardless of the priority of the rest of the views.

Figure 2-75: *View with a fixed size*

BASIC

Groups

Stack views create a structure of type **TupleView** to organize their content. This structure can manage up to 10 views and therefore that's the maximum number of views a stack can contain. Although it is not common to find this issue in a professional application, if necessary, we can avoid it by using **Group** views.

Group(content: Closure)

This initializer creates a **Group** view that contains the views defined by the closure assigned to the argument.

The purpose of **Group** views is to group views together. We can use them to split large lists of views into groups of 10 or less to avoid the issue mentioned above, but also for other purposes, such as applying styles to several views at the same time, as in the following example.

Listing 2-69: Arranging the views in groups

```
struct ContentView: View {
   var body: some View {
      VStack {
         Group {
            Text("This is the list of")
            Text("Cities")
         }.foregroundStyle(Color.gray)
         Group {
            Text("Manchester")
            Text("Viena")
         }.font(.largeTitle)
      }
   }
}
```

Each **Group** view defined in Listing 2-69 contains two **Text** views. To style these views, we apply modifiers to the **Group** views, not their content, so all the views within a group are affected by the same modifier.

Figure 2-76: *Modifiers applied to groups of views*

The **Group** view is also useful when we need to return one view or another depending on a condition. The closure assigned to the **body** property can return only one view, so the compiler can determine the data type of the view and process the value correctly. This means that if we try to use an **if else** statement to return different views depending on a condition, we will get an error. However, we can use a **Group** view to solve this issue. All we need to do is to place the conditional statement inside a **Group** view and return that view instead, as shown below.

Listing 2-70: Returning different views form the body property

```
struct ContentView: View {
   let valid = true

   var body: some View {
      Group {
         if valid {
            Image(systemName: "keyboard")
         } else {
            Text("The state is invalid")
         }
      }
   }
}
```

This code defines a Boolean constant to select the view. If the constant is **true**, we show an **Image** view with an SF Symbol, otherwise, we show a **Text** view. Therefore, the view displayed on the screen is selected at run time, depending on the value of the **valid** constant, but because we embedded the views in a **Group** view, the compiler can identify the value returned and therefore the code is functional. (We will learn how to make this selection dynamic in Chapter 3).

BASIC

Grids

We can embed one stack into another as many times as needed to achieve the design we are after, but SwiftUI defines an additional container view called **Grid** for this purpose. A **Grid** view can distribute static content in multiple rows and columns. The following is the view's initializer.

Grid(alignment: Alignment, **horizontalSpacing:** CGFloat, **verticalSpacing:** CGFloat, **content:** Closure)

This initializer creates a **Grid** view to define a grid-like layout. The **alignment** argument specifies the alignment of the content. It is a structure with the type properties **leading**, **center** (default), and **trailing**. The **horizontalSpacing** and **verticalSpacing** arguments define the space between cells. And the **content** argument provides the content for the grid.

The rows of the grid are defined by the **GridRow** structure.

GridRow(alignment: VerticalAlignment, **content:** Closure)

This initializer creates a row for a grid. The **alignment** argument specifies the vertical alignment of the content. It is a structure with the type properties **top**, **center**, **bottom**, **firstTextBaseline**, and **lastTextBaseline**. And the **content** argument provides the content for the row.

SwiftUI also includes the following modifiers to configure the rows.

gridCellColumns(Int)

This modifier specifies the number of columns the cell should occupy.

gridColumnAlignment(HorizontalAlignment)

This modifier overrides the horizontal alignment for a row. The argument is a structure with the type properties **leading**, **center**, and **trailing**.

gridCellUnsizedAxes(Axis)

This modifier returns a row that doesn't ask the grid for additional space in the axis specified by the argument. The argument is a structure with the type properties **horizontal** and **vertical**.

By default, the content of a grid is aligned to the center with a standard space between cells. If that's what we want, all we need to do is to declare the grid's content. The rows are defined by **GridRow** structures and the columns are determined by the views inside these structures, as shown below.

Listing 2-71: Defining a grid layout

```
struct ContentView: View {
   var body: some View {
      Grid {
         GridRow {
            Image(systemName: "message")
               .frame(width: 100, height: 100)
            Image(systemName: "mic")
               .frame(width: 100, height: 100)
         }.background(.red)
```

```
        GridRow {
            Image(systemName: "phone")
                .frame(width: 100, height: 100)
            Image(systemName: "envelope")
                .frame(width: 100, height: 100)
        }.background(.blue)
    }.font(.largeTitle)
  }
}
```

This example creates a grid with two rows and two columns. The rows are defined by two **GridRow** structures and the columns by two **Image** views per row displaying SF Symbols.

Figure 2-77: *Grid*

If we specify a different number of columns per row, the grid will generate empty columns to fill the gap. However, we can also use the **gridCellColumns()** modifier to make a row occupy multiple columns, as in the following example.

Listing 2-72: Defining a multicolumn cell

```
struct ContentView: View {
   var body: some View {
      Grid(verticalSpacing: 5) {
         GridRow {
            Text("Send us a Message")
         }
         .gridCellColumns(2)
         .padding(12)
         .background(.orange)
         GridRow {
            Image(systemName: "phone")
               .frame(width: 100, height: 100)
            Image(systemName: "envelope")
               .frame(width: 100, height: 100)
         }.background(.blue)
      }.font(.title2)
   }
}
```

In this example, the first row includes only one cell defined by a **Text** view, but because we apply the **gridCellColumns()** modifier with the value 2, the view occupies two columns.

Figure 2-78: *Multicolumn cell*

If what we want is for a cell to occupy two or more rows, we need to embed a grid within another grid, as shown below.

Listing 2-73: Embedding a grid within another grid

```
struct ContentView: View {
   var body: some View {
      Grid {
         GridRow {
            Image(systemName: "phone")
               .frame(width: 100, height: 100)
               .background(.blue)
            Grid(alignment: .leading) {
               GridRow {
                  Text("My Name")
               }
               GridRow {
                  Text("My Number")
               }
            }
         }
      }.font(.title2)
   }
}
```

In this example, the grid contains two columns, the one on the left with an image and the one on the right with another grid, which in turn contains two rows. Therefore, the two cells on the right share the same row with the cell on the left.

Figure 2-79: *Nested grids*

PRO

Generic Views

Views are of different data types, so if we want to pass different views around from a property or a method, we must wrap them in container views, such as the **Group** view introduced before. Although this is allowed, SwiftUI includes a structure called **AnyView** that we can use for that purpose.

AnyView(View)

This initializer creates an **AnyView** view to contain the views specified by the argument. The argument can be a single view or a hierarchy of views.

In the following example, we define a method inside the **ContentView** structure to produce the views for the interface. In this method, we check a condition and return an **AnyView** view with different content for each case.

Listing 2-74: Wrapping views in an AnyView view

```
struct ContentView: View {
   var body: some View {
      getView()
   }
   func getView() -> AnyView {
      let valid = true
      var myView: AnyView!

      if valid {
         myView = AnyView(Image(systemName: "keyboard"))
      } else {
         myView = AnyView(Text("The state is invalid"))
      }
      return myView
   }
}
```

The **getView()** method in this example returns an **AnyView** view depending on the value of the **valid** property. If the value is **true**, we create an **Image** view; otherwise, we create a **Text** view. In both cases, the views are wrapped in an **AnyView** view, so we always return the same type of view. When the content of the **body** property is processed, the method is called, and the view returned by the method is displayed on the screen.

The **AnyView** view is a wrapper we can use to pass different views around. The problem is that the views lose their identity. The system considers the views wrapped in an **AnyView** view to be the same, which affects performance. A better alternative is to process the views before they are returned by the method with the **@ContentBuilder** property wrapper. We have introduced this property wrapper before. It is used to construct the views returned by **Content** closures, such as the closures assigned to the **body** property, but we can also use it with our custom methods to be able to return different views without having to use a wrapper view, as in the following example.

Listing 2-75: Constructing views with the `@ContentBuilder` property wrapper

```
struct ContentView: View {
    var body: some View {
        getView()
    }
    @ContentBuilder
    func getView() -> some View {
        let valid = false

        if valid {
            Image(systemName: "keyboard")
        } else {
            Text("The state is invalid")
        }
    }
}
```

The code in Listing 2-75 applies the **@ContentBuilder** property wrapper to the **getView()** method, so now we can use this method as a **Content** closure and produce any type of view we want without using a wrapper.

We can also use the **@ContentBuilder** property wrapper to create reusable views. For example, if we need to present the same simple view in multiple parts of our code, we can define a computed property that returns that view, as shown below.

Listing 2-76: Constructing reusable views with the `@ContentBuilder` property wrapper

```
struct ContentView: View {
    var body: some View {
        myView
    }
    @ContentBuilder
    var myView: some View {
        Image(systemName: "envelope")
            .font(.system(size: 100))
    }
}
```

The code in Listing 2-76 defines a computed property called **myView** that returns an **Image** view. We can now use and display this view anywhere in our code by simply referencing the property name, as we did in the body of **ContentView**.

When the views returned by a method are dynamically selected, as we did in previous examples, we may not always be able to provide one. For cases like this, SwiftUI includes the **EmptyView** view.

EmptyView()

This initializer creates an **EmptyView** view with no content and no size.

The **EmptyView** view works like the rest, but it doesn't provide any content and it has no size, so it doesn't affect the interface. The following example creates an empty view when a condition is not met.

Listing 2-77: Returning an empty view

```
struct ContentView: View {
   var body: some View {
      VStack {
         Text("View Title")
         getView()
      }
   }
   @ContentBuilder
   func getView() -> some View {
      let valid = false

      if valid {
         Image(systemName: "keyboard")
      } else {
         EmptyView()
      }
   }
}
```

BASIC

Custom Views

So far, we have used views provided by the framework, but we can also define our own views. These custom views can contain other views, creating a hierarchy of nested views that helps us organize the interface and structure our app. We have already seen how to create these views. The **ContentView** structure defined in the template for the **App** project is a custom view that represents the app's initial screen, but we can define more. To create a custom view, we define a structure that conforms to the **View** protocol and implements the **body** property. For example, we can use a custom view to organize the content of a **VStack**.

Listing 2-78: Additional views

```
struct ContentView: View {
   var body: some View {
      VStack {
         MyCustomView()
      }
   }
}
struct MyCustomView: View {
   var body: some View {
      Group {
         Text("Manchester")
         Text("Viena")
      }.font(.largeTitle)
   }
}
```

After a custom view is defined, we can use it from other views. In this case, we define a view called **`MyCustomView`** that contains a **`Group`** view with two **`Text`** views, and then use it as the content of a **`VStack`**. When the system initializes the **`ContentView`** structure, it creates a **`VStack`**, then creates an instance of **`MyCustomView`**, and finally adds the **`Group`** view and its content to the stack. The result is the same as in previous examples, but the code is now better organized.

Figure 2-80: *Custom view*

> **IMPORTANT**
>
> If your custom view represents an entire screen, you should save it in a separate file, as explained in the **SwiftUI Files** section in Chapter 1. We will learn more about working with custom views and how to split the interface into multiple screens in further chapters.

BASIC

2.3 - Environment

As explained before, we can test different configurations from the Canvas. Using the Device Settings button at the bottom of the Canvas, we can change the orientation, font size or display mode (see Chapter 1, Figure 1-17, number 8), but we can also modify these settings directly in code by working with the environment. The environment is a data structure owned by the application that stores values shared across the app and its views. It acts as a centralized storage that any view can access. SwiftUI provides the **`EnvironmentValues`** structure to store these values, and the **`@Environment`** property wrapper to read them from the environment.

```
@Environment(KeyPath)
```

This property wrapper creates a binding with an environment property or an object stored in the environment. The argument is the key path of the property we want to read or a reference to the data type of the object we want to access.

The **`EnvironmentValues`** structure includes many properties to store the configuration of the system, the app and the views. The following are the most frequently used.

colorScheme

This property sets or returns the interface appearance. It is an enumeration of type **ColorScheme** with the values **light** and **dark**.

appearsActive

This property returns a Boolean value that indicates whether the app is active on the screen or another app has become active.

dynamicTypeSize

This property sets or returns the size for dynamic content. It is an enumeration with the values **large**, **medium**, **small**, **xLarge**, **xSmall**, **xxLarge**, and **xxxLarge**.

font

This property sets or returns the font by default.

accessibilityEnabled

This property sets or returns a Boolean value that determines whether any accessibility service has been enabled on the device.

calendar

This property sets or returns the calendar used by the views to process dates. It is a value of type **Calendar**.

locale

This property sets or returns the locale used by the views to process local data, such as language and currency. It is a value of type **Locale**.

timeZone

This property sets or returns the time zone used by the views to calculate dates and times. It is a value of type **TimeZone**.

To read these values, we need to create a property using the **@Environment** property wrapper and specify the property's key path. For instance, in the following example, we read the **colorScheme** property to get the current color scheme (appearance).

Listing 2-79: Responding to updates in the states of the environment

```
struct ContentView: View {
   @Environment(\.colorScheme) var mode

   var body: some View {
      Image(systemName: "trash")
         .font(Font.system(size: 100))
         .foregroundStyle(mode == .dark ? Color.yellow : Color.blue)
         .symbolVariant(mode == .dark ? .fill : .circle)
   }
}
```

In this example, we define a property called **mode** to read the environment's **colorScheme** property, and then assign different values to the modifiers of a **Text** view depending on the current appearance (**dark** or **light**). The **@Environment** property wrapper creates a binding between the **mode** property and the **colorScheme** property in the environment, so when the user changes the appearance from Settings, the value of the **colorScheme** property in the environment changes, this changes the value of the **mode** property in our view, and the view is updated according to the new state. The result is shown below.

Figure 2-81: *States in Light and Dark appearances*

Do It Yourself

Create a new App project. Update the **ContentView** structure with the code in Listing 2-79. You should see the blue trash can (Figure 2-81, left). Press the Device Settings button at the bottom of the canvas and activate the Dark appearance option in the Color Scheme section (Chapter 1, Figure 1-17, number 8). You should see the yellow trash can with a black background (Figure 2-81, right).

The values and objects stored in the environment can be modified or more values can be added. The following are the modifiers provided by SwiftUI for this purpose.

environment(KeyPath, Value)

This modifier sets a new value for a property in the environment. The first argument is a key path to the property we want to modify, and the second argument is the value we want to assign to that property.

environment(Object)

This modifier assigns an object to the environment. The argument is a reference to the object we want to share with the views.

Changing system values is useful when we need to pass values around, as we will see later, or when working with previews. For example, we can apply the **environment()** modifier to a view to change the color scheme for the preview, as shown below.

Listing 2-80: Activating dark mode in the preview from code

```
struct ContentView: View {
   var body: some View {
      Text("Hello World")
         .foregroundStyle(Color("MyColor"))
   }
}
#Preview {
   ContentView()
      .environment(\.colorScheme, .dark)
}
```

In this example, we assign a custom color called MyColor to the `Text` view, and then set the appearance for the preview to dark. The example assumes that we have added a **Color Set** to the Asset Catalog called MyColor and assigned different colors to the Any and Dark appearances, as we did before (see Figure 2-28). The `environment()` modifier assigns the value `dark` to the environment's `colorScheme` property, changing the view's appearance to dark, so the preview displays the text in the color we have selected for that appearance.

Do It Yourself

Create a Color Set in the Asset Catalog with the name MyColor and assign different colors for the Any and Dark appearances, as we did in the example in Figure 2-28. Update the **ContentView.swift** file with the code in Listing 2-80. On the canvas, you should see the text in the color selected for the dark appearance. Remove the `environment()` modifier. Now, you should see the text in the color selected for Any.

In addition to the values defined by the system, we can store our own. One way to do it is to create an extension for the `EnvironmentValues` structure and use it to add new properties. To simplify the creation of these properties, SwiftUI includes the following macro.

`@Entry`

This macro produces the code necessary to create properties for the environment and similar systems used to share information between the operating system, the app, and the views.

In the following example, we create an environment property to store a string, then read its value from the view and show it on the screen.

Listing 2-81: Adding custom properties to the environment

```
extension EnvironmentValues {
   @Entry var myValue: String = "Default value"
}
struct ContentView: View {
   @Environment(\.myValue) var value

   var body: some View {
      Text(value)
         .font(Font.system(size: 20))
   }
}
#Preview {
   ContentView()
}
```

IMPORTANT

Besides reading and storing properties, the environment can be used to access the user's data and respond to changes in the state of the app. We will learn how to work with this feature in the following chapter.

Chapter 3
Declarative User Interface

BASIC

3.1 - States

In the previous chapter, we introduced the main feature of SwiftUI, its declarative syntax. With SwiftUI, we can declare the views as we want them to appear on the screen and leave it to the system to create the code necessary to show them. However, declarative syntax is not just about organizing the views, but also about how they are updated when the state of the app changes. For example, we can have an interface like the one in Figure 3-1 below, with a `Text` view that displays a title, an input field where the user can type a new title, and a button to replace the old title with the new one. The `Text` view with the original title represents the initial state of our interface. The state is updated with each character the user types in the input field (Figure 3-1, left), and when the button is pressed, the interface enters a new state in which the title inserted by the user has replaced the original title (Figure 3-1, right).

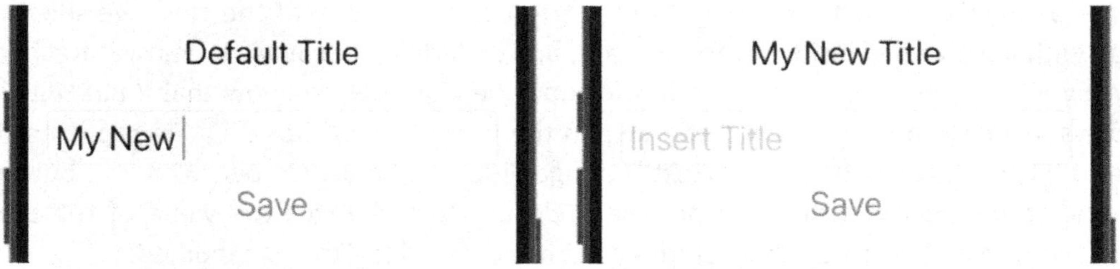

Figure 3-1: *User Interface at different states*

The possible states the interface can go through are determined by the information stored by the app. For example, the characters entered by the user in an input field are values stored by the app. Each time these values change, the app enters a new state, and the interface is updated to reflect it. Establishing this dependency between the app's data and the interface traditionally required a significant amount of code, but SwiftUI keeps it simple by using macros and property wrappers.

BASIC

@State

Macros and property wrappers allow us to define properties that generate code for us. SwiftUI relies heavily on these tools to store values and report changes to the views. To store the state of a single view, SwiftUI defines the **@State** macro. This macro generates all the code needed to store a value and notify the system when that value changes, so views are automatically updated to reflect the change on screen.

The **@State** macro is designed to store the state of a single view. Therefore, properties of this type should be declared as part of the view structure and marked **private**, so access is restricted to the structure in which they are declared, as shown in the following example.

Listing 3-1: Defining a state

```
struct ContentView: View {
   @State private var title: String = "Default Title"

   var body: some View {
      VStack {
         Text(title)
            .padding(10)
         Button(action: {
            title = "My New Title"
         }, label: {
            Text("Change Title")
         })
         Spacer()
      }.padding()
   }
}
```

The code in Listing 3-1 declares a **@State** property called **title** of type **String**. The property is initialized with the value "Default Title". In the body of the view, we show this value with a **Text** view inside a vertical stack, and include a **Button** view below it to change it. We will study **Button** views later, but for now we just need to know that a **Button** view displays a label and performs an action when the user clicks or taps on it. To represent the label, we use a **Text** view with the text "Change Title" so the user knows what the button is for, and to define the action, we provide a closure that changes the value of the **title** property to "My New Title" so when the button is pressed the title is modified.

The **title** property created with the **@State** macro is used in two places, first in the **Text** view to show the current value to the user, and then in the action for the **Button** view to modify its value. In consequence, when the button is pressed, the value of the **title** property changes, the code generated by the **@State** macro notifies the system that the state of the app has changed, and the content of the **body** property is automatically refreshed to display the new value on the screen.

Figure 3-2: *Initial state (left) and state after the button is pressed (right)*

Do It Yourself

Create a new App project. Update the **ContentView** structure with the code in Listing 3-1. Make sure that Live Preview is activated on the canvas (Chapter 1, Figure 1-17, number 1). Press the Change Title button to assign the string to the **Text** view. You should see something similar to Figure 3-2, right.

This entire process is automatic. We do not have to assign the new value to the **Text** view or notify the view that a new value is available. All of this is handled by the code generated by the **@State** macro. And we can include as many **@State** properties as needed. For instance, the following example adds a Boolean **@State** property to assign a different value to the **title** property each time the button is pressed.

Listing 3-2: Defining multiple states

```
struct ContentView: View {
    @State private var title: String = "Valid"
    @State private var isValid: Bool = true

    var body: some View {
        VStack {
            Text(title)
                .padding(10)
            Button(action: {
                isValid.toggle()
                title = isValid ? "Valid" : "Invalid"
            }, label: { Text("Change Validation") })
            Spacer()
        }.padding()
    }
}
```

The **isValid** property stores a Boolean value that determines the current validation state, allowing us to display the corresponding text on the screen. The string assigned to the **title** property is selected using a ternary operator. Using a ternary operator to set the state of a view is the recommended practice because it allows the system to determine all possible states the view can have and produce smooth transitions from one state to another. If the value of the **isValid** property is **true**, we assign the word "Valid" to the **title** property; otherwise, the text assigned to the property is "Invalid". Each time the button is pressed, the value of the **isValid** property changes, causing the view to display different text on the screen.

IMPORTANT

There are two states in the example of Listing 3-2, and both change at the same time, but the system takes into consideration these situations and makes sure that the interface is updated only when necessary.

A **@State** property creates a dependency between itself and the view and therefore the view is updated every time its value changes. It is said that the view is *bound* to the property. The binding we have used so far is unidirectional. If the property is modified, the view is updated. But there are views which values are modified by the user and therefore they must be able to store values back into the property without the code's intervention. For this purpose, SwiftUI allows us to define a bidirectional binding. Bidirectional bindings are declared by prefixing the name of the property with the **$** sign.

The views that usually require bidirectional binding are control views, such as those that create switches the user can turn on and off, or input fields to insert text. The following example implements a **TextField** view to illustrate this feature. A **TextField** view creates an input field. The values required by its initializer are a string with the text we want to show as placeholder and the binding property we are going to use to store the value inserted by the user. (We will learn more about **TextField** views and other control views later.)

Listing 3-3: Defining bidirectional binding

```
struct ContentView: View {
   @State private var title: String = "Default Title"
   @State private var titleInput: String = ""

   var body: some View {
      VStack {
         Text(title)
            .padding(10)
         TextField("Insert Title", text: $titleInput)
            .textFieldStyle(.roundedBorder)
         Button(action: {
            title = titleInput
            titleInput = ""
         }, label: { Text("Change Title") })
         Spacer()
      }.padding()
   }
}
```

This example reproduces the interface introduced in Figure 3-1. To process user input, we include two **@State** properties: one called **title** to store the string displayed on the screen, and another called **titleInput** to store the text entered by the user. The interface includes a **Text** view to show the value of the **title** property, a **TextField** view to let the user enter text, and a button to assign the text entered by the user to the **title** property. Note that the **TextField** view is initialized with the placeholder "Insert Title" and the **titleInput** property, but this property was declared as binding using the **$** symbol (**$titleInput**). This creates a permanent connection between the **TextField** view and the property, so each time the user types or removes a character in the input field, the new value is automatically assigned to the property.

Do It Yourself

Update the **ContentView** structure with the code in Listing 3-3. Run the application on the canvas or an iPhone simulator. Click on the text field and enter some text. Press the Change Title button. You should see your text appear on the screen, as shown in Figure 3-1.

IMPORTANT

The simulators on the Device Hub can receive input from either the computer's physical keyboard or the virtual keyboard. When a physical keyboard is used, the virtual keyboard is hidden. To display it again, open the Device menu, choose Keyboard, and select Toggle Software Keyboard.

BASIC

@Binding

The **@State** properties introduced in the previous section belong to the structure in which they are declared and should be accessible only from the code within that structure, which is why we declare them as **private**. However, as we saw in Chapter 2, when our views grow significantly, it is advisable to split them into independent structures (see Listing 2-78). The challenge with organizing the code this way is that the additional views lose access to the **@State** properties, so we can no longer read or modify their values. The solution is to create a bidirectional connection between the **@State** properties in one view and the code in another. For this purpose, SwiftUI provides the **Binding** structure and the **@Binding** property wrapper.

The following view is the same we defined in the previous example, but this time we move the **Text** and **TextField** views to a separate view called **HeaderView**. This additional view contains two **@Binding** properties to access the **@State** properties in the **ContentView** structure, so we always work with the same states.

Listing 3-4: Using `@Binding` properties

```
struct ContentView: View {
   @State private var title: String = "Default Title"
   @State private var titleInput: String = ""

   var body: some View {
      VStack {
         HeaderView(title: title, titleInput: $titleInput)
         Button(action: {
            title = titleInput
            titleInput = ""
         }, label: { Text("Change Title") })
         Spacer()
      }.padding()
```

```
    }
}
struct HeaderView: View {
    var title: String
    @Binding var titleInput: String

    var body: some View {
        VStack {
            Text(title)
                .padding(10)
            TextField("Insert Title", text: $titleInput)
                .textFieldStyle(.roundedBorder)
        }
    }
}
```

A **@Binding** property always receives its value from a **@State** property, so we don't have to assign a default value to it, but the connection created between them is bidirectional, so we always have to remember to prefix the **@State** properties with the **$** sign to connect them with the **@Binding** properties, as we did in this example (**HeaderView(title: title, titleInput: $titleInput)**).

Because of the bidirectional binding established between the **@Binding** property and the **@State** property, the value entered by the user is stored in one place, and each time the button is pressed, the changes are recognized by the system, the **body** property of the **HeaderView** structure is processed again, and the new value is displayed on the screen.

Do It Yourself

Update the **ContentView.swift** file with the code in Listing 3-4. Run the application on the canvas or an iPhone simulator. Insert a text in the text field, and press the Change Title button. Everything should work as before.

PRO

Binding Structures

Property wrappers are defined as structures and therefore they contain their own properties. SwiftUI allows access to the underlying structure of a property wrapper by prefixing the property's name with an underscore (e.g., **_title**). Once we gain access to the structure, we can work with its properties. The structure that defines the **@Binding** property wrapper is called **Binding**. This is a generic structure and therefore it can process values of any type. The following are the properties defined by this structure to store the state values.

wrappedValue

This property returns the value managed by the **@Binding** property.

projectedValue

This property returns a structure of type **Binding** that creates the bidirectional binding with the view.

The **wrappedValue** property stores the value assigned to the **@Binding** property, and the **projectedValue** property stores an additional **Binding** structure that creates the bidirectional binding needed to write a value back to the property. This means that from these properties, we can directly access and work with the value stored in the **@Binding** property. For instance, the following example implements a separate view again to manage the title and the input field, as we did in Listing 3-4, but this time we access and modify the values from the underlying **Binding** structure.

Listing 3-5: Accessing the values of a `Binding` structure

```
struct ContentView: View {
   @State private var title: String = "Default Title"
   @State private var titleInput: String = ""

   var body: some View {
      VStack {
         HeaderView(title: $title, titleInput: $titleInput)
         Button(action: {
            title = titleInput
            titleInput = ""
         }, label: { Text("Change Title") })
         Spacer()
      }.padding()
   }
}
struct HeaderView: View {
   @Binding var title: String
   @Binding var titleInput: String
   let counter: Int

   init(title: Binding<String>, titleInput: Binding<String>) {
      _title = title
      _titleInput = titleInput

      let sentence = _title.wrappedValue
      counter = sentence.count
   }
   var body: some View {
      VStack {
         Text("\(title) (\(counter))")
            .padding(10)
         TextField("Insert Title", text: _titleInput.projectedValue)
            .textFieldStyle(.roundedBorder)
      }
   }
}
```

In the **HeaderView** view of Listing 3-5, we define a property called **counter** and initialize it with the number of characters in the string returned by the **wrappedValue** property. Because the **@Binding** property doesn't have an initial value, we must also initialize it with the value received from the **ContentView** view (**_title = title**). Note that the value received by the **HeaderView** structure is a **Binding** structure that can manage values of type **String**, so the data type for the argument must be declared as **Binding<String>**.

In the view, we display the values of the properties with a **Text** view as before, but we also show how to update the **Binding** structure directly using the **projectedValue** property (this is the same as prefixing the property with the $ character). The title now shows the text inserted by the user along with the number of characters in that string, as shown below.

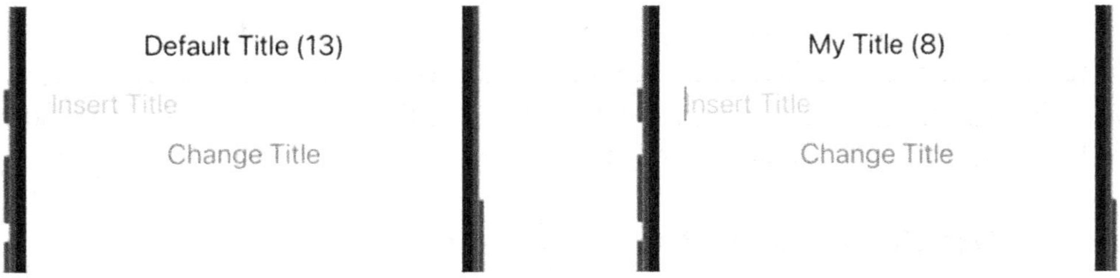

Figure 3-3: *Title defined with the values of the* `Binding` *structure*

The **`@Binding`** properties of the **`HeaderView`** view are connected to the **`@State`** properties of the **`ContentView`** view and therefore receive their values, but there are times when we need to provide the values ourselves. In cases like that, we can create the **`Binding`** structure ourselves with the following initializer.

`Binding(get:` `Closure`, **`set:`** `Closure)`

This initializer creates a **`Binding`** structure. The **get** argument is a closure that returns the current value, and the **set** argument is a closure that receives a new value for storage or processing.

There are many circumstances in which we may need a **`Binding`** value. For instance, if we want to create a preview of the **`HeaderView`**, we must provide values for the **`title`** and **`titleInput`** properties. The following example illustrates how to create new **`Binding`** structures to provide these values and how to define the preview for this view.

Listing 3-6: Creating a `Binding` structure

```
#Preview("Header") {
   let constantTitle = Binding<String>(
      get: { return "My Preview Title"},
      set: { value in
         print(value)
      })
   let constantInput = Binding<String>(
      get: { return ""},
      set: { value in
         print(value)
      })
   return HeaderView(title: constantTitle, titleInput: constantInput)
}
```

The initializer for the **`Binding`** structure includes a getter and a setter. The getter returns the current value and the setter receives the values assigned to the structure. In this example, we always return a string, and since we are not assigning new values to the structure, we just print the value on the console. The instances are assigned to the constants **`constantTitle`** and **`constantInput`** and then sent to the **`HeaderView`** structure, so the view has the values to show on the canvas.

There is not much use for the **Binding** structure of this example other than providing the values required by the **HeaderView** structure. In cases like this, we can simplify the code with the **constant()** method. This type method creates and returns a **Binding** structure with an immutable value, so we don't have to create the structures ourselves, as shown below.

Listing 3-7: Creating a `Binding` structure with an immutable value

```
#Preview("Header") {
   HeaderView(title: .constant("My Preview Title"), titleInput:
.constant(""))
}
```

Although we can create **Binding** properties or use the **constant()** method to provide the **Binding** values for a preview, sometimes it is better to create new state properties. For cases like this, SwiftUI includes the following macro.

@Previewable

This macro makes state properties available for previews.

The following example shows how to create state properties for a preview. The process is the same as before, but we must prefixed the property with the **@Previewable** macro.

Listing 3-8: Defining a state property for a preview

```
#Preview("Header") {
   @Previewable @State var title: String = "Default Title"
   @Previewable @State var titleInput: String = ""

   HeaderView(title: $title, titleInput: $titleInput)
}
```

BASIC

3.2 - Control Views

Controls are visual elements that users interact with to change the state of the interface, select options, and insert, modify, or delete information. We have already implemented some of these views, such as the **Button** and **TextField** views, but to define a useful interface, we need to learn more about these views and the rest of the controls provided by SwiftUI.

Button View

As we have already seen, the **`Button`** view creates a simple control that performs an action when clicked or tapped. The following are some of the structure's initializers.

`Button(action:` `Closure,` **`label:`** `Closure)`

This initializer creates a **`Button`** view. The **action** argument is a closure with the code to be executed when the button is pressed, and the **label** argument is a closure that returns the views used to create the label.

`Button(``String,` **`role:`** `ButtonRole?,` **`action:`** `Closure)`

This initializer creates a **`Button`** view with a string as the label. The first argument defines the button's label. The **role** argument is an optional structure with type properties to describe the purpose of the button. The properties available are **`cancel`**, **`destructive`**, **`close`** and **`confirm`**. And the **action** argument is a closure with the code to be executed when the button is pressed.

`Button(``String,` **`systemImage:`** `String,` **`action:`** `Closure)`

This initializer creates a **`Button`** view with a string and an SF Symbol as the label. The first argument defines the button's label, the **systemImage** argument specifies the SF Symbol used for the label, and the **action** argument is a closure that contains the code to be executed when the button is pressed.

We have already implemented the first initializer to create our buttons, but if we want to use only a string for the label, we can simplify the code by using the second initializer and a trailing closure for the action, as shown below.

Listing 3-9: Implementing `Button` views

```
struct ContentView: View {
   @State private var colorActive: Bool = false

   var body: some View {
      VStack(spacing: 10) {
         Text("Default Title")
            .padding()
            .background(colorActive ? Color.green : Color.clear)
         Button("Change Color") {
            colorActive.toggle()
         }
         Spacer()
      }.padding()
   }
}
```

This example includes a **`Text`** view and a **`Button`** view in a **`VStack`**. The **`Text`** view displays always the same string with a background color defined by the **`colorActive`** property. If the value of this property is **true**, we assign the **green** color to the background, otherwise the color assigned is **clear** (transparent). When the button is pressed, we toggle the value of this property, the **body** property is evaluated again, and the background of the text changes to the next color.

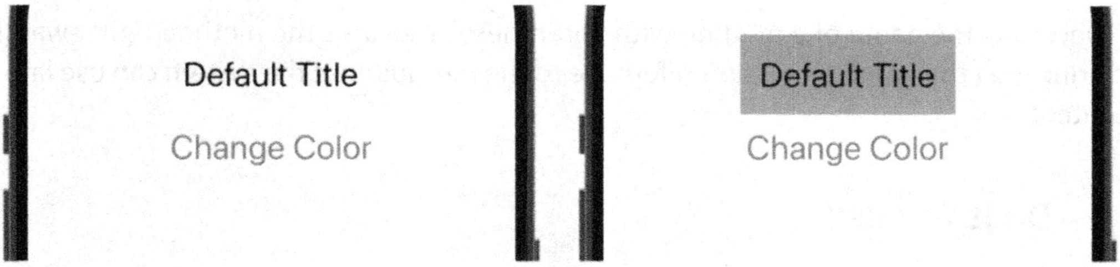

Figure 3-4: *Button view*

Do It Yourself

Update the **ContentView** structure with the code in Listing 3-9. Run the application on the Canvas or an iPhone simulator. Press the Change Color button. You should see the background color for the text change every time the button is pressed (Figure 3-4, right).

If we want to separate the views from the actions performed by the controls, we can move the statements to a method. For instance, we can add a method to the **ContentView** structure to toggle the value of the **colorActive** property and then call this method from the button. The application works the same way, but the code is better organized.

Listing 3-10: Using functions to perform the action for the button

```
struct ContentView: View {
   @State private var colorActive: Bool = false

   var body: some View {
      VStack(spacing: 10) {
         Text("Default Title")
            .padding()
            .background(colorActive ? Color.green : Color.clear)
         Button("Change Color") {
            changeColor()
         }
         Spacer()
      }.padding()
   }
   func changeColor() {
      colorActive.toggle()
   }
}
```

If the only action performed by the button is to call a method, we can simplify the definition of the view by declaring the **action** argument and specifying the name of the method as the action to perform, as shown below.

Listing 3-11: Referencing a method

```
Button("Change Color", action: changeColor)
```

Declaring the name of a method with parentheses executes the method right away, but declaring only the name provides a reference to the method that the system can use later to execute it.

Do It Yourself

Update the **ContentView** structure with the code in Listing 3-10. The application should work the same as before. Replace the **Button** view with the one in Listing 3-11. Press the button to confirm the action is performed.

In previous examples, we used a ternary operator to select the value for the **background()** modifier depending on the value of the **colorActive** property. This is the recommended practice, so SwiftUI can identify the views and effectively manage the transition between one state to another, but we can also use **if else** statements to respond to changes. This is useful when we need to show or hide a view when an action is performed, as in the following example.

Listing 3-12: Adding and removing views from the interface

```
struct ContentView: View {
    @State private var showInfo = false

    var body: some View {
        VStack(spacing: 10) {
            Button("Show Information") {
                showInfo.toggle()
            }.padding()
            if showInfo {
                Text("This is the information")
            }
            Spacer()
        }
    }
}
```

The button in this example toggles the value of a **@State** property called **showInfo**. Below the button, we check the current value of the property. If the value is **true**, we show a **Text** view, otherwise, we do nothing. Therefore, when the button is pressed, the value of the **showInfo** property changes, the content of the **body** property is drawn again, and the **Text** view appears or disappears, depending on the current value of the property.

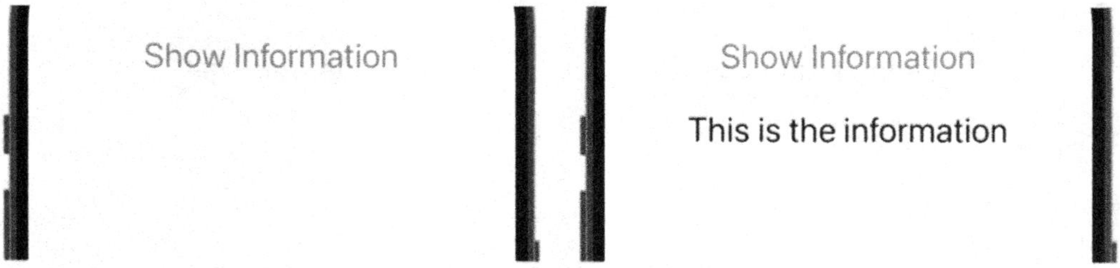

Figure 3-5: *Dynamic interface*

The **if else** statements can also be used to select whether or not to perform the action for the button, but SwiftUI provides the following modifier to disable the button altogether if that is what we are looking for.

disabled(Bool)

This modifier determines whether the control responds to the user interaction or not.

The following example applies this modifier to disable the button after it is pressed, so the user can perform the action only once.

Listing 3-13: Disabling a button

```
struct ContentView: View {
   @State private var color = Color.clear
   @State private var buttonDisabled = false

   var body: some View {
      VStack(spacing: 10) {
         Text("Default Title")
            .padding()
            .background(color)
         Button("Change Color") {
            color = Color.green
            buttonDisabled = true
         }
        .disabled(buttonDisabled)
         Spacer()
      }.padding()
   }
}
```

This view includes two **@State** properties, one to keep track of the color, and another to indicate whether the button is enabled or not. When the button is pressed, the action assigns the value **true** to the **buttonDisabled** property and the button stops working, so the user can press it only once.

Figure 3-6: *Button disabled*

Although we can assign styles to a button using the modifiers introduced earlier, SwiftUI defines standard styles that users are already familiar with. The following modifiers are provided by the framework to apply these styles.

buttonStyle(PrimitiveButtonStyle)

This modifier defines the style of the button. The argument is a structure that conforms to the **PrimitiveButtonStyle** protocol. To define the styles, the protocol includes the properties **automatic**, **accessoryBar**, **accessoryBarAction**, **bordered**, **borderedProminent**, **borderless**, **card**, **glass**, **glassProminent**, **glass(Glass)**, **link**, **plain**.

controlSize(ControlSize)

This modifier defines the scale of the button. The argument is an enumeration with the values **mini**, **small**, **regular**, **large** and **extraLarge**.

Some styles defined by the **PrimitiveButtonStyle** protocol, such as **accessoryBar** and **card**, are exclusive to specific platforms, while others, such as **borderedProminent** and **glass**, produce the same result across most platforms. Figure 3-7 shows the styles we can safely use in macOS and iOS.

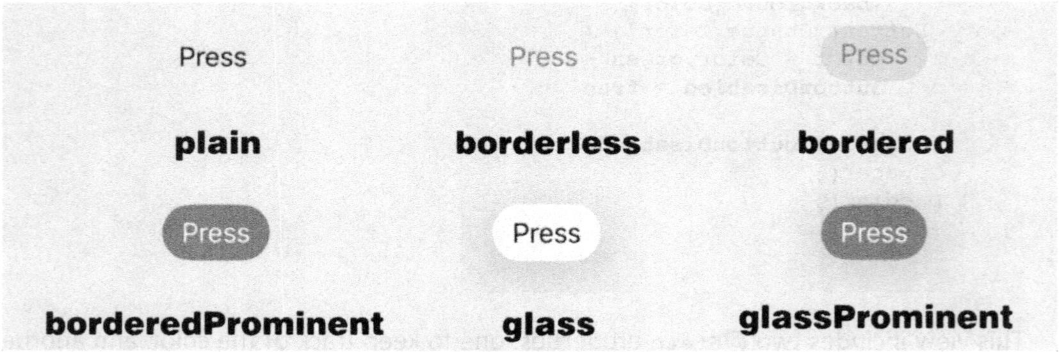

Figure 3-7: *Button styles*

These styles were designed with specific purposes in mind. For example, the **borderedProminent** style is used to represent a primary action, while the **bordered** style is used to represent a secondary or interrupting action. The following example shows how to implement these styles.

Listing 3-14: Styling buttons

```
struct ContentView: View {
   var body: some View {
      VStack(spacing: 10) {
         HStack {
            Button("Cancel") {
               print("Cancel Action")
            }.buttonStyle(.bordered)
            Spacer()
            Button("Send") {
               print("Send Information")
            }.buttonStyle(.borderedProminent)
         }
         Spacer()
      }.padding()
   }
}
```

This example creates two buttons at the top of the screen to represent typical actions in an application. We have a button on the right to perform an action and a button on the left to cancel it.

Figure 3-8: *Different styles depending on the action*

When the purpose of the button is to cancel a process or delete an item, we can assign that specific role to the button from the **`Button`**'s initializer. This allows the system to style the button according to the role and the device where the app is running. For instance, in mobile devices, a button with the **`destructive`** role is shown in red.

Listing 3-15: Assigning a role to a button

```
struct ContentView: View {
   var body: some View {
      VStack(spacing: 10) {
         HStack {
            Button("Delete", role: .destructive) {
               print("Delete Action")
            }.buttonStyle(.bordered)
            Spacer()
            Button("Send") {
               print("Send Information")
            }.buttonStyle(.borderedProminent)
         }
         Spacer()
      }.padding()
   }
}
```

Figure 3-9: *Destructive button*

If we have a rich background, we can use glass buttons to give our interface a modern look. In the following example, we apply the **`glass()`** method to give the Cancel button a clear, glass-like appearance.

Listing 3-16: Liquid glass buttons

```
struct ContentView: View {
   var body: some View {
      VStack {
         HStack {
            Button("Cancel", role: .destructive) {
               print("Cancel Action")
            }
            .buttonStyle(.glass(.clear))
            Spacer()
            Button("Send", role: .confirm) {
               print("Send Information")
            }
            .buttonStyle(.glassProminent)
         }
         Spacer()
      }.padding()
      .background(
         Image("Toronto")
            .resizable()
            .scaledToFill()
            .ignoresSafeArea()
      )
   }
}
```

The **`glass()`** method takes a structure of type **`Glass`** to define the effect. The properties provided by this structure are **`regular`** (regular glass effect), **`clear`** (clear glass), and **`identity`** (no effect). In this example, we use the **`clear`** value for the Cancel button, so it adopts a translucent glass appearance, as shown below.

Figure 3-10: *Liquid glass buttons*

Do It Yourself

Update the **`ContentView`** structure with the code in Listing 3-16. Download the **Toronto.jpg** image from our website and add it to an Asset Catalog (see Chapter 2, Figure 2-38). You should see an interface like the one shown in Figure 3-10 on the Canvas. Try other styles, like the **`glass`** style, to see how the buttons look like.

IMPORTANT

The glass effect we must apply depends on the button and its location in the interface. We will learn more about glass effects and how to create a Liquid Glass interface in Chapter 8.

In addition to the style, we can also specify the size of a button using the **`controlSize()`** modifier. There are several values available, depending on the platform. The following are the sizes available for **macOS** buttons.

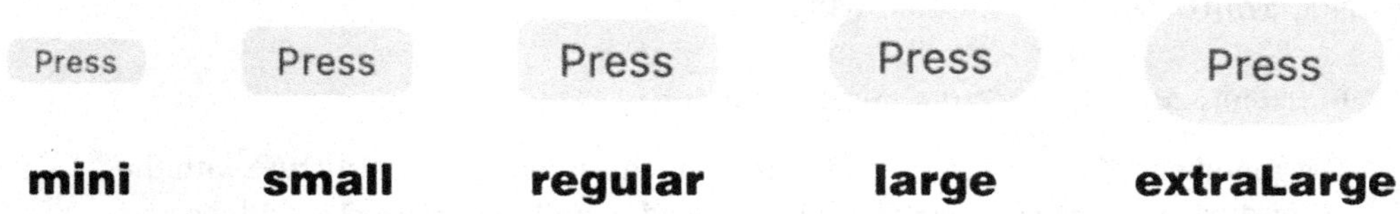

Figure 3-11: *Button sizes in macOS*

In iOS, many of these values produce the same result, so we effectively have only three possible sizes: small, regular, and large, as shown below.

Figure 3-12: *Button sizes in iOS*

Like standard styles, the standard sizes we can assign to buttons also serve a purpose. The idea is to give the user a visual hint about the importance of the action performed by the button. For example, if at the end of a form we need to place a button to submit an order, it is recommended to use a large size. The following example shows how these buttons look like when they are placed at the bottom of the screen.

Listing 3-17: Implementing large buttons

```
struct ContentView: View {
   var body: some View {
      VStack {
```

```
            Spacer()
            Button("Order") {
               print("Order Items")
            }
            .buttonStyle(.borderedProminent)
            .controlSize(.large)
         }
      }
   }
```

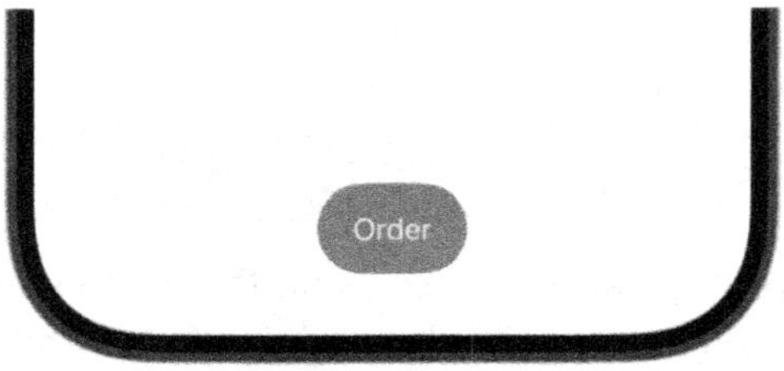

Figure 3-13: *Large button in iOS*

Standard buttons are displayed using the app's accent color and a shape that depends on their size. In macOS, buttons with the mini, small, and regular sizes are rectangular with rounded corners, while large and extra-large buttons are enclosed in capsules. In contrast, buttons in iOS are always displayed with a capsule shape. To customize this design and set the color, SwiftUI provides the following modifiers.

buttonBorderShape(ButtonBorderShape**)**

This modifier defines the shape of the button. The argument is a structure with the properties **automatic**, **capsule**, **circle**, and **roundedRectangle**, and the **roundedRectangle(radius: CGFloat)** method to define a specific corner radius.

tint(Color**)**

This modifier overrides the app's accent color with the color specified by the argument.

These modifiers work in both macOS and iOS buttons. For example, we can apply the **buttonBorderShape()** modifier to the previous Order button to give it a rectangular shape with a specific corner radius.

Listing 3-18: Changing the shape of a button

```
struct ContentView: View {
   var body: some View {
      VStack {
         Spacer()
         Button("Order") {
            print("Order Items")
         }
         .buttonStyle(.borderedProminent)
         .controlSize(.large)
         .buttonBorderShape(.roundedRectangle(radius: 10))
      }
   }
}
```

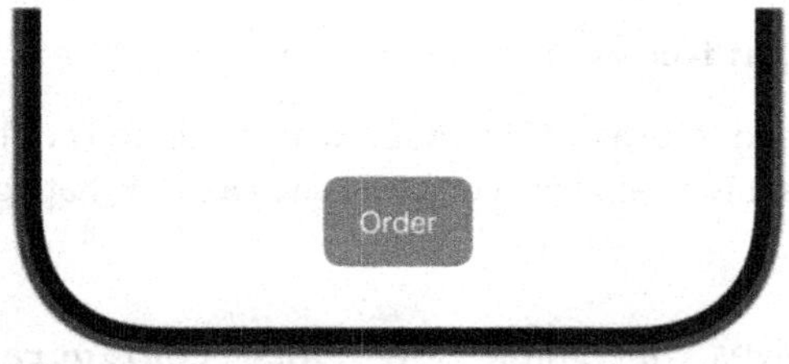

Figure 3-14: *Rectangular buttons in iOS*

These styles were designed to look good with SF Symbols. The advantage of using SF Symbols instead of custom images is that they scale automatically to match the font size assigned to the button, so we can create buttons of any size we want. For example, we can create a large circular button with a glass appearance that looks good on any platform.

Listing 3-19: Buttons with SF Symbols

```
struct ContentView: View {
   var body: some View {
      VStack {
         Spacer()
         Button(action: {
            print("Order Items")
         }, label: {
            Image(systemName: "cart.fill")
               .imageScale(.large)
               .padding()
         })
         .buttonStyle(.glassProminent)
         .buttonBorderShape(.circle)
         .tint(.orange)
      }
   }
}
```

In this example, we apply the **`imageScale()`** modifier to scale the SF Symbol, and the **`buttonBorderShape()`** and **`tint()`** modifiers to give the button a circular shape and an orange color. The result is shown below.

Figure 3-15: *Custom button with an SF Symbol*

The styles provided by SwiftUI are defined by structures that conform to the **`ButtonStyle`** protocol. Although the available options are sufficient to design any button we need, we can also create our own styles by defining a custom **`ButtonStyle`** structure. The protocol's only requirement is that the structure implements the following method.

makeBody(configuration: Configuration)

This method defines and returns a view that replaces the body of the button. The **configuration** argument is a value of type **Configuration** that contains information about the button.

This method receives a value of type **Configuration**, a typealias of **ButtonStyleConfiguration**, which contains properties that return information about the button. The following are the properties available.

isPressed

This property returns a Boolean value that indicates whether the button was pressed or not.

label

This property returns the view or views that define the button's current label.

The following example defines a button that expands when pressed. The styles include a padding and a green border. To apply these styles, we must create a structure that conforms to the **ButtonStyle** protocol, implement the **makeBody()** method, and return from this method the view we want to assign to the body of the button.

The views that make up the body of the button are provided by the **label** property of the **Configuration** structure, so we can read and modify the value of this property to apply the new styles, as shown below.

Listing 3-20: Defining custom styles for the button

```
struct MyStyle: ButtonStyle {
   func makeBody(configuration: MyStyle.Configuration) -> some View {
      let pressed = configuration.isPressed
      return configuration.label
         .padding()
         .border(Color.green, width: 5)
         .scaleEffect(pressed ? 1.2 : 1.0)
   }
}
struct ContentView: View {
   @State private var color = Color.gray

   var body: some View {
      VStack {
         Text("Default Title")
            .padding()
            .foregroundStyle(color)
         Button("Change Color") {
            color = Color.green
         }.buttonStyle(MyStyle())
         Spacer()
      }.padding()
   }
}
```

In this example, we define a structure called **`MyStyle`** and implement the required **`makeBody()`** method. This method gets the current configuration of the button from the type properties and then proceeds to modify and return the label. First, we read the value of the **`isPressed`** property to know if the button was pressed or not, and then apply the new styles to the **`label`** property. This property returns a copy of the views that create the button's current label, and therefore by modifying its value we are effectively modifying the label. In this case, we apply a padding, a border, and then assign a scale depending on the value of the **`isPressed`** property. If the value is **`true`**, which means the button is being pressed, we assign a scale of 1.2 to expand it, but if the value is **`false`**, we bring the scale back to 1.

In the **`ContentView`** view, we create an instance of this structure and assign it to the **`Button`** view with the **`buttonStyle()`** modifier. The result is shown below.

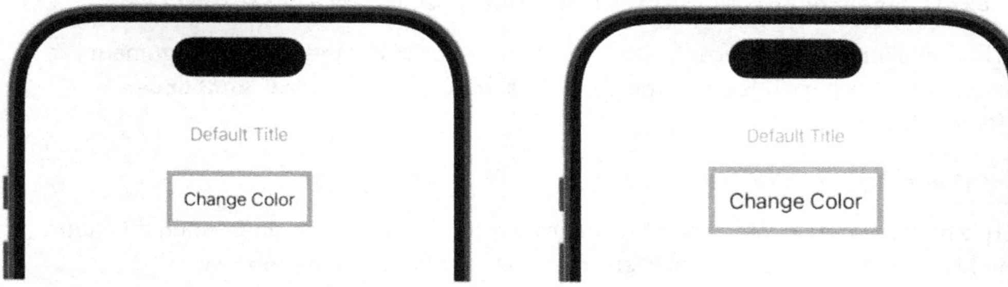

Figure 3-16: *Button with custom styles*

> **Do It Yourself**
>
> Update the **ContentView.swift** file with the code in Listing 3-20. Press the button. You should see the button expand, as shown in Figure 3-16, right. The button is automatically animated by SwiftUI. We will learn how to customize animations and create our own in Chapter 8.

BASIC

TextField View

The **`TextField`** view is another control we introduced earlier. This view creates an input field that the user can interact with to enter a value (a line of text). The following is one of the many initializers provided by the structure.

```
TextField(LocalizedStringKey, text: Binding, selection: Binding,
axis: Axis)
```

This initializer creates an input field. The first argument defines the field's placeholder, the **text** argument is the binding property of type **`String`** used to store the value inserted by the user, the **selection** argument is a binding property of type **`TextSelection`** used to store the range of the selection, and the **axis** argument defines the axis in which the content will scroll when it exceeds the bound of the view. It is an enumeration with the values **`horizontal`** and **`vertical`**.

The framework defines a few modifiers for **TextField** views. The following are the most frequently used.

textFieldStyle(TextFieldStyle)

This modifier defines the style of the text field. The argument is a structure that conforms to the **TextFieldStyle** protocol. The framework includes several structures to provide standard styles. These structures define the type properties **automatic**, **plain**, **roundedBorder**, and **squareBorder**.

autocorrectionDisabled(Bool)

This modifier enables or disables the system's autocorrection feature. By default, the value is **true** (disabled).

textInputAutocapitalization(TextInputAutocapitalization?)

This modifier defines the capitalization type used to format the text. The argument is a structure, which includes the type properties **characters**, **never**, **sentences** (default), and **words**.

keyboardType(UIKeyboardType)

This modifier defines the type of keyboard the system is going to open when the input field is selected. The argument is an enumeration with the values **default**, **asciiCapable**, **numbersAndPunctuation**, **URL**, **numberPad**, **phonePad**, **namePhonePad**, **emailAddress**, **decimalPad**, **twitter**, **webSearch**, **asciiCapableNumberPad**, and **alphabet**.

We have already seen how to include a simple **TextField** view in our interface to get input from the user, but we have only applied a few modifiers so far. The following example shows how to add a border and capitalize words.

Listing 3-21: Configuring a text field

```
struct ContentView: View {
   @State private var title: String = "Default Title"
   @State private var titleInput: String = ""

   var body: some View {
      VStack(spacing: 15) {
         Text(title)
            .lineLimit(1)
            .padding()
            .background(Color.yellow)
         TextField("Insert Title", text: $titleInput)
            .textFieldStyle(.roundedBorder)
            .textInputAutocapitalization(.words)
         Button("Save") {
            title = titleInput
            titleInput = ""
         }
         Spacer()
      }.padding()
   }
}
```

The style applied to the **TextField** view in Listing 3-21 is called **roundedBorder**. This adds a border to the input field that makes the area occupied by the view visible, as shown below.

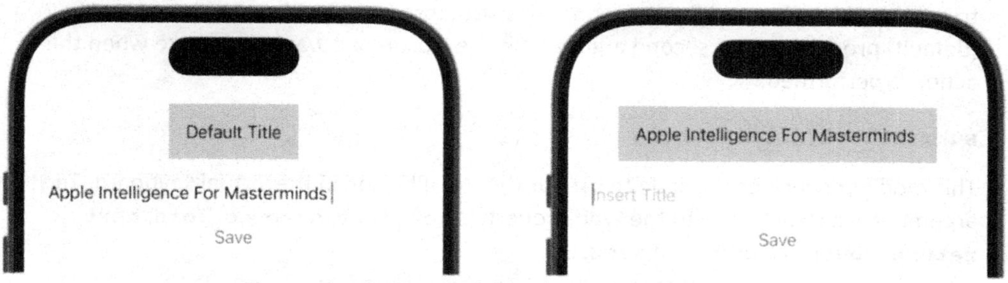

Figure 3-17: *Text field with a rounded border*

Do It Yourself

Update the **ContentView** structure with the code in Listing 3-21. Run the application on the Canvas or an iPhone simulator. Insert a text in the input field and press the Save button. You should see something like Figure 3-17.

In the previous example, we applied the **textFieldStyle()** modifier to give the view a predefined style that includes a light background and a gray border. To provide our own design, we can simply remove this modifier and apply the styles we want. In the following example, we show how to assign a custom background and add padding to the view to keep the text away from the edges.

Listing 3-22: Styling a text field

```
TextField("Insert Title", text: $titleInput)
   .padding(10)
   .background(.gray.opacity(0.2))
   .textInputAutocapitalization(.words)
```

Figure 3-18: *Customized text field*

In addition to having a button, the user normally expects to be able to save the value by pressing the Done button on the keyboard. The framework includes the following modifiers for this purpose.

onSubmit(of: SubmitTriggers, Closure)

This modifier performs an action when a trigger is fired, such as when the keyboard's Done button is pressed. The **of** argument is a structure that determines the type of trigger to which the modifier responds. This structure includes the **search** and **text** (default) properties. The second argument is the closure we want to execute when the action is performed.

submitLabel(SubmitLabel)

This modifier specifies the style to use for the Done button in the virtual keyboard. The argument is a structure with the type properties **continue**, **done**, **go**, **join**, **next**, **return**, **route**, **search**, and **send**.

submitScope(Bool)

This modifier determines whether the view will submit when is triggered.

The closure assigned to the **onSubmit()** modifier is executed when the view has focus, such as when the user is editing the input field. If we apply this modifier to a **TextField** view, the **of** argument can be omitted, as shown in the following example.

Listing 3-23: Responding to the Done button

```
struct ContentView: View {
   @State private var title: String = "Default Title"
   @State private var titleInput: String = ""

   var body: some View {
      VStack(spacing: 15) {
         Text(title)
            .lineLimit(1)
            .padding()
            .background(Color.yellow)
         TextField("Insert Title", text: $titleInput)
            .textFieldStyle(.roundedBorder)
            .submitLabel(.continue)
            .onSubmit {
               assignTitle()
            }
         HStack {
            Spacer()
            Button("Save") {
               assignTitle()
            }
         }
         Spacer()
      }.padding()
   }
   func assignTitle() {
      title = titleInput
      titleInput = ""
   }
}
```

The code in Listing 3-23 applies the **submitLabel()** modifier to the text field to change the style of the Done button to "Continue", and defines a method called **assignTitle()** to handle the action. This method is invoked from two places: the closure assigned to the **onSubmit()** modifier and the action of the **Button** view. As a result, the same operation is performed either when the user taps the button in the interface or presses the Done key on the keyboard. In both cases, the value entered in the text field is stored in the **title** property and shown on the screen.

Do It Yourself

Update the **ContentView** structure with the code in Listing 3-23 and run the app on the iPhone simulator. Click the input field, type some text using the virtual keyboard, and press the Done key. The text should be assigned to the title, as before. Remember that if the virtual keyboard is hidden in the simulator, you can force Device Hub to display it from the Device menu (**Device > Keyboard > Toggle Software Keyboard**).

When a view that can accept input or process feedback from the user is selected, the view is said to be in focus. SwiftUI includes several tools to manage this state. We can run a task when a view gains focus, determine whether the focus is on a specific view, or remove focus from a view. There are two property wrappers available for this purpose: **@FocusState** and **@FocusedBinding**. The **@FocusState** property wrapper stores a value that indicates where the focus is at a given moment, and **@FocusedBinding** is used to pass this state to other views. To manage focus, the framework provides the following modifiers.

focused(Binding, **equals:** Hashable**)**

This modifier stores the current state of the view in the binding property. The first argument is a reference to the **@FocusState** property, and the **equals** argument is the hashable value used to identify the view.

focusable(Bool**)**

This modifier determines if focus can be set on the view.

To track the state of the views, we need a **@FocusState** property whose type conforms to the **Hashable** protocol, so we can use this value to identify each view. In the following example, the property is defined using an enumeration. We declare two cases, **name** and **surname**, to track the focus state of two input fields and update their background color when the user starts typing.

Listing 3-24: Responding to changes in focus

```
enum FocusName: Hashable {
   case name
   case surname
}
struct ContentView: View {
   @FocusState var focusName: FocusName?
```

```
    @State private var title: String = "Default Name"
    @State private var nameInput: String = ""
    @State private var surnameInput: String = ""

    var body: some View {
        VStack(spacing: 10) {
            Text(title)
                .lineLimit(1)
                .padding()
                .background(Color.yellow)
            TextField("Insert Name", text: $nameInput)
                .textFieldStyle(.roundedBorder)
                .padding(4)
                .background(focusName == .name ? Color(white: 0.9) : .white)
                .focused($focusName, equals: .name)
            TextField("Insert Surname", text: $surnameInput)
                .textFieldStyle(.roundedBorder)
                .padding(4)
                .background(focusName == .surname ? Color(white: 0.9) :
                    .white)
                .focused($focusName, equals: .surname)
            HStack {
                Spacer()
                Button("Save") {
                    title = nameInput + " " + surnameInput
                }
            }
            Spacer()
        }.padding()
    }
}
```

The initial value of the **@FocusState** property is **nil**, which means no view is focused. When the user taps on a text field, the focus moves to that view and the value that identifies the view is assigned to the property. By comparing this value with the values in the enumeration, we know which **TextField** view is focused and can change the background color accordingly. Note that the **roundedBorder** style adds a border and a white background to the text field, so only the background of the padding is visible in this example.

Figure 3-19: *Focus*

On mobile devices, the virtual keyboard appears when a view that can accept input, such as a **TextField** view, gains focus. The keyboard remains visible as long as the focus stays on that view. To dismiss it, we must remove focus from the view. In SwiftUI, this is accomplished by assigning the value **nil** to the **@FocusState** property, as shown below.

Listing 3-25: Closing the keyboard

```
Button("Save") {
   title = nameInput + " " + surnameInput
   focusName = nil
}
```

This **Button** view replaces the **Button** view defined in Listing 3-24. Now, every time the Save button is pressed, the values are processed and the virtual keyboard is closed.

Do It Yourself

Update the **ContentView.swift** file with the code in Listing 3-24 and run the application on the iPhone simulator. Click on an input field. You should see the background color changing to gray, as illustrated in Figure 3-19. Replace the **Button** view with the view in Listing 3-25. Run the application again. Insert values in both fields and press the Save button. The values should be assigned to the title and the virtual keyboard should be closed.

In previous examples, we didn't check whether the user inserted a value or not, but usually applications must prevent the user from saving invalid or empty values. There are different ways to control this. One alternative is to check the values before storing them. We allow users to type whatever they want but only store the values accepted by the app.

Listing 3-26: Checking the values before storing

```
Button("Save") {
   let tempName = nameInput.trimmingCharacters(in: .whitespaces)
   let tempSurname = surnameInput.trimmingCharacters(in: .whitespaces)
   if !tempName.isEmpty && !tempSurname.isEmpty {
      title = tempName + " " + tempSurname
      focusName = nil
   }
}
```

In this example, we first trim the **nameInput** and **surnameInput** properties to remove spaces at the beginning and end, and then verify that the resulting values are not empty before assigning them to the **title** property. The Save button remains enabled, but the values are not stored until the user enters text in both fields.

Do It Yourself

Update the **Button** view in the **ContentView** structure with the code in Listing 3-26. You shouldn't be able to modify the title until you have inserted a name and a surname.

Another alternative is to disable the button using the **disabled()** modifier. We introduced this modifier before (see Listing 3-13). All it does is to enable or disable the control based on a condition, so we can use it in our example to enable the Save button only when the value entered by the user matches what the application expects, as shown below.

Listing 3-27: Disabling the button

```
Button("Save") {
    let tempName = nameInput.trimmingCharacters(in: .whitespaces)
    let tempSurname = surnameInput.trimmingCharacters(in: .whitespaces)

    if !tempName.isEmpty && !tempSurname.isEmpty {
        title = tempName + " " + tempSurname
        focusName = nil
    }
}
.disabled(nameInput.isEmpty || surnameInput.isEmpty)
```

In this example, we implement the **disabled()** modifier introduced before to disable the button until the user types a text in both fields. If one text field or both are empty, the button doesn't work.

Do It Yourself

Update the **Button** view with the code in Listing 3-27. You shouldn't be able to press the Save button until you have inserted a name and a surname.

Besides checking whether the properties contain a valid value, we can also limit what the user can type on the fields. For instance, we could only accept numbers or a specific amount of characters. For this, we need to check whether the value inserted by the user is valid or not every time the state of the view changes. The framework includes the following modifier for this purpose.

onChange(of: State, **initial:** Bool, Closure)

This modifier executes a closure when a state changes. The **of** argument is the property that stores the value to be checked, the **initial** argument is a boolean value that specifies whether the check should also be performed when the view appears, and the last argument is the closure to be executed when the system reports a change in the value. The closure can receive two values, one representing the property's old value and another representing the new one.

This modifier can only check one state, so we should apply it to every view we want to control. For instance, we can use it in the **TextField** views of our example to limit the number of characters the user is allowed to type. If the user goes over the limit, we remove the extra characters and assign the result back to the property, as shown below.

Listing 3-28: Controlling user's input

```
TextField("Insert Name", text: $nameInput)
   .textFieldStyle(.roundedBorder)
   .padding(4)
   .background(focusName == .name ? Color(white: 0.9) : .white)
   .focused($focusName, equals: .name)
   .onChange(of: nameInput, initial: false) { old, value in
      if value.count > 10 {
         nameInput = String(value.prefix(10))
      }
   }
TextField("Insert Surname", text: $surnameInput)
   .textFieldStyle(.roundedBorder)
   .padding(4)
   .background(focusName == .surname ? Color(white: 0.9) : .white)
   .focused($focusName, equals: .surname)
   .onChange(of: surnameInput, initial: false) { old, value in
      if value.count > 15 {
         surnameInput = String(value.prefix(15))
      }
   }
```

In this example, we monitor changes to the properties that store the state of the text fields (**`nameInput`** and **`surnameInput`**). When the user types or deletes a character, the value of the corresponding property changes and the closure assigned to the **`onChange()`** modifier is executed. This closure receives the updated value, so we can use it to determine whether the text entered by the user is valid and respond accordingly. In this case, we count the number of characters in the string and, if the value exceeds the limit, use the **`prefix()`** method to keep only the allowed portion of the text. As a result, once the character limit is reached, the user cannot enter additional characters.

Do It Yourself

Update the **`TextField`** views in your **`ContentView`** structure with the code in Listing 3-28. Run the application on the iPhone simulator. Insert a name and a surname. You shouldn't be able to add more than 10 characters for the name and 15 characters for the surname.

Of course, we can specify other conditions besides the number of characters. The following example creates a text field that accepts only integers.

Listing 3-29: Accepting only integer numbers

```
struct ContentView: View {
   @State private var title = "Default Name"
   @State private var numberInput = ""

   var body: some View {
      VStack(spacing: 10) {
```

```
            Text(title)
                .padding()
                .background(Color.yellow)
            TextField("Insert Number", text: $numberInput)
                .textFieldStyle(.roundedBorder)
                .padding(4)
                .keyboardType(.numbersAndPunctuation)
                .onChange(of: numberInput, initial: false) { old, value in
                    if !value.isEmpty && Int(value) == nil {
                            numberInput = old
                    }
                }
            HStack {
                Spacer()
                Button("Save") {
                    title = numberInput
                    numberInput = ""
                }
            }
            Spacer()
        }.padding()
    }
}
```

As before, the view contains a **TextField** with the **onChange()** modifier. The difference is in how we check the validity of the input. In this case, we need to make sure that the text field is not empty, and then see if we can convert it into an integer, which means that the user have only entered numbers. If this is not possible, we use the old value received by the closure and assign it to the **numberInput** property, returning the text field to its previous state. Note that we have also implemented the **keyboardType()** modifier to show the appropriate keyboard for the input we are expecting from the user (in this case, numbers).

Do It Yourself

Update the **ContentView** structure with the code in Listing 3-29. Run the application on the iPhone simulator. You should only be able to type numbers.

By default, a **TextField** view displays only one line of text, but we can allow it to expand by applying the **lineLimit()** modifier. (This is the same modifier used earlier to expand **Text** views.) This also requires enabling vertical scrolling for the view, as shown below.

Listing 3-30: Defining a multiline text field

```
struct ContentView: View {
    @State private var text: String = ""

    var body: some View {
        TextField("Insert Text", text: $text, axis: .vertical)
            .textFieldStyle(.roundedBorder)
            .padding(20)
```

```
            .lineLimit(5)
      }
   }
```

In this example, the **TextField** view expands until it reaches a height of 5 lines and then the text scrolls vertically to allow the user to keep typing. If we want to give the view a minimum and a maximum size, we can declare the modifier with a range, as in **lineLimit(3...5)**. The result is shown below.

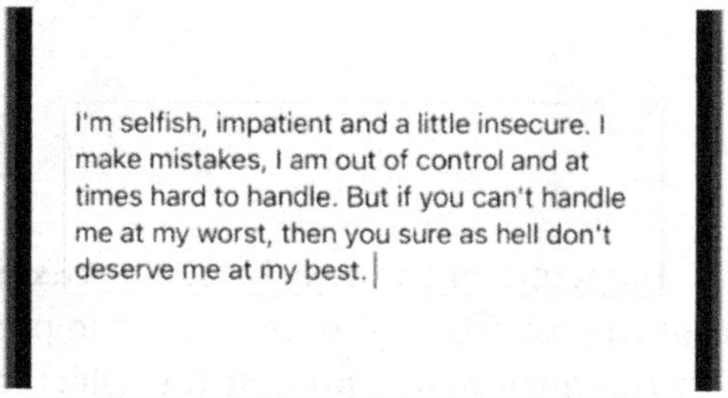

Figure 3-20: *Multiline text field*

The **TextField** view can also use a binding property to store information about the text selected by the user. The value stored in this property is a **TextSelection** structure, which includes the following properties to provide information about the selection.

indices

This property returns an enumeration of type **Indices** with two cases: **multiSelection()**, to return a set of **Range** values representing the locations of multiple selections, and **selection()**, to return a single **Range** representing the location of a single selection.

isInsertion

This property returns a Boolean value that indicates whether the selection represents the insertion point (**true**) or selected text (**false**).

To get the text selected by the user, we need to define a **@State** property to store the **TextSelection** structure, use this property to create the **TextField** view, and then process the value produced by the view by reading the **indices** property, as shown below.

Listing 3-31: Selecting text

```
struct ContentView: View {
   @State private var text = ""
   @State private var selected: TextSelection? = nil

   var body: some View {
      VStack {
         TextField("Insert Text", text: $text, selection: $selected, axis:
            .vertical)
            .textFieldStyle(.roundedBorder)
            .padding(20)
            .lineLimit(5)
```

```
            Text(getSelection() ?? "")
            Spacer()
        }
    }
    func getSelection() -> String? {
        if let selected = selected, !selected.isInsertion {
            if case .selection(let range) = selected.indices {
                let substring = text[range]
                return String(substring)
            }
        }
        return nil
    }
}
```

When the user selects characters in the text field, the **TextField** view automatically assigns a range to the **selected** property that determines the position of those characters. Once we have this range, we can retrieve and process the selected text. In this example, we define a method called **getSelection()** for this purpose. The method ensures that text has been selected by checking the value of the **selected** property, and then reads the value associated with the **selection()** case to obtain the range of characters. Using this range, we extract the corresponding substring from the **text** property and return it. Note that the method also checks the value of the **isInsertion** property to ensure that the ranges produced by the selection represent selected text and not just the insertion point (the location of the cursor). The string returned by the method is displayed on the screen with a **Text** view, as shown below.

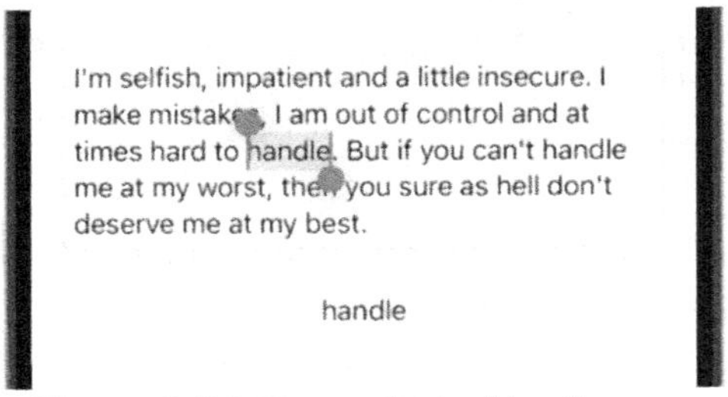

Figure 3-21: *Text selected by the user*

Do It Yourself

Update the **ContentView** structure with the code in Listing 3-31. Run the application on an iPhone simulator. Write a text and double-click on a word to select it. You should see the word below the text field, as shown in Figure 3-21.

BASIC

SecureField View

SwiftUI also includes a view to create a secure text field. The view replaces the characters inserted by the user with dots to hide sensitive information, such as passwords.

```
SecureField(String, text: Binding)
```

This initializer creates a secure input field. The first argument defines the placeholder, and the **text** argument is the binding property that stores the value inserted by the user.

The implementation is the same as with **TextField** views, and we can also apply some of the same modifiers, as shown below.

Listing 3-32: Using a secure text field

```
struct ContentView: View {
   @State private var pass: String = ""

   var body: some View {
      VStack(spacing: 15) {
         Text(pass)
            .padding()
         SecureField("Insert Password", text: $pass)
            .textFieldStyle(.roundedBorder)
         Spacer()
      }.padding()
   }
}
```

The **SecureField** view looks the same as the **TextField** view. The only difference is that the characters are hidden.

Figure 3-22: *Secure text field*

BASIC

TextEditor View

SwiftUI includes an additional view to allow users to insert multiple lines of text called **TextEditor**. The following is the view's initializer.

```
TextEditor(text: Binding, selection: Binding)
```

This initializer creates a text editor. The **text** argument is the binding property that stores the text inserted by the user, and the **selection** argument is a binding property of type **TextSelection** or **AttributedTextSelection** to store the range of the selection.

A **TextEditor** view only needs a binding property to store the text inserted by the user. This property can be of type **String** to store plain text, or **AttributedString** to store formatted text. In the following example, we show how to implement this view to allow the user to insert plain text.

Listing 3-33: Implementing a text editor

```
struct ContentView: View {
   @State private var text: String = ""

   var body: some View {
      TextEditor(text: $text)
   }
}
```

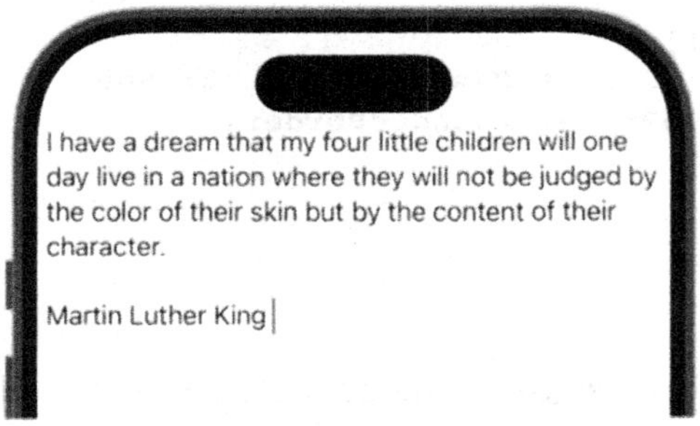

Figure 3-23: *Text editor*

By default, a **TextEditor** view appears with an opaque background. We can change this background using the **background()** modifier, just as we did for **TextField** and **Text** views, but there is one important detail to consider in this case. The background color of a text editor is controlled by an underlying view that provides scrolling behavior. As a result, to apply a custom background, we must first remove the default background added by the scroll view using the following modifier. (This applies to other scrolling views like **Lists** and **Tables**, as we will see later.)

scrollContentBackground(Visibility)—This modifier shows or hides the scroll view's background. The argument is an enumeration with the values **automatic**, **visible**, and **hidden**.

By applying this modifier, we can remove the default background of the **TextEditor** view and provide our own. In the following example, we show how to use this modifier together with those introduced earlier to configure the editor.

Listing 3-34: Customizing a text editor

```
struct ContentView: View {
   @State private var text: String = ""
```

```
   var body: some View {
      TextEditor(text: $text)
         .multilineTextAlignment(.leading)
         .lineSpacing(10)
         .autocorrectionDisabled(true)
         .padding(10)
         .scrollContentBackground(.hidden)
         .background(.gray.opacity(0.2))
         .padding(20)
   }
}
```

In this example, we align the text to the left, assign a spacing of 10 points between lines, disable autocorrection, and give the view a gray background. The result is shown below.

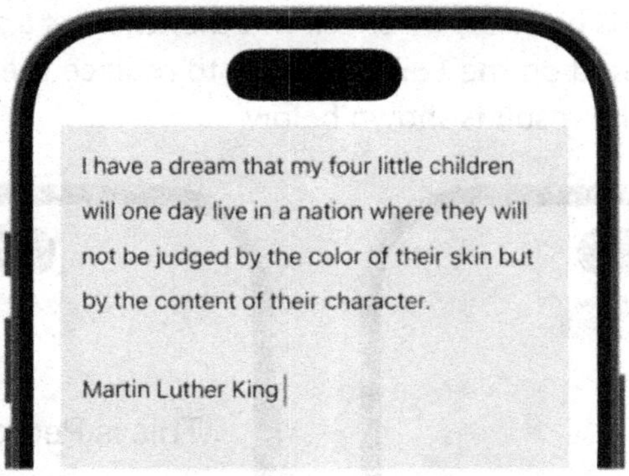

Figure 3-24: *Custom text editor*

Do It Yourself

Update the **ContentView** structure with the code in Listing 3-34. Run the application on an iPhone simulator and type some text. You should see something similar to Figure 3-24.

Selection in a **TextEditor** view works the same way as in a **TextField** view (see Listing 3-31). We need a **@State** property to store the **TextSelection** structure and then process the values produced by the view. In the following example, we add a button above the editor to retrieve the text selected by the user and show how it can be replaced with different text.

Listing 3-35: Selecting text in a text editor

```
struct ContentView: View {
   @State private var text: String = ""
   @State private var selected: TextSelection? = nil

   var body: some View {
      VStack {
         Button("Replace Selected") {
```

```
            if let selected = selected, !selected.isInsertion {
               if case .selection(let range) = selected.indices {
                  text.replaceSubrange(range, with: "Pedro")
               }
            }
         }.buttonStyle(.borderedProminent)

         TextEditor(text: $text, selection: $selected)
            .padding(10)
            .scrollContentBackground(.hidden)
            .background(.gray.opacity(0.2))
            .padding(20)
      }
   }
}
```

Every time the button is pressed, we check whether there is a selection and then call the **replaceSubrange()** method on the **text** property to replace the text selected by the user with the string "Pedro". The result is shown below.

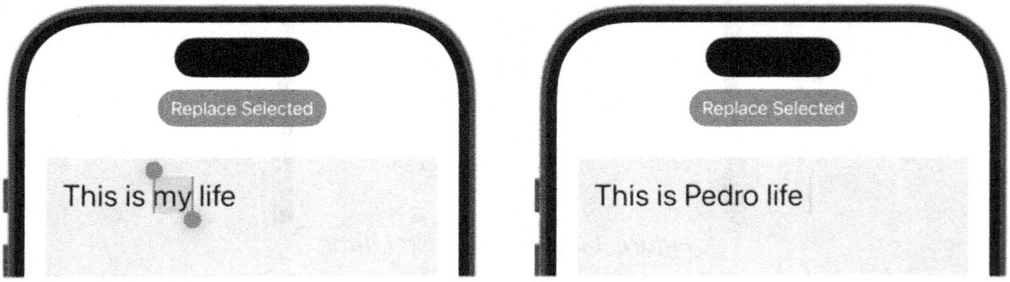

Figure 3-25: *Text selection*

PRO

Attributed String

In previous examples, we used a **String** property to store the text inserted by the user, but a **TextEditor** view can also work with attributed strings. Attributed text allows attributes to be applied to the characters, such as font styles, foreground and background colors, and alignment. To store and manage this information, the **Foundation** framework provides the **AttributedString** structure. The following are some of the structure's initializers.

AttributedString(String, **attributes:** AttributeContainer)

This initializer creates an **AttributedString** instance from the values provided by the arguments. The first argument specifies the text to store in the structure, and the **attributes** argument provides a container with the initial attributes we want to apply to the string.

AttributedString(NSAttributedString)

This initializer creates an **AttributedString** instance from an existing **NSAttributedString** object. It is commonly used to convert attributed text produced by legacy frameworks that still rely on **NSAttributedString** values.

To assign attributes, SwiftUI provides the **SwiftUIAttributes** structure. This structure exposes a wide range of properties, each returning a structure that represents a specific text attribute. The following are the most frequently used.

font

This property assigns a font to the characters. It receives a value of type **Font** that defines the characteristics of the font to apply.

foregroundColor

This property assigns a color to the characters. It receives a value of type **Color**.

backgroundColor

This property assigns a background color to the characters. It receives a value of type **Color**.

strikethroughStyle

This property applies a strikethrough to the characters. It receives a **LineStyle** structure that determines whether the characters are displayed with a line through them. We can use the **single** property provided by the structure to draw a single line, or the **none** value to represent the absence of a line.

underlineStyle

This property applies an underline to the characters. It receives a **LineStyle** structure that determines whether the characters are displayed with a line beneath them. We can use the **single** property provided by the structure to draw a single line, or the **none** value to represent the absence of a line.

alignment

This property aligns the text. It receives a value of type **TextAlignment**. The possible values are **center**, **left**, and **right**.

lineHeight

This property defines the height of the lines. It takes a structure of type **LineHeight**. The structure includes the properties **loose**, **normal**, **tight**, and **variable** to define standard line heights, as well as methods such as **exact(points: CGFloat)** to assign a specific height.

Working with these values is straightforward. We create an instance of the **AttributedString** structure with the desired text, apply the required styles, and present it to the user. In the following example, we define a computed property to style the text and then display the result on the screen using a **Text** view.

Listing 3-36: Creating attributed text

```
struct ContentView: View {
   var myText: AttributedString {
      var text1 = AttributedString("SwiftUI")
```

```
        text1.font = .body.bold()
        text1.foregroundColor = .blue
        let text2 = AttributedString(" can show ")
        var text3 = AttributedString("attributes")
        text3.font = .body.bold()
        text3.backgroundColor = .red
        let text4 = AttributedString(".")

        var finalText = text1 + text2 + text3 + text4
        finalText.font = .title
        return finalText
    }
    var body: some View {
        Text(myText)
            .padding(10)
    }
}
```

In this example, we define a computed property that creates four **AttributedString** structures, one to store each portion of the text we want to style. We leave the instances assigned to **text2** and **text4** with their default attributes, but assign a bold font and a blue foreground color to the text in **text1**, and a bold font and a red background color to the text in **text3**. This creates multiple texts with different styles. To recreate the sentence, we join these values into a single **AttributedString** and then assign the **title** font to it so the entire text uses the same font. The result is shown below.

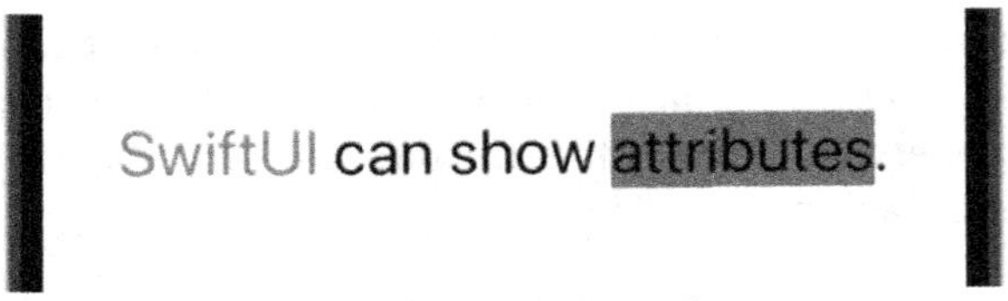

Figure 3-26: *Attributed text*

In this case, we assigned the attributes in code, but Apple platforms also provide users with tools to apply attributes to text. All we need to do is implement a **TextEditor** view with a binding property of type **AttributedString**, and the system handles the rest.

Listing 3-37: Allowing users to generate attributed text

```
struct ContentView: View {
    @State private var text: AttributedString = ""

    var body: some View {
        VStack {
            TextEditor(text: $text)
                .padding(10)
                .scrollContentBackground(.hidden)
                .background(.gray.opacity(0.2))
                .padding(20)
        }
    }
}
```

This is the same code we used earlier to present a text editor, but instead of storing the text in a **String** property, we use an **AttributedString** property, so now users can type text and apply any attributes they want using the system's tools. In iOS, these tools appear when we tap the editor or double-tap a word to select it, as shown below.

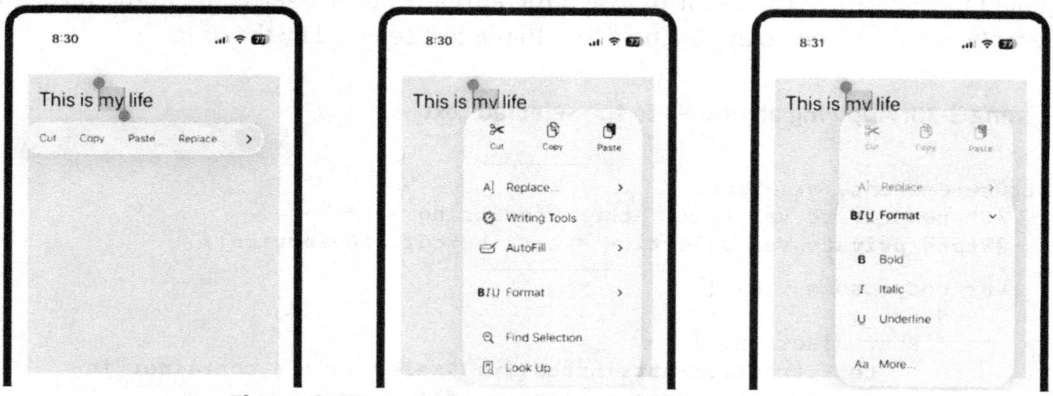

Figure 3-27: *Assigning attributes with system tools*

> **IMPORTANT**
>
> The tools provided by the system include controls to apply every available style, including alignment and colors. **AttributedString** values can also store special characters, such as emojis and Genmojis. To learn how to work with these characters, read our book *Apple Intelligence for Masterminds*.

Of course, we can provide our own tools to apply styles, but because attributed text stores not only the text itself but also its attributes and the ranges of characters to which they apply, instead of using a **TextSelection** value to store the selection, we must use an **AttributedTextSelection** structure. The following is the structure's initializer.

```
AttributedTextSelection(range: Range)
```

This initializer creates a structure used to store a selection of attributed text. The **range** argument is a **Range** of **Index** values that determines which characters are selected by default.

Attributed text is stored in a tree-like structure. When we modify the text or its attributes, this structure may change. To ensure that attributes are always applied to the characters selected by the user, the **AttributedString** structure includes the following method.

```
transformAttributes(in: inout AttributedTextSelection, body:
Closure)
```

This method applies attributes to the selected text. The **in** argument is a reference to the user's selection, and the **body** argument is the closure that applies the changes.

This method takes an **inout** value that references the **AttributedTextSelection** structure storing the selected text, so the selection is automatically updated whenever the text changes. To perform the modifications, the closure assigned to the **body** argument receives an **AttributeContainer** structure. This structure stores attributes that can later be applied to text, so we can use it to assign the attributes to the selection. In the following example, we show how to apply a bold font to the text selected by the user.

Listing 3-38: Applying attributes to the selected text

```
struct ContentView: View {
   @State private var text: AttributedString = ""
   @State private var selection = AttributedTextSelection()

   var body: some View {
      VStack {
         Button(action: {
            text.transformAttributes(in: &selection) { container in
               container.font = .body.bold()
            }
         }, label: {
            Image(systemName: "bold")
         }).buttonStyle(.glass)

         TextEditor(text: $text, selection: $selection)
            .padding(10)
            .scrollContentBackground(.hidden)
            .background(.gray.opacity(0.2))
            .padding(20)
      }
   }
}
```

In this example, we add a button to the interface. Each time the button is pressed, we call the **transformAttributes()** method to modify the selection. In this case, we assign a bold font to the **font** property, so the selected text becomes bold, as shown below.

Figure 3-28: *Assigning attributes to selection*

The **font** property takes a **Font** structure, not just individual font attributes. This means that every time we want to apply an attribute such as bold or italic, we must also specify the font to which those attributes will be applied. In our example, we use the **body** font, so every time the button is pressed, the font is reset to **body**, regardless of what the user had selected before. To avoid changing the font, instead of defining a specific one, we must retrieve the current font and apply the attributes to it.

Although we could read style information directly from the attributed string, as we will see later, the **AttributedString** structure only stores an abstract representation of those styles. The concrete fonts SwiftUI uses to render text on screen are stored in the environment. To access these values, the **Environment** structure includes the following property.

fontResolutionContext

This property returns a **Context** structure that allows us to resolve an abstract font into the concrete font used by SwiftUI.

To resolve a font, the **Font** structure provides the following method.

resolve(in: Context)

This method accesses the environment context to resolve a font into the concrete font SwiftUI uses to render text. The **in** argument is the **Context** structure used to perform the resolution.

The **resolve()** method returns a **Resolved** structure with the concrete representation of the font. From this structure, we can retrieve detailed information about the font. The following are some of the properties the structure defines for that purpose.

isBold

This property returns a Boolean value indicating whether the resolved font includes the bold trait.

isItalic

This property returns a Boolean value indicating whether the resolved font includes the italic trait.

weight

This property returns a value of type **Weight** that indicates the weight of the font. The possible values are **black**, **bold**, **heavy**, **light**, **medium**, **regular**, **semibold**, **thin**, and **ultraLight**.

width

This property returns a value of type **Width** to indicate the width of the font. The possible values are **compressed**, **condensed**, **expanded**, and **standard**.

To retrieve the current font and assign new attributes using these tools, we must get a reference to the **fontResolutionContext** property from the environment and use it with the **transformAttributes()** method to resolve the font of the text selected by the user. In the following example, we show how to follow this procedure to assign the bold style to the selected text based on its current state.

Listing 3-39: Applying attributes to the current font

```
struct ContentView: View {
   @State private var text: AttributedString = ""
   @State private var selection = AttributedTextSelection()
   @Environment(\.fontResolutionContext) var context

   var body: some View {
      VStack {
         Button(action: {
            text.transformAttributes(in: &selection) { container in
               let font = container.font ?? .body
               let bold = font.resolve(in: context).isBold

               if bold {
                  container.font = font.bold(false)
               } else {
                  container.font = font.bold(true)
               }
            }
         }, label: {
            Image(systemName: "bold")
         }).buttonStyle(.glass)

         TextEditor(text: $text, selection: $selection)
            .padding(10)
            .scrollContentBackground(.hidden)
            .background(.gray.opacity(0.2))
            .padding(20)
      }
   }
}
```

In this example, we want to determine whether the font has the bold attribute applied and add or remove it based on its current state. For this purpose, we first read the **font** property from the container to obtain the abstract description of the font, and then call the **resolve()** method to get its concrete representation. This method returns a **Resolved** structure, so we read the **isBold** property from this value to check the current state and apply the style accordingly. If the font is bold, we remove the style to make it regular, and vice versa, so every time the user presses the button, the style toggles, as shown below.

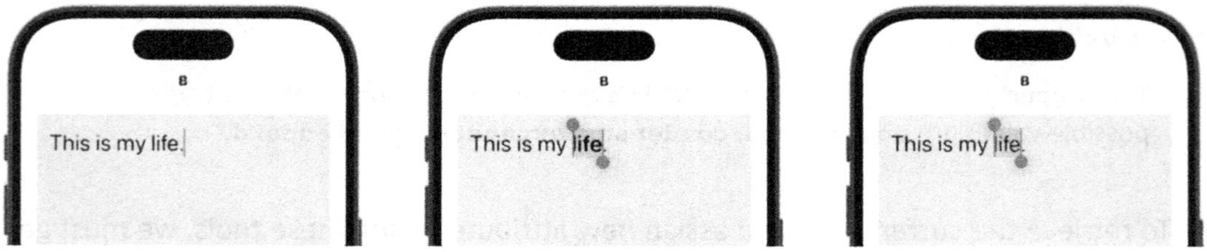

Figure 3-29: *Applying styles according to the current state*

Resolving a font into its concrete representation is only required when we need to apply new styles to the current font. If the styles we want to modify affect the text as a whole, we can update them directly on the container, as shown below.

Listing 3-40: Applying attributes to the text

```
Button(action: {
    text.transformAttributes(in: &selection) { container in
        if container.underlineStyle == .single {
            container.underlineStyle = .none
        } else {
            container.underlineStyle = .single
        }
    }
}, label: {
    Image(systemName: "underline")
}).buttonStyle(.glass)
```

In this example, we check the current value of the **underlineStyle** property to add or remove an underline from the text selected by the user. If the value is **single**, we change it to **none**, and vice versa, so every time the user presses the button, the style toggles as before.

> **Do It Yourself**
>
> Update the **ContentView** structure with the code in Listing 3-39. Run the application on an iPhone simulator, type some text, select a word, and press the button. The selected text should change to bold. Press the button again, and the text should return to regular. Update the **Button** view with the code in Listing 3-40 and repeat the process. Now, every time you press the button, an underline is added or removed to the text depending on the current state.

In addition to applying styles to the text selected by the user, we can also modify the attributed text directly. For this purpose, we can use the properties and methods provided by the **AttributedString** structure. The following are the properties provided by the structure to return collections of values that represent the characters in the string and their associated attributes.

characters

This property returns a **CharacterView** structure that provides access to the Unicode characters in the string.

runs

This property returns a collection of **Runs** structures that provide access to the contiguous ranges of characters sharing the same set of attributes in the string.

The collection of characters returned by the **characters** property conforms to the **BidirectionalCollection** protocol. This protocol defines a type called **Index** to represent the position of characters in the string, along with a set of properties and methods used to navigate and locate those positions. The following are the most frequently used.

startIndex

This property returns an **Index** structure that represents the location of the first character in the attributed string.

endIndex

This property returns an **Index** structure that represents the location of the last character in the attributed string.

index(after: Index)

This method returns an **Index** structure representing the location immediately after the index specified by the **after** argument.

index(before: Index)

This method returns an **Index** structure representing the location immediately before the index specified by the **before** argument.

index(Index, **offsetBy:** Int, **limitedBy:** Index)

This method returns an optional **Index** value representing the location determined by the arguments. The first argument specifies the starting location, the **offsetBy** argument defines how far to move from that location, and the **limitedBy** argument sets a boundary index that the result must not pass. If the calculated position exceeds that boundary, the method returns **nil**.

ranges(of: String)

This method returns a collection of **Range** values that represent the locations of characters in the string matching the value specified by the **of** argument.

Using these properties and methods, we can locate specific characters in a string and manually modify their attributes. For example, we can use the **ranges()** method to find all occurrences of a specific text and assign attributes to each one of them, as shown below.

Listing 3-41: Manually applying attributes to ranges of characters

```
struct ContentView: View {
   @State private var text: AttributedString = ""
   @State private var selection = AttributedTextSelection()

   var body: some View {
      VStack {
         Button(action: {
            let blueRanges = text.characters.ranges(of: "blue")
            let rangeSet = RangeSet(blueRanges)
            text[rangeSet].foregroundColor = .blue
         }, label: {
            Text("Set Blue")
         }).buttonStyle(.glass)

         TextEditor(text: $text, selection: $selection)
            .padding(10)
            .scrollContentBackground(.hidden)
```

```
            .background(.gray.opacity(0.2))
            .padding(20)
        }
    }
}
```

In this example, we use the **ranges()** method to find all occurrences of the word "blue" in the text. Once we have the **Range** values that indicate the location of each match, we use a subscript provided by **AttributedString** to assign the attributes (**text[rangeSet]**). This subscript covers all the ranges in the set, allowing us to read or modify attributes across multiple ranges at once. Note that because the **ranges()** method returns an array, we must first convert it into a **RangeSet** before applying the attributes. The result is shown below.

Figure 3-30: *Applying attributes to ranges of characters*

The collection returned by the **characters** property also includes the following property for working with character indices.

indices

This property returns a collection of indices representing the location of each character in the string.

There are many ways we can use these values to access and process the characters in a string. One common approach is to examine each character individually to determine its role or characteristics. For this purpose, we can use the properties provided by the **Character** structure, which return information about the nature of each character. The most frequently used are **isLetter**, **isPunctuation**, **isWhitespace**, **isSymbol**, **isCurrencySymbol**, **isUppercase**, **isLowercase**, and **isNumber**. In the following example, we show how to iterate over the characters and read the **isUppercase** property to apply attributes only to uppercase letters.

Listing 3-42: Applying attributes to specific characters

```
struct ContentView: View {
   @State private var text: AttributedString = ""
   @State private var selection = AttributedTextSelection()
```

```
    var body: some View {
        VStack {
            Button(action: {
                let indices = text.characters.indices
                for index in indices {
                    if text.characters[index].isUppercase {
                        let lastIndex = text.characters.index(after: index)
                        text[index..<lastIndex].foregroundColor = .orange
                    }
                }
            }, label: {
                Text("Set Characters")
            }).buttonStyle(.glass)

            TextEditor(text: $text, selection: $selection)
                .padding(10)
                .scrollContentBackground(.hidden)
                .background(.gray.opacity(0.2))
                .padding(20)
        }
    }
}
```

The **indices** property returns a collection of indices. Using these indices, we can access each character in the string. In this example, we iterate over all the characters, read their **isUppercase** property, and, if the value is **true**, assign a foreground color to make the character orange. Note that because the subscript operates on a range of indices, we call the **index(after:)** method to obtain the index immediately following the current character and then create an open range using those values. The result is shown below.

Figure 3-31: *Working with characters*

As we have already mentioned, we can also process the runs of a string. These represent contiguous sections of text that share the same set of attributes. Figure 3-32, below, illustrates how runs are defined within an attributed string.

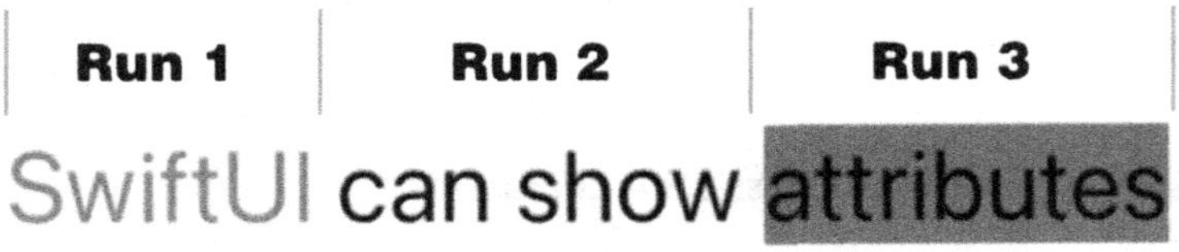

Figure 3-32: *Attribute runs*

As with characters, there are many operations we can perform on the runs of a string. One of the most common is checking whether a run includes a specific attribute. Since a run can contain multiple attributes, we must inspect it to determine whether that attribute is present. For this purpose, we can use a key-path subscript. In the following example, we show how to find runs that have the **foregroundColor** attribute applied to the text.

Listing 3-43: Inspecting runs to find if they apply a specific attribute

```
Button(action: {
   for (value, range) in text.runs[\.foregroundColor] {
      if value != nil {
         print(String(text.characters[range]))
      }
   }
}, label: {
   Text("Find Color")
}).buttonStyle(.glass)
```

This code inspects the **foregroundColor** property of the runs to determine whether each run contains that attribute. If the attribute is present, the property returns both its value and the range of characters to which it is applied; otherwise, the value returned is **nil**. In this case, we use this result to check for the attribute and if the attribute is found, we print the corresponding character to the console.

Do It Yourself

Update the **Button** view from the previous example with the code in Listing 3-43. Run the application on an iPhone simulator. Type some text, select a word, open the system tools, and assign a foreground color to it. Press the Find Color button. You should see the word printed in the console.

IMPORTANT

Using a **TextEditor** view with attributed text, you can build a fully functional text editor that provides all the tools users need to format content, including fonts, styles, alignment, and colors. The topic goes beyond the scope of this book. For more information, visit our website and follow the links for this chapter.

BASIC

Toggle View

The **Toggle** view creates a control to switch between two states. By default, it is displayed as a user-friendly switch on mobile devices and as a checkbox on Macs. The view includes the following initializer.

```
Toggle(String, isOn: Binding)
```

This initializer creates a **Toggle** view. The first argument defines the label, and the **isOn** argument is the binding property used to store the state. The view also includes an initializer to define the label with the views returned by a closure (**Toggle(isOn: Binding, label: Closure)**).

A **Toggle** view requires a Boolean binding property to store its current value. In the following example, we provide this property and also use its value to display the appropriate label.

Listing 3-44: Implementing a `Toggle`

```
struct ContentView: View {
   @State private var currentState: Bool = true

   var body: some View {
      VStack {
         Toggle(isOn: $currentState, label: {
            Text(currentState ? "On" : "Off")
         })
         Spacer()
      }.padding()
   }
}
```

This code uses a ternary operator to check the value of the **currentState** property and display the corresponding text ("On" or "Off"). By default, we set the value of this property to **true**, so the switch is activated and the "On" label is displayed on the screen. If we tap the switch, it is turned off, the view is updated, and the "Off" label is shown instead.

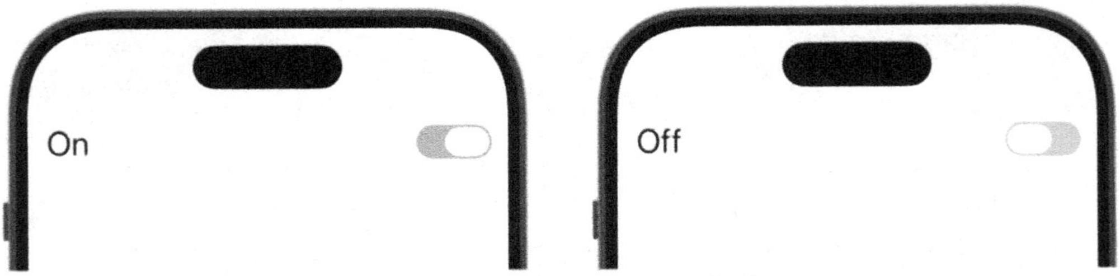

Figure 3-33: *Switch on and off*

The closure assigned to the **label** argument can include a second view to define a subtitle, as in the following example.

Listing 3-45: Including a subtitle

```
struct ContentView: View {
   @State private var currentState: Bool = true
```

```
    var body: some View {
        VStack {
            Toggle(isOn: $currentState, label: {
                Text(currentState ? "On" : "Off")
                Text("Enable or Disable")
            })
            Spacer()
        }.padding()
    }
}
```

Figure 3-34: *Switch with a title and subtitle*

The **`Toggle`** view creates a horizontal stack to contain the label and the control, with a flexible space in between. As a consequence, the view occupies all the horizontal space available in its container, and the label and the control are displaced to the sides. If we want to have absolute control over the position and size of the views, we can apply the **`fixedSize()`** modifier introduced before to reduce the view's size, or hide the label with the following modifier.

`labelsHidden()`

This modifier hides the labels assigned to controls.

This modifier works with several controls, but it is particularly useful with switches. The following example shows how to implement it to define a custom label for the control.

Listing 3-46: Defining a custom label for the `Toggle` view

```
struct ContentView: View {
    @State private var currentState: Bool = true

    var body: some View {
        HStack {
            Toggle("", isOn: $currentState)
                .labelsHidden()
            Text(currentState ? "On" : "Off")
                .padding()
                .background(Color(currentState ? .yellow : .gray))
        }.padding()
    }
}
```

The view is now the size of the control and centered on the screen. The label is no longer shown, so we declare it with an empty string, but include a **Text** view on the side to display the current value. The result is shown below.

Figure 3-35: *Custom label for the switch*

Like **Button** views, **Toggle** views also implement a modifier to define the style of the control.

> **toggleStyle(**ToggleStyle**)**
>
> This modifier defines the style of the toggle. The argument is a structure that conforms to the **ToggleStyle** protocol. To create standard structures, the framework includes the properties **automatic**, **button**, **checkbox**, and **switch**.

By default, the value is set to **automatic**, which means the system selects the style of the control (**switch** or **checkbox**), but we can also specify the **button** value to create a completely different type of control. When we apply this style to the view, the system displays a toggle button to represent the on and off states. When the button is on, it is highlighted; otherwise, it appears as a standard button.

Listing 3-47: Implementing a toggle button

```
struct ContentView: View {
   @State private var currentState: Bool = true

   var body: some View {
      HStack {
         Toggle(isOn: $currentState, label: {
            Label("Send", systemImage: "mail")
         })
         .toggleStyle(.button)
      }.padding()
   }
}
```

Figure 3-36: *Toggle button in the on and off state*

Slider View

A **Slider** view creates a control that lets the user select a value within a specified range. It appears as a horizontal bar with a movable knob that reflects the current value. The structure provides several initializers, with optional arguments that allow us to customize both the appearance and behavior of the control. The following is the most frequently used.

Slider(value: Binding, **in:** Range, **step:** Float, **label:** Closure, **minimumValueLabel:** Closure, **maximumValueLabel:** Closure, **tick:** Closure**)**

This initializer creates a **Slider** view from the values specified by the arguments. The **value** argument is a binding property that stores the current value, the **in** argument is a range that specifies the minimum and maximum values the user can choose from, the **step** argument indicates the number by which the current value will be incremented or decremented, the **label** argument is a view that describes the purpose of the control for accessibility, the **minimumValueLabel** and **maximumValueLabel** arguments define the labels to show at the beginning and end of the slider, and the **tick** argument defines the marks shown along the slider.

To create a slider, we must provide at least a binding property to store the value and a range to determine the minimum and maximum values allowed, as shown below.

Listing 3-48: Creating a basic slider

```
struct ContentView: View {
   @State private var currentValue: Float = 5

   var body: some View {
      VStack {
         Text("Current Value: \(currentValue.formatted(.number.
            precision(.fractionLength(0))))")
         Slider(value: $currentValue, in: 0...10, step: 1.0)
         Spacer()
      }.padding()
   }
}
```

This example creates a slider with a range from 0 to 10 and displays the current value using a **Text** view. The control works with values of type **Float** or **Double**, which means it supports floating point values. In this case, however, we specify a step of 1.0, so the user can only select integer values. Note that we format the value with the **formatted()** method to remove the decimal part. Since the **currentValue** property is initialized with the value **5**, the knob starts in the middle of the slider, as shown below.

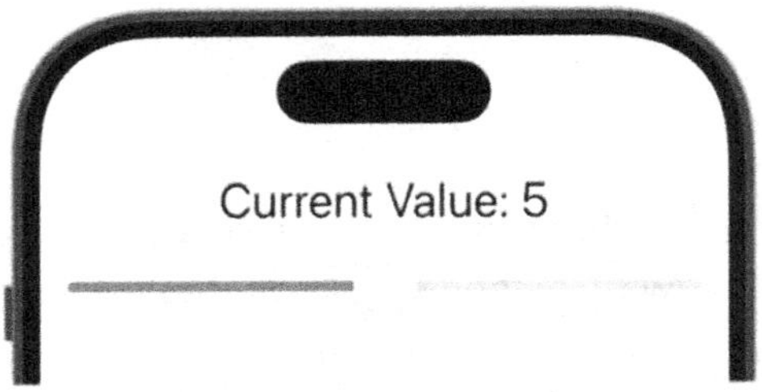

Figure 3-37: *Slider for integer values*

A slider can also include labels and images to clarify the purpose of the control and help the user select the appropriate value. In the following example, we add SF Symbols at the beginning and end of the slider to illustrate the design options available for this control.

Listing 3-49: Designing a slider

```
struct ContentView: View {
   @State private var currentValue: Float = 5

   var body: some View {
      VStack {
         Text("Current Value: \(currentValue.formatted(.number.
            precision(.fractionLength(0))))")
         Slider(value: $currentValue, in: 0...10, step: 1.0, label: {},
            minimumValueLabel: {
            Image(systemName: "backward.end.circle")
         }, maximumValueLabel: {
            Image(systemName: "forward.end.circle")
         })
         Spacer()
      }.padding()
   }
}
```

When we declare labels at the beginning and end of the slider, the view expects us to also provide the **label** argument to specify the purpose of the control. This label is displayed on Macs and is used for accessibility purposes on iOS. If we do not need it, we can declare it as an empty closure, as we did in this example. The result is shown below.

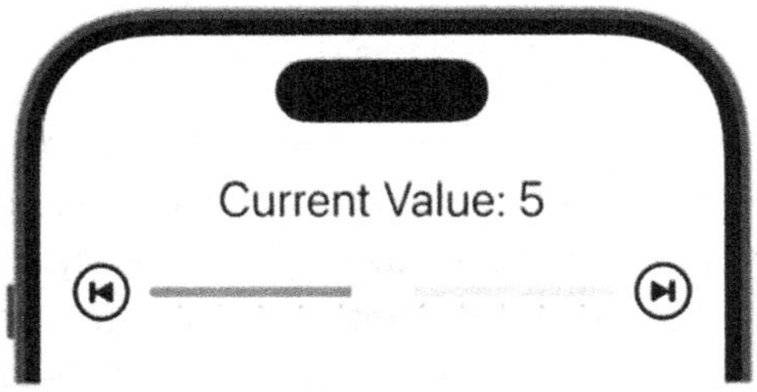

Figure 3-38: *Slider with custom design*

When we declare a label, the system automatically adds marks, commonly called ticks, along the slider to provide a visual cue that helps the user select values. These ticks are positioned according to the values specified by the **in** and **step** arguments. On iOS, ticks are automatically displayed and positioned by the system when all required arguments are provided. On Macs, however, we can customize them. For this purpose, the framework includes the **SliderTick** structure to create custom ticks. The following is the structure's initializer.

SliderTick(Value, **label:** Closure**)**

This initializer creates a single tick for a slider. The first argument is a value that indicates the location of the tick along the slider, and the **label** argument is an optional closure to provide the view we want to show in that location instead of the image by default.

There are several ways to customize ticks. We can declare individual **SliderTick** instances with fixed values to highlight specific positions, or filter the values provided by the slider to display only the ticks we want. In the following example, we show how to configure the slider with ticks at the beginning, middle, and end.

Listing 3-50: Customizing the slider

```
struct ContentView: View {
   @State private var currentValue: Float = 5

   var body: some View {
      VStack {
         Text("Current Value: \(currentValue.formatted(.number.
            precision(.fractionLength(0))))")
         Slider(value: $currentValue, in: 0...10, label: {}, ticks: {
            SliderTick(0)
            SliderTick(5)
            SliderTick(10)
         })
         Spacer()
      }.padding()
   }
}
```

The **SliderTick** view not only draws a dot at a specific position but also defines a step for the slider, so we no longer need to declare the **step** argument. In this case, we define three ticks at positions 0, 5, and 10, so the user can select only those values.

On iPhones and iPads, ticks are displayed as dots, but we can customize their appearance on Macs. In the following example, we show how to replace the default ticks with numbers.

Listing 3-51: Customizing the slider for Macs

```
struct ContentView: View {
   @State private var currentValue: Float = 5

   var body: some View {
```

```
   VStack {
      Text("Current Value: \(currentValue.formatted(.number.
         precision(.fractionLength(0))))")
      Slider(value: $currentValue, in: 0...10, step: 1.0, label: {},
         tick: { value in
         let position = Int(value)
         if position % 2 == 0 {
            return SliderTick(value, label: {
               Text(String(position))
            })
         } else {
            return nil
         }
      })
      Spacer()
   }.padding()
  }
}
```

The slider in this example allows the user to select a value between 0 and 10, as before, but now we include the **tick** argument to customize the ticks. The closure assigned to this argument receives a value that represents the current position for which the system is requesting a tick. In this case, we check whether the value is even using the modulo operator (**position % 2 == 0**) and return a tick with that value as the label, or **nil** otherwise. The result is shown below.

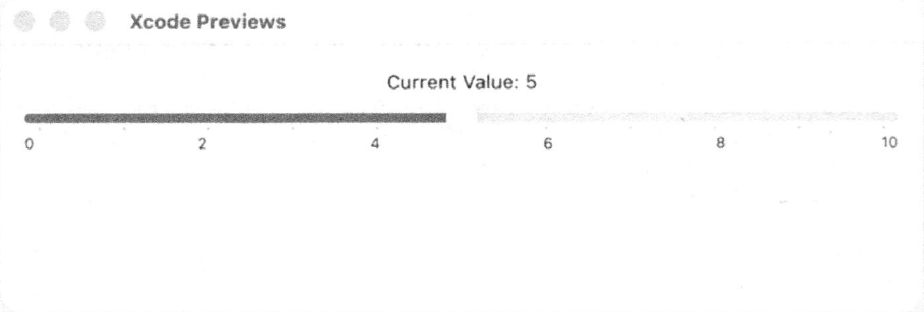

***Figure 3-39:** Custom ticks*

Do It Yourself

Update the **ContentView** structure with the code in Listing 3-51. Select My Mac from the device selector in Xcode's toolbar. Run the application on your Mac. You should see a slider similar to the one shown in Figure 3-39.

BASIC

ProgressView View

SwiftUI includes the **ProgressView** view to create a progress bar. The view was designed to show the progress of a task over time.

```
ProgressView(String, value: Binding, total: Double)
```

This initializer creates a progress bar. The first argument specifies the label, the **value** argument indicates the current progress, and the **total** argument specifies the value that determines the completion of the process.

The implementation of this view is straightforward. All we need is a property with the value that represents the current progress.

Listing 3-52: Showing progress

```
struct ContentView: View {
   @State private var currentValue: Float = 5

   var body: some View {
      VStack {
         ProgressView(value: currentValue, total: 10)
         Spacer()
      }.padding()
   }
}
```

This **ProgressView** view goes from 0.0 to 10.0 and starts at the value 5 (the initial value assigned to the **currentValue** property), so in this case the progress is set in the middle.

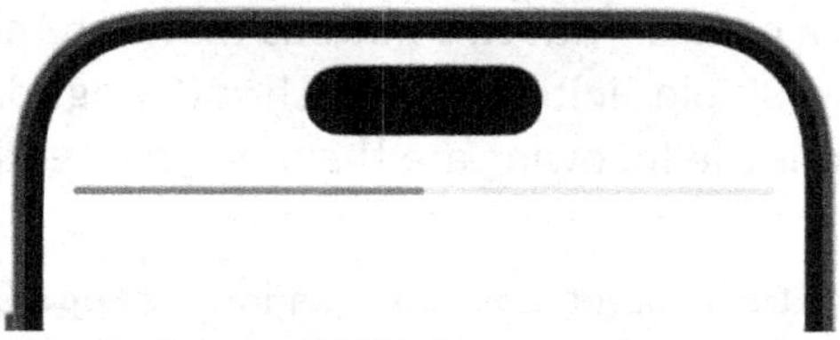

Figure 3-40: *Progress bar*

The **ProgressView** view is designed to display the progress of a task over time, such as how much data has been downloaded from a server or how close we are to completing a process. When the progress is not tied to a specific value, we can change the style of the view using the following modifier.

```
progressViewStyle(ProgressViewStyle)
```

This modifier specifies the style of a **ProgressView** view. The argument is a structure that conforms to the **ProgressViewStyle** protocol. The framework defines the properties **automatic**, **circular**, and **linear** to create standard views.

The style by default is **automatic**, which means that the view is going to be shown as a linear progress bar, but we can specify the **circular** value to create an activity indicator. This is a spinning wheel that indicates that a task is in progress, but unlike progress bars, this type of indicator has no implicit limitations, so we don't need to specify any values, as shown below.

Listing 3-53: Showing an activity indicator

```
struct ContentView: View {
   @State private var currentValue: Float = 5

   var body: some View {
      VStack {
         ProgressView()
            .progressViewStyle(.circular)
         Spacer()
      }.padding()
   }
}
```

***Figure 3-41:** Activity indicator*

BASIC

Stepper View

The **Stepper** view creates a control with two buttons that increment or decrement a value. The structure provides multiple initializers, each offering different combinations of arguments for configuration. The following are the most frequently used.

> **Stepper(**String, **value:** Binding, **in:** Range, **step:** Float, **onEditingChanged:** Closure)

This initializer creates a **Stepper** view configured with the values specified by the arguments. The first argument defines the label, the **value** argument is the binding property that stores the current value, the **in** argument is a range that determines the minimum and maximum values allowed, the **step** argument is a **Float** or a **Double** (depending on the binding property) that determines the amount by which the value is going to be incremented or decremented, and the **onEditingChanged** argument is a closure that is executed when the user begins and ends editing the value.

> **Stepper(**String, **onIncrement:** Closure?, **onDecrement:** Closure?, **onEditingChanged:** Closure)

This initializer creates a **Stepper** view that performs the actions specified by the arguments. The first argument defines the label, the **onIncrement** argument is a closure that is executed when the user taps on the **+** button, the **onDecrement** argument is a closure that is executed when the user taps on the **-** button, and the **onEditingChanged** argument is a closure that is executed when the user begins and ends editing the value.

To implement a **Stepper** view, we need a binding property to store the current value and define the range of values we want the user to choose from.

Listing 3-54: Creating a stepper

```
struct ContentView: View {
   @State private var currentValue: Float = 0

   var body: some View {
      VStack {
         Text("Current Value: \(currentValue.formatted(.number.
            precision(.fractionLength(0))))")
         Stepper("Counter", value: $currentValue, in: 0...100)
         Spacer()
      }.padding()
   }
}
```

The **Stepper** view works with floating-point values of type **Float** or **Double**, so we format the value to display only integers. The result is shown below.

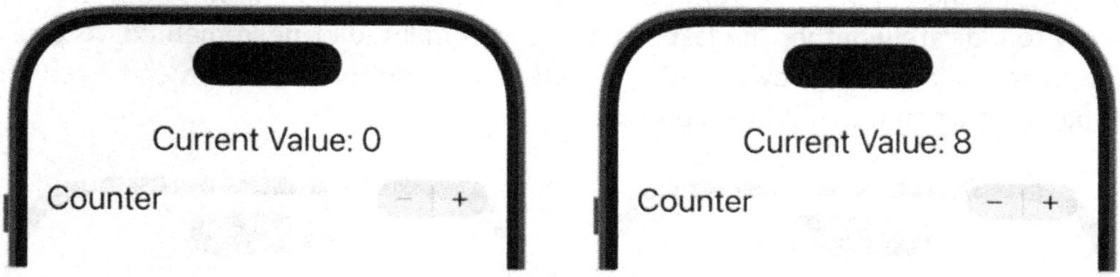

Figure 3-42: *Stepper*

Like the **Toggle** view, the **Stepper** view is implemented with a horizontal stack and a flexible space between the label and the control. If we want to provide our own label and define a custom position for the control, we need to apply the **labelsHidden()** modifier, as we did in Listing 3-46. The following example defines a custom label and creates the stepper with the **onIncrement** and **onDecrement** arguments to display an arrow on the screen that tells the user whether the last value was incremented or decremented.

Listing 3-55: Modifying the interface when the value is incremented or decremented

```
struct ContentView: View {
   @State private var currentValue: Float = 0
   @State private var goingUp: Bool = true

   var body: some View {
      VStack {
         HStack {
            Text("Current Value: \(currentValue.formatted(.number.
               precision(.fractionLength(0))))")
            Image(systemName: goingUp ? "arrow.up" : "arrow.down")
               .foregroundStyle(goingUp ? Color.green : Color.red)
            Stepper("", onIncrement: {
               currentValue += 5
               goingUp = true
            }, onDecrement: {
```

```
                currentValue -= 5
                goingUp = false
            }).labelsHidden()
        }
        Spacer()
    }.padding()
  }
}
```

In this example, we define two **@State** properties: **currentValue** to store the current value of the stepper, and a Boolean property called **goingUp** to indicate whether the last value was incremented or decremented. The views are included in an **HStack** to show them side by side. The first one is the same **Text** view used before to display the stepper's current value. After this view, we include an **Image** view that checks the **goingUp** property to show an SF Symbol of an arrow pointing up or down, depending on the property's value. The same property is used to determine the color of the arrows. Finally, we define the **Stepper** view with the **onIncrement** and **onDecrement** arguments. In the closures assigned to these arguments, we increment or decrement the value by 5 and change the value of the **goingUp** property to indicate whether the last value was incremented or decremented. As a result, the user can see a green arrow pointing up when the + button is pressed and a red arrow pointing down when the - button is pressed.

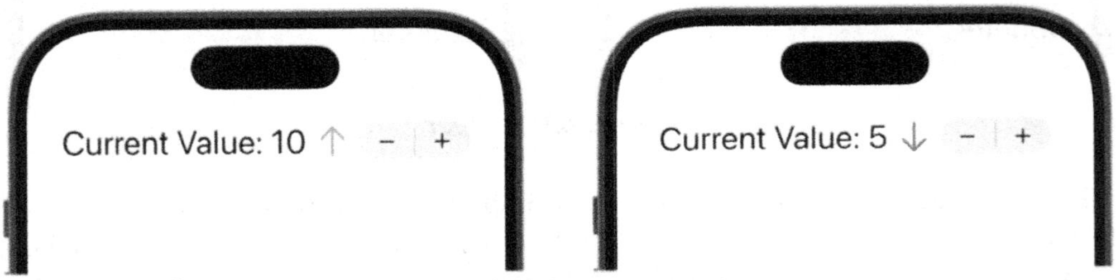

Figure 3-43: *Custom stepper*

BASIC

GroupBox View

SwiftUI includes a view called **GroupBox** that creates a container with styles by default. It is commonly used to present settings or configuration options. The view uses a background color and rounded corners to visually group related views and controls.

GroupBox(String, **content:** Closure)

This initializer creates a **GroupBox** view. The first argument defines the label to show at the top of the box, and the **content** argument is the closure that defines the views contained by the group.

The view is styled by default with a background color, so all we need to do is to implement it and provide the closure with all the views we want to include inside the box.

Listing 3-56: Defining a group box

```
struct ContentView: View {
    @State private var setting1: Bool = true
    @State private var setting2: Bool = true
    @State private var setting3: Bool = true

    var body: some View {
        GroupBox("Settings") {
            VStack(spacing: 10) {
                Toggle("Autocorrection", isOn: $setting1)
                Toggle("Capitalization", isOn: $setting2)
                Toggle("Editable", isOn: $setting3)
            }
        }.padding()
    }
}
```

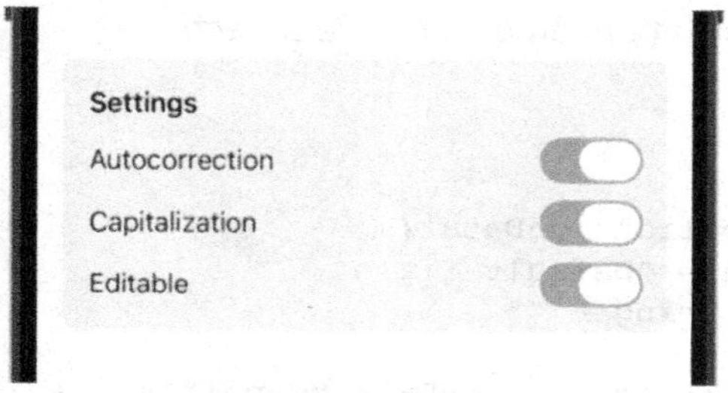

Figure 3-44: Group box

BASIC

3.3 - Data Model

Professional applications consist of multiple views, each representing a screen through which the user can navigate. These views must access the same data and respond to changes in the state of the application. For this reason, the application must provide a single source of data that can be accessed and modified by all views. This shared data source is usually referred to as the *model*, or *data model*.

The data model is part of the basic organization of an application. In this paradigm, a group of structures or objects defines the model, including the app's data and state, while the views connect to the model to present that data on the screen and update it based on user input.

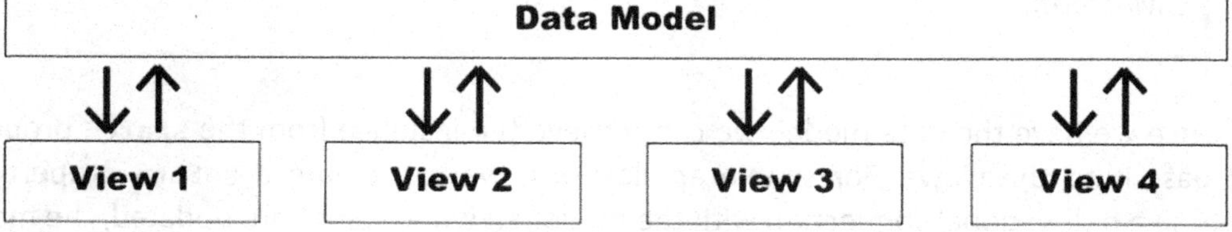

Figure 3-45: Data model

This organization cannot be created with **@State** properties. The code generated by the **@State** macro used in previous examples can only store values that control the states of a single view. What we need is an object that can be passed to the views and report any changes to the system. To define this object, SwiftUI includes the following macro.

@Observable

This macro adds to a class the code necessary to allow the properties to store and manage the states of the application.

With this macro, we can turn any class into an observable object, which means we can use the object's properties to store and manage the states of the application. The following example shows how to define this class. In this case, we call it **ApplicationData**, but it can take any name we want.

Listing 3-57: Storing our data in an observable object

```
import SwiftUI

@Observable class ApplicationData {
   var title: String = "Default Title"
   var titleInput: String = ""

   static let shared: ApplicationData = ApplicationData()
   private init() {}
}
```

This model includes two properties. We have a property called **title** to store the title of a book, and another called **titleInput** to allow the user to type a new one. But since we are modifying the class with the **@Observable** macro, we don't need to declare **@State** properties in the views anymore. The macro takes care of generating the code needed for the properties of the class to store the states and report the changes to the views.

IMPORTANT

In this case, we define the class as a singleton, which ensures that only one instance can be created. This is the recommended practice in SwiftUI because it makes the instance accessible from anywhere in the code, not just the views. To learn more about singletons, read our book *Swift for Masterminds*.

Once we have the data model, we can retrieve the instance from the **shared** property and pass it to the views. For simple applications, we can create a **@State** property to establish a bidirectional connection with the model, so when values are updated, the model and the view stay in sync, as shown below.

Listing 3-58: Working with an observable object

```
struct ContentView: View {
   @State private var appData = ApplicationData.shared

   var body: some View {
      VStack(spacing: 8) {
         Text(appData.title)
            .padding(10)
         TextField("Insert Title", text: $appData.titleInput)
            .textFieldStyle(.roundedBorder)
         Button(action: {
            appData.title = appData.titleInput
            appData.titleInput = ""
         }, label: { Text("Save") })
         Spacer()
      }.padding()
   }
}
```

This is similar to what we have done before, but instead of reading and storing values in `@State` properties, we store them in the properties of the `ApplicationData` object, so if we add other views to the interface later, they will also have access to these properties.

Do It Yourself

The classes defined to store the data are a central part of our application and can be large, so it makes sense to store them in a separate Swift file. Open your project. Open the File menu at the top of the screen and click on the **New > Empty File** option to create a new Swift file. Assign the name **ApplicationData.swift** to the file and copy the code in Listing 3-57. Update the `ContentView` structure with the code in Listing 3-58. Run the application on an iPhone simulator. Type a text and press the button. You should see the title change.

The properties of a model may be accessed from many views. If we need to provide a specific value for one of these properties in a view, we can do so from the view's initializer. For example, in the following view, we assign the value of the `title` property to the `titleInput` property so the user can edit the current title.

Listing 3-59: Initializing the properties of an observable object

```
struct ContentView: View {
   @State private var appData = ApplicationData.shared

   init() {
      appData.titleInput = appData.title
   }
```

```
    var body: some View {
        VStack(spacing: 8) {
            Text(appData.title)
                .padding(10)
            TextField("Insert Title", text: $appData.titleInput)
                .textFieldStyle(.roundedBorder)
            Button(action: {
                appData.title = appData.titleInput
                appData.titleInput = ""
            }, label: { Text("Save") })
            Spacer()
        }.padding()
    }
}
```

The initializer assigns the value of the model's **title** property to the **titleInput** property, so the **TextField** view shows the current value when the view appears.

Figure 3-46: *Text field initialized with the value in the model*

Another way to initialize properties of an observable object or **@State** properties is with the **onAppear()** modifier. As we have seen before, this modifier executes a closure when the view appears on the screen. For instance, we can apply it to the **VStack** view of our **ContentView** view to initialize the **titleInput** property as soon as the view is shown on the screen.

Listing 3-60: Initializing properties when the view appears

```
struct ContentView: View {
    @State private var appData = ApplicationData.shared

    var body: some View {
        VStack(spacing: 8) {
            Text(appData.title)
                .padding(10)
            TextField("Insert Title", text: $appData.titleInput)
                .textFieldStyle(.roundedBorder)
            Button(action: {
                appData.title = appData.titleInput
                appData.titleInput = ""
            }, label: { Text("Save") })
            Spacer()
        }.padding()
```

```
        .onAppear {
            appData.titleInput = appData.title
        }
    }
}
```

Although observable objects are useful for building an app's model and managing view states, a view does not always need to be updated when every value changes. If a property in an observable object does not require the view to refresh, we can apply the following macro.

@ObservationIgnored

This macro produces code that disables observation for a property.

For example, if our model contains a property that stores a value not required by the view, we can prefix that property with this macro, and the view will not be updated every time the value changes.

Listing 3-61: Disabling observation for a property

```
import SwiftUI

@Observable class ApplicationData {
    var title: String = "Default Title"
    var titleInput: String = ""
    @ObservationIgnored var defaultValue: Int = 0

    static let shared: ApplicationData = ApplicationData()
    private init() {}
}
```

Sometimes it is necessary to update the views when a new value is assigned to a non-observable property or when the system cannot recognize a change in the model. In such cases, we can assign a new identity to the view. For this purpose, SwiftUI provides the following modifier.

id(Value)

This modifier associates the view with a custom identifier. The argument is the **Hashable** value we want to use to identify the view.

Views are identified by a unique value so that the system can process and display them on the screen. The **id()** modifier associates the view with a custom value and can therefore be used to change the view's identity. Each time the identity of the view changes, the system thinks it is a new view and updates the interface to show it. For instance, we can apply the **id()** modifier with a unique value to the **Text** view from the previous examples and then change this identifier to manually update the view when the value of **defaultValue** changes, as shown below.

Listing 3-62: Updating the views manually

```
struct ContentView: View {
   @State private var appData = ApplicationData.shared
   @State private var textID: UUID = UUID()

   var body: some View {
      VStack(spacing: 8) {
         Text("\(appData.title) - \(appData.defaultValue)")
            .padding(10)
            .id(textID)
         TextField("Insert Title", text: $appData.titleInput)
            .textFieldStyle(.roundedBorder)
         Button(action: {
            appData.title = appData.titleInput
            appData.titleInput = ""
         }, label: { Text("Save") })
         Button(action: {
            appData.defaultValue = 100
            textID = UUID()
         }, label: { Text("Change Default Value") })
         Spacer()
      }.padding()
   }
}
```

In this case, we use a **UUID** structure to provide the identifier. This is a structure defined in the **Foundation** framework that generates a unique value every time it is created, so we can use it to make the system believe that the view has changed. In this example, we add a second button. The button updates the model's **defaultValue** property. This property is not observable, but because we assign a new **UUID** value to the **textID** property, the identity of the **Text** view changes and the entire view is refreshed to display the new value.

BASIC

3.4 - Environment

An application may include a view that presents a menu, another that displays a list of items, and another that shows information about the item selected by the user. All of these views must access the same data and therefore share a reference to the data model. Although we could create a binding property and pass the model instance to every view, as we did in previous examples, a better approach for large applications is to store a reference to the model in the environment and access it from there when needed.

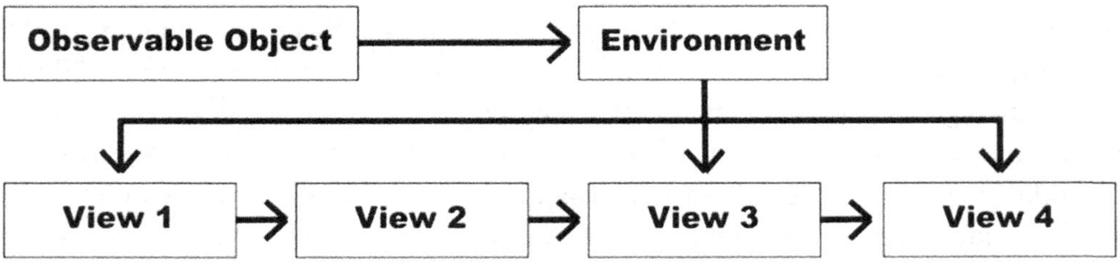

Figure 3-47: *Accessing the model through the environment*

We introduced the environment in Chapter 2. It is a general-purpose container that stores information about the application and its views, and it can also store custom data, including references to observable objects. In the example shown in Figure 3-47, an instance of an observable object is added to the environment and accessed only by the views that require it.

As mentioned earlier, to add a value to the environment we must apply the **environment()** modifier, and to read a value from the environment we need to create a property using the **@Environment** property wrapper (see Chapter 2, Listings 2-79 and 2-80). However, there are some important details to consider before accessing the data model from the environment. First, the **environment()** modifier assigns the object to the environment of a view hierarchy. This means that if we want all the views in our interface to have access to the property, we must apply it to the initial view, as shown below.

Listing 3-63: Assigning the observable object to the view's environment

```
@main struct MyApp: App {
   @State private var appData = ApplicationData.shared

   var body: some Scene {
      WindowGroup {
         ContentView()
            .environment(appData)
      }
   }
}
```

In this example, we apply the **environment()** modifier to the **ContentView** view created by the **WindowGroup** structure, so the data model is injected into the environment as soon as the app is launched. We store an instance of the **ApplicationData** class in a **@State** property to create a bidirectional connection between the model and the views, and then apply the modifier to the **ContentView** view, effectively injecting that instance into the environment.

The second detail we need to consider is that environment properties are not bidirectional by default. This means that if we want to use some of those properties in controls that allow the user to change their values (e.g., **$myinput**), we must turn the property into a bidirectional property. For this purpose, SwiftUI includes the following property wrapper.

@Bindable

This property wrapper creates bindings to the properties of an observable object.

The **@Bindable** property wrapper must be applied to the environment property when the view is created. The following example shows how to access the data model from the environment with an **@Environment** property, and how to turn that property into a bidirectional binding property with **@Bindable**.

Listing 3-64: Getting a reference to the observable object from the environment

```
struct ContentView: View {
   @Environment(ApplicationData.self) private var appData

   var body: some View {
      @Bindable var appData = appData

      VStack(spacing: 8) {
         Text(appData.title)
            .padding(10)
         TextField("Insert Title", text: $appData.titleInput)
            .textFieldStyle(.roundedBorder)
         Button(action: {
            appData.title = appData.titleInput
            appData.titleInput = ""
         }, label: { Text("Save") })
         Spacer()
      }.padding()
   }
}
#Preview {
   ContentView()
      .environment(ApplicationData.shared)
}
```

This example works like before, but now we access the data model through the environment. Note that because the view created for the preview belongs to a different hierarchy, we must apply the **environment()** modifier to this view as well.

Do It Yourself

Update the **App** structure with the code in Listing 3-63, and the **ContentView** structure with the code in Listing 3-64. The application works as before, but now the values are taken from the observable object through the environment and therefore they are available to all the views that belong to the **ContentView**'s hierarchy. We will learn how to add more views to this hierarchy in Chapter 5.

Chapter 4
Lists

BASIC

4.1 - Lists of Views

One of the main characteristics of computer systems is their ability to process sequential data. Due to their elementary structure, made up of sequences of switches on and off, computers excel at organizing information into lists of values, and this is the perfect format for displaying data to users. We can implement this type of organization with vertical and horizontal stacks, but SwiftUI provides additional tools to create dynamic lists of views and edit their content.

BASIC

ForEach View

The simplest tool provided by SwiftUI to create a list of views is the **`ForEach`** view. This view generates a loop that iterates through the values of a collection and creates a new view for each one of them. The structure includes the following initializer.

```
ForEach(Data, id: KeyPath, content: Closure)
```

This initializer creates a **`ForEach`** view. The first argument is the collection of values the loop is going to iterate through, the **id** argument is the key path that points to the unique identifier for each value, and the **content** argument is the closure that creates the views in each cycle.

A **`ForEach`** view needs two values: the collection from which it gets the data to build the list of views, and a key path that determines the value used to identify those views. This last value is important because the system needs to identify views to remove them or add new ones when the collection is updated. If the collection is made up of standard Swift values like **`Int`** or **`String`**, assigning an identifier is easy. These data types conform to the **`Hashable`** protocol and therefore they have a hash value that identifies each instance. To use this hash value as the identifier, we must specify the key path **`.self`**, as in the following example.

Listing 4-1: Creating a dynamic list of views

```
struct ContentView: View {
   var body: some View {
      VStack {
```

```
            ForEach(1...5, id: \.self) { value in
               Text("Value: \(value)")
            }
            Spacer()
         }
      }
   }
```

The **`ForEach`** view adds the content to its container, so we must declare it inside a container view like a **`VStack`** or an **`HStack`**, as we did in Listing 4-1. In this example, the loop is defined with a range of integers from 1 to 5, and the views are identified by the hash value (**`\.self`**). The **`ForEach`** view loops through the values in the range and sends them to the closure one by one. The closure receives each value and then creates a **`Text`** view with it to display it on the screen. The result is shown below.

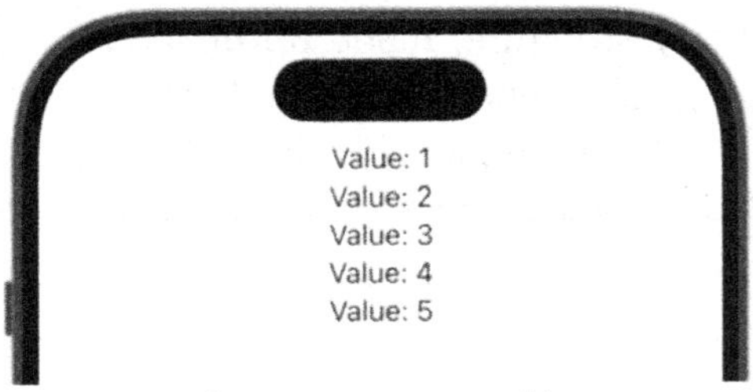

Figure 4-1: *List of views generated by a* `ForEach` *loop*

In this example, the values are presented on the screen with a **`VStack`** and the configuration by default (center alignment and a width determined by the widest view). Although we can use all the views at our disposal to present each value and apply any styles we want, there is a standard design that users immediately recognize in which the values are separated by a line. SwiftUI includes the following view to create this line.

`Divider()`
This initializer creates a **`Divider`** view. The view displays a line to separate content.

A **`Divider`** view is like any other view. If we want to position the line generated by this view below the value, we must embed the **`Text`** view and the **`Divider`** view in a **`VStack`**, as shown below.

Listing 4-2: Creating a list with a standard design

```
struct ContentView: View {
   let listCities: [String] = ["Paris", "Toronto", "Dublin"]

   var body: some View {
      VStack {
         ForEach(listCities, id: \.self) { value in
            VStack {
               Text(value)
               Divider()
            }
         }
```

```
            Spacer()
        }
    }
}
```

In this example, the **ForEach** view creates a list of views from an array of strings. Note that **String** values are hashable, so we can also identify them by the hash value with **.self**.

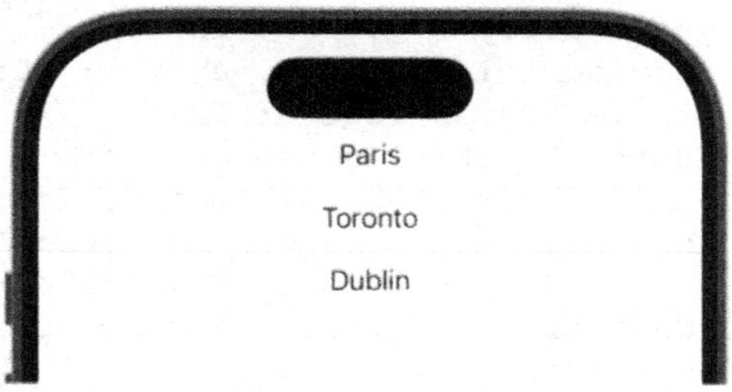

Figure 4-2: *List of views with a standard design*

Values of primitive data types like integers and strings conform to the **Hashable** protocol, so we can use their hash value to identify the views, as we did in the previous examples. However, when working with custom data types, we must provide our own identifier. For this purpose, SwiftUI offers the **Identifiable** protocol. This protocol requires the data type to define a property called **id** that stores a unique identifier for each instance. This is how we prepare the values in our data model to work with a list of views. For example, the following model defines a structure that includes all the properties required to store information about a book, along with an **id** property that uniquely identifies each book.

Listing 4-3: Defining a model to work with lists of views

```
import SwiftUI

struct Book: Identifiable, Hashable {
   let id = UUID()
   var title: String
   var author: String
   var cover: String
   var year: Int
   var selected: Bool

   var displayYear: String {
      get {
         return String(year)
      }
   }
}
@Observable class ApplicationData {
   var userData: [Book] = []

   static let shared: ApplicationData = ApplicationData()
   private init() {
      userData = [
         Book(title: "Apple Intelligence for Masterminds", author: "J.D
            Gauchat", cover: "book1", year: 2026, selected: false),
```

```
        Book(title: "Steve Jobs", author: "Isaacson", cover: "book2",
           year: 2011, selected: false),
        Book(title: "Swift for Masterminds", author: "J.D Gauchat",
           cover: "book3", year: 2026, selected: false),
        Book(title: "The C Programming Language", author: "Kernighan",
           cover: "book4", year: 1988, selected: false),
        Book(title: "Being Digital", author: "Negroponte", cover:
           "book5", year: 1996, selected: false),
        Book(title: "Only the Paranoid Survive", author: "Grove", cover:
           "book6", year: 1999, selected: false),
        Book(title: "Accidental Empires", author: "Cringely", cover:
           "book7", year: 1996, selected: false),
        Book(title: "Bobby Fischer Teaches Chess", author: "Fischer",
           cover: "book8", year: 1982, selected: false),
        Book(title: "New Guide to Science", author: "Asimov", cover:
           "book9", year: 1993, selected: false),
        Book(title: "Christine", author: "King", cover: "book10", year:
           1983, selected: false),
        Book(title: "IT", author: "King", cover: "book11", year: 1987,
           selected: false),
        Book(title: "Ending Aging", author: "Grey", cover: "book12",
           year: 2007, selected: false)
     ]
  }
}
```

The **Book** structure is the actual model. It contains the **id** property with a unique value to identify the book, as well as properties to store the title, the author, the name of the image for the cover, the year the book was published, a boolean property that indicates whether the book is currently selected or not, and a computed property that converts the year to a string so it can be displayed by a **Text** view.

Because the model to store the user's data is defined by the **Book** structure, all we need for the observable object is a property to store an array of these structures. In this example, we called this property **userData**, and initialize it with a total of 12 books to test the application.

> **IMPORTANT**
>
> The **Book** structure also conforms to the **Hashable** protocol. When a structure conforms to this protocol, the system creates a unique identifier that is used later to identify the instances of the structure within collections. Conformance to this protocol is required for navigation, as we will see in Chapter 5.

Once we have the model, we need to pass a reference to the views. As we saw in Chapter 3, it is best to inject the instance into the environment and then access it from the views using the **@Environment** property wrapper (see Listings 3-63 and 3-64). The following are the changes we need to introduce to the **App** structure.

Listing 4-4: Injecting the model into the environment

```
@main struct MyApp: App {
   @State private var appData = ApplicationData.shared

   var body: some Scene {
      WindowGroup {
         ContentView()
            .environment(appData)
      }
   }
}
```

The **Identifiable** protocol defines an associated type called **ID**, which the system can use to identify the items. This associated type represents the data type assigned to the **id** property in our model and it is used by the **ForEach** view to identify the views, so we only need to declare the collection and the list of views is automatically created from these values.

Listing 4-5: Creating a list of views with data from the model

```
struct ContentView: View {
   @Environment(ApplicationData.self) private var appData

   var body: some View {
      VStack {
         ForEach(appData.userData) { book in
            VStack {
               HStack(alignment: .top) {
                  Image(book.cover)
                     .resizable()
                     .scaledToFit()
                     .frame(width: 80, height: 100)
                  VStack(alignment: .leading, spacing: 2) {
                     Text(book.title)
                        .bold()
                     Text(book.author)
                     Text(book.displayYear)
                        .font(.caption)
                  }.padding(.top, 5)
                  Spacer()
               }
               Divider()
            }
         }
         Spacer()
      }
   }
}
#Preview {
   ContentView()
      .environment(ApplicationData.shared)
}
```

The **ForEach** view reads the array with all the books from the **userData** property of our observable object and sends the items one by one to the closure. The items are instances of the **Book** structure, each with the information of a book, so we use the values of the structure's properties to create the views. The result is shown below.

Figure 4-3: *List of views created from the data in the model*

Do It Yourself

Create a new App project. Download the book covers from our website. Create a new Asset Catalog and add the covers to it. Create a Swift file called **ApplicationData.swift** for the model in Listing 4-3. Update the **App** structure with the code in Listing 4-4, and the **ContentView** structure with the code in Listing 4-5. Run the application on the Canvas or an iPhone simulator. You should see a list of books, as illustrated in Figure 4-3.

IMPORTANT

The list of books used in this example is stored only in memory. Although we can modify the list by adding, removing, or updating books, as we will see later, every time the app launches, the **ApplicationData** object is recreated and all changes are lost. We will learn how to store data permanently on the device in Chapter 7.

BASIC

ScrollView View

The **ApplicationData** class defined in Listing 4-3 stores 12 books in the model for testing purposes. This creates a long list of books that extends beyond the edge of the screen and is therefore not completely visible to the user. For a list to actually display all the content available in the model, it must be scrollable. To convert a static list of views into a scrollable one, SwiftUI includes the **ScrollView** view.

```
ScrollView(Axes, content: Closure)
```

This initializer creates a container view that the user can scroll. The first argument is a set of values of type **Axis** that indicate the axes along which the content scrolls. The available values are **horizontal** and **vertical** (default). And the **content** argument is the closure that defines the scrollable content.

The **ScrollView** structure just creates a scrollable view, but the content is still generated by a vertical or a horizontal stack. SwiftUI defines the following views for this purpose.

```
LazyVStack(alignment: HorizontalAlignment, spacing: CGFloat?,
pinnedViews: PinnedScrollableViews, content: Closures)
```

This initializer creates a lazy vertical stack. The **alignment** argument determines the horizontal alignment of the views. It is a structure with the type properties **leading**, **center**, and **trailing**. The **spacing** argument determines the space between the views. The **pinnedViews** argument is a structure that determines which views will be momentarily pinned to the bounds of the scroll view while the content is scrolling. The structure defines the type properties **sectionFooters** and **sectionHeaders**. And the **content** argument is the closure that defines the list of views we want to show in the stack.

```
LazyHStack(alignment: VerticalAlignment, spacing: CGFloat?,
pinnedViews: PinnedScrollableViews, content: Closure)
```

This initializer creates a lazy horizontal stack. The arguments are the same as the lazy vertical stack, except for the **alignment** argument, which defines the vertical alignment of the views. It is a structure with the type properties **top**, **center**, **bottom**, **firstTextBaseline**, and **lastTextBaseline**.

Lazy stacks are similar to the normal stacks created by the **VStack** and **HStack** views, with the difference that the views in a lazy stack are created as needed. The system takes care of creating the views only before they are about to be rendered on the screen, consuming less resources and improving performance. Other than the use of lazy stacks, the list is defined as before, but embedded in a **ScrollView** view, as shown below.

Listing 4-6: Creating a scrollable list of views

```
struct ContentView: View {
   @Environment(ApplicationData.self) private var appData

   var body: some View {
      ScrollView {
         LazyVStack {
            ForEach(appData.userData) { book in
               VStack {
                  HStack(alignment: .top) {
                     Image(book.cover)
                        .resizable()
                        .scaledToFit()
                        .frame(width: 80, height: 100)
                     VStack(alignment: .leading, spacing: 2) {
                        Text(book.title).bold()
```

```
                    Text(book.author)
                    Text(book.displayYear).font(.caption)
                 }.padding(.top, 5)
                 Spacer()
              }.padding([.leading, .trailing], 10)
              .padding([.top, .bottom], 5)
              Divider()
           }
        }
      }
    }
  }
}
```

By default, the axis of the view is set to vertical and the content adapts to the size of the view, so all we had to do to allow the user to scroll the books was to replace the **VStack** views with a **LazyVStack** and embed the list in a **ScrollView**. The result is shown below.

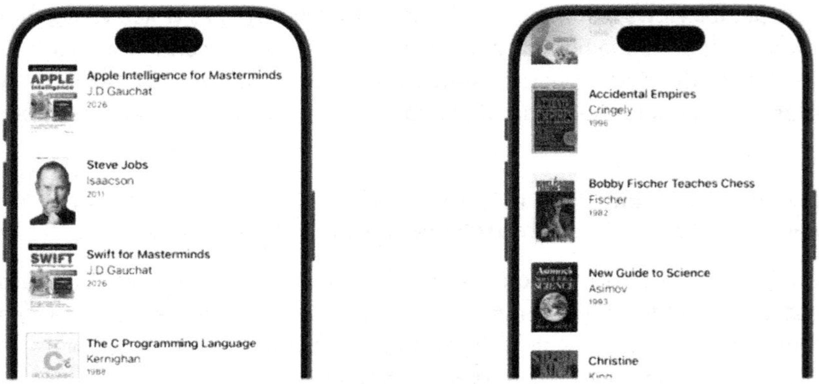

Figure 4-4: *Scroll View*

The **View** protocol includes the following modifiers to configure the scroll view.

scrollDisabled(Bool)

This modifier disables or enables scrolling.

scrollDismissesKeyboard(ScrollDismissesKeyboardMode)

This modifier determines the behavior of the keyboard when the drag gesture begins. The argument is a structure with the type properties **automatic**, **immediately**, **interactively**, and **never** (default).

scrollBounceBehavior(ScrollBounceBehavior, **axes:** Axes)

This modifier determines whether the scroll view bounces back when the user scrolls to the beginning or the end. The first argument determines the bounce behavior. It is a structure with the properties **automatic**, **always**, and **basedOnSize**. The **axes** argument is a set of values that determine the axis to which this behavior is applied. It is an enumeration with the values **horizontal** and **vertical**.

scrollClipDisabled(Bool)

This modifier determines whether or not the scroll view should clip the content that exceeds its boundaries.

The following are the modifiers available to control the scroll indicators.

scrollIndicators(ScrollIndicatorVisibility, **axes:** Axes**)**

This modifier sets the visibility of the scroll indicators. The first argument defines the visibility of the scroll indicators. It is a structure with the type properties **automatic**, **hidden**, **never**, and **visible**. And the **axes** argument defines the axis we want to affect. It is an enumeration with the values **vertical** and **horizontal**.

scrollIndicatorsFlash(onAppear: Bool**)**

This modifier determines if the indicators are going to flash when the view appears.

scrollIndicatorsFlash(trigger: Value**)**

This modifier determines if the indicators are going to flash when a value changes. The **trigger** argument is the value we want to check.

In the following example, we show how some of these modifiers work. At the top of the **ScrollView** view, we have added a **TextField** view so that the user can type text. Tapping on this text field opens the keyboard, but because we apply the **scrollDismisses-Keyboard()** modifier to the view, the keyboard is closed as soon as the user scrolls the view.

Listing 4-7: Configuring the scroll view

```
struct ContentView: View {
   @Environment(ApplicationData.self) private var appData
   @State private var title: String = ""

   var body: some View {
      VStack {
         TextField("Title", text: $title)
            .textFieldStyle(.roundedBorder)
            .padding()
         ScrollView {
            LazyVStack {
               ForEach(appData.userData) { book in
                  VStack {
                     HStack(alignment: .top) {
                        Image(book.cover)
                           .resizable()
                           .scaledToFit()
                           .frame(width: 80, height: 100)
                        VStack(alignment: .leading, spacing: 2) {
                           Text(book.title).bold()
                           Text(book.author)
                           Text(book.displayYear).font(.caption)
                        }.padding(.top, 5)
                        Spacer()
                     }
                     .padding([.leading, .trailing], 10)
                     .padding([.top, .bottom], 5)
                     Divider()
                  }
               }
            }
```

```
        }
        .scrollDismissesKeyboard(.immediately)
        .scrollIndicatorsFlash(onAppear: true)
      }
   }
}
```

Do It Yourself

Update the **ContentView** structure with the code in Listing 4-7. Run the application on an iPhone simulator. Tap on the text field to open the keyboard. You should be able to close the keyboard by scrolling the list.

The content of a **ScrollView** view has to be inside a vertical or a horizontal stack, depending on the axis. If we want to scroll the list of books horizontally, we must embed the **ForEach** view of our example in a **LazyHStack** view, as shown below.

Listing 4-8: Scrolling the list of views horizontally

```
struct ContentView: View {
   @Environment(ApplicationData.self) private var appData

   var body: some View {
      ScrollView(.horizontal, showsIndicators: false) {
         LazyHStack(spacing: 0) {
            ForEach(appData.userData) { book in
               CellBook(book: book)
            }
         }
      }
   }
}
struct CellBook: View {
   let book: Book

   var body: some View {
      VStack {
         Image(book.cover)
            .resizable()
            .scaledToFit()
            .frame(width: 80, height: 100)
         Text(book.title)
            .font(.caption)
      }.padding(10)
      .frame(width: 100, height: 150)
   }
}
```

In this example, we tell the **ScrollView** view to create a horizontal view without indicators, and then place the views inside a **LazyHStack** to display the list horizontally. Note that we have also moved the code that creates the views for each item to a separate view called **CellBook**. Moving the view that creates the rows to a separate view is not required but recommended because it improves the workflow and simplifies the code. The only thing we need to remember when we split the view this way is that the new view doesn't have access to the values processed by the loop, so we must pass the data, as we do in this example (**let book: Book**).

The application works the same way as before, but because of the changes we have introduced to the main view, the books are now displayed side by side.

Figure 4-5: *Horizontal scroll view*

The cells in this example have a fixed size that matches the look we were looking for in this application, but we can also resize the cells to fit the available space within the scroll view. For this purpose, the **View** protocol defines the following modifiers.

```
containerRelativeFrame(Axes, count: Int, span: Int, spacing: CGFloat, alignment: Alignment)
```

This modifier defines the size of the view relative to the size of its container. The first argument defines the axis according to which the size of the view is calculated. The available values are **horizontal** and **vertical**. The **count** argument determines how many columns or rows of views to create for the available space (one by default). The **span** argument determines how many columns or rows the view should take up (one by default). The **spacing** argument determines the amount of spacing between columns or rows. And the **alignment** argument specifies how the views should be aligned. It is an enumeration with the values **topLeading**, **top**, **topTrailing**, **leading**, **center** (default), **trailing**, **bottomLeading**, **bottom**, and **bottomTrailing**.

```
safeAreaPadding(Edges, Size)
```

This modifier sets a margin between the safe area and the content of the scroll view. The first argument determines the edges to be affected by the padding. The available values are **top**, **bottom**, **leading** and **trailing**.

```
contentMargins(Size, for: Placement)
```

This modifier adds a margin to the content of a scroll view. The first argument determines the size of the padding, and the **for** argument is a structure that determines whether the scroll indicators are affected. The structure includes the properties **automatic**, **scrollContent** and **scrollIndicators**.

Resizing the view to fit the available space within the scroll view is easy. All we need to do is apply the **containerRelativeFrame()** modifier to the view that generates the content for the scroll view, as shown in the following example.

Listing 4-9: Adapting the size of the views to the container

```
struct ContentView: View {
   @Environment(ApplicationData.self) private var appData

   var body: some View {
      ScrollView(.horizontal, showsIndicators: false) {
         LazyHStack(spacing: 0) {
            ForEach(appData.userData) { book in
               CellBook(book: book)
                  .containerRelativeFrame(.horizontal)
            }
         }
      }
   }
}
struct CellBook: View {
   let book: Book

   var body: some View {
      VStack {
         Image(book.cover)
            .resizable()
            .scaledToFit()
         Text(book.title)
            .font(.body)
      }.padding(10)
   }
}
```

In this case, we want each view to be the size of the scroll view, so we only need to specify the axis to create the columns and the **containerRelativeFrame()** modifier takes care of everything. Note that for the view to adapt to the available space, we had to remove the **frame()** modifiers that were applied before to the views inside the **CellBook** view. The result is shown below.

***Figure 4-6:** The views fit the available space*

Scroll views calculate the speed of the gesture performed by the user and the deceleration rate to determine how the content should be scrolled. By altering these parameters, we can change the scrolling behavior. The following are the modifiers provided for this purpose.

scrollTargetBehavior(ScrollTargetBehavior)

This modifier defines the scroll view's behavior. The argument is a structure that conforms to the **ScrollTargetBehavior** protocol. SwiftUI includes two structures to define common behaviors called **paging** and **viewAligned**.

scrollTargetLayout(isEnabled: Bool)

This modifier configures a view to become a scrolling target. The **isEnabled** argument determines if the views are considered scrolling targets or not.

The **ScrollTargetBehavior** protocol includes two properties called **paging** and **viewAligned** that return standard structures to define common behaviors. The structure returned by the **paging** property defines a scrolling behavior that calculates the deceleration rate based on the size of the views and the container, allowing the user to scroll view by view (page by page) instead of doing so continuously. If we apply the **scrollTargetBehavior()** modifier with the **paging** value to the **ScrollView** view of our example, we can scroll through the books one by one.

Listing 4-10: Scrolling the content page by page

```
struct ContentView: View {
   @Environment(ApplicationData.self) private var appData

   var body: some View {
      ScrollView(.horizontal, showsIndicators: false) {
         LazyHStack(spacing: 0) {
            ForEach(appData.userData) { book in
               CellBook(book: book)
                  .containerRelativeFrame(.horizontal)
            }
         }
      }
      .scrollTargetBehavior(.paging)
   }
}
```

On the other hand, the structure returned by the **viewAligned** property aligns the scrolling to individual views. This means that we can tell the scroll view how to scroll its views and when to decelerate. This behavior is usually required when two or more views fit in the space available within the container. For instance, if we apply the **containerRelativeFrame()** modifier with a count value of 2 and a span of 1 (one view per column), the scroll view displays two views at a time.

Listing 4-11: Scrolling two views at a time

```
struct ContentView: View {
   @Environment(ApplicationData.self) private var appData

   var body: some View {
```

```
      ScrollView(.horizontal, showsIndicators: false) {
         LazyHStack(spacing: 0) {
            ForEach(appData.userData) { book in
               CellBook(book: book)
                  .containerRelativeFrame(.horizontal, count: 2, span: 1,
                     spacing: 0)
            }
         }
      }
      .scrollTargetBehavior(.paging)
   }
}
```

Now, we can see two books per page, and every time we drag the books to one side or the other, the scroll view displays the next two.

Figure 4-7: *Two views per page*

If instead of scrolling two views at a time, we want to scroll them one by one, we need to define a **viewAligned** behavior and tell the scroll view when to stop. This is accomplished by using the **scrollTargetLayout()** modifier. This modifier identifies each view as a scroll target, so the scroll view will align the content to the container one view at a time.

Listing 4-12: Defining each view as a scroll target

```
struct ContentView: View {
   @Environment(ApplicationData.self) private var appData

   var body: some View {
      ScrollView(.horizontal, showsIndicators: false) {
         LazyHStack(spacing: 0) {
            ForEach(appData.userData) { book in
               CellBook(book: book)
                  .containerRelativeFrame(.horizontal, count: 2, span: 1,
                     spacing: 0)
            }
         }
         .scrollTargetLayout()
      }
      .scrollTargetBehavior(.viewAligned)
   }
}
```

Figure 4-8: *Scrolling one view at a time*

In addition to determining the scroll behavior, we can also programmatically scroll to a specific part of the content. To keep track of the scroll's position, SwiftUI includes the **`ScrollPosition`** structure.

> **`ScrollPosition(idType:`** `Type)`
>
> This initializer creates a structure to store the scrolling position of a **`ScrollView`** view. The **idType** argument is the data type of the value used to track the position.

The **`ScrollPosition`** structure includes the following property and method to control the scrolling.

> **`viewID`**
>
> This property returns a hashable value that represents the identifier of the view in the visible position.

> **`scrollTo(edge:`** `Edge)`
>
> This method scrolls the content of the **`ScrollView`** view to the position indicated by the argument. The **edge** argument is an enumeration that determines the side to which the content should scroll. The possible values are **`top`**, **`bottom`**, **`leading`** and **`trailing`**. There are also methods to scroll to a specific point in the view, like **`scrollTo(x: CGFloat, y: CGFloat)`**.

SwiftUI also includes the following modifier to configure the system and programmatically controlled the **`ScrollView`** view.

> **`scrollPosition(`**`Binding,` **`anchor:`** `UnitPoint?)`
>
> This modifier associates a binding property to the **`ScrollView`** view to store the content's position. The first argument is a binding property of type **`ScrollPosition`** that stores information about the current visible view, and the **anchor** argument determines what view is going to be used as a reference for alignment. Possible values are **`top`**, **`bottom`**, **`leading`** and **`trailing`**.

The **`scrollPosition()`** modifier requires a binding property to store the **`Scroll-Position`** structure used to control the current position. The **`ScrollPosition`** structure must be initialized with the data type used to identify each view in the **ScrollView** view. In our example, we can use the **UUID** data type assigned to the **id** property of our model or the associated type **ID**. As mentioned earlier, the associated type **ID** represents the data type of the **id** property in our model, so we can use it to represent the model's identifiers, as in the example below.

Listing 4-13: Scrolling the content programmatically

```
struct ContentView: View {
   @Environment(ApplicationData.self) private var appData
   @State private var position = ScrollPosition(idType: Book.ID.self)
   @State private var title: String = ""

   var body: some View {
      VStack {
         ScrollView(.horizontal, showsIndicators: false) {
            LazyHStack(spacing: 0) {
               ForEach(appData.userData) { book in
                  CellBook(book: book)
                     .containerRelativeFrame(.horizontal, count: 2,
                        span: 1, spacing: 0)
               }
               Button("< Back") {
                  position.scrollTo(edge: .top)
               }
               .buttonStyle(.glassProminent)
               .padding([.leading, .trailing], 55)
            }
            .scrollTargetLayout()
         }
         .scrollPosition($position)
         .scrollTargetBehavior(.viewAligned)
         .frame(height: 300)

         .onChange(of: position, initial: true, {
            if let selected = position.viewID as? UUID {
               if let book = appData.userData.first(where: { $0.id ==
                  selected }) {
                  title = book.title
               }
            }
         })
         Text(title)
            .font(.title)
            .padding()
         Spacer()
      }
   }
}
```

In this example, we create a **@State** property called **position** to store the **ScrollPosition** structure and then assign it to the **ScrollView** view with the **scrollPosition()** modifier. At the end of the list, we include a button that calls the **scrollTo()** method to allow the user to scroll back to the first book. To show how to read the values in the **ScrollPosition** structure, we have also implemented the **onChange()** modifier. Every time the user scrolls the list, the identifier of the prominent view is assigned to the **position** property, so we can read and process this value. To get the book's identifier, we cast the value returned by the **viewID** property of the **ScrollPosition** structure into a **UUID** value. If there is a value, we search for the book with that identifier and display the title on the screen.

Figure 4-9: *Button to scroll the list to the beginning*

Do It Yourself

Update the **ContentView** structure with the code in Listing 4-13. Run the application on an iPhone simulator. You should see the list of books as before. Scroll the list to the end. You should see the title of the visible book on the screen as you scroll and a Back button at the end. Press this button to go back to the beginning of the list.

Another thing we can do with the views in a scroll view is to determine how they appear on the screen when they become visible to the user. In other words, how they transition from one state to another. To customize the transition, SwiftUI includes the following modifier.

scrollTransition(ScrollTransitionConfiguration, **axis:** Axis, **transition:** Closure)

This modifier applies a visual effect to the transition of a view. The first argument determines how the transition will be applied. It is a structure with the properties **identity** (doesn't change the appearance of the view), **animated** (animates the transition when the view becomes visible), and **interactive** (interpolates the effect as the view becomes visible), and the methods **animated(Animation)** to apply a custom animation, and **interactive(timingCurve: UnitCurve)** to define a custom timing curve. The **axis** argument determines if the effect will be applied to the horizontal or vertical axis (**horizontal** or **vertical**). And the **transition** argument is the closure that defines the transition.

The transition effect is defined by a closure. This closure receives two values: an **EmptyVisualEffect** structure that defines a basic visual effect to which we can apply our custom effects, and a **ScrollTransitionPhase** enumeration that defines the current state of the view. The enumeration includes the values **identity** (the view is in the visible area), **topLeading** (the view is at the top or leading edge of the visible area), and **bottomTrailing** (the view is at the bottom or the trailing edge of the visible area). The enumeration also includes a Boolean property called **isIdentity** which indicates whether the view is visible, and the property **value** to return a value indicating the position of the view (-1.0 if the view is at the top of leading edge of the visible area, 0.0 if it is visible, and 1.0 if it is at the bottom or the trailing edge of the visible area).

Adding a visual effect to a transition is simple. We need to apply the **scrollTransition()** modifier to the view and then add the visual effect to the base effect received by the closure. Visual effects are created using common view modifiers, such as **opacity()**, **blur()**, or **grayscale()**, and also others we will introduce in Chapter 8, such as **offset()**, **rotationEffect()**, and **rotation3DEffect()**. The following example shows how to apply opacity to the views outside the visible area.

Listing 4-14: Applying a visual effect to the transition

```
struct ContentView: View {
   @Environment(ApplicationData.self) private var appData

   var body: some View {
      ScrollView(.horizontal, showsIndicators: false) {
         LazyHStack(spacing: 0) {
            ForEach(appData.userData) { book in
               CellBook(book: book)
                  .containerRelativeFrame(.horizontal)
                  .scrollTransition(axis: .horizontal) { effect, phase in
                     effect.opacity(phase.isIdentity ? 1 : 0)
                  }
            }
         }
         .scrollTargetLayout()
      }
      .scrollTargetBehavior(.paging)
   }
}
```

The system executes the closure passed to the **scrollTransition()** modifier for every view. Therefore, when applying the effect, we must determine the current state of the view. If the view is in the visible area, the **isIdentity** property of the **ScrollTransitionPhase** enumeration received by the closure returns **true**, otherwise **false**. By checking this value, we can apply different visual effects to the views that are inside or outside the visible area. In this example, we use a ternary operator to assign an opacity of 1 (fully opaque) to the visible view and an opacity of 0 (fully transparent) to the views outside the visible area. This creates an effect where views gradually appear on the screen as they scroll into the visible area, and fade out as they leave the area, as shown below.

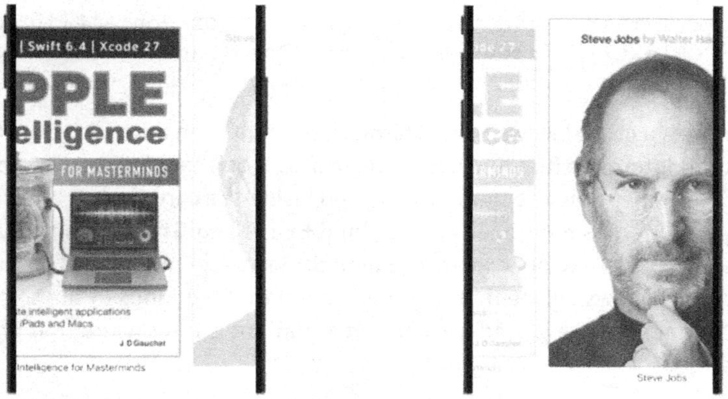

Figure 4-10: *Visual effect applied to the transition*

Many effects can be applied to the same transition. For instance, in the following example we change the opacity as before but also add a scaling effect with the **`scaleEffect()`** modifier.

Listing 4-15: Applying multiple visual effects to the transition

```
.scrollTransition(axis: .horizontal) { effect, phase in
   effect
      .opacity(phase.isIdentity ? 1 : 0)
      .scaleEffect(phase.isIdentity ? 1 : 0.5)
}
```

The **`scaleEffect()`** modifier takes a value representing the scale we want to assign to the view. A value of 1 represents the normal scale and values below or above 1 represent smaller or larger scales. In our example, when the view is visible, it has a scale of 1, but when it enters or leaves the visible area, the scale is reduced to 0.5.

Do It Yourself

Update the **`ContentView`** structure with the code in Listing 4-14 and scroll through the books. You should see the books fade in and out as they enter and leave the visible area, as shown in Figure 4-10. Update the **`scrollTransition()`** modifier with the code in Listing 4-15 and scroll through the books again. You should see the books getting larger and smaller as they enter or leave the visible area.

BASIC

Lazy Grids

The horizontal and vertical stack views presented earlier can only contain one item per row or column. If we want to include more, we need to create a grid. SwiftUI defines the following views for this purpose.

LazyVGrid(columns: [GridItem], **alignment:** HorizontalAlignment, **spacing:** CGFloat?, **pinnedViews:** PinnedScrollableViews, **content:** Closure)

This view creates a grid of views. The **columns** argument is an array of **GridItem** structures that determine how the items are arranged on the grid. The **alignment** argument determines how the items are aligned inside the container. It is a structure with the type properties **center**, **leading**, and **trailing**. The **spacing** argument determines the space between views. The **pinnedViews** argument is a structure that determines which views will be momentarily pinned to the bounds of the scroll view while the content is scrolling. And the **content** argument is the closure that provides the list of views.

LazyHGrid(rows: [GridItem], **alignment:** VerticalAlignment, **spacing:** CGFloat?, **pinnedViews:** PinnedScrollableViews, **content:** Closure)

This view is similar to the **LazyVGrid** view, but the items are arranged horizontally and the **alignment** argument determines the vertical alignment instead of the horizontal alignment. This is a structure with the type properties **bottom**, **center**, **firstTextBaseline**, **lastTextBaseline**, and **top**.

The **LazyVGrid** and **LazyHGrid** views create a grid of views arranged in rows and columns, but the size and quantity of views in a row or a column is determined by instances of the **GridItem** structure.

Griditem(Size, **spacing:** CGFloat?, **alignment:** Alignment?)

This structure defines the size, padding, and alignment of each item on the grid. The first argument determines the size. It is an enumeration with three associated values: **adaptive(minimum: CGFloat, maximum: CGFloat)**, **fixed(CGFloat)**, and **flexible(minimum: CGFloat, maximum: CGFloat)**. The **spacing** argument defines the space around the item. And the **alignment** argument defines the item's alignment. It is a structure with the type properties **bottom**, **bottomLeading**, **bottom-Trailing**, **center**, **leading**, **top**, **topLeading**, **topTrailing**, and **trailing**.

With a **GridItem** structure we can specify the number of views we want to display per row or column, or ask the grid to determine the number of items automatically from the space available. For this purpose, the structure can take three different associated values. The **fixed()** and **flexible()** values define a fixed or flexible size for a single view, and the **adaptive()** value defines a flexible size for multiple views. For instance, if we want to create a vertical grid with a specific number of items per row and a fixed size, we must create an array of **GridItem** structures with the **fixed()** value. The number of instances of the **GridItem** structure included in the array determine the number of items per row, as shown below.

Listing 4-16: Creating a grid with a fixed number of items

```
struct ContentView: View {
   @Environment(ApplicationData.self) private var appData
```

```
    let guides = [
        GridItem(.fixed(75)),
        GridItem(.fixed(75)),
        GridItem(.fixed(75))
    ]
    var body: some View {
        ScrollView {
            LazyVGrid(columns: guides) {
                ForEach(appData.userData) { book in
                    Image(book.cover)
                        .resizable()
                        .scaledToFit()
                }
            }
        }.padding()
    }
}
```

In this example, we define an array of three **GridItem** structures, all with a fixed size of 75 points, and use it to define a vertical grid of books. Because we use a fixed size, and include three instances of the structure, the **LazyVGrid** view creates a grid with three books per row, of a size of 75 points each, no matter the space available.

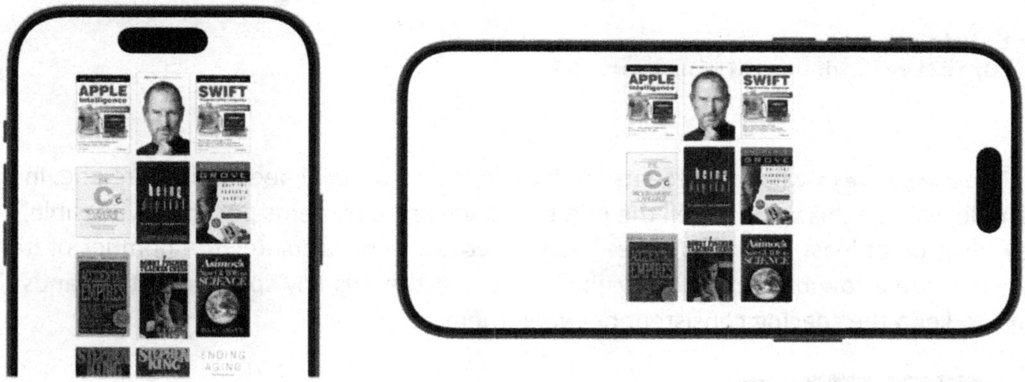

Figure 4-11: *Fixed grid*

In the previous example, the views are always 75 points wide. If what we want is to create three items per row but expand the items to occupy all the space available, we can turn them flexible with the **flexible()** value.

Listing 4-17: Defining flexible items

```
let guides = [
    GridItem(.flexible(minimum: 75), alignment: .top),
    GridItem(.flexible(minimum: 75), alignment: .top),
    GridItem(.flexible(minimum: 75), alignment: .top)
]
```

The **flexible()** value represents one single item, so we still must include three **GridItem** structures in the array to include three items per row, but because we are not declaring a fixed size, the items now expand to occupy all the space available in the container, as shown below.

Figure 4-12: *Flexible grid*

The **`flexible()`** value represents a single item, so the number of items per row is always the same. If what we want is to display as many items as possible per row but keeping the same proportions and space between views, we can use the **`adaptive()`** value.

Listing 4-18: Defining adaptive items

```
let guides = [
   GridItem(.adaptive(minimum: 75))
]
```

The **`adaptive()`** value represents multiple items, so we only need to declare one. In this example, we use this value to tell the grid to include as many items per row as possible, but they must be at least 75 points wide. The **`LazyVGrid`** view calculates the number of items that fit inside a row based on the available space. If there is any space left, it expands the items to keep the spacing consistent between them.

Figure 4-13: *Adaptive grid*

Do It Yourself

Update the **`ContentView`** structure with the code in Listing 4-16. Run the application on an iPhone simulator. You should see the grid of books illustrated in Figure 4-11. Update the **guides** array with the examples in Listings 4-17 and 4-18. Test different values to understand how the grid adapts and how the layout values work.

PRO

Reordering

SwiftUI also provides tools to let the user reorder items in a container. These tools work with standard containers such as **VStack**, **HStack**, and lazy stacks and grids. To enable this feature, reordering must be enabled and the container must be identified as reorderable. The framework provides the following modifiers for this purpose.

reorderable()

This modifier enables reordering for the views in a container.

reorderContainer(for: Type, **in:** Type, **isEnabled:** Bool, **move:** Closure)

This modifier defines a container as reorderable. The **for** argument specifies the data type of the values used to create the views, the **in** argument specifies the data type of the container's identifier, the **isEnabled** argument is a Boolean value that determines whether reordering is enabled, and the **move** argument is the closure executed after the user finishes reordering an item.

After the user drops an item in a new location in the container, the **reorderContainer()** modifier executes the closure assigned to the **move** argument. This closure receives a **ReorderDifference** structure with the identifiers of the items that have been moved. The structure includes the following properties.

sources

This property returns an array with the identifiers of the items to be moved.

destination

This property returns a **Destination** structure with information about the location where the items should be moved to.

The **Destination** structure includes information about the place in the collection where the items were dropped. To provide this information, the structure defines the following properties.

position

This property returns an enumeration of type **Position** with values that determine the location in the collection where the items were dropped. The values are **end** (the items were dropped at the end of the collection) and **before(ItemID)** (the items were dropped before the item with the identifier specified by the associated value).

collectionID

This property returns the identifier of the collection where the items were dropped.

SwiftUI provides the features needed for users to select an item on the screen, drag it, and drop it into a different position, but it is our responsibility to preserve that new order in the data model. To accomplish this, whenever the user completes a drag-and-drop operation, we must determine which items were moved and update the underlying data accordingly. The implementation depends on how the data is stored. The following example shows how to update our array of books, but the implementation may differ if the items are stored in a database or another type of collection.

Listing 4-19: Reordering the items in a grid

```
struct ContentView: View {
   @Environment(ApplicationData.self) private var appData

   let guides = [
      GridItem(.adaptive(minimum: 75))
   ]
   var body: some View {
      ScrollView {
         LazyVGrid(columns: guides) {
            ForEach(appData.userData) { book in
               Image(book.cover)
                  .resizable()
                  .scaledToFit()
            }
            .reorderable()
         }
         .reorderContainer(for: Book.self, move: { diff in
            guard let sourceIndex = appData.userData.firstIndex(where: {
               $0.id == diff.sources[0] }) else { return }
            let element = appData.userData.remove(at: sourceIndex)

            var destinationIndex: Int?
            switch diff.destination.position {
            case .end:
               destinationIndex = appData.userData.endIndex
            case .before(let id):
               destinationIndex = appData.userData.firstIndex(where: {
                  $0.id == id })
            }
            if let destinationIndex {
               appData.userData.insert(element, at: destinationIndex)
            }
         })
      }.padding()
   }
}
```

This is the same grid of books used in previous examples, but we made it reorderable. In our example, we use a **LazyVGrid** container to display the views and a **ForEach** view to list them, so we applied the **reorderable()** modifier to the **ForEach** view to enable reordering for every view in the grid, and the **reorderContainer()** modifier to the **LazyVGrid** container to define this container as reorderable.

Every time the user finishes reordering an item, the **reorderContainer()** modifier calls the closure assigned to the **move** argument, so we must use this closure to modify our array of books to match the new order selected by the user. For this purpose, there are two things we need to determine: the index of the item moved by the user and the index where we should move that item to. These values are returned by the **sources[]** and **position** properties included in the **ReorderDifference** structure received by the closure. Although these properties provide the information we need to move the items, they do not return the indexes of the items in the array, they return the item's identifiers, so we must first search for the items in the **userData** array to get the corresponding indexes. In our example, we first look for the index of the item to be moved. Because in this case selection is not enabled, the user is only able to move one item at a time, so we read the first value in the **sources** property and use the **firstIndex()** method to look for an item that matches that identifier (**$0.id == diff.sources[0]**). If found, we remove it from the array with the **remove()** method. This removes the item from the original location, but now we have to insert it in the new location. For this, we read the **position** property. This is an enumeration that returns the value **end** if the item should be inserted at the end of the array, and the value **before(itemID)** with the identifier of the item in whose place we should insert the item moved by the user. So, if the value is **end**, we insert the item at the last index (**endIndex**), and if the value is **before(itemID)**, we search for the location of the item again using the **firstIndex()** method and then insert it at the index returned by the method. The result is that every time the user reorders the items on the screen, the items in the **userData** array are reorganized to match those locations.

Do It Yourself

Update the **ContentView** structure with the code in Listing 4-19 and run the application on an iPhone simulator. You should see the same grid of books as before, but now, if you tap and hold a cover, you should be able to drag it and move it to a different location on the grid.

PRO

Swipe Actions

SwiftUI also includes built-in support for swipe actions. These are actions that the user can reveal by swiping a row to the left. The following is the modifier we need to apply to each row to enable this feature.

swipeActions(edge: HorizontalEdge, **allowsFullSwipe:** Bool, **content:** Closure)

This modifier defines swipe actions for a row on a list. The **edge** argument determines the side of the row where the buttons are going to be placed (left or right). It is an enumeration with the values **leading** and **trailing**. The **allowsFullSwipe** argument determines whether the first action is executed when the user swipes the row all the way to the side. And the **content** argument is a closure that provides the **Button** views that represent the actions the user can perform.

Some containers, like the **List** view we will study in the next section, limit the user to swiping one row at a time, but others allow the user to swipe as many rows as they want. If we want to always limit the user to one row, we can apply the following modifier to the container.

swipeActionsContainer()

This modifier declares the container as a swipe container, so the user is only allowed to swipe one row at a time.

By default, the swipe action is created on the trailing side and allows the user to perform the first action with a full swipe, so if that configuration works for our application, all we need to do is define the closure with the **Button** views we want to include, as shown below.

Listing 4-20: Adding swipe actions to the rows of a list

```
struct ContentView: View {
   @Environment(ApplicationData.self) private var appData

   var body: some View {
      ScrollView {
         LazyVStack(alignment: .leading) {
            ForEach(appData.userData) { book in
               HStack {
                  Text(book.title)
                     .padding(8)
                  Spacer()
               }
               .swipeActions {
                  Button(role: .destructive, action: {
                     if let index = appData.userData.firstIndex(where: {
                        $0.id == book.id }) {
                        appData.userData.remove(at: index)
                     }
                  }, label: {
                     Image(systemName: "trash")
                  })
               }
               Divider()
            }
         }
         .swipeActionsContainer()
      }.padding()
   }
}
```

In this example, we created a simple vertical list with the titles of our books. The **swipeActions()** modifier includes a single button that gets the index of the book in the **userData** array and removes it, so every time the button is pressed, the corresponding book is removed from the list. In this case, we also applied the **swipeActionsContainer()** modifier so the user can only swipe one row at a time. The result is shown below.

Figure 4-14: *Removing items with swipe actions*

Do It Yourself

Update the **ContentView** structure with the code in Listing 4-20 and run the application on an iPhone simulator. Drag an item to the left. You should see the delete button appear on the right. Press the button. The corresponding book should be removed from the list.

BASIC

4.2 - List View

Presenting information in a scrollable list of rows and columns is a common requirement in many applications. For this reason, SwiftUI includes a dedicated container called **List** to create scrollable lists of views. Like a **LazyVStack** view, a **List** view creates a vertical layout with a single column of items. However, the items are automatically separated by dividers, and the view provides built-in functionality to select, add, and remove content. The following is the view's initializer.

```
List(Data, id: KeyPath, selection: Binding, rowContent: Closure)
```

This initializer creates a list of views. The first argument is the collection of values used to create the rows, the **id** argument is the key path to the unique identifier of each value, the **selection** argument is a binding property that stores one or a set of identifiers to recognize the selected rows, and the **rowContent** argument is a closure that defines the views used to create the rows.

The **List** view works in the same way as the **ForEach** view. If our goal is simply to display the values of a collection, we only need to provide the data and a closure to create the views, as shown in the following example.

Listing 4-21: Creating a list of views with the `List` view

```
struct ContentView: View {
   @Environment(ApplicationData.self) private var appData

   var body: some View {
      List(appData.userData) { book in
         CellBook(book: book)
      }
   }
}
struct CellBook: View {
   let book: Book

   var body: some View {
      HStack(alignment: .top) {
         Image(book.cover)
            .resizable()
            .scaledToFit()
            .frame(width: 80, height: 100)
         VStack(alignment: .leading, spacing: 2) {
            Text(book.title).bold()
            Text(book.author)
            Text(book.displayYear).font(.caption)
            Spacer()
         }.padding(.top, 5)
         Spacer()
      }
   }
}
```

A **`List`** view automatically applies a predefined style to the views, which includes a line between rows and standard padding. The result is shown below.

***Figure 4-15:** List of rows created by a* List *view*

Do It Yourself

Update the **ContentView.swift** file with the code in Listing 4-21. Run the application on an iPhone simulator. You should see a scrollable list of books, as illustrated in Figure 4-15.

IMPORTANT

If you scroll down the list, you will see that the views go all to the top, behind the status bar. This is because **List** views were designed to work with the navigation bars provided by **NavigationStack** views. We will learn how to use these views and navigate between views in the next chapter.

In mobile devices, the list is shown with a style that generates a padding around the views. The **View** protocol defines the following modifier to customize the style.

listStyle(ListStyle)

This modifier assigns a style to the **List** view. The argument is a structure that conforms to the **ListStyle** protocol. SwiftUI defines multiple styling structures, and these structures include type properties to apply standard styles. The properties available are **automatic**, **plain**, **inset**, **grouped**, **insetGrouped**, and **sidebar**.

The style set by default in mobile devices is called **insetGrouped**, but we can change it with the **listStyle()** modifier. The **plain** style displays the views with no background or padding, the **inset** style adds padding to the list, the **insetGrouped** style adds a background and a padding around the views, and the **sidebar** style adds a background to the whole list. The following example shows how to apply a **plain** styling to the list.

Listing 4-22: Creating a plain list

```
struct ContentView: View {
   @Environment(ApplicationData.self) private var appData

   var body: some View {
      List(appData.userData) { book in
         CellBook(book: book)
      }.listStyle(.plain)
   }
}
```

The result is similar to what we achieved with the **ForEach** and **Divider** views before, but now the list has an inset on the left side that gives it a distinctive look.

Figure 4-16: *Plain list*

The **View** protocol includes the following modifiers to customize the list.

listRowBackground(View)

This modifier defines the background view for the row. The argument is a SwiftUI view, such as **Color**.

listRowInsets(EdgeInsets)

This modifier defines the paddings for the rows.

listRowSeparator(Visibility, **edges:** VerticalEdge)

This modifier configures the row separators. The first argument determines if the separators are visible or hidden. It is an enumeration with the values **automatic**, **hidden**, and **visible**. And the **edges** argument defines which separators are affected. It is a structure with the type properties **all**, **bottom**, and **top**.

listRowSeparatorTint(Color?, **edges:** VerticalEdge)

This modifier defines the separators' color. The first argument specifies the new color, and the **edges** argument determines which separator is affected. It is a structure with the type properties **all**, **bottom**, and **top**.

listItemTint(Color?)

This modifier defines a new tint color for the row. It overwrites the app's accent color.

These modifiers are applied to the rows, but by modifying the rows we can change the style of the entire list. For instance, we can remove the padding assigned to the rows by the **plain** style with the **listRowInsets()** modifier.

Listing 4-23: Customizing the rows

```
struct ContentView: View {
   @Environment(ApplicationData.self) private var appData

   var body: some View {
      List(appData.userData) { book in
         CellBook(book: book)
            .listRowInsets(EdgeInsets(top: 0, leading: 0, bottom: 10,
               trailing: 0))
            .listRowBackground(Color(white: 0.95))
            .listRowSeparator(.hidden)
      }.listStyle(.plain)
   }
}
```

In this example, we remove the insets on the sides, but assign an inset of 10 points to the bottom of each row. To demonstrate how other modifiers work, we have also assigned a background color and removed the separators. The result is shown below.

Figure 4-17: *Custom list*

The **`List`** view was designed to work along with the **`ForEach`** view to mix static and dynamic content. The advantage of using a **`ForEach`** view is that we can create a list of rows with the data from the model and at the same time include other rows with static content to incorporate additional information or for styling purposes, as in the following example.

Listing 4-24: Mixing static and dynamic content in a list

```
struct ContentView: View {
   @Environment(ApplicationData.self) private var appData

   var body: some View {
      List {
         HStack {
            Image(systemName: "book.circle")
               .font(.largeTitle)
            Spacer()
            Text("My Favorite Books")
               .font(.headline)
         }.frame(height: 50)
         ForEach(appData.userData) { book in
            CellBook(book: book)
         }
      }.listStyle(.plain)
   }
}
```

A **`List`** view takes a list of views, one or more **`ForEach`** loops, or a combination of both, and includes every view in a row. In Listing 4-24, we create one static view with an SF Symbol and some text, and then a **`ForEach`** view to list the data in the model. The static content is shown along with the dynamic content and even scrolls with the rest of the rows.

Figure 4-18: *Static and dynamic content*

Sections

A list can be organized into sections. Sections help the user identify values that have something in common. SwiftUI includes the **`Section`** view to create these sections.

`Section(content:` `Closure)`

This initializer creates a **`Section`** view to group related content. The **content** argument is the closure that defines the rows for the section.

`Section(content:` `Closure,` **`header:`** `View,` **`footer:`** `View)`

This initializer creates a **`Section`** view to group related content. The **content** argument is the closure that defines the rows for the section, the **header** argument is a view or a group of views that define the section's header, and the **footer** argument is a view or a group of views that define the section's footer.

`Section``(String,` **`isExpanded:`** `Binding,` **`content:`** `Closure)`

This initializer creates a **`Section`** view to group related content. The first argument defines the text for the header, the **isExpanded** argument is a Boolean binding property that determines whether the section is expanded or not, and the **content** argument is the closure that defines the rows for the section.

The text assigned to the section's header is displayed at the top of the section with a style that matches the style of the list, but we can make it more prominent with the following modifier.

`headerProminence``(Prominence)`

This modifier defines the prominence of the section's title. The argument is an enumeration with the values **`increased`** and **`standard`**.

Although a section may contain no header or footer, in most situations it is better to provide a visual cue of where a section begins and ends. The following example creates two sections with a prominent header defined by a **`Text`** view.

Listing 4-25: Dividing the content into sections

```
struct ContentView: View {
   @Environment(ApplicationData.self) private var appData

   var body: some View {
      List {
         Section(header: Text("Statistics")) {
            HStack {
               Text("Total Books:")
               Spacer()
               Text(String(appData.userData.count))
            }
         }.headerProminence(.increased)
```

```
         Section(header: Text("My Books")) {
            ForEach(appData.userData) { book in
               CellBook(book: book)
            }
         }.headerProminence(.increased)
      }
   }
}
```

This example creates two sections, one to show the total number of books in the model and another to list the books.

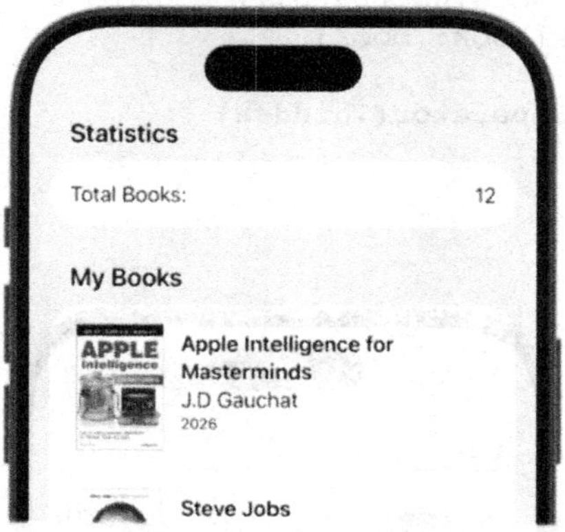

Figure 4-19: *Sections with headers*

If the style of the list is **`plain`** or **`inset`**, the sections show separators at the top and bottom. The **`View`** protocol includes the following modifiers to configure these lines.

`listSectionSeparator(``Visibility, `**`edges:`**` VerticalEdge)`

This modifier configures the sections separators. The first argument determines if the separators are visible or hidden. It is an enumeration with the values **`automatic`**, **`hidden`**, and **`visible`**. And the **edges** argument defines which separators are affected. It is a structure with the type properties **`all`**, **`bottom`**, and **`top`**.

`listSectionSeparatorTint(``Color?, `**`edges:`**` VerticalEdge)`

This modifier defines the color of the separators. The first argument specifies the new color, and the **edges** argument determines which separators are affected. It is a structure with the type properties **`all`**, **`bottom`**, and **`top`**.

These modifiers work in a similar way to those for rows. We can remove the top and bottom lines of the sections, or both, and change their colors. For example, in the following view, we remove the top line, change the color of the bottom line for the first section, and completely remove the lines for the second section.

Listing 4-26: Configuring the section separators

```
struct ContentView: View {
   @Environment(ApplicationData.self) private var appData
```

```
    var body: some View {
        List {
            Section(header: Text("Statistics")) {
                HStack {
                    Text("Total Books:")
                    Spacer()
                    Text(String(appData.userData.count))
                }
            }.listSectionSeparator(.hidden, edges: .top)
            .listSectionSeparatorTint(.blue)

            Section(header: Text("My Books")) {
                ForEach(appData.userData) { book in
                    CellBook(book: book)
                }
            }.listSectionSeparator(.hidden)
        }.listStyle(.plain)
    }
}
```

Figure 4-20: *Section separators*

By default, the height of headers and rows is determined by their content, but the environment includes two properties to modify those values.

defaultMinListHeaderHeight

This property defines the minimum height for the headers. It is a value of type **CGFloat**.

defaultMinListRowHeight

This property defines the minimum height for the rows. It is a value of type **CGFloat**.

To change the values of these properties, we must apply the **environment()** modifier to the **List** view. These properties are useful when the content of the headers or the rows is variable. For instance, we can assign a minimum size to the rows of our previous example so the row in the first section is of the same height as the rows with the books.

Listing 4-27: Configuring the rows from the environment

```
struct ContentView: View {
    @Environment(ApplicationData.self) private var appData
```

```
    var body: some View {
       List {
          Section(header: Text("Statistics")) {
             HStack {
                Text("Total Books:")
                Spacer()
                Text(String(appData.userData.count))
             }
          }
          Section(header: Text("My Books")) {
             ForEach(appData.userData) { book in
                CellBook(book: book)
             }
          }
       }.environment(\.defaultMinListRowHeight, 100)
    }
}
```

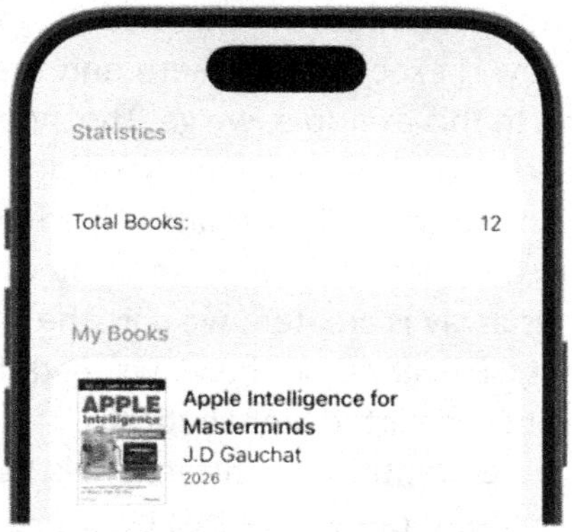

Figure 4-21: *Same height for all the rows*

So far, we have used sections to group different types of content. The first section of our example contains information about the model and the second section contains the list of books. However, sections are also useful when we need to divide content into groups, such as movies into categories, or when we want to arrange items alphabetically. For this purpose, we must prepare the data according to the organization we want to present to the user. An alternative is to define a computed property in the view that returns the items in the order required to organize them into sections. For example, we can define a property that returns the list of books in alphabetical order.

Listing 4-28: Providing an ordered list of values

```
struct ContentView: View {
   @Environment(ApplicationData.self) private var appData

   var orderList: [(key: String, value: [Book])] {
      let listGroup: [String: [Book]] = Dictionary(grouping:
         appData.userData, by: { value in
         let index = value.title.startIndex
         let initial = value.title[index]
         return String(initial)
      })
      return listGroup.sorted(by: { $0.key < $1.key })
```

```
    }
    var body: some View {
        List {
            ForEach(orderList, id: \.key) { sections in
                Section(header: Text(sections.key)) {
                    ForEach(sections.value) { book in
                        CellBook(book: book)
                    }
                }.headerProminence(.increased)
            }
        }
    }
}
```

Before defining the **body** property, the view in Listing 4-28 defines a computed property that returns an array of tuples with the books organized by the title's first letter. First, the closure applies the **Dictionary(grouping:, by:)** initializer to create a dictionary from the values of the **userData** array (the list of books in the model). The way this initializer works is that for every value in the array, it executes a closure and then groups the results by the values returned by the closure. In this example, we get the index of the first character in the book's title with the **startIndex** property, then use that index to extract the first character, and finally turn it into a string and return it. This creates an array with tuples which first value is a letter of the alphabet and the second value is an array with all the books which titles begin with that letter. After this array is created, we sort the values alphabetically with the **sorted()** method and return it, so every time the views read the **orderList** property, they get an array of tuples with the books sorted alphabetically.

The values of the tuples were identified with the labels **key** and **value**, so we can use these labels to read them and create our list. In this example, we define a **List** view with two **ForEach** loops inside, one to create the sections for each letter and another to list the books inside the sections. The first **ForEach** loop reads the content of the **orderList** property and creates a section with the value identified by the **key** label (the letter). Inside this section, another **ForEach** loop iterates through the array identified with the **value** label to create the list of books. As a result, we get a list of books organized alphabetically into sections.

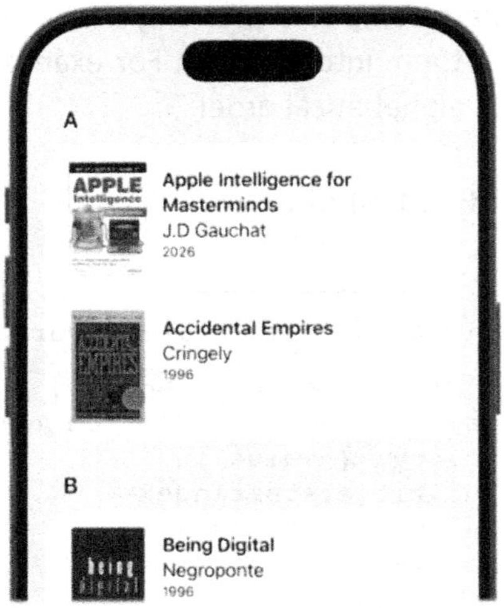

Figure 4-22: *Alphabetical sections*

When we organize a list into sections, as in this case, we can include an index. An index is a list of links that appears on the right side of the screen on iPhones and iPads to help users navigate through the list. The **View** protocol includes the following modifiers for this purpose.

sectionIndexLabel(Value)

This modifier adds a label to the section index. The argument can be a string or a **Text** view with a value that represents the section.

listSectionIndexVisibility(Visibility)

This modifier shows or hides the index. The argument is an enumeration with the values **automatic**, **visible** and **hidden**.

The **sectionIndexLabel()** modifier is applied to **Section** views, so we can reuse the same values declared for the section headers to build the index, as shown in the following example.

Listing 4-29: Adding an index to navigate the list

```
List {
   ForEach(orderList, id: \.key) { sections in
      Section(header: Text(sections.key)) {
         ForEach(sections.value) { book in
            CellBook(book: book)
         }
      }.headerProminence(.increased)
      .sectionIndexLabel(sections.key)
   }
}
```

The index is visible by default, so we do not need to apply the **listSectionIndexVisibility()** modifier to show it. As a result, an index appears on the right side of the screen with links that allow us to navigate through the list, as shown below.

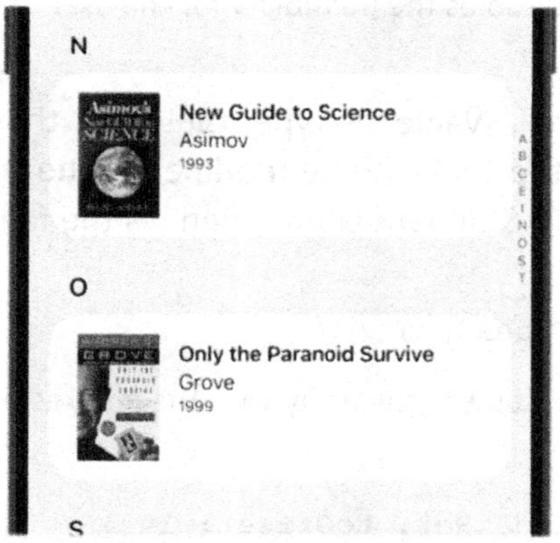

Figure 4-23: *Section index*

Do It Yourself

Update the **ContentView** structure with the code in Listing 4-28. Run the application on an iPhone simulator. You should see the list of books organized into alphabetical sections, as shown in Figure 4-22. Update the **List** view with the code in Listing 4-29 and run the application again. You should see an index appear on the right side of the screen, as shown in Figure 4-23. Tap the links to navigate through the list.

BASIC

Edit Mode

List views also provide tools to work with the values on the list. The following are the modifiers available to remove and sort views.

onDelete(perform: Closure)

This modifier executes the closure specified by the **perform** argument when the user tries to remove a row. The closure receives an **IndexSet** value with integers representing the indexes of the rows the user wants to delete.

deleteDisabled(Bool**)**

This modifier enables or disables the possibility for the user to delete a row.

onMove(perform: Closure)

This modifier executes the closure specified by the **perform** argument when the user tries to move a row to a different position on the list. The closure receives an **IndexSet** value with integers representing the indexes of the rows the user is moving, and an integer representing the index where the rows should be moved.

moveDisabled(Bool**)**

This modifier enables or disables the possibility for the user to move a row.

These modifiers produce a value of type **IndexSet** that contains a set of integers representing the indexes of the values to be modified in the collection. To work with these values from an array, the Swift Standard Library defines the following methods.

remove(atOffsets: IndexSet)

This method removes the items in the array with the indexes provided by the **atOffsets** argument.

move(fromOffsets: IndexSet, **toOffset:** Int)

This method moves the items of the array in the indexes specified by the **fromOffsets** argument to the index determined by the **toOffset** argument.

There are different ways to allow the user to modify the list. For instance, if we apply the **onDelete()** modifier to the list, the system automatically activates a swipe action that lets the user drag the rows to the left to expose a Delete button. When this button is pressed, the closure assigned to the modifier is executed and we can proceed accordingly.

Listing 4-30: Deleting rows

```
struct ContentView: View {
   @Environment(ApplicationData.self) private var appData

   var body: some View {
      List {
         ForEach(appData.userData) { book in
            CellBook(book: book)
         }.onDelete { indexes in
            appData.userData.remove(atOffsets: indexes)
         }
      }
   }
}
```

As shown in this example, the modifiers are implemented by the **ForEach** view, so we need to create the list with this view to be able to access these features. In this case, we use the **onDelete()** modifier to remove rows. The closure assigned to the modifier receives an **IndexSet** value with the index of the row to be deleted and calls the **remove()** method on the **userData** array to remove the item from the model. Now the user can delete the book by dragging the row to the left and pressing the Delete button.

Figure 4-24: *Delete feature*

Do It Yourself

Update the **ContentView** structure with the code in Listing 4-30. Drag a row to the left and press the Delete button, as shown in Figure 4-24. The row should be removed from the list.

In addition to allowing users to drag a row to delete it, **List** views include a set of tools that let users select, remove, and move rows. These tools are displayed when the list is in edit mode. To activate edit mode, SwiftUI provides the following view.

EditButton()

This initializer creates a view that toggles the edit mode for a list.

As we will see later, this button simply toggles the value of an environment property that enables or disables edit mode. For this reason, we can place it anywhere in the interface, as shown in the following example.

Listing 4-31: Activating the edit mode

```
struct ContentView: View {
   @Environment(ApplicationData.self) private var appData

   var body: some View {
      VStack {
         EditButton()
            .buttonStyle(.glassProminent)
         List {
            ForEach(appData.userData) { book in
               CellBook(book: book)
            }.onDelete { indexes in
               appData.userData.remove(atOffsets: indexes)
            }
         }.listStyle(.plain)
      }
   }
}
```

This view embeds the **List** view in a **VStack** view to add an **EditButton** at the top. When the button is pressed, the system activates the edit mode and the tools are shown according to the modifiers we have applied. For instance, in our example, we included the **onDelete()** modifier, so the view exposes buttons to let the user delete the row.

Figure 4-25: *Edit button*

The tool to move rows is included when the **onMove()** modifier is applied to the **ForEach** view, as in the following example.

Listing 4-32: Moving rows

```
struct ContentView: View {
   @Environment(ApplicationData.self) private var appData
```

```
    var body: some View {
        VStack {
            EditButton()
                .buttonStyle(.glassProminent)
            List {
                ForEach(appData.userData) { book in
                    CellBook(book: book)
                }.onDelete { indexes in
                    appData.userData.remove(atOffsets: indexes)
                }
                .onMove { source, destination in
                    appData.userData.move(fromOffsets: source,
                        toOffset: destination)
                }
            }.listStyle(.plain)
        }
    }
}
```

The system detects that we have implemented the **onMove()** modifier and automatically provides the tools for the user to move the rows and reorganize the list. After the user drops a row in the new location, the modifier sends the indexes of the rows and the new location to the closure, and here is where we have the chance to call the **move()** method to perform the change in the **userData** array, so the next time the list is redrawn, the rows remain in the position selected by the user.

Figure 4-26: *Move buttons*

Do It Yourself

Update the **ContentView** structure with the code in Listing 4-32. Run the application on an iPhone simulator. Press the Edit button. Use the tools to remove a row or move it to a different position. You should see the interface illustrated in Figure 4-26.

The edit mode also allows the user to select one or more rows. For single selection, the mode is enabled by default. All we need to do is to initialize the **List** view with the **selection** argument. The argument takes a binding property to store the identifier of the selected row, which we can use later to process the item, as shown below.

Listing 4-33: Selecting a row

```
struct ContentView: View {
   @Environment(ApplicationData.self) private var appData
   @State private var selectedRow: Book.ID? = nil

   var body: some View {
      VStack {
         HStack {
            Spacer()
            Button(action: {
               removeSelected()
            }, label: {
               Image(systemName: "trash")
            }).disabled(selectedRow == nil ? true : false)
         }.buttonStyle(.glass)
         .padding()

         List(selection: $selectedRow) {
            ForEach(appData.userData) { book in
               CellBook(book: book)
            }
         }.listStyle(.plain)
      }
   }
   func removeSelected() {
      if let index = appData.userData.firstIndex(where: {
         $0.id == selectedRow }) {
         appData.userData.remove(at: index)
         selectedRow = nil
      }
   }
}
```

The **@State** property must be of the same data type as the **id** property. In this example, we declare it using the associated type **ID** (see Listing 4-13). If the user selects an item, the **List** view assigns the value of the item's **id** property to the **selectedRow** property, so we can do whatever we want with it. In our example, we add a **Button** view at the top that calls a method to remove the selected book. The method gets the index of the selected item in the **userData** array, calls the **remove()** method to remove it, and assigns the value **nil** to the **selectedRow** property to cancel the selection. Note that we have applied the **disabled()** modifier to the button to only enable it when a book has been selected.

Figure 4-27: *Single selection*

To process multiple values, we can store the identifiers in an **IndexSet** structure and apply the same methods used before to move and remove rows. The **IndexSet** structure provides the following method for this purpose.

insert(Int)

This method adds the index specified by the argument to the set.

In the following example, we modify the **@State** property to take a **Set** of **UUID** values instead of just one (**Set<Book.ID>**) so the user can select multiple rows, and create an **IndexSet** structure with the indexes of the selected rows to remove the values from the model.

Listing 4-34: Selecting multiple rows

```
struct ContentView: View {
   @Environment(ApplicationData.self) private var appData
   @State private var selectedRows: Set<Book.ID> = []

   var body: some View {
      VStack {
         HStack {
            EditButton()
               .buttonStyle(.glassProminent)
            Spacer()
            Button(action: {
               removeSelected()
            }, label: {
               Image(systemName: "trash")
            }).disabled(selectedRows.count == 0 ? true : false)
         }.padding()

         List(selection: $selectedRows) {
            ForEach(appData.userData) { book in
               CellBook(book: book)
            }
         }.listStyle(.plain)
      }
   }
   func removeSelected() {
      var indexes = IndexSet()
      for item in selectedRows {
         if let index = appData.userData.firstIndex(where: {
            $0.id == item }) {
            indexes.insert(index)
         }
      }
      appData.userData.remove(atOffsets: indexes)
      selectedRows = []
   }
}
```

The view now includes two buttons at the top: the **EditButton** to activate or deactivate the edit mode, and the trash can button to remove the books selected by the user. When the user activates the edit mode, checkboxes appear on the left to select the rows. If the user selects a row, the **List** view adds the value of the **id** property to the **selectedRows** property, so we can call our **removeSelected()** method again to remove the books. In this case, the method creates an empty **IndexSet** structure and then iterates through the values in the **selectedRows** property to find the index of each book and add it to the set. Once all the indexes are found, we call the **remove()** method on the **userData** array to erase the books from the model, and then clean the **selectedRows** property to allow the user to start the process again.

Figure 4-28: *Selected rows*

Do It Yourself

Update the **ContentView** structure with the code in Listing 4-34. Run the application on an iPhone simulator and press the Edit button. Select a row and click the button on the right. The row should be removed.

If we want to disable the edit mode after removing a book or performing any other action, we need to control the mode programmatically. For this purpose, the environment provides the following property.

editMode

This property defines the state of the edit mode for the view. It is a binding property of type **EditMode**, an enumeration with the values **active**, **inactive**, and **transient**. The enumeration also includes the **isEditing** property to return a Boolean value that indicates whether the view is in edit mode or not.

To manage the mode, we need a binding property with a Boolean value that stores the state of the edit mode (active or inactive), set the mode according to the value of this property with the **environment()** modifier, as we did before for other environment properties, and also create a button to toggle this value, as shown below.

Listing 4-35: Customizing the edit mode

```
struct ContentView: View {
   @Environment(ApplicationData.self) private var appData
   @State private var selectedRows: Set<Book.ID> = []
   @State private var editActive: Bool = false
```

```
   var body: some View {
      VStack {
         HStack {
            Button(editActive ? "Done" : "Edit") {
               editActive.toggle()
            }.buttonStyle(.glassProminent)
            Spacer()
            Button(action: {
               removeSelected()
            }, label: {
               Image(systemName: "trash")
            }).buttonStyle(.glass)
            .disabled(selectedRows.count == 0 ? true : false)
         }.padding()

         List(selection: $selectedRows) {
            ForEach(appData.userData) { book in
               CellBook(book: book)
            }
         }.listStyle(.plain)
         .environment(\.editMode, .constant(editActive ? EditMode.active :
            EditMode.inactive))
      }
   }
   func removeSelected() {
      var indexes = IndexSet()
      for item in selectedRows {
         if let index = appData.userData.firstIndex(where: {
            $0.id == item }) {
            indexes.insert(index)
         }
      }
      appData.userData.remove(atOffsets: indexes)
      selectedRows = []
      editActive = false
   }
}
```

This code defines a **@State** property called **editActive** to keep track of the edit mode and replaces the **EditButton** view with a regular **Button** view. The value of the **editActive** property determines if the mode is active or not, so we use it to select the mode, to deactivate it after the selected books are deleted, and to set the title for the button ("Done" if **true**, "Edit" if **false**). Note that the environment's **editMode** property is a binding property and therefore we had to use the **constant()** method to provide a binding value of type **EditMode** (see Chapter 3, Listing 3-7).

The result is the same as before, but the process is now customized and therefore we can change the edit mode from code anytime we want by assigning the value **true** or **false** to the **editActive** property.

Do It Yourself

Update the **ContentView** structure with the code in Listing 4-35. Run the application on an iPhone simulator and press the Edit button. Select a row and click the Remove button. The row should be removed, as before, but now the edit mode is automatically deactivated.

The selection process can also be customized, but doing so requires us to keep track of the selected rows ourselves and detect selection using the **onTapGesture()** modifier. We will learn more about gesture modifiers in Chapter 9. For now, all we need to know is that this modifier executes a closure every time the user taps or clicks the view. In this case, we need to apply it to each **CellBook** view to assign the **id** value of the selected book to a binding property, as shown below.

Listing 4-36: Customizing the selection

```
struct ContentView: View {
   @Environment(ApplicationData.self) private var appData
   @State private var selectedRow: Book.ID? = nil

   var body: some View {
      List {
         ForEach(appData.userData) { book in
            CellBook(selected: $selectedRow, book: book)
               .background(.white)
               .onTapGesture {
                  if selectedRow == book.id {
                     selectedRow = nil
                  } else {
                     selectedRow = book.id
                  }
               }
         }
      }.listStyle(.plain)
   }
}
struct CellBook: View {
   @Binding var selected: Book.ID?
   let book: Book

   var body: some View {
      HStack(alignment: .top) {
         Image(book.cover)
            .resizable()
            .scaledToFit()
            .frame(width: 80, height: 100)
         VStack(alignment: .leading, spacing: 2) {
            Text(book.title).bold()
            Text(book.author)
            Text(book.displayYear).font(.caption)
            Spacer()
         }.padding(.top, 5)
         Spacer()
         if selected == book.id {
            Image(systemName: "checkmark")
               .foregroundStyle(Color.green)
               .frame(width: 25, height: 25)
         }
      }
```

```
    }
}
```

In this example, we allow the selection of one row at a time. If the user taps on a row, the **onTapGesture()** modifier checks whether the book's identifier was already stored in the **@State** property. If it was, it deselects the row by assigning the value **nil** to the property, otherwise, the value of the book's **id** property is assigned to the **@State** property to indicate that the row was selected. To show the selection to the user, we connect the **@State** property with a **@Binding** property in the **CellBook** view and then show an image if the value of this property is equal to the book's identifier. As a result, a checkmark is shown on the row selected by the user.

Figure 4-29: *Custom selection*

Do It Yourself

Update the **ContentView** and **CellBook** views with the code in Listing 4-36. Run the application on an iPhone simulator and click on a row. You should see the checkmark shown in Figure 4-29.

IMPORTANT

Note that we have applied the **background()** modifier to the **CellBook** view with a white color. This modifier generates a **Color** view that occupies the whole area, providing a surface for the **onTapGesture()** to detect the taps. This allows the user to select the row by tapping anywhere, not only on its content. SwiftUI also provides the **contentShape()** modifier for this purpose. We will learn more about this modifier and gesture recognizers in Chapter 9.

In the previous examples, the selection was stored in a **@State** property in the view. If for any reason the view is removed, the selection is removed with it. If we need to keep the selection active or access it from other views, we can save it in the model. The **Book** structure in our model already includes the **selected** property to store this value, so all we need is to change the value of this property every time the user taps on a row.

Listing 4-37: Storing the selection in the model

```
struct ContentView: View {
   @Environment(ApplicationData.self) private var appData

   var body: some View {
      @Bindable var appData = appData

      List {
         ForEach($appData.userData) { $book in
            CellBook(book: book)
               .background(.white)
               .onTapGesture {
                  book.selected.toggle()
               }
         }
      }.listStyle(.plain)
   }
}
struct CellBook: View {
   let book: Book

   var body: some View {
      HStack(alignment: .top) {
         Image(book.cover)
            .resizable()
            .scaledToFit()
            .frame(width: 80, height: 100)
         VStack(alignment: .leading, spacing: 2) {
            Text(book.title).bold()
            Text(book.author)
            Text(book.displayYear).font(.caption)
            Spacer()
         }.padding(.top, 5)
         Spacer()
         if book.selected {
            Image(systemName: "checkmark")
               .foregroundStyle(Color.green)
               .frame(width: 25, height: 25)
         }
      }
   }
}
```

Although we can access and modify the **Book** structures in the model through the array index, the **List** and **ForEach** views can take a binding value, which allows us to modify the model directly. To use this feature, we turn the app structure into a bindable property with the **@Bindable** macro so that we can change its values (see Chapter 3, Listing 3-64). In this example, the value of the **selected** property is toggled each time the user taps on a row. If the value is **true**, it becomes **false** and vice versa. The result is the same as before, but now we can select multiple books and each **Book** structure knows whether the book has been selected or not.

BASIC

Custom Buttons

In addition to the buttons generated by the system, we can include our own. Of course, when we use custom buttons to perform tasks on the list, there is no need to implement the methods defined for the edit mode. The following example illustrates how to include a remove button for each row.

Listing 4-38: Implementing a custom button to delete the rows

```
struct ContentView: View {
   @Environment(ApplicationData.self) private var appData

   var body: some View {
      List {
         ForEach(appData.userData) { book in
            CellBook(book: book)
         }
      }.listStyle(.plain)
   }
}
struct CellBook: View {
   @Environment(ApplicationData.self) private var appData
   let book: Book

   var body: some View {
      HStack(alignment: .top) {
         Image(book.cover)
            .resizable()
            .scaledToFit()
            .frame(width: 80, height: 100)
         VStack(alignment: .leading, spacing: 2) {
            Text(book.title).bold()
            Text(book.author)
            Text(book.displayYear).font(.caption)
            Spacer()
         }.padding(.top, 5)
         Spacer()
         Button(action: {
            removeBook(book: book)
         }, label: {
            Image(systemName: "trash")
               .foregroundStyle(.white)
               .frame(width: 30, height: 30)
         }).padding(.top, 5)
         .buttonStyle(.glassProminent)
         .tint(.red)
      }
   }
   func removeBook(book: Book) {
      if let index = appData.userData.firstIndex(where: {
         $0.id == book.id }) {
         appData.userData.remove(at: index)
      }
   }
}
```

In this example, we create a button on the right hand side of each row to delete it. The label is an SF Symbol of a trash can, and the action calls the **`removeBook()`** method implemented before. The result is shown below.

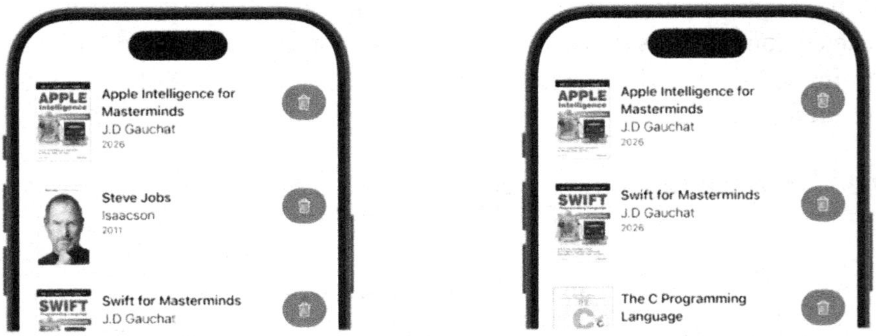

Figure 4-30: *Custom button to remove a row*

PRO

Refreshable

The **`List`** view can also support refresh behavior. This feature allows the user to refresh the data by pulling the list downward. When the user continues to scroll after reaching the top of the list, a spinning wheel appears to indicate that the system is refreshing the data. The **`View`** protocol includes the following modifier to add this feature.

```
refreshable(action: Closure)
```

This modifier adds a refreshable control to a list. The **action** argument is the closure to be executed when the user performs the action.

To add this feature to the list, we must implement the modifier on the **`List`** view and provide a closure with the task we want to perform, as in the following example.

Listing 4-39: Refreshing the list

```
struct ContentView: View {
   @Environment(ApplicationData.self) private var appData

   var body: some View {
      List {
         ForEach(appData.userData) { book in
            CellBook(book: book)
         }
      }.listStyle(.plain)
      .refreshable {
         sleep(3)
         print("Loading values")
      }
   }
}
```

When the user scrolls down the list, the closure is executed to perform the task. In this example, we simulate the time it takes for the task to complete by using the **sleep()** method and then print a message to the console, but in a real scenario the task usually involves accessing a server or a database to download and process information. While the system is waiting for the process to complete, an activity indicator is displayed on the screen, as shown below.

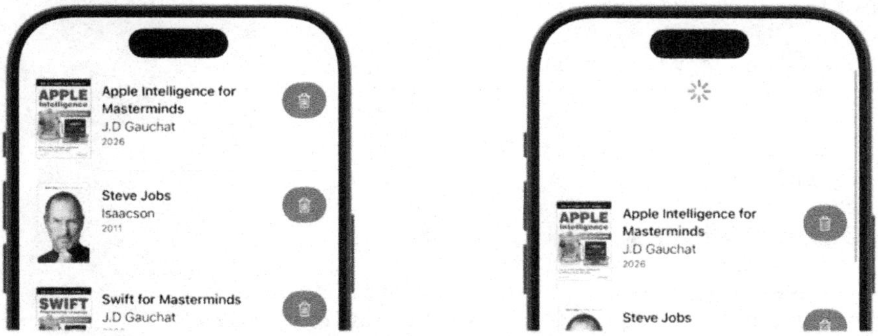

Figure 4-31: *Refresh control*

Do It Yourself

Update the **ContentView** structure with the code in Listing 4-39. Drag the list down. You should see a spinning wheel to indicate the list is refreshing its content, as shown in Figure 4-31.

PRO

Outline List

In addition to the lists of views we have created so far, SwiftUI also provides tools to create hierarchical lists. These are lists of views in which some rows can expand or collapse to display or hide other rows. The main views, also called parents, work as containers for other views, called children, which the user can reveal by tapping the top view's accessory. The **List** view provides the following initializer to create these lists.

List(Data, **children:** KeyPath, **rowContent:** Closure**)**

This initializer creates a hierarchical list. The first argument is the data used to create the views, the **children** argument is a key path to the property that contains the data to create the children views, and the **rowContent** argument is the closure with the views to create each row.

We don't need anything new to create these types of lists, all the functionality is provided by the **List** view, but the information in the model must be organized accordingly. For example, the following model includes a structure to store the items, which in turn contains a property with another array of instances of the same structure to store the items that will be displayed when the parent item is expanded.

Listing 4-40: Defining the model to create a hierarchical list

```
import SwiftUI

struct MainItems: Identifiable {
   var id = UUID()
   var name: String!
   var options: [MainItems]!
}
@Observable class ApplicationData {
   var items: [MainItems] = []

   static let shared: ApplicationData = ApplicationData()
   private init() {
      items = [
         MainItems(name: "Food", options: [
            MainItems(name: "Oatmeal", options: nil),
            MainItems(name: "Bagels", options: nil),
            MainItems(name: "Brownies", options: nil),
            MainItems(name: "Cheese", options: [
               MainItems(name: "Roquefort", options: nil),
               MainItems(name: "Mozzarella", options: nil),
               MainItems(name: "Cheddar", options: nil)
            ]),
            MainItems(name: "Cookies", options: nil),
            MainItems(name: "Donuts", options: nil)
         ]),
         MainItems(name: "Beverages", options: [
            MainItems(name: "Coffee", options: nil),
            MainItems(name: "Juice", options: nil),
            MainItems(name: "Lemonade", options: nil)
         ])
      ]
   }
}
```

The **MainItems** structure includes the **name** property to store the item's name, and the **options** property to store the children (also defined by **MainItems** structures). In this example, we define two parent items called "Food" and "Beverages", each with their own children assigned to the **options** property. There is also one item called "Cheese" with three more children, creating an additional hierarchy level. To represent this hierarchy, all we need is a **List** view with the **children** argument.

Listing 4-41: Displaying a hierarchical list

```
struct ContentView: View {
   @State private var appData = ApplicationData.shared
   var body: some View {
      List(appData.items, children: \.options) { item in
         Text(item.name)
      }
   }
}
```

When the user taps on a parent item, such as Food or Beverages, all the items stored in the **options** property are displayed, as shown below.

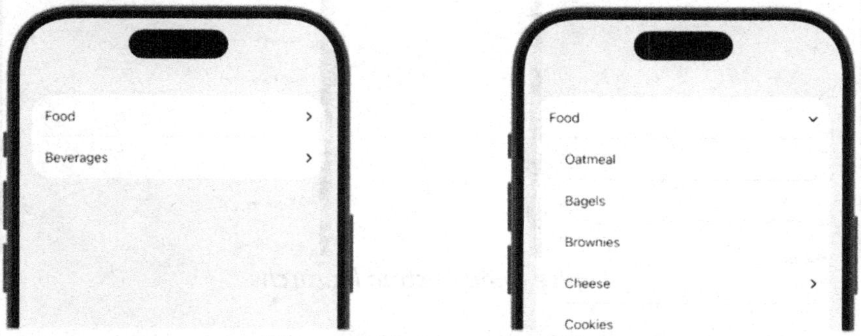

Figure 4-32: *Hierarchical list*

The **List** view implements another view in the background called **OutlineGroup** to create the hierarchical list of views, but we can declare this view ourselves to create more complex hierarchies. The **OutlineGroup** view includes the following initializer.

OutlineGroup(Data, **children:** KeyPath, **content:** Closure**)**

This view creates a hierarchical list. The first argument is the data used to create the views, the **children** argument is a key path to the property that contains the data to create the children view, and the **content** argument is the closure with the views for each row.

With an **OutlineGroup** view, we can present the hierarchy as we want. For example, we can include this view inside a **Section** view to divide the hierarchy in sections.

Listing 4-42: Implementing an `OutlineGroup` view

```
struct ContentView: View {
   @State private var appData = ApplicationData.shared

   var body: some View {
      List {
         ForEach(appData.items) { section in
            Section(header: Text(section.name)) {
               OutlineGroup(section.options ?? [], children: \.options)
               { item in
                  Text(item.name)
               }
            }
         }
      }
   }
}
```

In this example, we create the list with a **ForEach** view and the values of the **items** property. This property contains two items, "Food" and "Beverages", that we use to create the sections with a **Section** view. To display the content of the sections, we use an **OutlineGroup** view. This view takes the values in the **options** property of each item and creates an outline list.

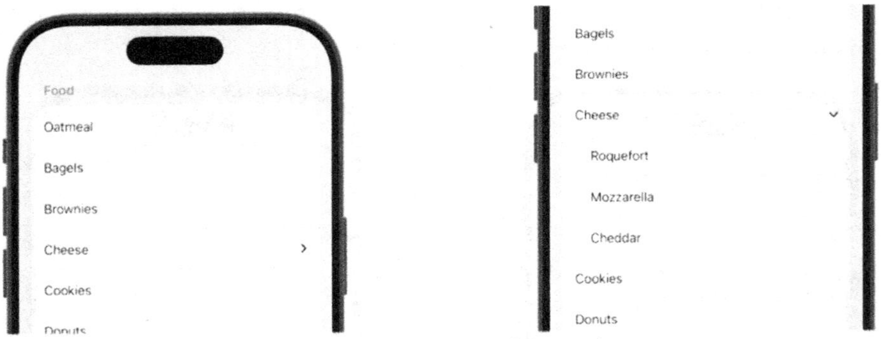

Figure 4-33: *Custom hierarchy*

Do It Yourself

Create a new App project. Create a Swift file called **ApplicationData.swift** for the model in Listing 4-40. Update the `ContentView` structure with the code in Listing 4-41. Run the application on an iPhone simulator. You should see the interface illustrated in Figure 4-32. Update the `ContentView` structure with the code in Listing 4-42. Now you should see the interface illustrated in Figure 4-33.

PRO

4.3 - Tables

`List` views were designed for the small screen of mobile devices like iPhones, but iPads and Macs have a larger screen and therefore more space to display content. If we only need one column of values, we can use a `List` view, as we have done so far, but to present more columns SwiftUI includes the `Table` view.

```
Table(Data, selection: Binding, sortOrder: Binding, columns:
Closure)
```

This initializer creates a `Table` view with the configuration specified by the arguments. The first argument is the data used to fill the table, the **selection** argument is a binding value with the identifiers of the selected rows, the **sortOrder** argument is a binding value with the sort descriptors used to sort the values on the table, and the **columns** argument provides the views to create the columns.

```
Table(of: Type, selection: Binding, sortOrder: Binding, columns:
Closure, rows: Closure)
```

This initializer creates a `Table` view with the configuration specified by the arguments. The first argument is a reference to the data type of the data we want to show, the **selection** argument is a binding value with the identifiers of the selected rows, the **sortOrder** argument is a binding value with the sort descriptors used to sort the values on the table, the **columns** argument provides the views to create the columns, and the **rows** argument provides the views to create the rows.

The framework includes the **TableColumn** structure to create columns and the **TableRow** structure in case we need to manually define rows. The following are the initializers for these views.

```
TableColumn(String, value: KeyPath, content: Closure)
```

This initializer defines a column for a table. The first argument specifies the column's title, the **value** argument is a key path to the property that provides the values for the column, and the **content** argument defines the views to display by the column.

```
TableRow(Value)
```

This initializer defines the rows of a table. The argument provides the value of a row for each column of the table.

By default, the columns are flexible, which means that the width is determined by the number of columns in the table and the space available, but the **TableColumn** structure includes the following modifiers to specify a custom width.

```
width(CGFloat?)
```

This modifier defines a fixed width for the column.

```
width(min: CGFloat?, ideal: CGFloat?, max: CGFloat?)
```

This modifier defines a flexible column but with constraints.

As always, we need a model with some data to test the app. The following is the one we are going to use for our examples. Our model includes a structure with a few properties to provide the values for the columns, an observable property to provide the values to the views, and some data for testing.

Listing 4-43: Defining a model to test tables

```
import SwiftUI

struct ConsumableItem: Identifiable {
   let id = UUID()
   nonisolated var name: String
   nonisolated var category: String
   nonisolated var calories: Int
   nonisolated var included: Bool
}
@Observable class ApplicationData {
   var listOfItems: [ConsumableItem] = []

   static let shared: ApplicationData = ApplicationData()
   private init() {
      listOfItems = [
         ConsumableItem(name: "Bagels", category: "Baked", calories: 250,
            included: false),
         ConsumableItem(name: "Brownies", category: "Baked", calories:
            466, included: false),
         ConsumableItem(name: "Butter", category: "Dairy", calories: 717,
            included: false),
```

```
         ConsumableItem(name: "Cheese", category: "Dairy", calories: 402,
            included: false),
         ConsumableItem(name: "Juice", category: "Beverages", calories:
            23, included: false),
         ConsumableItem(name: "Lemonade", category: "Beverages", calories:
            40, included: false)
      ]
   }
}
```

> **IMPORTANT**
>
> In this example, we have declared all the properties in our model as **`nonisolated`**. This is required to sort the values. As we will see later, sorting values in a table requires the use of key paths to reference these properties. In Swift 6, key paths are non-sendable by default, so declaring the properties as **`nonisolated`** is one way to avoid data race issues. For more information about data races and concurrency, read our book *Swift for Masterminds*.

The **`Table`** structure includes multiple initializers, each one with a different combination of arguments, so we can only implement those we need. Something similar happens with the **`TableColumn`** view. For instance, if the value presented by the column is a string, we can just specify the key path for the property and the view takes cares of creating the **`Text`** view to show the value. If not, we must provide a closure to the **content** argument, format the value, and create the view we want to use to show it.

The following example shows a possible implementation. The **`Table`** view is defined only with the data source (the **`listOfItems`** property) and a closure to create the columns. Some columns use a key path to provide the value and the last one a closure with a **`Text`** view.

Listing 4-44: Creating a table with multiple columns

```
struct ContentView: View {
   @State private var appData = ApplicationData.shared

   var body: some View {
      Table(appData.listOfItems) {
         TableColumn("Name", value: \.name)
         TableColumn("Category", value: \.category)
         TableColumn("Calories") { item in
            Text("\(item.calories)")
         }.width(100)
      }
   }
}
```

In this example, the first and second columns access the values of the **`name`** and **`category`** properties using key paths, but we use a closure for the **`calories`** property because its value is an integer that we need to convert into a string. We also assign a width of 100 points to this column using the **width()** modifier to always display it at that size, while keeping the rest of the columns flexible. On iPads and Macs, the system creates the Calories column with a width of 100 points and distributes the remaining space between the first two columns, while on iPhones only the first column is displayed, as shown below.

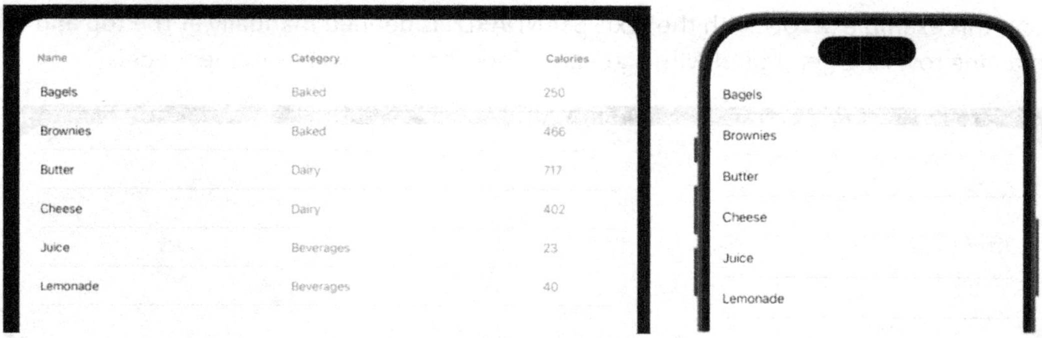

Figure 4-34: *Table in iPads and iPhones*

Do It Yourself

Create a new App project. Create a Swift file called **ApplicationData.swift** for the model in Listing 4-43 and update the **ContentView** structure with the code in Listing 4-44. Run the application on an iPad simulator or the Mac (My Mac). You should see a table with three columns, as shown in Figure 4-34, left. Run the application again on an iPhone simulator. You should see only one column, as illustrated in Figure 4-34, right.

The **Table** view creates the columns from the **TableColumn** views provided by the closure and the rows from the values in the model, but we can also define the rows manually. This is useful when we want to insert static rows into the table. For this purpose, we must implement the initializer that allows us to provide the **of** and **rows** arguments. The **of** argument tells the table the data type of the values we want to display, and the **rows** argument provides the values for the rows, as shown below.

Listing 4-45: Defining the rows manually

```
struct ContentView: View {
   @State private var appData = ApplicationData.shared

   var body: some View {
      Table(of: ConsumableItem.self, columns: {
         TableColumn("Name", value: \.name)
         TableColumn("Category", value: \.category)
         TableColumn("Calories") { item in
            Text("\(item.calories)")
         }.width(100)
      }, rows: {
         TableRow(ConsumableItem(name: "STANDARD", category: "",
            calories: 0, included: false))
```

```
            ForEach(appData.listOfItems)
        })
    }
}
```

In this example, a row with the text "STANDARD" is defined manually at the top and the remaining rows are generated with a **ForEach** loop from the values in the model.

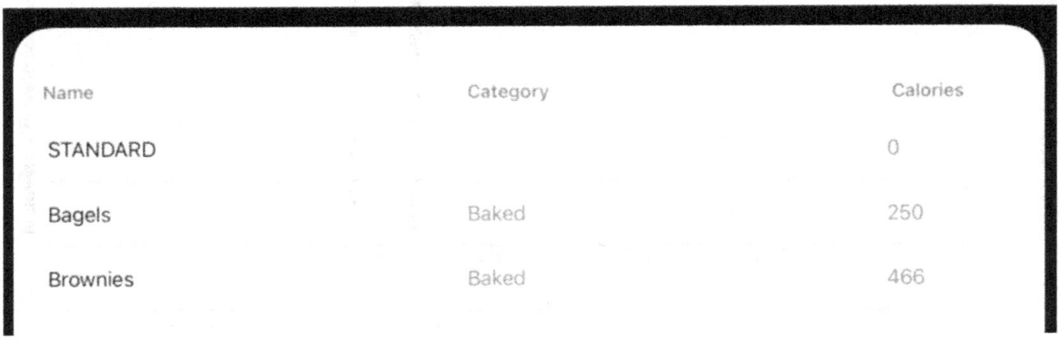

Figure 4-35: *Static rows*

On iPads and Macs, tables include a feature that allows the user to sort items by tapping or clicking a column's title. For instance, if we tap the header of the Name column in our example, the items will be sorted by name. This feature is added to the table when we include the **sortOrder** argument in the initializer. This argument takes a binding property that determines which column will be sorted. To compare values, the table uses a key path comparator. The following is the structure defined by the **Foundation** framework for this purpose.

KeyPathComparator(KeyPath, order: SortOrder)

This initializer defines a sort comparator for a property. The first argument is the key path of the property whose values we want to sort, and the **order** argument determines if the items will be sorted in ascending or descending order. It is an enumeration with the values **forward** and **reverse**.

The **KeyPathComparator** structure determines which values to sort, but we are responsible for sorting the values in the model. For this purpose, the Swift Standard Library includes the following method.

sort(using: Comparator)

This method sorts the items in a collection according to the sort comparator specified by the **using** argument.

To enable this feature, we need a binding property initialized with an array of **KeyPathComparator** structures, initialize the table with the **sortOrder** argument and a reference to this property, and then define the **value** argument for every column we want to sort. For instance, if we want to sort every column from our previous example, we must add the **value** argument to the Calories column, as shown below.

Listing 4-46: Sorting the values by column

```
struct ContentView: View {
   @State private var appData = ApplicationData.shared
   @State private var sort = [KeyPathComparator(\ConsumableItem.name)]

   var body: some View {
      Table(appData.listOfItems, sortOrder: $sort) {
         TableColumn("Name", value: \.name)
         TableColumn("Category", value: \.category)
         TableColumn("Calories", value: \.calories) { item in
            Text("\(item.calories)")
         }.width(100)
      }
      .padding(20)
      .onChange(of: sort) {
         appData.listOfItems.sort(using: sort)
      }
   }
}
```

When we click a column's name, the **Table** view stores a **KeyPathComparator** structure in the **sort** property with the key path for that column, so we use an **onChange()** modifier to track this change and call the **sort()** method on the **listOfItem** array to reorder the values in the model. This automatically sorts the items in ascending or descending order, depending on the previous state.

Do It Yourself

Update the **ContentView** structure with the code in Listing 4-46. Run the application on the iPad simulator or on your Mac (My Mac). Click the header of a column. You should see the items in that column sorted alphabetically.

Once we declare the **sortOrder** argument, the table enables sorting for every column, as long as it is defined with a key path. If we want to disable sorting for a column, we can define the row manually and omit the **value** argument, as in the following example.

Listing 4-47: Sorting only the calories

```
struct ContentView: View {
   @State private var appData = ApplicationData.shared
   @State private var sort = [KeyPathComparator(\ConsumableItem.name)]

   var body: some View {
      Table(appData.listOfItems, sortOrder: $sort) {
         TableColumn("Name") { item in
            Text("\(item.name)")
         }
         TableColumn("Category") { item in
```

```
            Text("\(item.category)")
        }
        TableColumn("Calories", value: \.calories) { item in
            Text("\(item.calories)")
        }.width(100)
    }
    .padding(20)
    .onChange(of: sort) {
        appData.listOfItems.sort(using: sort)
    }
  }
}
```

In this example, we manually define the value for the Name and Category columns and specify a key path only for the Calories column, so the user can sort the values only by calories.

> **Do It Yourself**
>
> Update the **ContentView** structure with the code in Listing 4-47. Run the application on an iPad simulator or on your Mac. You should only be able to sort the values by calories.

Tables also allow the user to select one or multiple rows. To enable this feature, we must provide a binding property to store the identifiers of the items selected by the user and assign that property to the table. For single selection, everything works out of the box, but iPads without a keyboard require the edit mode to be enabled. In the following example, we include an **EditButton** view to allow the user to enable this mode and also a **Text** view below to show the names of the items selected by the user.

Listing 4-48: Allowing the user to select items in a table

```
struct ContentView: View {
   @State private var appData = ApplicationData.shared
   @State private var selectedItems: Set<ConsumableItem.ID> = []

   var body: some View {
      VStack {
         EditButton()
            .buttonStyle(.glassProminent)
         Table(appData.listOfItems, selection: $selectedItems) {
            TableColumn("Name", value: \.name)
            TableColumn("Category", value: \.category)
            TableColumn("Calories") { item in
               Text("\(item.calories)")
            }.width(100)
         }
         Text(listSelected())
            .padding()
      }
   }
```

```
    func listSelected() -> String {
        let list: [String] = selectedItems.map({ id in
            let item = appData.listOfItems.first(where: { $0.id == id })
            return item?.name ?? ""
        })
        return String(list.sorted().joined(separator: " "))
    }
}
```

This example allows the user to select single items by just tapping on them, or enable the edit mode by pressing the **EditButton** to make a multiple selection. To show the names of the selected items, we created a method that maps the identifiers, gets the items from the **listOfItems** array, returns the value of the **name** property, and then sorts and joins the values to create a string with all the names.

Do It Yourself

Update the **ContentView** structure with the code in Listing 4-48. Run the application on an iPad simulator. Tap an item to select it. You should see the name of the item at the bottom of the screen.

In the last example, we display the selected names on the screen, but of course we can add buttons to the interface to process the values as needed. A useful tool provided by tables for this purpose are context menus. With context menus, the user can right-click the selected rows and perform an action. SwiftUI includes the following modifier to create the menu.

contextMenu(forSelectionType: Type, **menu:** Closure)

This modifier assigns a context menu to an item of a view. The **forSelectionType** argument specifies the data type of the values we want to associate with the menu, and the **menu** argument provides the options for the menu.

The closure assigned to the **menu** argument receives a copy of the set with the values selected by the user. By checking these values, we can configure the menu with options for when the user right-clicks on a single row, multiple rows, or the table's empty area. All we need to do to configure the menu is to count how many items are in the array, as shown below.

Listing 4-49: Using a context menu to process a row

```
struct ContentView: View {
    @State private var appData = ApplicationData.shared
    @State private var selectedItems: Set<ConsumableItem.ID> = []

    var body: some View {
        Table(appData.listOfItems, selection: $selectedItems) {
```

```
            TableColumn("Name", value: \.name)
            TableColumn("Category", value: \.category)
            TableColumn("Calories") { item in
               Text("\(item.calories)")
            }.width(100)
         }
         .contextMenu(forSelectionType: ConsumableItem.ID.self, menu: {
            selected in
            if selected.count <= 0  {
               Button("Create New Item") {
                  let newItem = ConsumableItem(name: "Test",
                     category: "Test", calories: 0, included: false)
                  appData.listOfItems.append(newItem)
               }
            } else if selected.count == 1 {
               Button("Remove Item") {
                  appData.listOfItems.removeAll(where: { item in
                     item.id == selected.first
                  })
               }
            } else {
               Button("Remove Selected Items") {
                  appData.listOfItems.removeAll(where: { item in
                     selected.contains(item.id)
                  })
               }
            }
         })
      }
   }
```

If there are no items in the set, which means that the user right-clicked on an empty area of the table, we show a button to add a new item to the model. If there is only one item in the set, we offer a button to remove the value from the model, and if there are multiple items, the option removes them all. The context menu is created by the same **`contextMenu()`** modifier, but it adapts based on where the user right-clicks (or taps and holds on iPads), as shown below.

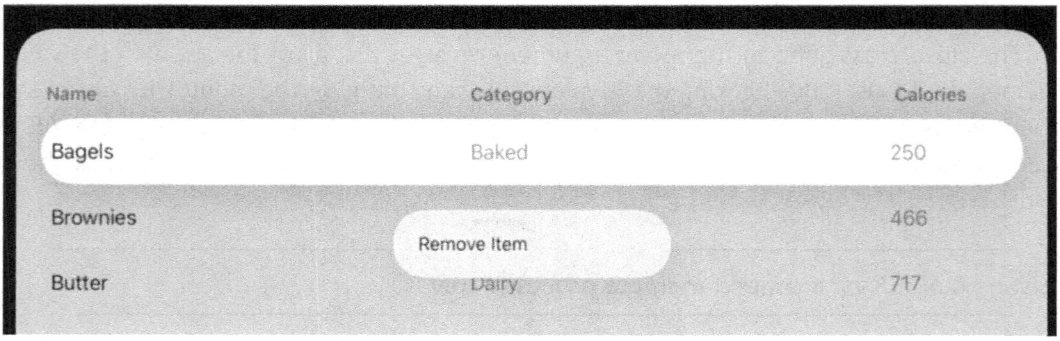

***Figure 4-36:** Contextual menu*

Do It Yourself

Update the **ContentView** structure with the code in Listing 4-49. Run the application on an iPad simulator or on your Mac. Right click on a row (Click and hold on the iPad simulator). Select the "Remove Item" option. The item should be removed. Do the same but in the table's empty area below and select the option "Create New Item". You should see a new item with the name "Test" at the bottom of the list. In this example, we always add the same item with the name "Test". We will learn how to open additional views to allow the user to insert custom values in Chapter 5.

In addition to **Text** views, tables can show other views, from images to control views. For instance, we can include a **Toggle** view, which is presented as a checkbox on the Mac, to allow the user to check or uncheck the items.

Listing 4-50: Defining the content of a column with a `Toggle` view

```
struct ContentView: View {
   @State private var appData = ApplicationData.shared

   var body: some View {
      Table(appData.listOfItems) {
         TableColumn("Name", value: \.name)
         TableColumn("Category", value: \.category)
         TableColumn("Calories") { item in
            Text("\(item.calories)")
         }.width(100)
         TableColumn("Included") { item in
            Toggle("", isOn: itemBinding(id: item.id).included)
               .labelsHidden()
         }.width(100)
      }
   }
   func itemBinding(id: UUID) -> Binding<ConsumableItem> {
      @Bindable var appData = appData

      let index = appData.listOfItems.firstIndex(where: {
         $0.id == id }) ?? 0
      return $appData.listOfItems[index]
   }
}
```

The **Toggle** view needs a bidirectional binding value to read and store the current value. The easiest way to provide this value is with a method. We call the method with the item's id, use this identifier to get the index of the item in the array, and return the item as a **Binding** value of type **ConsumableItem**. This creates the bidirectional connection between the **Toggle** view and the **ConsumableItem** structure, so every time the user clicks on the switch or the checkbox, the new value is stored directly into the item's **included** property.

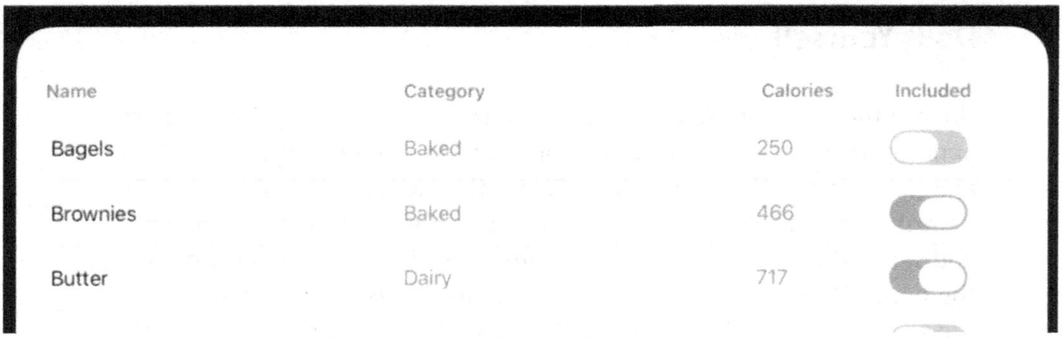

Figure 4-37: *Column of* `Toggle` *views*

The **`KeyPathComparator`** structure implemented before to sort the values conforms to the **`SortComparator`** protocol. This protocol defines the tools required to sort the values. The sort comparator implemented by that structure can compare and sort values of common data types like **`String`** and **`Int`** values, but it cannot sort custom data types or special values like Booleans. For instance, if we want to sort the **Included** column from our previous example, we must define our own **`SortComparator`** structure. The following are the protocol requirements.

`order`

This property defines the order of the values. It is a **`SortOrder`** enumeration with the values **`forward`** and **`reverse`**.

`compare(lhs:` `Value`, **`rhs:`** `Value)`

This method compares two values at a time and must return an enumeration value of type **`ComparisonResult`** to determine the order. The values available are **`orderedAscending`**, **`orderedDescending`**, and **`orderedSame`**.

In addition to these requirements, our structure also needs to define a typealias with the name **`Compared`** of the data type of the values we want to compare, as shown below.

Listing 4-51: Defining a custom sort comparator

```
struct CompareBool: SortComparator {
   typealias Compared = Bool
   var order: SortOrder = .forward

   func compare(_ lhs: Bool, _ rhs: Bool) -> ComparisonResult {
      if lhs && !rhs {
         return order == .forward ? .orderedAscending : .orderedDescending
      } else if !lhs && rhs {
         return order == .forward ? .orderedDescending : .orderedAscending
      } else {
         return .orderedSame
      }
   }
}
```

The **order** property determines the order of the values (ascending or descending). In this example, we provide an initial value, but the property is updated every time the user clicks on the column's header. In the **compare()** method, we compare the values received by the method and return a **ComparisonResult** value depending on the value of the **order** property (**orderedAscending** or **orderedDescending**).

Now that we have a comparator for Boolean values, we must apply it to the table. The **TableColumn** view includes the following initializer to apply a custom sort comparator.

```
TableColumn(String, value: KeyPath, comparator:
StandardComparator, content: Closure)
```

This initializer defines a column for a table. The first argument specifies the column's title, the **value** argument is the key path of the property that provides the values for the column, the **comparator** argument is a custom **SortComparator** structure to sort the values, and the **content** argument defines the views to display by the column.

This initializer is applied the same way as the previous ones, with the difference that now we must include an instance of our **CompareBool** structure to tell the table how to sort the values.

Listing 4-52: Sorting Boolean values on a table

```
struct ContentView: View {
   @State private var appData = ApplicationData.shared
   @State private var sort = [KeyPathComparator(\ConsumableItem.name)]

   var body: some View {
      Table(appData.listOfItems, sortOrder: $sort) {
         TableColumn("Name", value: \.name)
         TableColumn("Category", value: \.category)
         TableColumn("Calories") { item in
            Text("\(item.calories)")
         }.width(100)
         TableColumn("Included", value: \.included,
            comparator: CompareBool()) { item in
            Toggle("", isOn: itemBinding(id: item.id).included)
               .labelsHidden()
         }.width(100)
      }
      .onChange(of: sort) {
         appData.listOfItems.sort(using: sort)
      }
   }
   func itemBinding(id: UUID) -> Binding<ConsumableItem> {
      @Bindable var appData = appData

      let index = appData.listOfItems.firstIndex(where: {
         $0.id == id }) ?? 0
      return $appData.listOfItems[index]
   }
}
```

Do It Yourself

Add the structure in Listing 4-51 to the **ApplicationData.swift** file. Update the `ContentView` structure with the code in Listing 4-52. Run the application and turn some of the switches on. Click on the column's title. You should see the items sorted by the condition of the switches.

Tables can also display data in a hierarchical structure and reveal the information as needed. For this purpose, SwiftUI provides the following view.

DisclosureTableRow(Value, **isExpanded:** Binding?, **content:** Closure**)**

This initializer creates a view that displays rows containing other rows in a hierarchical structure. The first argument is the value containing the data for the rows, the **isExpanded** argument is a binding property that allows the rows to be expanded or collapsed programmatically, and the **content** argument is the closure that provides the rows to be displayed when the main row is expanded.

The purpose of the **DisclosureTableRow** view is to disclose rows that represent the same data but belong to a different hierarchy. For example, if we have a list of employees, some of whom are managers and some subordinates, we can use a **DisclosureTableRow** view to show the subordinate employees only when needed. The following is the data model for this example.

Listing 4-53: Defining a model with hierarchical data

```
import SwiftUI

struct Employees: Identifiable {
   let id = UUID()
   var name: String
   var position: String
   var subordinates: [Employees]
}
@Observable class ApplicationData {
   var listOfEmployees: [Employees] = []

   static let shared: ApplicationData = ApplicationData()
   private init() {
      let employee1 = Employees(name: "Sander", position: "Subordinate",
         subordinates: [])
      let employee2 = Employees(name: "Annie", position: "Subordinate",
         subordinates: [])
      let employee3 = Employees(name: "Charlie", position: "Subordinate",
         subordinates: [])
      let employee4 = Employees(name: "Sebastian", position:
         "Subordinate", subordinates: [])
      let employee5 = Employees(name: "Bill", position: "Subordinate",
         subordinates: [])

      listOfEmployees.append(Employees(name: "Robert", position:
         "Manager", subordinates: [employee1, employee2, employee3]))
```

```
        listOfEmployees.append(Employees(name: "Anna", position: "Manager",
           subordinates: [employee4, employee5]))
    }
}
```

This model defines the **Employees** structure to store the information about each employee in the company. The structure includes a property called **subordinates** to store the list of employees who are under the supervision of a manager. For testing purposes, we have created five employees who are subordinates to two managers. To display this information, we need to create the rows manually, as shown below.

Listing 4-54: Disclosing hierarchical data on a table

```
struct ContentView: View {
   @State private var appData = ApplicationData.shared

   var body: some View {
      Table(of: Employees.self, columns: {
         TableColumn("Name", value: \.name)
         TableColumn("Position ", value: \.position)
      }, rows: {
         ForEach(appData.listOfEmployees) { employee in
            if employee.subordinates.isEmpty {
               TableRow(employee)
            } else {
               DisclosureTableRow(employee) {
                  ForEach(employee.subordinates)
               }
            }
         }
      })
   }
}
```

In this example, we have a **ForEach** loop that goes through each employee in the **listOfEmployees** array and then determines whether or not the employee is a manager by checking the number of subordinates. If the **subordinates** property is empty, we show the employee's data, otherwise a **DisclosureTableRow** view is created to list the subordinates.

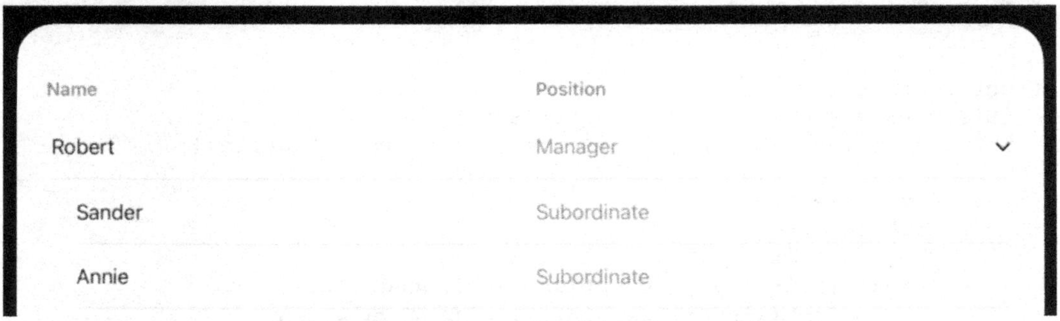

Figure 4-38: *Hierarchical data on a table*

Do It Yourself

Update the **ApplicationData.swift** file with the model in Listing 4-53 and the **`ContentView`** structure with the code in Listing 4-54. Run the application on an iPad simulator or on your Mac. Click on a manager's row to disclose the subordinates.

BASIC

4.4 - Pickers

SwiftUI also provides views to create pickers the user can interact with to select lists of values. A picker can present values in a wheel-style interface, in a list, or as a series of buttons, depending on the platform and configuration. The framework includes two views for this purpose: one to create a general-purpose list and another to generate lists of dates and times.

BASIC

Picker View

The **`Picker`** view creates a general-purpose picker to show a list of values. The structure includes the following initializer.

```
Picker(String, selection: Binding, content: Closure)
```

This initializer creates a **`Picker`** view with the label defined by the first argument. The **selection** argument is a binding property that stores the value selected by the user, and the closure assigned to the **content** argument provides the list of views required to present the values.

A **`Picker`** view needs a binding property to store the value currently selected by the user and a list of views to present the values available. The list of views can be created manually, one view per line, or dynamically with a **`ForEach`** view, as in the following example.

Listing 4-55: Defining a picker

```
struct ContentView: View {
   @State private var selectedValue: String = "No Value"
   let listCities: [String] = ["Paris", "Toronto", "Dublin"]

   var body: some View {
      VStack {
         Text(selectedValue)
         Picker("Cities:", selection: $selectedValue) {
            ForEach(listCities, id: \.self) { value in
               Text(value)
            }
         }
```

```
            Spacer()
        }.padding()
    }
}
```

By default, the picker is shown with a style of type **menu**. This creates a drop down menu on the Mac, and a button that opens a context menu when tapped in mobile devices. The label is not included on mobile devices, so if we test the application on an iPhone or iPad simulator, only the content of the picker is shown on the screen.

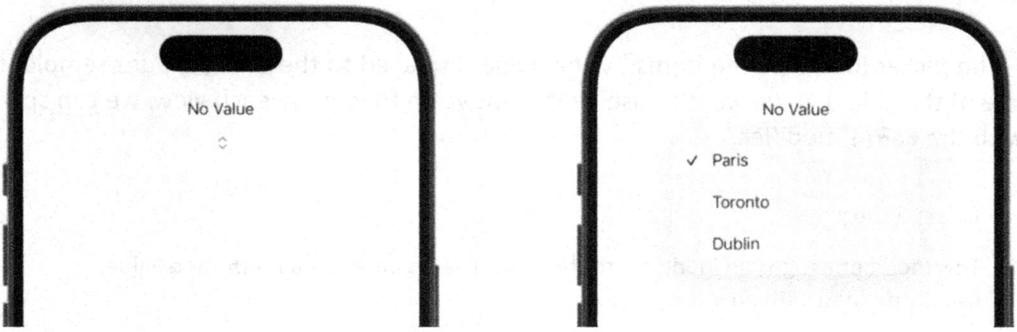

Figure 4-39: *Menu picker*

The value of the binding property is used to store the value selected by the user and also to initialize the picker. If the property contains a value, and the value is available in the model, the picker is shown with that value selected. There are several ways to provide this initial value. In the following example, we use the **onAppear()** modifier to select the second city on the list.

Listing 4-56: Selecting an initial value

```
struct ContentView: View {
   @State private var selectedValue: String = "No Value"
   let listCities: [String] = ["Paris", "Toronto", "Dublin"]

   var body: some View {
      VStack {
         Text(selectedValue)
         Picker("Cities:", selection: $selectedValue) {
            ForEach(listCities, id: \.self) { value in
               Text(value)
            }
         }
         Spacer()
      }.padding()
      .onAppear {
         selectedValue = listCities[1]
      }
   }
}
```

In this example, we initialize the **selectedValue** property with the second value in the **listCities** array and therefore this is the initial value selected by the **Picker** view (Toronto).

Do It Yourself

Create a new App project. Update the **ContentView** structure with the code in Listing 4-55. Run the application on the Canvas or an iPhone simulator. Press the button. You should see a context menu, as shown in Figure 4-39, right. Update the view with the code in Listing 4-56. Press the button again. You should see a context menu with the Toronto option already selected.

The picker identifies the items by the value displayed to the user (in our example, the name of the cities). If we want to use a different value to identify each view, we can specify it with the **tag()** modifier.

tag(Value)

This modifier assigns an identifier to the view. The argument is a **Hashable** value, usually defined with an integer.

An alternative is to use the indices of the array to represent the views. The Swift Standard Library provides the **indices** property to access these values. This property returns the indices of the collection, so we can use it to iterate through the values, as shown below.

Listing 4-57: Listing values by index

```
struct ContentView: View {
   @State private var selectedValue: Int = 0
   let listCities: [String] = ["Paris", "Toronto", "Dublin"]

   var body: some View {
      VStack {
         Text(listCities[selectedValue])
         Picker("Cities:", selection: $selectedValue) {
            ForEach(listCities.indices, id: \.self) { value in
               Text(listCities[value])
                   .tag(value)
            }
         }
         Spacer()
      }.padding()
   }
}
```

Because we are now working with the indexes of the array instead of the values, we define the **selectedValue** property of type **Int**. To get the index of each value, we define the **ForEach** view with the range of values returned by the **indices** property of the **listCities** array, and then assign the index to each value with the **tag()** modifier. When a value is selected, the picker assigns the value of the **tag()** modifier to the **selectedValue** property, and therefore we can use this property to get the name of the city from the array (**listCities[selectedValue]**).

Do It Yourself

Update the **ContentView** structure with the code in Listing 4-57. The application should work as before, but now the values processed by the picker are integers instead of strings.

The **Picker** view adopts a design according to the device and the conditions in which it is presented, but we can force the picker to adopt the design we want with the following modifier.

pickerStyle(Style)

This modifier sets the style of the picker. The argument is a structure that conforms to the **PickerStyle** protocol. The system defines a few structures with predefined styles. To declare these values, the structures include the type properties **automatic**, **menu**, **segmented**, and **wheel**.

The **automatic** style allows the picker to adapt the design to the device and conditions, and the **menu** style creates a context menu, as we have seen in the previous examples. But there are two additional styles. The **wheel** style displays the values in a virtual wheel the user can rotate to make a pick, and the **segmented** style defines a unique picker where the values are turned into buttons. The latter is frequently used to allow the user to select a value from a limited set of options, as illustrated by the following example.

Listing 4-58: Implementing a segmented picker

```
struct ContentView: View {
   @State private var selectedValue: String = "No Value"
   let listCities: [String] = ["Paris", "Toronto", "Dublin"]

   var body: some View {
      VStack {
         Text(selectedValue)
         Picker("Cities:", selection: $selectedValue) {
            ForEach(listCities, id: \.self) { value in
               Text(value)
            }
         }.pickerStyle(.segmented)
         Spacer()
      }.padding()
   }
}
```

The implementation of the picker is the same, but by applying a custom style we change the way the values are presented to the user. Below are the pickers we see when the style is set to **wheel** or **segmented**.

Figure 4-40: *Wheel and segmented pickers*

Do It Yourself

Update the **`ContentView`** structure with the code in Listing 4-58. Run the application on an iPhone simulator. You should be able to click on the buttons to select a different city. Assign the **`wheel`** value to the **`pickerStyle()`** modifier. You should be able to drag a wheel up or down to select a value.

BASIC

Date Picker

SwiftUI includes two picker views designed to simplify the creation of pickers that allow the user to select a date or a time: **`DatePicker`** for a single date and **`MultiDatePicker`** for multiple dates. The following are the most frequently used initializers.

```
DatePicker(String, selection: Binding, in: Range,
displayedComponents: Components)
```

This initializer creates a **`DatePicker`** view with the label defined by the first argument. The **selection** argument is a binding property of type **`Date`** that stores the date selected by the user, the **in** argument defines the range of dates the user can choose from, and the **displayComponents** argument is a structure of type **`DatePickerComponents`** that defines the type of values managed by the picker. The structure includes two type properties for this purpose: **`date`** and **`hourAndMinute`**.

```
MultiDatePicker(String, selection: Binding, in: Range)
```

This initializer creates a **`MultiDatePicker`** view with the label defined by the first argument. The **selection** argument is a binding property to a set of **`DateComponents`** values with the dates selected by the user, and the **in** argument defines the range of dates the user can choose from.

To define a **`DatePicker`** view, we must provide a binding property to store the value selected by the user and tell the picker the type of values we want to show. For dates, we must specify the **`date`** value, and for time the **`time`** value, but if we want the user to be able to select both, we must ignore the argument altogether, as we do in the following example.

Listing 4-59: Defining a `DatePicker` to select a date

```
struct ContentView: View {
    @State private var selectedDate: Date = Date()

    var body: some View {
        VStack {
            DatePicker("Date:", selection: $selectedDate)
            Spacer()
        }.padding()
    }
}
```

The **`@State`** property used to store the selected value was initialized with the current date (**`Date()`**) and therefore the picker shows it as the selected date and time, but we can initialize this value with any date we want. The picker is presented with the style by default, which in mobile devices shows buttons to open a calendar to select the date and a spinning wheel to select the time.

***Figure 4-41:** Picker for dates*

Do It Yourself

Update the **`ContentView`** structure with the code in Listing 4-59. Run the application on an iPhone simulator. You should see the interface in Figure 4-41, left. Add the **displayComponents** argument to the **`DatePicker`** view initializer with the value **`date`** or **`hourandminute`** to allow users to select only dates or times. You can also include the **`labelsHidden()`** modifier to remove the label.

By default, the **`DatePicker`** view presents a list with all the dates from a distant date in the past to a distant date in the future. To limit the list of values the user can select from, we must provide a range of dates. The range can be closed (from one date to another), or open. The following example shows a list of dates from the current date to a distant date in the future using an open range.

Listing 4-60: Limiting the `DatePicker` to a range of values

```
struct ContentView: View {
    @State private var selectedDate: Date = Date()

    var body: some View {
        VStack {
            DatePicker("Date:", selection: $selectedDate, in: Date()...,
                displayedComponents: .date)
            Spacer()
        }.padding()
    }
}
```

In this example, we limit the picker with a range of dates (**`Date()...`**) and therefore the user is not allowed to select a date before the current date. A range **`...Date()`** does the opposite, it only allows the user to select a date from the past. But we can also provide specific dates by creating custom **`Date`** structures.

A **`DatePicker`** view adopts a design according to the device and the conditions in which it is presented, but it includes the following modifier to specify the style we want.

`datePickerStyle``(Style)`

This modifier sets the style of the picker. The argument is a structure that conforms to the **`DatePickerStyle`** protocol. To provide standard styles, the system defines a few structures with the type properties **`automatic`**, **`compact`**, **`graphical`**, and **`wheel`**.

By default, the **`DatePicker`** view is configured with the **`compact`** style, which shows a button the user must press to reveal a calendar to select a date or a spinning wheel to select a time. But we can also show the calendar right away with the **`graphical`** style, or a spinning wheel with the **`wheel`** style, as we do in the following example.

Listing 4-61: Presenting a picker with a spinning wheel

```
struct ContentView: View {
    @State private var selectedDate: Date = Date()

    var body: some View {
        VStack {
            Text("Date: \(selectedDate.formatted(.dateTime.day().month()))")
            DatePicker("Date:", selection: $selectedDate,
                displayedComponents: .date)
                .labelsHidden()
                .datePickerStyle(.wheel)
            Spacer()
        }.padding()
    }
}
```

In addition to assigning the wheel style to the picker, this view also includes a **`Text`** view at the top to display the day and month selected by the user. The result is shown below.

Figure 4-42: Wheel picker

To allow the user to select multiple dates, we must create the picker with a **MultiDatePicker** view and a binding property that stores a set of **DateComponents** values, as shown below.

Listing 4-62: Picking multiple dates

```
struct ContentView: View {
   @State private var selectedDates: Set<DateComponents> = []
   @State private var mydates: String = ""

   var body: some View {
      VStack {
         MultiDatePicker("Dates:", selection: $selectedDates)
         Spacer()
         Text(mydates)
      }.padding()
      .onChange(of: selectedDates, initial: false) { old, values in
         let days = values.map({ value in String(value.day!) })
         mydates = days.joined(separator: ",")
      }
   }
}
```

A **MultiDatePicker** view works like the **DatePicker** view, but the selected values are stored in an array. In this example, we apply the **onChange()** modifier to show the days selected by the user in a **Text** view at the bottom of the screen.

Figure 4-43: Multiple date picker

Do It Yourself

Update the **ContentView** structure with the code in Listing 4-62. Run the application on an iPhone simulator and select a few dates. You should see the days displayed at the bottom (Figure 4-43).

BASIC

4.5 - Forms

Most applications include views with a list of options users can select to set the configuration of the app, the style of the interface, or the type of information they want to see. We can create these screens with a list of controls in a **VStack**, as we have done before, but SwiftUI provides a view specifically designed for this purpose called **Form**.

BASIC

Form View

A **Form** view is a container that organizes the views in a list, like the **List** view, but adapts the controls to the device and the platform in which the app is running. Creating a form in SwiftUI is easy, we just have to include the controls one after another inside the **Form** view, as shown below.

Listing 4-63: Defining a form

```
struct ContentView: View {
   @State private var setActive: Bool = false
   @State private var setShowPictures: Bool = false
   @State private var setTotal: Int = 10

   var body: some View {
      Form {
         Toggle("Active", isOn: $setActive)
         Toggle("Show Pictures", isOn: $setShowPictures)
         HStack {
            Text("Total")
            Spacer()
            Text(String(setTotal))
            Stepper("", value: $setTotal, in: 0...10)
               .labelsHidden()
         }
      }
   }
}
```

The style used to present the view depends on the system. In iOS, the **Form** view adds padding on the sides of the controls and presents the list with a **grouped** style.

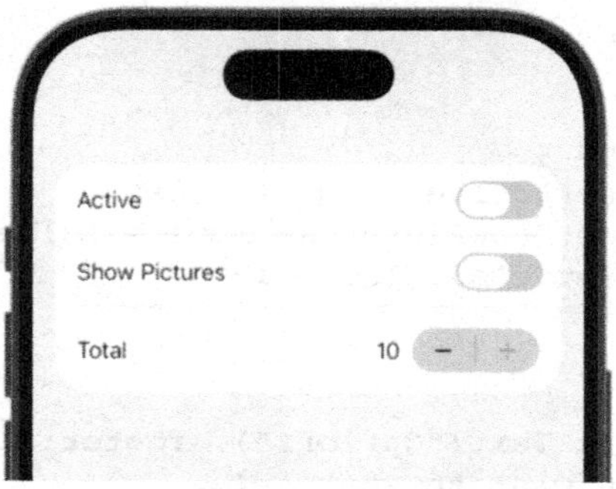

Figure 4-44: *Simple form*

Most views allow us to specify a string that the **Form** view can use to create the label for the control, but in some cases, we may need to hide the label and specify our own. To create custom labels, SwiftUI includes the **LabeledContent** view. This view attaches a label to another view. The following is the most frequently used initializer.

LabeledContent(String, **content:** Closure**)**

This initializer attaches a label to a view. The first argument specifies the label, and the **content** argument provides the views.

With this view, we can better organize our previous example and provide a custom label for the **Stepper** view.

Listing 4-64: Defining custom labels for a form

```
struct ContentView: View {
   @State private var setActive: Bool = false
   @State private var setShowPictures: Bool = false
   @State private var setTotal: Int = 10

   var body: some View {
      Form {
         Toggle("Active", isOn: $setActive)
         Toggle("Show Pictures", isOn: $setShowPictures)
         LabeledContent("Total") {
            HStack {
               Text(String(setTotal))
               Stepper("", value: $setTotal, in: 0...10)
                  .labelsHidden()
            }
         }
      }
   }
}
```

A **Form** view works like a **List** view, so we can separate the content in sections.

Listing 4-65: Styling a form

```
struct ContentView: View {
   @State private var setActive: Bool = false
   @State private var setShowPictures: Bool = false
   @State private var setTotal: Int = 10

   var body: some View {
      Form {
         Section(header: Text("Options"), footer: Text("Activate the
            options you want to see")) {
            Toggle("Active", isOn: $setActive)
            Toggle("Show Pictures", isOn: $setShowPictures)
         }
         Section(header: Text("Values"), footer: Text("Insert the number
            of items to display")) {
            LabeledContent("Total") {
               HStack {
                  Text(String(setTotal))
                  Stepper("", value: $setTotal, in: 0...10)
                     .labelsHidden()
               }
            }
         }
      }
   }
}
```

Figure 4-45: *Form with a standard design*

Do It Yourself

Create a new App project. Update the **ContentView** structure with the code in Listing 4-65. Run the application on the Canvas or an iPhone simulator. You should see the interface in Figure 4-45. Add controls to the **Form** view and create more sections to see how they look like.

IMPORTANT

In these examples, we have stored the values locally with **@State** properties. This means that the values inserted by the user are going to be available only for this view. To make them available to the rest of the app, we must store them in the model with observable properties, or send them to other views, as we will see in Chapter 5.

PRO

Disclosure Group

Some forms are extensive and hard to read. SwiftUI includes the **DisclosureGroup** view to expand and collapse a list of controls. This is similar to the **OutlineGroup** view implemented before to create hierarchical lists, but the **DisclosureGroup** view works with non hierarchical information, such as the one we find in a form. The structure includes the following initializer.

DisclosureGroup(String, **isExpanded:** Binding, **content:** Closure)

This initializer creates a **DisclosureGroup** view to hide or show content. The first argument is the view's label, the **isExpanded** argument is a binding property of type **Bool** that determines whether the view is expanded or collapsed, and the **content** argument is the closure that provides the views we want to show or hide.

With this view, we can organize the two sections of our form in expandable lists.

Listing 4-66: Disclosing controls

```
struct ContentView: View {
   @State private var setActive: Bool = false
   @State private var setShowPictures: Bool = false
   @State private var setTotal: Int = 10

   var body: some View {
      Form {
         DisclosureGroup("Controls") {
            Toggle("Active", isOn: $setActive)
            Toggle("Show Pictures", isOn: $setShowPictures)
         }
         DisclosureGroup("Values") {
            HStack {
               Text("Total")
               Spacer()
               Text(String(setTotal))
               Stepper("", value: $setTotal, in: 0...10)
                  .labelsHidden()
            }
         }
      }
   }
}
```

When the views are collapsed, all we see is the view's label. If we tap on these labels or the disclosure indicator, the content is expanded and we can interact with the controls.

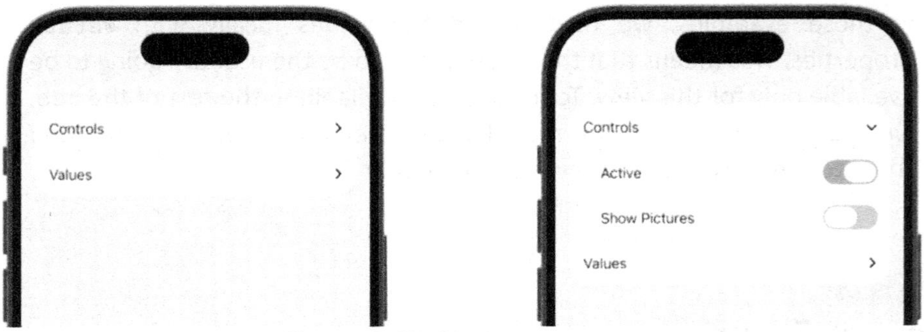

Figure 4-46: *Disclosure groups*

PRO

4.6 - Custom Containers

In addition to the predefined containers seen so far, we can also create our own. Custom containers allow us to change the design of the views and dynamically adapt it to the state of the app. To create a custom container, we need to define a structure that conforms to the **View** protocol, include a **@ContentBuilder** property to store and construct the views inside the container, and then read and design the views with a **ForEach** or a **Group** view. For this purpose, the **ForEach** and **Group** views include the following initializers.

ForEach(subviews: Views, **content:** Closure)

This initializer creates a **ForEach** view that can iterate over the views constructed by a **@ContentBuilder** property wrapper. The **subviews** argument is the **@ContentBuilder** property that provides the views, and the **content** argument is the closure used to process the views.

Group(subviews: Views, **transform:** Closure)

This initializer creates a group of views from the views constructed by a **@ContentBuilder** property wrapper. The **subviews** argument is the **@ContentBuilder** property that provides the views, and the **content** argument is the closure used to process the views.

The structure that defines the custom container must be generic to be able to process any type of views. In the following example, we define a structure for a custom container that creates a simple list of vertical views.

Listing 4-67: Defining a custom container

```
import SwiftUI

struct BoxListView<Content: View>: View {
   @ContentBuilder var content: Content
```

```
    var body: some View {
        VStack {
            ForEach(subviews: content) { subview in
                HStack {
                    subview
                        .padding()
                }
                .frame(minWidth: 0, maxWidth: .infinity)
                .border(.red, width: 5)
                .padding(5)
            }
        }
    }
}
#Preview {
    BoxListView {
        Text("Test")
    }
}
```

The **BoxListView** view defined in Listing 4-67 is a custom container. The container takes a list of views and then implements a **ForEach** view to process and style the views. Now we can use this container in our interface, as shown below.

Listing 4-68: Implementing a custom container

```
struct ContentView: View {
    var body: some View {
        BoxListView {
            Text("First")
            Text("Second")
            Text("Third")
        }
    }
}
```

In this example, we include three **Text** views, but we can also use a normal **ForEach** view to define the views from data, as we did before with **List** views.

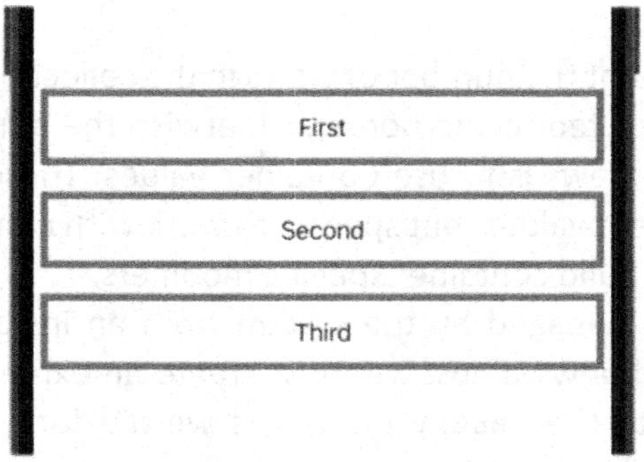

Figure 4-47: *Custom container*

Do It Yourself

Create a new App project. Create a Swift file called **BoxListView.swift** for the custom container in Listing 4-67. Update the **ContentView** structure with the code in Listing 4-68. Run the application on an iPhone simulator. You should see a list of views, as shown in Figure 4-47.

The **BoxListView** container processes the views one by one and always assigns the same style to each one of them, but there are ways to select a different design depending on the situation. One alternative is to use a **Group** view. This view creates a collection with the views in the container, so we can process them any way we want. For example, we can assign different styles depending on the number of views available.

Listing 4-69: Applying different styles to the views in a custom container

```
struct BoxListView<Content: View>: View {
   @ContentBuilder var content: Content

   var body: some View {
      VStack {
         Group(subviews: content) { subviews in
            let color = subviews.count > 2 ? Color.red : Color.blue

            ForEach(subviews) { subview in
               HStack {
                  subview
                     .padding()
               }
               .frame(minWidth: 0, maxWidth: .infinity)
               .border(color, width: 5)
               .padding(5)
            }
         }
      }
   }
}
```

In this example, we count the number of views in the collection. If the number is greater than 2, we assign the color red to the border, otherwise the border will be blue. Another alternative to modify the views is to use Container Values. These are values stored in the system, like the environment values, but specific to work with containers. One of their main functions is to allow us to build container specific modifiers.

Container values are managed by the system from an instance of a structure called **ContainerValues**. To add new values, we must create an extension of this structure and define the properties with the **@Entry** macro, as we did for environment properties in Chapter 2 (see Listing 2-81).

Listing 4-70: Adding a container value

```
extension ContainerValues {
   @Entry var showBorder: Bool = true
}
```

The extension in Listing 4-70 creates a new container value called **showBorder** with the value **true**. To change this value later, SwiftUI includes the following method.

containerValue(WritableKeyPath, Value**)**

This method sets the value of a container value. The first argument is the property's key path and the second argument is the value we want to assign to the property.

The best way to change a container value is to create a view modifier. For this purpose, we need to create an extension of the **View** protocol and define a new method, as shown below.

Listing 4-71: Modifying a container value

```
extension View {
   func showBorder(_ show: Bool) -> some View {
      containerValue(\.showBorder, show)
   }
}
```

Once we have the container values, we can use them in our custom container. To provide access to these values, the structure used to create container views include the following property.

containerValues

This property returns the **ContainerValues** structure associated with the view.

In the following example, we modify our custom container to adapt the views to the value of the **showBorder** property. If this container value is **true**, we show a border of 5 points, otherwise the width of the border is 0.

Listing 4-72: Using container values

```
struct BoxListView<Content: View>: View {
   @ContentBuilder var content: Content

   var body: some View {
      VStack {
         ForEach(subviews: content) { subview in
            let values = subview.containerValues

            HStack {
               subview
                  .padding()
            }
```

```
            .frame(minWidth: 0, maxWidth: .infinity)
            .border(.red, width: values.showBorder ? 5 : 0)
            .padding(5)
         }
      }
   }
}
```

Now that we have a container value and a custom container that can process the views according to that value, we can use it in our interface. In this case, all we need to do is to apply the new modifier to the view which value we want to change.

Listing 4-73: Changing the container value of a view

```
struct ContentView: View {
   var body: some View {
      BoxListView {
         Text("First")
         Text("Second")
            .showBorder(false)
         Text("Third")
      }
   }
}
```

In this example, we assign the **showBorder()** modifier to the second view. The first and third views in the custom container now include a border, but the second doesn't.

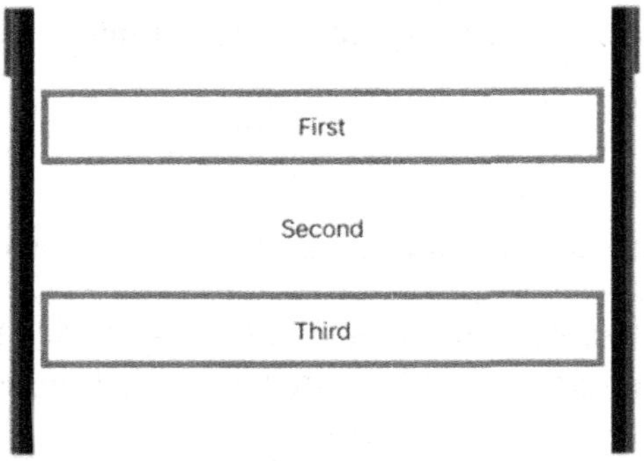

Figure 4-48: *Container values*

Do It Yourself

Add the extensions in Listings 4-70 and 4-71 to the **BoxListView.swift** file. Update the **BoxListView** view with the code in Listing 4-72 and the **ContentView** structure with the code in Listing 4-73. Run the application on an iPhone simulator. You should see the list of views as illustrated in Figure 4-48.

Chapter 5
Navigation

BASIC

5.1 - User Interface

The **ContentView** view used in previous examples defines the interface for the initial screen, but applications that rely on a single view and a simple interface are uncommon. On mobile devices, the limited screen size makes it necessary to use multiple views that replace one another in response to user interaction. Professional applications are typically composed of several views connected through predetermined paths that allow users to navigate the content. Figure 5-1, below, illustrates how these views work together to expand the user interface.

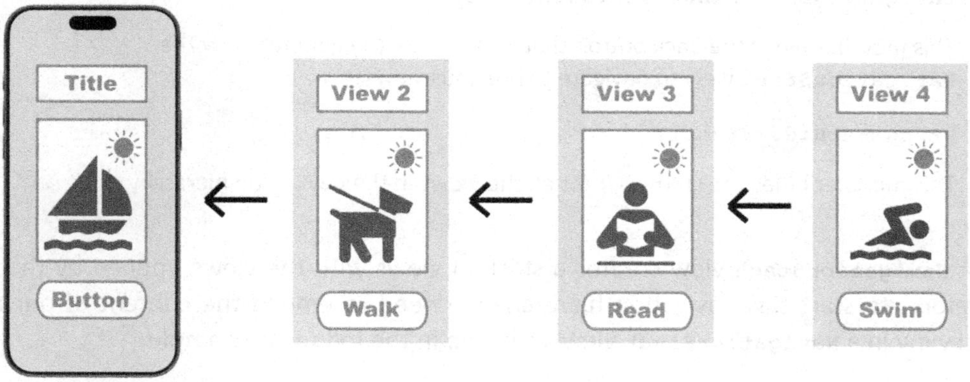

Figure 5-1: *Multiple views to expand the interface*

BASIC

Navigation Stack

The **ContentView** view included in the template for an App project represents the app's initial view, but we are responsible for creating the rest. The way these additional views are defined is always the same: we declare a structure that conforms to the **View** protocol and implement the **body** property, but there are different mechanisms to present them to the user. The approach recommended by Apple for mobile devices uses a transition in which views move from right to left, as illustrated in Figure 5-1. When the user navigates back, the current view is removed using a transition in the opposite direction. To create this navigation system, SwiftUI provides the **NavigationStack** view. The following is the view's initializer.

NavigationStack(path: Binding, **root:** Closure)

This initializer creates a navigation stack that manages the views through which the user can navigate. The **path** argument is a binding property that stores the navigation path followed by the user, and the **root** argument is a closure that returns the initial view presented by the navigation stack.

A **NavigationStack** view incorporates a navigation bar at the top of the interface to provide tools for navigation. The following are the modifiers available to configure this bar.

navigationTitle(String)

This modifier defines the title to show in the navigation bar.

navigationSubtitle(String)

This modifier adds a subtitle to the navigation bar.

toolbarTitleDisplayMode(ToolbarTitleDisplayMode)

This modifier determines the display mode for the title and subtitle. The argument is an enumeration with the values **automatic**, **inline**, **inlineLarge** and **large**.

navigationBarBackButtonHidden(Bool)

This modifier hides the Back button that is automatically generated by the **NavigationStack** view to navigate to previous views.

statusBarHidden(Bool)

This modifier hides the status bar for all the views in the navigation hierarchy.

A **NavigationStack** view creates a stack of views with the views opened by the user. Therefore, to start this navigation hierarchy we need to embed the content of our app's initial view in a **NavigationStack** view, as we do in the following example.

Listing 5-1: Initiating a navigation stack

```
struct ContentView: View {
   @Environment(ApplicationData.self) private var appData

   var body: some View {
      NavigationStack {
         List(appData.userData) { book in
            CellBook(book: book)
         }
         .navigationTitle(Text("Books"))
      }
   }
}
struct CellBook: View {
   let book: Book
```

```
    var body: some View {
        HStack(alignment: .top) {
            Image(book.cover)
                .resizable()
                .scaledToFit()
                .frame(width: 80, height: 100)
            VStack(alignment: .leading, spacing: 2) {
                Text(book.title).bold()
                Text(book.author)
                Text(book.displayYear).font(.caption)
                Spacer()
            }.padding(.top, 5)
            Spacer()
        }
    }
}
#Preview {
    ContentView()
        .environment(ApplicationData.shared)
}
```

This is the same application created in Chapter 4 to present a list of books, with the difference that now the list is embedded in a **`NavigationStack`** and therefore the interface includes a navigation bar at the top with the title provided by the **`navigationTitle()`** modifier.

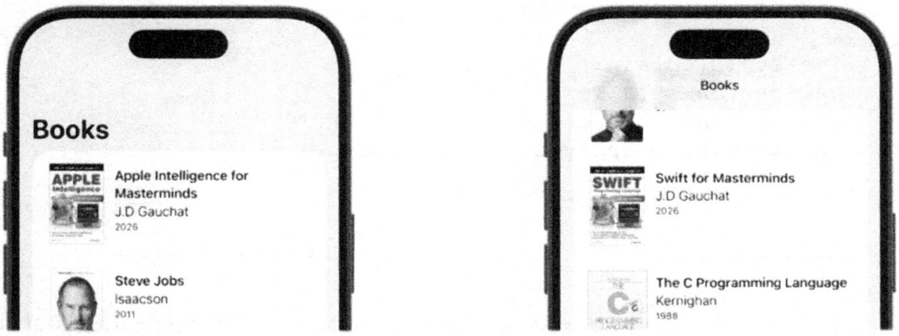

Figure 5-2: *Navigation stack*

Do It Yourself

Create a new App project. For this application to work, you need to create a Swift file called **ApplicationData.swift** with the data model introduced in Chapter 4, Listing 4-3, and inject an instance of the **`ApplicationData`** class into the environment and the previews, as we did in Chapter 4, Listing 4-4. Update the **`ContentView`** structure with the code in Listing 5-1. Download the book covers from our website. Create an Asset Catalog and add the covers to it. Run the application on an iPhone simulator. You should see an interface similar to Figure 5-2. Scroll down the list to see how the size of the navigation bar changes.

IMPORTANT

Note that most of the modifiers are applied to the content. For instance, the **navigationTitle()** modifier in our example is applied to the **List** view, not the **NavigationStack** view. This is because the rest of the views added to the stack are not going to be embedded in a **NavigationStack** view. This view is only required for the initial view to start building the stack. (This will become clear later.)

By default, the navigation bar displays a large title, but we can change this behavior using the **toolbarTitleDisplayMode()** modifier. For example, we can configure the bar to display a medium size title by specifying the **inlineLarge** mode.

Listing 5-2: Setting the title mode

```
struct ContentView: View {
   @Environment(ApplicationData.self) private var appData

   var body: some View {
      NavigationStack {
         List(appData.userData) { book in
            CellBook(book: book)
         }
         .listStyle(.plain)
         .navigationTitle(Text("Books"))
         .navigationSubtitle("My List of Books")
         .toolbarTitleDisplayMode(.inlineLarge)
      }
   }
}
```

In this example, we also include a subtitle to show how the navigation bar looks like when all the standard elements are included.

Figure 5-3: *Inline large mode*

BASIC

Toolbar

Besides the title and subtitle, the navigation bar can contain other elements, including images and buttons. SwiftUI provides the following modifiers to add items and configure the navigation bar.

toolbar(id: String, **content:** Closure)

This modifier adds elements to a toolbar or navigation bar. The **id** argument is an optional identifier used by the system to store the toolbar's last configuration, and the closure assigned to the **content** argument defines the views we want to include.

toolbarVisibility(Visibility, **for:** ToolbarPlacement)

This modifier shows or hides the bars. The first argument is an enumeration with the values **automatic**, **visible**, and **hidden**, and the **for** argument is a list of values representing the bars we want to modify, separated by comma. To specify the bars, the structure defines the type properties **automatic**, **bottomBar**, **navigationBar**, **tabBar**, and **windowToolbar**.

toolbar(removing: ToolbarDefaultItemKind)

This modifier removes items added to the toolbar by the system. The **removing** argument is a structure that determines the item to be removed. There are two properties available: **sidebarToggle** to remove the toggle button added to the sidebar by the **NavigationSplitView** view, **search** to remove the search bar, and **title** to remove the title and subtitle.

Items can be added to the left or right side of the toolbar, and to different toolbars, including the navigation bar generated by the **NavigationStack** view, a toolbar at the bottom of the screen, and a toolbar on top of the keyboard. For this reason, SwiftUI includes the **ToolbarItem** view to define the items.

ToolbarItem(id: String, **placement:** ToolbarItemPlacement, **content:** Closure)

This view defines an item for a toolbar. The **id** argument is an optional identifier used by the system to store the item's configuration. The **placement** argument is a structure that determines the place and the toolbar where the item will be located. The structure includes type properties to define standard configurations for every system. The properties available are **automatic**, **principal**, **status**, **primaryAction**, **secondaryAction**, **confirmationAction**, **cancellationAction**, **destructiveAction**, **navigation**, **topBarLeading**, **topBarTrailing**, **topBarPinnedTrailing**, **bottomBar**, **bottomOrnament**, **keyboard**, **largeSubtitle**, **largeTitle**, **title**, and **subtitle**. The closure assigned to the **content** argument defines the view we want to include in the toolbar.

As we already mentioned, the **toolbar()** modifier can add items to any toolbar in our interface. For instance, we can use it to add a button to the navigation bar of our example.

Listing 5-3: Adding a button to the navigation bar

```
struct ContentView: View {
   @Environment(ApplicationData.self) private var appData

   var body: some View {
      NavigationStack {
         List(appData.userData) { book in
            CellBook(book: book)
         }
         .navigationTitle(Text("Books"))
         .toolbar {
            ToolbarItem(placement: .topBarTrailing) {
               Button("Delete", systemImage: "trash", action: {
                  print("Delete Element")
               })
               .tint(.red)
            }
         }
      }
   }
}
```

The **toolbar()** modifier is applied to the views inside the **NavigationStack** view, and the toolbar items are then defined within its closure. In this case, we include a single **ToolbarItem** view with the **topBarTrailing** placement to position the item on the right side of the navigation bar. The item is defined using a **Button** view with an SF Symbol. By default, the system applies a **glass** style to buttons in a toolbar, but we use the **tint()** modifier to apply a red color. The result is shown below.

Figure 5-4: *Navigation bar button*

When placing two or more buttons in the same location, the system automatically groups them to indicate they are related. To separate these buttons, the framework provides the following view.

ToolbarSpacer(SpacerSizing, **placement:** ToolbarItemPlacement)

This view creates a standard space between toolbar items. The first argument determines the type of space to generate. It is a structure with the properties fixed and flexible. And the **placement** argument is a the same structure used by toolbar items to determine the place and the toolbar where the space will be located.

In the following example, we include two buttons on the right side of the navigation bar, but because we place a **ToolbarSpacerview** in between, the buttons are separated.

Listing 5-4: Adding multiple buttons to a toolbar

```
.toolbar {
   ToolbarItem(placement: .topBarTrailing) {
      Button("Save", systemImage: "folder", action: {
         print("Save")
      })
   }
   ToolbarSpacer(.fixed, placement: .topBarTrailing)
   ToolbarItem(placement: .topBarTrailing) {
      Button("Send", systemImage: "envelope", action: {
         print("Send Message")
      })
   }
}
```

As before, the buttons use the **glass** effect by default. This means that when they are placed next to each other, the system shows them as one single unit. Figure 5-5, below, shows how the buttons look with and without a spacer in between.

Figure 5-5 *Multiple buttons with and without a spacer*

When we include multiple buttons in the same location, the system still treats them as independent items. If we want the system to apply the appropriate visual effects and animations to related buttons, we must group them using the following view.

```
ToolbarItemGroup(placement: ToolbarItemPlacement, content: Closure)
```

This view defines multiple items for a toolbar. The **placement** argument is a the same structure used by toolbar items to determine the place and the toolbar where the items will be located, and the **content** argument is a closure with the views we want to include.

The **ToolbarItemGroup** view acts as a container for toolbar items, so all we need to do is define this view and add the items one after another, as shown below.

Listing 5-5: Grouping multiple related buttons

```
.toolbar {
   ToolbarItemGroup(placement: .topBarTrailing) {
      Button("Save", systemImage: "folder", action: {
         print("Save")
      })
      Button("Send", systemImage: "envelope", action: {
         print("Send Message")
      })
   }
}
```

Do It Yourself

Update the **ContentView** structure with the code in Listing 5-4. Run the application on an iPhone simulator. You should see two independent buttons on the toolbar, as shown in Figure 5-5, left. Remove the **ToolbarSpacer** view. The buttons should appear as a single unit, as shown in Figure 5-5, right. Update the **toolbar()** modifier with the code in Listing 5-5. The buttons should look the same as before, but now the system knows they are related and can apply the appropriate visual effects and animations, as we will see later.

As we have already mentioned, in addition to the navigation bar, the buttons may be added to a toolbar at the bottom of the screen or on top of the keyboard. These toolbars are automatically incorporated into the interface when a button is assigned to them. For instance, to show a toolbar at the bottom of the screen of our application, all we need to do is define a **ToolbarItem** view with the **bottomBar** placement value, as shown below.

Listing 5-6: Adding buttons to the bottom toolbar

```
struct ContentView: View {
   @Environment(ApplicationData.self) private var appData
   var body: some View {
      NavigationStack {
         List(appData.userData) { book in
            CellBook(book: book)
         }
         .navigationTitle(Text("Books"))
         .toolbar(.hidden, for: .navigationBar)
         .toolbar {
            ToolbarSpacer(.flexible, placement: .bottomBar)
            ToolbarItem(placement: .bottomBar) {
               Button("Show") {
                  print("Show Values")
               }
            }
         }
```

```
      }
   }
}
```

Buttons added to the bottom toolbar are displayed at the center. That is why, in our example, we include a flexible **ToolbarSpacer** view to move the button to the right. Note that, in this case, we also implement a second **toolbar()** modifier to hide the navigation bar. The result is shown below.

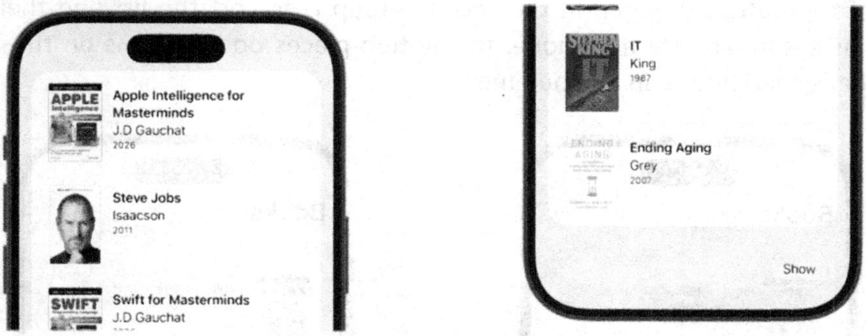

Figure 5-6: *Bottom toolbar*

Although we can position the buttons on the left or right side of the navigation bar with placement values like **topBarLeading** and **topBarTrailing**, the **ToolbarItemPlacement** structure also allows us to specify the intent of the buttons and let the system decide where and how to present them depending on the space available and the device. For instance, the structure returned by the **primaryAction** property usually places the buttons on the right, and the one returned by the **secondaryAction** property tells the system that the buttons are not essential for the application and therefore are placed inside a popup menu, as shown in the following example.

Listing 5-7: Defining the buttons intent

```
struct ContentView: View {
   @Environment(ApplicationData.self) private var appData

   var body: some View {
      NavigationStack {
         List(appData.userData) { book in
            CellBook(book: book)
         }
         .navigationTitle(Text("Books"))
         .toolbarTitleDisplayMode(.inlineLarge)
         .toolbar {
            ToolbarItemGroup(placement: .primaryAction) {
               Button("Add Book", systemImage: "plus.app", action: {
                  print("Adding Book...")
               })
            }
            ToolbarItemGroup(placement: .secondaryAction) {
               Button("Save", systemImage: "folder", action: {
                  print("Saving...")
               })
            }
```

```
            }
        }
    }
}
```

In the code in Listing 5-7, The **`toolbar()`** modifier includes two **`ToolbarItemGroup`** items with one button each. The purpose of the button in the first group is to add books to the list, which is a primary function and therefore we declare it as a primary action, but the purpose of the button included in the second group is to sort the list and therefore we declare it as secondary. On an iPhone, the system places both buttons on the right, but includes the second button in a popup menu.

Figure 5-7: *Primary and secondary buttons*

The location of primary and secondary buttons is automatically determined by the system. On iPhones and iPads, the buttons are grouped together and placed on the right, but on Macs, the title appears in the leading area, with the primary buttons on the right and the secondary buttons in the center, as shown below.

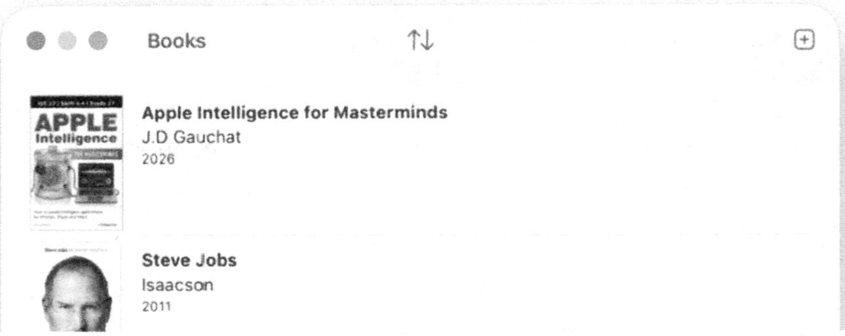

Figure 5-8: *Secondary buttons on a Mac*

The secondary button opens a pop-up menu with the available options. To manually add these menus to the toolbar, the framework provides the following view.

`Menu(String, content: Closure)`—This initializer creates a menu with the title specified by the first argument. The closure assigned to the **content** argument provides the **`Button`** views that represent the options. The view also includes the **`Menu(content: Closure, label: Closure)`** initializer to declare the title with a view.

Menu options are created using **`Button`** views. These buttons can include just a label or a label with an SF Symbol. When an SF Symbol is included, the icon appears on the left, as shown in the following example.

Listing 5-8: Creating a popup menu

```
struct ContentView: View {
   @Environment(ApplicationData.self) private var appData

   var body: some View {
      NavigationStack {
         List(appData.userData) { book in
            CellBook(book: book)
         }
         .navigationTitle(Text("Books"))
         .toolbar {
            Menu(content: {
               Button("Option 1", systemImage: "pencil.circle") {
                  print("Option 1")
               }
               Button("Option 2", systemImage: "trash") {
                  print("Option 2")
               }
               Button("Option 3", systemImage: "folder") {
                  print("Option 3")
               }
            }, label: {
               Image(systemName: "filemenu.and.selection")
            })
         }
      }
   }
}
```

The **`Menu`** view in our example includes three buttons that print messages to the console, but they can perform any task we want. The button used to open the menu is represented by an SF Symbol, and each option also includes an SF Symbol to help the user identify its function. The result is shown below.

Figure 5-9: *Custom popup menu*

In addition to defining individual options, we can group related options using **`Section`** views or declare **`Menu`** views instead of **`Button`** views to create submenus, as shown below.

Listing 5-9: Creating submenus

```
Menu(content: {
   Button("Option 1", systemImage: "pencil.circle") {
      print("Option 1")
   }
   Menu("Select") {
      Button("Option A") { print("Option A") }
      Button("Option B") { print("Option B") }
   }
   Button("Option 3", systemImage: "folder") {
      print("Option 3")
   }
}, label: {
   Image(systemName: "filemenu.and.selection")
})
```

Now the second option is called Select, and if we tap on it, a submenu opens with the options A and B, as shown below.

Figure 5-10: *Submenu*

The system automatically determines where to place the items in the toolbar. As explained earlier, if an item is declared as secondary, the system may decide to include an additional item that opens a menu to show the secondary actions (see Figure 5-7). This behavior is also repeated when there is not enough space in the toolbar to show all the items. The system displays the items that fit inside the toolbar and creates an additional item that opens a menu to select the rest, as shown below.

Figure 5-11: *Additional button to select more options*

The example in Figure 5-11 displays a total of seven items, but because they don't all fit inside the toolbar, two are shown in a popup menu. If we want to make sure that an item is always visible in the toolbar, we can apply the following modifier.

visibilityPriority(ToolbarItemVisibilityPriority)—This modifier determines the visibility of a toolbar item. The argument is a structure with the properties **automatic**, **low** and **high**.

To always show the item or group of items in the toolbar, we must apply this modifier with the value **high**, as shown below.

Listing 5-10: Changing the visibility priority of a toolbar item

```
.toolbar {
   ToolbarItemGroup {
      Button("Archive", systemImage: "archivebox", action: {
         print("Archive")
      })
      Button("Send", systemImage: "envelope", action: {
         print("Message")
      })
      Button("Save", systemImage: "externaldrive", action: {
         print("Store")
      })
      Button("Input", systemImage: "tray", action: {
         print("Input")
      })
      Button("Output", systemImage: "paperplane", action: {
         print("Output")
      })
      Button("Open", systemImage: "folder", action: {
         print("Open")
      })
   }
   ToolbarItem {
      Button("Shop", systemImage: "cart", action: {
         print("Shop")
      })
   }
   .visibilityPriority(.high)
}
```

This example includes the list of seven items used to create the toolbar in Figure 5-11, but we include the Shop button in a separate item and apply the **visibility()** modifier to it. Now that item is always visible in the toolbar, as shown below.

Figure 5-12: *Toolbar item with high visibility priority*

Priority items are always visible, but their location on the bar is determined by their position in the code. If we want a priority item to appear on the side of the toolbar, we can use the placement value **topBarPinnedTrailing**, as shown below.

Listing 5-11: Displaying a toolbar item on the trailing side

```
ToolbarItem(placement: .topBarPinnedTrailing) {
   Button("Shop", systemImage: "cart", action: {
      print("Shop")
   })
}
.visibilityPriority(.high)
```

Now the Shop button is placed on the right side of the toolbar, regardless of its location in the code.

Figure 5-13: *Toolbar item always on the trailing side*

If, on the other hand, what we want is to always hide the item in a popup menu, we can declare it with the following view.

ToolbarOverflowMenu(content: Closure)

This structure creates an item that displays a menu with secondary options. The **content** argument is the closure that provides the items to display by the menu.

The following example creates a toolbar with three items. The first two items are within a group, but the third item is included in a **ToolbarOverflowMenu** view, so it is only accessible from a popup menu.

Listing 5-12: Hiding a toolbar item

```
.toolbar {
   ToolbarItemGroup {
      Button("Archive", systemImage: "archivebox", action: {
         print("Archive")
      })
      Button("Send", systemImage: "envelope", action: {
         print("Message")
      })
   }
   ToolbarOverflowMenu {
      Button("Shop", systemImage: "cart", action: {
```

```
            print("Shop")
        })
    }
}
```

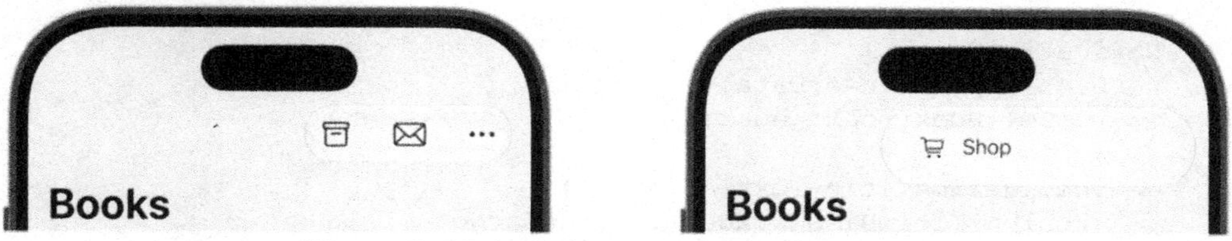

Figure 5-14: Item in custom overflow menu

So far, we have used the standard styles for the toolbar and the buttons, but the framework includes modifiers that allow us to customize their appearance. The following are the modifiers available for the bar.

toolbarBackgroundVisibility(Visibility, **for:** ToolbarPlacement**)**

This modifier determines the visibility of the toolbar's background. The first argument is an enumeration with the values **automatic**, **visible** and **hidden**, and the **for** argument is a structure that determines the toolbar that is going to be affected. The properties available are **automatic**, **bottomBar**, **navigationBar**, **tabBar**, and **windowToolbar**.

toolbarBackground(Color, **for:** ToolbarPlacement**)**

This modifier specifies the background color of the bar. The first argument is the color for the background, and the for argument is a structure that determines the toolbar that is going to be affected. The properties available are **automatic**, **bottomBar**, **navigationBar**, **tabBar**, and **windowToolbar**.

scrollEdgeEffectStyle(ScrollEdgeEffectStyle, **for:** Edge**)**

This modifier specifies the effect applied to the content when it is scrolled behind a toolbar. The first argument is a structure that defines the style. The properties available are **automatic**, **hard**, and **soft**. And the **for** argument determines which edges of the scroll view are affected.

toolbarMinimizationBehavior(ToolbarMinimizationBehavior, **for:** ToolbarPlacement**)**

This modifier defines the behavior of the toolbar when the content is scrolled. The first argument is a structure that determines if the toolbar is going to scroll along with the content and in which direction. The properties available are **automatic**, **never**, **onScrollDown** and **onScrollUp**. The **for** argument is a structure that determines the toolbar that is going to be affected. The properties available are **automatic**, **bottomBar**, **navigationBar**, **tabBar**, and **windowToolbar**.

By default, the toolbar is displayed with a translucent effect and no background. If we want to add a background, we must apply the **toolbarBackgroundVisibility()** modifier to make the background visible and then provide our own background using the **toolbarBackground()** modifier, as shown below.

Listing 5-13: Customizing the navigation bar

```
struct ContentView: View {
   @Environment(ApplicationData.self) private var appData

   var body: some View {
      NavigationStack {
         List(appData.userData) { book in
            CellBook(book: book)
         }
         .navigationTitle(Text("Books"))
         .toolbarTitleDisplayMode(.inlineLarge)
         .toolbarBackgroundVisibility(.visible, for: .navigationBar)
         .toolbarBackground(.cyan, for: .navigationBar)
         .scrollEdgeEffectStyle(.hard, for: .top)
         .toolbarMinimizationBehavior(.onScrollDown, for: .navigationBar)
         .toolbar {
            ToolbarItem(placement: .topBarTrailing) {
               Button("Email", systemImage: "envelope", action: {
                  print("Read Emails")
               })
            }
         }
      }
   }
}
```

In this example, we change the background to a cyan color and apply modifiers like **scrollEdgeEffectStyle()** and **toolbarMinimizationBehavior()** to show how they work. The navigation bar now looks different and is automatically minimized when the user scrolls the list.

Figure 5-15: *Custom navigation bar*

We can also customize the buttons. For this purpose, the framework includes the following modifiers.

sharedBackgroundVisibility(Visibility)

This modifier controls the visibility of the glass effect on toolbar items. The argument is an enumeration with the values **automatic**, **visible** and **hidden**.

badge(Value)

This modifier creates a badge for a button with the value provided by the argument. The argument can be an integer, a string, or a **Text** view.

By default, buttons in toolbars are rendered with a glass effect, but we can hide this effect using the **sharedBackgroundVisibility()** modifier and then style the item as needed, as shown below.

Listing 5-14: Customizing the items in a navigation bar

```
struct ContentView: View {
   @Environment(ApplicationData.self) private var appData

   var body: some View {
      NavigationStack {
         List(appData.userData) { book in
            CellBook(book: book)
         }
         .navigationTitle(Text("Books"))
         .toolbar {
            ToolbarItem(placement: .topBarTrailing) {
               Button("Email", systemImage: "envelope", action: {
                  print("Read Emails")
               })
               .buttonStyle(.plain)
               .foregroundStyle(.black)
               .padding(5)
               .background(.yellow)
               .badge(5)
            }
            .sharedBackgroundVisibility(.hidden)
         }
      }
   }
}
```

In this example, we hide the glass effect and then customize the button with some padding and foreground and background colors. Note that we also apply the **badge()** modifier to add a badge to the button. The result is shown below.

Figure 5-16: *Custom toolbar items*

Do It Yourself

Update the **ContentView** structure with the code in Listing 5-14. Try different styles to see how they are applied. In this example, the button is squared. We will learn how to define the shape of the button with a **`clipShape()`** modifier and how to create custom graphics in Chapter 8.

If we need absolute control over the navigation bar, we can remove it using the **`toolbarVisibility()`** modifier and create our own. In the following example, we show how to build a custom navigation bar with a title and a button.

Listing 5-15: Creating our own navigation bar

```
struct ContentView: View {
   @Environment(ApplicationData.self) private var appData

   var body: some View {
      NavigationStack {
         VStack(spacing: 0) {
            HStack {
               Text("Books")
                  .font(.largeTitle.bold())
               Spacer()
               Button(action: {
                  print("Read Emails")
               }, label: {
                  Image(systemName: "envelope")
               }).buttonStyle(.glass)
            }.padding()
            .background(.cyan)

            List(appData.userData) { book in
               CellBook(book: book)
            }
         }
         .toolbarVisibility(.hidden, for: .navigationBar)
      }
   }
}
```

When we create our own navigation bar, we lose the features provided by standard system navigation bars, such as built-in animations and styling, but we gain full control over every aspect of the interface. In this example, we embed the **`List`** view in a **`VStack`** view and place an **`HStack`** view at the top to display a title and a button. From there, we can add or remove any elements we want and style them to meet our needs. The result is shown below.

Figure 5-17: *Custom navigation bar*

Search

Navigation views, such as **`NavigationStack`**, can include a search bar that allows users to search for values in the model. The following modifier must be applied to the view to enable this feature.

> **searchable(text:** Binding, **tokens:** Binding, **placement:** SearchFieldPlacement, **prompt:** String, **token:** Closure)
>
> This modifier adds and configures a search bar. The **text** argument stores the value inserted by the user. The **tokens** argument keeps track of the search tokens shown to the user. The **placement** argument specifies the place where the bar will be located. For this purpose, the structure includes the type properties **`automatic`**, **`navigationBarDrawer`**, **`sidebar`**, and **`toolbar`**, and the method **`navigationBarDrawer(displayMode: NavigationBarDrawerDisplayMode)`** that can take the type properties **`always`** and **`automatic`** to always display or automatically hide the bar. The **prompt** argument specifies the bar's placeholder text. And the **token** argument provides the views to display the tokens.

The **`searchable()`** modifier displays the search bar, but how the search is performed depends on the characteristics of our model. In a model that stores values in an array, as the one we have used so far, the search can be performed by filtering the values with the **`filter()`** method. The following are the changes we need to introduce to the **`ApplicationData`** class in our model to filter books.

Listing 5-16: Filtering the data in the model

```
@Observable class ApplicationData {
   @ObservationIgnored var userData: [Book] {
      didSet {
         filterValues(search: "")
      }
   }
   var filteredItems: [Book] = []
   func filterValues(search: String) {
      if search.isEmpty {
         filteredItems = userData.sorted(by: { $0.title < $1.title })
      } else {
         let list = userData.filter( { item in
            return item.title.localizedStandardContains(search)
         })
         filteredItems = list.sorted(by: { $0.title < $1.title })
      }
   }
   static let shared: ApplicationData = ApplicationData()
   private init() {
      userData = [
         Book(title: "Apple Intelligence for Masterminds", author: "J.D
            Gauchat", cover: "book1", year: 2026, selected: false),
         Book(title: "Steve Jobs", author: "Isaacson", cover: "book2",
```

```
            year: 2011, selected: false),
         Book(title: "Swift for Masterminds", author: "J.D Gauchat",
            cover: "book3", year: 2026, selected: false),
         Book(title: "The C Programming Language", author: "Kernighan",
            cover: "book4", year: 1988, selected: false),
         Book(title: "Being Digital", author: "Negroponte", cover:
            "book5", year: 1996, selected: false),
         Book(title: "Only the Paranoid Survive", author: "Grove", cover:
            "book6", year: 1999, selected: false),
         Book(title: "Accidental Empires", author: "Cringely", cover:
            "book7", year: 1996, selected: false),
         Book(title: "Bobby Fischer Teaches Chess", author: "Fischer",
            cover: "book8", year: 1982, selected: false),
         Book(title: "New Guide to Science", author: "Asimov", cover:
            "book9", year: 1993, selected: false),
         Book(title: "Christine", author: "King", cover: "book10", year:
            1983, selected: false),
         Book(title: "IT", author: "King", cover: "book11", year: 1987,
            selected: false),
         Book(title: "Ending Aging", author: "Grey", cover: "book12",
            year: 2007, selected: false)
      ]
      filterValues(search: "")
   }
}
```

In this model, we have applied the **@ObservationIgnored** macro to the **userData** property so that changes to this property are not reported to the views. This is because this property is now used to store all the available books, but the data for the views is provided by a new property called **filteredItems**, which contains only the books that match the search performed by the user. To keep this property up to date, we define the **filterValues()** method that we call each time a new search is performed or books are added to or removed from the model.

The **filterValues()** method receives a string with the value inserted by the user in the search bar. If the value is empty, we assign all the books in the **userData** property to the **filteredItems** property to show the full list on the screen, but if there is a value to search, we filter the books in the **userData** property with the **filter()** method. This method receives a value and must return **true** or **false** to determine if it is going to be included in the result. In this case, we return **true** only when the book's title contains the value inserted by the user. The resulting array is assigned to the **filteredItems** property to make it available to the views. Note that in both cases, the arrays are sorted with the **sorted()** method, so the values are displayed in alphabetical order.

After we store the testing data in the **userData** property, we call the **filterValues()** method with an empty array to initialize the list. Now we can use the **filteredItems** property to show the books.

Listing 5-17: Displaying a search bar

```
struct ContentView: View {
   @Environment(ApplicationData.self) private var appData
   @State private var searchTerm: String = ""
```

```
    var body: some View {
        NavigationStack {
            List(appData.filteredItems) { book in
                CellBook(book: book)
            }.navigationTitle(Text("Books"))
        }
        .searchable(text: $searchTerm, prompt: Text("Insert title"))
        .onChange(of: searchTerm, initial: false) { old, value in
            let search = value.trimmingCharacters(in: .whitespaces)
            appData.filterValues(search: search)
        }
    }
}
```

This view includes a **@State** property to store the value inserted by the user, and two modifiers to manage the search. The **searchable()** modifier asks the system to display a search bar. For this example, we only need to provide two values, the binding property to store the value (**searchTerm**) and a **Text** view with the placeholder to show in the bar. This stores the value inserted by the user, but the search is performed by the **onChange()** modifier added below. This modifier executes a closure every time the value of the **searchTerm** property changes. In this closure, we trim the value to make sure there are no spaces at the beginning or the end, and then call the **filterValues()** method in the model. The method filters the values, assigns the result to the **filteredItems** property, and because we used this property to define the **List** view, only the books that match the search are shown on the screen.

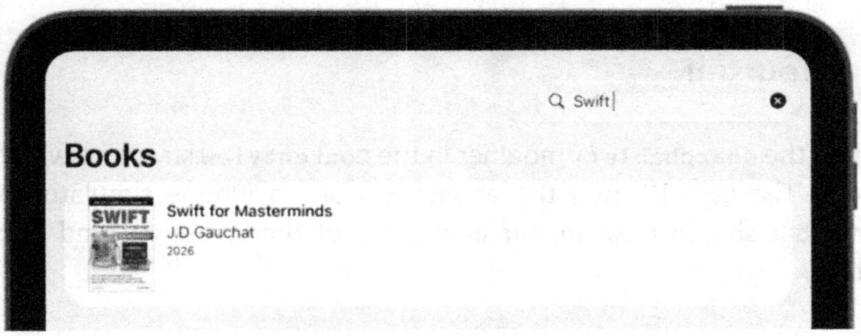

Figure 5-18: *Search bar*

Do It Yourself

Update the **ApplicationData** class with the code in Listing 5-16 and the **ContentView** structure with the code in Listing 5-17. Run the application on an iPhone or iPad simulator. Tap the search bar and enter a query. The list should display only the books whose titles match the text you type in the bar.

IMPORTANT

There are different programming patterns available to filter and update data. In this example, we use a method in the model, but we could also use a computed property to provide the data, or filter the data directly from the **onChange()** modifier. The key point to remember is that views read values from observable properties, so you must always ensure that these properties are up to date. We will learn more about filtering and permanently storing data on the device in Chapter 7.

The search bar appears at the bottom of the interface on iPhones and in the top-right corner on iPads and Macs, but we can customize this behavior by specifying its placement. There are several placement options available, and the appropriate choice depends on the platform and the current state of the bar. For example, if we want the search bar to appear at the top of the screen on iPhones, we can use the **navigationBarDrawer** placement, as shown below.

Listing 5-18: Moving the search bar to the navigation bar

```
.searchable(text: $searchTerm, placement: .navigationBarDrawer, prompt:
Text("Insert title"))
```

Do It Yourself

Update the **searchable()** modifier in the **ContentView** structure with the code in Listing 5-18. Run the application on an iPhone simulator. The search bar should now appear at the top of the screen instead of the bottom.

By default, the search bar appears expanded and ready for the user to type. However, if the toolbar that contains the navigation bar also includes other items and there is not enough space to display the search bar in its full form, the system automatically collapses it into a single button. When search is not a primary feature of our application, we can force this behavior using the following modifier.

searchToolbarBehavior(SearchToolbarBehavior)

This modifier defines the behavior of a search bar in a toolbar. The argument is a structure with the properties **automatic** and **minimize**.

The **automatic** value lets the system decide how to display the search bar, but we can specify the **minimize** value to collapse it whenever possible, as shown below.

Listing 5-19: Minimizing the search bar

```
.searchable(text: $searchTerm, prompt: Text("Insert title"))
.searchToolbarBehavior(.minimize)
```

When we apply these modifiers to our example, the system keeps the search bar open on iPhones but collapses it on iPads, as shown below.

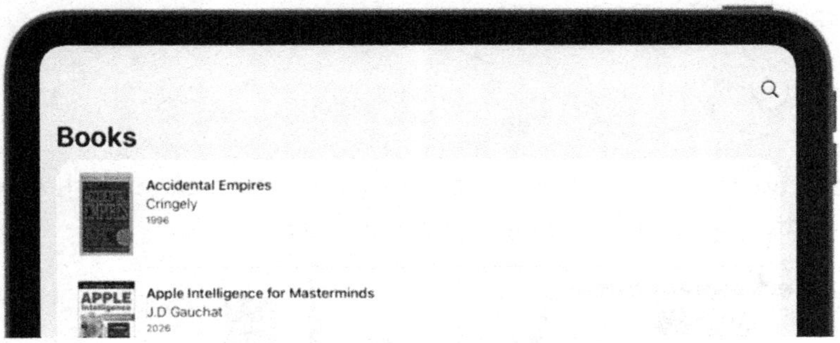

***Figure 5-19:** Collapsed search bar*

The search bar becomes active when the user taps on it, but we can also activate it from code by setting the focus state. The **View** protocol defines the following modifier to assign a **FocusState** property to the field.

searchFocused(FocusState)

This modifier associates a **FocusState** property of type **Bool** to the search field to control its focus state.

In the following example, we define a property to store the state of the field with the **@FocusState** property wrapper (see Chapter 3, Listing 3-24), assign this property to the field with the **searchFocused()** modifier, and create a button that allows the user to set the state to **true**.

Listing 5-20: Activating the search field

```
struct ContentView: View {
   @Environment(ApplicationData.self) private var appData
   @State private var searchTerm: String = ""
   @FocusState private var isFocused: Bool

   var body: some View {
      NavigationStack {
         List {
            ForEach(appData.filteredItems) { book in
               CellBook(book: book)
            }
         }
         .navigationTitle(Text("Books"))
         .toolbarTitleDisplayMode(.inlineLarge)
         .toolbar {
            ToolbarItem(placement: .topBarTrailing) {
```

```
                Button("Search") {
                    isFocused = true
                }
            }
        }
    }
    .searchable(text: $searchTerm, prompt: Text("Insert title"))
    .searchFocused($isFocused)
    .onChange(of: searchTerm, initial: false) { old, value in
        let search = value.trimmingCharacters(in: .whitespaces)
        appData.filterValues(search: search)
    }
  }
}
```

When the Search button is pressed, the focus is set on the search field, the cursor appears to allow the user to type, and the keyboard opens.

Figure 5-20: *Focus on the search field*

The **`searchable()`** modifier automatically stores every character typed by the user into the binding property. This means that the search is performed for each character typed or removed from the bar. If we want the user to decide when the search takes place, we can include the **`onSubmit()`** modifier. We have implemented this modifier before with **`TextField`** views to process a value when the Return/Done key is pressed on the keyboard, but if we declare it with the **`search`** value, we can use it to perform a search, as shown below.

Listing 5-21: Performing the search only when the Return/Done key is pressed

```
struct ContentView: View {
    @Environment(ApplicationData.self) private var appData
    @State private var searchTerm: String = ""

    var body: some View {
        NavigationStack {
            List(appData.filteredItems) { book in
                CellBook(book: book)
            }
```

```
            .navigationTitle(Text("Books"))
        }
        .searchable(text: $searchTerm, prompt: Text("Insert title"))
        .onSubmit(of: .search) { performSearch() }
        .onChange(of: searchTerm, initial: false) { old, value in
            if value.isEmpty {
                performSearch()
            }
        }
    }
    func performSearch() {
        let search = searchTerm.trimmingCharacters(in: .whitespaces)
        appData.filterValues(search: search)
    }
}
```

Since we need to perform the search from two different modifiers, we move the process to a new method called **performSearch()**. When the Return/Done key is pressed, the closure assigned to the **onSubmit()** modifier is executed and the **performSearch()** method is called to trim the text and filter the books. This method is also called from the **onChange()** modifier, but only when the search is empty. This is because we don't want to update the list every time the user types or removes a character, as we did before, but still need to do it when the user cancels the search. If the user presses the Cancel button, the system assigns an empty string to the **searchTerm** property, so we check this condition and update the list accordingly.

Do It Yourself

Update the **ContentView** structure with the code in Listing 5-21. Run the application on an iPhone simulator and search for a book. The search should not be performed until you press the Return or Done key.

Another important feature of search bars is the ability to display a list of suggested values to guide user input. For this purpose, SwiftUI provides the following modifier.

searchSuggestions(Closure)

This modifier creates a list of values that are displayed to the user as a suggestion. The argument is a closure that provides the list of **Text** views we need to present the values.

The suggestions are provided with a list of **Text** views defined in a closure. If the views are created with the same model used to create the **List** view, only values that match the search are shown. The user can close the suggestion list by pressing the Return/Done key or by selecting one of the values. To allow selection, the framework includes the following modifier.

searchCompletion(String)

This modifier associates a search value with a view. The argument is the value we want the search bar to contain when the view is selected.

The **Text** views for the suggestions may be declared manually to create a static list, or with a **ForEach** loop to create a dynamic list. In our case, we want to show suggestions according to the value inserted by the user, so we create a dynamic list with a **ForEach** loop.

Listing 5-22: Suggesting terms to the user

```
struct ContentView: View {
   @Environment(ApplicationData.self) private var appData
   @State private var searchTerm: String = ""

   var body: some View {
      NavigationStack {
         List(appData.filteredItems) { book in
            CellBook(book: book)
         }
         .navigationTitle(Text("Books"))
      }
      .searchable(text: $searchTerm, prompt: Text("Insert title"))
      .searchSuggestions({
         ForEach(appData.filteredItems) { item in
            Text("\(item.title) - \(item.author)")
               .searchCompletion(item.title)
         }
      })
      .onChange(of: searchTerm, initial: false) { old, value in
         let search = value.trimmingCharacters(in: .whitespaces)
         appData.filterValues(search: search)
      }
   }
}
```

In this example, we applied the **searchable()** modifier, as before, but also included the **searchSuggestions()** modifier to display a list of suggested values. The closure assigned to this modifier creates a list of **Text** views with the values of the **filteredItems** property, so only the books that match the current search are included. To help the user identify the books, the **Text** view shows the book's title and author, but when the user selects a suggestion, only the title is assigned to the search bar by the **searchCompletion()** modifier.

Figure 5-21: *Suggestions*

On iPhones, the search bar includes two buttons, one to clear the bar and another to allow the user to cancel the search, but we can also do it programatically. The environment includes the following values to control the process.

isSearching

This is a Boolean value that determines if the user is currently performing a search or not.

dismissSearch

This property creates an action to cancel the search. It is a **DismissSearchAction** structure. The structure exposes a handler we can call to perform the action.

The **searchable()** modifier passes information down the view hierarchy through the environment, allowing the system to determine when and where to display the search bar. As a result, these environment values are only accessible to views lower in the hierarchy. To read them, we must embed the list of books in a custom view. In the following example, we name this view **SearchableView**.

Listing 5-23: Cancelling the search programmatically

```
struct ContentView: View {
   @Environment(ApplicationData.self) private var appData
   @State private var searchTerm: String = ""

   var body: some View {
      NavigationStack {
         SearchableView()
            .navigationTitle(Text("Books"))
      }
      .searchable(text: $searchTerm, prompt: Text("Insert title"))
      .onChange(of: searchTerm, initial: false) { old, value in
         let search = value.trimmingCharacters(in: .whitespaces)
         appData.filterValues(search: search)
      }
   }
}
struct SearchableView: View {
   @Environment(ApplicationData.self) private var appData
   @Environment(\.isSearching) var isSearching
   @Environment(\.dismissSearch) var dismissSearch

   var body: some View {
      List(appData.filteredItems) { book in
         CellBook(book: book)
         .background(.white)
         .onTapGesture {
            if isSearching {
               dismissSearch()
            }
         }
      }
   }
}
```

To illustrate how to work with these properties, we apply the **onTapGesture()** modifier to each cell. As mentioned earlier, this modifier executes a closure when the user taps the view, so we use it to cancel the search. Inside the closure, we first check whether a search is in progress using the **isSearching** property, and then cancel it by calling the **dismissSearch** property. Note that **dismissSearch** returns a structure that exposes a closure, which we can invoke just like any other closure or function.

Do It Yourself

Update the **ContentView.swift** file with the code in Listing 5-23. Run the application on an iPhone simulator. Tap the search bar to activate it, and then tap a cell. The search should be canceled.

Another feature we can add to a search bar are scope buttons. These are buttons that appear at the top of the list to allow the user to specify the scope of the search. To incorporate these buttons, SwiftUI includes the following modifier.

searchScopes(Binding, scopes: Closure)—This modifier defines a list of search scopes. The first argument is a binding property to store the currently selected scope, and the **scopes** argument provides the views to create the buttons.

In the following example, we show how to use this modifier to let users search by title or author.

Listing 5-24: Adding scope buttons

```
enum Scopes {
   case title, author
}
struct ContentView: View {
   @Environment(ApplicationData.self) private var appData
   @State private var searchTerm: String = ""
   @State private var searchScope: Scopes = .title

   var body: some View {
      NavigationStack {
         List(appData.filteredItems) { book in
            CellBook(book: book)
         }.navigationTitle(Text("Books"))
      }
      .searchable(text: $searchTerm, prompt: Text("Insert title"))
      .searchScopes($searchScope, scopes: {
         Text("Title").tag(Scopes.title)
         Text("Author").tag(Scopes.author)
      })
      .onChange(of: searchTerm, initial: false) { _, _ in
         performSearch()
```

```
        }
        .onChange(of: searchScope, initial: false) { _, _ in
            performSearch()
        }
    }
    func performSearch() {
        let search = searchTerm.trimmingCharacters(in: .whitespaces)
        appData.filterValues(search: search, scope: searchScope)
    }
}
```

There are many ways to identify the scopes. In this case, we use an enumeration with two values: **title** and **author**. The **@State** property is initialized with the **title** value, so the searches are first performed by title. The closure assigned to the **searchScopes()** modifier includes two **Text** views to create two scope buttons, one to select the **title** scope and another to select the **author** scope. To perform the search in the current scope, we send the value of the **searchScope** property to the **filterValues()** method in the model. The method must now check the selected scope and search the value accordingly, as shown below.

Listing 5-25: Searching by title and author

```
func filterValues(search: String, scope: Scopes = .title) {
    if search.isEmpty {
        filteredItems = userData.sorted(by: { $0.title < $1.title })
    } else {
        let list = userData.filter( { item in
            let value = scope == .title ? item.title : item.author
            return value.localizedStandardContains(search)
        })
        filteredItems = list.sorted(by: { $0.title < $1.title })
    }
}
```

Now, when the user begins typing, a bar with two buttons appears at the top of the list, allowing the user to select whether to search by title or author, as shown below.

Figure 5-22: *Search scopes*

Another feature we can incorporate to a search bar are search tokens. These are values that appear inside the bar to help the user perform complex search queries. For instance, if we want to allow the user to search books by author, we can create a token that shows the current selected author so the user knows the current constraint applied to the search and can also remove it.

As with scopes, we need a binding property to store the current tokens, but to define the tokens we need a data type that conforms to the **`Identifiable`** and **`Equatable`** protocols (Conformance to the **`Equatable`** protocol is necessary to track changes with the **`onChange()`** modifier). In the following example, we define a structure to create tokens from the authors' names.

Listing 5-26: Adding tokens

```
struct Tokens: Identifiable, Equatable {
   let id = UUID()
   let name: String
}
struct ContentView: View {
   @Environment(ApplicationData.self) private var appData
   @State private var searchTerm: String = ""
   @State private var searchTokens: [Tokens] = []

   var body: some View {
      NavigationStack {
         List(appData.filteredItems) { book in
            CellBook(book: book)
         }.navigationTitle(Text("Books"))
         .toolbar {
            let list = appData.userData.map { $0.author }
            let authors = Set(list).sorted()
            Menu(content: {
               ForEach(authors, id: \.self) { author in
                  Button(author) {
                     let token = Tokens(name: author)
                     searchTokens = [token]
                  }
               }
            }, label: {
               Image(systemName: "pencil.circle")
            })
         }
      }
      .searchable(text: $searchTerm, tokens: $searchTokens, token: {
         token in
         Text(token.name)
      })
      .onChange(of: searchTerm, initial: false) { _, _ in
         performSearch()
      }
      .onChange(of: searchTokens, initial: false) { _, _ in
         performSearch()
      }
   }
   func performSearch() {
      let search = searchTerm.trimmingCharacters(in: .whitespaces)
```

```
        appData.filterValues(search: search, author: searchTokens.first?.
           name ?? "")
    }
}
```

The **searchable()** modifier stores the tokens in an array, so we define the **@State** property as an array of **Tokens** structures. To create the tokens, we have added a **toolbar()** modifier with a **Menu** view. The menu's options are defined with the name of the authors available in the model. This creates a button in the navigation bar the user can press to select an author. Note that to get the list of authors, we map the **userData** array, extract the author's name, turn the array into a **Set** to remove duplicates, and sort them in alphabetical order.

Once an author is selected, we create an instance of the **Tokens** structure with the author's name and assign it to the **searchTokens** property. This adds a token to the search bar, which tells the user that the search will be performed on the books written by that author. As always, we need to modify the **filterValues()** method in the data model for this search to work.

Listing 5-27: Filtering books by author

```
func filterValues(search: String, author: String = "") {
   if search.isEmpty && author.isEmpty {
      filteredItems = userData.sorted(by: { $0.title < $1.title })
   } else {
      let list = userData.filter( { item in
         var valid = true
         if !author.isEmpty && author != item.author {
            valid = false
         }
         if valid && !search.isEmpty && !item.title.
            localizedStandardContains(search) {
            valid = false
         }
         return valid
      })
      filteredItems = list.sorted(by: { $0.title < $1.title })
   }
}
```

In this new method, we must check if the user has selected an author and then filter the array by author and title. The easiest way to do it is to start with a valid condition (**valid = true**) and then invalidate it if something doesn't match. We first check if the user selected an author and compare it with the author of the book. If they don't match, the condition becomes invalid. Next, we do the same for the title, but only if the condition was not already invalidated by the author. As a result, when the user selects an author, a token with the author's name appears in the search bar and the search is only performed on the books written by that author.

Figure 5-23: Using tokens

BASIC

Navigation Link

The **NavigationStack** view can manage a stack of views (screens). To allow the user to open additional views, SwiftUI includes the **NavigationLink** view. This is a control view that creates a button the user can press to replace the current view with another. The following are the view's initializers.

NavigationLink(String, **destination:** View**)**

This initializer creates a button for navigation. The first argument is the text we want to assign to the button's label, and the **destination** argument is the view we want to open when the button is pressed. If we want to define a complex label for the button, we can use the initializer **NavigationLink(destination: View, label: Closure)** instead.

NavigationLink(String, **value:** Value**)**

This initializer creates a button for dynamic navigation. The first argument is the text we want to assign to the button's label, and the **value** argument is a value that identifies the link. If we want to define a complex label for the button, we can use the initializer **NavigationLink(value: Value, label: Closure)** instead.

The **NavigationLink** view requires a view to open and a label the user can tap to perform the action. For instance, the following example adds a link to the navigation bar to open a view the user can use to change the app's settings.

Listing 5-28: Including a navigation link

```
struct ContentView: View {
   @Environment(ApplicationData.self) private var appData

   var body: some View {
      NavigationStack {
         List(appData.filteredItems) { book in
            CellBook(book: book)
         }.navigationTitle(Text("Books"))
         .toolbar {
```

```
            ToolbarItem(placement: .topBarTrailing) {
               NavigationLink(destination: SettingsView(), label: {
                  Image(systemName: "gearshape")
               })
            }
         }
      }
   }
}
```

Like the **Button** view, the **NavigationLink** view creates a button but with the purpose of replacing the current view with another one. In this case, we create the button with an SF Symbol image of a gear, and set the destination view to be a custom view that we call **SettingsView**. The following is the definition of this view.

Listing 5-29: Defining a second view

```
import SwiftUI

struct SettingsView: View {
   @State private var showPictures: Bool = true
   @State private var showYear: Bool = true

   var body: some View {
      Form {
         Toggle("Show Pictures", isOn: $showPictures)
         Toggle("Show Year", isOn: $showYear)
      }.navigationTitle("Settings")
   }
}
#Preview{
   NavigationStack {
      SettingsView()
   }
}
```

The **SettingsView** view is opened from the **ContentView** view and therefore it is part of its hierarchy, so we don't have to embed it in a **NavigationStack** view, but we still need to apply the **navigationTitle()** modifier to define its title. Other than that, the view is designed as any other. When the user taps the button in the **ContentView** view, an instance of the **SettingsView** view is created and presented on the screen transitioning from right to left.

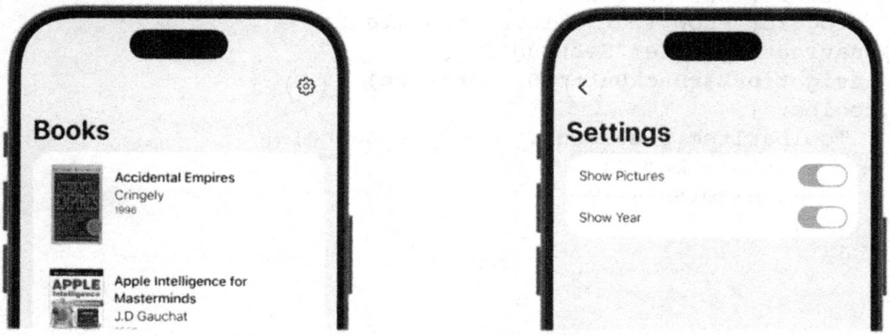

Figure 5-24: *Interface with two views*

Do It Yourself

Update the **ContentView** structure with the code in Listing 5-28. Create a new SwiftUI file called **SettingsView.swift** with the code in Listing 5-29. Run the application on an iPhone simulator and press the button on the navigation bar. You should see the **SettingsView** view appear on the screen, transitioning from right to left, as shown in Figure 5-24.

A view opened by a **NavigationLink** view includes a button in the navigation bar that allows the user to return to the previous view. This button is automatically generated by SwiftUI and is part of the standard navigation tools provided by the framework. If we need to change the style of this button, we must remove it using the **navigationBarBackButtonHidden()** modifier and create our own. For this purpose, the environment provides the following values.

dismiss

This property creates an action to dismiss the view. It is a **DismissAction** structure. The structure exposes a handler we can call to perform the action.

isPresented

This is a Boolean value that determines whether the view is being presented or not.

To create a custom back button, all we need to do is declare an **@Environment** property for the **dismiss** value and then call its handler, as shown below.

Listing 5-30: Creating a custom back button

```
struct SettingsView: View {
   @Environment(\.dismiss) var dismiss
   @State private var showPictures: Bool = true
   @State private var showYear: Bool = true

   var body: some View {
      Form {
         Toggle("Show Pictures", isOn: $showPictures)
         Toggle("Show Year", isOn: $showYear)
      }.navigationTitle("Settings")
      .navigationBarBackButtonHidden(true)
      .toolbar {
         ToolbarItem(placement: .topBarLeading) {
            Button("Back") {
               dismiss()
            }
         }
      }
   }
}
```

As always, it is recommended to use the name of the environment value when defining the property. In this example, we name it **dismiss**. To add a custom back button, we first remove the one provided by the system using the **navigationBarBackButtonHidden()** modifier, and then add a new button to the left side of the navigation bar with the **toolbar()** modifier. When the button is pressed, we execute the closure exposed by the **DismissAction** structure through the **dismiss** property, and the view is dismissed.

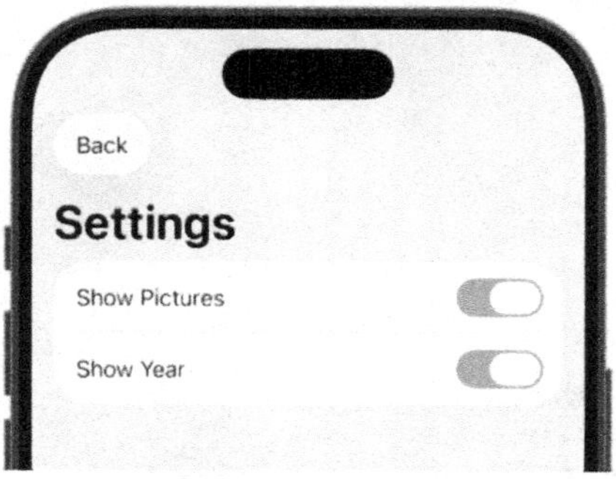

Figure 5-25: *Custom back button*

Do It Yourself

Update the **SettingsView** structure with the code in Listing 5-30. Run the application on an iPhone simulator. Press the button to open the Settings view and then press the Back button to close it. The back button should remove the view as before.

In the previous example, we used an **Image** view with an SF Symbol as the label for the **NavigationLink** view, but a navigation link can be created using any view, including custom ones. In the following example, we embed the **CellBook** view inside a **NavigationLink** view so that, when the user taps a cell, we can open another view with additional information about the book.

Listing 5-31: Selecting rows with a navigation link

```
struct ContentView: View {
   @Environment(ApplicationData.self) private var appData

   var body: some View {
      NavigationStack {
         List(appData.userData) { book in
            NavigationLink(destination: {
               DetailView(book: book)
            }, label: {
               CellBook(book: book)
            })
         }.navigationTitle(Text("Books"))
      }
   }
}
```

The view that opens when a row is selected is typically used to display information about the selected item. In our example, we call this view **DetailView** and use it to show information about the book selected by the user. To display this information, we pass a copy of the **Book** structure to the view. The view receives this instance and displays its values on the screen, as shown below.

Listing 5-32: Defining a Detail view

```
import SwiftUI

struct DetailView: View {
   let book: Book

   var body: some View {
      VStack {
         Text(book.title)
            .font(.title)
         Text(book.author)
         Image(book.cover)
            .resizable()
            .scaledToFit()
      }.padding()
      .navigationTitle("Book")
      .toolbarTitleDisplayMode(.inline)
   }
}
#Preview {
   NavigationStack {
      DetailView(book: ApplicationData.shared.userData[0])
   }
}
```

When the user selects a row in the **ContentView** view, an instance of the **DetailView** view is created and presented on the screen transitioning from right to left, and the values of the book are shown to the user.

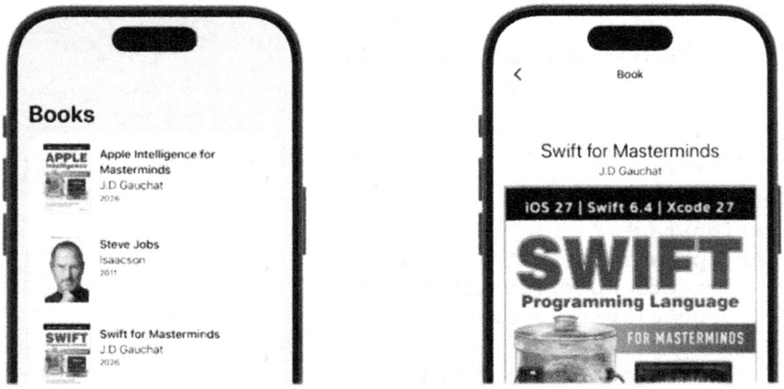

Figure 5-26: Detail view

Do It Yourself

Update the **ContentView** structure with the code in Listing 5-31. Create a new SwiftUI file called **DetailView.swift** for the code in Listing 5-32. Run the application on an iPhone simulator. Tap on a book. You should see the information of the book on the screen, as shown in Figure 5-26.

BASIC

Navigation Path

Although the navigation approach we have used so far is perfectly valid, it gives us limited control over how users move through the interface. Navigating through the views one by one, as we did in previous examples, is tedious and time-consuming. To have more control over the navigation path, we can use the tools provided by the **NavigationStack** view. This view can keep track of all the views opened by the user and store references to those views in a binding property. By changing the values stored in this property, we can navigate through the views programmatically.

There are a few steps we need to follow to control the navigation path. First, we must create the navigation links with the **NavigationLink(String, value: Value)** initializer. This initializer identifies the link with the value provided by the **value** argument. Once the link is identified, we must add the following modifier to tell the system what to open.

navigationDestination(for: Type, **destination:** Closure**)**

This modifier specifies the destination view for a **NavigationLink** view. The **for** argument is the data type of the values used by the **NavigationLink** view to identify the link, and the **destination** argument creates an instance of the destination view to present it on the screen.

The **NavigationLink** view and the **navigationDestination()** modifier are connected by the data type of the value used by the view to identify the link. When the user taps on a **NavigationLink** view identified with a value, the **navigationDestination()** modifier associated to that data type creates a destination view and presents it on the screen. Once the destination view is presented on the screen, the **NavigationStack** view stores it in a navigation stack and the value assigned to the **NavigationLink** is added to a binding property that we can modify later to control the navigation path. The values in this property are stored in a collection, but because they can be of different data types, SwiftUI provides the following structure to manage them.

NavigationPath(Path**)**

This initializer creates a structure used to store values associated with views in a navigation path. The argument determines the current path. If the argument is omitted, the structure starts with an empty path, but we can also provide a collection of values to define a predefined path or a **CodableRepresentation** structure to restore a previous path. (We will learn more about **CodableRepresentation** in Chapter 9.)

The **NavigationPath** structure includes the following properties and methods to manage the values.

isEmpty

This property returns a Boolean value that indicates if the path is empty.

count

This property returns the number of values (views) in the path.

append(Value**)**

This method adds a value (a view) to the path.

removeLast(Int**)**

This method removes the last value from the path. The argument is the number of values (views) to remove. By default, only the last value is removed.

When we add a value to the **NavigationPath** structure, the view associated to that value is shown on the screen, and when we remove a value, the view is removed from the navigation path (and the screen if it is currently active). For this process to work, we need to define a binding property with a **NavigationPath** structure, initialize the **NavigationStack** view with a reference to this property, create the **NavigationLink** views with a value, and implement the **navigationDestination()** modifier to tell the system which view to open when a link is followed by the user. The next example shows how to implement these changes to control navigation.

Listing 5-33: Using custom navigation

```
struct ContentView: View {
   @Environment(ApplicationData.self) private var appData
   @State private var viewPath = NavigationPath()

   var body: some View {
      NavigationStack(path: $viewPath) {
         List(appData.userData) { book in
            NavigationLink(value: book, label: {
               CellBook(book: book)
            })
         }
         .navigationTitle(Text("Books"))
         .toolbarTitleDisplayMode(.inline)
         .toolbar {
            ToolbarItem(placement: .topBarTrailing) {
               NavigationLink(value: "Settings View", label: {
                  Image(systemName: "gear")
               })
            }
         }
         .navigationDestination(for: Book.self, destination: { book in
            DetailView(viewPath: $viewPath, book: book)
         })
         .navigationDestination(for: String.self, destination: { viewID in
```

```
            if viewID == "Settings View" {
               SettingsView(viewPath: $viewPath)
            }
         })
      }
   }
}
```

As we already mentioned, the **NavigationLink** view and the **navigationDestination()** modifier are connected by the data type of the value that identifies the link. In this example, we define two **NavigationLink** views, one to open a detail view with information about the selected book and another to open a settings view. The navigation link for the detail view is identified with the **Book** structure that represents the book selected by the user, and the one for the settings view is identified with a string. To tell the system which view to open when a link is activated by the user, we implement two **navigationDestination()** modifiers, one associated with the **Book** data type to open the **DetailView** view and another associated with the **String** data type to open the **SettingsView** view. When a link is activated, the system finds the right destination based on the data type and opens the corresponding view.

The **NavigationPath** structure can be stored in a **@State** property or in the data model. In this case, we store it in a **@State** property within the view, so we must pass a reference of this property to the rest of the views. The views must receive this reference and use it to remove themselves from the navigation path. The following example shows how this process works in the **DetailView** view.

Listing 5-34: Adding and removing views from the path

```
struct DetailView: View {
   @Binding var viewPath: NavigationPath
   var book: Book

   var body: some View {
      VStack {
         Text(book.title)
            .font(.title)
         Text(book.author)
         Image(book.cover)
            .resizable()
            .scaledToFit()
            .frame(width: 100)
         Spacer()
      }.padding()
      .navigationTitle(Text("Book"))
      .navigationBarBackButtonHidden(true)
      .toolbar {
         ToolbarItem(placement: .topBarLeading) {
            Button("Back") {
               viewPath.removeLast()
            }
         }
      }
   }
}
```

```
#Preview {
   @Previewable @State var navigation = NavigationPath()

   NavigationStack {
      DetailView(viewPath: $navigation, book: ApplicationData.shared.
userData[0])
   }
}
```

In this example, we add a button that allows the user to remove the view. The button calls the **removeLast()** method, which removes the last value from the **NavigationPath** structure. In this case, the value is the **Book** structure representing the **DetailView** view, so the **DetailView** view is removed from the screen.

We do something similar in the **SettingsView** view. In this case, the view is opened when a button in the navigation bar is pressed, but the procedure for removing the view is the same.

Listing 5-35: Removing a view from the path

```
struct SettingsView: View {
   @Binding var viewPath: NavigationPath
   var body: some View {
      VStack {
         Text("My Settings")
         Spacer()
      }.padding()
      .navigationBarBackButtonHidden(true)
      .toolbar {
         ToolbarItem(placement: .topBarLeading) {
            Button("Back") {
               viewPath.removeLast()
            }
         }
      }
   }
}
#Preview {
   @Previewable @State var navigation = NavigationPath()
   NavigationStack {
      SettingsView(viewPath: $navigation)
   }
}
```

Do It Yourself

Update the **ContentView** structure with the code in Listing 5-33, the **DetailView** structure with the code in Listing 5-34, and the **SettingsView** structure with the code in Listing 5-35. Run the application. Select a book to open the detail view or tap on the button in the navigation bar to open the Settings view. You should see a Back button at the top of the screen to go back to the initial view.

Removing a value from the navigation path with the **removeLast()** method is similar to what we can do with the **dismiss** value (see Listing 5-30), but a navigation path can span multiple views. In these cases, we need to keep two things in mind. First, if we store the navigation path in a **@State** property, as we did in the **ContentView** view of our example, we must pass a reference of this property to each view we want to control. This can be tedious and error-prone, so it is better to store the path in the model instead. Second, the **NavigationStack** view gives precedence to the **navigationDestination()** modifier that is higher in the view hierarchy. For example, if we define two **navigationDestination()** modifiers to process **String** values, the **NavigationStack** view will process only the one that is higher in the view hierarchy, which means that all the navigation links identified with a string will be processed from the same place.

The following example shows an alternative way to control a long navigation path. For this purpose, we create two properties in the model: one to store the navigation path, and another to store a reference to the book selected by the user.

Listing 5-36: Controlling the navigation path from the model

```
@Observable class ApplicationData {
   var userData: [Book] = []
   var viewPath = NavigationPath()
   var selectedBook: Book? = nil

   static let shared: ApplicationData = ApplicationData()
   private init() {
      userData = [
         Book(title: "Apple Intelligence for Masterminds", author: "J.D
            Gauchat", cover: "book1", year: 2026, selected: false),
         Book(title: "Steve Jobs", author: "Isaacson", cover: "book2",
            year: 2011, selected: false),
         Book(title: "Swift for Masterminds", author: "J.D Gauchat",
            cover: "book3", year: 2026, selected: false),
         Book(title: "The C Programming Language", author: "Kernighan",
            cover: "book4", year: 1988, selected: false),
         Book(title: "Being Digital", author: "Negroponte", cover:
            "book5", year: 1996, selected: false),
         Book(title: "Only the Paranoid Survive", author: "Grove", cover:
            "book6", year: 1999, selected: false),
         Book(title: "Accidental Empires", author: "Cringely", cover:
            "book7", year: 1996, selected: false),
         Book(title: "Bobby Fischer Teaches Chess", author: "Fischer",
            cover: "book8", year: 1982, selected: false),
         Book(title: "New Guide to Science", author: "Asimov", cover:
            "book9", year: 1993, selected: false),
         Book(title: "Christine", author: "King", cover: "book10", year:
            1983, selected: false),
         Book(title: "IT", author: "King", cover: "book11", year: 1987,
            selected: false),
         Book(title: "Ending Aging", author: "Grey", cover: "book12",
            year: 2007, selected: false)
      ]
   }
}
```

Now we can store the path in the observable object and manage the whole navigation from the **ContentView** view, as shown below.

Listing 5-37: Controlling the navigation path from the initial view

```
struct ContentView: View {
   @Environment(ApplicationData.self) private var appData

   var body: some View {
      @Bindable var appData = appData

      NavigationStack(path: $appData.viewPath) {
         List(appData.userData) { book in
            NavigationLink(value: book, label: {
               CellBook(book: book)
            })
         }
         .navigationTitle(Text("Books"))
         .toolbarTitleDisplayMode(.inlineLarge)
         .toolbar {
            ToolbarItem(placement: .topBarTrailing) {
               NavigationLink(value: "Settings View", label: {
                  Image(systemName: "gear")
               })
            }
         }
         .navigationDestination(for: Book.self, destination: { book in
            DetailView(book: book)
         })
         .navigationDestination(for: String.self, destination: { viewID in
            if viewID == "Settings View" {
               SettingsView()
            } else if viewID == "Picture View" {
               PictureView()
            }
         })
      }
   }
}
```

The **navigationDestination()** modifier declared to process navigation links identified with a **String** value now opens two views: the **SettingsView** view, as before, and the **PictureView** view that opens when the user taps the book's cover. Below are the changes we need to introduce to the **DetailView** view to create this link.

Listing 5-38: Adding views to the navigation path programmatically

```
struct DetailView: View {
   @Environment(ApplicationData.self) private var appData
   var book: Book

   var body: some View {
      VStack {
         Text(book.title)
            .font(.title)
```

```
            Text(book.author)
            Button(action: {
               appData.selectedBook = book
               appData.viewPath.append("Picture View")
            }, label: {
               Image(book.cover)
                  .resizable()
                  .scaledToFit()
                  .frame(width: 100)
            })
            Spacer()
         }.padding()
         .navigationBarBackButtonHidden(true)
         .toolbar {
            ToolbarItem(placement: .topBarLeading) {
               Button("Back") {
                  appData.viewPath.removeLast()
               }
            }
         }
      }
   }
#Preview {
   NavigationStack {
      DetailView(book: ApplicationData.shared.userData[0])
         .environment(ApplicationData.shared)
   }
}
```

To create the navigation link, we use a **Button** view instead of the **NavigationLink** view implemented before. This is to be able to assign the book selected by the user to the **selectedBook** property in the model, so that the **PictureView** view knows which cover to display. To open the **PictureView** view, we add the string **"Picture View"** to the **NavigationPath** structure using the **append()** method. Below is our implementation of this view.

Listing 5-39: Returning to different views

```
import SwiftUI

struct PictureView: View {
   @Environment(ApplicationData.self) private var appData

   var body: some View {
      VStack {
         Image(appData.selectedBook?.cover ?? "nopicture")
            .resizable()
            .scaledToFit()
         Spacer()
      }.padding()
      .navigationBarBackButtonHidden()
      .toolbar {
         ToolbarItem(placement: .topBarLeading) {
            Button("Back") {
               appData.viewPath.removeLast()
```

```
            }
         }
         ToolbarItem(placement: .topBarTrailing) {
            Button("Back to List") {
               appData.viewPath = NavigationPath()
            }
         }
      }
   }
}
#Preview {
   NavigationStack {
      PictureView()
         .environment(ApplicationData.shared)
   }
}
```

When the user taps the book cover in the **DetailView** view, the string "Picture View" is added to the **NavigationPath** structure, the **NavigationStack** view then looks for a **navigationDestination()** modifier that responds to **String** values, and that modifier opens the **PictureView** view. At this point, the **NavigationPath** structure contains two values: the **Book** structure, which represents the **DetailView** view, and the string "Picture View", which represents the **PictureView** view. This means that we now have two views to return to: the **DetailView** view and the **ContentView** view.

To demonstrate how to navigate back to previous views, the navigation bar of the **PictureView** view defined in Listing 5-39 includes two buttons. The first button removes the last value from the **NavigationPath** structure using the **removeLast()** method. In this case, that value is the string "Picture View", so the **PictureView** view is removed from the screen. The second button returns the user to the initial view, but the process is slightly different. As mentioned earlier, the values stored in the **NavigationPath** structure represent the views opened by the user. In our example, an empty **NavigationPath** structure represents the **ContentView** view (the initial view), the **Book** structure stored first represents the **DetailView** view, and the string "Picture View" stored second represents the **PictureView** view. Therefore, to return to the initial view, we can remove these two values using the **removeLast()** method by calling **removeLast(2)**, or we can assign a new **NavigationPath** structure with an empty path to the **viewPath** property. The latter approach is recommended and is the one used in this example, as it prevents errors caused by removing too many values and going out of range.

We now have a button in the **DetailView** view to open the **PictureView** view with the book cover, as well as buttons in that view to return to any other view in the hierarchy. The only thing left to do is apply the same changes to the **SettingsView** view, so we can also control the navigation path from there.

Listing 5-40: Working with the navigation path from the model

```
struct SettingsView: View {
   @Environment(ApplicationData.self) private var appData

   var body: some View {
      VStack {
```

```
            Text("My Settings")
            Spacer()
         }.padding()
         .navigationBarBackButtonHidden(true)
         .toolbar {
            ToolbarItem(placement: .topBarLeading) {
               Button("Back") {
                  appData.viewPath.removeLast()
               }
            }
         }
      }
   }
#Preview {
   NavigationStack {
      SettingsView()
         .environment(ApplicationData.shared)
   }
}
```

The application is now complete. The detail view displays a small image that the user can tap to expand, and the picture view includes two buttons that allow the user to navigate back. The result is shown below.

***Figure 5-27:** Custom navigation path*

Do It Yourself

Update the **ApplicationData** class with the code in Listing 5-36, the **ContentView** structure with the code in Listing 5-37, the **DetailView** structure with the code in Listing 5-38, and the **SettingsView** structure with the code in Listing 5-40. Create a new SwiftUI file called **PictureView.swift** for the code in Listing 5-39. Run the application on an iPhone simulator. Select a book and tap on the cover. You should see the **PictureView** view on the screen with an enlarged image of the cover. If you press the Back button, you should go back to the **DetailView** view, but if you press the Back to List button, the interface should transition back to the list of books.

PRO

Zoom Transition

By default, a **NavigationStack** view transitions the views from side-to-side, but we can change it to a zoom transition. This type of transition zooms a view in and out relative to another view. To configure this behavior, we must specify which view is being presented and which view serves as the starting point for the animation. SwiftUI provides the following modifiers for this purpose.

> **navigationTransition**(NavigationTransition)
>
> This modifier sets the navigation style for the view. The argument is a protocol with the property **automatic** to set the transition by default and the method **zoom(sourceID: Value, in: Namespace.ID)** to set a zoom transition.

> **matchedTransitionSource(id:** Value, **in:** Namespace.ID)
>
> This modifier determines which view is the origin for the animation. The **id** argument is a value that associates the source view with the view to be presented, and the **in** argument is the namespace used by the system to coordinate the transition.

The **navigationTransition()** modifier specifies which view is to be opened, and the **matchedTransitionSource()** modifier specifies the view from which the animation is to be performed. To connect these two views, we need to provide an identifier, usually a string, and a namespace. A namespace is a name that objects and structures use to work together. SwiftUI defines the following property wrapper to create a namespace.

> **@Namespace**
>
> This property wrapper defines a new namespace.

To open a view with a zoom transition, we need to define a property with the **@Namespace** property wrapper and then apply the modifiers to the views involved. If there are multiple views participating in the process, we need to identify each animation with different values. For example, if we want to open the **DetailView** view for each book in our project with a zoom transition, we can identify each animation with the book's **id** property, as shown below.

Listing 5-41: Opening a view with a zoom transition

```
struct ContentView: View {
   @Environment(ApplicationData.self) private var appData
   @Namespace var zoomBooks

   var body: some View {
      @Bindable var appData = appData

      NavigationStack(path: $appData.viewPath) {
```

```
            List(appData.userData) { book in
               NavigationLink(value: book, label: {
                  CellBook(book: book)
                     .matchedTransitionSource(id: book.id, in: zoomBooks)
               })
            }
            .navigationTitle(Text("Books"))
            .toolbarTitleDisplayMode(.inlineLarge)
            .toolbar {
               ToolbarItem(placement: .topBarTrailing) {
                  NavigationLink(value: "Settings View", label: {
                     Image(systemName: "gear")
                  })
               }
            }
            .navigationDestination(for: Book.self, destination: { book in
               DetailView(book: book)
                  .navigationTransition(.zoom(sourceID: book.id,
                     in: zoomBooks))
            })
            .navigationDestination(for: String.self, destination: { viewID in
               if viewID == "Settings View" {
                  SettingsView()
               } else if viewID == "Picture View" {
                  PictureView()
               }
            })
         }
      }
   }
```

Do It Yourself

Update the **ContentView** structure with the code in Listing 5-41. Run the application on an iPhone simulator and select a row. You should see the **DetailView** view zoom into the screen, with an animation that starts from the selected book.

BASIC

5.2 - Modal Views

In addition to the views opened by navigation links, we can extend the interface with modal views. Modal views are normal views but are presented on top of the rest of the views.

BASIC

Sheets

Sheets are general-purpose modal views. On iPhones, they occupy the full width of the screen, while on iPads and Mac computers they appear as a rectangular view centered on the screen. The **View** protocol defines the following modifiers to present a sheet.

sheet(isPresented: Binding, **onDismiss:** Closure?, **content:** Closure)

This modifier displays a sheet. The **isPresented** argument is a binding property of type **Bool** that determines whether the sheet has to be presented (**true**) or removed (**false**), the **onDismiss** argument is a closure that is executed when the sheet is removed, and the **content** argument is a closure that defines the view to be shown on the screen.

sheet(item: Binding, **onDismiss:** Closure?, **content:** Closure)

This modifier displays a sheet. The **item** argument is an optional binding value that determines whether the sheet has to be presented or removed (**nil**), the **onDismiss** argument is a closure that is executed when the sheet is removed, and the **content** argument is a closure that defines the view to be shown on the screen. The closure receives the value stored in the binding property.

On iPhones, these modifiers create sheets that partially cover the interface. SwiftUI also includes the following modifiers to create full-screen sheets.

fullScreenCover(isPresented: Binding, **onDismiss:** Closure, **content:** Closure)

This modifier displays a full-screen sheet. The arguments are the same used by the **sheet()** modifier.

fullScreenCover(item: Binding, **onDismiss:** Closure, **content:** Closure)

This modifier displays a full-screen sheet. The arguments are the same used by the **sheet()** modifier.

Sheets are controlled from a binding property. When the property contains a value or the value is **true**, the modifier opens the view on top of the current interface, and we can use this view for anything we want. A common practice is opening sheets to allow the user to add values to the model. For instance, we can open a sheet to allow the user to add a book to the list.

Listing 5-42: Displaying a sheet

```
struct ContentView: View {
   @Environment(ApplicationData.self) private var appData
   @State private var showSheet: Bool = false

   var body: some View {
      NavigationStack {
         List(appData.userData) { book in
            CellBook(book: book)
         }
         .navigationTitle(Text("Books"))
         .toolbarTitleDisplayMode(.inlineLarge)
         .toolbar {
            ToolbarItem(placement: .topBarTrailing) {
```

```
                Button("Add Book", systemImage: "plus", action: {
                    showSheet = true
                })
            }
        }
        .sheet(isPresented: $showSheet) {
            AddBookView()
        }
    }
}
}
```

This view defines a **@State** property to control the state of the sheet and adds a **Button** view to the navigation bar that assigns the value **true** to this property to open the sheet when pressed. The sheet is managed by the **sheet()** modifier applied to the **List** view. The modifier is connected to the **showSheet** property, so when the value of this property is **true** a custom view called **AddBookView** is presented on the screen. This is the view we are using to allow the user to add new books. The view includes **TextField** views to insert the book's title, author and year, and a button to store the values in the model.

Listing 5-43: Defining the view for the sheet

```
import SwiftUI

struct AddBookView: View {
   @Environment(ApplicationData.self) private var appData
   @Environment(\.dismiss) var dismiss
   @State private var titleInput: String = ""
   @State private var authorInput: String = ""
   @State private var yearInput: String = ""

   var body: some View {
      VStack(alignment: .trailing, spacing: 10) {
         HStack {
            Button("Close") {
               dismiss()
            }
            .buttonStyle(.glass)
            .padding([.top, .bottom], 10)
            Spacer()
            Button("Save") {
               storeBook()
               dismiss()
            }.buttonStyle(.borderedProminent)
         }
         TextField("Insert Title", text: $titleInput)
            .textFieldStyle(.roundedBorder)
         TextField("Insert Author", text: $authorInput)
            .textFieldStyle(.roundedBorder)
         TextField("Insert Year", text: $yearInput)
            .textFieldStyle(.roundedBorder)
            .keyboardType(.numbersAndPunctuation)
         Spacer()
      }.padding()
   }
```

```
    func storeBook() {
        let title = titleInput.trimmingCharacters(in: .whitespaces)
        let author = authorInput.trimmingCharacters(in: .whitespaces)
        if let year = Int(yearInput), !title.isEmpty && !author.isEmpty {
            let newBook = Book(title: title, author: author,
                cover: "nocover", year: year, selected: false)
            appData.userData.append(newBook)
        }
    }
}
#Preview {
    NavigationStack {
        AddBookView()
            .environment(ApplicationData.shared)
    }
}
```

There is nothing new in this view, all we do is to take the input from the user, trim the values to remove additional space, check whether the values are valid, and store a new book in the model. For this purpose, we create a new **Book** structure with the values inserted by the user and add it to the **userData** array in the model. After the process is over, we perform the **dismiss** handler, the view is closed, and the new book appears at the end of the list.

Figure 5-28: *Sheet to insert new books*

Do It Yourself

Update the **ContentView** structure with the code in Listing 5-42. Create a new SwiftUI file called **AddBookView.swift** for the code in Listing 5-43. Run the application on an iPhone simulator. Press the + button in the navigation bar. You should see a sheet with three input fields. Insert the values of the book and press Save. The book should be added at the end of the list.

IMPORTANT

The views opened in a sheet are not part of the hierarchical structure created by the **NavigationStack** view, and therefore they do not participate in the path created by this view. To remove it, we must implement the **dismiss** property, as we did in Listing 5-43.

In this example, we have included a button to close the view, but there is a built-in feature that allows the user to remove the view by dragging it down with the finger. SwiftUI includes the following modifier to enable or disable this tool.

interactiveDismissDisabled(Bool)

This modifier enables or disables the possibility of dragging down the view to close it (**true** disabled, **false** enabled).

There are also modifiers to configure the sheet. The following are the most frequently used.

presentationDetents(Set, **selection:** Binding)

This modifier determines the sheet's height. The first argument is a set of values that determine all the different sizes the sheet can take. The values are defined by a structure of type **PresentationDetent**. The structure includes the type properties **large** and **medium** to set predefined sizes, and the type methods **custom(Type)**, **fraction(CGFloat)**, and **height(CGFloat)** to set custom sizes. The **selection** argument is a binding property we can use to keep track of the current height.

presentationBackground(ShapeStyle)

This modifier defines the sheet's background. The argument specifies a color or a pattern, such as those provided by **Color** views or **Material** structures.

presentationCornerRadius(CGFloat?)

This modifier defines the sheet's corner radius.

presentationBackgroundInteraction(PresentationBackgroundInteraction)

This modifier determines if the user can interact with the content behind the sheet.

navigationTransition(NavigationTransition)

This modifier defines the navigation transition for the view. The argument is a structure with the properties **automatic** (uses the transition by default) and **crossFade** (fades out the old view and fades in the new one).

By default, the sheet's height is set to **large**, which means that the view will take up as much space as possible, but we can declare a specific size with the **presentationDetents()** modifier. In the following example, we give the sheet a height of 250 points.

Listing 5-44: Assigning a predefined height

```
.sheet(isPresented: $showSheet) {
   AddBookView()
      .presentationDetents([.height(250)])
}
```

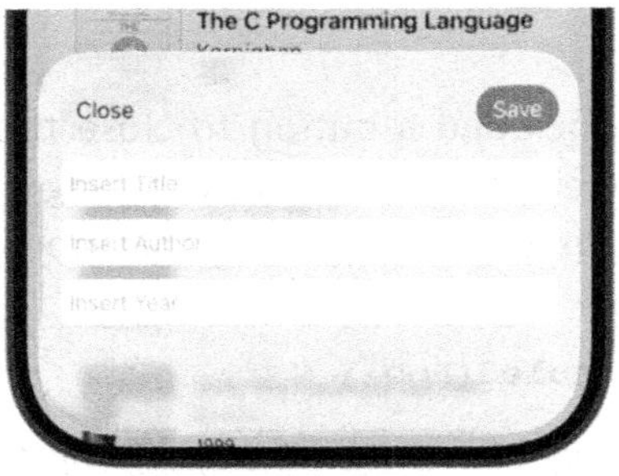

***Figure 5-29:** Sheet's custom height*

As illustrated by the previous examples, the background of a sheet changes depending on its size. Larger sheets are shown with an opaque background, while shorter views use a liquid glass effect. Apple recommends using this effect, but we can change it with the **presentationBackground()** modifier if necessary. In the following example, we apply a material to the background to make it more opaque.

Listing 5-45: Assigning a custom background

```
.sheet(isPresented: $showSheet) {
   AddBookView()
      .presentationDetents([.height(250)])
      .presentationBackground(.thinMaterial)
}
```

Do It Yourself

Replace the **sheet()** modifier in the **ContentView** structure with the modifier you want to try. Run the application on an iPhone simulator and press the + button to open the sheet. Assign different values to the first argument of the **presentationDetents()** modifier to see how the sheet adapts to different heights.

On iPhones, the sheets are displayed full screen, but on iPads and Mac computers they partially cover the screen. The size and shape of the view is determined by the system, but we can change it with the following modifier.

presentationSizing(PresentationSizing)

This modifier determines the shape of the sheet and how it is going to adapt to the size of its content. The argument is a structure that conforms to the **PresentationSizing** protocol. The framework includes properties to return predefined structures that conform to this protocol. The currently available are **automatic**, **fitted**, **form** and **page**.

The structure returned by the **page** property is the one used by default. It presents a view over the content with a size determined by the space available on the screen. The one returned by the **form** property presents a narrow view, which is ideal to display forms. And the structure returned by the **fitted** property adapts the view to the size of the content. For example, if we are designing the sheet for an iPad, we can assign a fixed width and height to the view with the **frame()** modifier and then ask the sheet to adapt to that size.

Listing 5-46: Declaring the size of the sheet

```
.sheet(isPresented: $showSheet) {
   AddBookView()
      .frame(width: 350, height: 250)
      .presentationSizing(.fitted)
}
```

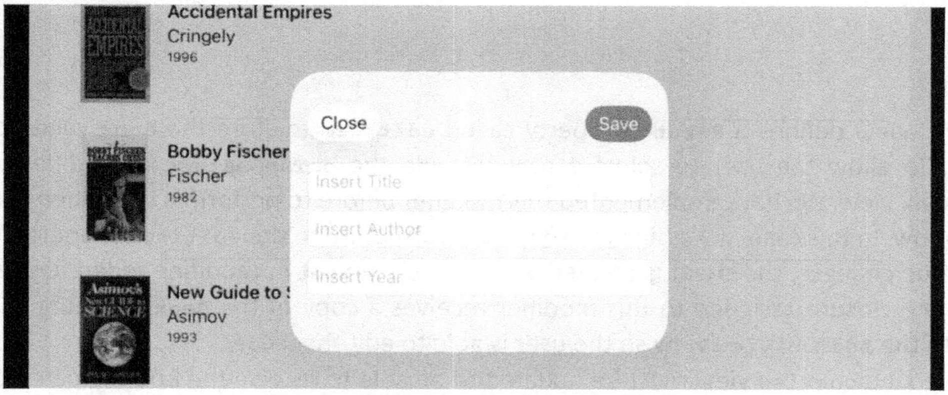

Figure 5-30: *Custom sheet on iPads*

There is a second **sheet()** modifier designed to open a sheet for each of the values in the model. It is usually implemented to open a sheet for each row on a list. The modifier needs an optional binding property of the same data type of the items in our model (the data type must conform to the **Identifiable** protocol). If the property contains a value, a sheet is opened with that value, and when the value **nil** is assigned to the property, the sheet is closed.

In the following example, we implement this modifier to allow the user to edit the values of the books. When a row is selected, we assign the **Book** structure that represents the book to the **@State** property, so the sheet is opened with this value.

Listing 5-47: Presenting a sheet for every value on the list

```
struct ContentView: View {
   @Environment(ApplicationData.self) private var appData
   @State private var showSheet: Bool = false
   @State private var editItem: Book?
```

```
    var body: some View {
        NavigationStack {
            List(appData.userData) { book in
                CellBook(book: book)
                    .background(.white)
                    .onTapGesture {
                        editItem = book
                    }
            }.navigationTitle(Text("Books"))
            .toolbar {
                ToolbarItem(placement: .topBarTrailing) {
                    Button("Add Book", systemImage: "plus", action: {
                        showSheet = true
                    })
                }
            }
            .sheet(isPresented: $showSheet) {
                AddBookView()
            }
            .sheet(item: $editItem) { item in
                AddBookView(book: item)
            }
        }
    }
}
```

This view defines a **@State** property called **editItem** to store the **Book** value for the sheet. To allow the user to select a row, we add the **onTapGesture()** modifier to the **CellBook** view. We have implemented this modifier before to perform a task when the user taps a row. In this case, we assign the row's **Book** structure to the **editItem** property. When this value changes, the sheet is opened with a second **sheet()** modifier added to the **List** view. The closure assigned to this modifier receives a copy of the **Book** structure that we send to the **AddBookView** view so the user is able to edit the values.

The **AddBookView** view must be updated to be able to receive the book selected by the user and show the current values in the input fields. But we also must contemplate that the view might be opened by the user to insert a new book. The following are the modifications we need to introduce to the view for this purpose.

Listing 5-48: Editing a book

```
struct AddBookView: View {
    @Environment(ApplicationData.self) private var appData
    @Environment(\.dismiss) var dismiss
    @State private var titleInput: String = ""
    @State private var authorInput: String = ""
    @State private var yearInput: String = ""
    var book: Book?

    var body: some View {
        VStack(alignment: .trailing, spacing: 10) {
            HStack {
                Button("Close") {
                    dismiss()
                }.buttonStyle(.glass)
                .padding([.top, .bottom], 10)
```

```
            Spacer()
            Text(book == nil ? "Add Book" : "Edit Book")
               .font(.body.weight(.bold))
            Spacer()
            Button("Save") {
               storeBook()
               dismiss()
            }.buttonStyle(.glassProminent)
         }
         TextField("Insert Title", text: $titleInput)
            .textFieldStyle(.roundedBorder)
         TextField("Insert Author", text: $authorInput)
            .textFieldStyle(.roundedBorder)
         TextField("Insert Year", text: $yearInput)
            .textFieldStyle(.roundedBorder)
            .keyboardType(.numbersAndPunctuation)
         Spacer()
      }.padding()
      .onAppear {
         titleInput = book?.title ?? ""
         authorInput = book?.author ?? ""
         yearInput = book?.displayYear ?? ""
      }
   }
   func storeBook() {
      let title = titleInput.trimmingCharacters(in: .whitespaces)
      let author = authorInput.trimmingCharacters(in: .whitespaces)
      if let year = Int(yearInput), !title.isEmpty && !author.isEmpty {
         if let index = appData.userData.firstIndex(where: {
            $0.id == book?.id }) {
            let newBook = Book(title: title, author: author, cover:
               appData.userData[index].cover, year: year, selected: false)
            appData.userData[index] = newBook
         } else {
            let newBook = Book(title: title, author: author,
               cover: "nocover", year: year, selected: false)
            appData.userData.append(newBook)
         }
      }
   }
}
```

There are a few differences in this view from the one defined in Listing 5-43. First, we added an optional property called **book** to receive the book. If the user opens the view to add a new book, the value of this property will be **nil**, but if the view is opened by selecting a row, the property will contain the **Book** structure with the information about the selected book. By checking this value, we can perform tasks for each situation. For instance, at the top of the view, we added a **Text** view to display the texts "Add Book" or "Edit Book" depending on the value of this property. At the bottom, the **onAppear()** modifier was included to load the values. If the **book** property contains a book, we assign the values to the input fields so the user can change them.

The **storeBook()** method updates or adds the book to the model. We first get the index of the selected book with the **firstIndex()** method. If an index is returned, we create a new **Book** structure with the values inserted by the user and the current image, otherwise, we create the structure with an image by default and add it to the **userData** array.

Figure 5-31: *Sheet to edit values*

Do It Yourself

Update the **ContentView** structure with the code in Listing 5-47 and the **AddBookView** structure with the code in Listing 5-48. Run the application on an iPhone simulator and select a row. You should see the values of the book on the screen. Edit a value and press Save. You should see the new value on the list.

IMPORTANT

In addition to the presentation styles available for sheets, we can also present sheets using the zoom transition introduced earlier for navigation (see Listing 5-41). In this case, we must apply the **matchedTransition-Source()** modifier to the button that opens the sheet and the **navigationTransition()** modifier to the view. The sheet then opens using a zoom transition.

PRO

Inspector

SwiftUI also provides a modal view, similar to sheets, that opens on the right side of the screen on iPads and Macs and as a sheet on iPhones. This view is called *Inspector* and is used to provide additional information and functionality related to the content selected by the user. Below is the modifier we need to implement to present this view.

inspector(isPresented: Binding, **content:** Closure)

This modifier presents the inspector. The **isPresented** argument is a Boolean property that determines whether the view is presented or not, and the **content** argument is the closure that provides the view to be presented.

SwiftUI also provides a modifier to determine the size of the inspector.

```
inspectorColumnWidth(min: CGFloat?, ideal: CGFloat, max:
CGFloat?)
```

This modifier defines the inspector's width. The **min** argument determines the minimum width possible, the **ideal** argument determines the initial width (it can be changed by the user), and the **max** argument determines the maximum width possible.

The **inspector()** modifier works like the **sheet()** modifier; it takes a binding property to determine whether the inspector should be open or not, and a closure to define its content.

Listing 5-49: Presenting the inspector

```
struct ContentView: View {
   @Environment(ApplicationData.self) private var appData
   @State private var presentInspector: Bool = false

   var body: some View {
      NavigationStack {
         List(appData.userData) { book in
            CellBook(book: book)
         }
         .navigationTitle(Text("Books"))
         .toolbarTitleDisplayMode(.inlineLarge)
         .inspector(isPresented: $presentInspector) {
            InspectorView()
         }
         .toolbar {
            Button(action: {
               presentInspector.toggle()
            }, label: {
               Image(systemName: presentInspector ? "xmark.circle" :
                  "info.circle")
            })
         }
      }
   }
}
```

In this example, we include a Boolean property called **presentInspector** to determine whether the inspector is open or not, and a button in the navigation bar to toggle the value. When the button is pressed, the **inspector()** modifier opens the **InspectorView** view. For this example, we defined the view with a **VStack** and three **Text** views to show some content. On an iPad or Mac, this view is displayed on the right side of the screen, while on iPhones it is presented as a sheet, as shown below.

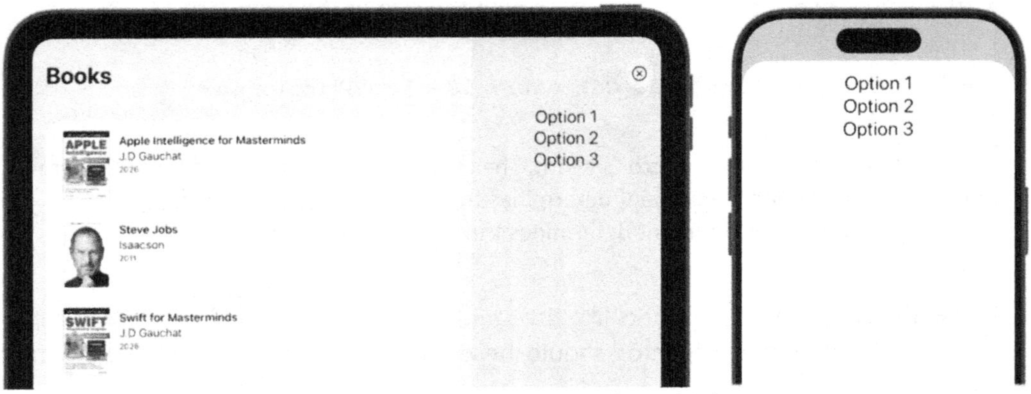

Figure 5-32: *Inspector on iPads and iPhones*

The inspector adopts a size depending on the system, but we can specify the width we want with the **`inspectorColumnWidth()`** modifier. This modifier is applied to the view and can take a specific width or specify a maximum, minimum, and ideal size, as shown below.

Listing 5-50: Defining the size of the inspector

```
.inspector(isPresented: $presentInspector) {
   InspectorView()
      .inspectorColumnWidth(min: 200, ideal: 250, max: 300)
}
```

BASIC

Popovers

Another type of views we can add to our interface are popovers. Popovers are presented like sheets on iPhones, but as small views on iPads and Mac computers. The **`View`** protocol defines the following modifier to present them.

> **`popover(isPresented:`** `Binding,` **`attachmentAnchor:`** `PopoverAttachmentAnchor,` **`arrowEdge:`** `Edge,` **`content:`** `Closure)`

> This modifier displays a popover. The **isPresented** argument is a binding property of type **`Bool`** that determines whether the popover has to be displayed (**`true`**) or removed (**`false`**). The **attachmentAnchor** argument is an enumeration of type **`PopoverAttachmentAnchor`** that includes the **`point()`** and **`rect()`** methods to determine the part of the view to which the popover should be anchored. The **arrowEdge** argument is an enumeration of type **`Edge`** that determines the side in which the popover's arrow should be placed. The values available are **`bottom`**, **`leading`**, **`top`**, and **`trailing`**. And the **content** argument is a closure that defines the view to be shown on the screen.

On iPhones, a popover is presented as a sheet, while on iPads it appears as a smaller view whose size is determined by its content. If we want the view to always be presented as a popover, regardless of the device, we must apply the following modifier.

presentationCompactAdaptation(PresentationAdaptation)

This modifier adapts the view to the size of the screen. The argument specifies the type of adaptation we want. It is a structure with the properties **automatic**, **none**, **fullScreenCover**, **popover** and **sheet**.

The position of the popover is determined by the view to which the **popover()** modifier is applied and the location of the popover's arrow (top, left, right, or bottom). For instance, the following example shows a popover anchored to a **Button** view with a **top** arrow, so the view appears below the button.

Listing 5-51: Showing a popover

```
struct ContentView: View {
   @State private var showPopover: Bool = false

   var body: some View {
      VStack {
         Button("Show Popover") {
            showPopover = true
         }
         .popover(isPresented: $showPopover, arrowEdge: .top) {
            HelpView()
               .presentationCompactAdaptation(.popover)
         }
         Spacer()
      }.font(.title)
   }
}
```

The **popover()** modifier in this example has two arguments: the **isPresented** argument to control when the popover is shown, and the **arrowEdge** argument to determine the side where the arrow is placed, which in turn determines the position of the popover relative to the anchor view. When the value of the **showPopover** property is **true**, the modifier creates an instance of the **HelpView** view and shows it on the screen. The following is our implementation of this view.

Listing 5-52: Defining the content of the popover

```
import SwiftUI

struct HelpView: View {
   @Environment(\.dismiss) var dismiss

   var body: some View {
      VStack {
         HStack {
            Spacer()
            Button("X") {
               dismiss()
            }.buttonStyle(.glass)
            .padding(.trailing, 16)
```

```
      }
      Text("Press this button when you need help")
        .font(.title)
        .padding()
    }.frame(width: 250, height: 250)
  }
}
```

In this example, we give the view a size of 250 by 250 points. Because we have applied the **`presentationCompactAdaptation()`** modifier to the view, it is displayed at that size on every device, as shown below.

Figure 5-33: *Popover*

Do It Yourself

Create a new App project. Update the **`ContentView`** structure with the code in Listing 5-51. Create a SwiftUI file called **HelpView.swift** for the code in Listing 5-52. Run the application on an iPad simulator and press the Show Popover button. You should see the popover illustrated in Figure 5-33. Remove the **`resentationCompactAdaptation()`** modifier to see how the popover is shown on iPhones.

BASIC

Alert Views

Alert views are predefined modal views that can display messages and receive input from the user. Their purpose is to deliver to the user important information that requires immediate attention. For example, an alert view may be used to ask confirmation from the user before deleting data from the model. The following are the most frequently used modifiers provided by the framework to create these views.

alert(String, isPresented: Binding, actions: Closure, message: Closure)

This modifier presents an alert view. The first argument is the view's title, the **isPresented** argument is a binding value of type **Bool** that determines whether the alert view has to be presented (**true**) or removed (**false**), the **actions** argument is a closure with **Button** views to create the buttons for the view, and the **message** argument is a closure with the view that provides the message.

alert(String, item: Binding, actions: Closure, message: Closure)

This modifier presents an alert view. The first argument is the view's title, the **item** argument is an optional binding value that determines whether the sheet has to be presented or removed (**nil**), the **actions** argument is a closure with **Button** views to create the buttons for the view, and the **message** argument is a closure with the view that provides the message. The closures receive the value assigned to the **item** argument for processing.

The process to open alert views is the same as with sheets. We have to define a **@State** property to manage the state of the view and then apply the **alert()** modifier.

Listing 5-53: Displaying an alert view

```
struct ContentView: View {
   @State private var name: String = ""
   @State private var openAlert: Bool = false

   var body: some View {
      VStack(spacing: 10) {
         TextField("Insert your Name", text: $name)
            .textFieldStyle(.roundedBorder)
         HStack {
            Spacer()
            Button("Save") {
               openAlert = name.isEmpty
            }
         }
         Spacer()
      }.padding()
      .alert("Error", isPresented: $openAlert, actions: {
         Button("Cancel", role: .cancel, action: {
            openAlert = false
         })
      }, message: { Text("Insert your name") })
   }
}
```

The **@State** property for this view is called **openAlert**. The view includes a **TextField** view and a button. When the button is pressed, the code checks whether the user inserted a value. If not, the value **true** is assigned to the **openAlert** property to present the alert view. The view was defined with the title "Error", the message "Insert your name", and a **Button** view that allows the user to dismiss it. Note that the button has been assigned a role that corresponds to the action performed (in this case, **cancel**) so that the system knows its purpose and can style it appropriately.

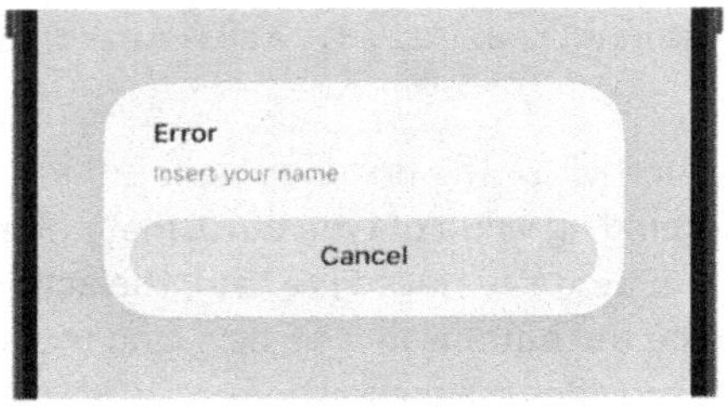

Figure 5-34: *Alert view*

Do It Yourself

Update the **ContentView** structure in your project with the code in Listing 5-53. Press the Save button. If you didn't insert anything in the text field, you should see the alert view illustrated in Figure 5-34.

Our current view contains only one button, but we can include more. If there are two buttons, they are shown side by side, but three or more are displayed on a list, with the Cancel button at the end, as shown next.

Listing 5-54: Defining an Alert view with multiple buttons

```
.alert("Error", isPresented: $openAlert, actions: {
   Button("Cancel", role: .cancel, action: {})
   Button("Delete", role: .destructive, action: {
      name = ""
   })
   Button("Save Anyway", role: .none, action: {
      print("Save value")
   })
}, message: { Text("Insert your name") })
```

This modifier includes three buttons. A button to cancel the action and two more to perform other tasks. The Cancel button was defined first, but because the role is set to **cancel**, the system places it at the end of the list.

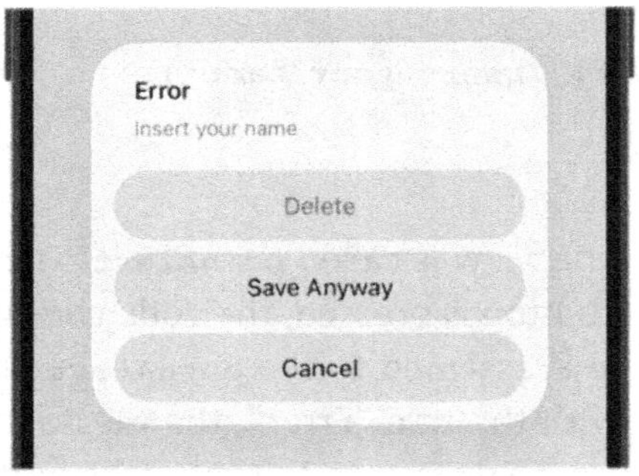

Figure 5-35: *Alert view with multiple buttons*

Confirmation Dialog

SwiftUI includes another type of alert views called *Confirmation Dialogs* (also known as Action Sheets). These views are usually presented when our application needs the user to make a decision and there is more than one option available. The following are the modifiers we need to apply to create this view.

confirmationDialog(String, **isPresented:** Binding, **titleVisibility:** Visibility, **actions:** Closure, **message:** Closure)

This modifier creates a confirmation dialog. The first argument is the text for the title, the **isPresented** argument is a binding value of type **Bool** that determines whether the view has to be presented (**true**) or removed (**false**), the **titleVisibility** argument is an enumeration with the values **automatic**, **hidden**, and **visible** that determines the visibility of the title, the **actions** argument defines the buttons to include in the view, and the **message** argument provides the text for the message.

confirmationDialog(String, **item:** Binding, **titleVisibility:** Visibility, **actions:** Closure, **message:** Closure)

This modifier creates a confirmation dialog. The first argument is the text for the title, the **item** argument is an optional binding value that determines whether the sheet has to be presented or removed (**nil**), the **titleVisibility** argument is an enumeration with the values **automatic**, **hidden**, and **visible** that determines the visibility of the title, the **actions** argument defines the buttons to include in the view, and the **message** argument provides the text for the message. The closures receive the value assigned to the **item** argument for processing.

Confirmation dialogs are displayed as alert views on Macs and as popovers on iPhones and iPads. To ensure that they are anchored to the correct view, we must apply the modifier to the view that triggers the action, as shown below.

Listing 5-55: Defining an action sheet

```
struct ContentView: View {
   @State private var openDialog: Bool = false

   var body: some View {
      VStack(spacing: 10) {
         Button("Open Confirmation Dialog") {
            openDialog = true
         }
         .confirmationDialog("Email", isPresented: $openDialog, actions: {
            Button("Move to Inbox", role: .none, action: {})
            Button("Delete", role: .destructive, action: {})
            Button("Cancel", role: .cancel, action: {})
         }, message: {
            Text("What do you want to do with the message?")
         })
         Spacer()
```

```
        }.padding()
    }
}
```

In this example, we apply the **`confirmationDialog()`** modifier to the button that opens the dialog, ensuring that the popover is anchored to this view on iPhones and iPads, as shown below.

Figure 5-36: *Confirmation dialog on iPhones*

PRO

Tip Views

Tip views are small views we can show to help users find features in our app and learn how they work. They can be displayed along with the rest of the views in the interface or as popups.

Figure 5-37: *Tip View*

Tip views and all the tools required to configure and display tips are defined by a framework called **TipKit**. To define the tips, the framework provides the **`Tip`** protocol. This protocol includes the following properties to declare the content of the tip.

`title`

This property returns a **`Text`** view to display the title of the tip.

`message`

This property returns a **`Text`** view to display the message of the tip.

`image`

This property returns an **`Image`** view with the image to display with the tip.

id

This property returns a **String** value with the tip's identifier.

options

This property returns an array of structures that conform to the **TipOption** protocol and are used to configure the tip. There are two structures available: The **IgnoresDisplayFrequency** structure is initialized with a Boolean value that determines if the tip is going to ignore the display frequency set by the system, and the **MaxDisplayCount** is initialized with an integer value that determines the maximum number of times the tip will be displayed to the user.

rules

This property returns an array of **Rule** structures that determine the condition to meet before displaying a tip.

actions

This property returns an array of **Action** structures that define the buttons to include with the tip to allow users to perform actions.

To create a tip, we need to import the **TipKit** framework, create a structure that conforms to the **Tip** protocol, and define the properties. The **title** property is required for the tip to be valid, but the rest are optional. In the following example, we define the **title** and **message** properties to specify the tip's title and message (recommended).

Listing 5-56: Defining a tip

```
import SwiftUI
import TipKit

struct TipButton: Tip {
   var title: Text {
      Text("Press to Save")
   }
   var message: Text? {
      Text("Press this button to save your progress.")
   }
}
```

TipKit defines an enumeration called **Tips** that provides access to configuration options and the following method to configure the tips.

configure([ConfigurationOption])

This type method configures the tips. The argument is an array of **ConfigurationOption** structures. The framework includes two methods to return these structures: The **datastoreLocation(DatastoreLocation)** method determines where the state of the tips is going to be stored, and the **displayFrequency()** method determines when the tips are eligible to be displayed.

After the tips are defined and the system is configured, we can show the tips with a **TipView** view. The following is the view's initializer.

> **TipView(**Tip, **arrowEdge:** Edge?, **action:** Closure)
>
> This initializer creates a view to show a tip. The first argument is the **Tip** structure that defines the tip, the **arrowEdge** argument is an enumeration that determines the direction of the view's indicator (**top**, **bottom**, **leading** and **trailing**), and the **action** argument is a closure with the code we want to execute when a tip button is pressed. The closure receives a reference of the **Action** structure that represents the button pressed by the user.

To display a tip, we need to create an instance of the **Tip** structure and use it to initialize a **TipView** view. It is recommended to store the instance in a constant so we can reference the tip later and work with it. In the following example, we store an instance of our **TipButton** structure in a constant called **tipButton** and present it using a **TipView** view below a button to indicate the purpose of that button.

Listing 5-57: Presenting a tip

```
import SwiftUI
import TipKit

struct ContentView: View {
   let tipButton = TipButton()

   var body: some View {
      VStack {
         Button("Save") {
            print("Action Performed")
         }
         TipView(tipButton)
      }
      .padding()
      .task {
         try? Tips.configure([
            .displayFrequency(.immediate),
            .datastoreLocation(.applicationDefault)
         ])
      }
      Spacer()
   }
}
```

For the tips to appear, we must configure the system. In this example, we use a **task()** modifier. This modifier executes the code in a closure as soon as the view is loaded, like the **onAppear()** modifier, but it runs the code in the background. There are two options for configuration. First, we can determine the frequency in which the tip is going to appear with the **displayFrequency()** method. This method takes the values **immediate**, **daily**, **hourly**, **weekly** and **monthly**. In this example we use the value **immediate** to show the tip when the view appears on the screen for the first time. The second configuration option is provided by the **datastoreLocation()** method. With this method we can determine where the states of the tips are going to be stored. Depending on the frequency, a tip can be shown one or multiple times. To know if the tip is eligible to be shown to the user, the system stores the states of the tips in a file. There are three options available: We can store the states in a file inside the application's support directory, in a specific file, or in CloudKit. In this example, we use the **applicationDefault** property to store the states in a file selected by the system (default), but the **DatastoreLocation** structure also includes the methods **url(URL)** to select our own file and **groupContainer(identifier: String)** to select a container in CloudKit to share the state with other devices. (We will learn how to work with files and share information between devices in Chapter 7.)

Do It Yourself

Create a new App project. Create a new file called **Tips.swift** for the code in Listing 5-56. Update the **ContentView.swift** file with the code in Listing 5-57. You should see the tip on the screen, as shown in Figure 5-37.

The example in Listing 5-57 displays the tip view along with the rest of the views in the interface. If instead of a view, we want to show the tip over the interface in a popup window, we can use the following modifier.

popoverTip(Tip, arrowEdge: Edge, action: Closure)

This modifier creates a popover to show a tip. The first argument is the **Tip** structure that defines the tip, the **arrowEdge** argument is an **Edge** enumeration that determines the direction of the arrow of the popover (**top**, **bottom**, **leading** and **trailing**), and the **action** argument is a closure with the code we want to execute when a tip button is pressed. The closure receives the **Action** structure that represents the button pressed by the user.

To present the tip as a popover, we need to remove the **TipView** view and assign the **popoverTip()** modifier to the view associated with the tip, as shown below.

Listing 5-58: Presenting a tip in a popover

```
Button("Save") {
   print("Action Performed")
}
.popoverTip(tipButton)
```

Tips only appear when they are eligible according to the frequency set by the system. In our example, we set the frequency to **immediate** and therefore the tip is shown when the view appears on the screen for the first time and never again. This means that if we introduce changes to the tip or the interface, we won't be able to see it again. To help us work with tips and design the interface, the framework includes the following methods.

showAllTipsForTesting()

This method configures the system to show all the tips as soon as the view appears on the screen.

hideAllTipsForTesting()

This method configures the system to never show the tips.

Like the configuration options, these methods are also accessible from the **Tips** enumeration. In the following example, we show how to call the **showAllTipsForTesting()** method to always show the tips on the screen.

Listing 5-59: Showing the tips for testing

```
.task {
   try? Tips.configure([
      .displayFrequency(.immediate)
   ])
   Tips.showAllTipsForTesting()
}
```

Do It Yourself

Update the **ContentView** structure with the code in Listing 5-59. You should see the tip on the canvas again. Update the **ContentView** structure again with the code in Listing 5-58. You should now see the tip in a popover.

The **immediate** value configures the tips to appear the first time the view is shown to the user and then never again, but we can get the tip to appear every hour, day, week or month with the values **daily**, **hourly**, **immediate**, **monthly** and **weekly**. This means that a tip will appear over and over again at the frequency determined by the system. To stop showing a tip, the **Tip** protocol defines the following method.

invalidate(reason: InvalidationReason)

This method invalidates the tip. The **reason** argument determines the reason why the tip was invalidated. It is an enumeration with the values **actionPerformed**, **displayCountExceeded**, and **tipClosed**.

In the following example, we configure the tips to be shown daily and then invalidate the tip when a button is pressed.

Listing 5-60: Invalidating a tip

```
struct ContentView: View {
   let tipButton = TipButton()
```

```
    var body: some View {
        VStack {
            Button("Save") {
                print("Action Performed")
                tipButton.invalidate(reason: .actionPerformed)
            }
            .popoverTip(tipButton)
        }
        .padding()
        .task {
            try? Tips.configure([
                .displayFrequency(.daily)
            ])
        }
        Spacer()
    }
}
```

We can also control the display frequency from the tip itself. There are two options available: we can configure the tip to ignore the display frequency set by the system with a **IgnoresDisplayFrequency** structure, or limit the times the tip is displayed with the **MaxDisplayCount** structure. In the following example, we configure our tip to be shown only one time.

Listing 5-61: Showing the tip only once

```
struct TipButton: Tip {
    var title: Text {
        Text("Press to Save")
    }
    var message: Text? {
        Text("Press this button to save your progress.")
    }
    var options: [any TipOption] {
        [MaxDisplayCount(1)]
    }
}
```

Tips can also include buttons that perform actions. The actions are defined by the **Action** structure and assigned to the **actions** property of the **Tip** structure, as shown below.

Listing 5-62: Adding actions to a tip

```
struct TipButton: Tip {
    var title: Text {
        Text("Press to Save")
    }
    var message: Text? {
        Text("Press this button to save your progress.")
    }
    var actions: [Action] {
        [Action(id: "tipButton", title: "More Into")]
```

```
    }
}
```

There are two ways to perform an action. We can assign a closure to the **Action** structure with the code we want to execute when the button is pressed, or assign an identifier to the action and then run the code from the view. In this example, we identified the action with the string "tipButton", so we can perform the action from the view.

Listing 5-63: Performing an action

```
.popoverTip(tipButton, action: { action in
    if action.id == "tipButton" {
        print("Help")
    }
})
```

When the button in the tip view is pressed, the system calls the closure assigned to the tip view. In this closure, we check if the action's identifier is equal to "tipButton" and execute the code.

Figure 5-38: *Tip action*

Do It Yourself

Update the **TipButton** structure with the code in Listing 5-62 and the **popoverTip()** modifier in the **ContentView** structure with the code in Listing 5-63. Remember to call the **showAllTipsForTesting()** method on the **Tips** enumeration to get the tip to show again, as we did in Listing 5-59. You should see a popover like the one in Figure 5-38. Press the button. The string "Help" should be printed on the console.

IMPORTANT

TipKit also offers the possibility to set rules that determine conditions for the tip to appear, it can allow the app to display multiple tips for the same view, and define custom styles. The topic is beyond the scope of this book. For more information, visit our website.

5.3 - Tab Views

Another way to organize multiple views (screens), is with a Tab view. This view offers the user several options for opening views. By default, the view creates a toolbar with buttons that users can tap to open the view they want. On iPhones, the buttons are displayed at the bottom of the screen, whereas on iPads they are displayed in a bar at the top.

Figure 5-39: *Tab View with three views*

SwiftUI includes the **`TabView`** and **`Tab`** structures to create a Tab view and the tabs. The following are the initializers.

`TabView(selection:` `Binding,` **`content:`** `Closure)`

This initializer creates a **`TabView`** view. The **selection** argument returns the value that identifies the view currently open, and the **content** argument is a closure with the list of **`Tab`** views the **`TabView`** view is going to include.

`Tab(value:` `Value,` **`role:`** `TabRole?,` **`content:`** `Closure)`

This initializer creates a Tab view. The **value** argument identifies the tab for selection purposes. The **role** argument is a structure that defines the purpose of the tab. The possible values are **`search`**, to declare that the tab is used for searching, and **`prominent`**, to specify that the tab should be displayed separately from the rest. And the **content** argument is a closure that provides the view to be shown when the tab is selected.

A **`TabView`** can have many configurations. The user can select views using tabs at the bottom or top of the screen, as shown in Figure 5-39, but also as a sidebar or like the pages of a book. The following is the modifier used to select the configuration.

`tabViewStyle(``TabViewStyle)`

This modifier defines the appearance of a **`TabView`** view. The argument is a structure that conforms to the **`TabViewStyle`** protocol. The framework includes many prede-fined structures with properties to configure the view. The most frequently used are **`automatic`**, **`page`**, **`verticalPage`**, **`grouped`**, **`sidebarAdaptable`** and **`tabBarOnly`**.

The following example shows how to create a standard Tab view with two tabs, one for the main content and another for settings.

Listing 5-64: Defining a `TabView` view with two tabs

```
struct ContentView: View {
    var body: some View {
        TabView {
            Tab("Home", systemImage: "book.circle") {
                Text("Main Screen")
            }
            Tab("Settings", systemImage: "gear") {
                Text("Settings")
            }
        }
    }
}
```

The **`TabView`** view defined in this example includes two tabs to present two views. The first tab is created with an SF Symbol called "book.circle" and the text "Home" and the second tab with an SF Symbol called "gear" and the text "Settings". The purpose of the tabs is to present fully functional views, as we did with the **`NavigationStack`** view before, but in this case we use simple **`Text`** views to simplify the example. When a tab is selected, the Tab view creates a new view with the corresponding **`Text`** view at the center of the screen, as shown below.

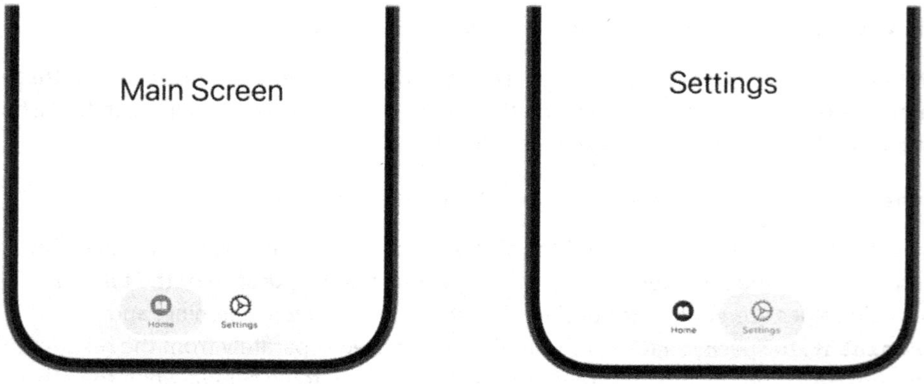

Figure 5-40: *Views in a* `TabView` *view*

Do It Yourself

Create a new App project. Update the **`ContentView`** structure with the code in Listing 5-64. Run the application on an iPhone simulator. You should see the screen illustrated in Figure 5-40. Click on the tabs to switch between the views.

We can include all the **Tab** views we want in a **TabView** view. If there is no space in the toolbar to display all of them, the system shows an additional button so that the user can select the remaining tabs, as shown below.

Figure 5-41: *More tabs*

If we want to highlight a tab, we can declare it as prominent. Prominent tabs are displayed separately from the rest. For this purpose, we must declare the tab's role as **prominent**, as shown below.

Listing 5-65: Defining a prominent tab

```
struct ContentView: View {
   var body: some View {
      TabView {
         Tab("Home", systemImage: "book.circle") {
            Text("Main Screen")
         }
         Tab("Settings", systemImage: "gear") {
            Text("Settings")
         }
         Tab("Shopping Cart", systemImage: "cart", role: .prominent) {
            Text("Shopping")
         }
      }
   }
}
```

The tab works like any other, when selected it opens a view, but because we declared it as prominent, it is displayed on the right side of the Tab view.

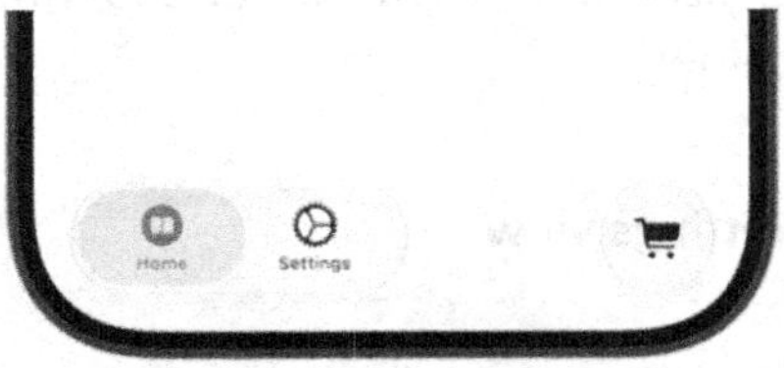

Figure 5-42: *Prominent tab*

A **TabView** view shows one view at a time. This means that the user may not be aware when the content of a view has been updated. To alert the user that new information is available, we can display a badge over the button using the **`badge()`** modifier introduced earlier for navigation items (see Listing 5-14). In the following example, we apply this modifier to the Settings tab to indicate how many issues require the user's attention.

Listing 5-66: Displaying a badge on a tab

```
struct ContentView: View {
   var body: some View {
      TabView {
         Tab("Home", systemImage: "book.circle") {
            Text("Main Screen")
         }
         Tab("Settings", systemImage: "gear") {
            Text("Settings")
         }
         .badge(12)
      }
   }
}
```

In this case, the badge is created with the number 12, so it will always show that value, but badges are usually defined with values from properties or counters used to alert the user of important issues that need attention.

Figure 5-43: *Badge*

The user can tap on the buttons to open a view, but we can also do it from code. The **`TabView`** view can use a binding property to store a value that determines which view is currently opened. By modifying the value of this property, we can open a view programmatically. For this to work, we must assign the binding property to the **selection** argument of the **`TabView`** initializer and assign the tab's identifier to the **value** argument of the **`Tab`** initializer, as shown below.

Listing 5-67: Selecting the Settings view

```
struct ContentView: View {
   @State private var selectedView: Int = 2

   var body: some View {
      TabView(selection: $selectedView) {
         Tab("Home", systemImage: "book.circle", value: 1) {
            Text("Main Screen")
```

```
            }
            Tab("Settings", systemImage: "gear", value: 2) {
               Text("Settings")
            }
         }
      }
}
```

Every time a new value is assigned to the **@State** property, the tab with that identifier is shown on the screen. This also means that we can determine the view to show by default by initializing the property with that view's identifier. In our example, we assign the value **2** to the property, so the Settings view is shown first.

When the user scrolls content on an iPhone, the buttons of a **TabView** view may get in the way. The framework provides the following modifier to reduce their size.

tabBarMinimizeBehavior(TabBarMinimizeBehavior)

This modifier controls whether the tab bar is minimized when content is scrolled. The argument specifies when the bar should be minimized. It is a structure with the properties **automatic**, **never**, **onScrollDown**, and **onScrollUp**.

This modifier responds to the state of the scroll view. To test it, we can create a simple list of values for the main screen, as shown in the following example.

Listing 5-68: Minimizing the tabs

```
struct ContentView: View {
   var body: some View {
      TabView {
         Tab("Home", systemImage: "book.circle") {
            List(1..<50) { value in
               Text("Item \(value)")
            }
         }
         Tab("Settings", systemImage: "gear") {
            Text("Settings")
         }
      }
      .tabBarMinimizeBehavior(.onScrollDown)
   }
}
```

Because in this example we apply the modifier with the **onScrollDown** value, the tabs are minimized when the user scrolls down the content. The result is shown below.

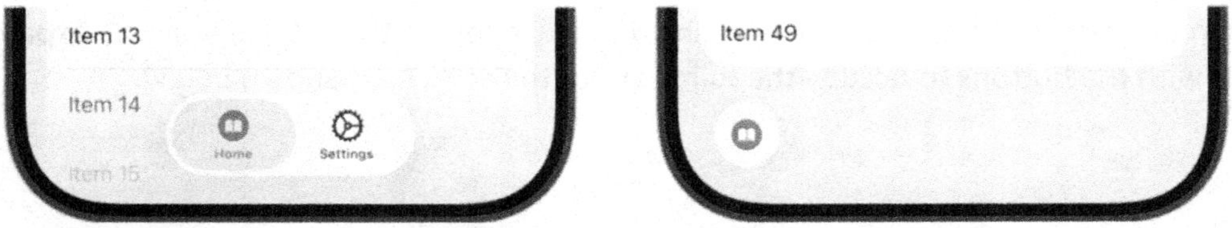

Figure 5-44: *Minimized tabs*

Tab views can include a view at the top to show additional content. The framework defines the following modifier for this purpose.

tabViewBottomAccessory(Closure)

This modifier adds an accessory view on top of the Tab view. The argument is the closure that provides the views.

When we include an accessory view and the tab view is minimized, the system automatically inserts the accessory view into the tab view. If we need to know whether the accessory view was minimized along with the tab view, we can read the following environment property.

tabViewBottomAccessoryPlacement

This property returns an enumeration of type **TabViewBottomAccessoryPlacement** to indicate whether the accessory view was minimized or not. The values available are **expanded** and **inline** (minimized).

In the following example, we create a simple accessory view to display a message. Note that we also include the **tabBarMinimizeBehavior()** modifier to show how the system integrates the accessory view into the tab view when the content is scrolled.

Listing 5-69: Adding an accessory view

```
struct ContentView: View {
   var body: some View {
      TabView {
         Tab("Home", systemImage: "book.circle") {
            List(1..<50) { value in
               Text("Item \(value)")
            }
         }
         Tab("Settings", systemImage: "gear") {
            Text("Settings")
         }
      }
      .tabViewBottomAccessory {
         Text("Additional Content")
      }
      .tabBarMinimizeBehavior(.onScrollDown)
   }
}
```

On iPhones, the accessory view is shown at the top of the tab view and is expanded along with the buttons to occupy the full width of the screen, as shown below.

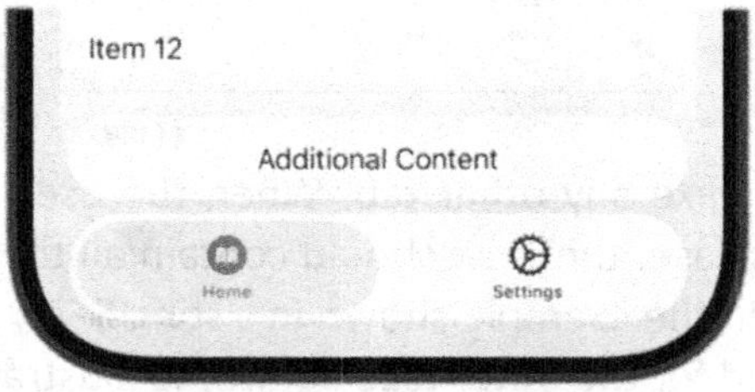

Figure 5-45: *Accessory view on iPhones*

BASIC

Search

In addition to creating custom tabs, the **`Tab`** view also offers the option of creating a predefined tab that the user can open to search for information. This tab contains the icon of a magnifying glass, which makes it perfect for the compact design of iPhones and iPads, as shown below.

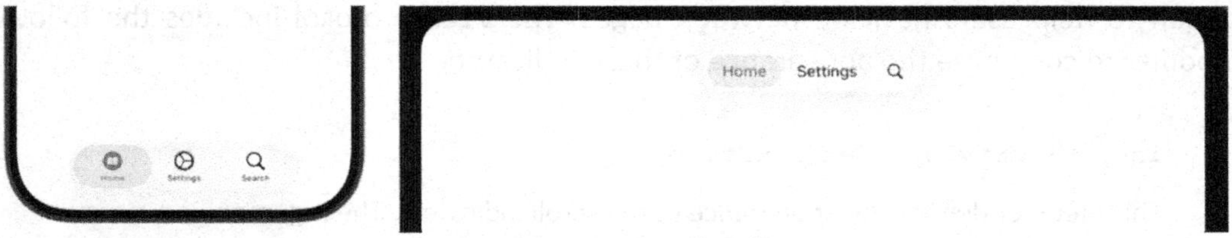

Figure 5-46: *Search tab*

The search tab is created by assigning the value **`search`** to the **role** argument of the **`Tab`** view's initializer. In the following example, we add a search tab to our **`TabView`** view to reproduce the design in Figure 5-46.

Listing 5-70: Adding a search tab

```
struct ContentView: View {
   var body: some View {
      TabView {
         Tab("Home", systemImage: "book.circle") {
            Text("Main Screen")
         }
         Tab("Settings", systemImage: "gear") {
            Text("Settings")
         }
         Tab(role: .search) {
            Text("Search")
         }
      }
   }
}
```

IMPORTANT

A search tab works like any other tab. When the user selects the tab, a view opens. In this case, the view should contain all the tools required to perform a search. In the example shown in Listing 5-70, we open a simple **`Text`** view, as we did for the other tabs before, to illustrate how a **`TabView`** view works. We will develop a more realistic example later in this chapter.

BASIC

Pages

By default, a **`TabView`** view displays its tabs as a series of buttons, but we can change this behavior using the **`tabViewStyle()`** modifier. On iOS devices, an alternative is to present the views as the pages of a book by applying the **`page`** style. When a **`TabView`** view uses this presentation, the toolbars are hidden and page indicators appear at the bottom of the screen to help users navigate between pages. The **`View`** protocol includes the following modifier to customize the appearance of these indicators.

`indexViewStyle``(IndexViewStyle)`

This modifier defines the appearance of the scroll indicators. The argument is a structure that includes the type method **`page(backgroundDisplayMode: BackgroundDisplayMode)`** to specify the style. The method takes a structure of type **`BackgroundDisplayMode`**. This structure includes the type properties **`always`**, **`automatic`**, **`interactive`**, and **`never`**.

The **`page`** style is usually implemented when we need to provide easy access to visual content, such as images, as shown below.

Listing 5-71: Configuring the `TabView` view to show content in pages

```
struct ContentView: View {
   var body: some View {
      TabView {
         Tab {
            Image("spot1")
               .resizable()
               .scaledToFill()
               .ignoresSafeArea(.all)
         }
         Tab {
            Image("spot2")
               .resizable()
               .scaledToFill()
               .ignoresSafeArea(.all)
         }
      }
      .tabViewStyle(.page)
      .indexViewStyle(.page(backgroundDisplayMode: .always))
```

```
            .ignoresSafeArea(.all)
        }
    }
```

This view creates a **TabView** view with two tabs, but because we declare the **tabViewStyle()** modifier with the value **page**, instead of showing the tabs at the bottom, the **TabView** view allows the user to swipe the views to the left or the right, as shown below.

Figure 5-47: *Pages*

Do It Yourself

Update the **ContentView** structure with the code in Listing 5-71. Download the **spot1.jpg** and **spot2.jpg** files from our website. Create an Asset Catalog and add the images to it. Run the application on an iPhone simulator. You should be able to swipe the images to the left to reveal the next one, as shown in Figure 5-47.

PRO

Sidebar

The **tabViewStyle()** modifier also provides the option on iPads to access the buttons in a sidebar with the **sidebarAdaptable** style. On iPhones, the tabs are added to the tab bar as always, but on iPads the **TabView** view includes an additional button on the left to open the sidebar.

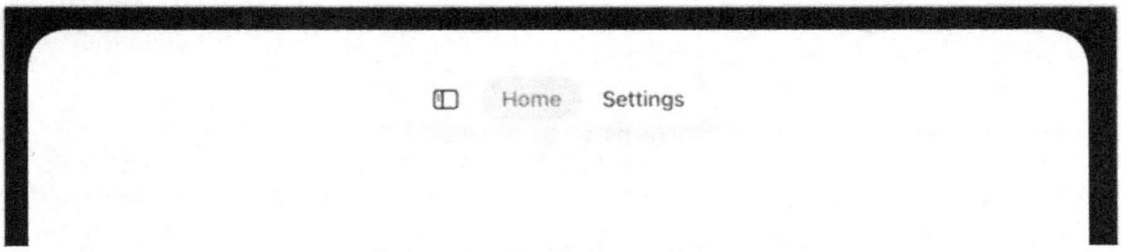

Figure 5-48: *Sidebar button*

To add this button and allow the user to open the sidebar, all we need to do is to apply the modifier to the **TabView** view, as shown below.

Listing 5-72: Expanding the `TabView` view with a sidebar

```
struct ContentView: View {
    var body: some View {
        TabView {
            Tab("Home", systemImage: "book.circle") {
                Text("Main Screen")
            }
            Tab("Settings", systemImage: "gear") {
                Text("Settings")
            }
        }
        .tabViewStyle(.sidebarAdaptable)
    }
}
```

When the button is pressed, the **TabView** view replaces the toolbar with a sidebar. If there is enough space, the sidebar is placed on the left side of the screen and the content on the right, otherwise, the sidebar is displayed over the content, as shown below.

Figure 5-49: *Sidebar*

In addition to the buttons, the sidebar can include a header, a footer, and a toolbar at the bottom. The **View** protocol includes the following modifiers for this purpose.

tabViewSidebarHeader(content: Closure)

This modifier inserts a view above the buttons. The **content** argument is the closure that provides the view to be displayed.

tabViewSidebarFooter(content: Closure)

This modifier inserts a view below the buttons. The **content** argument is the closure that provides the view to be displayed.

tabViewSidebarBottomBar(content: Closure)

This modifier inserts a view at the bottom of the sidebar. The **content** argument is the closure that provides the view to be displayed.

In the following example, we show how to create a header with a simple **Text** view.

Listing 5-73: Adding a header to the sidebar

```
struct ContentView: View {
   var body: some View {
      TabView {
         Tab("Home", systemImage: "book.circle") {
            Text("Main Screen")
         }
         Tab("Settings", systemImage: "gear") {
            Text("Settings")
         }
      }
      .tabViewStyle(.sidebarAdaptable)
      .tabViewSidebarHeader {
         Text("My Menu")
            .padding()
      }
   }
}
```

Figure 5-50: *Sidebar header*

The toolbar can only display a short list of buttons at a time, but the sidebar can display more buttons to help users find additional content. For this purpose, SwiftUI includes the **TabSection** structure. With this structure, we can create sections with tabs that can only be selected in the sidebar. The following is the structure's initializer.

TabSection(Closure, **header:** Closure**)**

This initializer creates a container for sidebar tabs. The first argument is the closure that provides the tabs, and the **header** argument is the closure that provides the view for the section's header.

The **TabSection** structure creates a container for **Tab** views. In the following example, we add a section called More Info below the Settings tab of our previous example. The section includes two **Tab** views and therefore two new buttons are added to the sidebar.

Listing 5-74: Creating a section for the sidebar

```
struct ContentView: View {
    var body: some View {
        TabView {
            Tab("Home", systemImage: "book.circle") {
                Text("Main Screen")
            }
            Tab("Settings", systemImage: "gear") {
                Text("Settings")
            }
            TabSection("More Info") {
                Tab("Additional One", systemImage: "plus") {
                    Text("Additional Tab One")
                }
                Tab("Additional Two", systemImage: "pencil") {
                    Text("Additional Tab Two")
                }
            }
        }
        .tabViewStyle(.sidebarAdaptable)
    }
}
```

The contents of the sections are only visible in the sidebar and the Sections are displayed below individual tabs, as shown below.

Figure 5-51: *Sidebar section*

Because the sidebar can contain additional buttons, the **TabView** view offers the possibility for the users to select the buttons they want to include in the sidebar and toolbar. To store the current selection, the framework defines the **TabViewCustomization** structure and the following modifiers to enable customization, and also to identify and configure the tabs.

tabViewCustomization(TabViewCustomization)

This modifier applies the configuration selected by the user to the **TabView** view. The argument is the binding property used to store and read the current configuration.

customizationID(String)

This modifier set the identifier for a tab.

customizationBehavior(TabCustomizationBehavior, **for:** AdaptableTabBarPlacement**)**

This modifier sets the configuration behavior for a tab. The first argument determines what the user is allowed to do with the tab. It is a structure with the properties **automatic**, **disabled**, and **reorderable**. The **for** argument determines where the behavior is going to be applied. It is a structure with the properties **automatic**, **sidebar**, and **tabBar**. (More than one value can be declared separated by comma.)

defaultVisibility(Visibility, **for:** AdaptableTabBarPlacement**)**

This modifier determines whether the tab is going to be included or not. The first argument is an enumeration with the values **automatic**, **visible**, and **hidden**, and the **for** argument determines where the behavior is going to be applied. It is a structure with the properties **automatic**, **sidebar**, and **tabBar**. (More than one value can be declared separated by comma.)

To enable customization, we need a binding property to store the **TabViewCustomization** structure, apply the **tabViewCustomization()** modifier to tell the **TabView** view to use this property to save and read the configuration, and finally apply the **customizationID()** modifier with a unique identifier to each tab we want the user to be able to modify.

Listing 5-75: Customizing the `TabView` view

```
struct ContentView: View {
   @State private var configuration = TabViewCustomization()

   var body: some View {
      TabView {
         Tab("Home", systemImage: "book.circle") {
            Text("Main Screen")
         }
         Tab("Settings", systemImage: "gear") {
            Text("Settings")
         }
         TabSection("More Info") {
            Tab("Additional One", systemImage: "plus") {
               Text("Additional Tab One")
            }
            .customizationID("com.formasterminds.additional1")

            Tab("Additional Two", systemImage: "pencil") {
               Text("Additional Tab Two")
            }
            .customizationID("com.formasterminds.additional2")
         }
         .customizationID("com.formasterminds.more")
      }
      .tabViewStyle(.sidebarAdaptable)
      .tabViewCustomization($configuration)
   }
}
```

When customization is enabled, the sidebar shows a button at the top to edit the tabs. After activating the editing mode, the user can drag tabs from the sidebar to the toolbar, remove tabs, or decide which tabs are going to be shown in the sidebar.

IMPORTANT

In this example, we use a **`@State`** property to save the configuration selected by the user. This means that every time the application is closed, the configuration is lost. To permanently store the changes made by the user, we can create an **`@AppStorage`** property. This type of property stores its values in a database so that they are preserved even after the application is closed. We will learn more about this property wrapper in Chapter 7.

BASIC

Tab View Implementation

A **`TabView`** view is no different from a **`NavigationStack`** view except for the way it presents the views to the user, so we can use it with our model to present a list of books and define each screen as before. For instance, we can define a **`TabView`** view that opens three views: one to show the list of books, another to configure the list, and one more to allow the user to search for a book. The following is the **`TabView`** view we need for this example.

Listing 5-76: Designing a `TabView` view to manage books

```
struct ContentView: View {
   var body: some View {
      TabView {
         Tab("Home", systemImage: "book.circle") {
            BooksView()
         }
         Tab("Settings", systemImage: "gear") {
            SettingsView()
         }
         Tab(role: .search) {
            SearchView()
         }
      }
      .tabViewStyle(.sidebarAdaptable)
   }
}
#Preview {
    ContentView()
      .environment(ApplicationData.shared)
}
```

To allow the user to change the app's configuration, we need to store the values in the model. The following are the changes we need to introduce to our previous model.

Listing 5-77: Updating the model

```
import SwiftUI

struct Book: Identifiable, Hashable {
   let id = UUID()
   var title: String
   var author: String
   var cover: String
   var year: Int
   var selected: Bool

   var displayYear: String {
      get {
         return String(year)
      }
   }
}
@Observable class ApplicationData {
   var showPictures: Bool = true
   var showYear: Bool = true

   @ObservationIgnored var userData: [Book] {
      didSet {
         filterValues(search: "")
      }
   }
   var filteredItems: [Book] = []

   func filterValues(search: String) {
      if search.isEmpty {
         filteredItems = []
      } else {
         let list = userData.filter( { item in
            return item.title.localizedStandardContains(search)
         })
         filteredItems = list.sorted(by: { $0.title < $1.title })
      }
   }
   static let shared: ApplicationData = ApplicationData()
   private init() {
      userData = [
         Book(title: "Apple Intelligence for Masterminds", author: "J.D
            Gauchat", cover: "book1", year: 2026, selected: false),
         Book(title: "Steve Jobs", author: "Isaacson", cover: "book2",
            year: 2011, selected: false),
         Book(title: "Swift for Masterminds", author: "J.D Gauchat",
            cover: "book3", year: 2026, selected: false),
         Book(title: "The C Programming Language", author: "Kernighan",
            cover: "book4", year: 1988, selected: false),
         Book(title: "Being Digital", author: "Negroponte", cover:
            "book5", year: 1996, selected: false),
         Book(title: "Only the Paranoid Survive", author: "Grove", cover:
            "book6", year: 1999, selected: false),
         Book(title: "Accidental Empires", author: "Cringely", cover:
            "book7", year: 1996, selected: false),
         Book(title: "Bobby Fischer Teaches Chess", author: "Fischer",
            cover: "book8", year: 1982, selected: false),
```

```
        Book(title: "New Guide to Science", author: "Asimov", cover:
           "book9", year: 1993, selected: false),
        Book(title: "Christine", author: "King", cover: "book10", year:
           1983, selected: false),
        Book(title: "IT", author: "King", cover: "book11", year: 1987,
           selected: false),
        Book(title: "Ending Aging", author: "Grey", cover: "book12",
           year: 2007, selected: false)
     ]
     filterValues(search: "")
   }
}
```

This model is based on the one introduced in Listing 5-16, but now we include two new properties to store Boolean values that users can change from the Settings tab, and assign an empty array to the **filteredItems** property when there is nothing to search, so the user only see results when a value is inserted into the field.

The values stored in the **showPictures** and **showYear** properties from the Settings view determine whether the list of books should include the book's cover and year of publication, so we must use them in the **BooksView** view to configure the rows, as shown below.

Listing 5-78: Designing the rows according to the app's configuration

```
import SwiftUI

struct BooksView: View {
   @Environment(ApplicationData.self) private var appData

   var body: some View {
      List(appData.userData) { book in
         CellBook(book: book)
      }
   }
}
struct CellBook: View {
   @Environment(ApplicationData.self) private var appData
   let book: Book

   var body: some View {
      HStack(alignment: .top) {
         if appData.showPictures {
            Image(book.cover)
               .resizable()
               .scaledToFit()
               .frame(width: 80, height: 100)
         }
         VStack(alignment: .leading, spacing: 2) {
            Text(book.title).bold()
            Text(book.author)
            if appData.showYear {
               Text(book.displayYear).font(.caption)
            }
            Spacer()
         }.padding(.top, 5)
         Spacer()
```

```
        }
    }
}
#Preview {
    BooksView()
        .environment(ApplicationData.shared)
}
```

The list is created from the values in the **userData** array, as always, but the rows are now designed according to the app's configuration. If the value of the **showPictures** property is **true**, we show the book's cover, and if the value of the **showYear** property is **true**, we show the year of publication. To allow the user to set these values, we must provide a form in the **SettingsView** view, as shown below.

Listing 5-79: Configuring the app

```
import SwiftUI

struct SettingsView: View {
    @Environment(ApplicationData.self) private var appData

    var body: some View {
        @Bindable var appData = appData

        Form {
            Section(header: Text("Settings"), footer: Text("Select what you
                want to see")) {
                Toggle("Show Pictures", isOn: $appData.showPictures)
                Toggle("Show Year", isOn: $appData.showYear)
            }
        }
    }
}
#Preview {
    SettingsView()
        .environment(ApplicationData.shared)
}
```

This view includes two **Toggle** views to set the values in the model. Now the user can decide what to show on the list. To complete the application, we need a view with a **TextField** view to allow the user to search for a book when the search tab is selected.

Listing 5-80: Searching for books

```
import SwiftUI

struct SearchView: View {
    @Environment(ApplicationData.self) private var appData
    @State private var searchBook: String = ""

    var body: some View {
        VStack {
```

```
         TextField("Insert Title", text: $searchBook)
            .textFieldStyle(.roundedBorder)
            .padding()
         List(appData.filteredItems) { book in
            CellBook(book: book)
         }
      }
      .onChange(of: searchBook, initial: true, {
         appData.filterValues(search: searchBook)
      })
   }
}
#Preview {
   SearchView()
      .environment(ApplicationData.shared)
}
```

Every time the user inserts a character in the field, we call the **`filterValues()`** method in the model. This method finds the books whose titles contain the text inserted by the user and adds them to the **`filteredItems`** array, so only the books that match the search appear on the list.

The application now includes a view to show the whole list of books, another to select the information we want to see on the list, and another to search for books.

Figure 5-52: `TabView` *application*

Do It Yourself

Create a new App project. Download the book covers from our website. Create an Asset Catalog and add the covers to it. Update the **`ContentView`** structure with the code in Listing 5-76. Create a new Swift file called **ApplicationData.swift** with the code in Listing 5-77. Remember to inject the **`ApplicationData`** object into the environment, as we did in Chapter 4, Listing 4-4. Create new files called **BooksView.swift**, **SettingsView.swift** and **SearchView.swift** for the codes in Listings 5-78, 5-79 and 5-80. Run the application on an iPhone simulator. Select the Settings tab and turn off the switches. You should see the books on the list without the cover and year of publication, as shown in Figure 5-52.

BASIC

5.4 - Universal Interface

Working with one view per screen is enough for small devices such as iPhones, but iPads and Macs require a more elaborate design. SwiftUI provides a container view called `NavigationSplitView` that can present two or three views on the screen at the same time. The main advantage of using this container is not only that multiple views can share the available space, but also that it automatically adapts to smaller screens or windows. As a result, we can use it to build universal interfaces that work seamlessly across iPhones, iPads, and Macs.

```
NavigationSplitView(columnVisibility: Binding, sidebar: Closure,
content: Closure, detail: Closure)
```

This initializer creates a container view to present two or three views on the screen simultaneously. The **columnVisibility** argument is a binding property that determines the visibility of the columns. This value is determined by a **`NavigationSplitViewVisibility`** structure, which includes the type properties **`automatic`**, **`all`**, **`doubleColumn`**, and **`detailOnly`**. And the **sidebar**, **content**, and **detail** arguments return the views we want to present in each column. (If we only want to present two columns, we must omit the **content** argument.)

The columns are called Sidebar, Content, and Detail, and they are interconnected. A `NavigationLink` view in the Sidebar column updates the content of the Content column, and a `NavigationLink` view in the Content column updates the content of the Detail column.

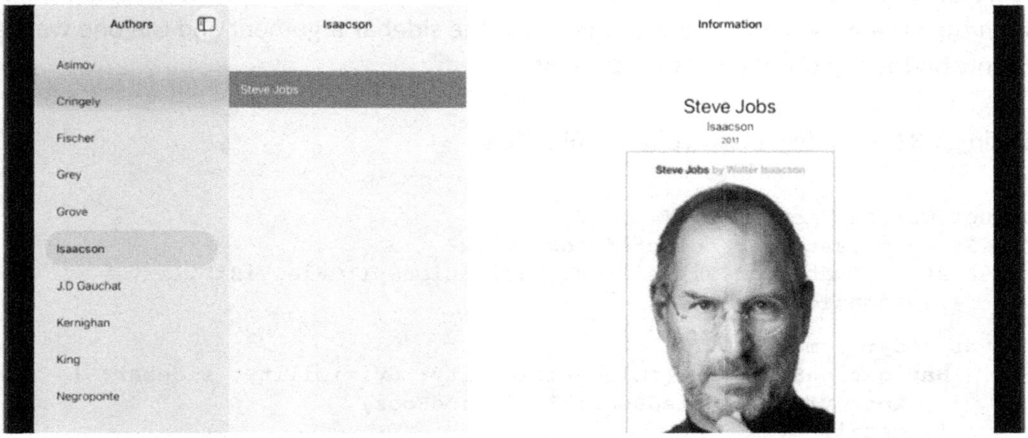

Figure 5-53: *iPad app configured with three columns*

The Sidebar and Content columns are removable, and are presented on the screen depending on the number of columns and the space available. By default, on iPads we get two columns in landscape mode and only one in portrait mode, and on iPhones, the columns are displayed as in a `NavigationStack` view, as shown below.

Figure 5-54: `NavigationSplitView` view *on iPhones in portrait mode*

The Content and Detail columns display the content selected by the user. If no content has been selected yet, these columns remain empty. In this situation, it is recommended to present a view that clearly communicates the absence of content to the user. For this purpose, the framework provides the **`ContentUnavailableView`**. The following is the view's initializer.

> **`ContentUnavailableView(label:`** `Closure,` **`description:`** `Closure,` **`actions:`** `Closure)`

This initializer creates placeholder view. The **label** argument generates the view used as the label, the **description** argument generates the view used as the description, and the **actions** argument generates the views that present the actions the user can perform from this view.

A **`NavigationSplitView`** view may contain two or three columns. A two columns design is very common. The interface is simple. We define the **`NavigationSplitView`** view and assign the view we want to show on the left to the **sidebar** argument and the one we want to show on the right to the **detail** argument.

Listing 5-81: Defining a two-column split view

```
struct ContentView: View {
   @State private var selectedBook: Book?
   @State private var visibility: NavigationSplitViewVisibility =
      .automatic

   var body: some View {
      NavigationSplitView(columnVisibility: $visibility, sidebar: {
         BooksView(selectedBook: $selectedBook)
      }, detail: {
         if let book = selectedBook {
            DetailView(book: book)
         } else {
            ContentUnavailableView {
               Label("No Book", systemImage: "book.fill")
            } description: {
               Text("Select a book from the list.")
            }
         }
```

```
        })
    }
}
#Preview {
    ContentView()
        .environment(ApplicationData.shared)
}
```

To keep track of the selected items, the **NavigationSplitView** view works with **List** selection. In our example, we include a **@State** property called **selectedBook** to store the book selected by the user, another for the **NavigationSplitView** view to store the columns' visibility state, and the view itself with two columns. The column on the left (Sidebar) opens the **BooksView** view with a list of books, and the column on the right (Detail) opens the **DetailView** view with information about the selected book (or a placeholder view if no book was selected yet).

When a book is selected, the **Book** structure that represents the book is assigned to the **selectedBook** property, the content of the **ContentView** view is recreated, and a new **DetailView** view opens on the right column to present the book on the screen. To know when a new row has been selected, we pass a reference of the **selectedBook** property to the **BooksView** view. Therefore, every time the user selects a book in the **BooksView** view, the value is stored in the **selectedBook** property, and the interface is updated.

For the selection to work, the **BooksView** view must include a **List** view connected to the **selectedBook** property and also create the rows with a **NavigationLink** view identified with a value that matches the value stored in that property, as shown below.

Listing 5-82: Defining the view for the left column

```
import SwiftUI

struct BooksView: View {
    @Environment(ApplicationData.self) private var appData
    @Binding var selectedBook: Book?

    var body: some View {
        List(appData.userData, selection: $selectedBook) { book in
            NavigationLink(value: book, label: {
                Text(book.title)
            })
        }
        .listStyle(.sidebar)
        .navigationTitle("Books")
    }
}
#Preview {
    @Previewable @State var selected: Book? = nil

    BooksView(selectedBook: $selected)
        .environment(ApplicationData.shared)
}
```

The **DetailView** view for this example is similar to the one we created earlier for an iPhone application. We need to receive the **Book** structure representing the book selected by the user and display it on the screen.

Listing 5-83: Defining the Detail view

```
import SwiftUI

struct DetailView: View {
   let book: Book

   var body: some View {
      VStack {
         Text(book.title)
            .font(.title)
         Text(book.author)
         Text(book.displayYear)
            .font(.caption)
         Image(book.cover)
            .resizable()
            .scaledToFit()
            .frame(maxWidth: 300)
         Spacer()
      }.padding()
      .navigationTitle(Text("Information"))
   }
}
#Preview {
   DetailView(book: ApplicationData.shared.userData[1])
}
```

The result is the same as before, but the interface is now presented according to the device on which the app is running, as shown below.

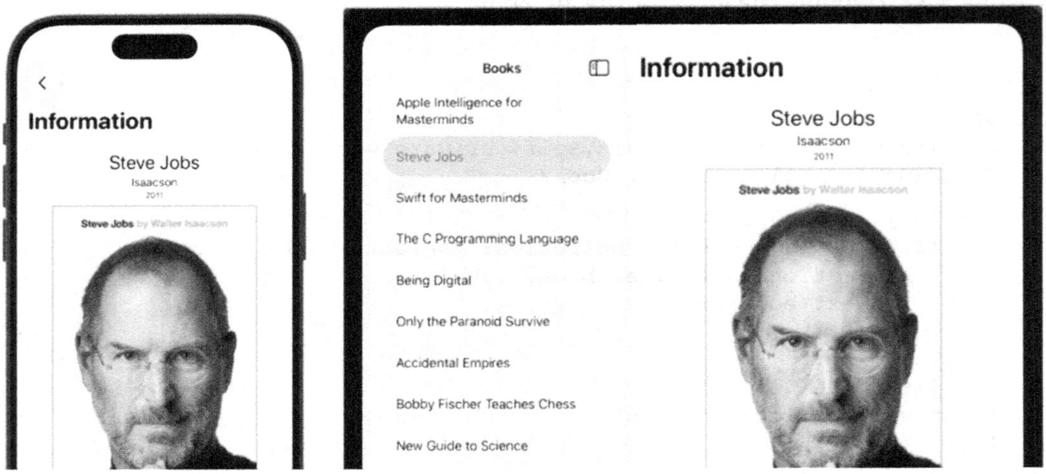

***Figure 5-55:** Different design for iPhones and iPads*

Do It Yourself

Create a new App project. Download the book covers from our website. Create an Asset Catalog and add the covers to it. Update the **ContentView.swift** file with the code in Listing 5-81. Create a new SwiftUI file called **BooksView.swift** for the code in Listing 5-82, and another called

DetailView.swift for the code in Listing 5-83. Create a Swift file called **ApplicationData.swift** for the model in Chapter 4, Listing 4-3. Remember to inject the `ApplicationData` object into the environment, as we did in Chapter 4, Listing 4-4. Run the application on an iPad simulator and select a book. You should see the interface illustrated in Figure 5-55, right. Repeat the process on the iPhone simulator to see how it looks on that device.

IMPORTANT

In this example, we use the same detail view on every device, so the interface looks identical regardless of where the app is running. However, a well-designed interface should adapt to the available space. We will learn how to build multi-platform applications that adjust to each device in Chapter 6.

When our app is launched on a device with a large screen, the interface is presented in two columns. The column on the left shows the list of books, and the column on the right shows the placeholder view. This view is replaced by the `DetailView` view when a book is selected from the list. Depending on the characteristics of our application, sometimes it might be better to show an item by default. For instance, we can show the `DetailView` view instead of the placeholder view when there are books available in the model, as shown below.

Listing 5-84: Showing an item by default

```
struct ContentView: View {
   @Environment(ApplicationData.self) private var appData
   @State private var selectedBook: Book?
   @State private var visibility: NavigationSplitViewVisibility =
      .automatic

   var body: some View {
      NavigationSplitView(columnVisibility: $visibility, sidebar: {
         BooksView(selectedBook: $selectedBook)
      }, detail: {
         if let book = selectedBook {
            DetailView(book: book)
         } else {
            ContentUnavailableView {
               Label("No Book", systemImage: "book.fill")
            } description: {
               Text("Select a book from the list.")
            }
         }
      })
      .onAppear {
         if let book = appData.userData.first {
            selectedBook = book
         }
```

```
            }
        }
    }
```

Although we could get a book from the model and show the **DetailView** view with it, it is better to assign that book to the **selectedBook** property instead. This way, the item is also selected in the **List** view. In our example, we use the **onAppear()** modifier for this purpose. On iPhones in portrait, the application works as before, but on iPads, the first row is selected and the book is shown on the screen.

Do It Yourself

Update the **ContentView** structure with the code in Listing 5-84. Run the application on an iPad simulator. You should see the first book found in the **userData** array on the screen.

The view on the right is just one view, but we can allow the user to navigate to other views by embedding the **DetailView** view in a **NavigationStack** view. To control the navigation, we need to add a **NavigationPath** property, as shown below.

Listing 5-85: Enabling navigation in the right column

```
struct ContentView: View {
    @State private var selectedBook: Book?
    @State private var path = NavigationPath()
    @State private var visibility: NavigationSplitViewVisibility =
        .automatic

    var body: some View {
        NavigationSplitView(columnVisibility: $visibility, sidebar: {
            BooksView(selectedBook: $selectedBook)
        }, detail: {
            NavigationStack(path: $path) {
                if let book = selectedBook {
                    DetailView(path: $path, book: book)
                } else {
                    ContentUnavailableView {
                        Label("No Book", systemImage: "book.fill")
                    } description: {
                        Text("Select a book from the list.")
                    }
                }
            }
        })
        .onChange(of: selectedBook, initial: false) { _, _ in
            path = NavigationPath()
        }
    }
}
```

The procedure is the same one we used earlier to control the navigation path. We declare a **NavigationPath** property and use it to initialize the **NavigationStack** view. However, because we are enabling navigation for the right column, we must pass a reference to this path to the **DetailView** view. To ensure that the navigation path always starts with the **DetailView** view, we clear the **NavigationPath** structure when a book is selected, that is, when the value of the **selectedBook** property changes. As a result, when this application is launched, the **DetailView** view becomes the initial view of the navigation stack, so the rest of the navigation is managed from this view. We can, for instance, allow the user to tap on the cover to expand it, as shown below.

Listing 5-86: Creating a navigation path for the right column

```
import SwiftUI

struct DetailView: View {
   @Binding var path: NavigationPath
   let book: Book

   var body: some View {
      VStack {
         Text(book.title)
            .font(.title)
         Text(book.author)
         Text(book.displayYear)
            .font(.caption)
         Button(action: {
            path.append("Picture View")
         }, label: {
            Image(book.cover)
               .resizable()
               .scaledToFit()
               .frame(maxWidth: 300)
         })
         Spacer()
      }.padding()
      .navigationTitle(Text("Information"))
      .navigationDestination(for: String.self, destination: { _ in
         PictureView(book: book)
      })
   }
}
#Preview {
   @Previewable @State var navigation = NavigationPath()
   DetailView(path: $navigation, book: ApplicationData.shared.userData[1])
}
```

This **DetailView** view receives a reference to the **path** property so it can add or remove views from the navigation stack. To modify the path, we embed the book's cover in a **Button** view. When the user presses the button, the **append()** method adds a **String** value to the **path** property, the **navigationDestination()** modifier detects this value, and the **NavigationStack** view then opens the **PictureView** view to display the expanded cover on the screen. The following is our implementation of this view.

Listing 5-87: Expanding the cover

```
import SwiftUI

struct PictureView: View {
    let book: Book

    var body: some View {
        VStack {
            Image(book.cover)
                .resizable()
                .scaledToFit()
                .padding(20)
            Spacer()
        }
    }
}
#Preview {
    NavigationStack {
        PictureView(book: ApplicationData.shared.userData[0])
    }
}
```

Do It Yourself

Update the `ContentView` structure with the code in Listing 5-85 and the **DetailView.swift** file with the code in Listing 5-86. Create a SwiftUI file called **PictureView.swift** for the code in Listing 5-87. Run the application on an iPad simulator, select a book and tap the cover. You should see the `PictureView` view on the right column transitioning from right to left. Select another book. You should see the `DetailView` view again in the right column.

We can also add navigation to the left column (Sidebar). The problem is that `NavigationLink` views in the left column always open the destination view in the right column. To change this behavior, the framework provides the following modifier.

isDetailLink(Bool)

This modifier determines whether the link will open in the Detail column or not (`true` or `false`).

If we apply this modifier with the value `false` to a `NavigationLink` view in the left column, the view will open in the same column. For instance, we can embed the `BooksView` view in a `NavigationStack` view and add a button to the navigation bar to allow the user to configure the list of books.

Listing 5-88: Adding navigation to the left column

```
struct ContentView: View {
   @State private var selectedBook: Book?
   @State private var path = NavigationPath()
   @State private var visibility: NavigationSplitViewVisibility =
.automatic

   var body: some View {
      NavigationSplitView(columnVisibility: $visibility, sidebar: {
         NavigationStack {
            BooksView(selectedBook: $selectedBook)
         }
      }, detail: {
         NavigationStack(path: $path) {
            if let book = selectedBook {
               DetailView(path: $path, book: book)
            } else {
               ContentUnavailableView {
                  Label("No Book", systemImage: "book.fill")
               } description: {
                  Text("Select a book from the list.")
               }
            }
         }
      })
      .onChange(of: selectedBook, initial: false) { _, _ in
         path = NavigationPath()
      }
   }
}
```

To open the view, we must add the button in the **BooksView** view with a **NavigationLink** associated to a value. In this case, we use a string and open a view called **SettingsView** when the button is pressed.

Listing 5-89: Opening a view on the left column

```
struct BooksView: View {
   @Environment(ApplicationData.self) private var appData
   @Binding var selectedBook: Book?

   var body: some View {
      List(appData.userData, selection: $selectedBook) { book in
         NavigationLink(value: book, label: {
            Text(book.title)
         })
      }
      .listStyle(.sidebar)
      .navigationTitle("Books")
      .toolbar {
         ToolbarItem(placement: .topBarTrailing) {
            NavigationLink(value: "Settings View", label: {
               Image(systemName: "gear")
            })
```

```
                .isDetailLink(false)
            }
        }
        .navigationDestination(for: String.self, destination: { _ in
            SettingsView()
        })
    }
}
```

The **BooksView** view now includes an item in the navigation bar defined by a **NavigationLink** view and an SF Symbol that opens a view to configure the application, but because we applied the **isDetailLink()** modifier with the value **false**, the **SettingsView** view opens in the same column, as shown below.

Figure 5-56: *Link opens the view in the left column*

Do It Yourself

Update the **ContentView** structure with the code in Listing 5-88 and the **BooksView** structure with the code in Listing 5-89. Create a SwiftUI file called **SettingsView.swift** with just a **Text** view to show the message "Settings View". Run the application on an iPad simulator. Press the Settings button in the navigation bar. You should see the **SettingsView** view open in the left column, as shown in Figure 5-56 (right).

PRO

Three-Columns Layout

A **NavigationSplitView** view can present up to three columns. So far, we have been using the two-column layout, but we can add one more by including the **content** argument in the **NavigationSplitView**'s initializer. In a three-column layout, the links in the Sidebar column update the content in the Content column, and the links in the Content column update the content in the Detail column. Therefore, we have two columns on the left to select information and a column on the right to show it.

This process is not automatic, we need to prepare the data in the model to feed the views. For instance, if we want to show a list of authors in the first column, and the books that belong to the selected author in the second column, as we do in the example in Figure

5-53, the model must provide the list of values in that order. How we organize and store this data in our model depends on the characteristics of the application. For our example, we are going to store the list of books in an array and implement a method that extracts the names of the authors from it.

Listing 5-90: Providing the list of authors

```
@Observable class ApplicationData {
   @ObservationIgnored var userData: [Book] = [] {
      didSet {
         updateAuthors()
      }
   }
   var listAuthors: [String] = []

   func updateAuthors() {
      var list: [String] = []
      for name in userData.map({ $0.author }) {
         if !list.contains(name) {
            list.append(name)
         }
      }
      listAuthors = list.sorted(by: { $0 < $1 })
   }
   static let shared: ApplicationData = ApplicationData()
   private init() {
      userData = [
         Book(title: "Apple Intelligence for Masterminds", author: "J.D
            Gauchat", cover: "book1", year: 2026, selected: false),
         Book(title: "Steve Jobs", author: "Isaacson", cover: "book2",
            year: 2011, selected: false),
         Book(title: "Swift for Masterminds", author: "J.D Gauchat",
            cover: "book3", year: 2026, selected: false),
         Book(title: "The C Programming Language", author: "Kernighan",
            cover: "book4", year: 1988, selected: false),
         Book(title: "Being Digital", author: "Negroponte", cover:
            "book5", year: 1996, selected: false),
         Book(title: "Only the Paranoid Survive", author: "Grove", cover:
            "book6", year: 1999, selected: false),
         Book(title: "Accidental Empires", author: "Cringely", cover:
            "book7", year: 1996, selected: false),
         Book(title: "Bobby Fischer Teaches Chess", author: "Fischer",
            cover: "book8", year: 1982, selected: false),
         Book(title: "New Guide to Science", author: "Asimov", cover:
            "book9", year: 1993, selected: false),
         Book(title: "Christine", author: "King", cover: "book10", year:
            1983, selected: false),
         Book(title: "IT", author: "King", cover: "book11", year: 1987,
            selected: false),
         Book(title: "Ending Aging", author: "Grey", cover: "book12",
            year: 2007, selected: false)
      ]
      updateAuthors()
   }
}
```

This new **ApplicationData** class implements the **userData** property to store the books, as before, but now also includes a new observable property called **listAuthors** to store the authors' names. To extract the authors from the data, we created a method named **updateAuthors()**. This method retrieves the authors' names using the **map()** method and assigns them to the **listAuthors** property in alphabetical order. Note that before adding a name, we check whether it already exists to avoid duplicates (**!list.contains(name)**).

The **updateAuthors()** method should be called every time the values in the **userData** property change to keep the views up to date. In our example, we call it after the property is initialized with testing values, and also with a property observer applied to the **userData** property, so the authors are updated every time a book is added or removed from the model.

Now that we have the values for the first column, it is time to define the three-column layout in the **ContentView** view.

Listing 5-91: Defining a three-column layout

```
struct ContentView: View {
   @State private var selectedAuthor: String?
   @State private var selectedBook: Book?
   @State private var visibility: NavigationSplitViewVisibility =
      .automatic

   var body: some View {
      NavigationSplitView(columnVisibility: $visibility, sidebar: {
         AuthorsView(selectedAuthor: $selectedAuthor)
      }, content: {
         BooksView(selectedBook: $selectedBook, selectedAuthor:
            selectedAuthor)
      }, detail: {
         if let book = selectedBook {
            DetailView(book: book)
         } else {
            ContentUnavailableView {
               Label("No Book", systemImage: "book.fill")
            } description: {
               Text("Select a book from the list.")
            }
         }
      })
   }
}
```

Because we now have two columns with lists of values the user can choose from, we need two properties to store the selection. In this example, we call them **selectedAuthor** and **selectedBook**. The view in the first column, called **AuthorsView**, presents the list of authors available, so we pass a reference to the **selectedAuthor** property to capture the user's selection. On the other hand, the view in the second column, called **BooksView**, presents the list of books that belong to the selected author, so we need to pass a reference to the **selectedBook** property to control selection and also the value of the **selectedAuthor** property to filter the books by author.

The **AuthorsView** view must create a list of authors and allow the user to select one. The code is similar to previous examples, as shown below.

Listing 5-92: Showing the authors

```
import SwiftUI

struct AuthorsView: View {
   @Environment(ApplicationData.self) private var appData
   @Binding var selectedAuthor: String?

   var body: some View {
      List(appData.listAuthors, id: \.self, selection: $selectedAuthor) {
         author in
         NavigationLink(value: author, label: {
            Text(author)
         })
      }
      .listStyle(.sidebar)
      .navigationTitle("Authors")
   }
}
#Preview {
   @Previewable @State var selected: String? = nil
   AuthorsView(selectedAuthor: $selected)
      .environment(ApplicationData.shared)
}
```

The `BooksView` view is also similar to previous examples, but now we must show only the list of books that belong to the author selected by the user. To filter the values, we define a computed property called `listBooks` and use it to feed the `List` view.

Listing 5-93: Showing the books

```
struct BooksView: View {
   @Environment(ApplicationData.self) private var appData
   @Binding var selectedBook: Book?
   let selectedAuthor: String?

   var listBooks: [Book] {
      let list = appData.userData.filter({ item in
         return item.author == selectedAuthor
      })
      return list.sorted(by: { $0.title < $1.title })
   }
   var body: some View {
      List(listBooks, selection: $selectedBook) { book in
         NavigationLink(value: book, label: {
            Text(book.title)
         })
      }.listStyle(.grouped)
      .toolbarTitleDisplayMode(.inline)
      .navigationTitle(selectedAuthor ?? "Undefined")
   }
}
#Preview {
   @Previewable @State var selected: Book? = nil
```

```
    BooksView(selectedBook: $selected, selectedAuthor: nil)
        .environment(ApplicationData.shared)
}
```

The **listBooks** property gets the author's books and returns them in alphabetical order. The rest of the view is the same as before. We create a **List** view with these values and embed the rows in a **NavigationLink** view to allow the user to select them.

Do It Yourself

Update the **ApplicationData.swift** file with the code in Listing 5-90 and the **ContentView** structure with the code in Listing 5-91. Create a new SwiftUI file called **AuthorsView.swift** for the code in Listing 5-92. Update the **BooksView** structure with the code in Listing 5-93. The **DetailView** view used in this example is the same defined for previous examples (see Listing 5-83). Run the application on an iPad simulator in landscape orientation. Press the button on the top-left corner. You should see the three columns on the screen, as shown in Figure 5-53. Run the application again on the iPhone simulator to see how the columns are presented on that device.

BASIC

Configuration

The width of the columns, which columns are visible, and how they are presented on the screen are determined by the available space. However, we can suggest a specific configuration, and the system will try to honor it when possible. One option is to suggest how many columns should be visible by modifying the value of the binding property assigned to the **columnVisibility** argument. We can ask the system to display all columns (**all**), only the Content and Detail columns (**doubleColumn**), or only the Detail column (**detailOnly**). For example, we can hide the left column when an item is selected.

Listing 5-94: Hiding columns programmatically

```
struct ContentView: View {
    @State private var selectedAuthor: String?
    @State private var selectedBook: Book?
    @State private var visibility: NavigationSplitViewVisibility =
        .automatic

    var body: some View {
        NavigationSplitView(columnVisibility: $visibility, sidebar: {
            AuthorsView(selectedAuthor: $selectedAuthor)
        }, content: {
            BooksView(selectedBook: $selectedBook, selectedAuthor:
                selectedAuthor)
        }, detail: {
```

```
            if let book = selectedBook {
               DetailView(book: book)
            } else {
               ContentUnavailableView {
                  Label("No Book", systemImage: "book.fill")
               } description: {
                  Text("Select a book from the list.")
               }
            }
         })
         .onChange(of: selectedBook, initial: false) { _, _ in
            visibility = .detailOnly
         }
      }
   }
```

This example applies the **onChange()** modifier to change the value of the **visibility** property to **detailOnly** when a book is selected. This closes the columns on the left and expands the column on the right to take up all the space available.

Do It Yourself

Update the **ContentView** structure with the code in Listing 5-94. Run the application on an iPad simulator. Press the button to open the columns on the left. Select an author and a book. You should see the selected book on the right and the rest of the columns should be removed from the screen.

In a three-column design, the Detail column is displaced to the right when the columns on the left become visible. The **NavigationSplitView** view implements the following modifiers to configure this behavior and define the width of the columns.

navigationSplitViewStyle(NavigationSplitViewStyle**)**

This modifier defines how the Detail column is displayed when other columns are present. The argument is a structure that conforms to the **NavigationSplitViewStyle** protocol. The protocol defines the type properties **automatic** (default), **balanced** (the size of the Detail column is reduced to make room for the rest of the columns), and **prominentDetail** (the size of the Detail column is maintain and the rest of the columns are overlaid on top).

navigationSplitViewColumnWidth(CGFloat**)**

This modifier defines a fixed width for the column.

navigationSplitViewColumnWidth(min: CGFloat?, **ideal:** CGFloat, **max:** CGFloat?**)**

This modifier defines a flexible column but with constraints.

The style is applied to the **NavigationSplitView** view, but the width is applied to the columns. In the following example, we set the width for the Sidebar and Content columns to

200 points, and apply the **prominentDetail** style to the view, so the columns on the left open over the Detail column but take up only a portion of the screen.

Listing 5-95: Configuring the columns

```
struct ContentView: View {
    @State private var selectedAuthor: String?
    @State private var selectedBook: Book?
    @State private var visibility: NavigationSplitViewVisibility =
       .automatic

    var body: some View {
       NavigationSplitView(columnVisibility: $visibility, sidebar: {
          AuthorsView(selectedAuthor: $selectedAuthor)
             .navigationSplitViewColumnWidth(200)
       }, content: {
          BooksView(selectedBook: $selectedBook, selectedAuthor:
             selectedAuthor)
             .navigationSplitViewColumnWidth(200)
       }, detail: {
          if let book = selectedBook {
             DetailView(book: book)
          } else {
             ContentUnavailableView {
                Label("No Book", systemImage: "book.fill")
             } description: {
                Text("Select a book from the list.")
             }
          }
       })
       .navigationSplitViewStyle(.prominentDetail)
    }
}
```

Do It Yourself

Update the **ContentView** structure with the code in Listing 5-95. Run the application on an iPad simulator and press the button to reveal the left columns. The columns are now only 200 points wide. Select a book. You should see the book displayed in the detail view, below the other columns. Tap the detail view to remove the columns. Try different configurations to see how the columns are shown and how they respond to user interaction.

Chapter 6

Multiplatform Applications

BASIC

6.1 - Adaptivity

SwiftUI allows us to build applications that run on devices with very different characteristics, including iPhones, iPads, and Macs. For many years, developers designed user interfaces specifically for each device. If an app ran on both iPhones and iPads, it typically included different views optimized for each one of those devices. This approach began to change with the introduction of resizable windows on iPad. Instead of designing interfaces for a fixed screen size, developers were encouraged to create layouts that adapt to the available space. At first, this was optional, and apps could still rely on full-screen interfaces that ignored window resizing. Today, however, adaptive layouts have become the standard. As Apple's ecosystem continues to expand with devices that support different screen sizes and window configurations, applications are expected to present interfaces that fully adapt to the available space, regardless of the device on which they are running. SwiftUI provides several tools to build adaptive interfaces, but the primary mechanism recommended by Apple is Size Classes.

BASIC

Size Classes

Size classes are a way to measure variations in the space available. Instead of relying on specific devices or screen dimensions, SwiftUI classifies the available horizontal and vertical space into two categories: **Compact** and **Regular**. A Compact size class indicates limited space, while a Regular size class indicates enough space to present a large interface. To detect the current size class, SwiftUI provides the following environment properties.

`horizontalSizeClass`

This property contains a **`UserInterfaceSizeClass`** value that represents the current horizontal size class of the window. Possible values are **`compact`** and **`regular`**.

`verticalSizeClass`

This property contains a **`UserInterfaceSizeClass`** value that represents the current vertical size class of the window. Possible values are **`compact`** and **`regular`**.

Usually, all we need in order to adapt an interface is to determine whether the available horizontal space is compact or regular. The following example shows a basic implementation. We read the **horizontalSizeClass** from the environment and present one view or another depending on its value.

Listing 6-1: Adapting the interface to the horizontal space available

```
struct ContentView: View {
   @Environment(\.horizontalSizeClass) var HSize

   var body: some View {
      Group {
         if HSize == .compact {
            Text("Small Interface")
         } else {
            Text("Large Interface")
         }
      }
   }
}
```

Do It Yourself

Create a new App project. Update the **ContentView** structure with the code in Listing 6-1. Enable resizable windows in the Canvas (see Chapter 1, Figure 1-17, number 2), or run the application in the iPad simulator. Resize the window. You should see the text on the screen change according to the available horizontal space.

Although we can perform this process for every view and every screen, the approach depends on the application. If all we need is to present the same views on every device and adjust only certain aspects of the layout, we can use a **NavigationSplitView** container (see Universal Interface in Chapter 5). However, if the application must provide a different interface or different functionality for each size class, this approach is not enough. In these cases, we can define two separate interfaces: one for the compact size class and another for the regular size class.

When we need to adapt many aspects of the interface, it is better to control the state from the data model, so we can check these values anywhere we want. The following example implements a data model that keeps track of the current size class and includes properties to inform the views of every change.

Listing 6-2: Managing the app's current state

```
import SwiftUI

enum LayoutMode: Equatable {
   case small
   case large
}
```

```
@Observable class ApplicationData {
   var mode: LayoutMode = .small

   func update(horizontalSizeClass: UserInterfaceSizeClass?) {
      let newMode: LayoutMode = horizontalSizeClass == .regular ? .large
         : .small
      guard mode != newMode else { return }
      mode = newMode
   }
   static let shared: ApplicationData = ApplicationData()
   private init() { }
}
```

This model includes an enumeration to define values that represent each type of interface (**small** and **large**), a property to store this value, and a method called **update()** to update it. Now, we need to call this method from the main view every time the horizontal size class changes, so we can keep the value and all the views updated, as shown below.

Listing 6-3: Updating the app's interface to the horizontal size class

```
struct ContentView: View {
   @Environment(ApplicationData.self) private var appData
   @Environment(\.horizontalSizeClass) private var hSize

   var body: some View {
      Group {
         switch appData.mode {
         case .small:
            NavigationStack {
               Text("Interface for small window")
            }
         case .large:
            NavigationSplitView {
               Text("Menu for large window")
            } detail: {
               Text("Content for large window")
            }
         }
      }
      .onAppear {
         appData.update(horizontalSizeClass: hSize)
      }
      .onChange(of: hSize) { _, new in
         appData.update(horizontalSizeClass: new)
      }
   }
}
#Preview {
   ContentView()
      .environment(ApplicationData.shared)
}
```

As before, we read the **horizontalSizeClass** property to get the current horizontal size class, but now we apply the **onAppear** and **onChange** modifiers to send this value to the model. To create the interface, we read the value of the **mode** property from the model and present a **NavigationStack** container if the space is narrow or a **NavigationSplitView** container if there is room for two or more columns, defining two completely different interfaces for each class. The result is shown below.

Figure 6-1: *Adaptive interface*

Do It Yourself

Create a new Swift file called **ApplicationData.swift** for the model in Listing 6-2. Update the **ContentView** structure with the code in Listing 6-3. Remember to inject the **ApplicationData** object into the environment, as we did in Chapter 4, Listing 4-4. Enable resizable windows in the Canvas (see Chapter 1, Figure 1-17, number 2), or run the application in the iPhone and iPad simulators. You should see a different interface depending on the horizontal space available, as shown in Figure 6-1.

IMPORTANT

In this example, we use **Text** views as placeholders for the different views, but you can display a menu view, a detail view, a settings view, or any other views needed to define the navigation path for each type of interface. By reading the **mode** property, you can also control which views appear in the containers and customize every aspect of the layout depending on the space available.

PRO

Geometry Reader

In most situations, size classes provide enough information to adapt the interface to work on every screen, but sometimes we may need to fine-tune the interface to more specific sizes. For this purpose, SwiftUI includes the **GeometryReader** view. This view measures the size of its container and provides that information to its child views, allowing them to adapt their layout accordingly.

GeometryReader(content: Closure)

This initializer creates a **GeometryReader** view. The closure assigned to the **content** argument contains the views we want to adapt. This closure receives a **GeometryProxy** value with the container's position and dimensions.

The **GeometryReader** view adapts to the size of its container and then passes a **GeometryProxy** structure to the closure with the container's size and position. The structure includes the following properties and method.

size

This property returns a **CGSize** value with the width and height of the **GeometryReader** view.

safeAreaInsets

This property returns an **EdgeInsets** value with the insets of the safe area.

frame(in: CoordinateSpace)

This method returns a **CGRect** value with the position and size of the **GeometryReader** view. The values are returned according to the coordinate space specified by the **in** argument. The argument is an enumeration with the values **global**, **local**, and **named(String)**.

By combining size classes with a **GeometryReader**, we can adapt our interface to every situation. The following is a possible implementation. We first need to add a property and a method to the data model to keep track of the information, as shown below.

Listing 6-4: Using a GeometryReader **to fine tune the interface**

```
@Observable class ApplicationData {
   var mode: LayoutMode = .small
   var isLandscape: Bool = false
   var columnVisibility: NavigationSplitViewVisibility = .detailOnly

   func update(horizontalSizeClass: UserInterfaceSizeClass?) {
      let newMode: LayoutMode = horizontalSizeClass == .regular ? .large
         : .small
      guard mode != newMode else { return }
      mode = newMode
   }
   func updateGeometry(size: CGSize) {
      let newIsLandscape = size.width > size.height
      let newVisibility: NavigationSplitViewVisibility = newIsLandscape ?
         .all : .detailOnly
      guard isLandscape != newIsLandscape || columnVisibility !=
         newVisibility else { return }
      isLandscape = newIsLandscape
      columnVisibility = newVisibility
   }
   static let shared: ApplicationData = ApplicationData()
   private init() { }
}
```

This model includes two new properties. The **isLandscape** property is used to report to the views whether the interface is in landscape or portrait mode, and the **columnVisibility** property stores the current state of the **NavigationSplitView**. To update these values, we define the **updateGeometry()** method. This method receives the current size, compares the width with the height to determine the current orientation (portrait or landscape), and then updates the properties accordingly.

In this example, if the interface is in portrait mode, we assign the **detailOnly** mode to the **NavigationSplitView**, so the left column is hidden. Now, we must update the main view to respond to this value, as shown below.

Listing 6-5: Adapting the interface to the current orientation

```
struct ContentView: View {
   @Environment(ApplicationData.self) private var appData
   @Environment(\.horizontalSizeClass) private var hSize

   var body: some View {
      @Bindable var appData = appData

      Group {
            switch appData.mode {
            case .small:
                 NavigationStack {
                    VStack {
                       Text("Interface for small window")
                          .font(.system(size: 26))
                          .padding(.top, 150)
                       Spacer()
                    }
                 }
            case .large:
               NavigationSplitView(columnVisibility: $appData.
                  columnVisibility) {
                    VStack {
                       Text("Menu for large window")
                          .font(.system(size: 26))
                          .padding(.top, 150)
                       Spacer()
                    }
                 } detail: {
                    VStack {
                       Text("Content for large window")
                          .font(.system(size: 36))
                          .padding(.top, 150)
                       Spacer()
                    }
                 }
            }
         }
         .onAppear {
            appData.update(horizontalSizeClass: hSize)
         }
         .onChange(of: hSize) { _, new in
            appData.update(horizontalSizeClass: new)
         }
```

```
        .background {
            GeometryReader { proxy in
                Color.clear
                    .onAppear {
                        appData.updateGeometry(size: proxy.size)
                    }
                    .onChange(of: proxy.size) { _, size in
                        appData.updateGeometry(size: size)
                    }
            }
        }
    }
}
```

There are two additions to this view from the previous example. Now the **NavigationSplitView** container responds to the visibility state set by the **columnVisibility** property, and we apply a **background()** modifier to the **Group** view to determine its size. For this purpose, we implement the **GeometryReader** with a clear **Color** view. The **GeometryReader** expands to occupy the space available (all the space occupied by the **Group** view), and the **Color** view does the same, so by measuring the size of this view, we get the size of the interface. These values are sent to the model, and the model compares them to determine the orientation. As a result, now we have three different interfaces. When the app is displayed in a small window, we show a single view within a **NavigationStack**; when the window is large, we show two columns with a **NavigationSplitView**; but when the app is displayed on a large window but in a narrow space, such as an iPad in portrait mode, the left column is hidden, as shown below.

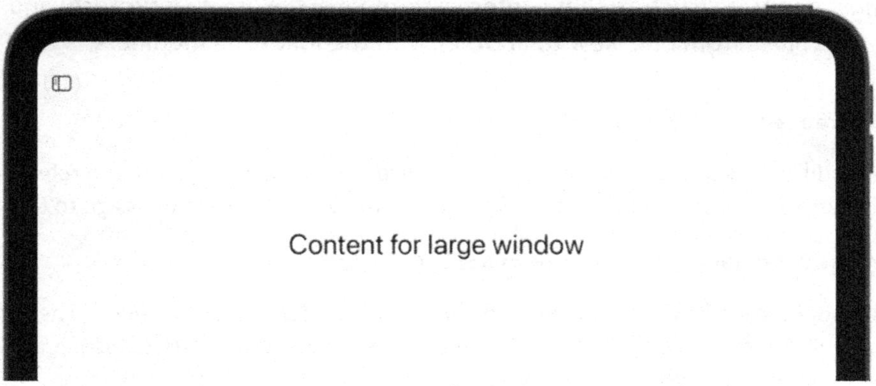

Figure 6-2: *Large interface in portrait mode*

Do It Yourself

Update the **ApplicationData** class with the code in Listing 6-4 and the **ContentView** structure with the code in Listing 6-5. Run the application on an iPad simulator in portrait mode. You should see the content for a large window, but with the left column hidden, as shown in Figure 6-2.

PRO

Preferences

The **GeometryReader** view sends the information down the hierarchy. Only the views within the **GeometryReader** view can read and use these values. If we need to send the values up the hierarchy, we must use Preferences. Despite what the name suggests, Preferences are just named values that we can generate from a view and read from the rest of the views in the hierarchy. For instance, if we have a **Text** view inside a **VStack** view, the preference values generated by the **Text** view are accessible from the **VStack** view.

Preference values are stored in what is called a Preference Key. This is a structure that conforms to the **PreferenceKey** protocol. The protocol has the following requirements.

Value

This property is an associated type that defines the data type of the values we are going to work with.

defaultValue

This property defines the value the Preference Key is going to have by default.

reduce(value: Value, **nextValue:** Closure**)**

This method adds a new value to the structure. The **value** argument is a reference to the values stored in the structure from previous calls, and the **nextValue** argument is a closure that returns the new value.

We must define a structure that conforms to the **PreferenceKey** protocol and then use it to pass the values from one view to another with the following modifiers.

preference(key: Type, **value:** Value)

This modifier sets a value for a specific preference key. The **key** argument is a reference to the key's data type, and the **value** argument is the value we want to assign to that key.

onPreferenceChange(Type, **perform:** Closure)

This modifier executes a closure when the value of a preference key changes. The first argument is a reference to the key's data type, and the **perform** argument is the closure to be executed when the value changes.

The process of passing a value from one view to another begins by defining a structure that conforms to the **PreferenceKey** protocol. Once this structure is in place, we must apply the **preference()** modifier to the view that produces the value and the **onPreferenceChange()** modifier to the view that receives it. The following example illustrates how this process works. We use a **GeometryReader** view to determine the size of an image, as in the previous example, but instead of handling the values locally, we propagate them to other views using a **PreferenceKey** structure.

Listing 6-6: Setting and reading preferences

```
struct BoxPreference: PreferenceKey {
   typealias Value = CGSize
   static let defaultValue: CGSize = .zero

   static func reduce(value: inout CGSize, nextValue: () -> CGSize) {
      value = nextValue()
   }
}
struct ContentView: View {
   @State private var size: CGSize = .zero

   var body: some View {
      VStack {
         Image("spot1")
            .resizable()
            .scaledToFit()
            .background(
               GeometryReader { geometry in
                  Color.clear
                     .preference(key: BoxPreference.self, value:
                        geometry.size)
               })
         Text("\(Int(size.width)) x \(Int(size.height))")
      }.padding()
      .onPreferenceChange(BoxPreference.self) { value in
         size = value
      }
   }
}
```

The first thing we do in this example is to define the structure to store the values. To conform to the **PreferenceKey** protocol, this structure must meet some requirements. First, we must define a typealias called **Value**. Because we are going to store the **CGSize** value returned by the **size** property of the **GeometryProxy** structure, we define **Value** as a typealias of **CGSize**. Next comes a type property called **defaultValue**. This property defines the value of the structure by default. Since we are working with a **CGSize** structure, we define it as a **CGSize** structure with its values set to 0 (**zero**). Finally, we implement the **reduce()** method. This method receives a reference to the values already stored in the structure and a closure that returns the new value. To store this new value, we must execute the closure and add the value returned to the values already stored in the structure. In this case, we are working only with one value (a **CGSize** structure), so we assign it directly to the property (**value = nextValue()**).

In the view, we embed an **Image** view in a **VStack** view and apply a **GeometryReader** view to the background, as before, but this time we store the values in an instance of our **BoxPreference** structure with the **preference()** modifier. Now, this value is defined as a Preference and therefore we can read it from the views in the hierarchy with the **onPreferenceChange()** modifier. In this example, the modifier is applied to the **VStack** view. When a new value is received, we assign it to a **@State** property to update the view. As a result, the view always shows the current size of the image on the screen.

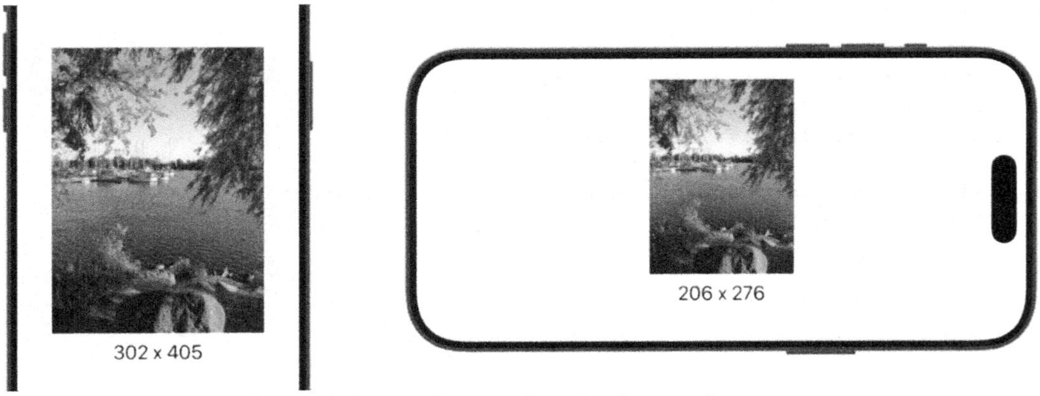

Figure 6-3: *Interface updated using preferences*

Do It Yourself

Create a new App project. Update the **ContentView.swift** file with the code in Listing 6-6. Download the **spot1.jpg** image from our website or provide your own. Create an Asset Catalog and add the image to it. Run the application on an iPhone simulator. Rotate the screen. You should see the size of the image change according to the orientation.

PRO

Alignment Guides

Another way to adapt an interface to different screen sizes and window configurations is by adjusting the alignment of its views. By default, horizontal stacks align their content vertically, while vertical stacks align their content horizontally. These default behaviors are sufficient for many layouts, but more complex or polished interfaces often require finer control over how views are positioned relative to one another. To achieve this, the **View** protocol provides the following modifier.

alignmentGuide(Alignment, **computeValue:** Closure)

This modifier defines the values of the horizontal or vertical alignment. The first argument determines the type of alignment we want to customize. It is defined with the type properties **center**, **leading**, and **trailing** from the **HorizontalAlignment** structure, or the type properties **bottom**, **center**, **firstTextBaseline**, **lastTextBaseline**, and **top** from the **VerticalAlignment** structure. The **computeValue** argument is a closure that receives the current dimensions of the view and returns a **CGFloat** with the new value for the alignment.

The following example applies a standard alignment to three images of different sizes. They are all 100 points wide, but the **signbus.png** image is 200 points tall, the **signplane.png** image is 170 points tall, and the **signphone.png** image is 220 points tall.

Listing 6-7: Aligning images to the center with standard values

```
struct ContentView: View {
   var body: some View {
      HStack(alignment: .center) {
         Image("signbus")
         Image("signplane")
         Image("signphone")
      }.border(Color.blue, width: 2)
   }
}
```

A stack view determines a common point of alignment according to its alignment type and the dimensions of the views. For instance, if the alignment of a vertical stack is **`center`**, the stack gets the position of the **`center`** alignment of each view and from that value it calculates a common point of alignment (usually the point of alignment of its tallest view) and then repositions all the views to match that common point, as shown below.

Figure 6-4: *Images aligned at the center*

Do It Yourself

Download the **signbus.png**, **signplane.png** and **signphone.png** images from our website and add them to an Asset Catalog. Update the **`ContentView`** structure with the code in Listing 6-7. Run the application on an iPhone simulator. You should see the images aligned by their vertical centers, as shown in Figure 6-4.

The alignment values are determined by the stack's coordinates system, starting from the top-left corner. The value at the top is 0 and the value at the bottom of the view depends on the children's height. Every view has an alignment guide with values that determine their points of alignment. The value associated with the **`top`** alignment is 0, the value associated with the **`bottom`** alignment is equal to the view's height, and the value associated with the **`center`** alignment is the height divided by two (the formula is: **`top`** + (**`bottom`** - **`top`**) / 2).

The views return these alignment guides by default, but we can change them with the **`alignmentGuide()`** modifier. For instance, the wheels of the bus in our example are below the common point of alignment (see Figure 6-4). This image is 200 points tall, so the center alignment returned by the image is at 100 points, but the wheels are 18 points below.

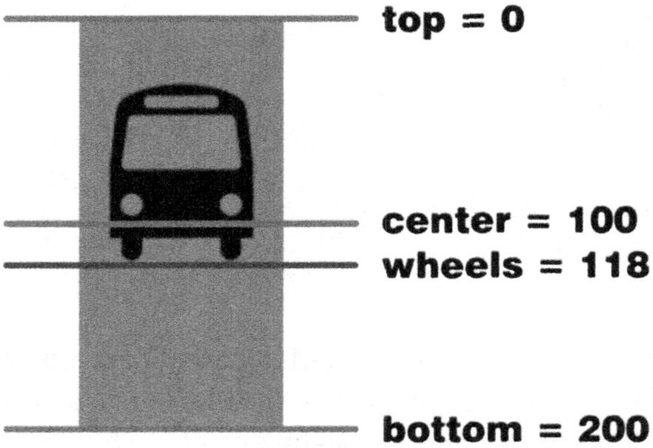

Figure 6-5: *Alignment guides for the bus*

As illustrated in Figure 6-5, the **`center`** alignment by default for the bus is 100 points (half its height), but the wheels are positioned at 118 points. If we want to center the image at this point, we must add 18 points to the image's natural center, as shown below.

Listing 6-8: Aligning an image to the center with custom values

```
struct ContentView: View {
    var body: some View {
        HStack(alignment: .center) {
            Image("signbus")
                .alignmentGuide(VerticalAlignment.center, computeValue: {
                    dimension in
                    return dimension[VerticalAlignment.center] + 18
                })
            Image("signplane")
            Image("signphone")
        }.border(Color.blue, width: 2)
    }
}
```

The **`alignmentGuide()`** modifier requires two values. The first value specifies the alignment we want to modify and the second value is a closure that returns the adjusted value for that alignment. In this case, we are aligning the views by their center, so we modify the **`VerticalAlignment.center`** alignment. The closure receives a **`ViewDimensions`** value, which provides the **`width`** and **`height`** properties to report the current size of the view, as well as a subscript that lets us access the values of individual alignment guides using square brackets and the alignment as the key, so we use these tools to add 18 points to the **`VerticalAlignment.center`** guide and return the result. From that point on, the center alignment for this view returns 118 instead of 100, which causes the view to be aligned 18 points higher, as shown below.

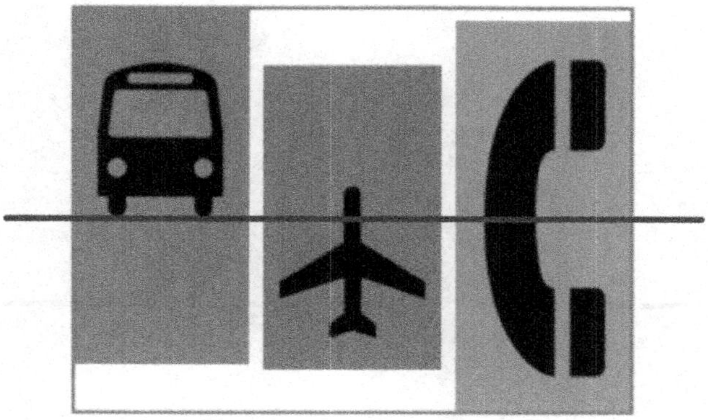

Figure 6-6: *Bus aligned with custom values*

If we want to align all the images by the bottom of the graphic, we must modify the alignment guide for each `Image` view, as in the following example.

Listing 6-9: Aligning all images to the center with custom values

```
struct ContentView: View {
  var body: some View {
     HStack(alignment: .center) {
        Image("signbus")
           .alignmentGuide(VerticalAlignment.center) { dimension in
              dimension[VerticalAlignment.center] + 18 }
        Image("signplane")
           .alignmentGuide(VerticalAlignment.center) { dimension in
              dimension[VerticalAlignment.center] + 68 }
        Image("signphone")
           .alignmentGuide(VerticalAlignment.center) { dimension in
              dimension[VerticalAlignment.center] + 89 }
     }.border(Color.blue, width: 2)
  }
}
```

The bus image is 200 points tall, so its default center is at 100 points, but the base of the bus is at 118 points, so we add 18 points to the current center alignment (118 - 100). The plane image is 170 points tall, placing its default center at 85 points, but the base of the plane is at 153 points, so we add 68 points to the center alignment (153 - 85). The phone image is 220 points tall, with a default center of 110 points, but the base of the phone is at 199 points, so we add 89 points to the center alignment (199 - 110). As a result, all images are aligned by the baseline of their graphics.

Figure 6-7: *Images aligned by the baselines*

PRO

Custom Layout

Standard views such as stacks and grids provide predefined rules for sizing and aligning views, allowing us to organize our interfaces quickly and efficiently. In many cases, these built-in layouts are sufficient to create clear and adaptive designs. However, there are situations where the default behavior does not offer enough control over how views are positioned within a container. To address these cases, SwiftUI provides support for custom layouts. Custom layouts let us define the exact position and size of each view inside a container, giving us full control over the layout process. They are implemented by creating structures that conform to the **`Layout`** protocol, which requires the implementation of the following two methods.

sizeThatFits(proposal: ProposedViewSize, **subviews:** Subviews, **cache:** Cache)

This method is called on the layout structure when the system needs to know the size of the container view. The method must calculate the size and return a **`CGSize`** value with the container's width and height. The **proposal** argument is a structure that determines the proposed size for the container. The structure defines three type properties to return a proposal: **`zero`**, **`infinity`**, and **`unspecified`**. The **subviews** argument is a collection of structures that represent each view in the container. And the **cache** argument is a storage space to share the calculated values between methods.

placeSubviews(bounds: CGRect, **proposal:** ProposedViewSize, **subviews:** Subviews, **cache:** Cache)

This method is called on the layout structure when the system needs to know the position of each view inside the container. The **bounds** argument is the bounds of the container. The **proposal** argument is a structure that determines the proposed size for the container. The structure defines three type properties to return a proposal: **`zero`**, **`infinity`**, and **`unspecified`**. The **subviews** argument is a collection of structures that represent each view in the container. And the **cache** argument is a storage space to share the calculated values between methods.

The **sizeThatFits()** method receives a collection of **LayoutSubview** structures. This is a proxy between our code and the views we need to allocate inside the container. To provide information about the views, the **LayoutSubview** structure includes the following properties and methods.

spacing

This property returns a **ViewSpacing** structure with values that determine the space preferred by the view between itself and other views. The structure defines the **distance(to: ViewSpacing, along: Axis)** method to return a **CGFloat** value with the preferred spacing between two views.

priority

This property returns a **Double** value with the view's layout priority.

sizeThatFits(ProposedViewSize)

This method returns a **CGSize** value with the size of the view the structure is representing. The argument is a structure that determines the proposed size we want to read. The structure defines three type properties to represent a proposal: **zero**, **infinity**, and **unspecified**.

dimensions(proposal: ProposedViewSize)

This method returns a **ViewDimensions** structure with the view's size and alignment guides. The **proposal** argument is a structure that determines the proposed size we want to read. The structure defines three type properties to represent a proposal: **zero**, **infinity**, and **unspecified**.

On the other hand, the **placeSubviews()** method is called on the layout structure when the system needs to know the position of each view within the container. This method receives similar values to allow us to calculate the right position for each view. To assign the position to the view, the **LayoutSubview** structure includes the following method.

place(at: CGPoint, **anchor:** UnitPoint, **proposal:** ProposedViewSize)

This method sets the position of the view. The **at** argument specifies the position in **x** and **y** coordinates. The **anchor** argument determines what point within the view is positioned at those coordinates. It is a structure returned by the type properties **bottom**, **bottomLeading**, **bottomTrailing**, **center**, **leading**, **top**, **topLeading** (default), **topTrailing**, **trailing**, and **zero**. And the **proposal** argument is the proposed size for which we want to set the position.

To define a custom layout, all we need to do is to define a structure that conforms to the **Layout** protocol and implement the protocol methods. In the **sizeThatFits()** method, we must use the size of each view to calculate the size of the container, and in the **placeSubviews()** method, we must calculate and assign the position of each view. The following example shows a possible implementation.

Listing 6-10: Defining a custom layout

```
struct ContentView: View {
   var body: some View {
      MyLayout {
         Group {
            Text("First")
               .padding(10)
               .background(.red)
            Text("Second")
               .padding(10)
               .background(.red)
            Text("Third")
               .padding(10)
               .background(.red)
         }.font(.title)
      }
   }
}
struct MyLayout: Layout {
   func sizeThatFits(proposal: ProposedViewSize, subviews: Subviews,
      cache: inout ()) -> CGSize {
      var totalWidth: CGFloat = 0
      var totalHeight: CGFloat = 0

      for (index, view) in subviews.enumerated() {
         if index > 0 {
            totalHeight += 10
         }
         let viewSize = view.sizeThatFits(.unspecified)
         totalWidth += viewSize.width + CGFloat(30 * index)
         totalHeight += viewSize.height
      }
      return CGSize(width: totalWidth, height: totalHeight)
   }
   func placeSubviews(in bounds: CGRect, proposal: ProposedViewSize,
      subviews: Subviews, cache: inout ()) {
      var posX: CGFloat = bounds.origin.x
      var posY: CGFloat = bounds.origin.y

      for (index, view) in subviews.enumerated() {
         if index > 0 {
            posY += 10
            posX += 30
         }
         view.place(at: CGPoint(x: posX, y: posY), proposal: .unspecified)
         posY += view.sizeThatFits(.unspecified).height
      }
   }
}
```

In this example, we define a layout structure called **MyLayout** and use it in the **ContentView** view to create the interface. The content of the layout structure must be embedded in a container view, such as a **Group** view or a **ForEach** view for dynamic lists. In this case, we use a **Group** view to show three **Text** views, so the work of the layout structure is to determine the position of these three views. We begin by calculating the size of the container in the **sizeThatFits()** method. For this purpose, we define two variables to store the width and height and then create a **for in** loop to get the size of each view and add it to the total. Because the views will be vertically separated by 10 points, we add this value to the **totalHeight** variable for the second and third views (when the view's index is greater than 0). Then, we get the view's size with the **sizeThatFits()** method and add the view's width and height to the total. To calculate the container's height, we add the height of each view, but for the width we add the width plus 30 points per view because we are going to displace each view 30 points to the right from the previous one. And finally, the total values are returned in a **CGSize** structure.

Note that the **sizeThatFits()** method returns a proposed size. Views can take any size they want, but first they receive a proposal from the container, so we can calculate the size of the view according to the size proposed by the container. There are three types of proposals: **zero**, **infinity**, and **unspecified**. The **zero** proposal returns the minimum size the view can take (in our case, it is 20 by 20 points because of the padding), the **infinity** proposal returns the maximum size the view can take, and the **unspecified** proposal returns the view's ideal size (the size determined by the size of the content, padding, and border). In our example, we always returned the size we want for the **unspecified** proposal, but we can do it for each proposal by checking the value of the method's **proposal** argument.

In the **placeSubviews()** method, we must calculate the position of each view. The process is similar than before, we must loop through the subviews collection and get the size of each view, but this time we use it to calculate their positions. The position of the view is calculated from the container's position, returned by the **bounds** argument. To those values, we add the vertical and horizontal displacements for the second and third views, and assign the final values back to the views with the **place()** method. The result is shown below.

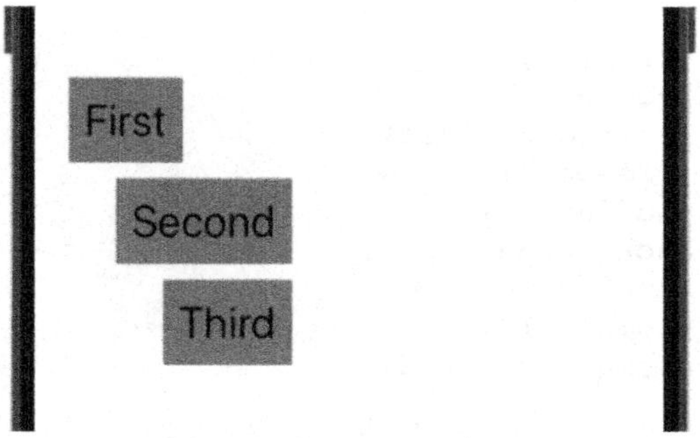

Figure 6-8: *Custom layout*

Although we can present different interfaces with conditional statements, this requires the system to recreate the views. SwiftUI includes the **AnyLayout** structure to create a wrapper that makes it easy to swap layouts without recreating the views. To show how we can switch layouts with the **AnyLayout** structure, we are going to use the custom layout defined in the previous example along with layouts provided by the system. SwiftUI includes the following structures to define horizontal and vertical layouts.

VStackLayout(alignment: HorizontalAlignment, **spacing:** CGFloat?)

This structure creates a layout that arranges a group of views vertically. The **alignment** argument determines the horizontal alignment of the views. It is a structure with the type properties **center**, **leading**, and **trailing**. And the **spacing** argument determines the space between the views.

HStackLayout(alignment: VerticalAlignment, **spacing:** CGFloat?)

This structure creates a layout that arranges a group of views horizontally. The **alignment** argument determines the vertical alignment of the views. It is a structure with the type properties **bottom**, **center**, **firstTextBaseline**, **lastTextBaseline**, and **top**. And the **spacing** argument determines the space between the views.

These structures work like the **VStack** and **HStack** structures, but they conform to the **Layout** protocol and are therefore used to define a layout. For instance, we can use a **VStackLayout** structure to replace our custom layout when the value of a property changes. To switch between layouts, we need to assign them to a property, as shown below.

Listing 6-11: Selecting a layout

```
struct ContentView: View {
   @State private var selected: Bool = true
   var body: some View {
      let SelectedLayout = selected ? AnyLayout(MyLayout()) :
         AnyLayout(HStackLayout())
      VStack {
         Button("Change Layout") {
            selected.toggle()
         }.buttonStyle(.glass)
         .padding()
         SelectedLayout {
            Group {
               Text("First")
                  .padding(10)
                  .background(.red)
               Text("Second")
                  .padding(10)
                  .background(.red)
               Text("Third")
                  .padding(10)
                  .background(.red)
            }
         }
         Spacer()
      }.padding()
      .font(.title)
   }
}
```

This code defines a property of type **Bool** to select the layout and stores the current layout in a variable inside the **body** closure. Every time the value of the **selected** property changes, the corresponding layout is assigned to the **SelectedLayout** property with a ternary operator, and then the layout is applied to the interface. When the value of the property is **true**, we show the custom layout, otherwise, we show the views with a standard **HStackLayout**. The result is shown below.

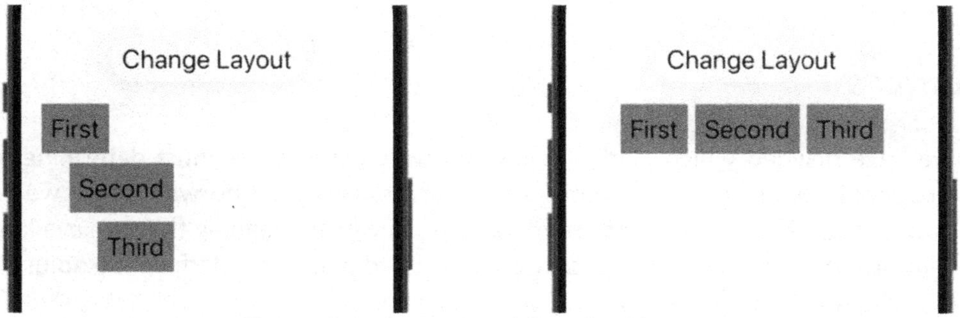

Figure 6-9: *Custom and Standard layouts*

BASIC

6.2 - Platform Specific Tools

SwiftUI is available on every Apple platform, allowing us to build applications for iPhones, iPads, Macs, Apple Watch, Apple TV, and Vision Pro. However, this does not mean that the same code can be used unchanged everywhere. While iPhones and iPads share the same underlying system, Macs, Apple Watch, Apple TV, and Vision Pro rely on different frameworks and interaction models. The good news is that Xcode can compile a single project for multiple devices. By organizing our Swift files as we have done so far and introducing platform-specific code where needed, we can adapt one application to multiple platforms without duplicating the entire codebase.

BASIC

Platforms

The first step is to configure the app's targets so Xcode knows which platforms the app supports. When we create an App project, it is already configured to run on iPhones, iPads, Macs, and Apple Vision, but we can change that from the General panel in the project's settings, as shown below.

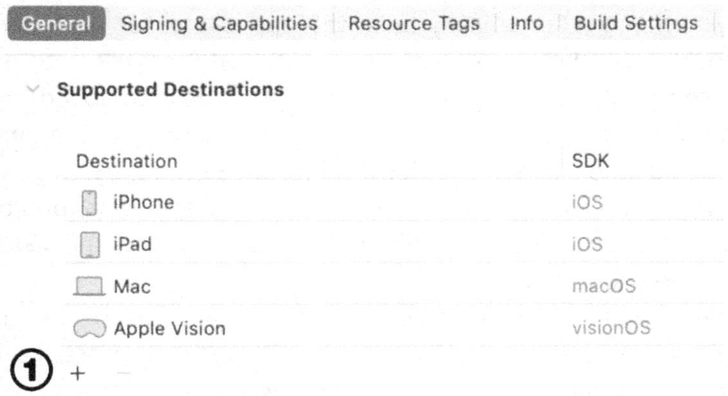

Figure 6-10: *Supported platforms*

The panel includes two buttons at the bottom of the list to edit the platforms (Figure 6-10, number 1). We can press the + button to add a platform, or select a platform from the list and press the - button to remove it.

BASIC

Resources

Once we have decided which platforms our app will support, we must determine which resources should be used on each platform. This process is straightforward when we use an Asset Catalog. By default, resources are marked as Universal, meaning they are available on every platform. However, we can restrict a resource to a specific platform by adjusting its settings in the Attributes inspector panel, as shown below.

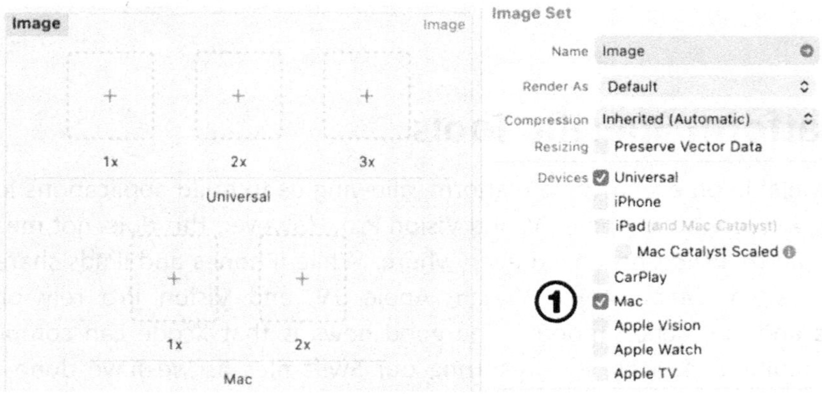

Figure 6-11: *Mac images*

Every time we select a platform from the panel, the Asset Catalog adds placeholders for platform-specific resources. In this example, we select the Mac option (Figure 6-11, number 1), so the Asset Catalog displays additional placeholders for Mac, allowing us to provide resources that are available only on that platform.

BASIC

Conditional Code

Although the system can automatically build the application for each platform, it is our responsibility to define platform-specific code. An alternative is to use conditional compilation. These conditionals are checked before the code is compiled, and therefore we can use them to select the code we want to implement according to the target platform.

Conditional compilation in Swift is done using the **`#if`**, **`#else`**, **`#elseif`** and **`#endif`** keywords. The **`#if`**, **`#else`** and **`#elseif`** keywords work like the Swift conditionals **`if else`**, but because the statements are not delimited by curly braces, the **`#endif`** keyword is required to signal the end of the block.

There are several parameters we can use to set the condition. For example, we can use the statement **`targetEnvironment()`** to tell the compiler to process the code only on a specific environment. The values available are **`simulator`** and **`macCatalyst`**. Another useful statement is **`os()`**. With this statement, we can tell the compiler to process the code only on a specific system. The values available are **`macOS`**, **`iOS`**, **`watchOS`**, **`tvOS`**, **`visionOS`**, **`Linux`**, **`Windows`** and **`anyAppleOS`**. In the following example, we use the value **`macOS`** to show a **`Text`** view only when the application is compiled for a Mac.

Listing 6-12: Detecting the platform before compiling

```
struct ContentView: View {
   var body: some View {
      VStack {
         #if os(macOS)
            HStack {
               Text("Mac Application")
                  .frame(width: 500, height: 350)
            }
         #else
            Text("Mobile Application")
         #endif
      }
   }
}
```

This is a very simple example, but it illustrates how to work with these types of conditionals. When we run this project on a mobile device, we get the message "Mobile Application", but on the Mac, we get a window with a size of 500 by 350 points and the message "Mac Application".

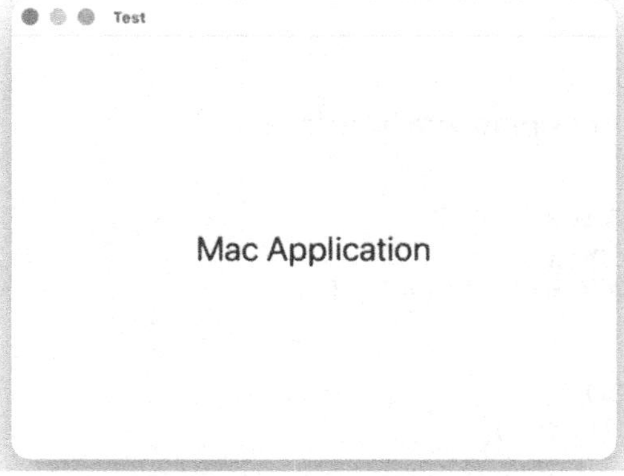

Figure 6-12: *Mac application*

Do It Yourself

Create a new App project. Update the **ContentView** structure with the code in Listing 6-12. From the Xcode's toolbar, click on the My Mac option and press the Play button to run the application. You should see a window with a message at the center, as illustrated in Figure 6-12.

When the differences between platforms are significant, instead of adapting individual views or modifiers, we can load entire views designed specifically for each system. SwiftUI files are created as usual, and we can use conditional compilation to control which views are loaded, but to avoid Xcode reporting errors, we must also assign each file to the platforms it is intended for. This configuration is performed in the Build Phases section of the project settings. Within the Compile Sources section, we can select a file and specify the platforms for which it should be compiled, as shown below.

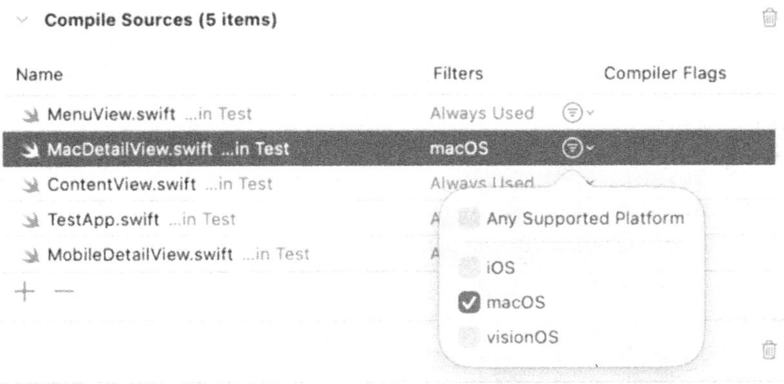

Figure 6-13: *Assigning a file to a platform*

In this example, we define a view called **`MobileDetailView`** that is intended to be used on all platforms, and another view called **`MacDetailView`** that is designed specifically for macOS. After configuring Xcode to compile the **MacDetailView.swift** file only for macOS, as shown in Figure 6-13, we must instruct the compiler which view to include in the interface by using **`#if`** and **`#else`** statements. In the following example, the application defines a universal two-column interface, but loads a different view in the second column depending on the platform.

Listing 6-13: Defining a multiplatform interface

```
struct ContentView: View {
   var body: some View {
      NavigationSplitView(sidebar: {
         MenuView()
      }, detail: {
         #if os(macOS)
            MacDetailView()
         #else
            MobileDetailView()
         #endif
      })
   }
}
```

When we open this application on an iPad or a Mac, the system first loads the **`ContentView`** view and then creates two columns. The content of the left column is defined by the **`MenuView`** view, but the content of the right column depends on the platform. If the app is compiled for Mac computers, the system displays the **`MacDetailView`**, but if it is compiled for iPhones and iPads, the system loads the **`MobileDetailView`** instead.

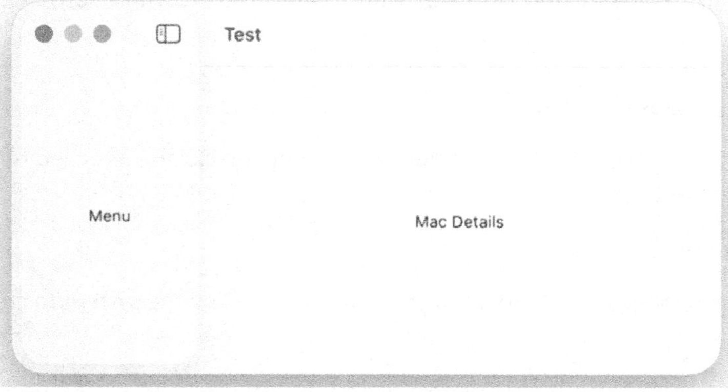

Figure 6-14: *Multiplatform interface*

We can also compile code specific for a version of an operating system. To specify the minimum required version of a system to run the code, Swift includes the **#available()** statement. This statement is checked by the compiler but the condition is determined by Swift, so we must use it with Swift **if else** statements. In the following example, we show the first **Text** view when the app is running on devices with iOS 26 and macOS 26 or newer, and the second **Text** view is shown in older systems.

Listing 6-14: Detecting the version of the operating system

```
struct ContentView: View {
   var body: some View {
      VStack {
         if #available(iOS 26, macOS 26, *) {
            Text("New Version")
         } else {
            Text("Old Version")
         }
      }.frame(width: 300, height: 350)
   }
}
```

BASIC

Menu

Mac and iPad applications include a menu bar that provides quick access to the app's main features. On Macs, the menu bar automatically appears at the top of the screen. On iPads, however, the user must click or swipe downward to reveal it. By default, the menu bar includes a set of standard menus and options, as shown below.

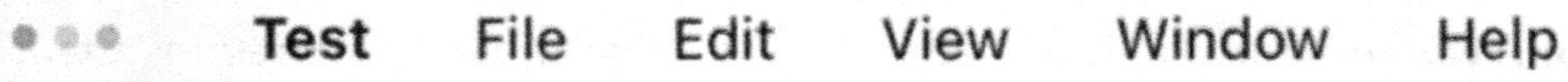

Figure 6-15: *Standard menu*

The menu bar includes the app's own menu, which provides information about the app, followed by standard menus for managing windows, editing content, accessing views, and more. To customize the bar and add our own commands, SwiftUI provides the following modifiers.

commands(content: Closure)

This modifier adds the menus and options defined by the closure assigned to the **content** argument.

commandsRemoved()

This modifier removes the standard menu option created by the system to create new windows.

The **commands()** modifier is applied to the scene (the **WindowGroup** structure in the **App** structure) and returns a new scene with the menu bar configured by the closure. To define the menus and the options from this closure, SwiftUI includes the **CommandMenu** and **CommandGroup** structures. The **CommandMenu** structure is used to create new menus. The following is the structure's initializer.

CommandMenu(String, **content:** Closure)

This structure creates a menu to add to the menu bar. The first argument specifies the menu's title, and the closure assigned to the **content** argument defines the menu's options. The new menu is inserted between the View and Window menus.

To modify the options of standard menus, we can use the **CommandGroup** structure instead. The following are the structure's initializers.

CommandGroup(after: CommandGroupPlacement, **addition:** Closure)

This structure defines a menu option. The **after** argument is a structure that specifies the option after which the new option will be added. The option is defined by the closure assigned to the **addition** argument.

CommandGroup(before: CommandGroupPlacement, **addition:** Closure)

This structure defines a menu option. The **before** argument is a structure that specifies the option before which the new option will be added. The option is defined by the closure assigned to the **addition** argument.

CommandGroup(replacing: CommandGroupPlacement, **addition:** Closure)

This structure defines a menu option. The **replacing** argument is a structure that specifies the option that will be replaced by the new option. The option is defined by the closure assigned to the **addition** argument.

The **CommandGroup** structure determines the position of the new option based on the position of a standard option. The standard options are represented by a **Command-GroupPlacement** structure. The structure includes type properties to return instances that represent all the standard options available. The properties are **appInfo**, **appSettings**, **appTermination**, **appVisibility**, **systemServices**, **importExport**, **newItem**, **printItem**, **saveItem**, **pasteboard**, **textEditing**, **textFormatting**, **undoRedo**, **sidebar**, **toolbar**, **singleWindowList**, **windowArrangement**, **windowList**, **windowSize**, and **help**.

Because the **commands()** modifier applies to the scene, we can only implement it in the **App** structure. For instance, in the following example we use it to add a new menu to the menu bar.

Listing 6-15: Adding a menu to the menu bar

```
@main struct MyApp: App {
   var body: some Scene {
      WindowGroup {
         ContentView()
      }
      .commands {
         CommandMenu("Options") {
            Button("Option 1", systemImage: "1.circle", action: {
               print("This is the option 1")
            }).labelStyle(.titleAndIcon)
            Button("Option 2", systemImage: "2.circle", action: {
               print("This is the option 2")
            }).labelStyle(.titleAndIcon)
         }
      }
   }
}
```

Menu options are created with **Button** views, as in any other menu, but only the label is shown. If we want to display an icon, we must apply the **labelStyle()** modifier with the value **titleAndIcon**, as we did in this example. The new menu is inserted between the View and Window menus, as shown below.

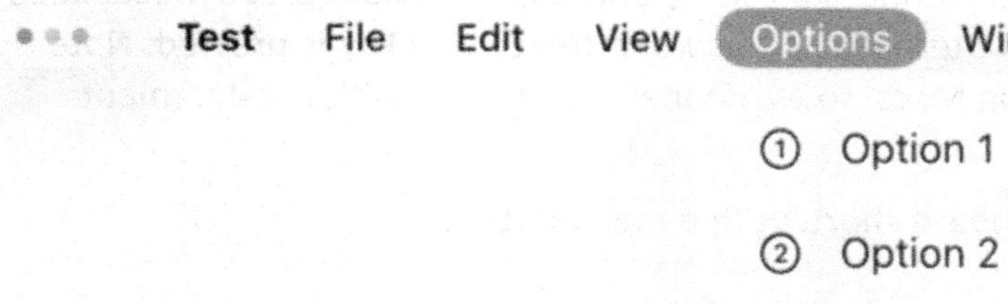

Figure 6-16: *Custom menu*

Do It Yourself

Create a new App project. Update the **App** structure with the code in Listing 6-15. Run the application on an iPad simulator or on a Mac. On iPads, swipe downward from the top of the screen to open the menu bar. You should see the Options menu with two commands, as shown in Figure 6-16. When selected, these commands print a message to the console, but you can use them for anything you want, such as modifying observable properties to update the interface or executing a method in the model, as we will see later.

Menu options can be associated with keys on the keyboard so that when the keys are pressed, the action assigned to the option is performed. SwiftUI provides the following modifiers to create these keyboard shortcuts.

keyboardShortcut(KeyEquivalent, **modifiers:** EventModifiers)

This modifier assigns a keyboard shortcut to a menu option. The first argument can be a string representation of the key (e.g., "A") or a function key represented by a **KeyEquivalent** structure. The **modifiers** argument is an array of key modifiers that must be pressed along with the main key to perform the action. The structure includes type properties to return instances for every modifier key available. The properties are **all**, **capsLock**, **command**, **control**, **numericPad**, **option**, and **shift**.

modifierKeyAlternate(EventModifiers, Closure)

This modifier offers an alternate menu option when a modifier key is pressed. The first argument is a structure that represents the key that must be pressed to activate the alternate option. The structure includes type properties to return instances for every modifier key available. The properties are **all**, **capsLock**, **command**, **control**, **numericPad**, **option** and **shift**. The second argument is the closure that provides the **Button** view that represents the alternate option.

The **KeyEquivalent** structure used by the **keyboardShortcut()** modifier to identify the key can be represented by a string (a letter, a number, or a punctuation character) or by type properties that return instances of the structure that represent function keys. The properties available are **upArrow**, **downArrow**, **leftArrow**, **rightArrow**, **clear**, **delete**, **deleteForward**, **end**, **escape**, **home**, **pageDown**, **pageUp**, **return**, **space**, and **tab**.

In the following example, we use the **keyboardShortcut()** modifier to create a shortcut for the second option with the A and Shift keys, and use the **modifierKeyAlternate()** modifier as well to provide an alternate option when the Option key is pressed. Note that this modifier is only available on Macs, so we define it inside a conditional statement.

Listing 6-16: Assigning a keyboard shortcut to a menu option

```
.commands {
   CommandMenu("Options") {
      Button("Option 1", systemImage: "1.circle", action: {
         print("This is the option 1")
      }).labelStyle(.titleAndIcon)
      Button("Option 2", systemImage: "2.circle", action: {
         print("This is the option 2")
      }).labelStyle(.titleAndIcon)
      .keyboardShortcut("A", modifiers: [.shift])
      #if os(macOS)
      .modifierKeyAlternate(.option, {
         Button("Option 3", systemImage: "3.circle", action: {
            print("Alternate Option 3")
         }).labelStyle(.titleAndIcon)
      })
      #endif
   }
}
```

Do It Yourself

Update the **commands()** modifier with the code in Listing 6-16. Run the application on an iPad simulator or on a Mac. Press the Shift + A keys. You should see the message produced by Option 2 in the console. If you run the application on a Mac, you will also be able to press the Option key to select Option 3 instead of Option 2.

IMPORTANT

You can add as many options as you want to a menu. If you need to organize those options into groups, use a **Section** view to group related commands or a **Divider** view to draw a line between them.

In addition to our own menus, we can also add options to the standard menus or replace the options provided by the system with the **CommandGroup** structure. This structure defines three initializers that we can use to insert a new option before or after a system option, and also replace an existing one. For instance, on Macs, the system includes an option in the File menu called New Window. This option is represented by the **newItem** property defined by the **CommandGroupPlacement** structure. The following example shows how to use this property to add an option to the File menu after the New Window option.

Listing 6-17: Adding options to a standard menu

```
.commands {
   CommandGroup(after: .newItem, addition: {
      Button("Option 1", systemImage: "1.circle", action: {
         print("This is the option 1")
      }).labelStyle(.titleAndIcon)
   })
}
```

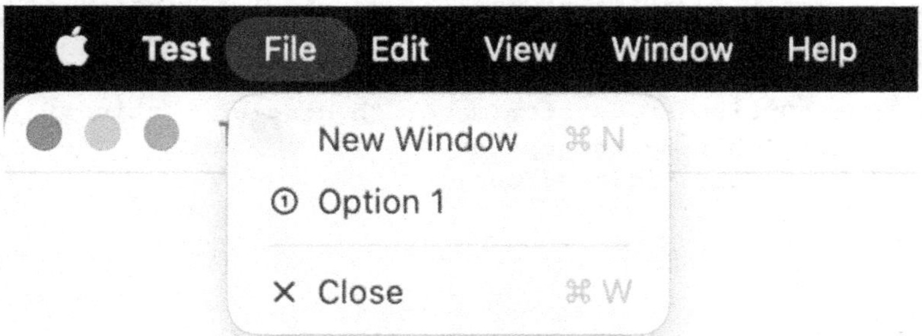

Figure 6-17: *Custom option added to a standard menu on Macs*

If instead of adding an option we want to remove one, we just need to assign an empty closure to the **addition** argument. For instance, the following example adds a new option after the **newItem** option and removes that option from the menu.

Listing 6-18: Removing options

```
.commands {
   CommandGroup(replacing: .newItem, addition: {})
   CommandGroup(after: .newItem, addition: {
      Button("Option 1", systemImage: "1.circle", action: {
         print("This is the option 1")
      }).labelStyle(.titleAndIcon)
   })
}
```

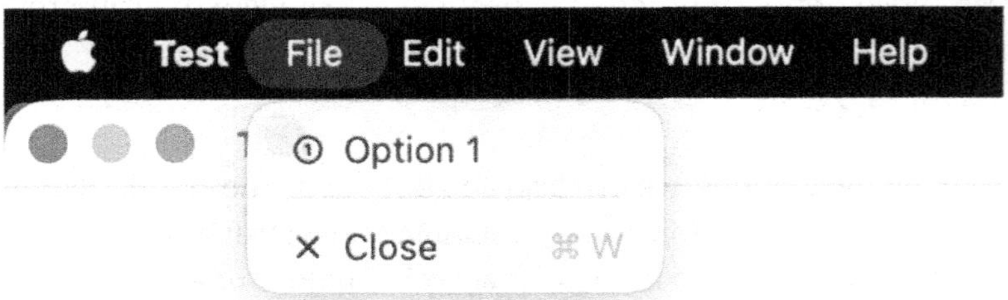

Figure 6-18: *Standard option removed on Macs*

We can also add submenus to a menu by using a **Menu** view to define the options (see Chapter 5, Listing 5-8). In the following example, we add a custom menu named Options with two commands: one that performs an action and another that opens a submenu.

Listing 6-19: Adding a submenu

```
.commands {
   CommandMenu("Options") {
      Button("Option 1", systemImage: "1.circle", action: {
         print("This is the option 1")
      }).labelStyle(.titleAndIcon)
      Menu("Option 2", systemImage: "2.circle", content: {
         Button("Option A", systemImage: "a.circle", action: {
            print("This is the option A")
         }).labelStyle(.titleAndIcon)
         Button("Option B", systemImage: "b.circle", action: {
            print("This is the option B")
         }).labelStyle(.titleAndIcon)
      })
   }
}
```

The custom menu shows two options, but if we tap the second option, a submenu opens with two additional options, Option A and Option B, as shown below.

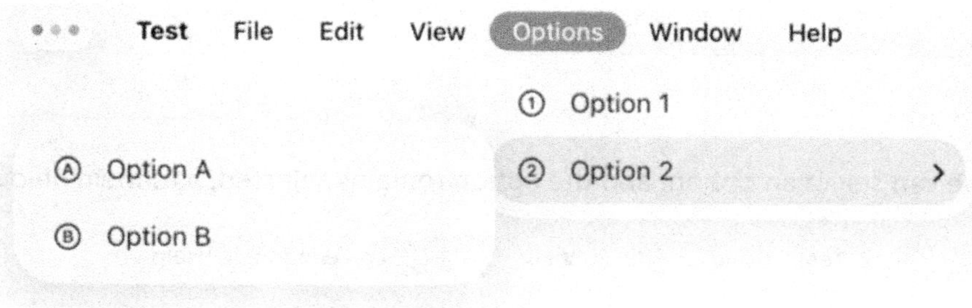

Figure 6-19: *Submenu*

We can also make menu options selectable. When an option is selected, the system displays a checkmark next to it to indicate whether the option is enabled or disabled. To support this behavior, we must replace the **Button** views with a **Picker** view and define a property in the data model to track the current state, as shown in the following example.

Listing 6-20: Defining a property in the model to store the index of the selected option

```
import SwiftUI

@Observable class ApplicationData {
   var selectedOption: Int = 1

   static let shared: ApplicationData = ApplicationData()
   private init() { }
}
```

The observable property in this model stores the integer value that we use to identify the picker options. When an option is selected, the value specified by its **tag()** modifier is assigned to the observable property, so we can then read this value from the views to determine which option is currently selected.

Listing 6-21: Selecting options

```
@main struct MyApp: App {
   @State private var appData = ApplicationData.shared

   var body: some Scene {
      WindowGroup {
         ContentView()
      }
      .commands {
         CommandMenu("Options") {
            Button("Option 1", systemImage: "1.circle", action: {
               print("This is the option 1")
            }).labelStyle(.titleAndIcon)
            Picker("Option 2", selection: $appData.selectedOption) {
               Text("Option A").tag(1)
               Text("Option B").tag(2)
            }
         }
```

```
        }
     }
  }
```

Now we can select an option, and the option remains selected, as shown below.

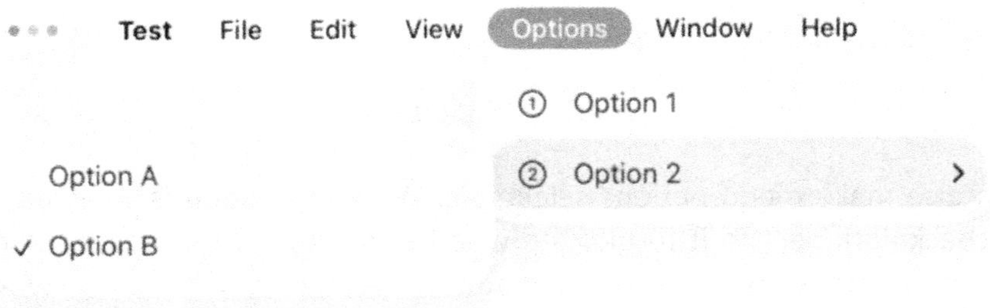

Figure 6-20: *Submenu with selectable options*

Do It Yourself

Create a Swift file called **ApplicationData.swift** for the model in Listing 6-20. Update the **`App`** structure with the code in Listing 6-21. Run the application on an iPad simulator or the Mac. Open the Options menu and select an option. The option should remain selected.

The options in a menu can be disabled. To disable an option, we apply the **`disabled()`** modifier to the **`Button`** view that represents it and connect the modifier to a state in the model that controls whether the option is enabled or disabled. For instance, we can disable the option when no text has been entered into a **`TextField`** view. The following are the changes required in our data model for this example.

Listing 6-22: Defining a state to enable and disable a menu option

```
@Observable class ApplicationData {
   var inputMessage: String = ""

   static let shared: ApplicationData = ApplicationData()
   private init() { }
}
```

Now we can disable the option in the menu when the **`inputMessage`** property is empty.

Listing 6-23: Enabling and disabling a menu option

```
.commands {
   CommandMenu("Options") {
      Button("Option 1", systemImage: "1.circle", action: {
         print("This is the option 1")
```

```
        }).labelStyle(.titleAndIcon)
        Button("Option 2", systemImage: "2.circle", action: {
            print("This is the option 2")
        }).labelStyle(.titleAndIcon)
        .disabled(appData.inputMessage.isEmpty)
    }
}
```

To complete the example, we need to include a **TextField** view in our view that works with the observable property in the model.

Listing 6-24: Defining a `TextField` view to enable and disable the option

```
struct ContentView: View {
    @State private var appData = ApplicationData.shared

    var body: some View {
        VStack {
            TextField("Insert your Name", text: $appData.inputMessage)
                .textFieldStyle(.roundedBorder)
            Spacer()
        }.padding()
    }
}
```

When the user inserts a value in the text field, the option is enabled, but it is immediately disabled when the field is empty, as shown below.

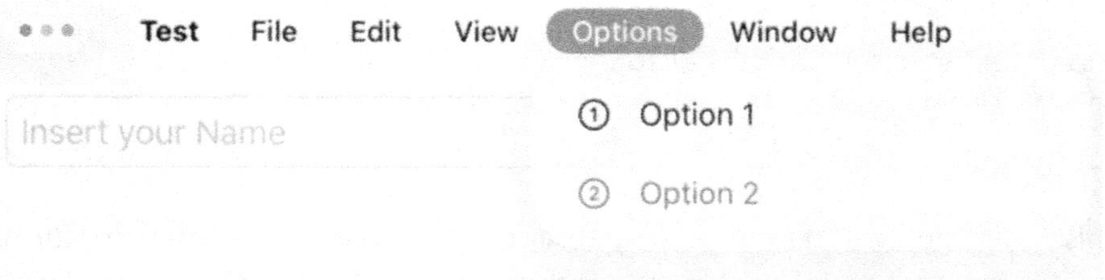

Figure 6-21: *Option disabled*

Do It Yourself

Update the **ApplicationData** class with the code in Listing 6-22, the **commands()** modifier in the **App** structure with the code in Listing 6-23, and the **ContentView** structure with the code in Listing 6-24. Run the application on an iPad simulator or your Mac. Open the File menu. The option should be disabled. Insert a text in the text field and open the menu again. Now the option should be enabled.

In the last example, the option is disabled if a condition is not met, but often options are enabled or disabled depending on which element is focused on the interface. For example, we can have two **TextField** views, but the action can only be performed when the user is working on one of them (the text field is focused). In Chapter 3, we learned how to handle focus changes for a view (see Listing 3-24), but to pass the focus state from one view to another, or as in this case from one view to the menu bar, we need to implement a structure called **FocusedValues**.

The **FocusedValues** structure is a collection of values managed by the system that contains the state of the focused view. Each state is identified by a structure that conforms to the **FocusedValueKey** protocol, which only requirement is to have a typealias named **Value** with a data type of the value managed by the view being monitored. Once we have this structure, we need to add a property of this type to the **FocusedValues** structure with an extension, as in the following example.

Listing 6-25: Storing a focus state in the `FocusedValues` structure

```
import SwiftUI

struct AddressKey : FocusedValueKey {
   typealias Value = String
}
extension FocusedValues {
   var address: AddressKey.Value? {
      get { self[AddressKey.self] }
      set { self[AddressKey.self] = newValue }
   }
}
@Observable class ApplicationData {
   var inputMessage: String = ""
   var inputAddress: String = ""

   static let shared: ApplicationData = ApplicationData()
   private init() { }
}
```

In this example, we define a structure called **AddressKey** that conforms to the **FocusedValueKey** protocol. The structure includes a typealias of **String** called **Value**, so we can store the values managed by the **TextField** view. After the structure is defined, we define an extension of the **FocusedValues** structure to include our own property of this type. We call this property **address**. The data type is the **Value** type defined in the previous structure, but set as an optional. This allows the system to assign the value **nil** to the property when the view is not focused. The **address** property includes a setter and a getter to set and return the value in the collection with our structure as the key.

Now we need to set and read this focus state from the view and the **App** structure. To set the focus state, SwiftUI includes the following modifier.

focusedValue(WritableKeyPath, Value)

This modifier stores a value in the **FocusedValues** structure. The first argument is the key path of the property in the **FocusedValues** structure we want to use to store the value, and the second argument is the value we want to store.

To observe the value from the focused view, SwiftUI includes the **@FocusedValue** property wrapper. This property wrapper is created from the **FocusedValue** structure, which includes the following initializer.

FocusedValue(KeyPath)

This initializer creates a structure to observe the values from a focused view. The argument is the key path of the property in the **FocusedValues** structure that stores the state we want to observe.

To store the focus state of a view in the **FocusedValues** structure, all we need to do is to apply the **focusedValue()** modifier to the view. In the following example, we do it to the **TextField** view that allows the user to insert an address.

Listing 6-26: Passing the focus state to the FocusedValues structure

```
struct ContentView: View {
   @State private var appData = ApplicationData.shared

   var body: some View {
      VStack {
         TextField("Insert your Name", text: $appData.inputMessage)
            .textFieldStyle(.roundedBorder)
         TextField("Insert Address", text: $appData.inputAddress)
            .textFieldStyle(.roundedBorder)
            .focusedValue(\.address, appData.inputAddress)
         Spacer()
      }.padding()
   }
}
```

When the second **TextField** view is focused, the **focusedValue()** modifier assigns the value of the **inputAddress** property to the **address** property of the **FocusedValues** structure, so the value is available for other views. Now we can observe this value from the **App** structure with the **@FocusedValue** property wrapper.

Listing 6-27: Disabling a menu option according to the focus state of a view

```
@main struct MyApp: App {
   @State private var appData = ApplicationData.shared
   @FocusedValue(\.address) var addressValue: String?

   var body: some Scene {
      WindowGroup {
         ContentView()
      }
      .commands {
         CommandMenu("Options") {
            Button("Option 1", systemImage: "1.circle", action: {
               print("This is the option 1")
            }).labelStyle(.titleAndIcon)
```

```
            Button("Option 2", systemImage: "2.circle", action: {
               print("This is the option 2")
            }).labelStyle(.titleAndIcon)
            .disabled(addressValue == nil)
         }
      }
   }
}
```

The view defines a property called **addressValue**, which contains the value of the address property of the **FocusedValues** structure. If the **TextField** view that allows the user to insert an address is focused (the user is typing on it), this property contains the value inserted by the user, otherwise, the property returns **nil**, so we can enable or disable the menu option accordingly.

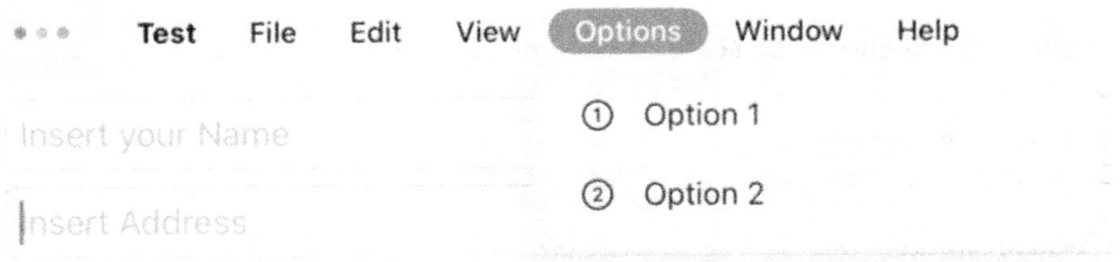

Figure 6-22: *Option enabled when the text field is focused*

Do It Yourself

Update the **ApplicationData.swift** file with the code in Listing 6-25, the **ContentView** structure with the code in Listing 6-26, and the **App** structure with the code in Listing 6-27. Run the application on an iPad simulator or your Mac. Click on the first text field. Open the Options menu. Option 2 should be disabled. Click on the second text field to select it. Now the option should be enabled, as shown in Figure 6-22.

IMPORTANT

SwiftUI also includes the **@FocusedBinding** property wrapper to observe the value of a binding property. This is useful when we need to change the state of a view from the menu. There is also a modifier called **focusedSceneValue()** to store the focus of a scene (a window) instead of a single view. For more information, visit our website and follow the links for this chapter.

BASIC

Toolbars on Macs

Instead of navigation bars, Mac applications use a toolbar at the top of the window to host the controls and actions the app requires, but the overall behavior is very similar. This allows us to reuse many of the same modifiers available on iOS, with only a few platform-specific differences. For example, in macOS there are no placement values designed specifically for navigation bars, such as **topBarLeading** and **topBarTrailing**, and placements like **primaryAction** and **secondaryAction** behave differently. Another difference is that, in Mac applications, the toolbar appears only when the interface is defined with a **NavigationSplitView** view. In the following example, we implement this view to create a multi-platform application and show how toolbar buttons are defined for each platform.

Listing 6-28: Defining a two-column interface for a multi-platform application

```
struct ContentView: View {
   var body: some View {
      NavigationSplitView(sidebar: {
         MenuView()
      }, detail: {
         DetailView()
      })
   }
}
```

The **MenuView** view defines the left column and doesn't require any special content for this example. The **DetailView** view, on the other hand, displays the toolbar, and here is where we should define the toolbar items, as in the following example.

Listing 6-29: Adding items to the toolbar for a multi-platform application

```
import SwiftUI

struct DetailView: View {
   var body: some View {
      VStack {
         Text("Details")
            .padding()
         Spacer()
      }
      .navigationTitle("My Title")
      .navigationSubtitle("My Subtitle")
      .toolbarTitleDisplayMode(.inlineLarge)
      .toolbar {
         #if os(macOS)
         ToolbarItem(placement: .primaryAction) {
            Button("Add Item", systemImage: "plus", action: {
               print("Add Item")
            })
         }
         #else
```

```
            ToolbarItem(placement: .topBarTrailing) {
               Button("Add Item", systemImage: "plus", action: {
                  print("Add Item")
               })
            }
            #endif
         }
      }
   }
```

This view defines the title and subtitle and adds a button with an SF Symbol to the bar, but the placement of the button depends on the platform. On macOS, we position the button using the **`primaryAction`** placement, while on iOS devices we use the **`topBarTrailing`** value. As a result, the button appears in the intended location regardless of the platform on which the app is running.

Figure 6-23: *Mac toolbar*

If we want to hide the toolbar on the Mac, we can remove it using the **`toolbarVisibility()`** modifier introduced in Chapter 5. The only difference is that, in macOS, the toolbar is identified by the **`windowToolbar`** value. In the following example, we show how to remove the toolbar from our application.

Listing 6-30: Hiding the toolbar on the Mac

```
struct DetailView: View {
   var body: some View {
      VStack {
         Text("Details")
            .padding()
         Spacer()
      }
      .navigationTitle("My Title")
      .navigationSubtitle("My Subtitle")
      .toolbarTitleDisplayMode(.inlineLarge)
      #if os(macOS)
      .ignoresSafeArea()
      .toolbarVisibility(.hidden, for: .windowToolbar)
      #endif
   }
}
```

This example shows a title and a subtitle on iPads and iPhones, but when the app runs on a Mac, the toolbar is completely hidden, as shown below.

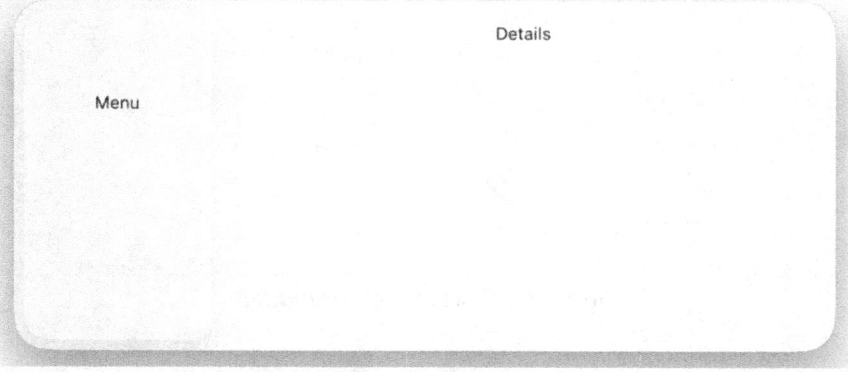

Figure 6-24: *Mac toolbar and title bar hidden*

As this example shows, when we remove the toolbar, the title bar and the window buttons are removed as well. This happens because, on macOS, the toolbar is part of the title bar, so removing one also removes the other. If we want to keep the title bar, instead of removing the toolbar entirely, we can hide it by using the **`toolbar(removing:)`** and **`toolbarBackgroundVisibility()`** modifiers, as shown in the following example.

Listing 6-31: Hiding only the toolbar on the Mac

```
struct DetailView: View {
   var body: some View {
      VStack {
         Text("Details")
            .padding()
         Spacer()
      }
      .navigationTitle("My Title")
      .navigationSubtitle("My Subtitle")
      .toolbarTitleDisplayMode(.inlineLarge)
      #if os(macOS)
      .ignoresSafeArea()
      .toolbar(removing: .title)
      .toolbarBackgroundVisibility(.hidden, for: .windowToolbar)
      #endif
   }
}
```

The **`toolbar(removing:)`** modifier hides the elements in the bar, and the **`toolbarBackgroundVisibility()`** modifier hides the toolbar background, effectively removing the toolbar from the window while preserving the title bar, as shown below.

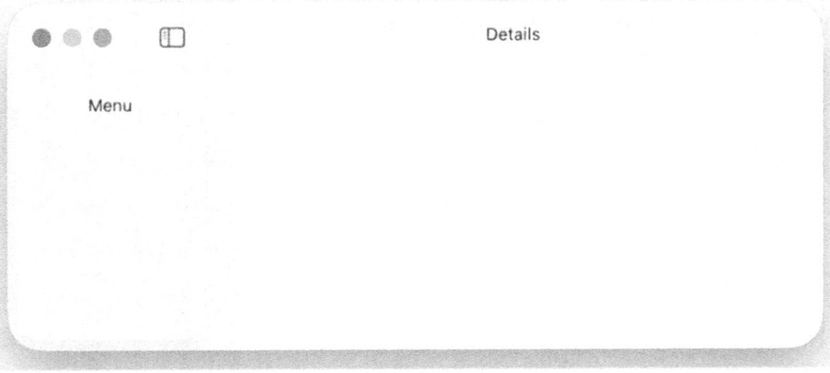

Figure 6-25: *Mac toolbar hidden*

Do It Yourself

Update the **`ContentView`** structure with the code in Listing 6-28. Create two SwiftUI files called **MenuView.swift** and **DetailView.swift**. Leave the **`MenuView`** structure with a single **`Text`** view, but modify the **`DetailView`** structure with the code in Listing 6-29. Run the application on your Mac. You should see a toolbar with a title and a subtitle, as illustrated in Figure 6-23. Update the **`DetailView`** structure with the codes in Listing 6-30 or 6-31 to see the effect of the modifiers in both cases.

BASIC

Mac Modifiers

SwiftUI also defines modifiers specific to Mac applications. The following are the most frequently used.

`help``(String)`

This modifier creates a tooltip. A tooltip is a message that appears next to a view when the pointer remains positioned over it for a short time.

`pointerStyle``(PointerStyle)`

This modifier changes the style of the mouse's pointer. The argument is a structure with properties and methods to define the style. The most useful are **`columnResize`**, **`default`**, **`grabActive`**, **`grabIdle`**, **`horizontalText`**, **`link`**, **`rectSelection`**, **`rowResize`**, **`verticalText`**, **`zoomIn`** and **`zoomOut`**.

`pointerVisibility``(Visibility)`

This modifier determines whether the mouse's pointer is visible or not. The argument is an enumeration with the values **`automatic`**, **`visible`** and **`hidden`**.

textInputSuggestions(Closure)

This modifier creates a list of suggestions for a **TextField** view. The argument is the closure that provides the list of **Text** views with the suggestions. This modifier works along with the **textInputCompletion(String)** modifier to specify the value to assign to the text field when an option is selected.

alternatingRowBackgrounds(AlternatingRowBackgroundBehavior)

This modifier displays the views in a list or a table with alternative backgrounds. The argument is a structure that enables or disables the feature. The structure includes the properties **automatic**, **enabled** (default) and **disabled**.

Applying some of this modifiers is straightforward. In the following example, we show how to use the **help()** modifier to show a message to the user when the mouse is over a view and the **pointerStyle()** modifier to change the style of the pointer.

Listing 6-32: Showing a tooltip for a button

```
struct DetailView: View {
   var body: some View {
      VStack {
         Text("Details")
      }
      .toolbar {
         ToolbarItem(placement: .automatic) {
            Button("Add Book", systemImage: "plus", action: {
               print("Adding Book")
            })
            #if os(macOS)
            .help("Press this button to add a book")
            .pointerStyle(.link)
            #endif
         }
      }
      .navigationTitle("My Title")
   }
}
```

If we position the mouse over the button, we can see the pointer changing into a hand and a message appearing after a few seconds.

Figure 6-26: *Tooltip*

Another useful modifier is **textInputSuggestions()**. With this modifier we can show suggestions for a text field. The suggestions are created with **Text** views that can be declared as static or dynamic with a **ForEach** loop, as in the following example.

Listing 6-33: Showing suggestions for a text field

```
struct DetailView: View {
   @State private var text = ""
   let listSuggestions = ["Red", "Green", "Blue"]

   var body: some View {
      VStack {
         TextField("Insert Text", text: $text)
            .textFieldStyle(.roundedBorder)
            #if os(macOS)
            .textInputSuggestions({
               ForEach(listSuggestions, id: \.self) { suggestion in
                  Text(suggestion)
                     .textInputCompletion(suggestion)
               }
            })
            #endif
         Spacer()
      }.padding()
   }
}
```

In this case, we use a simple array to provide the values and then assign those values to each suggestion using the **`textInputCompletion()`** modifier, so when a suggestion is selected, the corresponding value is inserted into the search bar, as shown below.

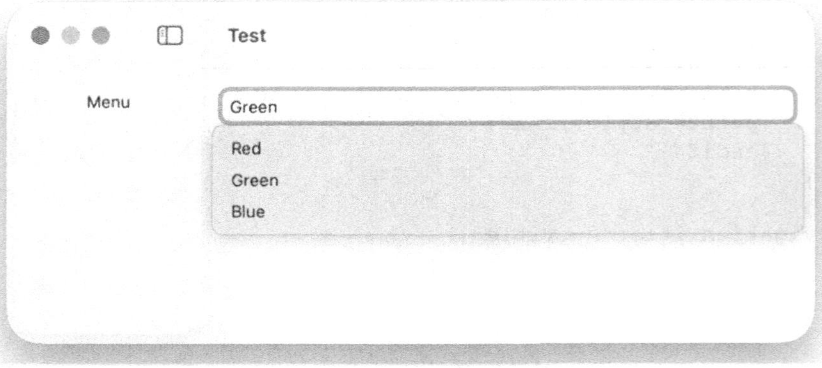

Figure 6-27: *Suggestions*

The **`alternatingRowBackgrounds()`** modifier highlights alternate rows so they can be easily identified. The following example includes a model with a list of values to show how this modifier works.

Listing 6-34: Defining a model to test alternate backgrounds

```
import SwiftUI

@Observable class ApplicationData {
   var foodList: [String]
```

```
    static let shared: ApplicationData = ApplicationData()
    private init() {
        foodList = ["bagels", "brownies", "butter", "cheese", "coffee",
            "cookies", "donuts", "granola", "juice", "lemonade", "lettuce",
            "milk", "oatmeal", "potato", "tomato", "yogurt"]
    }
}
```

The following are the changes we need to introduce to the **`DetailView`** view to display a list with alternate backgrounds.

Listing 6-35: Creating a list with alternate background

```
struct DetailView: View {
    @State private var appData = ApplicationData.shared

    var body: some View {
        List {
            ForEach(appData.foodList, id: \.self) { item in
                Text(item)
            }
        }
        .navigationTitle("Food List")
        #if os(macOS)
        .alternatingRowBackgrounds()
        #endif
    }
}
```

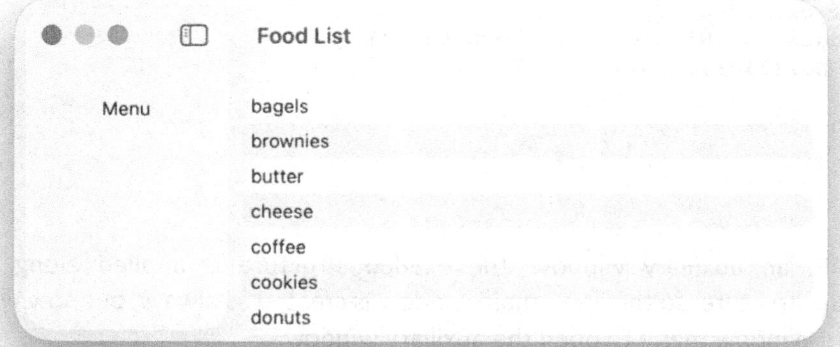

Figure 6-28: *Highlighted rows*

Do It Yourself

Create a Swift file called **ApplicationData.swift** for the code in Listing 6-34. Update the **`DetailView`** view with the code in Listing 6-35. Run the application on your Mac. You should see something like Figure 6-28.

BASIC

Scenes

As explained in Chapter 2, to create an application, we must first define a scene (a window). SwiftUI includes several structures to create standard scenes for every system. We have already implemented the **WindowGroup** structure to create multi-platform applications, but there are more available. For example, SwiftUI includes the **Window** structure to create a scene on Macs with only one window. The following is the structure's initializer.

Window(String, id: String, content: Closure)

This structure creates a scene to present a single window. The first argument defines the window's title, the **id** argument defines the window's identifier, and the **content** argument is a closure that provides the view for the Scene.

The **Window** structure creates a single independent scene and is therefore useful for applications that cannot allow the user to open multiple windows, such as video games, or when we need to present auxiliary windows, as in the following example.

Listing 6-36: Opening an auxiliary window

```
@main struct MyApp: App {
   var body: some Scene {
      WindowGroup {
         ContentView()
      }
      #if os(macOS)
      Window("My Window", id: "mywindow") {
         AuxiliaryView()
      }
      #endif
   }
}
```

To create an auxiliary window, the **Window** structure is applied along with the **WindowGroup** structure, so the app's main window is created as always, but now we have an option in the Window menu to open the auxiliary window.

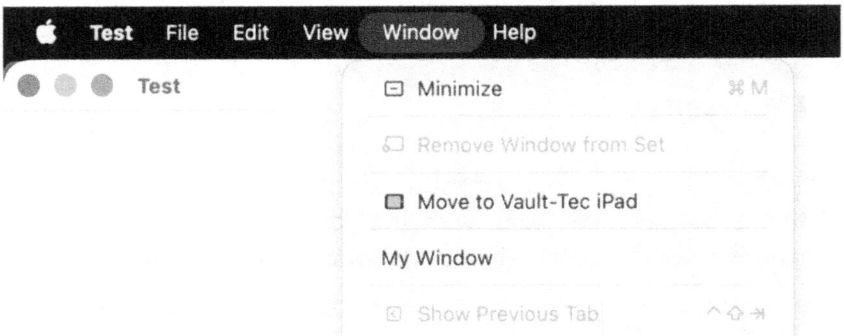

Figure 6-29: *Option to open an auxiliary window*

Do It Yourself

Create a new App project. Update the **App** structure with the code in Listing 6-36. Create a new SwiftUI file called **AuxiliaryView.swift** with a single **Text** view. Run the application on your Mac. Open the Window menu. You should see an option with the name of the window, as shown in Figure 6-29 (My Window). Click on this option to open the auxiliary window.

The menu option is automatically added to the Window menu when we add a **Window** scene to the **App** structure, but most users don't know that the option even exists. To provide a better alternative, the Environment includes the following properties to open and close windows programmatically.

openWindow

This property creates an action that presents a window. The property contains an instance of the **OpenWindowAction** structure that exposes a handler we can call to perform the action. There are two options available: we can call it with the **id** argument to open a window with a specific identifier (**openWindow(id: String)**), or with the **value** argument to open a window presented by the **WindowGroup** structure that can process that value type (**openWindow(value: Value)**).

dismissWindow

This property creates an action that dismisses a window. The property contains an instance of the **DismissWindowAction** structure that exposes a handler we can call to perform the action. There are two options available: we can call it with the **id** argument to close a window with a specific identifier (**dismissWindow(id: String)**), or with the **value** argument to close a window presented by the **WindowGroup** structure that can process that value type (**dismissWindow(value: Value)**).

As with other Environment properties, such as **dismiss** and **dismissSearch**, we must define an **@Environment** property and then call its handler to perform the action. The following **ContentView** view shows how to define a property to access the **openWindow** value and how to use it to open the auxiliary view created in the previous example.

Listing 6-37: Opening a window programmatically

```
struct ContentView: View {
   @Environment(\.openWindow) var openWindow

   var body: some View {
      VStack {
         Text("Hello, world!")
         Button("Open Auxiliary Window") {
            openWindow(id: "mywindow")
         }.buttonStyle(.borderedProminent)
      }
```

```
        .frame(minWidth: 500, maxWidth: .infinity, minHeight: 300,
maxHeight: .infinity)
    }
}
```

This interface includes a **Button** view to open the auxiliary window. When the button is pressed, we perform the action with the **id** argument to open the window identified with the string "mywindow". We can add a similar button in the **AuxiliaryView** view to dismiss it.

Listing 6-38: Closing a window programmatically

```
import SwiftUI

struct AuxiliaryView: View {
   @Environment(\.dismissWindow) var dismissWindow

   var body: some View {
      VStack {
         Text("Auxiliary View")
            .padding()
         Button("Close Window") {
            dismissWindow(id: "mywindow")
         }.buttonStyle(.bordered)
      }
      .frame(minWidth: 300, maxWidth: .infinity, minHeight: 200,
         maxHeight: .infinity)
   }
}
```

When we press the button in the **ContentView** view, the window with the "mywindow" identifier is opened, and if we press the button in the **AuxiliaryView** view, the same window is closed.

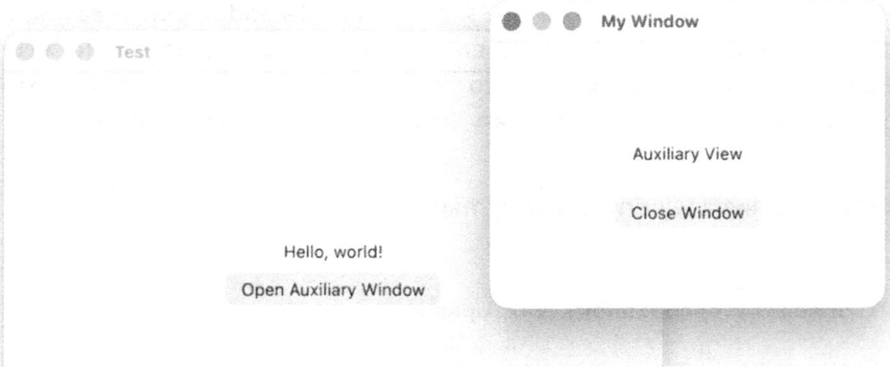

Figure 6-30: *Opening and closing windows*

In the previous example, we used the **frame()** modifier to set a minimum size for the views. The maximum size was declared with the value **infinity**, which means that the views will always take up the size of the window. This is the recommended approach, but it may not be suitable for our application. For example, if we set a maximum size for the view, this determines how large the view can be, but does not stop the user from expanding the window further. By default, the minimum size of the view determines the minimum size of the window, but users can expand the window as they wish, no matter the maximum size we set for the views. There are many ways to change this behavior. One alternative is to set the size of the window according to the size of the content with the following modifiers.

windowResizability(WindowResizability**)**

This modifier determines the strategy followed by the system to resize the window. The argument is a structure with the properties **automatic**, **contentMinSize** and **contentSize**.

windowResizeAnchor(UnitPoint**)**

This modifier determines the side to which a view is anchored when its size changes. The argument is a structure with the properties **topLeading**, **top**, **topTrailing**, **leading**, **center**, **trailing**, **bottomLeading**, **bottom**, and **bottomTrailing**.

By default, the resizability behavior is set to **automatic**, which means that the window is going to respect the minimum size of the view but ignore the maximum size. If we want the window to respect these values, we can set the behavior to **contentSize** (the window determines its size according to the content).

Listing 6-39: Configuring the window to adopt the size of the content

```
@main struct MyApp: App {
   var body: some Scene {
      WindowGroup {
         ContentView()
      }
      #if os(macOS)
      Window("My Window", id: "mywindow") {
         AuxiliaryView()
      }
      .windowResizability(.contentSize)
      #endif
   }
}
```

Now we can give the **AuxiliaryView** view a minimum and maximum size or a fixed size, as in the following example.

Listing 6-40: Assigning a fixed size to a view

```
struct AuxiliaryView: View {
   @Environment(\.dismissWindow) var dismissWindow

   var body: some View {
      VStack {
         Text("Auxiliary View")
```

```
            .padding()
        Button("Close Window") {
            dismissWindow(id: "mywindow")
        }
    }
    .frame(width: 300, height: 200)
  }
}
```

The **AuxiliaryView** view now has a fixed size of 300 x 200 points, and because we applied the **windowResizability()** modifier, the window adopts the same size and the user can't change it.

Do It Yourself

Update the **App** structure with the code in Listing 6-39 and the **AuxiliaryView** view with the code in Listing 6-40. Run the application on your Mac. Click the button to open the **AuxiliaryView** view. The window should be of a size of 300 x 200 points and you shouldn't be able to resize it.

Unless we specify otherwise, the initial position and size of the windows are determined by the system. If we want to change these values, we can apply the following modifiers.

defaultPosition(UnitPoint**)**

This modifier specifies the window's initial position relative to the screen. The argument is a structure with the type properties **topLeading**, **top**, **topTrailing**, **leading**, **center**, **trailing**, **bottomLeading**, **bottom**, and **bottomTrailing**.

defaultSize(width: CGFloat, **height:** CGFloat**)**

This modifier specifies the window's size by default. The arguments determine the width and height.

Regardless of the position and size we choose, these values can be changed by the user. This means that we can only determine the position and size of a window when it is opened for the first time, but from that moment on the system will use the values selected by the user. If we want the window to always have the same initial position and size when the app is launched, we can use the following modifiers.

restorationBehavior(SceneRestorationBehavior**)**

This modifier determines how the system restores previous opened windows. The argument is a structure with the properties **automatic** and **disabled**.

defaultLaunchBehavior(SceneLaunchBehavior**)**

This modifier determines the window to be opened when the application is launched for the first time. The argument is a structure with the properties **automatic**, **presented** and **suppressed**.

In the following example, we ask the system to position the window for the **AuxiliaryView** view at the bottom-left corner of the screen, and to ignore any changes performed by the user every time the app is launched.

Listing 6-41: Assigning a position by default

```
@main struct MyApp: App {
   var body: some Scene {
      WindowGroup {
         ContentView()
      }
      #if os(macOS)
      Window("My Window", id: "mywindow") {
         AuxiliaryView()
      }
      .windowResizability(.contentSize)
      .defaultPosition(.bottomLeading)
      .restorationBehavior(.disabled)
      #endif
   }
}
```

Do It Yourself

Update the **App** structure with the code in Listing 6-41. Run the application on your Mac. Click on the button to open the **AuxiliaryView** view. The window should appear at the bottom-left corner of the screen.

Other than specifying a standard position and default size for the window, we can calculate them dynamically with the following modifiers.

defaultWindowPlacement(Closure)

This modifier runs a closure that we can use to calculate the position and size of the window. The closure receives two values: a **WindowLayoutRoot** structure that represents the content of the window, and a **WindowPlacementContext** structure that provides information about the screen and the windows.

windowIdealPlacement(Closure)

This modifier runs a closure that we can use to calculate the position and size of the window when it is zoomed in. The closure receives two values: a **WindowLayoutRoot** structure that represents the content of the window, and a **WindowPlacementContext** structure that provides information about the screen and the windows.

The closures assigned to these modifiers must return a **WindowPlacement** structure with the new position and size of the window. The following is one of the structure's initializers.

WindowPlacement(CGPoint, **size:** CGSize)

This initializer creates a structure that represents the position and size of a window. The first argument determines the window's preferred position, and the **size** argument its size.

To calculate the position and size of the window, the **WindowLayoutRoot** structure includes the **sizeThatFits()** method that returns a **CGSize** value with the width and height of the window's content, and the **WindowPlacementContext** structure includes the **defaultDisplay** property to return information about the screen. This property stores a **DisplayProxy** structure, which in turn includes the properties **bounds** to return a **CGRect** value with the dimensions of the screen, the **safeAreaInsets** property to return an **EdgeInsets** value with the insets of the safe area, and the **visibleRect** property to return a **CGRect** value with the dimensions of the portion of the screen where it is safe to place the window.

In the following example, we position the window for the **AuxiliaryView** view 100 points from the upper-left corner of the screen and give it a size that is half the width and height of the screen.

Listing 6-42: Defining a custom position and size for the window

```
@main struct MyApp: App {
   var body: some Scene {
      WindowGroup {
         ContentView()
      }
      #if os(macOS)
      Window("My Window", id: "mywindow") {
         AuxiliaryView()
      }
      .defaultWindowPlacement { content, context in
         let bounds = context.defaultDisplay.bounds
         let position = CGPoint(x: 100, y: 100)
         let size = CGSize(width: bounds.width / 2, height:
            bounds.height / 2)
         return WindowPlacement(position, size: size)
      }
      .restorationBehavior(.disabled)
      #endif
   }
}
```

So far, we have opened the windows with a default configuration, but we can specify some attributes by applying the following modifiers to the views.

windowMinimizeBehavior(WindowInteractionBehavior)

This modifier enables or disables the window's minimize functionality. The argument is a structure with the properties **automatic**, **disabled** and **enabled**.

windowDismissBehavior(WindowInteractionBehavior)

This modifier enables or disables the window's dismiss functionality. The argument is a structure with the properties **automatic**, **disabled** and **enabled**.

windowFullScreenBehavior(WindowInteractionBehavior)

This modifier enables or disables the window's full screen mode. The argument is a structure with the properties **automatic**, **disabled** and **enabled**.

windowResizeBehavior(WindowInteractionBehavior)

This modifier enables or disables the window's resizing capabilities. The argument is a structure with the properties **automatic**, **disabled** and **enabled**.

windowBackgroundDragBehavior(WindowInteractionBehavior)

This modifier enables or disables the possibility of dragging the window by the background. The argument is a structure with the properties **automatic**, **disabled** and **enabled**.

These modifiers are applied to the views, except for the **windowBackgroundDrag-Behavior()** modifier that is applied to the window. In the following example, we use the **windowResizeBehavior()** and **windowMinimizeBehavior()** modifiers with the **AuxiliaryView** view, so the only thing the user can do with this window is to close it.

Listing 6-43: Disabling window controls

```
@main struct MyApp: App {
   var body: some Scene {
      WindowGroup {
         ContentView()
      }
      #if os(macOS)
      Window("My Window", id: "mywindow") {
         AuxiliaryView()
            .windowResizeBehavior(.disabled)
            .windowMinimizeBehavior(.disabled)
      }
      #endif
   }
}
```

The windows we have used so far are presented with the design provided by the operating system, but SwiftUI offers modifiers to change the window's aspect and style. The following are the most frequently used.

windowStyle(WindowStyle)

This modifier changes the window's style. The argument is a protocol with properties that determine the type of window to create. The properties available are **automatic** (default), **hiddenTitleBar**, **plain**, **titleBar** and **volumetric**.

windowLevel(WindowLevel)

This modifier determines if the window is going to be shown on top or behind other windows. The argument is a structure with the properties **automatic**, **desktop**, **floating** and **normal**.

containerBackground(Style, **for:** ContainerBackgroundPlacement)

This modifier defines the background style for the container. It works with many containers, including **NavigationStack** views, **NavigationSplitView** views, **TabView** views and windows. The first argument is the style to apply to the background, and the **for** argument is a structure that determines the container to be affected. Some of the properties provided by the structure are **navigation**, **tabView**, **widget**, **navigationSplitView** and **window**.

The two styles used in macOS to create the entire window are **automatic** and **plain**. The **automatic** style creates a standard view, while the **plain** style removes control bars, buttons and borders. The latter is the one used when we want to provide our own design, as in the following example.

Listing 6-44: Applying a custom design to a window

```
@main struct MyApp: App {
   var body: some Scene {
      WindowGroup {
         ContentView()
      }
      #if os(macOS)
      Window("My Window", id: "mywindow") {
         AuxiliaryView()
            .background(.yellow)
      }
      .windowStyle(.plain)
      #endif
   }
}
```

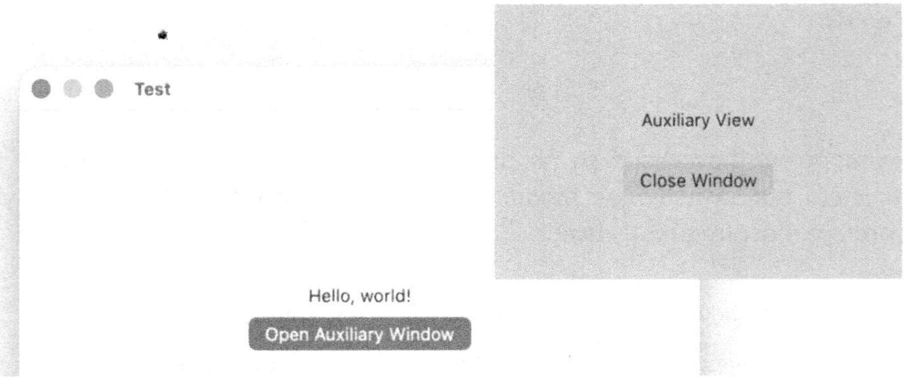

Figure 6-31: *Custom window style*

A **plain** window doesn't include a navigation or a title bar and therefore it is not possible for the user to drag it or change its size. For a normal window, we can use the **windowBackgroundDragBehavior()** modifier to allow the user to drag the window by positioning the mouse over the background, but because the plain style also removes the window's background, we need to apply the gesture to the view. SwiftUI includes the following structure for this purpose.

WindowDragGesture()

This initializer creates a gesture recognizer to allow the user to drag a view.

Because we already assigned a yellow background to the **AuxiliaryView** view in the previous example, all we need to do to allow the user to drag it is apply the **gesture()** modifier with a **WindowDragGesture** structure. We will explore this modifier in more detail in Chapter 9. For now, all we need to know is that the modifier adds the ability for a view to process user gestures, so we can use it to detect a drag gesture and allow the user to move the view, as shown in the following example.

Listing 6-45: Dragging a view

```
@main struct MyApp: App {
   var body: some Scene {
      WindowGroup {
         ContentView()
      }
      #if os(macOS)
      Window("My Window", id: "mywindow") {
         AuxiliaryView()
            .background(.yellow)
            .gesture(WindowDragGesture())
      }
      .windowStyle(.plain)
      #endif
   }
}
```

Another structure provided by SwiftUI for creating a scene for macOS applications is **Settings**. This structure creates a scene that opens when the user selects the Settings option from the app's menu. The following is the structure's initializer.

Settings(content: Closure)

This structure creates a scene to present the app's settings. The **content** argument is a closure with the views for the scene.

In the following example, we create a simple **Settings** scene with a **Text** view to show how the scene works.

Listing 6-46: Defining a `Settings` scene

```
@main struct MyApp: App {
   var body: some Scene {
      WindowGroup {
         ContentView()
      }
      #if os(macOS)
      Settings {
         VStack {
            Text("Settings")
         }.frame(width: 200, height: 150)
      }
      #endif
   }
}
```

Do It Yourself

Update the **App** structure with the code in Listing 6-46. Run the application on your Mac. Open the app's menu and click on the Settings option. You should see a small window appear on the screen with the text "Settings". A Settings scene is used to show the current settings and allow the user to change them. We will learn how to permanently store these values in Chapter 7.

There is one more useful structure for creating a scene in macOS applications called **MenuBarExtra**. This structure creates a scene that adds an icon to the menu bar, which provides access to additional functionality. The following is the structure's initializer.

```
MenuBarExtra(String, systemImage: String, isInserted: Binding,
content: Closure)
```

This structure creates a scene that adds a control to the system's menu bar. The first argument is the control's title, the **systemImage** argument is the SF Symbol we want to use to represent the control, the **isInserted** argument is a Boolean binding property that determines if the control is displayed or not, and the **content** argument is the closure that defines the menu or the view to show when the control is selected.

There are two different styles for the control. We can open a menu with options created by **Button** views, or a view with a custom interface. To select the style, the framework includes the following modifier.

```
menuBarExtraStyle(MenuBarExtraStyle)
```

This modifier specifies the style of the content shown by the control. The argument is a structure that conforms to the **MenuBarExtraStyle** protocol. The framework defines three structures to define the styles. These structures include the type properties **automatic**, **menu**, and **window**.

By default, the style is set to **automatic**, which means the control opens a menu. In the following example, we show how to create an icon that opens a menu with three options, two to perform actions and one to close the app.

Listing 6-47: Inserting a control in the system's menu bar

```
@main struct MyApp: App {
   var body: some Scene {
      WindowGroup {
         ContentView()
      }
      #if os(macOS)
      MenuBarExtra("My Control", systemImage: "phone") {
         Button("Option 1") {
            print("Option 1")
         }
         Button("Option 2") {
            print("Option 2")
         }
         Divider()
         Button("Quit") {
            NSApplication.shared.terminate(nil)
         }
      }
      #endif
   }
}
```

Most scenes contain a predefined menu with default options, including an option to close the application. This is not the case with the scene created by the **MenuBarExtra** structure. In this case, we need to add the option to close the window programmatically. Applications in macOS are managed by an instance of the **NSApplication** class. The class includes a type property called **shared** to return this instance, and the instance includes the **terminate()** method to close the application. And that's all we need to create our own option to allow the user to terminate the app. The result is shown below.

Figure 6-32: *Control with a menu*

To show a view instead of a menu, we must apply the **menuBarExtraStyle()** modifier with the **window** value and replace the buttons with a single view and its content, as shown below.

Listing 6-48: Defining the control to open a view

```
MenuBarExtra("My Menu", systemImage: "phone") {
   VStack {
      HStack {
         Spacer()
         Button(action: {
            NSApplication.shared.terminate(nil)
         }, label: {
            Image(systemName: "xmark.circle")
         }).buttonBorderShape(.circle)
      }.padding()
      Button("Option 1") {
         print("Option 1")
      }.buttonStyle(.borderedProminent)
      Button("Option 2") {
         print("Option 2")
      }.buttonStyle(.borderedProminent)
      Spacer()
   }.frame(width: 200, height: 180)
}.menuBarExtraStyle(.window)
```

Figure 6-33: *Control with a view*

Chapter 7

Data Storage

BASIC

7.1 - User Defaults

Up to this point, all data has been stored in arrays defined in the model, with values hard-coded into the application. As a result, the data is always the same each time the user launches the app. Any changes made to the model persist only while the application is running and are lost as soon as it is closed. To preserve values and retain all user-generated changes across launches, we must store data permanently on the device. Apple provides several systems for data storage, ranging from simple text files to fully indexed databases.

BASIC

App Storage

The simplest storage system available on Apple devices is called User Defaults. This system is designed to store user preferences, including values set by the user to control how the app behaves and values set by the app to restore previous states. These values are stored in a system-managed database and persist after the app is closed for as long as they are needed by the user or the application. SwiftUI provides the following property wrapper for storing and retrieving User Defaults values.

@AppStorage(String)

This property wrapper stores or retrieves a value from User Defaults. The argument is a string with the key of the value we want to access.

The User Defaults system can store any type of data, but it is recommended for short strings and small values. Its main purpose is to store the app's settings. For example, we can use it to let the user define a limit on the number of items managed by the app and then restore that limit each time the app is launched. To achieve this, all we need to do is define a property using the **@AppStorage** property wrapper, as shown below.

Listing 7-1: Storing and reading values from User Defaults

```
struct ContentView: View {
   @AppStorage("counter") var mycounter: Double = 0
```

```
    var body: some View {
        HStack {
            Stepper("", value: $mycounter)
                .labelsHidden()
            Text("\(mycounter.formatted(.number.precision(.
                fractionLength(0))))")
                .font(.title)
        }
    }
}
```

An **@AppStorage** property is used in the same way as a **@State** property, but its value is stored in the User Defaults system. As a result, the value persists even after the app is closed. In this example, we use a **Stepper** view to let the user select a value and store it in a property called **mycounter**. Because the property is defined with the **@AppStorage** property wrapper, the value remains in User Defaults when the app is closed and is automatically retrieved when the app is launched again.

Figure 7-1: *Value stored in User Defaults*

Do It Yourself

Create a new App project. Update the **ContentView** structure with the code in Listing 7-1. Run the application on an iPhone simulator. Press the buttons on the stepper to change the value. Wait a few seconds. Stop the execution of the app from the Stop button in Xcode. Run the application again. The value displayed on the screen should be the same one you selected before.

IMPORTANT

The **@AppStorage** property wrapper can only store simple values like strings and numbers, but you can also store other types of values, including custom data types, by converting them into **Data** structures, as we will see later.

7.2 - SwiftData

The User Defaults system was designed to store the app's state and configuration, and is therefore not suitable for large amounts of data. To offer a better solution, Apple created the **SwiftData** framework. This framework can store any amount of data in a database and provides all the tools needed to manage it. It includes a container to manage the data, a context to insert and fetch values, and an API to interact with the context to persist and retrieve that data, as shown below.

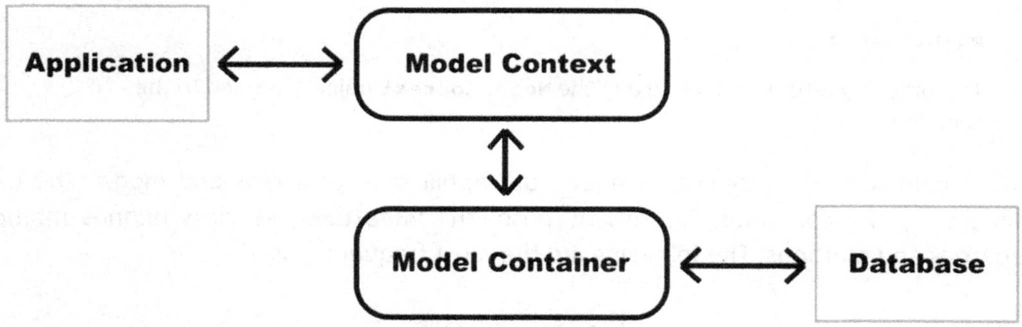

Figure 7-2: *Model structure*

The **Model Container** is the object in charge of managing the database and storing the data permanently on file. This object is created from the **`ModelContainer`** class, which includes the following initializer.

```
ModelContainer(for: Types, migrationPlan: Type, configurations: ModelConfiguration)
```

This initializer creates a container for the models specified by the arguments. The **for** argument is a list of references to the data types used to create the models. The **migrationPlan** argument is a reference to the data type that describes how to migrate to a new version of the container. And the **configurations** argument is a list of **`ModelConfiguration`** structures that specify the container's configuration.

To configure the container, the framework includes the **`ModelConfiguration`** structure. The following are some of the structure's initializers.

```
ModelConfiguration(isStoredInMemoryOnly: Bool)
```

This initializer creates a structure to configure a model container. The **isStoredInMemoryOnly** argument determines whether the data is stored permanently on disk or temporarily in memory.

```
ModelConfiguration(String, schema: Schema?, url: URL, allowsSave: Bool, cloudKitDatabase: CloudKitDatabase)
```

This initializer creates a structure to configure a model container. The first argument is the name we want to give the configuration, the **schema** argument is an object that maps the classes describing the model to the container, the **url** argument determines where the database is stored, the **allowsSave** argument specifies whether the changes in the context are automatically saved to the container (`true` by default), and the **cloudKitDatabase** argument is a structure that specifies the identifier of the CloudKit container used to share data with other devices. The structure defines the properties `automatic` and `none` to determine how the system is going to find the container, and the method `private(String)` to declare a specific container.

The container takes care of managing the data, but our application accesses that data through the **Model Context**. This is an object created by the `ModelContext` class. Although we can create the context manually, every container provides its own context. Below is the property included by the `ModelContainer` class to return a reference to this object.

`mainContext`

This property returns a reference to the `ModelContext` object assigned to the container.

The context is the object that allows our application to access and modify the data managed by the container. For this purpose, the `ModelContext` class defines multiple properties and methods. The following are the most frequently used.

`fetch(FetchDescriptor, batchSize: Int)`

This method retrieves from the container the objects that match the description specified by the arguments. The first argument is a structure that specifies the criteria and sort order used to retrieve the objects, and the **batchSize** argument specifies the maximum number of objects to retrieve.

`fetchCount(FetchDescriptor)`

This method returns an `Int` value with the number of objects found by the container that match the description specified by the argument. The argument is a structure that specifies the criteria and sort order used to find the objects.

`insert(Object)`

This method inserts an object into the context.

`delete(Object)`

This method removes an object from the context.

`save()`

This method saves the changes in the context to the container.

BASIC

Model

The first step when working with a database is to tell the system which types of values we want to store. In SwiftData, this procedure is straightforward. We define a class that includes all the properties required to store the user's data and use it to represent the data model. For this purpose, SwiftData provides the following macro.

`@Model`

This macro adds to a class all the code necessary to permanently store any object created from that class in a database.

To create a SwiftData model, all we need is to apply the **`@Model`** macro to a class. For example, we can convert the **`Book`** structure from our previous examples into a class and apply the **`@Model`** macro to turn it into a SwiftData model, as shown below.

Listing 7-2: Defining a SwiftData model

```
import SwiftUI
import SwiftData

@Model
class Book: Identifiable {
   var id: UUID = UUID()
   var title: String = ""
   var author: String = ""
   var cover: String = ""
   var year: Int = 0

   init(title: String, author: String, cover: String, year: Int) {
      self.title = title
      self.author = author
      self.cover = cover
      self.year = year
   }
   var displayYear: String {
      get {
         let value = year > 0 ? String(year) : "Undefined"
         return value
      }
   }
}
```

The **`@Model`** macro is defined in the **SwiftData** framework. After importing this framework, we apply the macro to the **`Book`** class and define the properties as before. The class includes a property to store a unique identifier for each book, along with all the properties required to store the information, including the title, author, cover, and year. Note that SwiftData requires properties to have a default value or be optional, so we assign an initial value to each one of them.

Store properties are used to define the structure of the data stored in the database, but we can also include any computed properties and methods we need to prepare and process that data. In this example, we include a computed property called **`displayYear`** to format the value of the **`year`** property for the views (**`Text`** views can only display strings).

BASIC

Container

The **@Model** macro uses a class to define the structure of the data our app can store, so we can create objects from this class, insert them into the context, and they will be permanently stored in the database. But we still need to create the container that will process the data and manage the database. Although we can do this manually by creating an instance of the **ModelContainer** class, as we will see later, SwiftUI includes the following modifier to create the container and inject it into the environment.

```
modelContainer(for: [Type], inMemory: Bool, isAutosaveEnabled: Bool, isUndoEnabled: Bool, onSetup: Closure)
```

This modifier creates a container with the configuration specified by the arguments and injects it into the environment. The **for** argument is a set with references to all the classes that make up the data model, the **inMemory** argument specifies whether the data is stored permanently on disk or temporarily in memory (**false** by default), the **isAutosaveEnabled** argument specifies whether the changes in the context are automatically saved to the container (**true** by default), the **isUndoEnabled** argument specifies whether the user should be able to undo and redo changes (**false** by default), and the **onSetup** argument provides a closure that is executed after the container is set up.

Like any data model, the SwiftData model must be injected into the environment from the window or the main view to make it available to all the views in the interface. The following example shows how to work with a SwiftData model along with the observable data models introduced in previous chapters.

Listing 7-3: Creating the container

```
import SwiftUI
import SwiftData

@main struct MyApp: App {
   @State private var appData = ApplicationData.shared

   var body: some Scene {
      WindowGroup {
         ContentView()
            .environment(appData)
            .modelContainer(for: [Book.self])
      }
   }
}
```

Unless we want to provide a specific configuration, the only argument required to create the container is a set with the data types of the classes we want to store in the database. In our example, this is the **Book** class defined in Listing 7-2. Now we have access to the data model to store any value required by the app (**ApplicationData**), and to the Model Container to store books in the database.

BASIC

Context

The **modelContainer()** modifier creates a container, but our application must interact with the context. To access the context assigned to the container, the environment includes the following property.

modelContext

This environment property returns a reference to the context assigned to the container.

When a value is modified, the system detects the change and automatically stores it in the container. When reading data, the process is reversed. The container retrieves the objects from the database and then moves them to the context. Once the objects are in the context, we can read their properties, change their values, or delete them. The problem with retrieving data from a database is that thousands or even millions of objects may be available. Getting all this information at once takes time and consumes resources. Therefore, we must retrieve only the objects that the user needs at any given time. For this purpose, SwiftData defines the **Query** macro.

@Query(filter: Predicate?, **sort:** KeyPath, **order:** SortOrder, **transaction:** Transaction?, **sectionBy:** KeyPath**)**

This macro performs a query on the container and keeps the objects synchronized. The **filter** argument provides a predicate for filtering the objects, the **sort** argument specifies the property used to sort the objects, the **order** argument is an enumeration with the values **forward** and **reverse** to determine whether the objects are listed in ascending or descending order, the **transaction** argument specifies the type of animation used to insert or remove objects from the list, and the **sectionBy** argument is a key path pointing to the property used to create the sections.

@Query(FetchDescriptor, **transaction:** Transaction?**)**

This macro performs a query on the container and keeps the objects synchronized. The first argument is a structure that defines the criteria to filter and sort the objects, and the **transaction** argument specifies the type of animation used to insert or remove objects from the list.

BASIC

Implementation

Using SwiftData to store user data in a database is straightforward. We define the model using the **@Model** macro to describe the data structure (Listing 7-2), create a container and inject it into the environment with the **modelContainer(for:)** modifier (Listing 7-3), and then access the context from the views to read, create, and modify objects.

The following example demonstrates how to use these tools to store and manage a list of books. The books are managed by the SwiftData model, but we still use an observable object to control the app's state. In this first example, the observable object requires only a single property to store the navigation path, as shown below.

Listing 7-4: Controlling the navigation path from an observable object

```
import SwiftUI

@Observable class ApplicationData {
   var viewPath = NavigationPath()

   static let shared: ApplicationData = ApplicationData()
   private init() { }
}
```

From the `ContentView` view, we read the books in the database with a `@Query` property and allow the user to open an additional view to add more.

Listing 7-5: Fetching books from the database

```
struct ContentView: View {
   @Environment(ApplicationData.self) private var appData
   @Environment(\.modelContext) var dbContext
   @Query var listBooks: [Book]

   var body: some View {
      @Bindable var appData = appData

      NavigationStack(path: $appData.viewPath) {
         List(listBooks) { book in
            CellBook(book: book)
         }
         .listStyle(.plain)
         .navigationTitle("Books")
         .toolbarTitleDisplayMode(.inline)
         .toolbar {
            ToolbarItem(placement: .topBarTrailing) {
               NavigationLink(value: "Add Book", label: {
                  Image(systemName: "plus")
               })
            }
         }
         .navigationDestination(for: String.self, destination: { viewID in
            if viewID == "Add Book" {
               AddBook()
            }
         })
      }
   }
}
struct CellBook: View {
   let book: Book

   var body: some View {
      HStack(alignment: .top) {
         Image(book.cover)
            .resizable()
            .scaledToFit()
```

```
            .frame(width: 80, height: 100)
         VStack(alignment: .leading, spacing: 2) {
            Text(book.title).bold()
            Text(book.author)
            Text(book.displayYear).font(.caption)
            Spacer()
         }
         Spacer()
      }.padding([.top], 10)
   }
}
#Preview {
   ContentView()
      .environment(ApplicationData.shared)
      .modelContainer(for: [Book.self], inMemory: true)
}
```

The list of values is created using a **List** view, as before, but this time we use the **@Query** macro to fetch the list of books from the database. Because we want to retrieve all objects stored in the database, the query does not require any parameters other than the property used to store the values.

The **@Query** macro automatically accesses the context and fetches the books from the database. In this example, however, we also define a property called **dbContext** to obtain a reference to the context from the environment, so we can use it later to manually modify or delete values. Note that we also apply the **modelContainer()** modifier to the preview to give the view access to the database. In this case, the data is stored in memory, so it is automatically discarded each time the preview is recreated.

The view in Listing 7-5 also includes a **NavigationLink** view and a **navigationDestination()** modifier to navigate to a view called **AddBook()**, where users can insert new books. In that view, we must create an instance of the **Book** class using the information provided by the user and then call the **insert()** method of the **ModelContext** object to add it to the database, as shown below.

Listing 7-6: Storing a book in the database

```
import SwiftUI
import SwiftData

struct AddBook: View {
   @Environment(ApplicationData.self) private var appData
   @Environment(\.modelContext) var dbContext

   @State private var titleInput: String = ""
   @State private var authorInput: String = ""
   @State private var yearInput: String = ""

   var body: some View {
      VStack(alignment: .trailing, spacing: 10) {
         TextField("Insert Title", text: $titleInput)
            .textFieldStyle(.roundedBorder)
         TextField("Insert Author", text: $authorInput)
            .textFieldStyle(.roundedBorder)
         TextField("Insert Year", text: $yearInput)
```

```
            .textFieldStyle(.roundedBorder)
            .keyboardType(.numbersAndPunctuation)
         Button("Save") {
            storeBook()
         }.buttonStyle(.glassProminent)
         Spacer()
      }.padding()
   }
   func storeBook() {
      let title = titleInput.trimmingCharacters(in: .whitespaces)
      let author = authorInput.trimmingCharacters(in: .whitespaces)
      if let year = Int(yearInput), !title.isEmpty && !author.isEmpty {
         let newBook = Book(title: title, author: author, cover:
            "nocover", year: year)
         dbContext.insert(newBook)
         try? dbContext.save()
         appData.viewPath.removeLast()
      }
   }
}
#Preview {
   AddBook()
      .environment(ApplicationData.shared)
      .modelContainer(for: [Book.self], inMemory: true)
}
```

This view contains three **TextField** views to allow the user to enter the title, author, and the year the book was published. Below the text fields there is also a button to store the book. For this purpose, the **Button** view calls a method that we use to trim the values, check that they are valid, and then save them to the database. To save the data in the database, we need to create an instance of the class we are using as a model (in our case, this is the **Book** class), insert it into the context using the **insert()** method, and finally call the **save()** method to save the changes in the context to the database. The **@Query** macro detects the change and updates the views with the new entry. The result is shown below.

Figure 7-3: *Interface to save and list books stored in a database*

Do It Yourself

Create a new App project. Update the **App** structure with the code in Listing 7-3. Create a Swift file called **ApplicationData.swift** for the code in Listing 7-4 and another called **BookModel.swift** for the SwiftData model in

Listing 7-2. Update the **ContentView.swift** file with the code in Listing 7-5. Create a SwiftUI file called **AddBook.swift** for the code in Listing 7-6. Remember to inject the **ApplicationData** object into the environment, as we did in Chapter 4, Listing 4-4. Download the book covers from our website. Create a new Asset Catalog and add the covers to it. Run the application. Press the + button to add a book. Insert the information and press Save. You should see something similar to Figure 7-3.

BASIC

Attributes

The properties in the **Book** class tell the database the type of values we want to store, but not how to store them. The database can store the values as they are, but it can also assign special attributes to them. For example, a value may be encrypted for security reasons or stored in a separate file for efficiency. To apply these attributes, SwiftData includes the following macros.

@Attribute(Option, **originalName:** String?, **hashModifier:** String?)

This macro assigns attributes to the properties of the model. The first argument is a structure with properties that determine the type of attribute we want to assign to the value, the **originalName** argument is used to migrate a value to a different name, and the **hashModifier** argument identifies the new version for migration.

@Transient

This macro marks a property as non-persistent, indicating that its value should not be stored in the database.

The **@Attribute** macro works with an **Option** structure. This structure determines the type of attribute to assign to the property. For this purpose, the structure includes the properties **allowsCloudEncryption** (it stores the value in an encrypted form), **externalStorage** (it stores the value in an external file), **preserveValueOnDeletion** (it preserves the value in the persistent history after deletion), **spotlight** (it indexes the value so it can appear in Spotlight search results), **ephemeral** (it tells the system not to store the value in the database), **unique** (it ensures the value is unique), and **codable** (it encodes and decodes values for storage) The structure also includes the **transformable(by: Type)** method to transform a value of a custom data type into a form that can be stored in the database.

Probably the most useful of these attributes are the **allowsCloudEncryption** attribute, used to store encrypted data, the **externalStorage** attribute, used to store images in external files to improve database performance, and the **unique** attribute, used to avoid duplicate values. For example, with the **unique** attribute we can ensure that the identifiers for each book are unique.

Listing 7-7: Storing unique values

```
@Model
class Book: Identifiable {
    @Attribute(.unique) var id: UUID = UUID()
    var title: String = ""
    var author: String = ""
    var cover: String = ""
    var year: Int = 0

    init(title: String, author: String, cover: String, year: Int) {
        self.title = title
        self.author = author
        self.cover = cover
        self.year = year
    }
    var displayYear: String {
        get {
            let value = year > 0 ? String(year) : "Undefined"
            return value
        }
    }
}
```

The **UUID** structure guarantees that each value is unique, but we can make the mistake of using the identifier of one book to store another. By implementing the **@Attribute** macro with the value **unique**, we ensure that this can never happen. The database will refuse to store a book with the same identifier as another book.

Do It Yourself

Update the **Book** class with the code in Listing 7-7. The application should work as before, but now SwiftData checks for duplicates and does not allow you to store books with the same identifier. We will see more examples on how to apply attributes later.

If the uniqueness of an object is determined by multiple values, we can use the **#Unique** macro. This macro ensures that the objects are unique based on all the required values.

#Unique([PartialKeyPath])

This macro determines which properties SwiftData has to check to make sure that the objects are unique. The argument is an array of key paths that specify the properties involved.

For example, books may have the same title, author or year of publication, but we don't want those three values to be the same. If we want to make sure that the user doesn't insert two books with the same title, author and year, we can include a **#Unique** macro, as shown below.

Listing 7-8: Using the `#Unique` macro to avoid duplicates

```
@Model
class Book: Identifiable {
   #Unique<Book>([\.title, \.author, \.year])

   @Attribute(.unique) var id: UUID = UUID()
   var title: String = ""
   var author: String = ""
   var cover: String = ""
   var year: Int = 0

   init(title: String, author: String, cover: String, year: Int) {
      self.title = title
      self.author = author
      self.cover = cover
      self.year = year
   }
   var displayYear: String {
      get {
         let value = year > 0 ? String(year) : "Undefined"
         return value
      }
   }
}
```

When multiple properties are used to determine the uniqueness of an object, the system must search the database and compare those values against every existing entry. This process consumes resources and can become expensive as the database grows. To improve performance, we can create indexes. Indexes are auxiliary data structures that store selected values to speed up queries. SwiftData provides the following macro to define these indexes.

`#Index``([PartialKeyPath])`

This macro creates indexes for a SwiftData model. The argument is an array of key paths that specify the properties we want to create the indexes for.

The syntax for the **`#Index`** macro is the same used for the **`#Unique`** macro. So if we want to use the title, author and year as unique values, as we did in the previous example, we can create an **`#Index`** macro with these properties too, as shown below.

Listing 7-9: Creating indexes for better performance

```
@Model
class Book: Identifiable {
   #Unique<Book>([\.title, \.author, \.year])
   #Index<Book>([\.title, \.author, \.year])

   @Attribute(.unique) var id: UUID = UUID()
   var title: String = ""
   var author: String = ""
   var cover: String = ""
   var year: Int = 0
```

```
    init(title: String, author: String, cover: String, year: Int) {
        self.title = title
        self.author = author
        self.cover = cover
        self.year = year
    }
    var displayYear: String {
        get {
            let value = year > 0 ? String(year) : "Undefined"
            return value
        }
    }
}
```

BASIC

Relationships

The **Book** class includes properties to store all the values we need for a book, including the author's name. This approach has a significant drawback: users must re-enter the author's name every time they add a new book. This process is error-prone and time-consuming, and when multiple books share the same author, there is no guarantee that the name will be entered consistently. For example, one book might include the author's middle name, while another might include only the first and last name. Without consistent author names, it becomes difficult to support features such as sorting books by author or listing only the books written by a specific author. The problem becomes more pronounced when we want to store additional information about the author beyond the name, such as the biography or the date of birth. Properly organizing this data requires separate models, which means creating new classes to represent them. In our example, we can create a new class called **Author** to store the author's name, as shown below.

Listing 7-10: Creating a second model to store the authors

```
import SwiftUI
import SwiftData
@Model
class Author: Identifiable {
    @Attribute(.unique) var id: UUID = UUID()
    var name: String = ""
    var books: [Book]? = []

    init(name: String, books: [Book]) {
        self.name = name
        self.books = books
    }
}
```

Since an author can have multiple books, we need to tell the system which **Book** objects the author is associated with. For this purpose, the **Author** class includes a property called **books** to store an array of **Book** objects. This establishes a relationship between the **Author** class and the **Book** class, but it is not enough for the system to recognize the connection; we also need a property in the **Book** class to establish the reverse relationship with the **Author** class, as shown below.

Listing 7-11: Creating a relationship with the Author class

```
@Model
class Book: Identifiable {
   @Attribute(.unique) var id: UUID = UUID()
   var title: String = ""
   var author: Author?
   var cover: String = ""
   var year: Int = 0

   init(title: String, author: Author?, cover: String, year: Int) {
      self.title = title
      self.author = author
      self.cover = cover
      self.year = year
   }
   var displayYear: String {
      get {
         let value = year > 0 ? String(year) : "Undefined"
         return value
      }
   }
}
```

In this example, we have turned the **author** property into an optional property of type **Author** to store an instance of the **Author** class. This creates a connection between the **Book** object and the **Author** object. From this property and the **books** property in the **Author** class, the system can see what **Author** object is associated with each book, and which **Book** objects are associated with each author. (In this example, we assume that our app only stores books written by one author.)

The connection between the **Book** and **Author** class we just created is called a *Relationship*. Relationships are created automatically by SwiftData when an instance of one class references an instance of another. However, since there can be different types of relationships, SwiftData provides the following macro to define them explicitly.

@Relationship(Option, **deleteRule:** DeleteRule, **minimumModelCount:** Int?, **maximumModelCount:** Int?, **originalName:** String?, **inverse:** AnyKeyPath?, **hashModifier:** String?**)**

This macro establishes a relationship between models. The first argument is used to assign an attribute to the property (these are the same attributes applied by the **@Attribute** macro). The **deleteRule** argument is an enumeration with values to specify the rule to follow when an object in a relationship is deleted. The possible values are **cascade**, **deny**, **noAction**, and **nullify**. The **minimumModelCount** and **maximumModelCount** arguments define the minimum and maximum objects allowed in the relationship. The **originalName** argument is used to migrate a value to a different name. The **inverse** argument tells SwiftData which property in the other object is participating in the relationship. And the **hashModifier** argument identifies the version for migration purposes.

The most important values in a relationship are the deletion rule and the inverse property. The deletion rule determines what happens to the destination of a relationship when the object is deleted. For example, if we delete a **Book** object, should the **Author** object assigned to the **author** property also be deleted? There are four deletion rules available: **cascade** (the **Author** object is deleted when the **Book** object is deleted), **deny** (the **Book** object is not deleted when it is linked to an **Author** object), **noAction** (the **Author** object is not affected by what happens to the **Book** object), and **nullify** (when a **Book** object is deleted, the **Author** object linked to that book loses the connection with the book, but is not deleted). On the other hand, the inverse property helps the system determine the bidirectional connection between objects so that the system knows what to do with the other side of the relationship when an object is changed or removed.

By default, the system defines the deletion rule as **nullify**, which means that the value of the property involved in the relationship is set to **nil** but the object is not deleted. For example, if we delete an **Author** object, the **author** property in the **Book** object is set to **nil**, but the **Book** object is not deleted. This is usually the best approach, because it gives us absolute control over what is deleted and what is not.

Although we can use the relationships set by default, it is always recommended to declare them explicitly with the **@Relationship** macro, especially if we are working in a team, so that everyone knows what properties are involved in the relationship and what kind of relationship we are working with. For our example, we should declare the **author** property in the **Book** class as follows.

Listing 7-12: Defining the relationship in the `Book` **class**

```
@Relationship(deleteRule: .nullify, inverse: \Author.books) var author:
Author?
```

The inverse relationship is only declared on one side of the relationship, so all we need to do in the **Author** class is to declare the delete rule for the relationship, as shown below.

Listing 7-13: Defining the relationship in the `Author` **class**

```
@Relationship(deleteRule: .nullify) var books: [Book]? = []
```

Now our model is ready to store books and authors, we just need to provide the interface for the user to create and associate these objects. For this example, we will create two additional views, one to list the available authors and another to add more.

Figure 7-4: *Interface to add and select authors*

How we build this interface depends on the type of navigation we use and how our application is organized. In our example, we need to add two properties to the data model, one to store a reference to the book selected by the user, and another for the author.

Listing 7-14: Controlling the values selected by the user from the model

```
@Observable class ApplicationData {
   var viewPath = NavigationPath()
   var selectedBook: Book? = nil
   var selectedAuthor: Author? = nil

   static let shared: ApplicationData = ApplicationData()
   private init() { }
}
```

As shown in Figure 7-4, we need two new views to allow the user to associate an author with a book. One view lists the existing authors, and the other allows the user to add more. Because we use strings to identify the links, we need to open these views from the **navigationDestination()** modifier defined in the **ContentView** view, as we did earlier for the **AddBook** view (see Listing 7-6).

Listing 7-15: Opening additional views for navigation

```
.navigationDestination(for: String.self, destination: { viewID in
   if viewID == "Add Book" {
      AddBook()
   } else if viewID == "List Authors" {
      ListAuthors()
   } else if viewID == "Add Author" {
      AddAuthor()
   }
})
```

The option to select an author must be added to the **AddBook** view. For this purpose, we need to replace the text field used before to enter the author's name with a button that opens the **ListAuthors** view, as shown below.

Listing 7-16: Assigning an author to a book

```
struct AddBook: View {
   @Environment(ApplicationData.self) private var appData
   @Environment(\.modelContext) var dbContext
   @State private var titleInput: String = ""
   @State private var yearInput: String = ""

   var body: some View {
      VStack(alignment: .leading, spacing: 10) {
         TextField("Insert Title", text: $titleInput)
            .textFieldStyle(.roundedBorder)
         TextField("Insert Year", text: $yearInput)
            .textFieldStyle(.roundedBorder)
            .keyboardType(.numbersAndPunctuation)
```

```
        VStack(alignment: .leading) {
            Text("Author")
            NavigationLink(value: "List Authors", label: {
                Text(appData.selectedAuthor?.name ?? "Select")
            })
        }
        HStack {
            Spacer()
            Button("Save") {
                storeBook()
            }.buttonStyle(.borderedProminent)
        }
        Spacer()
    }.padding()
  }
  func storeBook() {
    let title = titleInput.trimmingCharacters(in: .whitespaces)
    if let year = Int(yearInput), !title.isEmpty {
        let newBook = Book(title: title, author: appData.selectedAuthor,
            cover: "nocover", year: year)
        dbContext.insert(newBook)
        try? dbContext.save()
        appData.selectedAuthor = nil
        appData.viewPath.removeLast()
    }
  }
}
```

In this application, we use the **selectedAuthor** property in the observable object to keep a reference to the **Author** object selected by the user, so in addition to adding the **NavigationLink** to get the list of authors, we also modify the **storeBook()** method to initialize the **Book** structure with this value instead of a string. After the book is stored, we clear the selection by assigning **nil** to the **selectedAuthor** property and then navigate back to the previous view.

When the user taps the **NavigationLink** in the **AddBook** view, the **ListAuthors** view opens to let the user select an author. To fetch the list of authors from this view, we need to define a property using the **@Query** macro and display the results in a **List** view. In this case, we also use a **@State** property to track the selection, so we can determine which author was chosen and assign it to the **selectedAuthor** property in the observable object.

Listing 7-17: Listing the authors

```
import SwiftUI
import SwiftData

struct ListAuthors: View {
    @Environment(ApplicationData.self) private var appData
    @Query private var authorsList: [Author]
    @State private var selection: Author.ID? = nil

    var body: some View {
        List(authorsList, selection: $selection) { author in
            Text(author.name)
        }
        .onChange(of: selection, initial: false) { old, idAuthor in
```

```
            appData.selectedAuthor = authorsList.first(where: {
               $0.id == idAuthor })
            appData.viewPath.removeLast()
         }
         .toolbar {
            ToolbarItem(placement: .topBarTrailing) {
               NavigationLink(value: "Add Author", label: {
                  Image(systemName: "plus")
               })
            }
         }
      }
}
#Preview {
   NavigationStack {
      ListAuthors()
         .environment(ApplicationData.shared)
         .modelContainer(for: [Book.self, Author.self], inMemory: true)
   }
}
```

When the user selects an author, we retrieve the reference from the **authorsList** property, assign it to the **selectedAuthor** property in the observable object, and then dismiss the view so the user can continue entering the remaining information for the book. But if the author the user wants to associate with the book is not listed, we must provide a way to add one. For this purpose, we include a button in the navigation bar. The **NavigationLink** for this button is identified by the string "Add Author," so the **AddAuthor** view opens when the button is pressed.

The **AddAuthor** view must provide a text field to enter the author's name and create the **Author** object using that information, as shown below.

Listing 7-18: Adding new authors

```
import SwiftUI
import SwiftData

struct AddAuthor: View {
   @Environment(ApplicationData.self) private var appData
   @Environment(\.modelContext) var dbContext
   @State private var nameInput: String = ""

   var body: some View {
      VStack(alignment: .leading, spacing: 10) {
         TextField("Insert Name", text: $nameInput)
            .textFieldStyle(.roundedBorder)
         HStack {
            Spacer()
            Button("Save") {
               storeAuthor()
            }.buttonStyle(.borderedProminent)
         }
         Spacer()
      }.padding()
   }
```

```
    func storeAuthor() {
        let name = nameInput.trimmingCharacters(in: .whitespaces)
        if !name.isEmpty {
            let newAuthor = Author(name: name, books: [])
            dbContext.insert(newAuthor)
            try? dbContext.save()
            appData.selectedAuthor = newAuthor
            appData.viewPath.removeLast(2)
        }
    }
}
#Preview {
    NavigationStack {
        AddAuthor()
            .environment(ApplicationData.shared)
            .modelContainer(for: [Book.self, Author.self], inMemory: true)
    }
}
```

The procedure for adding a new author to the database is the same as for books. We create an object (in this case an instance of the **Author** class), insert it into the context using the **insert()** method, and then save the change to the container with the **save()** method. Note that, since the author has not yet been associated with any books, we initialize the **books** property with an empty array. After the **Author** object is created and inserted into the context, we assign it to the **selectedAuthor** property to indicate that the newly created author is now selected. We then remove two views from the navigation path, which takes the user directly back to the **AddBook** view and avoids the extra step of selecting the new author from the list.

Once the remaining information is entered and the user saves the new book, the **listBooks** property in the **ContentView** view is updated and the book appears in the list on the screen. This update happens automatically, but because the author's name is no longer stored as a string, we must update the **CellBook** view to display the value of the **name** property of the **Author** object instead, as shown below.

Listing 7-19: Displaying the author's name

```
struct CellBook: View {
    let book: Book
    var body: some View {
        HStack(alignment: .top) {
            Image(book.cover)
                .resizable()
                .scaledToFit()
                .frame(width: 80, height: 100)
            VStack(alignment: .leading, spacing: 2) {
                Text(book.title).bold()
                Text(book.author?.name ?? "Undefined")
                Text(book.displayYear).font(.caption)
                Spacer()
            }
            Spacer()
        }.padding([.top], 10)
    }
}
```

Because a book may not have an author (the value of the **author** property may be **nil**), we check the value with the nil-coalescing operator and display the string "Undefined" if no author is found.

There is only one more change we need to perform for this example to be ready. When we add a new model to our application, as we did with the **Author** class in this example, SwiftData can recognize it based on the relationships and automatically add it to the container, but it is always recommended to do this explicitly via the **modelContainer()** modifier. The new modifier for the **App** structure should be declared as follows.

Listing 7-20: Including all the models in the container

```
WindowGroup {
    ContentView()
        .environment(appData)
        .modelContainer(for: [Book.self, Author.self])
}
```

Do It Yourself

Create a new Swift file called **AuthorModel.swift** for the code in Listing 7-10. Update the **Book** class with the code in Listing 7-11, the **author** property in the **Book** class with the code in Listing 7-12, and the **books** property in the **Author** class with the code in Listing 7-13. Update the **ApplicationData** class with the code in Listing 7-14, the **navigation-Destination()** modifier of the **ContentView** view with the code in Listing 7-15, and the **AddBook** view with the code in Listing 7-16. Create two SwiftUI files called **ListAuthors.swift** and **AddAuthor.swift** for the codes in Listings 7-17 and 7-18. Update the **CellBook** view with the code in Listing 7-19 and the **App** structure with the code in Listing 7-20. Run the application on an iPhone simulator. Press the + button to add a book. You should see the interface in Figure 7-4 (left). Press the Select button to select an author for the book. You should see an empty list. Press the + button to add an author. Enter the author's name and press Save. Enter the title for the book and the year of publication, and press Save. You should see the book on the list, including the name of the author.

BASIC

Deleting Objects

Deleting an object from the database is no different than any other value (see Chapter 4, Listing 4-30). We need to implement a **ForEach** view to list the values, apply the **onDelete()** modifier to this view, and then remove the objects from the context with the **delete()** method.

Listing 7-21: Deleting objects

```
List {
   ForEach(listBooks) { book in
      CellBook(book: book)
   }
   .onDelete { indexes in
      for index in indexes {
         dbContext.delete(listBooks[index])
      }
      try? dbContext.save()
   }
}
```

The indexes received by the **onDelete()** modifier are the indexes of the objects the user wants to delete from the array in the **listBooks** property. Therefore, to remove the objects selected by the user, we iterate through the indexes with a **for in** loop, get the objects from the **listOfBooks** array in those indexes, and remove them from the context with the **delete()** method. Once the objects are removed from the context, the **listOfBooks** property is automatically updated and the changes are displayed on the screen.

Do It Yourself

Update the **List** view in the **ContentView** structure with the code in Listing 7-21. Press the + button to add a new book. After the book is added to the list, drag it to the left. You should see the Delete button. Press the button to remove the book. The system automatically includes a swipe action to allow the user to delete the rows, but you can create custom actions with the **swipeActions()** modifier, as we did in the example in Chapter 4, Listing 4-38.

BASIC

Sorting Objects

Objects returned by a query are typically ordered by their creation time, but this behavior is not guaranteed. To enforce a specific order, the **@Query** macro accepts two arguments. The **sort** argument specifies the key path of the property used for sorting, and the **order** argument determines whether the results are returned in ascending or descending order (**forward** or **reverse**). For example, the following query retrieves books sorted by title in ascending order.

Listing 7-22: Sorting objects

```
@Query(sort: \Book.title, order: .forward) private var listBooks: [Book]
```

To sort the objects, the **@Query** macro uses the values provided by its arguments to create a **SortDescriptor** structure. If we need more control over the sorting behavior, we can create and supply this structure ourselves. The following is the structure's initializer.

SortDescriptor(KeyPath, comparator: StandardComparator, order: SortOrder)—This initializer creates a **SortDescriptor** structure that sorts the objects according to the value of the property specified by the first argument. The **comparator** argument determines how to compare the values. It is a structure with the type properties **lexical**, **localized**, and **localizedStandard** (default). And the **order** argument determines if the objects will be sorted in ascending or descending order. It is an enumeration with the values **forward** and **reverse**.

The **@Query** macro can take an array of **SortDescriptor** structures to determine the sort order of the objects. The advantage of using **SortDescriptor** structures is that we can specify multiple conditions for sorting the list. The final order is determined based on the position of the **SortDescriptor** structures in the array. For example, the following query sorts the books first by author and then by year.

Listing 7-23: Sorting books by author and year

```
@Query(sort: [SortDescriptor(\Book.author?.name, order: .forward),
SortDescriptor(\Book.year)]) private var listBooks: [Book]
```

The values are sorted according to a comparator. The **String** structure defines the **StandardComparator** structure to create a comparator for those types of values. The structure includes type properties to create instances for common comparators. The ones currently available are **lexical**, **localizedStandard** (default), and **localized**. The structure returned by the **lexical** property sorts the values alphabetically. For instance, if we have an array with the values 1, 2, and 10, the order will be 1, 10, 2 (the value 10 begins with 1, which comes before 2). This also applies to letters. Uppercase letters come before lowercase letters, so words beginning with a lowercase letter are moved to the end of the list. On the other hand, the structure returned by the **localizedStandard** property sorts the values numerically (1, 2, 10), which is also true for letters (words beginning with uppercase letters are sorted along with lowercase letters). And finally, the structure returned by the **localized** property sorts the values alphabetically like the **lexical** structure, but uppercase and lowercase letters are sorted together, as with the **localizedStandard** structure.

By default, the values are sorted with the **localizedStandard** structure. The following example shows how to apply a **lexical** sorting instead.

Listing 7-24: Sorting with a lexical comparator

```
@Query(sort: [SortDescriptor(\Book.title, comparator: .lexical, order:
.forward)]) private var listBooks: [Book]
```

Do It Yourself

Update the **@Query** macro in the **ContentView** structure with the example you want to try. Run the application on an iPhone simulator and insert books with different values to see if they are sorted as specified by the query.

BASIC

Filtering Objects

So far we have retrieved all the books in the database, but the **@Query** macro can take an additional argument to filter the objects. The argument is called **filter** and takes a structure called **Predicate** to specify the condition for the filter. SwiftData includes the following macro to create this structure.

#Predicate(Closure)

This macro produces the code to create a predicate. The argument is a closure that specifies the condition to filter the objects.

The closure assigned to the **#Predicate** macro receives a value representing the object to be filtered, so we can use that value to set the condition. For instance, in the following example, we use a predicate to filter the books by year.

Listing 7-25: Filtering books by year

```
@Query(filter: #Predicate<Book> { $0.year == 1986 }) private var
listBooks: [Book]
```

The **Predicate** structure is generic, so we need to specify the data type of the values we want to filter. In this case, it is the **Book** class. Inside the closure, we get the instance of the **Book** class and compare the value of the **year** property with the number 1986. If the values match, the condition returns **true** and the book is included in the list, otherwise the book is ignored.

The condition in Listing 7-25 implements the == operator to compare the values, but all other comparison operators are available, including <, <=, >, >=, ==, and !=, and also logical operators such as && (AND), || (OR), and ! (NOT). For example, we can look for books that have been assigned an author and were published after the year 2000.

Listing 7-26: Filtering books by author and year

```
@Query(filter: #Predicate<Book> {
   $0.author != nil && $0.year > 2000
}) private var listBooks: [Book]
```

For collections and sequences of values, we can also implement the methods **allSatisfy()**, **filter()**, **contains()**, **contains(where:)**, and **starts(with:)**. And to perform a case-insensitive search, we can use the **localizedStandardContains()** method. For example, we can use this method to get only the books whose author name is "Stephen" without considering lowercase or uppercase letters.

Listing 7-27: Filtering books by text

```
@Query(filter: #Predicate<Book> {
   $0.author?.name.localizedStandardContains("Stephen") == true
}) private var listBooks: [Book]
```

BASIC

Dynamic Query

The **@Query** macro is built on a structure defined in the **SwiftData** framework called **Query**. This means that we can replace the **Query** structure generated by the macro to change the sorting and filtering criteria at any time. As we have seen in Chapter 3 (see Binding Structures), this is achieved by prefixing the property name with an underscore, as in _ **myQuery**. For example, the following code shows how to replace the **Query** structure associated with a **@Query** property when the view is initialized.

Listing 7-28: Defining a dynamic query

```
@Query private var listBooks: [Book]

init() {
   _listBooks = Query(sort: \Book.title, order: .reverse)
}
```

In this example, we define a simple **@Query** property that fetches all the books from the database with no specific order, but when the view is initialized, we assign a new **Query** structure to the property to sort the books by title in reverse alphabetical order, so the books are displayed on the screen using that criterion.

Do It Yourself

Update the **@Query** property in the **ContentView** structure with the code in Listing 7-28 and add the initializer below it. Run the application on an iPhone simulator. You should see the list of books ordered by title in reverse alphabetical order, as specified by the **Query** structure created in the initializer.

The ability to assign a new **Query** structure to a **@Query** property allows us to change the sorting or filtering criteria in response to user input. For instance, the following example shows how to initialize a new **Query** structure to sort the values according to the order selected by the user.

Listing 7-29: Defining a dynamic query

```
struct ContentView: View {
   @Environment(ApplicationData.self) private var appData
   @Environment(\.modelContext) var dbContext
   @State private var orderBooks: SortOrder = .forward

   var body: some View {
      @Bindable var appData = appData

      NavigationStack(path: $appData.viewPath) {
         ListBooksView(orderBooks: orderBooks)
            .listStyle(.plain)
            .navigationTitle("Books")
            .toolbarTitleDisplayMode(.inline)
            .toolbar {
               ToolbarItem(placement: .topBarTrailing) {
                  Button("Sort", systemImage: "gear", action: {
                     orderBooks = orderBooks == .forward ? .reverse :
                        .forward
                  })
               }
               ToolbarSpacer(placement: .topBarTrailing)
               ToolbarItem(placement: .topBarTrailing) {
                  NavigationLink(value: "Add Book", label: {
                     Image(systemName: "plus")
                  })
               }
            }
            .navigationDestination(for: String.self, destination: {
               viewID in
               if viewID == "Add Book" {
                  AddBook()
               } else if viewID == "List Authors" {
                  ListAuthors()
               } else if viewID == "Add Author" {
                  AddAuthor()
               }
            })
      }
   }
}
struct ListBooksView: View {
   @Query var listBooks: [Book]

   init(orderBooks: SortOrder) {
      _listBooks = Query(sort: \Book.title, order: orderBooks)
   }
   var body: some View {
      List {
         ForEach(listBooks) { book in
            CellBook(book: book)
         }
```

```
        }
    }
}
```

The user selection is handled in the **ContentView** view, but to be able to create a new **Query** structure based on that selection, we move the **List** view into a separate view called **ListBooksView**. To store the **SortOrder** value chosen by the user, the **ContentView** view includes a **@State** property called **orderBooks**. When the user taps the button in the navigation bar, the **orderBooks** property is toggled, the views are updated, the value of the property is passed to the **ListBooksView** view, the **Query** structure is recreated, and the order of the list changes, as shown below.

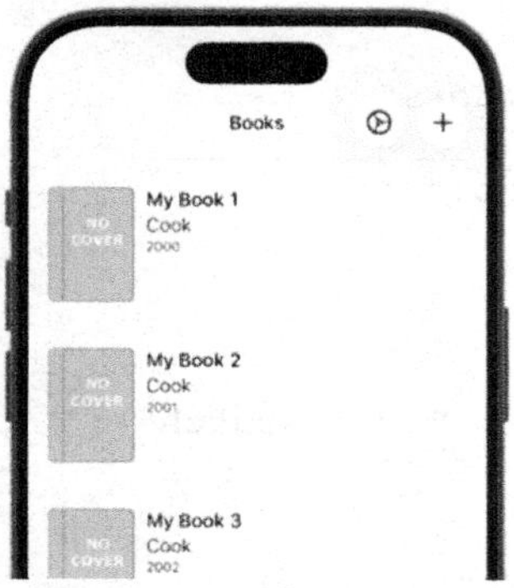

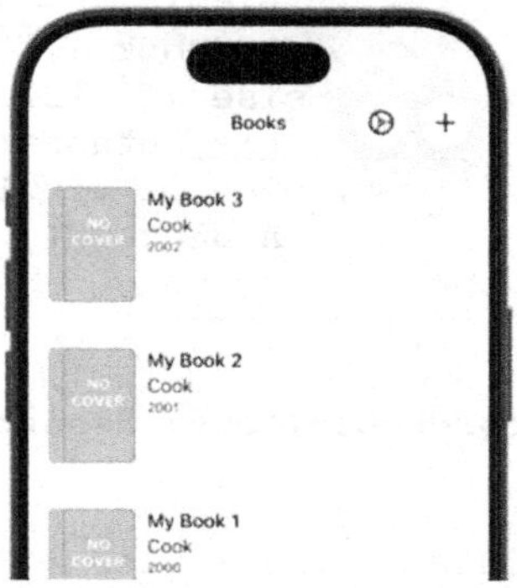

Figure 7-5: *Order of objects set by the user*

Do It Yourself

Update the **ContentView.swift** file with the code in Listing 7-29. Run the application on an iPhone simulator. Add a few books and press the button in the navigation bar. You should see the list of books alternate between ascending and descending order.

BASIC

Search

With a dynamic query we can also search for values provided by the user. For example, we can allow the user to search books by title.

Listing 7-30: Searching books by title

```
struct ContentView: View {
   @Environment(ApplicationData.self) private var appData
   @Environment(\.modelContext) var dbContext
   @State private var searchValue: String = ""

   var body: some View {
      @Bindable var appData = appData
```

```swift
        NavigationStack(path: $appData.viewPath) {
            ListBooksView(search: searchValue)
                .listStyle(.plain)
                .navigationTitle("Books")
                .toolbarTitleDisplayMode(.inline)
                .toolbar {
                    ToolbarItem(placement: .topBarTrailing) {
                        NavigationLink(value: "Add Book", label: {
                            Image(systemName: "plus")
                        })
                    }
                }
                .navigationDestination(for: String.self, destination: {
                    viewID in
                    if viewID == "Add Book" {
                        AddBook()
                    } else if viewID == "List Authors" {
                        ListAuthors()
                    } else if viewID == "Add Author" {
                        AddAuthor()
                    }
                })
        }
        .searchable(text: $searchValue, prompt: Text("Search"))
    }
}
struct ListBooksView: View {
    @Query private var listBooks: [Book]

    init(search: String) {
        var predicate = #Predicate<Book> { _ in true }
        if !search.isEmpty {
            let searching = search.lowercased()
            predicate = #Predicate<Book> { book in
                book.title.localizedStandardContains(searching)
            }
        }
        _listBooks = Query<Book, [Book]>(filter: predicate, sort:
            \Book.title, order: .forward)
    }
    var body: some View {
        List {
            ForEach(listBooks) { book in
                CellBook(book: book)
            }
        }
    }
}
```

To allow the user to search for a value, we implement the **searchable()** modifier (see Chapter 5, Listing 5-17). This modifier displays a search field and stores the text entered by the user in a binding property, so we can pass the value of this property to the **ListBooksView** view to create the query. When the view is initialized, we build a predicate that searches for books whose title contains the text entered by the user. The result is shown below.

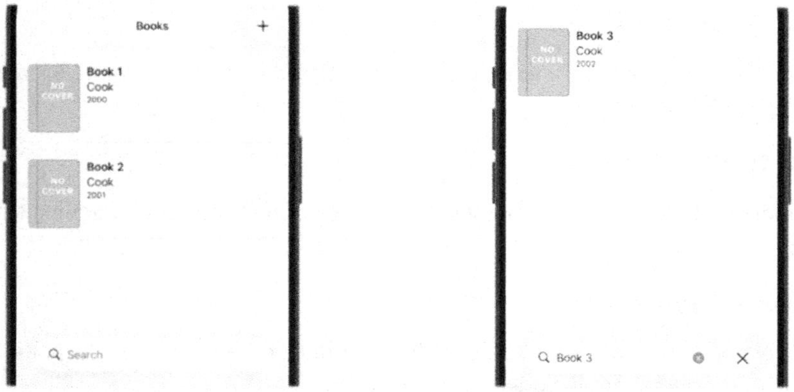

Figure 7-6: *User search*

Do It Yourself

Update the **ContentView.swift** file with the code in Listing 7-30. Run the application on an iPhone simulator, add new books, and perform a search. You should see only the books whose titles contain the string entered in the search bar.

PRO

Fetching Objects

So far we have used the tools provided by SwiftData to work with SwiftUI views, but there are situations where we need to access the objects in the database from outside a view. The **`ModelContext`** class includes the **`fetch()`** and **`fetchCount()`** methods to fetch objects, but to specify the predicate and sort descriptors, we need to implement a structure provided by SwiftData called **`FetchDescriptor`**. The following is the structure's initializer.

`FetchDescriptor(predicate:` `Predicate?,` **`sortBy:`** `[SortDescriptor])`

This initializer creates a structure for filtering and sorting objects. The **predicate** argument is a **`Predicate`** structure to filter the objects, and the **sortBy** argument is an array of **`SortDescriptor`** structures to sort them.

The **`FetchDescriptor`** structure includes the following properties to change the values or provide additional configuration.

`predicate`

This property sets or returns the **`Predicate`** structure assigned to the fetch descriptor.

`sortBy`

This property sets or returns the array of **`SortDescriptor`** structures assigned to the fetch descriptor.

fetchLimit

This property sets or returns an **Int** value that determines the maximum number of objects to fetch.

fetchOffset

This property sets or returns an **Int** value that determines where the fetching should begin.

includePendingChanges

This property sets or returns a Boolean value that determines whether the pending changes in the context are included in the result.

We can use a fetch descriptor to prepare the information for the views or to process objects in the background. The following example creates a fetch descriptor to retrieve all the books that haven't yet been assigned an author and prints the titles on the console.

Listing 7-31: Fetching objects manually

```
.onAppear {
   let predicate = #Predicate<Book> { book in
      book.author?.name == nil
   }
   let sort = SortDescriptor<Book>(\.title, order: .forward)

   let descriptor = FetchDescriptor<Book>(predicate: predicate,
      sortBy: [sort])
   if let list = try? dbContext.fetch(descriptor) {
      for book in list {
         print(book.title)
      }
   }
}
```

Although we could use the same approach to count objects in the database, doing so would load the objects into memory and unnecessarily consume resources. To avoid this issue, the **ModelContext** class provides the **fetchCount()** method. This method returns an integer representing the number of objects that would be returned if we executed the same request using the **fetch()** method.

Listing 7-32: Counting objects

```
.onAppear {
   let predicate = #Predicate<Book> { book in
      book.author == nil
   }
   let sort = SortDescriptor<Book>(\.title, order: .forward)
   let descriptor = FetchDescriptor<Book>(predicate: predicate,
      sortBy: [sort])
```

```
    if let count = try? dbContext.fetchCount(descriptor) {
        print(count)
    }
}
```

Do It Yourself

Apply the **onAppear()** modifier in Listing 7-31 to the **ListBooksView** view. Run the application on an iPhone simulator. Insert a book without an author. You should see the title of the book in the console. Update the modifier with the code in Listing 7-32. Now you should see the number of books without an author printed on the console.

Another practical use of fetch descriptors and the **fetchCount()** method is to check for duplicates. Although we can modify a property in the model with the **@Attribute** macro and the value **unique** to ensure that no object with the same value is stored in the database, sometimes we need to be able to warn the user before a duplicate is created or have more control over the situation. In such cases, we can use a fetch descriptor with a predicate that searches for existing objects with the same values before creating a new one. In the following example, the **AddAuthor** view checks if the author entered by the user already exists in the database before storing the new **Author** object.

Listing 7-33: Checking for duplicates

```
struct AddAuthor: View {
    @Environment(ApplicationData.self) private var appData
    @Environment(\.modelContext) var dbContext
    @State private var nameInput: String = ""
    @State private var openAlert: Bool = false

    var body: some View {
        VStack(alignment: .leading, spacing: 10) {
            TextField("Insert Name", text: $nameInput)
                .textFieldStyle(.roundedBorder)
            HStack {
                Spacer()
                Button("Save") {
                    storeAuthor()
                }.buttonStyle(.borderedProminent)
            }
            Spacer()
        }.padding()
        .alert("Error", isPresented: $openAlert, actions: {
            Button("OK", role: .cancel, action: {})
        }, message: { Text("The author already exists") })
    }
    func storeAuthor() {
        let name = nameInput.trimmingCharacters(in: .whitespaces)
        if !name.isEmpty {
            let predicate = #Predicate<Author> { $0.name == name }
            let descriptor = FetchDescriptor<Author>(predicate: predicate)
```

```swift
            if let count = try? dbContext.fetchCount(descriptor), count > 0 {
               openAlert = true
            } else {
               let newAuthor = Author(name: name, books: [])
               dbContext.insert(newAuthor)
               try? dbContext.save()
               appData.selectedAuthor = newAuthor
               appData.viewPath.removeLast(2)
            }
         }
      }
   }
```

This example creates a fetch descriptor for the **Author** model with a predicate that searches for objects whose name matches the value entered by the user. Using this descriptor, we call the **fetchCount()** method on the context to get the total number of objects that satisfy the condition. If the returned value is 0, we know there are no authors with that name, and we can create a new one.

> **Do It Yourself**
>
> Update the **AddAuthor** view with the code in Listing 7-33. Run the application on an iPhone simulator. Press the + button to add a book. Press the Select button to select an author. Press the + button to add an author. You should only be able to insert a new author if there is no other with the same name in the database.

BASIC

Previews

So far, we have created the container for the previews in memory with the **modelContainer()** modifier. This is enough to make the preview work on the canvas, but it's not good for testing. Every time we update the view, the preview is recreated and all data is deleted. To always have values to work with, we can create a custom container with some sample data, but recreating the container and the data every time the view is updated can affect performance. To avoid these issues, SwiftUI provides the **PreviewModifier** protocol. With this protocol, we can create a structure that preprocess content and then provides that content to any preview that needs it. The protocol requires the implementation of the following methods.

makeSharedContext()

This type method is used to create the content we want to assign to the previews.

body(content: Content, **context:** Context)

This method is called to assign the content to the preview. The **content** argument is a reference to the view the preview is going to show, and the **context** attribute is the context we want to associate with the view.

The first step to preprocess data for previews is to define a structure that conforms to the **PreviewModifier** protocol and implement its methods. In our example, we need to create a custom SwiftData container with the **ModelContainer** class and then apply it to the preview with the **modelContainer()** modifier, as shown below.

Listing 7-34: Providing sample data for the previews

```
struct PreviewData: PreviewModifier {
   static func makeSharedContext() throws -> ModelContainer {
      let config = ModelConfiguration(isStoredInMemoryOnly: true)
      let container = try ModelContainer(for: Book.self, Author.self,
         configurations: config)

      let author = Author(name: "Stephen King", books: [])
      container.mainContext.insert(author)

      let book1 = Book(title: "Christine", author: author, cover:
         "book10", year: 1987)
      let book2 = Book(title: "IT", author: author, cover: "book11",
         year: 1986)
      container.mainContext.insert(book1)
      container.mainContext.insert(book2)

      return container
   }
   func body(content: Content, context: ModelContainer) -> some View {
      content.modelContainer(context)
   }
}
```

The **PreviewData** structure defines the two methods required by the protocol. In the **makeSharedContext()** method, we create a **ModelConfiguration** structure with the **isStoredInMemoryOnly** argument set to **true** to store the data in memory, then use that configuration to create the **ModelContainer** object for the **Book** and **Author** models, create a new **Author** object and two **Book** objects to have something to work with, and finally return the container so we can assign it later to the previews.

Every time a preview needs the information created by the **makeSharedContext()** method, it calls the **body()** method in our structure with a reference to the view (**content**). In this method, we can assign the content to the view as we did before. In our example, we assign the container to the view with the **modelContainer()** modifier.

When working with preprocessed data, the previews are defined as before, but the data is provided as a trait using the **modifier()** method, as shown below.

Listing 7-35: Implementing a custom container in the preview

```
#Preview(traits: .modifier(PreviewData())) {
   ContentView()
      .environment(ApplicationData.shared)
}
```

This preview is for the **ContentView** view of our previous example, but we should apply the modifier to every view in the interface, so they all work with the same container. The preview is now created from the container returned by the **PreviewData** structure and therefore it includes two books and an author.

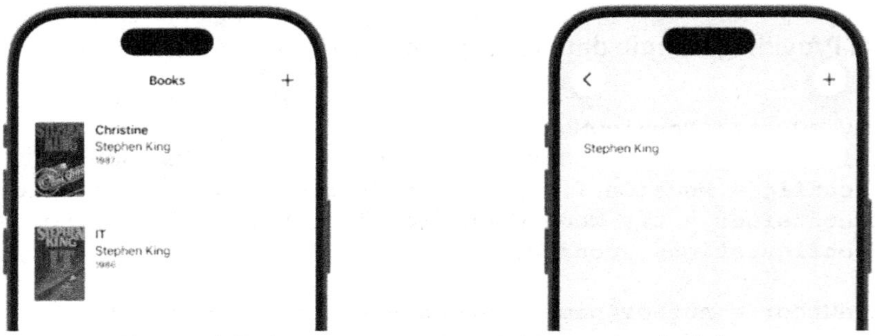

Figure 7-7: *Custom container with pre-loaded data*

> ### Do It Yourself
>
> Add the **PreviewData** structure in Listing 7-34 at the bottom of the **ApplicationData.swift** file. For this code to work, you also need to import the **SwiftData** framework. Update the preview of the **ContentView** view with the code in Listing 7-35. Remember to update the previews for the other views as well so they all use the same container, and also to download the books covers from our website and add them to an Asset Catalog. You should see the preview on the canvas with two books and an author, as shown in Figure 7-7.

BASIC

Modifying Objects

Usually, users need to modify the values of objects stored in the database. With SwiftData, this is quite simple. All we need to do is get the object from the container, as we have done so far, and then pass it to the view that allows the user to change the values of its properties. Once a property is updated, SwiftData takes care of saving the object back to the database and reporting the change to the system so that the views are updated with the new values.

Although we can provide a new view to modify the values, we can also use our **AddBook** view to serve both purposes: add new books and edit the values of those already stored in the database. For this purpose, we can check the value of the **selectedBook** property added to the model in Listing 7-14. If the property contains a **Book** object, it means that the user has selected a book and wants to edit its values, otherwise it means that the user wants to add a new book. Figure 7-8, below, shows the interface we need to build for this example.

Figure 7-8: *Editing values*

For this to work, we need to update the + button in the navigation bar of the **ContentView** view so we can make sure that the value of the **selectedBook** property is **nil** every time the user wants to add a new book.

Listing 7-36: Preparing the `selectedBook` property to add new books

```
struct ContentView: View {
   @Environment(ApplicationData.self) private var appData
   @Environment(\.modelContext) var dbContext
   @Query private var listBooks: [Book]

   var body: some View {
      @Bindable var appData = appData
      NavigationStack(path: $appData.viewPath) {
         List {
            ForEach(listBooks) { book in
               NavigationLink(value: book, label: {
                  CellBook(book: book)
               })
            }
         }
         .listStyle(.plain)
         .navigationTitle("Books")
         .toolbarTitleDisplayMode(.inline)
         .toolbar {
            ToolbarItem(placement: .topBarTrailing) {
               Button("Add Book", systemImage: "plus", action: {
                  appData.selectedBook = nil
                  appData.viewPath.append("Add Book")
               })
            }
         }
         .navigationDestination(for: String.self, destination: { viewID in
            if viewID == "Add Book" {
               AddBook()
            } else if viewID == "List Authors" {
               ListAuthors()
            } else if viewID == "Add Author" {
               AddAuthor()
            }
         })
         .navigationDestination(for: Book.self, destination: { book in
            DetailView(book: book)
         })
```

```
        }
    }
}
```

In this example, we also embedded the **CellBook** view into a **NavigationLink** view and added an additional **navigationDestination()** modifier at the bottom to open a view called **DetailView** when a book is selected. This view displays the book's data, but it must also include a button in the navigation bar to open the **AddBook** view to allow the user to edit the values, as shown below.

Listing 7-37: Opening the view to edit a book

```
import SwiftUI
import SwiftData

struct DetailView: View {
    @Environment(ApplicationData.self) private var appData
    let book: Book

    var body: some View {
        VStack {
            Text(book.title)
                .font(.title)
            Text(book.author?.name ?? "Undefined")
            Image(book.cover)
                .resizable()
                .scaledToFit()
                .frame(width: 100)
            Spacer()
        }.padding()
        .navigationTitle(Text("Book"))
        .toolbar {
            ToolbarItem(placement: .topBarTrailing) {
                Button("Add Book", systemImage: "pencil.circle", action: {
                    appData.selectedBook = book
                    appData.selectedAuthor = book.author
                    appData.viewPath.append("Add Book")
                })
            }
        }
    }
}
#Preview(traits: .modifier(PreviewData())) {
    @Previewable @Query var listBooks: [Book]

    NavigationStack {
        DetailView(book: listBooks[0])
            .environment(ApplicationData.shared)
    }
}
```

When the button that opens the **AddBook** view is pressed, we assign the **Book** object and the **Author** object of the selected book to the **selectedBook** and **selectedAuthor** properties in the observable object, so that the **AddBook** view knows that a book has been selected and can show the values to the user. The following are the changes for this view.

Listing 7-38: Editing a book

```
struct AddBook: View {
   @Environment(ApplicationData.self) private var appData
   @Environment(\.modelContext) var dbContext
   @State private var titleInput: String = ""
   @State private var yearInput: String = ""

   var body: some View {
      VStack(alignment: .leading, spacing: 10) {
         TextField("Insert Title", text: $titleInput)
            .textFieldStyle(.roundedBorder)
         TextField("Insert Year", text: $yearInput)
            .textFieldStyle(.roundedBorder)
            .keyboardType(.numbersAndPunctuation)
         VStack(alignment: .leading) {
            Text("Author")
            NavigationLink(value: "List Authors", label: {
               Text(appData.selectedAuthor?.name ?? "Select")
            })
         }
         HStack {
            Spacer()
            Button("Save") {
               storeBook()
            }.buttonStyle(.borderedProminent)
         }
         Spacer()
      }.padding()
      .onAppear {
         if let selectedBook = appData.selectedBook, titleInput.isEmpty &&
            yearInput.isEmpty {
            titleInput = selectedBook.title
            yearInput = selectedBook.displayYear
         }
      }
   }
   func storeBook() {
      let title = titleInput.trimmingCharacters(in: .whitespaces)
      if let year = Int(yearInput), !title.isEmpty {
         if let oldBook = appData.selectedBook {
            oldBook.title = title
            oldBook.year = year
            oldBook.author = appData.selectedAuthor
            try? dbContext.save()
         } else {
            let newBook = Book(title: title, author:
               appData.selectedAuthor, cover: "nocover", year: year)
            dbContext.insert(newBook)
            try? dbContext.save()
         }
         appData.selectedAuthor = nil
         appData.selectedBook = nil
         appData.viewPath.removeLast()
      }
   }
}
```

To determine if the user wants to edit a book or create a new one, we check the value of the **selectedBook** property (see the **onAppear()** modifier). If the property contains a value and the text fields are empty, we assign the title and year of the book to these fields to show them to the user. We do the same thing when the Save button is pressed. In this case, if the **selectedBook** property contains a **Book** object, we modify the properties with the values entered by the user, otherwise we create a new book. Note that at the end we clear the values of both properties, **selectedBook** and **selectedAuthor**, to reset the system.

Do It Yourself

Update the **ContentView.swift** file with the code in Listing 7-36. Create a SwiftUI file called **DetailView.swift** for the code in Listing 7-37. Update the **AddBook** view with the code in Listing 7-38. Run the application on an iPhone simulator and select a book. Tap on the button in the navigation bar to edit the book. Modify the values and press Save. The changes should be visible in the **DetailView** view and in the list.

BASIC

Images

In the previous examples, we loaded an image from an Asset Catalog to represent the cover of the book (**nocover.png**). However, the images supplied by users are stored as data and come from a variety of sources, such as the camera, the network, or a storage device. Therefore, to store an image in a database, we need to convert it into data, and to load it and display it on the screen, we must perform the reverse process and convert the data back into an image. For this purpose, the **Foundation** framework provides the **Data** structure and the UIKit framework provides the **UIImage** class (**NSImage** for Mac applications). The **Data** structure stores the data, while the **UIImage** class provides all the tools to perform the conversions and prepare the images for the views. The following are some of the initializers provided by this class.

UIImage(named: String)

This initializer creates an object that contains the image from the file specified by the **named** argument. The argument is a string with the name of the file or the image set in the Asset Catalog.

UIImage(data: Data, **scale:** CGFloat)

This initializer creates an object that contains an image generated from the data provided by the **data** argument and with an associated scale specified by the **scale** argument. If the last argument is ignored, the image is assigned a scale of 1.

UIImage(contentsOfFile: String)

This initializer creates an object that contains the image stored in the file indicated by the **contentsOfFile** argument. The argument is a string with a path that determines the location of the file.

```
UIImage(cgImage: CGImage, scale: CGFloat, orientation: Orientation)
```

This initializer creates an object that contains an image generated from a **CGImage** object and with a scale and orientation defined by the arguments. The **CGImage** class is defined by the Core Graphics framework to store a low-level representation of an image, and the **orientation** argument is an enumeration with the values **up**, **down**, **left**, **right**, **upMirrored**, **downMirrored**, **leftMirrored**, and **rightMirrored**.

The **UIImage** class includes properties and methods to get information about the image and process it. The following are the most frequently used.

```
size
```

This property returns a **CGSize** value with the size of the image.

```
scale
```

This property returns a **CGFloat** value with the scale of the image.

```
imageOrientation
```

This property returns a value that identifies the image's orientation. It is an enumeration called **Orientation**. The values available are **up**, **down**, **left**, **right**, **upMirrored**, **downMirrored**, **leftMirrored**, and **rightMirrored**.

```
cgImage
```

This property returns the image in the Core Graphic format. It is of type **CGImage**, a Core Graphic data type.

The size of photographs taken by the camera or images loaded from the Photo Library are often too large for processing and storage. Storing these images in files and databases can consume too much storage space and memory. The **UIImage** class includes the following methods to optimize an image and reduce its size.

```
preparingThumbnail(of: CGSize)
```

This method returns a new image created from the original and with a size determined by the **of** argument.

```
byPreparingThumbnail(ofSize: CGSize)
```

This asynchronous method creates a new image from the original. The **ofSize** argument determines the size of the image.

```
preparingForDisplay()
```

This method decompresses the original image and returns a new one ready to be shown on the screen.

```
byPreparingForDisplay()
```

This asynchronous method decompresses the original image.

To convert an image into data, the **UIImage** class includes the following methods.

pngData()

This method converts the image into raw data in the PNG format and returns a **Data** structure with it.

jpegData(compressionQuality: CGFloat)

This method converts the image into raw data in the JPEG format and returns a **Data** structure with it. The **compressionQuality** argument is a value between 0.0 and 1.0 to determine the level of compression.

Images are represented by large amounts of data. Storing this data in a database can affect performance and slow down essential processes such as searching for values or migrating the model. An alternative is to store the images in separate files and keep a link to the file in the database. However storing and synchronizing this information can be tedious and error-prone when hundreds or even thousands of images are available. Fortunately, SwiftData can take care of this process for us. All we have to do is define a property that can store a **Data** structure, and then modify it with the **externalStorage** attribute, as shown below.

Listing 7-39: Storing images externally

```
@Model
class Book: Identifiable {
   @Attribute(.unique) var id: UUID = UUID()
   var title: String = ""
   @Relationship(deleteRule: .nullify, inverse: \Author.books) var
      author: Author?
   @Attribute(.externalStorage) var cover: Data?
   var year: Int = 0

   init(title: String, author: Author?, cover: Data?, year: Int) {
      self.title = title
      self.author = author
      self.cover = cover
      self.year = year
   }
   var displayYear: String {
      get {
         let value = year > 0 ? String(year) : "Undefined"
         return value
      }
   }
   var displayCover: UIImage {
      if let data = cover, let image = UIImage(data: data) {
         return image
      } else {
         return UIImage(named: "nocover")!
      }
   }
}
```

The image for the cover is now stored as a **Data** structure in an external file. This means that every time we want to process or show this image to the user, we have to convert the **Data** structure into a **UIImage** object. For this purpose, we added an additional computer property to the model called **displayCover**. This property checks if there is data stored in the **cover** property and converts it to a **UIImage** object using the **UIImage(data:)** initializer. If no data is found, we create a **UIImage** object with the **nocover.png** image from the Asset Catalog, and return that instead.

Once we have the **UIImage** object with the image we want to show, we can turn it into an **Image** view using the **Image(uiImage:)** initializer introduced earlier. In the following example, we update the **CellBook** view with this initializer to show the covers on the screen.

Listing 7-40: Displaying an image from a `UIImage` object

```
struct CellBook: View {
    let book: Book

    var body: some View {
        HStack(alignment: .top) {
            Image(uiImage: book.displayCover)
                .resizable()
                .scaledToFit()
                .frame(width: 80, height: 100)
            VStack(alignment: .leading, spacing: 2) {
                Text(book.title).bold()
                Text(book.author?.name ?? "Undefined")
                Text(book.displayYear).font(.caption)
                Spacer()
            }
            Spacer()
        }.padding([.top], 10)
    }
}
```

The same change is required in the **DetailView** view. Instead of providing a string to load the image from the Asset Catalog, we now get it from the **UIImage** object returned by the **displayCover** property.

Listing 7-41: Displaying the image in the `DetailView` view

```
Image(uiImage: book.displayCover)
    .resizable()
    .scaledToFit()
    .frame(width: 100)
```

The **displayCover** property converts image data from the database into an image that can be shown on the screen. To perform the opposite process, that is, storing an image in the database, we must convert it into data using the **pngData()** or **jpegData(compressionQuality:)** methods provided by the **UIImage** class. The images we need to store in the database typically come from the camera or the Photo Library. We will learn how to work with these systems in Chapter 14. For now, we can convert an image from the Asset Catalog instead. For example, when the user creates a new book in our application, we can load the **nocover.png** image from the Asset Catalog with a **UIImage** object, convert it to data using the **pngData()** method, and then use the resulting **Data** value to create the **Book** object. The following shows the changes required in the **storeBook()** method of the **AddBook** view for this purpose.

Listing 7-42: Converting a UIImage object into data

```
func storeBook() {
    let title = titleInput.trimmingCharacters(in: .whitespaces)
    if let year = Int(yearInput), !title.isEmpty {
        if let oldBook = appData.selectedBook {
            oldBook.title = title
            oldBook.year = year
            oldBook.author = appData.selectedAuthor
            try? dbContext.save()
        } else {
            let cover = UIImage(named: "nocover")?.pngData()
            let newBook = Book(title: title, author: appData.selectedAuthor,
               cover: cover, year: year)
            dbContext.insert(newBook)
            try? dbContext.save()
        }
        appData.selectedAuthor = nil
        appData.selectedBook = nil
        appData.viewPath.removeLast()
    }
}
```

Since the cover of the book is now stored as a **Data** structure instead of a string, we also need to modify the objects inserted into the database in the **PreviewData** structure. The following are the changes we need to make to the **makeSharedContext()** method.

Listing 7-43: Creating Book objects with images from the Asset Catalog

```
struct PreviewData: PreviewModifier {
    static func makeSharedContext() throws -> ModelContainer {
        let config = ModelConfiguration(isStoredInMemoryOnly: true)
        let container = try ModelContainer(for: Book.self, Author.self,
           configurations: config)

        let author = Author(name: "Stephen King", books: [])
        container.mainContext.insert(author)

        let book10 = UIImage(named: "book10")?.pngData()
        let book11 = UIImage(named: "book11")?.pngData()
        let book1 = Book(title: "Christine", author: author, cover: book10,
           year: 1987)
        let book2 = Book(title: "IT", author: author, cover: book11,
           year: 1986)
        container.mainContext.insert(book1)
        container.mainContext.insert(book2)

        return container
    }
```

```
    func body(content: Content, context: ModelContainer) -> some View {
        content.modelContainer(context)
    }
}
```

Do It Yourself

Update the **Book** model with the code in Listing 7-39, the **CellBook** view in the **ContentView.swift** file with the code in Listing 7-40, the **Image** view in the **DetailView** view with the code in Listing 7-41, the **storeBook()** method in the **AddBook** view with the code in Listing 7-42, and the **makeSharedContext()** method in the **PreviewData** structure with the code in Listing 7-43. Run the application on an iPhone simulator. Add a new book. You should see that the book is created with the image **nocover.png**, as before, but this time it is stored in the database as a **Data** structure. We will learn how to work with the camera and load images from the Photo library in Chapter 14.

BASIC

Sections

As we have seen in Chapter 4, SwiftUI allows us to divide lists and other containers into sections, each with its own header and footer. To reproduce this organization with SwiftData, the **@Query** macro includes the **sectionBy** argument. This argument takes a key path to the property we want to use to define the sections, so the query returns the list of items organized according to this value. For example, if we want to organize the items by category, we must use a key path to the property in the model that stores the category's name.

The query macro can only take a key path to a property in the model, and this property must be of type **String**, so if we don't have a property in our model that we can use to define the sections, we must add it. For example, if we want to organize our books in alphabetical sections, we need to add a property to the **Book** model to store the initial letter of the book's title, as shown below.

Listing 7-44: Adding a property to organize the items in sections

```
@Model
class Book: Identifiable {
    @Attribute(.unique) var id: UUID = UUID()
    var title: String = "" {
        didSet {
            sectionLetter = title.prefix(1).uppercased()
        }
    }
    @Relationship(deleteRule: .nullify, inverse: \Author.books) var author:
Author?
```

```
    @Attribute(.externalStorage) var cover: Data?
    var year: Int = 0
    var sectionLetter: String

    init(title: String, author: Author?, cover: Data?, year: Int) {
        self.title = title
        self.author = author
        self.cover = cover
        self.year = year
        self.sectionLetter = title.prefix(1).uppercased()
    }
    var displayYear: String {
        get {
            let value = year > 0 ? String(year) : "Undefined"
            return value
        }
    }
    var displayCover: UIImage {
        if let data = cover, let image = UIImage(data: data) {
            return image
        } else {
            return UIImage(named: "nocover")!
        }
    }
}
```

This model includes a new property called **sectionLetter**. Every time a new object is created (a new book is added to the database), we get the first letter from the title, uppercase it, and assign it to this property. Note that to keep the value of this property up to date, we also define the **didSet** method for the **title** property, so every time the user modifies the title of the book, the **sectionLetter** property is updated as well.

When we specify the **sectionBy** argument, the **@Query** macro takes care of organizing the items in sections based on the value of the argument. To return this list, the **Query** structure includes the following property.

sections

This property returns a **ResultsSectionCollection** structure with the objects from the current result organized by section.

To organize the information, the **ResultsSectionCollection** structure returns a collection of **ResultsSection** structures with the values for each section. The following is the property provided by this structure to return the section's name.

name

This property returns a string with the section's name.

Since the values are now returned by the **sections** property, we must read this property from the macro's underlying structure. This means that we need to prefix the **listBooks** property with an underline character to access the underlying structure and then read the **sections** property to list the values, as shown below.

Listing 7-45: Displaying the books in sections

```
struct ContentView: View {
   @Environment(ApplicationData.self) private var appData
   @Environment(\.modelContext) var dbContext
   @Query(sort: \Book.title, sectionBy: \Book.sectionLetter) private var
      listBooks: [Book]

   var body: some View {
      @Bindable var appData = appData

      NavigationStack(path: $appData.viewPath) {
         List {
            ForEach(_listBooks.sections) { section in
               Section {
                  ForEach(section) { book in
                     NavigationLink(value: book, label: {
                        CellBook(book: book)
                     })
                  }
               } header: {
                  Text(section.name)
                     .font(.system(size: 24).bold())
               }
            }
         }
         .listStyle(.plain)
         .navigationTitle("Books")
         .toolbarTitleDisplayMode(.inline)
         .toolbar {
            ToolbarItem(placement: .topBarTrailing) {
               Button(action: {
                  appData.selectedBook = nil
                  appData.viewPath.append("Add Book")
               }, label: {
                  Image(systemName: "plus")
               })
            }
         }
         .navigationDestination(for: String.self, destination: { viewID in
            if viewID == "Add Book" {
               AddBook()
            } else if viewID == "List Authors" {
               ListAuthors()
            } else if viewID == "Add Author" {
               AddAuthor()
            }
         })
         .navigationDestination(for: Book.self, destination: { book in
            DetailView(book: book)
         })
      }
   }
}
```

Because we are organizing the books in alphabetical sections, we also need to sort them in that order. In this example, we declare a **@Query** macro that sorts the books by title and then organizes them by sections from the value of the **sectionLetter** property. To create the sections, we need two **ForEach** loops, one to list the sections, and another to list the content of each section. As before, the sections are defined by the **Section** view. We read the **name** property to show the section's title, and then iterate over the content to display the books. The result is shown below.

Figure 7-9: *Alphabetical sections*

Do It Yourself

Update the **Book** model with the code in Listing 7-44 and the **ContentView** structure with the code in Listing 7-45. Run the application on the Canvas. You should see the books organized in alphabetical sections, as shown in Figure 7-9.

PRO

Archiving

Although we can add as many properties to a model as we want and define as many models as we need, professional applications usually rely on more sophisticated models that include collection of values and custom data types. To give us more flexibility, the **Foundation** framework provides the **NSCoder** class. This class can encode and decode values into **Data** structures for storage in a process called *Archiving*.

Archiving works with Property List values. These are values that can be converted into raw data and reconstructed later. All Swift primitive data types qualify as Property List values, but custom data types must be converted before they can be archived. For this purpose, Foundation provides the **PropertyListEncoder** and **PropertyListDecoder** classes, which include the following methods for encoding and decoding values.

encode(Value)

This method of the **PropertyListEncoder** class encodes a value into a Property List value.

decode(Type, from: Data)

This method of the **PropertyListDecoder** class decodes a Property List value into a value of the type specified by the first argument. The **from** argument is a **Data** structure with the data to be decoded.

Another requirement for custom structures is that they must implement the initializers and methods defined in a protocol called **NSCoding**. These initializers and methods tell the system how to encode and decode data for storage or distribution. Fortunately, the Swift Standard Library defines a protocol called **Codable** that simplifies our work by turning a structure into an encodable and decodable data type. All we have to do is to get our structure to conform to this protocol, and the compiler takes care of adding all the methods needed to encode and decode the values.

In the following example, we store the author's date and place of birth, but archive the data and assign it to a single property. For this purpose, we need to create a **Codable** structure and encode/decode the values as needed. We call this structure **AuthorInfo**.

Listing 7-46: Defining a `Codable` structure

```
import SwiftUI

struct AuthorInfo: Codable {
   var birthday: Date?
   var placeOfBirth: String = ""
}
```

To store an instance of this structure, we need to add a property to the **Author** model, as shown below.

Listing 7-47: Storing and decoding data

```
@Model
class Author: Identifiable {
   @Attribute(.unique) var id: UUID = UUID()
   var name: String = ""
   @Relationship(deleteRule: .nullify) var books: [Book]? = []
   var info: Data?

   init(name: String, books: [Book], info: Data?) {
      self.name = name
      self.books = books
      self.info = info
   }
   var listBooks: [Book] {
      get {
         let sortList = books?.sorted(by: { $0.title < $1.title }) ?? []
         return sortList
      }
   }
   @MainActor
   var showBirthday: String? {
      let decoder = PropertyListDecoder()
```

```
        if let info, let authorInfo = try? decoder.decode(AuthorInfo.self,
           from: info) {
           if let date = authorInfo.birthday, date < Date() {
              return authorInfo.birthday?.formatted(date: .abbreviated,
                 time: .omitted)
           }
        }
        return nil
     }
     @MainActor
     var showPlaceOfBirth: String? {
        let decoder = PropertyListDecoder()
        if let info, let authorInfo = try? decoder.decode(AuthorInfo.self,
           from: info) {
           if !authorInfo.placeOfBirth.isEmpty {
              return authorInfo.placeOfBirth
           }
        }
        return nil
     }
}
```

This model includes a new property called **info** that stores a **Data** structure, and two computed properties to prepare the values for the views. To decode the **Data** structure into an **AuthorInfo** structure, we create an instance of the **PropertyListDecoder** class and call the **decode()** method. This method takes the **Data** structure in the **info** property and creates an instance of the **AuthorInfo** class with that data. Once we have this structure, we format the values and return them so that the view can show them on the screen.

The next step is to provide the controls for the user to be able to enter the author's date and place of birth, and then to encode these values before creating the new **Author** object. The following are the changes we need to make to the **AddAuthor** view.

Listing 7-48: Encoding data

```
struct AddAuthor: View {
   @Environment(ApplicationData.self) private var appData
   @Environment(\.modelContext) var dbContext
   @State private var nameInput: String = ""
   @State private var openAlert: Bool = false
   @State private var birthday: Date = Date()
   @State private var placeOfBirth: String = ""

   var body: some View {
      VStack(alignment: .leading, spacing: 10) {
         TextField("Insert Name", text: $nameInput)
            .textFieldStyle(.roundedBorder)
         DatePicker("Birthday", selection: $birthday, displayedComponents:
            .date)
         TextField("Insert Address", text: $placeOfBirth)
            .textFieldStyle(.roundedBorder)
         HStack {
            Spacer()
            Button("Save") {
               storeAuthor()
```

```
         }.buttonStyle(.borderedProminent)
      }
      Spacer()
   }.padding()
      .alert("Error", isPresented: $openAlert, actions: {
         Button("OK", role: .cancel, action: {})
      }, message: { Text("The author already exists") })
   }
   func storeAuthor() {
      let name = nameInput.trimmingCharacters(in: .whitespaces)
      if !name.isEmpty {
         let predicate = #Predicate<Author> { $0.name == name }
         let descriptor = FetchDescriptor<Author>(predicate: predicate)
         if let count = try? dbContext.fetchCount(descriptor), count > 0 {
            openAlert = true
         } else {
            let newAuthor = Author(name: name, books: [],
               info: archiveInfo())
            dbContext.insert(newAuthor)
            try? dbContext.save()
            appData.selectedAuthor = newAuthor
            appData.viewPath.removeLast(2)
         }
      }
   }
   func archiveInfo() -> Data? {
      var newBirthday = Date.distantFuture
      if birthday < Date(timeIntervalSinceNow: -86400) {
         newBirthday = birthday
      }
      let authorInfo = AuthorInfo(birthday: newBirthday,
         placeOfBirth: placeOfBirth)
      let encoder = PropertyListEncoder()
      let infoData = try? encoder.encode(authorInfo)
      return infoData
   }
}
```

This view includes two new **@State** properties called **birthday** and **placeOfBirth** to store the values entered by the user. As always, when the user presses the Save button, we create the **Author** object and insert it into the context, but this time we call an additional method to encode the data for the **info** property. In this method, we check if the date is older than the current date (minus one day) to confirm that the user has selected a date of birth. If no date is selected, we store a **distantFuture** date to later determine if a date is available or not, and then create the **AuthorInfo** structure with that value. To encode the structure, we create an instance of the **PropertyListEncoder** class and call the **encode()** method.

The values are now encoded and stored in the database, so we can read them from the stored properties defined in the model and show them on the screen. The following are the changes we need to make to the **DetailView** view.

Listing 7-49: Displaying encoded data

```
struct DetailView: View {
   @Environment(ApplicationData.self) private var appData
   let book: Book

   var body: some View {
      VStack {
         Text(book.title)
            .font(.title)
         Image(uiImage: book.displayCover)
            .resizable()
            .scaledToFit()
            .frame(width: 100)
         Text(book.author?.name ?? "Undefined")
         Text(book.author?.showBirthday ?? "Undefined")
         Text(book.author?.showPlaceOfBirth ?? "Undefined")
         Spacer()
      }.padding()
      .navigationTitle(Text("Book"))
      .toolbar {
         ToolbarItem(placement: .topBarTrailing) {
            Button("Add Book", systemImage: "pencil.circle", action: {
               appData.selectedBook = book
               appData.selectedAuthor = book.author
               appData.viewPath.append("Add Book")
            })
         }
      }
   }
}
```

***Figure 7-10:** Encoded data*

Do It Yourself

Create a Swift file called **AuthorInfo.swift** for the code in Listing 7-46. Update the **`Author`** model with the code in Listing 7-47, the **`AddAuthor`** view with the code in Listing 7-48, and the **`DetailView`** view with the code in Listing 7-49. You also need to add the **`info`** argument to the **`Author`** initializer in the **`PreviewData`** structure for the previews to work (**`let author = Author(name: "Stephen King", books: [], info: nil)`**).

Run the application. Press the + button to add a new book. Press the Select button to select the author. Press the + button to add a new author. You should see the form in Figure 7-10 (left). Enter the information and press Save. Select the book from the list. You should see the values on the screen, as in Figure 7-10 (right).

Another way to encode and decode custom data types is by using JSON (JavaScript Object Notation). Although this format was originally developed for transmitting information over the Internet, its readability and simplicity have made it suitable for storing application data as well. The **Foundation** framework provides the **`JSONDecoder`** class to decode JSON data into Swift structures and the **`JSONEncoder`** class to encode Swift structures into JSON data. The following are the methods defined by these classes to decode and encode values.

decode(Type, **from:** Data**)**

This method returns a value of the type specified by the first argument with the information provided by the **from** argument. The **from** argument is a **`Data`** structure that contains the JSON data we want to decode.

encode(Value**)**

This method returns a **`Data`** structure with the JSON representation of the value provided by the argument.

A JSON file is just a text file that stores the data in a specific syntax. The syntax includes the values of an object or structure as key/value pairs separated by a colon, like dictionaries. The property name becomes the key for the value, and each object or structure is enclosed in curly braces. The following example shows how a JSON file looks like when we store an instance of our **`AuthorInfo`** structure.

Listing 7-50: JSON file

```
{
   "placeOfBirth": "Toronto",
   "birthday": 271479840
}
```

As always, the objects or structures we want to encode must conform to the **`Codable`** protocol, and the data must be encoded and decoded before it can be stored or read. Therefore, adapting our application to work with JSON is simple. We just have to replace the Property List encoders and decoders with those defined for the JSON format. Below are the computed properties that were previously defined for the **`Author`** model, but now the values are decoded by the **`JSONDecoder`** class.

Listing 7-51: Decoding with JSON

```
@MainActor
var showBirthday: String? {
   let decoder = JSONDecoder()
   if let info, let authorInfo = try? decoder.decode(AuthorInfo.self,
      from: info) {
      if let date = authorInfo.birthday, date < Date() {
         return authorInfo.birthday?.formatted(date: .abbreviated,
            time: .omitted)
      }
   }
   return nil
}
@MainActor
var showPlaceOfBirth: String? {
   let decoder = JSONDecoder()
   if let info, let authorInfo = try? decoder.decode(AuthorInfo.self,
      from: info) {
      if !authorInfo.placeOfBirth.isEmpty {
         return authorInfo.placeOfBirth
      }
   }
   return nil
}
```

The changes in the **AddAuthor** view are also simple. We just need to update the **archiveInfo()** method to encode the data with the **JSONEncoder** class.

Listing 7-52: Encoding with JSON

```
func archiveInfo() -> Data? {
   var newBirthday = Date.distantFuture
   if birthday < Date(timeIntervalSinceNow: -86400) {
      newBirthday = birthday
   }
   let encoder = JSONEncoder()
   let authorInfo = AuthorInfo(birthday: newBirthday, placeOfBirth:
      placeOfBirth)
   let infoData = try? encoder.encode(authorInfo)
   return infoData
}
```

Do It Yourself

Update the computed properties in the **Author** model with the code in Listing 7-51, and the **archiveInfo()** method in the **AddAuthor** view with the code in Listing 7-52. The app should work as before, but now the information is encoded and decoded with JSON.

PRO

7.3 - Files

Although the User Defaults system and SwiftData are effective storage solutions, we can also work directly with files stored on the device. For this purpose, the **Foundation** framework provides the **`FileManager`** class. With this class, we can create, delete, copy, and move files and directories within the storage space reserved for the app. The system automatically creates an instance of this class for the application. The following is the type property defined by the class to access this instance.

`default`

This type property returns a reference to the **`FileManager`** object assigned to the app.

The **`FileManager`** class provides several properties and methods for managing files and directories. The following are the most frequently used.

`urls(for:` `SearchPathDirectory,` **`in:`** `SearchPathDomainMask)`

This method returns an array with the locations of a directory. The **for** argument is an enumeration with values that represent common system directories. The most frequently used are **`documentDirectory`** to represent the Documents directory, and **`applicationSupportDirectory`** to reference the Application Support directory. The **in** argument is an enumeration with values that determine the domain in which the files are located. The most frequently used is **`userDomainMask`** to represent the user's home directory.

`createFile(atPath:` `String,` **`contents:`** `Data?,` **`attributes:`** `Dictionary?)`

This method creates a file. The **atPath** argument specifies the location of the file, including its name and extension, the **contents** argument represents the content of the file, and the **attributes** argument is a dictionary with values that determine the file's attributes. The value **`nil`** sets the attributes by default.

`createDirectory(at:` `URL,` **`withIntermediateDirectories:`** `Bool,` **`attributes:`** `Dictionary?)`

This method creates a new directory. The **at** argument specifies the location of the directory, including its name, the **withIntermediateDirectories** argument indicates whether intermediate directories will also be created or not, and the **attributes** argument is a dictionary with values that determine the directory's attributes. The value **`nil`** sets the attributes by default.

`contents(atPath:` `String)`

This method returns the contents of the file at the path specified by the **atPath** argument. The value returned is an optional of type **`Data`**.

`contentsOfDirectory(atPath:` `String)`

This method returns an array with the paths of the files and directories inside the directory indicated by the **atPath** argument.

`copyItem(atPath: String, toPath: String)`

This method copies the file or directory at the path specified by the **at** argument to the path specified by the **to** argument.

`moveItem(atPath: String, toPath: String)`

This method moves the file or directory at the path specified by the **at** argument to the path specified by the **to** argument.

`removeItem(atPath: String)`

This method removes the file or directory at the path indicated by the **atPath** argument.

`fileExists(atPath: String)`

This method returns a Boolean value that determines if the file or the directory at the path specified by the **atPath** argument exists.

`attributesOfItem(atPath: String)`

This method returns a dictionary with the attributes of the file or directory at the location indicated by the **atPath** argument. The **`FileManager`** class includes constants to define the attributes, including **`creationDate`**, **`modificationDate`**, **`size`**, and **`type`**, among others.

PRO

URLs and Paths

As in any other operating system, files in iOS and macOS are organized in directories (folders). There is a directory called root, which can contain other files and directories in a tree-like structure. To specify the location of a file, Apple systems use a conventional syntax that separates each component with a slash (/) and begins with a single slash to indicate the root directory (e.g., /Pictures/Travels/Hawaii.png). This is called a path and can be used to access any file on the system. Paths are an easy way to access files, but they are not enough to determine the location of a file in the storage system. This is because in practice, files are usually not stored in a single storage location, but in multiple units or even on remote servers. Tracing a long path to find a file also takes time and consumes resources. For these reasons, storage locations are always identified with URLs (Uniform Resource Locator). To define URLs, the **Foundation** framework includes the **`URL`** structure. The following are some of the initializers, properties, and methods included in this structure to work with local files and directories.

`URL(fileURLWithPath: String)`

This initializer returns a **`URL`** object referencing a local file or directory. The **fileURLWithPath** argument is a string with the file's path.

`URL(fileURLWithPath: String, relativeTo: URL)`

This initializer returns a **`URL`** object referencing a local file or directory. The **fileURLWithPath** argument is a string with the file's path, and the **`relativeTo`** argument is a **`URL`** object referencing the base URL.

path

This property returns the path of a URL. It is a conditional of type **String**.

pathComponents

This property returns an array of **String** values that represent the components of a path extracted from a URL (the strings between forward slashes).

lastPathComponent

This property returns a string with the last component of a path extracted from a URL. It is usually used to get the file's name and extension.

pathExtension

This property returns a string with the extension of the path extracted from a URL. It is used to get the file's extension.

appendingPathComponent(String)

This method returns a new **URL** structure with the URL of the original object plus the component specified by the argument.

> **IMPORTANT**
>
> The **FileManager** class includes methods that work with both paths and URLs. For example, there are two versions of the **createDirectory()** method, one for creating the directory from a path and another to do it from a URL. The methods that work with paths take care of converting the path to a URL and are usually easier to implement. For a complete list, visit our website and follow the links for this chapter.

PRO

Files and Directories

Apple's operating systems allow users to create and access files and directories freely, but applications are sandboxed and restricted to their own storage space so they cannot interfere with each other. On iPhones and iPads, apps can read and write files only within directories assigned to them by the system. On Macs, apps can read and write files outside their sandbox only when the user explicitly grants permission, typically through open and save panels or shared locations.

When an application is installed on a device, the system creates a set of standard directories that the app can use to store files. On mobile devices, the most relevant are the **Documents** directory, which is intended for user-generated content, and the **Application Support** directory, which is used for files created by the app at runtime that are not directly produced by the user. The physical location of these directories is not guaranteed and may change, so we must always ask the system for the current URL that points to the directory or file we want to access.

To locate common directories such as **Documents**, the **FileManager** class provides the **urls()** method. This method takes two arguments: one that identifies the directory we want to access, and another that specifies the domain in which the directory resides. The user's home directory domain is represented by the **userDomainMask** value. Therefore, to obtain the URL of a system-provided directory and create files to store user data, we first get a reference to the **FileManager** object and then call the **urls()** method with the appropriate directory and domain values. In the following example, we define a data model that shows how to access the **Documents** directory and save files to it.

Listing 7-53: Saving files

```
import SwiftUI

@Observable class ApplicationData {
   @ObservationIgnored let manager: FileManager
   @ObservationIgnored let directories: [URL]?

   static let shared: ApplicationData = ApplicationData()
   private init() {
      manager = FileManager.default
      directories = manager.urls(for: .documentDirectory,
         in: .userDomainMask)
   }
   func saveFile(name: String) {
      if let docURL = directories?.first {
         let newFileURL = docURL.appendingPathComponent(name)
         let path = newFileURL.path

         if let contentData = UIImage(named: "husky")?.pngData() {
            manager.createFile(atPath: path, contents: contentData,
               attributes: nil)
         }
      }
   }
}
```

This model includes two non-observable properties, one to store a reference to the **FileManager** object assigned to the application and another to store the directories returned by the **urls()** method. After initializing these properties, we define a method called **saveFile()** that the views are going to call to create a file. This method receives a string and creates a file with that name. First, we get the URL of the Documents directory from the **directories** property (the Documents directory is always the first item in the array), and then use the **appendingPathComponent()** method to add the name of the file to the URL. Once we have this URL, we get the path from the **path** property and create the file.

For this example, we define the contents of the file as an image that we get from the Assets Catalog. (We will learn how to get images from the Photo Library and the camera in Chapter 14) Files can only store data, so we convert the image to a **Data** structure with the **pngData()** method and then use that value to call the **createFile()** method to create the file. Note that if the file already exists, the method updates its contents.

Since in this example we are storing the same image in every file, the interface only needs a view to list the files and another with a text field to allow the user to create more, as shown below.

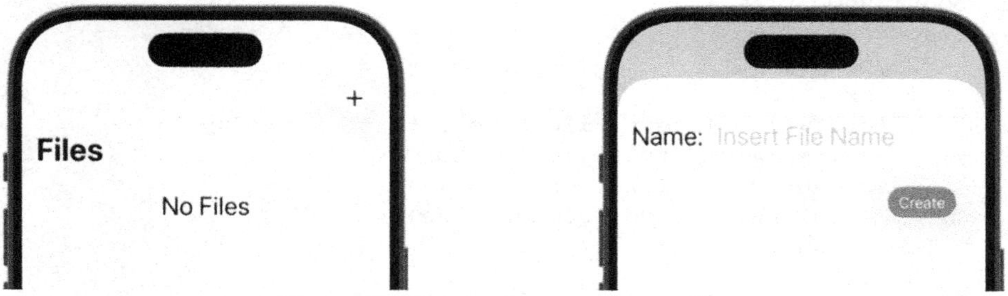

Figure 7-11: *Interface to create files*

The following is the code for the initial view.

Listing 7-54: Opening a sheet to add files to the model

```
struct ContentView: View {
   @Environment(ApplicationData.self) private var appData
   @State private var openSheet: Bool = false

   var body: some View {
      NavigationStack {
         VStack {
            Text("No Files")
            Spacer()
         }.padding()
         .navigationBarTitle("Files")
         .toolbar {
            ToolbarItem(placement: .topBarTrailing) {
               Button("Add File", systemImage: "plus", action: {
                  openSheet = true
               })
            }
         }
         .sheet(isPresented: $openSheet) {
            AddFileView()
         }
      }
   }
}
```

At the moment, this view only displays a message on the screen, but it provides a button in the navigation bar to open a sheet with a view called **AddFileView**, which allows the user to create new files.

Listing 7-55: Creating new files

```
import SwiftUI

struct AddFileView: View {
   @Environment(ApplicationData.self) private var appData
   @Environment(\.dismiss) var dismiss
   @State private var nameInput: String = ""
```

```
    var body: some View {
        VStack {
            HStack {
                Text("Name:")
                TextField("Insert File Name", text: $nameInput)
                    .textFieldStyle(.roundedBorder)
                    .autocapitalization(.none)
                    .disableAutocorrection(true)
            }.padding(.top, 25)
            HStack {
                Spacer()
                Button("Create") {
                    var fileName = nameInput.trimmingCharacters(in:
                        .whitespaces)
                    if !fileName.isEmpty {
                        fileName += ".dat"
                        appData.saveFile(name: fileName)
                        dismiss()
                    }
                }.buttonStyle(.glassProminent)
                .padding()
            }
            Spacer()
        }.padding()
    }
}
```

This view includes a **TextField** view where the user can enter the name of the file, and a **Button** view to create it. When the button is pressed, the string is truncated to remove spaces at the beginning and the end, the extension ".dat" is appended to the name (adding an extension is not necessary), and then the **saveFile()** method is called in the model to create the file.

Do It Yourself

Create a new App project. Create a Swift file called **ApplicationData.swift** for the model in Listing 7-53. Update the **ContentView** structure with the code in Listing 7-54. Create a SwiftUI View file called **AddFileView.swift** for the code in Listing 7-55. Remember to inject the **ApplicationData** object into the environment for the app and the previews (Chapter 4, Listing 4-4). Download the image **husky.png** from our website and add it to an Asset Catalog. Run the application on an iPhone simulator and press the button on the toolbar. Insert the name of the file and press the Create button. The file is created, and the sheet is closed.

At the moment, regardless of how many files we create, the initial view always displays the message "No Files." However, the goal of this application is to allow the user to create multiple files and display them on the screen. For this purpose, we can implement the methods provided by the **FileManager** class to list the contents of a directory. For example, we can use the **contentsOfDirectory()** method to retrieve an array containing the names of the files and directories at a given path. We can store these values in an array and then present them on the screen using a **List** view. To support this behavior, we need to update our data model to store the file names along with a unique identifier, as we did earlier with books, and expose a property that provides this list to the views, as shown below.

Listing 7-56: Getting the list of files

```
import SwiftUI

struct File: Identifiable, Hashable {
   let id: UUID = UUID()
   var name: String
}
@Observable class ApplicationData {
   var listOfFiles: [File] = []
   @ObservationIgnored let manager: FileManager
   @ObservationIgnored let directories: [URL]?

   static let shared: ApplicationData = ApplicationData()
   private init() {
      manager = FileManager.default
      directories = manager.urls(for: .documentDirectory,
         in: .userDomainMask)
      if let docURL = directories?.first {
         if let list = try? manager.contentsOfDirectory(atPath:
            docURL.path) {
            for name in list {
               let newFile = File(name: name)
               listOfFiles.append(newFile)
            }
         }
      }
   }
   func saveFile(name: String) {
      if let docURL = directories?.first {
         let newFileURL = docURL.appendingPathComponent(name)
         let path = newFileURL.path

         if let contentData = UIImage(named: "husky")?.pngData() {
            if manager.createFile(atPath: path, contents: contentData,
               attributes: nil) {
               let newFile = File(name: name)
               listOfFiles.append(newFile)
            }
         }
      }
   }
}
```

The first structure, called **File**, is the model we use to store the name of each file. The structure conforms to the **Identifiable** protocol so that it can be easily managed by the views, and also the **Hashable** protocol so that we can later use these values to identify the links with the **NavigationLink** view.

When the observable object is initialized, we initialize the properties as before and then retrieve the list of files in the directory with the **contentsOfDirectory()** method. This method returns an array of strings with the names of the files, so we create a loop, initialize an instance of the **File** structure with each name, and add it to an observable property called **listOfFiles** to make it available to the views.

The **saveFile()** method remains the same, but after calling the **createFile()** method, we now verify that the file was created and add a **File** structure to the **listOfFiles** property only if no other file with the same name already exists in the list.

After the **ApplicationData** structure is initialized, the **listOfFiles** property contains the names of all the files in the directory, so we can show them to the user.

Listing 7-57: Listing the files created by the user

```
struct ContentView: View {
   @Environment(ApplicationData.self) private var appData
   @State private var openSheet: Bool = false

   var body: some View {
      NavigationStack {
         List {
            ForEach(appData.listOfFiles) { file in
               Text(file.name)
            }
         }
         .navigationBarTitle("Files")
         .toolbar {
            ToolbarItem(placement: .topBarTrailing) {
               Button("Add File", systemImage: "plus", action: {
                  openSheet = true
               })
            }
         }
         .sheet(isPresented: $openSheet) {
            AddFileView()
         }
      }
   }
}
```

Now, every time we create a file, it is added to the list and displayed on the screen, as shown below.

Figure 7-12: *List of files*

Do It Yourself

Update the **ApplicationData.swift** file with the code in Listing 7-56 and the **ContentView** structure with the code in Listing 7-57. Remember to include the **husky.png** image in an Assets Catalog or the files won't be created. Run the application on an iPhone simulator. Press the button on the toolbar to add a file. Insert the name of the file and press the Create button. You should see the list of all the files you have created so far, as shown in Figure 7-12.

Creating and listing files is only the first step, we must also allow the user to read their contents. To read files, we need to check if the file exists and then read its contents with the **contents()** method. The following is the function we need to include in our model for this purpose.

Listing 7-58: Reading the content of a file

```
func loadFile(name: String) -> UIImage? {
   if let docURL = directories?.first {
      let fileURL = docURL.appendingPathComponent(name)
      let filePath = fileURL.path

      if manager.fileExists(atPath: filePath) {
         if let content = manager.contents(atPath: filePath) {
            return UIImage(data: content)
         }
      }
   }
   return nil
}
```

To read the contents of a file, we get the URL as before, then use the **fileExists()** method to check if the file exists, and read the contents with the **contents()** method. Since in this case we know that the file contains an image, we create the **UIImage** object and return it.

In the views, we need a way to allow users to open the files. For this example, we will add a **NavigationLink** to the items in the list to open an additional view that displays the contents of the file. The following are the changes we need to make to the **ContentView** view.

Listing 7-59: Allowing the user to open a file

```
struct ContentView: View {
   @Environment(ApplicationData.self) private var appData
   @State private var openSheet: Bool = false

   var body: some View {
      NavigationStack {
         List {
```

```
            ForEach(appData.listOfFiles) { file in
               NavigationLink(value: file, label: {
                  Text(file.name)
               })
            }
         }
         .navigationBarTitle("Files")
         .toolbar {
            ToolbarItem(placement: .topBarTrailing) {
               Button("Add File", systemImage: "plus", action: {
                  openSheet = true
               })
            }
         }
         .navigationDestination(for: File.self, destination: { file in
            ShowFile(file: file)
         })
         .sheet(isPresented: $openSheet) {
            AddFileView()
         }
      }
   }
}
```

When the user selects a file from the list, the `navigationDestination()` modifier receives a `File` structure and opens the `ShowFile` view with that value. In this view, we need to call the `loadFile()` method in the model and display the image returned by the method on the screen.

Listing 7-60: Displaying the contents of a file

```
import SwiftUI

struct ShowFile: View {
   @Environment(ApplicationData.self) private var appData
   @State private var imageContent: UIImage?
   let file: File

   var body: some View {
      VStack {
         Text(file.name)
         Image(uiImage: imageContent ?? UIImage(named: "nopicture")!)
            .resizable()
            .scaledToFit()
         Spacer()
      }.padding(.horizontal)
      .toolbarTitleDisplayMode(.inline)
      .task {
         imageContent = appData.loadFile(name: file.name)
      }
   }
}
#Preview {
   ShowFile(file: File(name: "Test File"))
      .environment(ApplicationData.shared)
}
```

This view includes a **@State** property to store a **UIImage** object. When the view appears, the **task()** modifier calls the **loadFile()** method with the name of the file selected by the user, the method reads the file, converts the contents to a **UIImage** object, returns it, and the object is assigned to the property to display the image on the screen. The result is shown below.

Figure 7-13: *File content*

Do It Yourself

Add the method in Listing 7-58 to the **ApplicationData** class. Update the **ContentView** structure with the code in Listing 7-59. Create a SwiftUI file called **ShowFile.swift** for the code in Listing 7-60. Download the **nopicture.png** file from our website and add it to the Asset Catalog. Run the application on an iPhone simulator and select a file. You should see the picture of the husky, as shown in Figure 7-13.

Of course, we can also delete files. For this purpose, we just need to implement the **onDelete()** modifier introduced before and use it to remove the file from the Documents directory and the **File** structure from the **listOfFiles** array. The following is the method we need to add to our model for this purpose.

Listing 7-61: Deleting a file

```
func deleteFile(index: Int) {
   let file = listOfFiles[index]
   let name = file.name

   if let docURL = directories?.first {
      let fileURL = docURL.appendingPathComponent(name)
      do {
         try manager.removeItem(atPath: fileURL.path)
         listOfFiles.remove(at: index)
      } catch {
         print("File was not removed")
      }
   }
}
```

This method receives the index of the file the user wants to delete, retrieves the corresponding **File** structure, builds the file's URL, and then updates the model. We first remove the file from the Documents directory using the **removeItem()** method, and then remove the **File** structure from the **listOfFiles** array.

To allow the user to select the file to delete, we apply the **onDelete()** modifier to the **ForEach** view and then call the **deleteFile()** method in the model each time the user presses the Delete button.

Listing 7-62: Allowing the user to delete files

```
List {
   ForEach(appData.listOfFiles) { file in
      NavigationLink(value: file, label: {
         Text(file.name)
      })
   }
   .onDelete { indexSet in
      for index in indexSet {
         appData.deleteFile(index: index)
      }
   }
}
```

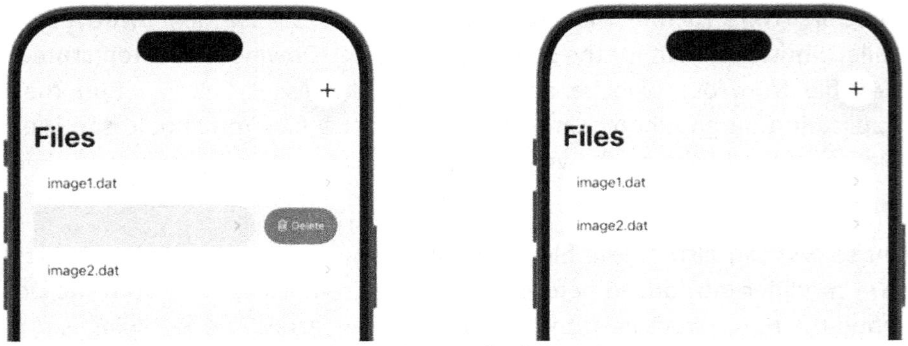

Figure 7-14: *File deleted*

Files can store any kind of information as long as we convert it to raw data. For custom data types, we can use Property List values or JSON encoding, as discussed earlier, but if we just want to store a string, we can implement the tools provided by the **String** structure. The following are the initializer and method defined by this structure to convert a string into **Data** and recreate a string from a **Data** value.

String(data: Data, **encoding:** Encoding)

This initializer creates a **String** value with the text in the **Data** structure provided by the **data** argument. The **encoding** argument determines the type of encoding used to generate the string. It is a structure of type **Encoding**, which includes properties such as **ascii**, **unicode**, **utf16** and **utf8**, among others.

```
data(using: Encoding, allowLossyConversion: Bool)
```

This method returns a **Data** structure containing the string from a **String** value. The **using** argument determines the type of encoding used to generate the string. It is a structure of type **Encoding**, which includes properties such as **ascii**, **unicode**, **utf16** and **utf8**, among others. The **allowLossyConversion** argument determines the precision of the conversion.

The **String** structure also includes the following method to turn a string into data and store it in a file, all at once.

```
write(to: URL, atomically: Bool, encoding: Encoding)
```

This method converts a string into a **Data** structure and stores it in the file located at the URL specified by the **to** argument. The **atomically** argument determines if we want the data to be stored in an auxiliary file first to ensure that the original file is not corrupted (recommended). And the **encoding** argument determines the type of encoding used to generate the string. It is a structure of type **Encoding**, which includes properties such as **ascii**, **unicode**, **utf16** and **utf8**, among others.

There is also a similar method provided by the **Data** structure to save the data directly into a file.

```
write(to: URL, options: WritingOptions)
```

This method stores the **Data** structure in the file located at the URL specified by the **to** argument. The **options** argument is a structure that determines how the file should be saved. The structure includes the type properties **atomic**, **withoutOverwriting**, **noFileProtection**, **completeFileProtection**, **completeFileProtection-UnlessOpen**, **completeFileProtectionUntilFirstUserAuthentication**, and **fileProtectionMask**.

As an example, we can create an application that allows the user to write text and save it to a file. The goal of the app is to load the content of a file, display it on the screen, and write the text back to the file each time the user makes a change. The following is the data model required to perform this process.

Listing 7-63: Storing text in a file

```
import SwiftUI

@Observable class ApplicationData {
   var textInFile: String = "" {
      didSet {
         if let docURL = directories?.first {
            let fileURL = docURL.appendingPathComponent("textdata.dat")
            let filePath = fileURL.path
            if let textData = textInFile.data(using: .utf8,
               allowLossyConversion: true) {
               manager.createFile(atPath: filePath, contents: textData,
                  attributes: nil)
            }
         }
```

```
        }
    }
    @ObservationIgnored var manager: FileManager
    @ObservationIgnored var directories: [URL]?
    static let shared: ApplicationData = ApplicationData()
    private init() {
        manager = FileManager.default
        directories = manager.urls(for: .documentDirectory,
            in: .userDomainMask)
        if let docURL = directories?.first {
            let fileURL = docURL.appendingPathComponent("textdata.dat")
            let filePath = fileURL.path
            if manager.fileExists(atPath: filePath) {
                if let content = manager.contents(atPath: filePath) {
                    if let text = String(data: content, encoding: .utf8) {
                        textInFile = text
                    }
                }
            }
        }
    }
}
```

When the model is initialized, we load a file named **textdata.dat**, and then assign its contents to an observable property called **textInFile** to make it available for the views. This property implements the **didSet()** method, so each time the user modifies the text, we convert the string to **Data** using the **data()** method and call the **createFile()** method to persist the changes to the file.

The view for this example must include a **TextEditor** view to show the text currently stored in the file and allow the user to change it.

Listing 7-64: Editing the content of a file

```
struct ContentView: View {
    @State private var appData = ApplicationData.shared

    var body: some View {
        GroupBox("Editor") {
            TextEditor(text: $appData.textInFile)
        }.padding()
    }
}
```

Figure 7-15: *Interface to insert and store text*

Do It Yourself

Create a new App project. Create a Swift file called **ApplicationData.swift** for the model in Listing 7-63. Update the **ContentView** structure with the code in Listing 7-64. Run the application on an iPhone simulator. Type a text. Stop the application from Xcode and run it again. You should see the same text on the screen.

PRO

Bundle

In the previous examples, we worked with files created by the user. However, if we want to load files that were added to the project during development, we need to read them from the bundle. Bundles are directories assigned to each application by the system. They define a hierarchical structure that organizes all the files and resources for the application. To create and manage bundles, the **Foundation** framework provides the **Bundle** class. This class includes properties and methods to work with bundles and determine their location. The following is the type property we can use to get a reference to the bundle created by default for the application.

main

This type property returns a reference to the app's bundle.

The problem with accessing the files in the bundle is that the bundle is created by the system after the app is installed on the device. Therefore, we don't know what URLs are assigned to the files. To get these URLs, we need to retrieve them from the **Bundle** object. For this purpose, the class provides the following methods.

url(forResource: String?, **withExtension:** String?)

This method returns a **URL** structure with the URL of a file or directory inside the bundle. The first argument specifies the name of the file or directory we are looking for, and the **withExtension** argument specifies the extension.

path(forResource: String?, **ofType:** String?)

This method returns the path of a file or directory inside the bundle. The first argument specifies the name of the file or directory we are looking for, and the **ofType** argument specifies the extension.

Files stored in the bundle are typically used to load initial data or restore the application's default state. The following example illustrates this process by loading a single file that contains some text. When the application launches, it reads a text file called **quote.txt** from the bundle. This file must be added to the project during development by dragging it from Finder into the Navigator, as we did for other files before.

Listing 7-65: Loading a file from the bundle

```
import SwiftUI

@Observable class ApplicationData {
   var textInFile: String = ""

   static let shared: ApplicationData = ApplicationData()
   private init() {
      let manager = FileManager.default
      let bundle = Bundle.main
      if let path = bundle.path(forResource: "quote", ofType: "txt") {
         if let data = manager.contents(atPath: path) {
            if let message = String(data: data, encoding: .utf8) {
               textInFile = message
            }
         }
      } else {
         textInFile = "File Not Found"
      }
   }
}
```

The model's initializer gets a reference to the app's bundle and then calls the **`path()`** method to find the path for a file called **quote.txt**. Once we get the path, we can read the file as before. The value is stored in an observable property to update the view. The view for this example just needs to read this property and display the text on the screen.

Listing 7-66: Displaying the content of a file stored in the bundle

```
struct ContentView: View {
   @State private var appData = ApplicationData.shared

   var body: some View {
      VStack {
         Text(appData.textInFile)
            .lineLimit(nil)
            .padding(15)
            .frame(minWidth: 0, maxWidth: .infinity)
            .background(Color(white: 0.8))
         Spacer()
      }.padding()
   }
}
```

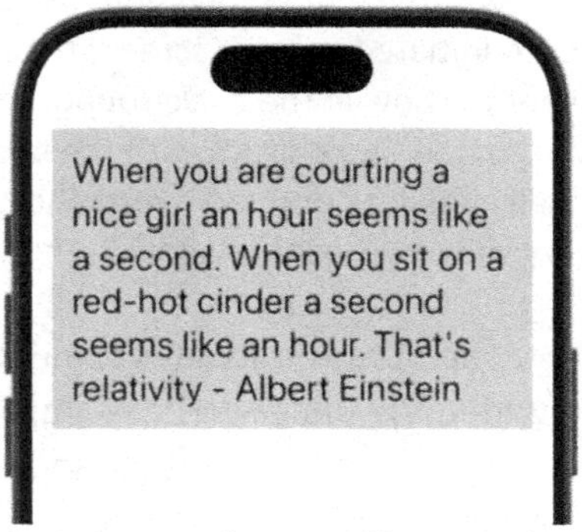

Figure 7-16: *Content of a text file stored in the bundle*

Do It Yourself

Create a new App project. Create a Swift file called **ApplicationData.swift** for the model in Listing 7-65. Update the **ContentView** structure with the code in Listing 7-66. Download the file **quote.txt** from our website or create your own and add it to the project. Run the application on an iPhone simulator. You should see the text loaded from the file on the screen, as shown in Figure 7-16.

BASIC

Documents

The **FileManager** class provides the tools needed to create and store files in the storage space designated by the system for the application. However, there are situations in which users need to share that information with other apps. To support this workflow, Apple platforms allow users to create and share documents. Documents are containers designed to process and store a specific type of information in a file. They can be stored on the device, shared with other apps, sent to servers, or saved in iCloud to make them available across devices.

Creating, editing, and sharing documents has become important enough that SwiftUI includes two **Scene** types specifically designed for building document-based applications. The following are the initializers.

DocumentGroup(newDocument: Closure, **editor:** Closure)

This initializer creates a **DocumentGroup** structure that defines a scene with all the tools required to open, create, edit, and save documents. The **newDocument** argument is a closure that returns a document model to create the documents, and the **editor** argument is a closure that provides the view used to edit the document's content.

DocumentGroupLaunchScene(String, Closure, **background:** Closure, **backgroundAccessoryView:** Closure, **overlayAccessoryView:** Closure)

This initializer creates a **DocumentGroupLaunchScene** structure to use along with a **DocumentGroup** structure to define the launch screen for a **DocumentGroup** scene.

The first argument is the window's title, the second argument is a closure that provides the actions we want the user to initiate from this screen, the **background** argument is a closure with the views we want to show in the background, the **backgroundAccessoryView** argument is a closure with the accessory views we want to show in the background (usually images), and the **overlayAccessoryView** argument is the closure with the accessory views we want to show in the overlay.

The **`DocumentGroup`** structure replaces the **`WindowGroup`** structure we have been using so far to create the scene (the window). Once we have implemented the **`DocumentGroup`** structure, the system presents an interface for creating and loading documents, as shown below.

***Figure 7-17:** Document app*

The documents are created from a document model. This is a structure or class that defines the type of data managed by the document and how the information is converted into a format that the application can process. The model is defined using a structure that conforms to the **`FileDocument`** protocol or a class that conforms to the **`ReferenceFileDocument`** protocol. Which protocol to use depends on the requirements of our application, but both define similar properties and methods for configuration. For example, below are the requirements of the **`FileDocument`** protocol.

`readableContentTypes`

This property returns an array of **`UTType`** structures to indicate the type of values managed by the document.

`init(configuration:` `ReadConfiguration)`

This initializer is used by the Document app to get the data when the user wants to read it. The **configuration** argument is a structure with information about the document. The structure includes the **`file`** property to return a **`FileWrapper`** structure, which in turn includes properties to return information about the document. The most frequently used are **`filename`** and **`preferredFilename`** to return the file's name and extension, **`fileAttributes`** to return the file's attributes, and **`regularFileContents`** to return the file's content.

fileWrapper(configuration: WriteConfiguration)

This method is called by the Document app to get the content we want to include in the document. The **configuration** argument is a structure with information about the current document. The structure includes the **existingFile** property to return a **FileWrapper** structure with this information or the value **nil** if the document was not saved yet. The method must return a **FileWrapper** structure with the content we want to save.

The content of the document is managed by an instance of the **FileWrapper** structure. The following is the structure's initializer.

FileWrapper(regularFileWithContents: Data)

This initializer creates a file wrapper for a document with the data provided by the argument.

To allow the user to work with documents, we need to define the document model using the tools presented above. This can be a structure or a class, depending on what we need for our application. The following example shows how to define a document model with a structure that conforms to the **FileDocument** protocol.

Listing 7-67: Defining a document model

```
import SwiftUI
import UniformTypeIdentifiers

struct TextDocument: FileDocument {
   static let readableContentTypes: [UTType] = [.plainText]

   var documentText: String
   init() {
      documentText = ""
   }
   init(configuration: ReadConfiguration) throws {
      if let data = configuration.file.regularFileContents {
         if let text = String(data: data, encoding: .utf8) {
            documentText = text
         } else {
            throw CocoaError(.fileReadCorruptFile)
         }
      } else {
         throw CocoaError(.fileReadCorruptFile)
      }
   }
   func fileWrapper(configuration: WriteConfiguration) throws ->
      FileWrapper {
      let data = documentText.data(using: .utf8)
      let wrapper = FileWrapper(regularFileWithContents: data!)
      return wrapper
   }
}
```

Among other responsibilities, the document model defines the type of data the document can process. This is specified by a **UTType** structure. Although we can define custom types, the structure includes type properties for the most common formats, such as **png**, **gif**, **jpeg**, **pdf**, **mp3**, **avi**, **json**, **image**, **text**, and **plainText**. In this example, we assign the **plainText** type to the **readableContentTypes** property to configure the document to store plain text. Note that to use the **UTType** data type, we must import the **UniformTypeIdentifiers** framework, where this structure is defined.

The rest of the model implements the tools required to process the document. We define a property called **documentText** to store the string, initialize it with an empty value, and then implement the protocol requirements. This includes the initializer the system uses to read the contents of the file and the **fileWrapper()** method, which writes the text back to the document.

> **IMPORTANT**
>
> Note that we must return an error if the process of reading the document fails. The **Foundation** framework defines a class called **CocoaError** that returns common error codes. The class includes an initializer to create an object from a **Code** structure and several type properties to return **Code** values. The most commonly used for reading files are **fileReadCorruptFile**, **fileReadNoSuchFile**, and **fileReadUnknown**.

Now that the document model is ready, we can create the scene with the **DocumentGroup** structure. The structure's initializer requires an instance of our document model and a closure with the view we want to use to edit the document. This closure receives a **FileDocumentConfiguration** structure with a reference to the document and its properties. The structure includes the following properties to return these values.

document

This is a binding property with a reference to the document.

fileURL

This property returns a **URL** structure with the file's URL.

isEditable

This property returns a Boolean value that indicates whether the user is allowed to edit the document or not.

The **DocumentGroup** structure creates a scene for processing documents and therefore it can replace the **WindowGroup** structure implemented in previous examples, as shown below.

Listing 7-68: Creating a Document app

```
@main struct MyApp: App {
   var body: some Scene {
      DocumentGroup(newDocument: TextDocument(), editor: { config in
         ContentView(document: config.$document)
      })
   }
}
```

This **App** structure creates an app for managing documents. We initialize the **DocumentGroup** structure with an instance of our **TextDocument** structure to tell the app how to create the documents, and a closure that returns a **ContentView** view to provide a view for editing the documents. Note that we take the property from the **FileDocumentConfiguration** structure received by the closure and pass it to the view so that the view can access the document and edit its content. For the view to receive this value, it must contain a binding property, as shown below.

Listing 7-69: Editing the document

```
struct ContentView: View {
   @Binding var document: TextDocument

   var body: some View {
      GroupBox("Editor") {
         TextEditor(text: $document.documentText)
      }.padding()
      .toolbarTitleDisplayMode(.inline)
   }
}
#Preview {
   @Previewable @State var document = TextDocument()
   ContentView(document: $document)
}
```

With a document app, users can save and share documents on the device, in iCloud, or on a server. The user interface consists of a home screen with a button at the top to create a new document and a sheet at the bottom with tabs to select recent documents and create new ones. When we press a button to create or open a document, the app opens the **ContentView** view to edit the content, as shown below.

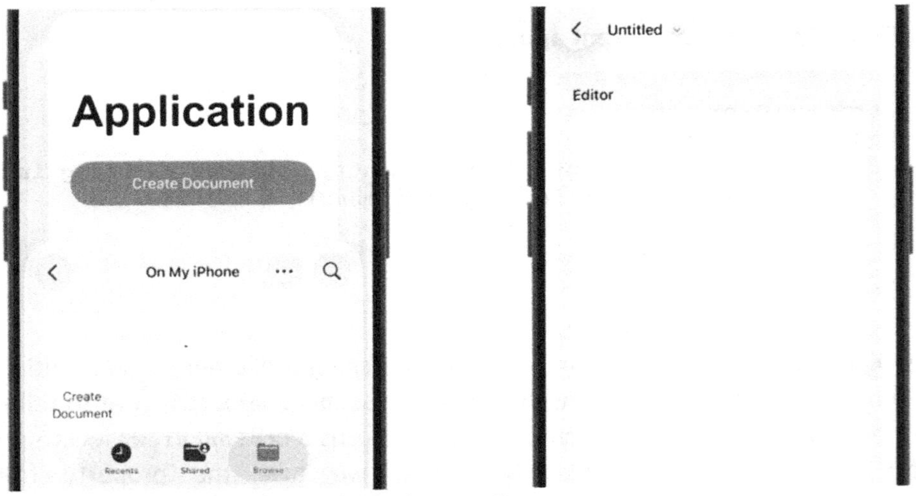

Figure 7-18: *Custom Document app*

Do It Yourself

Create a new App project. Create a Swift file called **TextDocument.swift** for the structure in Listing 7-67. Update the **App** structure with the code in Listing 7-68 and the **ContentView** structure with the code in Listing 7-69. Run the application on an iPhone simulator. Select the Browse tab and tap the Create Document button (Figure 7-18, left). You should see the document editor (Figure 7-18, right).

The **DocumentGroup** structure provides an interface with all the tools the user needs to create, modify, and remove documents, but sometimes all we need is to allow the user to export or import documents from our own custom interface. For this purpose, SwiftUI includes the following modifiers.

fileExporter(isPresented: Binding, **document:** FileDocument, **contentType:** UTType, **defaultFilename:** String, **onCompletion:** Closure)

This modifier presents an interface to allow the user to save a document on the device, iCloud, or a remote location. The **isPresented** argument is a binding property of type **Bool** that indicates whether the interface is shown or hidden. The **document** argument is the document model we want to use to create the document. The **contentType** argument determines the type of content the document is going to handle. The **defaultFilename** argument is the name we want to assign to the document. And the **onCompletion** argument is the closure to execute when the process is over. The closure receives a **Result** value with the document's URL and an **Error** value to report errors.

fileImporter(isPresented: Binding, **allowedContentTypes:** [UTType], **onCompletion:** Closure)

This modifier presents an interface to allow the user to open a document. The **isPresented** argument is a binding property of type **Bool** that indicates whether the interface is shown or hidden. The **allowedContentTypes** argument determines the type of document we want to allow the user to open. And the **onCompletion** argument is the closure to execute when the process is over. The closure receives a **`Result`** value with the document's URL and an **`Error`** value to report errors.

`fileMover(isPresented:` `Binding,` **`file:`** `URL,` **`onCompletion:`** `Closure)`

This modifier presents an interface to allow the user to move a document. The **isPresented** argument is a binding property of type **`Bool`** that indicates whether the interface is shown or hidden. The **file** argument is the URL of the document we want to move. And the **onCompletion** argument is the closure to execute when the process is over. The closure receives a **`Result`** value with the document's URL and an **`Error`** value to report errors.

These modifiers open their own interface, so we no longer need to create the window using the **`DocumentGroup`** structure. For example, the **`fileExporter()`** modifier opens an interface that allows the user to export and share a file. This modifier creates a document from a document model, as before, but from our own application, as shown below.

Listing 7-70: Exporting a document

```
import SwiftUI
import UniformTypeIdentifiers

struct ContentView: View {
   @State private var document = TextDocument()
   @State private var openExport: Bool = false

   var body: some View {
      NavigationStack {
         GroupBox("Editor") {
            TextEditor(text: $document.documentText)
         }.padding()
         .navigationTitle("Document")
         .toolbarTitleDisplayMode(.inline)
         .toolbar {
            ToolbarItem(placement: .topBarTrailing) {
               Button(action: {
                  openExport = true
               }, label: {
                  Image(systemName: "square.and.arrow.up")
               })
            }
         }
      }
      .fileExporter(isPresented: $openExport, document: document,
         contentType: .plainText, defaultFilename: "My Document",
         onCompletion: { result in
         print("Document exported")
      })
   }
}
```

To create the document, we need an instance of the document model. In this example, we create a **`@State`** property called **`document`** and initialize it with an instance of the same **`TextDocument`** structure used in the previous example. The view includes a **`TextEditor`** view so that the user can edit the contents of the document, and for exporting, we provide a button in the navigation bar. When the button is pressed, we assign the value **`true`** to a **`@State`** property and the **`fileExporter()`** modifier opens the interface to save the document, as shown below.

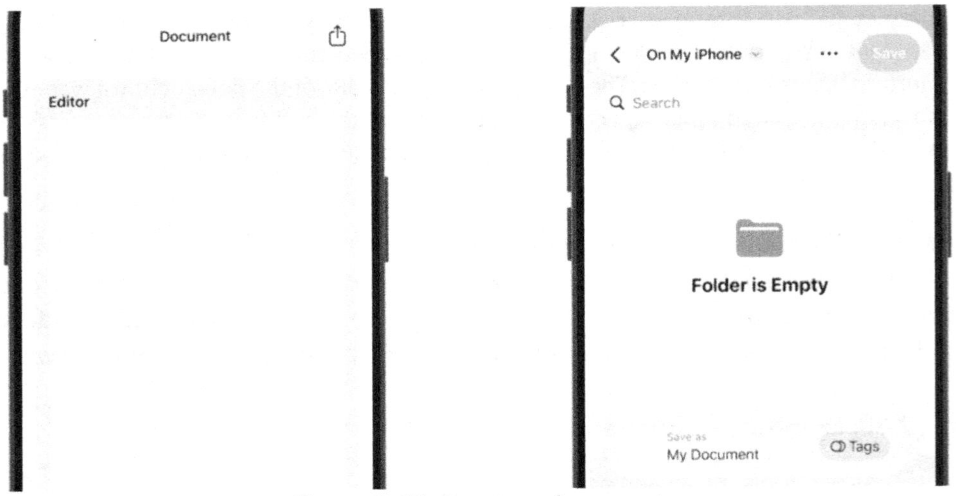

Figure 7-19: *Export a document*

Do It Yourself

Create a new App project. Create a Swift file called **TextDocument.swift** for the document model in Listing 7-67. Update the **`ContentView`** structure with the code in Listing 7-70. Run the application on the simulator. Type some text. Press the button on the navigation bar to export the text as a document. You should see an interface similar to the one in Figure 7-19, right.

In the same way that we can create and export a document with the text inserted by the user, we can import a document, read it, and display the text to the user by implementing the **`fileImporter()`** modifier. The only difference is that in this case we do not work with a document but with the file associated with the document. The **`fileImporter()`** modifier returns a **`URL`** structure with the location of the file. To read the file at this URL and extract the data, the **`Data`** structure includes the following initializer.

`Data(contentsOf:` `URL)`

This initializer creates a **`Data`** structure with the content of the file at the location specified by the **contentsOf** argument.

Since the files we access with the **`fileImporter()`** modifier are not stored in our app's storage space but in the file system, they are protected and inaccessible by default. To allow our app to access these files, the **`URL`** structure includes the following methods.

startAccessingSecurityScopedResource()

This method grants access to the resource referenced by the **URL** structure. The method returns a Boolean value to report whether access was granted or not.

stopAccessingSecurityScopedResource()

This method revokes the access granted to the application for the resource referenced by the **URL** structure.

The implementation of the **fileImporter()** modifier is very similar to the **fileExporter()** modifier. We must apply it to a view and define a Boolean state to indicate when we want to open the interface. In the following example, we add an additional button to the navigation bar. When the button is pressed, we assign the value **true** to the **@State** property to open the interface, then read the document selected by the user and assign the text to the **TextEditor** view to show it on the screen.

Listing 7-71: Importing a document

```
struct ContentView: View {
   @State private var document = TextDocument()
   @State private var openExport: Bool = false
   @State private var openImport: Bool = false

   var body: some View {
      NavigationStack {
         GroupBox("Editor") {
            TextEditor(text: $document.documentText)
         }.padding()
         .navigationTitle("Document")
         .toolbarTitleDisplayMode(.inline)
         .toolbar {
            ToolbarItem(placement: .topBarLeading) {
               Button(action: {
                  openImport = true
               }, label: {
                  Image(systemName: "square.and.arrow.down")
               })
            }
            ToolbarItem(placement: .topBarTrailing) {
               Button(action: {
                  openExport = true
               }, label: {
                  Image(systemName: "square.and.arrow.up")
               })
            }
         }
      }
      .fileExporter(isPresented: $openExport, document: document,
contentType: .plainText, defaultFilename: "My Document", onCompletion: {
result in
         print("Document exported")
      })
      .fileImporter(isPresented: $openImport, allowedContentTypes:
[.plainText], onCompletion: { result in
```

```
            if let fileURL = try? result.get() {
               if fileURL.startAccessingSecurityScopedResource() {
                  if let data = try? Data(contentsOf: fileURL) {
                     if let text = String(data: data, encoding: .utf8) {
                        document.documentText = text
                     }
                  }
                  fileURL.stopAccessingSecurityScopedResource()
               }
            }
         })
   }
}
```

The **fileImporter()** modifier imports the document and calls the closure assigned to the **onCompletion** argument to report the result. This closure receives a **Result** value that we can read to get the file's URL. In this example, we use the **get()** method to get the URL and then read the file with the **Data(contentsOf:)** initializer. The data is converted to a string and assigned to the document so that the text is shown on the screen.

Figure 7-20: *Interface to import a document*

Do It Yourself

Update the **ContentView** structure with the code in Listing 7-71. Run the application on an iPhone simulator. Press the Import button and select the document created before. You should see the content of the document on the screen.

IMPORTANT

The **FileDocument** protocol we used in these examples to create and manage our documents works with value types (structures), but SwiftUI also includes protocols to work with reference types (classes), including specific protocols for reading and writing documents. The topic is beyond the scope of this book. For more information, visit our website and follow the links for this chapter.

Chapter 8
Graphics & Animations

BASIC

8.1 - Shapes

All the views we have used so far are containers or are designed to display predefined content on the screen, but SwiftUI also includes graphical views to create custom controls or to use them for decoration. These views work like the ones introduced before and can use most of the modifiers presented so far, but are specifically designed to draw custom graphics on the screen.

BASIC

Standard Shapes

SwiftUI allows us to create predefined or custom shapes. The following are the views available for creating standard shapes.

Rectangle()

This initializer creates a **Rectangle** view. The size of the rectangle is determined by the view's frame.

RoundedRectangle(cornerRadius: CGFloat, **style:** RoundedCornerStyle**)**

This initializer creates a **RoundedRectangle** view. The **cornerRadius** argument determines the radius of the curvature of the corners, and the **style** argument is an enumeration of type **RoundedCornerStyle** that determines the type of curvature to use. The values available are **circular** and **continuous**. The view also includes the following initializer to define the radius with a **CGSize** value: **RoundedRectangle(cornerSize: CGSize, style: RoundedCornerStyle)**.

Circle()

This initializer creates a **Circle** view. The diameter of the circle is determined by the view's frame.

Ellipse()

This initializer creates an **Ellipse** view. The size of the ellipse is determined by the width and height of the view's frame.

Capsule(style: RoundedCornerStyle)

This initializer creates a **Capsule** view. The **style** argument is an enumeration that determines the type of curvature to apply to the corners. The values available are **circular** and **continuous**.

Like many other views, graphical views adopt the size of their container when no explicit size is specified, but we can define a specific size using the **frame()** modifier. The following example shows all the standard shapes available. We place the views inside a horizontal **ScrollView** so the list can be scrolled.

Listing 8-1: Drawing standard shapes

```
struct ContentView: View {
   var body: some View {
      VStack {
         ScrollView(.horizontal, showsIndicators: true) {
            HStack {
               Rectangle()
                  .frame(width: 100, height: 100)
               RoundedRectangle(cornerRadius: 25, style: .continuous)
                  .frame(width: 100, height: 100)
               Circle()
                  .frame(width: 100, height: 100)
               Ellipse()
                  .frame(width: 100, height: 50)
               Capsule()
                  .frame(width: 100, height: 50)
            }.padding()
         }
         Spacer()
      }
   }
}
```

Figure 8-1: *Standard shapes*

Do It Yourself

Create a new App project. Update the **ContentView** structure with the code in Listing 8-1. Run the application on the Canvas or an iPhone simulator. You should see a list of shapes displayed on the screen, as shown in Figure 8-1. Use this project to test the rest of the examples in this chapter.

By default, views are rendered with a color that depends on the appearance mode (black for Light and white for Dark), but we can specify the colors we want with the following modifiers.

fill(View)

This modifier fills the shape with the view specified by the argument. The argument is a view that represents a color, a gradient or an image.

stroke(View, **lineWidth:** CGFloat)

This modifier defines the border of the shape. The first argument is a view that represents a color, a gradient, or an image, and the **lineWidth** argument defines the border's width.

stroke(View, **style:** StrokeStyle)

This modifier defines the border of the shape. The first argument is a view that represents a color, a gradient or an image, and the **style** argument is a structure of type **StrokeStyle** that defines the border's width, cap, join, miter limit, dash, and dash phase.

strokeBorder(View, **lineWidth:** CGFloat)

This modifier defines the inner border of the shape. The first argument is a view that represents a color, a gradient, or an image, and the **lineWidth** argument defines the border's width.

strokeBorder(View, **style:** StrokeStyle)

This modifier defines the inner border of the shape. The first argument is a view that represents a color, a gradient or an image, and the **style** argument is a structure of type **StrokeStyle** that defines the border's width, cap, join, miter limit, dash, and dash phase.

There are two aspects of a shape that we can change with these modifiers: the fill and the border. In the following example, we show how to fill a shape with a solid color using the **fill()** modifier.

Listing 8-2: Filling a shape with a color

```
struct ContentView: View {
   var body: some View {
      RoundedRectangle(cornerRadius: 25)
         .fill(Color.red)
         .frame(width: 100, height: 100)
   }
}
```

The **fill()** modifier works with shapes, so we must apply it first, before any other modifier, as we did in our example. The result is shown below.

Figure 8-2: *Red rectangle*

We can also modify the border of a shape. In this case, there are two modifiers that produce slightly different results. The **stroke()** modifier expands the border both inward and outward, while the **strokeBorder()** modifier creates an inner border.

Listing 8-3: Defining a border

```
struct ContentView: View {
   var body: some View {
      HStack {
         RoundedRectangle(cornerRadius: 25)
            .stroke(Color.red, lineWidth: 20)
            .frame(width: 100, height: 100)
            .padding()
         RoundedRectangle(cornerRadius: 25)
            .strokeBorder(Color.red, lineWidth: 20)
            .frame(width: 100, height: 100)
            .padding()
      }
   }
}
```

This view includes two **RoundedRectangle** views with a border of 20 points, but because we are using different modifiers, the borders are different. Half of the border for the first rectangle is drawn outside the shape, while the other half is drawn inside the view's frame, but the border for the second rectangle is all inside the frame, as shown below.

Figure 8-3: *Rectangles with different strokes*

These two modifiers can also take a **StrokeStyle** structure to fine-tune the border. The structure provides the following initializer.

```
StrokeStyle(lineWidth: CGFloat, lineCap: CGLineCap, lineJoin: CGLineJoin, miterLimit: CGFloat, dash: [CGFloat], dashPhase: CGFloat)
```

This initializer creates a **StrokeStyle** structure to configure a stroke. The **lineWidth** argument determines the width. The **lineCap** argument determines the style of the end of the lines. It is an enumeration with the values **butt** (squared end), **round** (rounded end), and **square** (squared end). The **lineJoin** argument sets the style of the joint of two connected lines. It is an enumeration with the values **miter** (sharp end), **round** (rounded end), and **bevel** (squared end). The **miterLimit** argument determines how long the lines extend when the **lineJoin** argument is set to **miter**. The **dash** argument determines the length of the segments for a dashed stroke. And the **dashPhase** argument determines where the dashed line begins.

The following example creates a **RoundedRectangle** view where the outline is configured as a dashed line with a width of 15 points and rounded tips.

Listing 8-4: Defining a custom border

```
struct ContentView: View {
   let lineStyle = StrokeStyle(lineWidth: 15, lineCap: .round, lineJoin: .round, miterLimit: 0, dash: [20], dashPhase: 0)

   var body: some View {
      RoundedRectangle(cornerRadius: 25)
         .stroke(Color.red, style: lineStyle)
         .frame(width: 100, height: 100)
   }
}
```

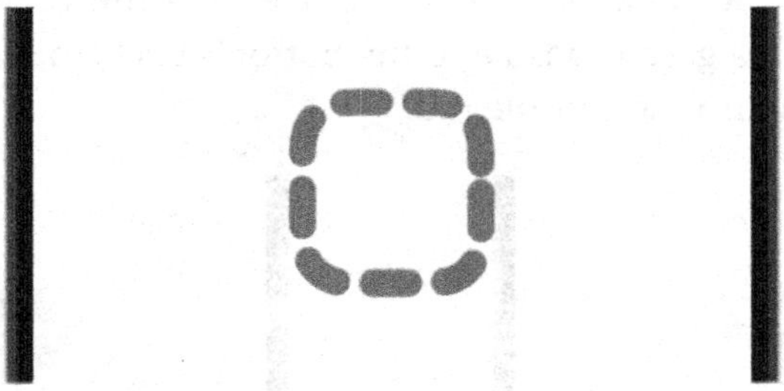

Figure 8-4: *Rectangle with a custom stroke*

Shapes are views and therefore can be combined with other SwiftUI views and controls. For instance, the following example assigns a **Capsule** shape as the background of a button.

Listing 8-5: Combining shapes with other views

```
struct ContentView: View {
   @State private var setActive: Bool = true

   var body: some View {
      Button(action: {
```

```
            setActive.toggle()
        }, label: {
            Text(setActive ? "Active" : "Inactive")
                .font(.title)
                .foregroundStyle(Color.white)
                .padding(.horizontal, 30)
                .padding(.vertical, 10)
        })
        .background(
            Capsule()
                .fill(setActive ? Color.green : Color.red)
        )
        .padding()
    }
}
```

There is also a version of the **background()** modifier specifically designed for shapes.

background(Color, **in:** Shape)

This modifier assigns a shape to the background of a view. The first argument specifies the color, and the **in** argument the shape.

Using this modifier, we can declare the background of the button in the previous example with a single line of code.

Listing 8-6: Assigning a shape as the background of a button

```
.background(setActive ? Color.green : Color.red, in: Capsule())
```

The button toggles the value of a **@State** property. If the value is **true**, we show the label "Active" and assign a green capsule to the button's background, otherwise we display the label "Inactive" and turn the capsule red.

Figure 8-5: *Graphic button*

BASIC

Gradients

We can also use color gradients to fill the shapes and the borders. SwiftUI includes four structures for creating gradients: **LinearGradient**, **RadialGradient**, **AngularGradient**, and **EllipticalGradient**. These structures conform to the **ShapeStyle** protocol, which defines the following methods to create customized instances.

```
linearGradient(Gradient, startPoint: UnitPoint, endPoint: UnitPoint)
```

This method returns a linear gradient. The **gradient** argument is the gradient of colors to be used, and the **startPoint** and **endPoint** arguments determine the points inside the shape where the gradient starts and ends.

```
radialGradient(Gradient, center: UnitPoint, startRadius: CGFloat, endRadius: CGFloat)
```

This method returns a circular gradient. The **gradient** argument is the gradient of colors to be used. The **center** argument determines the position of the center of the circle, and the **startRadius** and **endRadius** arguments determine where the gradient starts and ends.

```
ellipticalGradient(Gradient, center: UnitPoint, startRadiusFraction: CGFloat, endRadiusFraction: CGFloat)
```

This method returns a radial gradient with the shape of an ellipse. The **gradient** argument is the gradient of colors to be used. The **center** argument determines the center of the ellipse, and the **startRadiusFraction** and **endRadiusFraction** argument determine the radius of the ellipse.

```
angularGradient(Gradient, center: UnitPoint, startAngle: Angle, endAngle: Angle)
```

This method returns an angular gradient. The **gradient** argument is the gradient of colors to be used. The **center** argument determines the center of the shape, the **startAngle** argument determines the angle at the beginning of the gradient and the **endAngle** determines the angle at the end.

```
conicGradient(Gradient, center: UnitPoint, angle: Angle)
```

This method returns a conic gradient. The **gradient** argument is the gradient of colors to be used. The **center** argument determines the position of the tip of the cone, and the **angle** argument determines the angle where the gradient begins.

These methods return an instance of one of the gradient structures introduced before, but the gradient of colors is defined by the `Gradient` structure.

```
Gradient(colors: [Color])
```

This initializer creates a gradient with the colors specified by the argument. The **colors** argument is an array of `Color` views.

```
Gradient(stops: [Gradient.Stop])
```

This initializer creates a gradient with the colors specified by the argument. The **stops** argument is an array of `Stop` structures that determine the colors and when they stop.

Another value required to present a gradient is the `UnitPoint` structure. This is like the `CGPoint` structure but specifically designed to work with graphical structures.

```
UnitPoint(x: CGFloat, y: CGFloat)
```

This initializer creates a **UnitPoint** structure. The **x** and **y** arguments determine the x and y coordinates of the point. For gradients, these arguments are defined with values from 0.0 to 1.0.

The **UnitPoint** structure also includes the type properties **bottom**, **bottomLeading**, **bottomTrailing**, **center**, **leading**, **top**, **topLeading**, **topTrailing**, **trailing**, and **zero** to define common points. For example, we can apply a linear gradient with the values **bottom** and **top** to draw the gradient from the bottom to the top of the shape.

Listing 8-7: Defining a linear gradient

```
struct ContentView: View {
   let gradient = Gradient(colors: [Color.red, Color.green])

   var body: some View {
      RoundedRectangle(cornerRadius: 25)
         .fill(.linearGradient(gradient, startPoint: .bottom,
            endPoint: .top))
         .frame(width: 100, height: 100)
   }
}
```

This example defines a gradient with two colors, red and green, and then applies the gradient to a **RoundedRectangle** view with the structure returned by the **linearGradient()** method. Because we declare the value **bottom** as the starting point and the value **top** as the ending point, the colors are displayed from bottom to top in the order declared by the **Gradient** structure.

Figure 8-6: *Linear gradient*

When a gradient is created without specifying color stops, the colors are distributed evenly over the entire area occupied by the gradient. If we want to adjust the distribution, we must define the colors for the gradient with **Stop** structures.

```
Stop(color: Color, location: CGFloat)
```

This initializer creates a color with a stop value. The **color** argument determines the color, and the **location** argument determines the position in the gradient where the color begins (it's a value from 0.0 to 1.0).

The following example reproduces the previous gradient, but this time the green color begins at the position 0.4 (40% of the area occupied by the gradient).

Listing 8-8: Defining a linear gradient with custom stops

```
struct ContentView: View {
   let gradient = Gradient(stops: [
      Gradient.Stop(color: Color.red, location: 0.0),
      Gradient.Stop(color: Color.green, location: 0.4)
   ])
   var body: some View {
      RoundedRectangle(cornerRadius: 25)
         .fill(.linearGradient(gradient, startPoint: .bottom,
            endPoint: .top))
         .frame(width: 100, height: 100)
   }
}
```

Figure 8-7: Linear gradient with custom stops

In addition to the linear gradient, we can also create gradients with different shapes. For example, radial and elliptical gradients are created with circular layers drawn outward from the center of a circle, as shown below.

Listing 8-9: Defining a circular gradient

```
struct ContentView: View {
   let gradient = Gradient(colors: [Color.red, Color.white])

   var body: some View {
      RoundedRectangle(cornerRadius: 25)
         .fill(.radialGradient(gradient, center: .center, startRadius: 0,
            endRadius: 120))
         .frame(width: 100, height: 100)
   }
}
```

This example illustrates how to create a radial gradient. The values required are the `Gradient` structure, the center of the circle, and the position within the shape where the gradient begins and ends. These values determine where the gradient begins and ends, but only the part of the gradient that is inside the shape is drawn. In our example, the **endRadius** argument was specified as 120, but because the size of the shape is 100 x 100, only part of the gradient is visible.

Figure 8-8: *Circular gradient*

SwiftUI also includes the **`MeshGradient`** view for creating two-dimensional color gradients. The gradient is created from a grid of points. Each point is associated with a color, so the system can mix the colors between each point and change the gradient as the points are moved.

> **MeshGradient(width:** Int, **height:** Int, **points:** [Float], **colors:** [Color], **background:** Color, **smoothsColors:** Bool, **colorSpace:** Gradient.ColorSpace)
>
> This initializer creates a view for displaying a two-dimensional gradient. The **width** and **height** arguments determine the number of horizontal and vertical points in the grid. The **points** argument is an array of vectors with **`Float`** values representing the coordinates of the points on the grid. The **colors** argument is an array of **`Color`** views that represent the colors for each point. The **background** argument determines the background color of the grid (**`clear`** by default). The **smoothsColors** argument determines whether the transition between the colors is smooth or not (**`true`** by default). And the **`colorSpace`** argument determines the color space used to display the colors.

The **width** and **height** arguments define the side of the grid. For example, a grid of 3 by 3 points includes a total of 9 points. The position of the points is defined with values from 0.0 to 1.0 (left to right and top to bottom) and the colors for each point are declared with **`Color`** views, as shown below.

Listing 8-10: Defining a mesh gradient

```
struct ContentView: View {
   var body: some View {
      MeshGradient(width: 3, height: 3, points: [
         [0.0, 0.0], [0.5, 0.0], [1.0, 0.0],
         [0.0, 0.5], [0.8, 0.8], [1.0, 0.6],
         [0.0, 1.0], [0.5, 1.0], [1.0, 1.0]
      ], colors: [
         .red, .purple, .indigo,
         .orange, .white, .blue,
         .yellow, .green, .mint
      ])
      .ignoresSafeArea(.all)
   }
}
```

Figure 8-9: Mesh gradient

BASIC

Effects

The **ShapeStyle** protocol, which defines the type methods used in the previous section to create gradient structures, also specifies methods for applying additional effects to a view. The following are the most frequently used.

shadow(ShadowStyle)

This method applies a shadow to the view. The argument is a structure with two type methods to create drop and inner shadows: **drop(color: Color, radius: CGFloat, x: CGFloat, y: CGFloat)** and **inner(color: Color, radius: CGFloat, x: CGFloat, y: CGFloat)**.

opacity(Double)

This method assigns a level of opacity to the view. The argument takes values from 0.0 (fully transparent) to 1.0 (fully opaque).

blendMode(BlendMode)

This method determines how the view is going to blend with the background and other views. The argument is an enumeration with the values **normal**, **darken**, **multiply**, **colorBurn**, **plusDarker**, **lighten**, **screen**, **colorDodge**, **plusLighter**, **overlay**, **softLight**, **hardLight**, **difference**, **exclusion**, **hue**, **saturation**, **color**, **luminosity**, **sourceAtop**, **destinationOver**, and **destinationOut**.

Many modifiers can take a structure that conforms to the **ShapeStyle** protocol to assign a style to a view. When working with shapes, these styles work better with the **foregroundStyle()** modifier. For instance, if we want to apply a shadow to a rectangular shape, we can apply this modifier for the shadow and then again for the fill color, as shown in the following example.

Listing 8-11: Adding a shadow to a shape

```
struct ContentView: View {
   var body: some View {
      RoundedRectangle(cornerRadius: 25)
```

```
            .foregroundStyle(.shadow(.drop(color: .black, radius: 3, x: 4,
               y: 4)))
            .foregroundStyle(.red)
            .frame(width: 100, height: 100)
      }
   }
```

Figure 8-10: *Shadow*

BASIC

Patterns

In addition to colors and gradients, we can also use images to fill a shape. SwiftUI includes the **ImagePaint** structure for this purpose. The structure includes the following type method to create a custom instance.

> **image(**Image, **sourceRect:** CGRect, **scale:** CGFloat**)**
>
> This method returns an **ImagePaint** structure with the image and configuration specified by the arguments. The first argument provides the **Image** view with the image we want to use, the **sourceRect** argument determines the part of the image to be drawn (by default, the entire image), and the **scale** argument defines the scale of the image (by default, the original scale).

By default, the **ImagePaint** structure uses the entire image at its original scale, so in most cases, specifying the image is enough for the system to create the pattern, as in the following example.

Listing 8-12: Filling a shape with an image

```
struct ContentView: View {
   var body: some View {
      Rectangle()
         .fill(.image(Image("pattern")))
         .frame(width: 100, height: 100)
   }
}
```

The image repeats to fill the entire shape. In this example, we define a square measuring 100 by 100 points and paint it with an image that is 25 by 25 points. Because the image is smaller than the shape, it is drawn multiple times to cover the area.

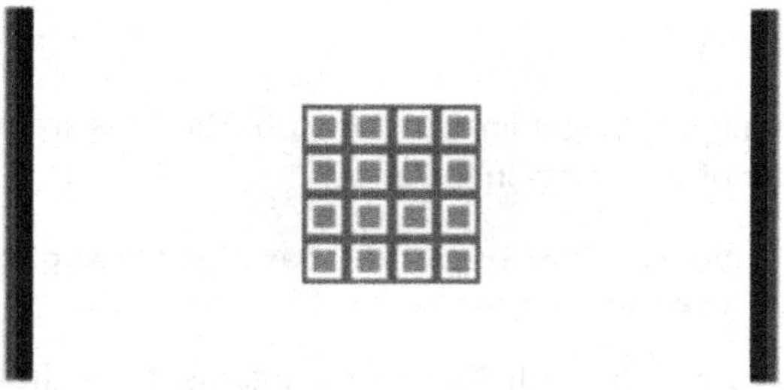

Figure 8-11: *Pattern*

BASIC

8.2 - Paths

The shapes we have implemented so far are defined by paths. A path is a set of instructions that define the outline of a 2D shape. In addition to the paths defined by the standard shapes, we can create our own.

BASIC

Path View

The **Path** view is designed to create a view that contains a custom path. The following are some of the initializers.

Path()—This initializer creates an empty **Path** view. The path is created by applying modifiers to this instance.

Path(Closure)—This initializer creates an empty **Path** view. The argument is a closure to define the path. The closure receives a reference to the **Path** structure that we can use to create the path.

A path is created by combining lines and curves. Each stroke moves from one point to another within the view's coordinate space, much like the motion of a pencil drawing on paper. The **Path** structure provides a set of methods to control the position of the pencil and construct the path. The following are the most frequently used.

move(to: CGPoint)—This modifier moves the pencil to the coordinates determined by the **to** argument.

addLine(to: CGPoint)—This modifier adds a straight line to the path, from the pencil's current position to the coordinates indicated by the **to** argument.

addLines([CGPoint])

This modifier adds multiple straight lines to the path. The lines are added in sequence according to the order of the points in the array.

addArc(center: CGPoint, **radius:** CGFloat, **startAngle:** Angle, **endAngle:** Angle, **clockwise:** Bool)

This modifier adds an arc to the path. The **center** argument specifies the coordinates of the center of the circle formed by the arc, the **radius** argument is the radius of the circle, the **startAngle** and **endAngle** arguments are the angles in which the arc starts and ends, and the **clockwise** argument determines the orientation in which the arc is calculated (**true** clockwise and **false** counterclockwise).

addArc(tangent1End: CGPoint, **tangent2End:** CGPoint, **radius:** CGFloat)

This modifier adds an arc to the path using tangent points. The **tangent1End** argument defines the coordinates of the end of the first tangent line, the **tangent2End** argument defines the coordinates of the end of the second tangent line, and the **radius** argument determines the radius of the circle.

addCurve(to: CGPoint, **control1:** CGPoint, **control2:** CGPoint)

This modifier adds a cubic Bezier curve to the path with two control points. The **to** argument defines the coordinates of the ending point, and the **control1** and **control2** arguments define the coordinates of the first and second control points, respectively.

addQuadCurve(to: CGPoint, **control:** CGPoint)

This modifier adds a quadratic Bezier curve to the path with a control point. The **to** argument defines the coordinates of the ending point, and the **control** argument defines the coordinates of the control point.

addEllipse(in: CGRect)

This modifier adds an ellipse to the path. The **in** argument determines the area of the ellipse. If the rectangle is a square, the ellipse becomes a circle.

addRect(CGRect)

This modifier adds the rectangle defined by the argument to the path. There is a version of this modifier that takes an array of **CGRect** values to add multiple rectangles at a time (**addRects([CGRect])**).

addRoundedRect(in: CGRect, **cornerSize:** CGSize, **style:** RoundedCornerStyle)

This modifier adds a rounded rectangle to the path. The **in** argument determines the dimensions of the rectangle, the **cornerRadius** argument determines the radius of the curvature of the corners, and the **style** argument is an enumeration with the values **circular** and **continuous**.

A custom path works the same way as a predefined path. If we don't specify the fill or stroke, the path is drawn with a color that depends on the appearance mode (black for Light and white for Dark), but we can change that with the **fill()** and **stroke()** modifiers, as we did before for standard shapes. If we draw the path with the **fill()** modifier, the path is automatically closed, but if we do it with the **stroke()** modifier, it stays open. To close the path and ensure that the lines are connected, the **Path** structure includes the following modifier.

closeSubpath()

This modifier closes the current path. If the path is not a closed path, the modifier adds a line between the end and the beginning of the path to close it.

To create a path, we must apply the modifiers in order, following the line of an imaginary pencil. In the following example, a path is created in the shape of a triangle.

Listing 8-13: Defining a custom path

```
struct ContentView: View {
   var body: some View {
      Path { path in
         path.move(to: CGPoint(x: 100, y: 150))
         path.addLine(to: CGPoint(x: 200, y: 150))
         path.addLine(to: CGPoint(x: 100, y: 250))
         path.closeSubpath()
      }.stroke(Color.blue, lineWidth: 5)
   }
}
```

By default, the initial position of the pencil is at coordinates 0, 0 (upper-left corner of the container view). If we want to start drawing from a different position, we must first apply the **move()** modifier. In Listing 8-13, we move the pencil to the coordinates 100, 150 before adding the first line. Subsequent lines are drawn from the current position of the pencil to the coordinates specified by the modifier. For example, after we set the starting point in our example, we create a line from that point to the point 200, 150, so the next line starts at that point and ends at 100, 250. Notice that we only created two lines. The line that goes from point 100, 250 to point 100, 150 is automatically created by the **closeSubpath()** modifier to close the path. If we want to create an open path, we can ignore this modifier. The result is shown below.

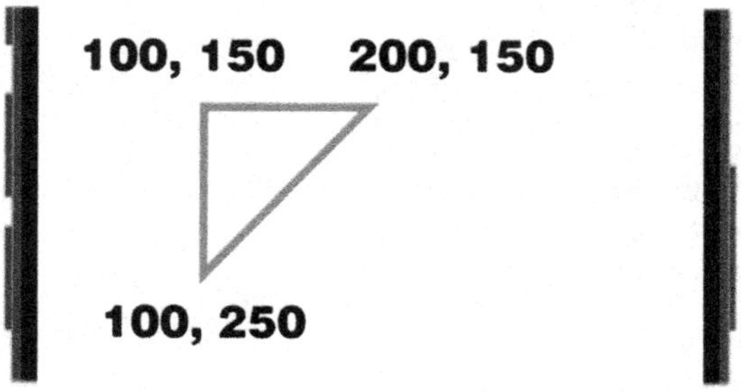

Figure 8-12: *Custom path*

By combining different modifiers, we can create complex paths. The following path is defined with two lines and an arc.

Listing 8-14: Combining lines and arcs

```
struct ContentView: View {
   var body: some View {
      Path { path in
         path.move(to: CGPoint(x: 100, y: 150))
         path.addLine(to: CGPoint(x: 200, y: 150))
         path.addArc(center: CGPoint(x: 200, y: 170), radius: 20,
            startAngle: .degrees(270), endAngle: .degrees(90),
            clockwise: false)
         path.addLine(to: CGPoint(x: 100, y: 190))
      }.stroke(Color.blue, lineWidth: 5)
   }
}
```

Since arcs are calculated from the coordinates of the center of the circle and the radius, we must consider these two values to connect the arc to the previous line. If the initial coordinates of the arc do not match the current position of the pencil, a line is automatically created between these two points to connect the path. Figure 8-13 below shows the path we get with the example in Listing 8-14, and what we see when we move the center of the arc up 10 points (**y: 160**).

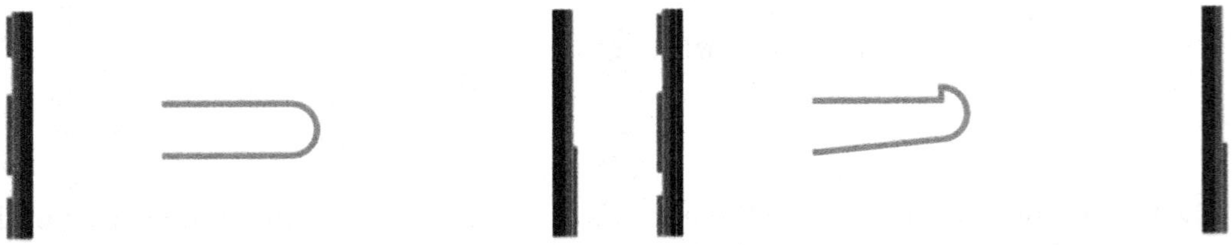

***Figure 8-13:** Lines and arcs*

The **addRect()** and **addEllipse()** modifiers allow us to add rectangles and circles to the path. The modifiers add the shapes to the current path, but they move the pencil to the position indicated by the **CGRect** value, so they are considered by the system as independent shapes.

Listing 8-15: Combining lines and ellipses

```
struct ContentView: View {
   var body: some View {
      Path { path in
         path.move(to: CGPoint(x: 100, y: 150))
         path.addLine(to: CGPoint(x: 200, y: 150))
         path.addEllipse(in: CGRect(x: 210, y: 140, width: 20,
            height: 20))
      }.stroke(Color.blue, lineWidth: 5)
   }
}
```

In this example, we draw a line and then an ellipse positioned 10 points to the right. Because the ellipse is treated as an independent shape, no additional line is drawn to connect the two shapes. The result is shown below.

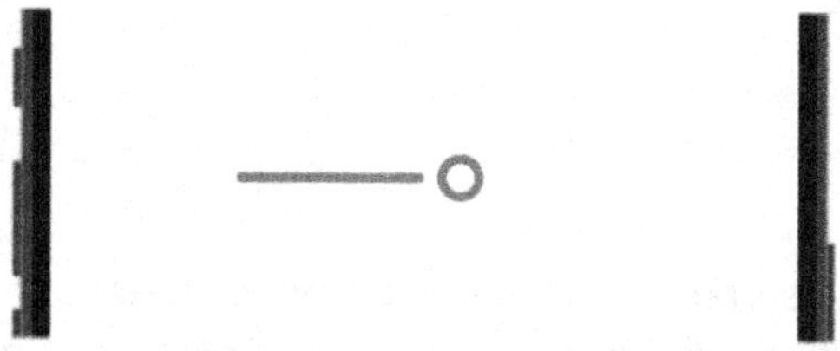

Figure 8-14: *Lines and ellipses*

In addition to **addArc()** and **addEllipse()**, we have two other modifiers to draw curves: The **addQuadCurve()** modifier generates a quadratic Bezier curve, and the **addCurve()** modifier generates a cubic Bezier curve. The difference between these modifiers is that the first one has only one control point and the second has two, creating different types of curves.

Listing 8-16: Creating complex curves

```
struct ContentView: View {
   var body: some View {
      Path { path in
         path.move(to: CGPoint(x: 50, y: 50))
         path.addQuadCurve(to: CGPoint(x: 50, y: 200), control: CGPoint(x:
100, y: 125))
         path.move(to: CGPoint(x: 250, y: 50))
         path.addCurve(to: CGPoint(x: 250, y: 200), control1: CGPoint(x:
200, y: 125), control2: CGPoint(x: 300, y: 125))
      }.stroke(Color.blue, lineWidth: 5)
   }
}
```

To create a quadratic curve, we move the pencil to the point 50, 50, finish the curve at 50, 200, and place the control point at 100, 125. The cubic curve, created with the **addCurve()** method, is more complex. This curve uses two control points, the first at 200, 125 and the second at 300, 125. These points define the shape of the curve, as shown below.

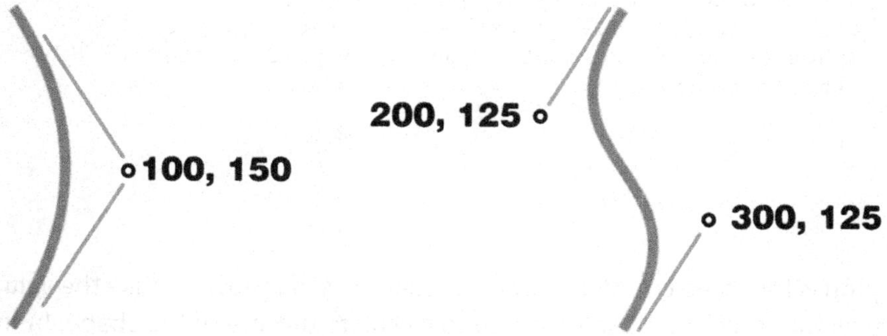

Figure 8-15: *Complex curves*

PRO

Custom Shapes

The paths we have created so far use fixed values, which means the resulting shapes always have the same size, regardless of the size of the view. To adjust a path to the size of its view, we need to create a structure that conforms to the **Shape** protocol. The advantage of defining **Shape** structures instead of directly using **Path** views is that a **Shape** structure receives a **CGRect** value representing the size of the view in which it is drawn, allowing us to adapt the shape to the size of its container. To create and return the path, the **Shape** protocol requires the implementation of the following method.

path(in: CGRect)

This method receives a **CGRect** value with the dimensions of the view and must return a **Path** view with the path we want to assign to the shape.

Creating a custom shape is easy. We must define a structure that conforms to the **Shape** protocol, implement the **path()** method, and create and return a **Path** view. The following example defines a shape structure called **Triangle** that draws a triangle.

Listing 8-17: Creating a custom shape view

```
import SwiftUI

struct Triangle: Shape {
   func path(in rect: CGRect) -> Path {
      var path = Path()
      let width = rect.width
      let height = rect.height
      let posX = rect.origin.x
      let posY = rect.origin.y

      path.move(to: CGPoint(x: posX, y: posY))
      path.addLine(to: CGPoint(x: posX + width, y: posY))
      path.addLine(to: CGPoint(x: posX, y: posY + height))
      path.closeSubpath()

      return path
   }
}
```

The path is the same created in previous examples, but now we take the values from the **CGRect** structure received by the method to calculate the size of the shape. In this case, we expand the triangle from left to right and top to bottom to cover the entire view.

Once the **Shape** view is defined, we can implement it in our interface like any other view. To illustrate how this works, we can instantiate multiple **Triangle** views of different sizes, as shown below.

Listing 8-18: Implementing custom shape views

```
struct ContentView: View {
    var body: some View {
        VStack {
            ScrollView(.horizontal, showsIndicators: true) {
                HStack {
                    Triangle()
                        .fill(Color.blue)
                        .frame(width: 170, height: 150)
                    Triangle()
                        .fill(Color.green)
                        .frame(width: 170, height: 100)
                    Triangle()
                        .fill(Color.yellow)
                        .frame(width: 150, height: 180)
                    Triangle()
                        .fill(Color.red)
                        .frame(width: 100, height: 150)
                }
            }.padding()
            Spacer()
        }
    }
}
```

When a **`Triangle`** view is created, the **`path()`** method is called with the dimensions of the view and the triangle is drawn according to those values. Therefore, if we define **`Triangle`** views of different sizes, we will get triangles of different shapes on the screen.

Figure 8-16: *Custom shape views*

Do It Yourself

Create a new Swift file in your project called **Triangle.swift** for the code in Listing 8-17. Update the **`ContentView`** structure with the code in Listing 8-18. Run the application on an iPhone simulator. You should see the shapes shown in Figure 8-16. Change the sizes of the **`Triangle`** views to see how the shapes adapt.

8.3 - Transformations

SwiftUI provides a variety of tools to modify the appearance of a view or a **Shape** view, including the orientation, perspective, and position of its content. The following are some of the modifiers available for this purpose.

offset(CGSize)

This modifier displaces the content of the view to the horizontal and vertical distance defined by the argument.

rotationEffect(Angle)

This modifier rotates the content of the view to the angle determined by the argument.

rotation3DEffect(Angle, Tuple)

This modifier rotates the content of the view in three dimensions. The first argument declares the angle in degrees or radians, and the second argument is a tuple with three values to represent the axes to be affected (**(x: Double, y: Double, z: Double)**). Values different than 0 rotate the image in that axis.

clipShape(Shape)

This modifier clips the view with the shape specified by the argument.

These modifiers affect the content of the view, not the view itself. For example, if we apply an offset to an **Image** view, the image within the view is moved by the distance determined by the modifier, but the frame of the view is not affected.

Listing 8-19: Displacing an image

```
struct ContentView: View {
    var body: some View {
        Image("spot1")
            .resizable()
            .scaledToFit()
            .frame(width: 150, height: 200)
            .offset(CGSize(width: 75, height: 0))
    }
}
```

The code in Listing 8-19 moves the image 75 points to the right, which is half the width of the Image view, but the view's frame remains in the same location, as shown below.

Figure 8-17: *Image displaced to the right*

Do It Yourself

Update the **`ContentView`** structure with the code in Listing 8-19. Download the **spot1.jpg** image from our website and add it to an Asset Catalog. Run the application on an iPhone simulator. You should see the image shifted 75 points to the right, as shown in Figure 8-17.

The rotation modifiers work in a similar way. They rotate the content of the view in 2D or 3D. The most interesting is the **`rotation3DEffect()`** which can rotate the content around any axis.

Listing 8-20: Rotating the image

```
struct ContentView: View {
   var body: some View {
      Image("spot1")
         .resizable()
         .scaledToFit()
         .frame(width: 150, height: 200)
         .scaleEffect(CGSize(width: 0.9, height: 0.9))
         .rotation3DEffect(.degrees(30), axis: (x: 0, y: 1, z: 0))
   }
}
```

The **`rotation3DEffect()`** modifier requires a tuple with values that determine the axes about which the content should be rotated. A value of 0 means that there is no rotation, and a value other than 0 indicates the direction of rotation, negative to one side and positive to the other.

Figure 8-18: *Image rotated in the y axis*

Another transformation we can perform is clipping the view with the **`clipShape()`** modifier. This modifier overlays the view with a shape and preserves only the parts of the view that are covered by the shape. This is especially useful for images. For example, we can clip our image with a **`Circle`** shape to create a nice thumbnail.

Listing 8-21: Clipping the image

```
struct ContentView: View {
   var body: some View {
      Image("spot1")
         .resizable()
         .scaledToFit()
         .frame(width: 150, height: 200)
         .clipShape(Circle())
   }
}
```

Figure 8-19: *Image clipped with a* Circle *shape*

When a view is clipped, its shape changes. This means that if we want to apply a border, it won't match the shape of the view. To apply a border to a view with an irregular shape, we need to create an overlay using the **`overlay()`** modifier and draw a view that matches the shape of the original view. For example, we can create a border for the previous image with a **`Circle`** view and the **`stroke()`** modifier.

Listing 8-22: Adding a border to an irregular shape

```
struct ContentView: View {
   var body: some View {
      Image("spot1")
         .resizable()
```

```
            .scaledToFit()
            .frame(width: 150, height: 200)
            .clipShape(Circle())
            .overlay {
               Circle().stroke(Color.blue, lineWidth: 10)
            }
      }
}
```

Figure 8-20: *Irregular view with a border*

SwiftUI also includes modifiers specifically designed for transforming **Shape** views. The following are the most frequently used.

> **rotation(**Angle, **anchor:** UnitPoint**)**

This modifier rotates the shape to the angle specified by the first argument. The **anchor** argument determines the point around which the shape will rotate. The point is specified with values between 0.0 and 1.0.

> **scale(**CGFloat, **anchor:** UnitPoint**)**

This modifier changes the scale of the shape. The first argument determines the new scale (1.0 by default), and the **anchor** argument determines the point from which the shape is scaled. There is an additional modifier to change the scale independently for the x and y axes: **scale(x: CGFloat, y: CGFloat, anchor: UnitPoint)**.

> **trim(from:** CGFloat, **to:** CGFloat**)**

This modifier trims the shape from the point determined by the **from** argument to the point determined by the **to** argument.

These modifiers are implemented by **Shape** views and therefore must be applied before other modifiers, as in the following example.

Listing 8-23: Rotating a shape

```
struct ContentView: View {
   var body: some View {
      RoundedRectangle(cornerRadius: 20)
         .rotation(.degrees(45))
         .fill(Color.red)
         .frame(width: 100, height: 100)
   }
}
```

As we already mentioned, the transformation modifiers affect the content of the view, in this case the shape, but the view remains the same, as shown below.

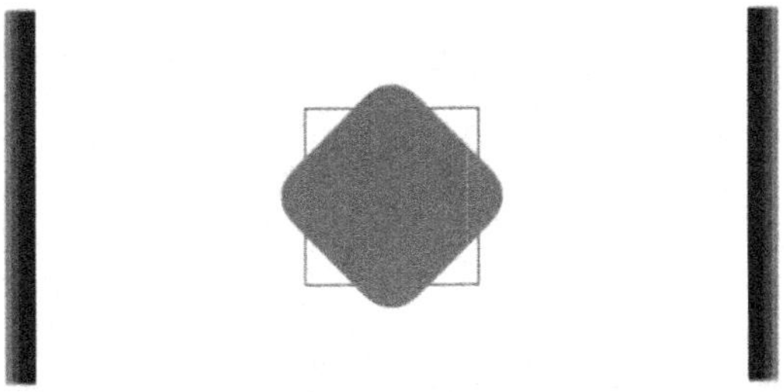

Figure 8-21: *Shape rotation*

The **scale()** modifier is used not only to change the size of a shape, but also to create interesting visual effects. For example, we can contract or expand shapes by specifying different horizontal and vertical scale values, or use a negative value to create a mirrored image. The following example applies this last technique to invert the coordinate system and draw an inverted shape.

Listing 8-24: Inverting a shape with the scale() modifier

```
struct ContentView: View {
   var body: some View {
      HStack {
         Triangle()
            .fill(Color.blue)
            .frame(width: 100, height: 100)
         Triangle()
            .scale(x: -1, y: 1)
            .fill(Color.blue)
            .frame(width: 100, height: 100)
      }
   }
}
```

This example implements the **Triangle** view defined in Listing 8-17. The first instance is displayed with a normal scale, but the second instance is transformed with the **scale()** modifier and a horizontal scale of **-1**, inverting the coordinate system and creating a mirror image.

Figure 8-22: *Mirror shapes*

As mentioned earlier, paths are drawn from one point to another as if following the movement of a pencil. We can remove part of the process with the **trim()** modifier. This modifier determines which part of the path is drawn with values from 0.0 to 1.0, where 0.0 is the beginning of the path and 1.0 is the end.

Listing 8-25: Trimming a path

```
struct ContentView: View {
   var body: some View {
      HStack {
         Triangle()
            .trim(from: 0, to: 0.70)
            .stroke(Color.blue, lineWidth: 10)
            .frame(width: 100, height: 100)
      }
   }
}
```

This example creates a **Triangle** view, but the path is truncated at the point 0.70, which represents the 70% of the drawing. This allows the system to draw the first and second lines completely, but the process is interrupted so that the triangle is never completed.

Figure 8-23: *Incomplete shape*

BASIC

Concentric Shapes

Another transformation we can apply to views is making them concentric. Concentric shapes have corners that are rounded relative to the corner radius of their container and to the distance between each shape's corners, as shown below.

Figure 8-24: *Concentric shapes*

In this example, we have two rectangles: a gray rectangle in the background and a white rectangle inside it. The rounded corners of the white rectangle adapt based on the corner radius of the container and the distance between the corners. In the image on the left, the corner radius of the white rectangle is reduced to account for the distance to the container's corners, but in the image on the right, the white rectangle was expanded, so its corner radius is automatically increased to create a more balanced and visually pleasing shape.

To create these concentric shapes, the container view must have a shape determined by a data type that conforms to the **RoundedRectangularShape** protocol. To assign these shapes to a container, the **View** protocol includes the following modifier.

containerShape(Shape**)**

This modifier assigns a concentric shape to a view. The argument is a structure that conform to the **Shape** protocol.

The **Shape** protocol includes several properties and methods for defining shapes. We can use properties such as **capsule**, **circle**, or **ellipse** to assign standard shapes, but to give a view a concentric shape, we must use the following method.

rect(cornerRadius: CGFloat, **style:** RoundedCornerStyle**)**

This method returns a rectangular shape with rounded corners. The **cornerRadius** argument specifies the radius of the corners, and the **style** argument determines how the corners are rendered. This argument is an enumeration with the values **circular** and **continuous**.

The **containerShape()** modifier assigns a shape to the container. To assign a shape to the content, we can use the **clipShape()** modifier introduced before. To define a concentric shape, the framework provides the **ConcentricRectangle** view. The following is the view's initializer.

ConcentricRectangle(corners: Style, **isUniform:** Bool**)**

This initializer creates a concentric rectangular shape. The **corners** argument is a structure that includes the **concentric** property to enable concentric behavior, and the **concentric(minimum: CGFloat)** method to specify a minimum corner radius. The **isUniform** argument determines whether all corners use the same radius (**true**) or adapt to the corresponding corners of the container (**false**).

The following example shows how to use these tools to recreate the concentric shapes introduced in Figure 8-24.

Listing 8-26: Creating concentric views

```
struct ContentView: View {
   var body: some View {
      VStack {
         ConcentricRectangle()
            .padding(40)
```

```
            .foregroundStyle(.white)
        }
        .frame(height: 200)
        .background(.gray)
        .containerShape(.rect(cornerRadius: 60))
        .padding()
    }
}
```

This example creates a **VStack** to use as a container and applies the **containerShape()** modifier to give it a concentric rectangular shape with a corner radius of 60. For the content, we use a **ConcentricRectangle** view. This is a standard shape view, similar to those we used earlier, but it produces a concentric rectangle. As a result, the corners of the view adapt to the container's corners based on the radius and the distance between them, reproducing the shapes shown in Figure 8-24.

Do It Yourself

Update the **ContentView** structure with the code in Listing 8-26. Run the application on an iPhone simulator. You should see the same concentric rectangles shown in Figure 8-24, left. Change the value of the **padding()** modifier applied to the **ConcentricRectangle** view to 20. The corner radius of the **ConcentricRectangle** view should update automatically to adapt to the new distance from the container, as shown in Figure 8-24, right.

In the previous example, we used a **ConcentricRectangle** view for the content, but in most cases the content consists of additional containers or standard views that present text or images. In these situations, we can give the view a concentric rectangular shape by applying the **clipShape()** modifier, as shown below.

Listing 8-27: Assigning a concentric shape to an image

```
struct ContentView: View {
   var body: some View {
      VStack {
         Image("spot1")
            .resizable()
            .scaledToFit()
            .clipShape(ConcentricRectangle())
            .padding(40)
      }
      .background(.gray)
      .containerShape(.rect(cornerRadius: 60))
      .padding()
   }
}
```

In this example, the container is the same as before, but the content is now defined by an **Image** view. To round the corners, we apply the **clipShape()** modifier using a **ConcentricRectangle** shape. This modifier overlays the view with a shape and preserves only the portions that fall within it. Because the shape is a concentric rectangle, the view's corners adapt to the container's corners. Figure 8-25, below, shows the result when the image uses a padding of 40 points and how the corner radius changes when the value is decreased to 20.

Figure 8-25: *Concentric views*

Do It Yourself

Update the **ContentView** structure with the code in Listing 8-27. Download the **spot1.jpg** and **spot2.jpg** images from our website and add them to an Asset Catalog (We will use **spot2.jpg** next). Run the application on an iPhone simulator. You should see the concentric image shown in Figure 8-25, left. Change the value of the **padding()** modifier applied to the image to 20. The corner radius of the **Image** view should update automatically to adapt to the new distance from the container, as shown in Figure 8-25, right.

The corners of a concentric shape are calculated by the system based on the container's corner radius and the distance between the corresponding corners. When that distance varies, the radius applied to the content's corners varies as well. For example, if the content consists of two images instead of one, the corners of the image that are farther from the container's corners become straight, as shown below.

Listing 8-28: Concentric shapes with different corners

```
struct ContentView: View {
   var body: some View {
      HStack {
         Image("spot1")
            .resizable()
            .scaledToFit()
            .clipShape(ConcentricRectangle())
            .padding(20)
         Image("spot2")
            .resizable()
            .scaledToFit()
            .clipShape(ConcentricRectangle())
            .padding(20)
      }
      .background(.gray)
      .containerShape(.rect(cornerRadius: 60))
      .padding()
   }
}
```

In this example, we have two images displayed side by side, so their inner corners are not close to the container's corners and are therefore not influenced by its corner radius, as shown below.

Figure 8-26: *Different concentric corners*

If we want all corners to use the same radius, we can initialize the **ConcentricRectangle** view with the **isUniform** argument set to **true**, as shown in the following example.

Listing 8-29: Concentric shapes with uniform corners

```
struct ContentView: View {
   var body: some View {
      HStack {
         Image("spot1")
            .resizable()
            .scaledToFit()
            .clipShape(ConcentricRectangle(corners: .concentric,
               isUniform: true))
```

```
            .padding(20)
        Image("spot2")
            .resizable()
            .scaledToFit()
            .clipShape(ConcentricRectangle(corners: .concentric,
               isUniform: true))
            .padding(20)
      }
      .background(.gray)
      .containerShape(.rect(cornerRadius: 60))
      .padding()
   }
}
```

The initializer for the `ConcentricRectangle` view includes the **corners** and **isUniform** arguments. The **corners** argument can take the `concentric` property to create a shape with concentric corners, or the `concentric(minimum: CGFloat)` method to specify concentric corners with a minimum radius. In this case, we use the `concentric` property and set the **isUniform** argument to `true`, so the radius for all corners is calculated from the container's corner radius and the distance to the closest corner. The result is shown below.

Figure 8-27: *Uniform corners*

PRO

8.4 - Image Renderer

All the graphics defined in the previous examples are created on the spot. If we want to recreate a graphic or a complex view, we have to redraw every line and circle. But sometimes we need to reuse a graphic or save it to a file or a database. In such cases, we can convert the view into an image. SwiftUI includes the `ImageRenderer` class for this purpose.

ImageRenderer(content: View)

This initializer creates an image from the view specified by the **content** argument.

The image is created by the `ImageRenderer` object and then returned by its properties. Three properties are available: `uiImage` returns a `UIImage` object (UIKit), `cgImage` returns a `CGImage` object (Core Graphics), and `nsImage` returns an `NSImage` object (Appkit).

To convert a view into an image, we need to store the view in a property so we can use that property to reference the view from the **ImageRenderer**'s initializer. For instance, the following example defines a separate view called **NewPictureView** with an **Image** view that presents a circular image. The view is stored in a property called **newPicture** which we use to display it on the screen and then convert it to a **UIImage** object.

Listing 8-30: Creating an image from a view

```
struct ContentView: View {
   @State private var pattern: UIImage?
   let newPicture = NewPictureView()

   var body: some View {
      VStack {
         newPicture
         Button("Export Image") {
            let renderer = ImageRenderer(content: newPicture)
            if let image = renderer.uiImage {
               pattern = image
            }
         }.buttonStyle(.glassProminent)
         if let pattern {
            Image(uiImage: pattern)
               .resizable(resizingMode: .tile)
               .frame(width: 300, height: 200)
         }
         Spacer()
      }
   }
}
struct NewPictureView: View {
   var body: some View {
      Image("spot1")
         .resizable()
         .scaledToFit()
         .frame(width: 150, height: 200)
         .clipShape(Circle())
   }
}
```

The interface includes a button. When the button is pressed, we create an **ImageRenderer** object from the view stored in the **newPicture** property and read its **uiImage** property to obtain a **UIImage** instance containing the rendered image. Once we have this image, we can process it like any other. In this example, we simply assign it to the **pattern** property and use it to create a pattern, as shown below.

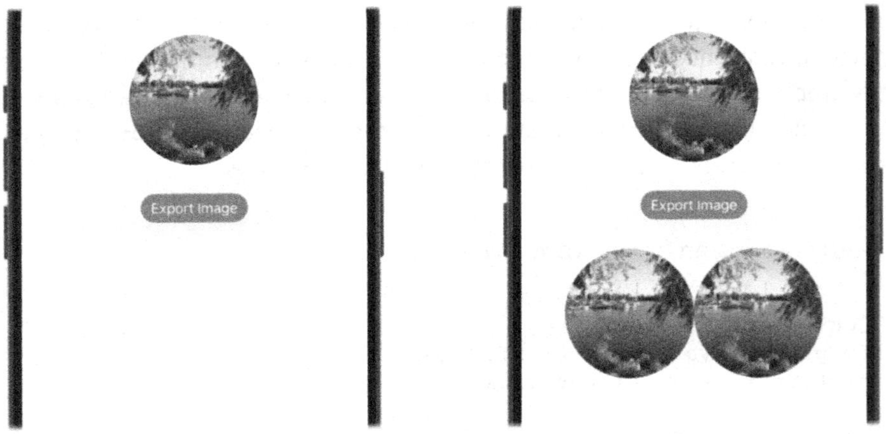

Figure 8-28: *Processing a view as an image*

BASIC

8.5 - Canvas

With standard and custom shapes, we can add as many graphics as needed to the interface, but performance can degrade when too many views are involved. To address this limitation, SwiftUI provides the **`Canvas`** view, which is designed specifically for efficient, dynamic 2D drawing.

```
Canvas(opaque: Bool, colorMode: ColorRenderingMode,
rendersAsynchronously: Bool, renderer: Closure)
```

This initializer creates a **`Canvas`** view. The **opaque** argument determines whether the canvas is opaque (**`true`**) or transparent (**`false`**). The **colorMode** argument defines the color space used to draw the graphics. It is an enumeration with the values **`extendedLinear`**, **`linear`**, and **`nonLinear`**. The **rendersAsynchronously** argument determines whether the drawing is going to be made synchronously or asynchronously. And the **renderer** argument provides the graphics to be drawn. The closure receives two values, a **`GraphicsContext`** structure that represents the graphic context where all the drawing is performed, and a **`CGSize`** value with the canvas' width and height.

The closure assigned to the **`Canvas`** view provides an instance of the **`GraphicsContext`** structure that represents the drawing context. All the drawing is performed in this context from methods provided by the structure. The following are some of the methods available for drawing images.

```
draw(Image, at: CGPoint, anchor: UnitPoint)
```

This method draws the image specified by the first argument. The **at** argument determines the position of the image in the context, and the **anchor** argument determines the origin of the image.

```
draw(Image, in: CGRect, style: FillStyle)
```

This method draws the image specified by the first argument in the area specified by the **in** argument. The **style** argument determines the style of the image. It is a structure with the initializer **`FillStyle(eoFill: Bool, antialiased: Bool)`**.

The following are some of the methods available for drawing text.

```
draw(Text, at: CGPoint, anchor: UnitPoint)
```

This method draws the text specified by the first argument. The **at** argument determines the position in the context, and the **anchor** argument determines the origin of the text.

```
draw(Text, in: CGRect)
```

This method draws the text specified by the first argument within the area specified by the **in** argument. If there is not enough space in the area, the text is truncated.

And the following are the methods available for drawing paths.

```
stroke(Path, with: Shading, lineWidth: CGFloat)
```

This method draws the path specified by the first argument. The **with** argument specifies the color or pattern used to stroke the path, and the **lineWidth** argument determines the width.

```
stroke(Path, with: Shading, style: StrokeStyle)
```

This method draws the path specified by the first argument. The **with** argument specifies the color or pattern used to stroke the path, and the **style** argument determines the style.

```
fill(Path, with: Shading, style: FillStyle)
```

This method draws the path specified by the first argument. The **with** argument specifies the color or pattern used to fill the shape, and the **style** argument determines the style. It is a structure with the initializer `FillStyle(eoFill: Bool, antialiased: Bool)`.

Paths are drawn with the colors and patterns specified by a `Shading` structure. The structure includes the following type methods to produced custom styles.

```
color(Color)
```

This method returns a color. The argument is the `Color` view with the color we want to assign to the path.

```
color(red: Double, green: Double, blue: Double, opacity: Double)
```

This method returns a color. The **red**, **green**, and **blue** arguments determine the levels of red, green, and blue with values from 0.0 (no color) to 1.0 (full color).

```
color(white: Double, opacity: Double)
```

This method returns a color. The **white** argument determines the level of white with a value from 0.0 to 1.0 (black to white), and the **opacity** argument determines the level of opacity with a value from 0.0 (transparent) to 1.0 (opaque).

```
linearGradient(Gradient, startPoint: CGPoint, endPoint: CGPoint)
```

This method returns a linear gradient. The first argument is the gradient of colors to be used, and the **startPoint** and **endPoint** arguments determine the points inside the shape where the gradient starts and ends.

```
radialGradient(Gradient, center: CGPoint, startRadius: CGFloat,
endRadius: CGFloat)
```

This method returns a circular gradient. The first argument is the gradient of colors to be used. The **center** argument determines the position of the center of the circle, and the **startRadius** and **endRadius** arguments determine where the gradient starts and ends.

```
conicGradient(Gradient, center: CGPoint, angle: Angle)
```

This method returns a conic gradient. The first argument is the gradient of colors to be used. The **center** argument determines the position of the tip of the cone, and the **angle** argument determines the angle where the gradient begins.

```
tiledImage(Image, origin: CGPoint, sourceRect: CGRect, scale:
CGFloat)
```

This method draws the image specified by the first argument over and over again to cover the shape. The **origin** argument determines the point in the shape where the initial image is placed. The **sourceRect** argument determines the region of the original image we want to draw. And the **scale** argument defines the scale of the image.

By default, the canvas is non-opaque (the **opaque** argument is assigned the value **false**), the color mode is set to **nonLinear**, and the rendering is performed synchronously. If this configuration is sufficient for our application, we only need to declare the closure to render the graphics, as in the following example.

Listing 8-31: Drawing an image on the canvas

```
struct ContentView: View {
   var body: some View {
      Canvas { context, size in
         let imageFrame = CGRect(origin: .zero, size: size)
         context.draw(Image("spot1"), in: imageFrame)
      }.ignoresSafeArea()
   }
}
```

This example creates a **Canvas** view of the size of the screen. The **draw()** method takes a **CGRect** value and draws the image in that area. In this case, we decided to use the entire canvas, so we define a **CGRect** value with origin 0,0 and the size of the canvas, but we can also declare a specific size. For example, the image we are using in this example is 644 pixels wide and 864 pixels high. Using these values, we can define the **CGRect** value required to display the image at a smaller size.

Listing 8-32: Drawing an image of a custom size

```
struct ContentView: View {
   var body: some View {
      Canvas { context, size in
         let imageSize = CGSize(width: 161, height: 216)
         let posX = (size.width - imageSize.width) / 2
         let posY = posX

         let imageFrame = CGRect(x: posX, y: posY, width: imageSize.width,
            height: imageSize.height)
         context.draw(Image("spot1"), in: imageFrame)
      }.ignoresSafeArea()
   }
}
```

In this example, we define an area that is one quarter the size of the original image and divide the remaining horizontal space by two to determine its position. As a result, the image is centered on the canvas.

Figure 8-29: *Image of a custom size*

Of course, we can also draw shapes, including standard and custom shapes and paths. For example, we can combine our image with graphics and text.

Listing 8-33: Drawing shapes and text

```
struct ContentView: View {
   var body: some View {
      Canvas { context, size in
         let imageFrame = CGRect(x: 60, y: 75, width: 215, height: 288)
         context.draw(Image("spot1"), in: imageFrame)

         let circleFrame = CGRect(x: 20, y: 50, width: 60, height: 60)
         context.fill(Circle().path(in: circleFrame),
            with: .color(.yellow))

         let rectFrame = CGRect(x: 50, y: 60, width: 250, height: 40)
         context.fill(RoundedRectangle(cornerRadius: 25).path(in:
            rectFrame), with: .color(.yellow))
```

```
        let textPos = CGPoint(x: 80, y: 80)
        context.draw(Text("My Picture").font(.title.bold()), at: textPos,
           anchor: .leading)
      }.ignoresSafeArea()
   }
}
```

In this example we create a banner over the image with a circle, a rounded rectangle and a text. The result is shown below.

***Figure 8-30:** Shapes and text on the canvas*

The **GraphicsContext** structure also includes methods to perform transformations on the canvas. The following are the most frequently used.

scaleBy(x: CGFloat, **y:** CGFloat)

This method determines the horizontal and vertical scale of the canvas. By default, the scale is 1.0.

rotate(by: Angle)

This method rotates the canvas the angle specified by the **by** argument.

translateBy(x: CGFloat, **y:** CGFloat)

This method moves the point of origin of the canvas to the position determined by the **x** and **y** arguments.

These methods work like those previously implemented for shapes, but they only affect the matrix that the context uses to calculate the position and size of the graphics. For example, if we call the **rotate()** method on the context, the graphics already on the canvas will remain unchanged, only the graphics drawn afterwards will be rotated. As an example, we can draw two copies of the same image on the canvas. The first one is drawn on the default canvas and the second one is drawn after the canvas is rotated by 20 degrees.

Listing 8-34: Rotating the canvas

```
struct ContentView: View {
   var body: some View {
```

```
        Canvas { context, size in
            let imageFrame = CGRect(x: 160, y: 150, width: 161, height: 216)
            context.draw(Image("spot1"), in: imageFrame)

            context.rotate(by: .degrees(20))
            context.draw(Image("spot1"), in: imageFrame)
        }.ignoresSafeArea()
    }
}
```

As Figure 8-31 below shows, only the image drawn after applying the **rotate()** method is affected by the rotation; the previous image remains unchanged. This is because the transformation methods do not affect the canvas, it affects the matrix that the context uses to calculate how to draw the graphics.

Figure 8-31: *Canvas rotation*

The rotation is about the origin of the canvas, which by default is at coordinates 0, 0 (upper left corner). If instead we want to rotate a graphic around its center, we must first move the origin to that position using the **translateBy()** method, as shown below.

Listing 8-35: Rotating an image

```
struct ContentView: View {
    var body: some View {
        Canvas { context, size in
            context.translateBy(x: size.width/2, y: size.height/2)
            context.rotate(by: .degrees(45))

            let width = 161
            let height = 216
            let imageFrame = CGRect(x: -width/2, y: -height/2, width: width,
                height: height)
            context.draw(Image("spot1"), in: imageFrame)
        }.ignoresSafeArea()
    }
}
```

In this example, we position the image at the center of the canvas and then rotate the context by 45 degrees. Since the origin of the image is at the position 0, 0 (upper-left corner) and we want to rotate the image around its center, we need to specify values that place the center of the image at the origin of the canvas, and this means using negative values. The horizontal position is minus half the width of the image (-85) and the vertical position is minus half the height (-108), so that the center of the image coincides with the origin of the canvas, and therefore the image is rotated around the center, as shown below.

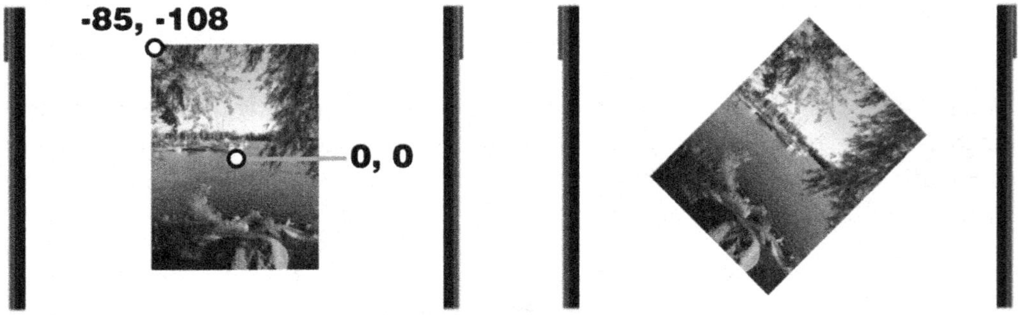

Figure 8-32: *Custom rotation*

Transformations are cumulative. This means that the transformations performed on the canvas are superimposed on the previous transformations. For example, if we rotate the canvas 45 degrees and then another 45 degrees, the final rotation is 90 degrees.

Listing 8-36: Performing multiple transformations

```
struct ContentView: View {
   var body: some View {
      Canvas { context, size in
         let imageFrame = CGRect(x: 0, y: 0, width: 100, height: 100)
         context.translateBy(x: size.width/2, y: size.height/2)
         for _ in 0..<10 {
            context.rotate(by: .degrees(36))
            context.draw(Image("spot1"), in: imageFrame)
         }
      }.ignoresSafeArea()
   }
}
```

In this example, we create a loop with 10 cycles (from 0 to 9). With each cycle, the context is rotated 36 degrees and then an image is drawn. Because the rotations are cumulative, each rotation adds to the previous rotation, forming a complete circle.

Figure 8-33: *Multiple rotations*

Drawing the same image multiple times affects performance. The system must prepare the image each time it is about to be drawn. To improve performance, we can prepare the image beforehand using the following method.

```
resolve(Image)
```

This method returns an image that is configured according to the current context.

This method can also be used to prepare **Text** views and **Shading** values, but it is especially useful with images. The following example is the same as the previous one, but the image is resolved before drawing.

Listing 8-37: Preparing images

```
struct ContentView: View {
   var body: some View {
      Canvas { context, size in
         let imageReady = context.resolve(Image("spot1"))
         let imageFrame = CGRect(x: 0, y: 0, width: 100, height: 100)
         context.translateBy(x: size.width/2, y: size.height/2)
         for _ in 0..<10 {
            context.rotate(by: .degrees(36))
            context.draw(imageReady, in: imageFrame)
         }
      }.ignoresSafeArea()
   }
}
```

The **GraphicsContext** structure also includes the following method for creating a clipping mask that specifies which part of the canvas is available for drawing.

```
clip(to: Path)
```

This method creates a clipping mask. Only the parts of the graphics inside the mask are drawn.

The following code applies a circular clipping mask to the canvas of the previous example, so that only the parts of the images that lie within the circle are drawn.

Listing 8-38: Clipping the canvas

```
struct ContentView: View {
   var body: some View {
      Canvas { context, size in
         let imageFrame = CGRect(x: 0, y: 0, width: 100, height: 100)
         context.translateBy(x: size.width/2, y: size.height/2)

         let clipFrame = CGRect(x: -100, y: -100, width: 200, height: 200)
         context.clip(to: Circle().path(in: clipFrame))
```

```
            for _ in 0..<10 {
                context.rotate(by: .degrees(36))
                context.draw(Image("spot1"), in: imageFrame)
            }
        }.ignoresSafeArea()
    }
}
```

Figure 8-34: *Clipping mask*

The **GraphicsContext** structure also allows us to filter the graphics. With filters, we can add effects and configure different aspects of the graphics, such as brightness, contrast, blur, and more. The structure includes the following method for applying a filter.

addFilter(Filter)

This method applies a filter to the context. The argument defines the type of filter and its configuration. The structure includes multiple type methods to define standard filters. The most frequently used are **brightness(Double)**, **contrast(Double)**, **saturation(Double)**, **colorInvert(Double)**, **colorMultiply(Color)**, **hueRotation(Angle)**, **grayscale(Double)**, **blur(radius: CGFloat)**, and **shadow(color: Color, radius: CGFloat, x: CGFloat, y: CGFloat, blendMode: BlendMode, options: ShadowOptions)**.

Applying a filter is simple. We call the **addFilter()** method in the context for each effect we want to apply, and all the graphics drawn afterwards will be affected. The following example colors an image and blurs it.

Listing 8-39: Applying filters to the graphics

```
struct ContentView: View {
    var body: some View {
        Canvas { context, size in
            context.addFilter(.colorMultiply(Color.red))
            context.addFilter(.blur(radius: 5))

            let margin = (size.width - 161) / 2
            let imageFrame = CGRect(x: margin, y: margin, width: 161, height:
216)
            context.draw(Image("spot1"), in: imageFrame)
        }.ignoresSafeArea()
    }
}
```

Figure 8-35: *Graphic filters*

BASIC

8.6 - Charts

In addition to the tools SwiftUI provides to create and display graphics on the screen, there is also a framework called **Swift Charts** that we can use to create a graphical representation of the user's data. The following is the structure provided by the framework to create these charts.

```
Chart(Data, content: Closure)
```

This initializer creates a view to display a chart. The first argument specifies the data to be represented, and the **content** argument is the closure that returns the views required to create the chart.

BASIC

Mark Views

There are several predefined charts available. We can create a bar chart, a line chart, a point chart, and more. The graphics used to create these charts are called *Marks*. The following are the views that are included in the framework to create these marks and some of their initializers.

```
BarMark(x: PlottableValue, y: PlottableValue)
```

This initializer creates a mark that represents the data with a bar. The **x** and **y** arguments represent the position and size of the bar in the chart's coordinates.

```
LineMark(x: PlottableValue, y: PlottableValue)
```

This initializer creates a mark that represents the data with lines between points. The **x** and **y** arguments represent the position of the point that is going to be used to connect the lines.

```
PointMark(x: PlottableValue, y: PlottableValue)
```

This initializer creates a mark that represents the data with points. The **x** and **y** arguments represent the position of the point in the chart's coordinates.

```
RectangleMark(x: PlottableValue, y: PlottableValue, width: MarkDimension, height: MarkDimension)
```

This initializer creates a mark that represents the data with a rectangle. The **x** and **y** arguments represent the position of the rectangle, and the **width** and **height** arguments determine the size.

```
AreaMark(x: PlottableValue, y: PlottableValue)
```

This initializer creates a mark that represents the data by filling the area below or between the points. The **x** and **y** arguments represent the position of the points used to calculate the area.

```
SectorMark(angle: PlottableValue, innerRadius: MarkDimension, outerRadius: MarkDimension, angularInset: CGFloat?)
```

This initializer creates a mark that represents the data with a pie chart. The **angle** argument is a value that determines the proportional size of the sector, or a range of values that specifies the start and end angles, the **innerRadius** argument specifies the inner radius of the pie chart, the **outerRadius** argument specifies the outer radius of the pie chart, and the **angularInset** argument determines the corner radius for each section.

```
RuleMark(x: PlottableValue, yStart: PlottableValue, yEnd: PlottableValue)
```

This initializer creates a view that represents data with a single line. The **x** argument determines the position of the line in the **x** axis, and the **yStart** and **yEnd** arguments determine the position where the line begins and ends in the **y** axis.

The positions in the chart's coordinate system are determined by an instance of the **PlottableValue** structure. The structure includes the following type methods to return these values.

```
value(String, Value)
```

This type method creates a value for a mark that represents quantitative data. The first argument is a custom string to describe the value, and the second argument is the value itself.

```
value(String, Date, unit: Component, calendar: Calendar?)
```

This type method creates a value for a mark that represents dates. The first argument is a custom string to describe the value. The second argument specifies the date we are representing. The **unit** argument determines the component of the date we want to use to represent the data. And **calendar** is an optional argument we can use to specify the calendar that should be used to determine the date.

A chart can take quantitative values, such as integers, nominal values, such as strings, and temporal values, such as dates. Therefore, we can usually create charts directly from the user's data. For instance, we can use a model that includes food items and their calorie content.

Listing 8-40: Providing the data for a chart

```
import SwiftUI

struct Consumables: Identifiable {
   let id = UUID()
   var name: String
   var category: String
   var calories: Int
}
@Observable class ApplicationData {
   var listOfItems: [Consumables]

   static let shared: ApplicationData = ApplicationData()
   private init() {
      listOfItems = [
         Consumables(name: "Bagels", category: "Baked", calories: 250),
         Consumables(name: "Brownies", category: "Baked", calories: 466),
         Consumables(name: "Butter", category: "Dairy", calories: 717),
         Consumables(name: "Cheese", category: "Dairy", calories: 402),
         Consumables(name: "Cookies", category: "Baked", calories: 502),
         Consumables(name: "Donuts", category: "Baked", calories: 452),
         Consumables(name: "Granola", category: "Baked", calories: 471)
      ]
   }
}
```

The syntax of the **Chart** view is similar to that of the **List** view. We can provide the data in the view initializer or use a **ForEach** loop and then build the views with the value received by the closure, as shown below.

Listing 8-41: Visualizing data with a bar chart

```
import SwiftUI
import Charts

struct ContentView: View {
   @State private var appData = ApplicationData.shared

   var body: some View {
      VStack {
         Chart(appData.listOfItems) { item in
            BarMark(x: .value("Name", item.name), y: .value("Calories",
               item.calories))
         }.frame(height: 300)
         .padding()
         Spacer()
      }
   }
}
```

The **Chart** view generates a loop with the data in the model. In each cycle, the closure assigned to the **content** argument receives a value and creates the view that represents that value. In this example, we use a **BarMark** view to represent the values with bars. The value of the **name** property is assigned to the **x** axis and the number of calories is assigned to the **y** axis. This creates vertical bars, with the names of the foods under the bars and the calories on the side. However, we can easily reverse the axes by swapping the values. (The calories are assigned to the **x** axis and the name to the **y** axis). The result of both configurations is shown below.

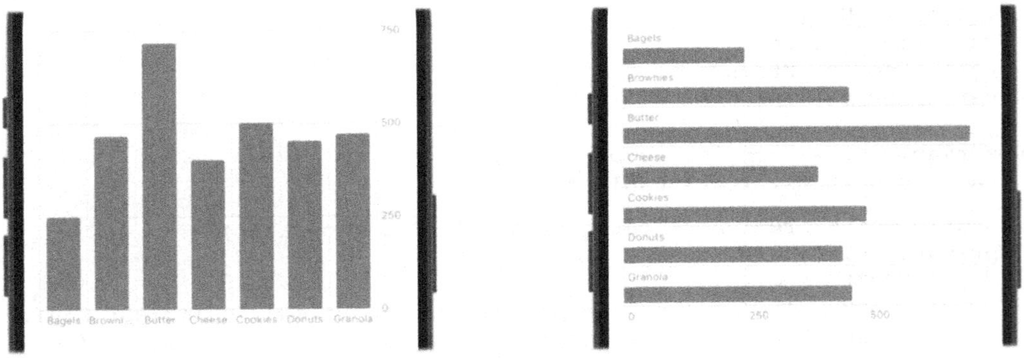

Figure 8-36: *Bar Charts*

If we want to create a different type of chart, we just need to replace the **BarMark** view with the desired view. For example, we can plot the same data with lines.

Listing 8-42: Visualizing data with a line chart

```
struct ContentView: View {
   @State private var appData = ApplicationData.shared

   var body: some View {
      VStack {
         Chart(appData.listOfItems) { item in
            LineMark(x: .value("Name", item.name), y: .value("Calories",
item.calories))
         }.frame(height: 300)
         .padding()
         Spacer()
      }
   }
}
```

This chart draws a line connecting the points created by the names and calorie values. Figure 8-37, below, shows the graphic produced by this example and the variations we can obtain by replacing the **LineMark** view with a **PointMark**, **RectangleMark**, or **AreaMark** view.

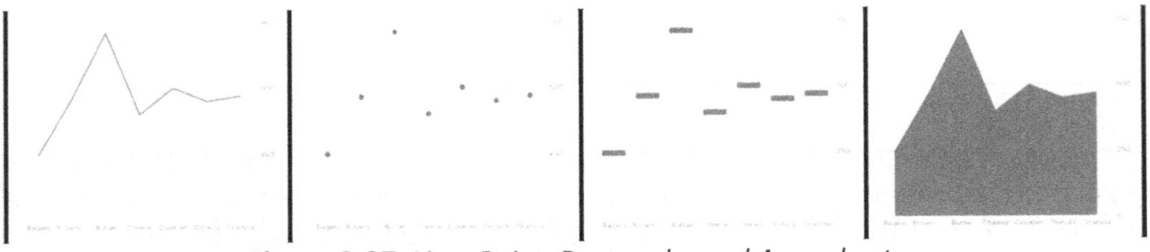

Figure 8-37: *Line, Point, Rectangle, and Area charts*

Do It Yourself

Create a new App project. Add a Swift file called **ApplicationData.swift** for the model in Listing 8-40. Update the **ContentView.swift** file with the code in Listing 8-41. Run the application on an iPhone simulator. You should see a bar chart, as shown in Figure 8-36. Replace the **`BarMark`** view with a **`LineMark`**, **`PointMark`**, **`RectangleMark`**, or **`AreaMark`** view. You should see the charts illustrated in Figure 8-37.

PRO

Chart Modifiers

The **`View`** protocol includes modifiers to customize the chart. The following are those defined to configure the scale of the chart.

`chartXScale(domain:` `Domain,` **`range:`** `Range,` **`type:`** `ScaleType?)`

This modifier defines the scale for the **`x`** axis. The **domain** argument specifies the possible values with a range for quantitative values and an array for nominal values, the **range** argument defines the positions corresponding to the scale values in the plot area, and the **type** value is a structure that determines the type of scale to use. The structure includes the type properties **`category`**, **`date`**, **`linear`**, and **`log`**.

`chartYScale(domain:` `Domain,` **`range:`** `Range,` **`type:`** `ScaleType?)`

This modifier defines the scale for the **`y`** axis. The arguments are the same as those used by the **`chartXScale()`** modifier.

`chartZScale(domain:` `Domain,` **`range:`** `Range,` **`type:`** `ScaleType?)`

This modifier defines the scale for the **`z`** axis. The arguments are the same as those used by the **`chartXScale()`** modifier.

`chartForegroundStyleScale``(Dictionary)`

This modifier assigns specific foreground styles to a scale of values. The argument is a dictionary with items that map the values to the styles.

The scale used to plot values is automatically calculated by the **`Chart`** view based on the data. In the previous examples, the system set a scale from 0 to 800 based on the calories values in our model. If we do not want the scale to adapt to the data, we can apply the **`chartXScale()`** or **`chartYScale()`** modifiers. For example, if we know that all foods in our model have a maximum of 1,000 calories, we can define a fixed scale from 0 to 1,000.

Listing 8-43: Defining a custom scale for the y axis

```
struct ContentView: View {
   @State private var appData = ApplicationData.shared
```

```
    var body: some View {
        VStack {
            Chart(appData.listOfItems) { item in
                BarMark(x: .value("Name", item.name), y: .value("Calories",
                    item.calories))
            }
            .chartYScale(domain: 0...1000)
            .frame(height: 300)
            .padding()
            Spacer()
        }
    }
}
```

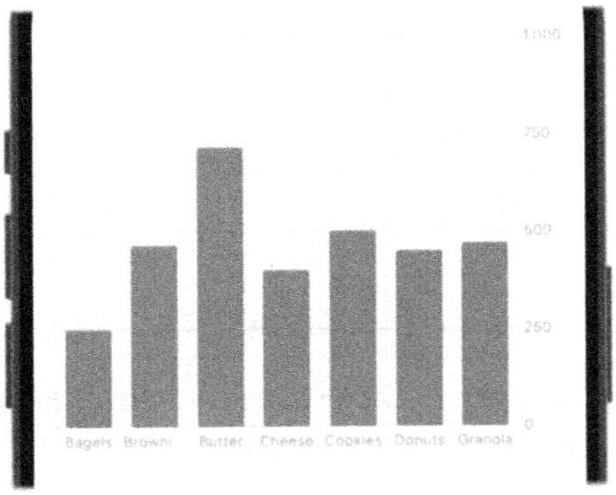

Figure 8-38: *Custom scale*

The views used to create the chart conform to the **ChartContent** protocol. This protocol defines many modifiers for configuring and styling the views. The following are the most frequently used.

foregroundStyle(Style)

This modifier sets the color or style of the mark.

foregroundStyle(**by:** PlottableValue)

This modifier assigns different foreground styles to the marks based on a value. The **by** argument specifies the value to consider when assigning the styles.

opacity(Double)

This modifier sets the mark's opacity.

cornerRadius(CGFloat, **style:** RoundedCornerStyle)

This modifier sets the mark's corner radius. The first argument determines the radius, and the **style** argument specifies the style. It is an enumeration with the values **circular** and **continuous**.

The **ChartContent** protocol also defines modifiers to style the elements in a chart, such as the lines and symbols. The following are the most frequently used.

symbol(by: PlottableValue)

This modifier assigns different symbols to the points in a chart based on a value. The **by** argument specifies the value to consider when assigning the symbols.

symbolSize(CGFloat)

This modifier sets the size of the symbols that represent the points in the chart. The argument specifies the size of the area occupied by the symbol.

lineStyle(StrokeStyle)

This modifier defines the style of the line.

interpolationMethod(InterpolationMethod)

This modifier determines the style used to join the points when the chart contains lines or area marks. The argument is a structure with the type properties **cardinal**, **catmullRom**, **linear**, **monotone**, **stepCenter**, **stepEnd**, and **stepStart**.

chartLegend(Visibility)

This modifier displays or hides the labels below the chart. The argument is an enumeration with the values **automatic**, **visible** and **hidden**.

There are also modifiers to set the position of the content. The following are the most frequently used.

position(by: PlottableValue, **axis:** Axis?, **span:** MarkDimension)

This modifier assigns a position for the marks. The **by** argument determines the value used to identify the marks. The **axis** argument specifies the axis used to position the marks. It is an enumeration with the values **horizontal** and **vertical**. And the **span** argument determines the space available for the marks. It is a structure with the type methods **fixed(CGFloat)**, **inset(CGFloat)**, and **ratio(CGFloat)**.

offset(x: CGFloat, **y:** CGFloat)

This modifier moves the marks by the offset specified by the arguments.

The protocol also includes modifiers to add labels and views to the chart. The following is the most frequently used.

annotation(position: AnnotationPosition, **alignment:** Alignment, **spacing:** CGFloat?, **content:** Closure)

This modifier adds an annotation to the line. The **position** argument specifies the position of the annotation in the plot area. It is a structure with the type properties **automatic**, **bottom**, **bottomLeading**, **bottomTrailing**, **leading**, **overlay**, **top**, **topLeading**, **topTrailing**, and **trailing**. The alignment argument aligns the annotation in relation to the line. It is a structure with the type properties **leading**, **center**, and **trailing**. The **spacing** argument defines the space between the line and the annotation. And the **content** argument provides the views to create the annotation.

Some of these modifiers apply to any view but others are more specific. For example, the **foregroundStyle(by:)** modifier is particularly useful with the **SectorMark** structure. This structure creates a pie chart, and therefore the sectors are only distinguishable if they are drawn in different colors. In the following example, we use this modifier and the names of the foods to determine the colors of the sectors.

Listing 8-44: Assigning different styles based on a value

```
struct ContentView: View {
   @State private var appData = ApplicationData.shared

   var body: some View {
      VStack {
         Chart(appData.listOfItems) { item in
            SectorMark(angle: .value("Value", item.calories))
               .foregroundStyle(by: .value("Product category", item.name))
         }.frame(height: 300)
         .padding()
         Spacer()
      }
   }
}
```

The **Chart** view checks the values and assigns a different color to each one of them (the colors are automatically assigned by the system). Note that the chart also creates labels at the bottom to inform the user what the colors represent.

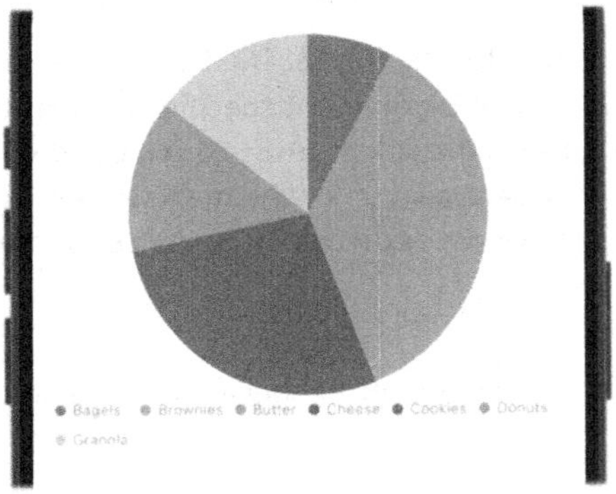

***Figure 8-39:** Different styles per value*

Some of the modifiers provided by the **ChartContent** protocol are useful when multiple types of marks are used to represent the values. For example, if lines and points are to be used, the graphics representing the points can be enlarged to make them more visible.

Listing 8-45: Representing the values with different types of marks

```
struct ContentView: View {
   @State private var appData = ApplicationData.shared

   var body: some View {
```

```
        VStack {
            Chart(appData.listOfItems) { item in
                LineMark(x: .value("Name", item.name), y: .value("Calories",
                    item.calories))
                    .interpolationMethod(.catmullRom)
                PointMark(x: .value("Name", item.name), y: .value("Calories",
                    item.calories))
                    .foregroundStyle(by: .value("Category", item.category))
                    .symbol(by: .value("Category", item.category))
                    .symbolSize(200)
            }.frame(height: 300)
            .padding()
            Spacer()
        }
    }
}
```

In this example, we apply an interpolation of type **catmullRom** to the **LineMark** view to smooth the lines. For the points, we apply a different color for each category using the **foregroundStyle(by:)** modifier, just as we did for the pie chart in the previous example. We also assign a different symbol to each category with the **symbol()** modifier, and finally enlarge the symbols with the **symbolSize()** modifier.

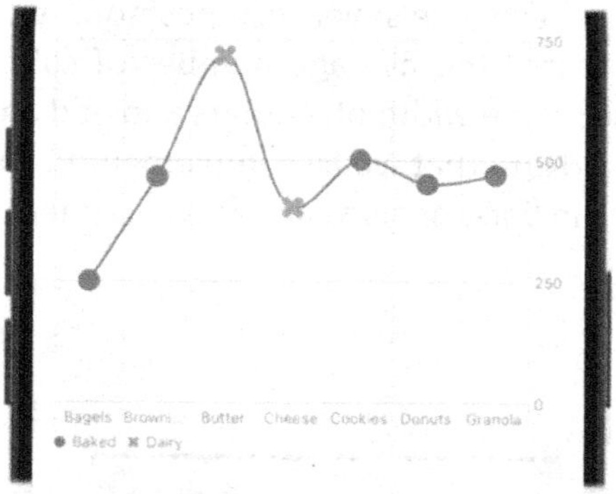

Figure 8-40: *Multiple mark styles*

Some modifiers are designed to work together. For example, the **RuleMark** view draws a line above or behind the chart and relies on additional modifiers to convey information, such as the **lineStyle()** and **annotation()** modifiers, as shown below.

Listing 8-46: Drawing a line in the plot area

```
struct ContentView: View {
    @State private var appData = ApplicationData.shared

    var body: some View {
        VStack {
            Chart {
                ForEach(appData.listOfItems) { item in
                    BarMark(x: .value("Name", item.name), y: .value("Calories",
                        item.calories))
                        .foregroundStyle(.cyan)
```

```
               .opacity(0.5)
               .cornerRadius(20)
         }
         RuleMark(y: .value("Average", averageCalories()))
            .foregroundStyle(.black)
            .lineStyle(StrokeStyle(lineWidth: 5))
            .annotation(position: .top, alignment: .leading) {
               Text("Average Calories")
            }
      }.frame(height: 300)
      .padding()
      Spacer()
   }
}
func averageCalories() -> Int {
   let total = appData.listOfItems.reduce(0, { $0 + $1.calories })
   return total / appData.listOfItems.count
}
}
```

In this example, the **Chart** view creates the chart, but the marks are generated by a **ForEach** loop. After this loop, we define a **RuleMark** view to draw a horizontal line across the chart. (To draw the line behind the chart, we need to declare the **RuleMark** view before the **ForEach** view.) To calculate the line's vertical position, we define a method called **averageCalories()** that returns the average number of calories of all the items in the model. For the design, we set a line width of 5 points and add an annotation at the top with the string "Average Calories". Note that we also implemented some modifiers to design the marks, including a color for the bars, opacity, and round corners. The result is shown below.

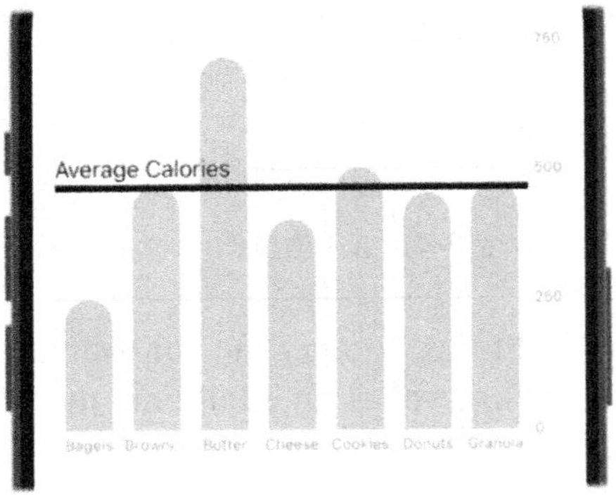

Figure 8-41: *Horizontal line*

PRO

Selection

A **Chart** view can also allow the user to select a value. The selection is made by pressing and holding or dragging the finger over the plot area or, on Mac computers, by moving the mouse over the chart. The view determines where the finger or mouse is currently located and stores the value in a binding property that we can later use to perform a task or display additional information to the user. The **View** protocol includes the following modifiers to enable this feature.

chartXSelection(value: Binding)

This modifier allows the selection of values on the **x** axis. The **value** argument is the binding property to be used to store the selected value. The protocol also defines the **chartYSelection(value:)** modifier for the **y** axis and the **chartZSelection (value:)** modifier for the **z** axis.

chartXSelection(range: Binding)

This modifier allows the selection of a range of values on the **x** axis. The **range** argument is the binding property to be used to store the range of selected values. The protocol also defines the **chartYSelection(range:)** modifier for the **y** axis and the **chartZSelection(range:)** modifier for the **z** axis.

chartAngleSelection(value: Binding)

This modifier allows selection of values on pie charts. The **value** argument is the binding property to be used to store the selected value.

The implementation is simple. We need a **@State** property to store the value selected by the user, apply the modifier with this property to enable selection, and then do something with the value. In the following example, we use the property's value to change the color of the selected bar.

Listing 8-47: Selecting a value

```
struct ContentView: View {
   @State private var appData = ApplicationData.shared
   @State private var selectedFood: String? = nil

   var body: some View {
      VStack {
         Chart(appData.listOfItems) { item in
            BarMark(x: .value("Name", item.name), y: .value("Calories",
               item.calories))
               .foregroundStyle(item.name == selectedFood ? .yellow :
                  .blue)
         }
         .frame(height: 300)
         .padding()
         .chartXSelection(value: $selectedFood)
         Spacer()
      }
   }
}
```

In our model, the values for the **x** axis are names of food, so we declare a **@State** property of type **String** to store this value, and then compare the value used to create each bar with the value selected by the user. If they match, the bar is colored yellow, otherwise the bar is blue.

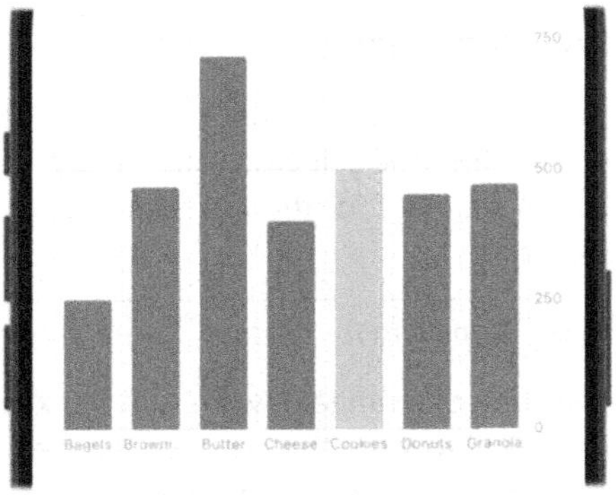

***Figure 8-42:** Selection*

PRO

Plot Views

Mark views are well suited for small data sets. To display large amounts of data, SwiftUI includes the following views to create vectorized plots.

BarPlot(Collection, **x:** PlottableProjection, **y:** PlottableProjection, **width:** MarkDimensions, **height:** MarkDimensions, **stacking:** MarkStackingMethod)

This initializer creates a plot view to represent a large dataset with bars. The first argument is the dataset with the values we want to display, the **x** and **y** arguments represent the position of the point in the chart's coordinates, the **width** and **height** arguments determine the thickness of the bars in horizontal and vertical orientation, and the **stacking** argument is a structure with the properties **center**, **normalized**, **standard** and **unstacked** to determine the way the graphics are stacked.

LinePlot(Collection, **x:** PlottableProjection, **y:** PlottableProjection, **series:** PlottableProjection)

This initializer creates a plot view to represent a large dataset with lines. The first argument is the dataset with the values we want to display, the **x** and **y** arguments represent the position of the point in the chart's coordinates, and the **series** argument is the value used to create regions in the chart.

PointPlot(Collection, **x:** PlottableProjection, **y:** PlottableProjection)

This initializer creates a plot view to represent a large dataset with points. The first argument is the dataset with the values we want to display, and the **x** and **y** arguments represent the position of the point in the chart's coordinates.

RectanglePlot(Collection, **x:** PlottableProjection, **y:** PlottableProjection, **width:** MarkDimensions, **height:** MarkDimensions)

This initializer creates a plot view to represent a large dataset with rectangles. The first argument is the dataset with the values we want to display, the **x** and **y** arguments represent the position of the point in the chart's coordinates, and the **width** and **height** arguments determine the size of the rectangles.

```
AreaPlot(Collection, x: PlottableProjection, y:
PlottableProjection, series: PlottableProjection, stacking:
MarkStackingMethod)
```

This initializer creates a plot view to represent a large dataset by filling the area below or between the points. The first argument is the dataset with the values we want to display, the **x** and **y** arguments represent the position of the point in the chart's coordinates, the **series** argument is the value used to create regions in the chart, and the **stacking** argument is a structure with the properties **`center`**, **`normalized`**, **`standard`**, and **`unstacked`** to determine how the regions are going to be stacked.

```
SectorPlot(Collection, angle: PlottableProjection, innerRadius:
MarkDimensions, outerRadius: MarkDimensions, angularInset:
CGFloat?)
```

This initializer creates a plot view that represents a large dataset with a pie chart. The first argument is the dataset with the values we want to display, the **angle** argument determines the proportional size of the sector, the **innerRadius** argument specifies the inner radius of the pie chart, the **outerRadius** argument specifies the outer radius of the pie chart, and the **angularInset** argument determines the corner radius for each section.

```
RulePlot(Collection, xStart: PlottableProjection, xEnd:
PlottableProjection, y: PlottableProjection)
```

This initializer creates a plot view that represents a large dataset with a single line. The first argument is the dataset with the values we want to display, the **xStart** and **xEnd** arguments determine the position where the line begins and ends in the **`x`** axis, and the **y** argument determines the vertical position of the line.

These views are applied in the same way as the mark views we have seen before, but they take care of reading and processing the values, as shown in the following example.

Listing 8-48: Visualizing large datasets with a point plot

```
struct ContentView: View {
   @State private var appData = ApplicationData.shared

   var body: some View {
      VStack {
         Chart {
            PointPlot(appData.listOfItems, x: .value("Food", \.name), y:
               .value("Calories", \.calories))
         }.frame(height: 300)
         .padding()
         Spacer()
      }
   }
}
```

The **`LinePlot`** and **`AreaPlot`** views can not only display large datasets, but also plot mathematical functions. The following are the initializers we need for this purpose.

```
LinePlot(x: String, y: String, domain: Range, Closure)
```

This initializer creates a plot view to visualize a single mathematical function. The **x** and **y** arguments provide the labels for the **x** and **y** axes, the **domain** argument limits the domain of the function, and the last argument is a closure that provides the function to be plotted.

```
AreaPlot(x: String, yStart: String, yEnd: String, domain: Range,
Closure)
```

This initializer creates a plot view to visualize the area covered by a mathematical function. The **x**, **yStart**, and **yEnd** arguments provide the labels for the chart, the **domain** argument limits the domain of the function, and the last argument is a closure that provides the function to be plotted.

The following example plots a mathematical function that returns the sine of every given value.

Listing 8-49: Plotting a mathematical function

```
struct ContentView: View {
   var body: some View {
      VStack {
         Chart {
            LinePlot(x: "x", y: "y") { x in
               sin(x)
            }
         }
         .chartXScale(domain: -5...5)
         .chartYScale(domain: -5...5)
         .frame(width: 300, height: 300)
         Spacer()
      }
   }
}
```

To display the part of the function we want, we need to apply the `chartXScale()` and `chartYScale()` modifiers with the **domain** argument. In this case, we limit the function in both axes to the values -5 and 5. The result is shown below.

Figure 8-43: *Chart representing a mathematical function*

PRO

Multiple Marks

A **Chart** view can present multiple series of values. The process is similar than before, but we need to organize the data in the model depending on what we want to achieve. The following example shows a possible implementation. In this model, there is a structure to store the date and number of items sold (**Sales**), and another to store the sales per item (**Products**). To test the application, we initialize it with two products, Bagels and Brownies, and one week of sales each.

Listing 8-50: Representing the values with different types of marks

```
import SwiftUI

struct Sales: Identifiable {
   let id = UUID()
   var date: Date
   var amount: Int
}
struct Products: Identifiable {
   let id = UUID()
   var name: String
   var sales: [Sales]
}
@Observable class ApplicationData {
   var sales: [Products]

   static let shared: ApplicationData = ApplicationData()
   private init() {
      let salesBagels = [
         Sales(date: Date(timeInterval: -86400 * 7, since: Date()),
            amount: 10),
         Sales(date: Date(timeInterval: -86400 * 6, since: Date()),
            amount: 12),
         Sales(date: Date(timeInterval: -86400 * 5, since: Date()),
            amount: 8),
         Sales(date: Date(timeInterval: -86400 * 4, since: Date()),
            amount: 13),
         Sales(date: Date(timeInterval: -86400 * 3, since: Date()),
            amount: 9),
         Sales(date: Date(timeInterval: -86400 * 2, since: Date()),
            amount: 7),
         Sales(date: Date(timeInterval: -86400 * 1, since: Date()),
            amount: 8) ]
      let salesBrownies = [
         Sales(date: Date(timeInterval: -86400 * 7, since: Date()),
            amount: 3),
         Sales(date: Date(timeInterval: -86400 * 6, since: Date()),
            amount: 5),
         Sales(date: Date(timeInterval: -86400 * 5, since: Date()),
            amount: 2),
         Sales(date: Date(timeInterval: -86400 * 4, since: Date()),
            amount: 8),
         Sales(date: Date(timeInterval: -86400 * 3, since: Date()),
            amount: 6),
```

```
        Sales(date: Date(timeInterval: -86400 * 2, since: Date()),
           amount: 5),
        Sales(date: Date(timeInterval: -86400 * 1, since: Date()),
           amount: 9) ]
      sales = [
        Products(name: "Bagels", sales: salesBagels),
        Products(name: "Brownies", sales: salesBrownies) ]
   }
}
```

To create the chart, we must iterate through the items and then through the sales for each item, so we need two **ForEach** loops, as shown below.

Listing 8-51: Visualizing two series of values

```
struct ContentView: View {
   @State private var appData = ApplicationData.shared

   var body: some View {
      VStack {
         Chart {
            ForEach(appData.sales) { product in
               ForEach(product.sales) { sale in
                  LineMark(x: .value("Date", sale.date, unit: .day), y:
                     .value("Sales", sale.amount))
               }.foregroundStyle(by: .value("Products", product.name))
            }
         }.frame(height: 300)
         .padding()
         Spacer()
      }
   }
}
```

This example creates a line chart. The first **ForEach** loop gets the products from the **sales** property in the model and then reads the **sales** property of each product to visualize the sales. Because we use dates to define the **x** axis, we implement the **value()** method to specify the date and the unit we want to use to represent the value (**day**). As a result, we get two line charts, one for Bagels and another for Brownies.

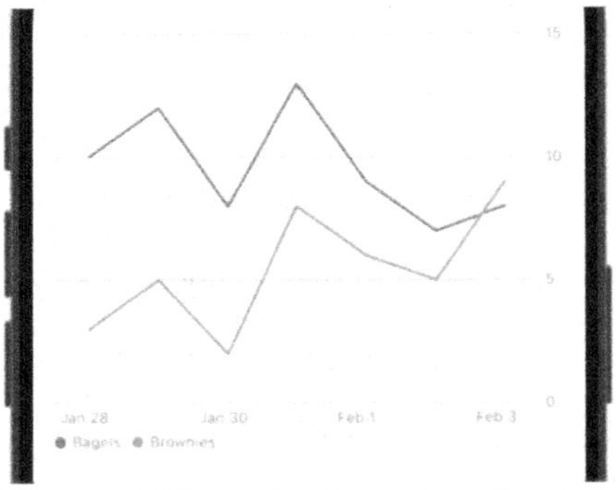

Figure 8-44: *Multiple series of values*

In a line chart, the series of values are independent, but bar and area charts add the marks on top of each other to display the total per value, as shown in the following example.

Listing 8-52: Visualizing two series of values with a bar chart

```
struct ContentView: View {
   @State private var appData = ApplicationData.shared

   var body: some View {
      VStack {
         Chart {
            ForEach(appData.sales) { product in
               ForEach(product.sales) { sale in
                  BarMark(x: .value("Date", sale.date, unit: .day), y:
                     .value("Sales", sale.amount))
               }.foregroundStyle(by: .value("Products", product.name))
            }
         }.chartForegroundStyleScale([
            "Bagels": .red,
            "Brownies": .orange
         ])
         .frame(height: 300)
         .padding()
         Spacer()
      }
   }
}
```

In this chart, we replace the **LineMark** view with a **BarMark** view, but we also implement the **chartForegroundStyleScale()** modifier to assign custom colors to the bars. In this case, we set the color red for Bagels and orange for Brownies. The result is shown below.

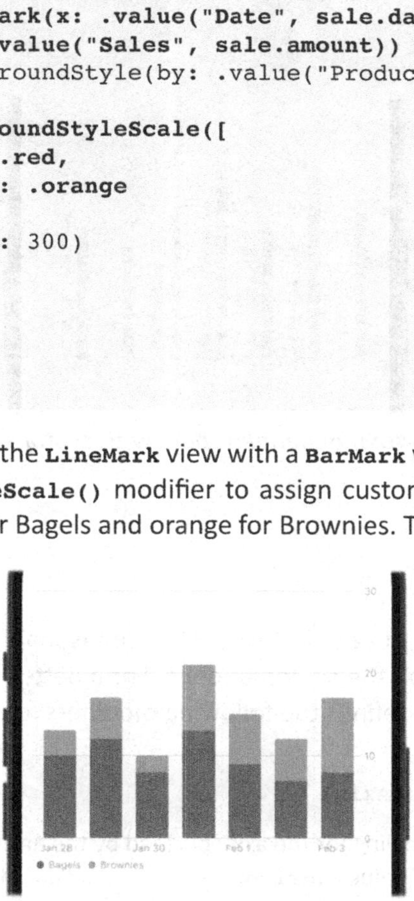

Figure 8-45: *Bar chart with two series of values*

By default, the bars are added to show the total, but we can use the **position()** modifier to adjust the position of the bars. In the following example, we specify a different position for each product and separate the bars with a space.

Listing 8-53: Defining the positions of the bars

```
struct ContentView: View {
   @State private var appData = ApplicationData.shared
```

```
var body: some View {
    VStack {
        Chart {
            ForEach(appData.sales) { product in
                ForEach(product.sales) { sale in
                    BarMark(x: .value("Date", sale.date, unit: .day), y:
                        .value("Sales", sale.amount))
                }.foregroundStyle(by: .value("Products", product.name))
                .position(by: .value("Product", product.name))
            }
        }.frame(height: 300)
        .padding()
        Spacer()
    }
  }
}
```

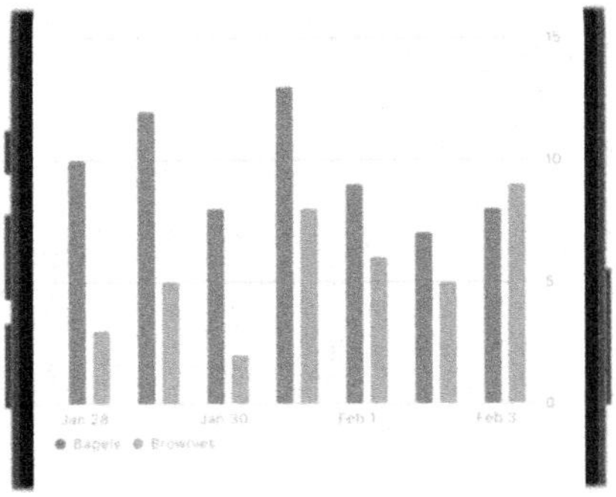

Figure 8-46: *Independent bars with custom positions*

PRO

Scrolling

Models often store long lists of values. It would be unreasonable to try to create a chart that displays all of these values on the screen at once. For a better presentation, we can enable scrolling. The **View** protocol defines the following modifiers for this purpose.

chartScrollableAxes(Axis**)**

This modifier enables scrolling for the axis specified by the argument. The argument is an enumeration with the values **horizontal** and **vertical**. It can take a set to enable scrolling for both axes.

chartXVisibleDomain(length: Value**)**

This modifier determines the number of values to present per screen on the **x** axis. The **length** argument determines the length of the range of values to be displayed. The protocol defines the **chartYVisibleDomain(length:)** modifier for the **y** axis.

chartScrollPosition(x: Binding**)**

This modifier determines the scrolling position in the **x** axis and stores it in a binding property. The protocol includes the **chartScrollPosition(y:)** modifier for the **y** axis.

chartScrollTargetBehavior(ChartScrollTargetBehavior)

This modifier determines the scrolling behavior. The argument is a structure that conforms to the **ChartScrollTargetBehavior** protocol. The protocol includes several type methods called **valueAligned()** with different parameters to determine the behavior according to the values represented by the chart.

The last example in the previous section displays the bars side by side, and so the width of the bars is reduced to fit the available space, but we can make them look better by displaying a few at a time and allowing the user to scroll the chart, as shown below.

Listing 8-54: Scrolling the chart

```
struct ContentView: View {
   @State private var appData = ApplicationData.shared

   var body: some View {
      VStack {
         Chart {
            ForEach(appData.sales) { product in
               ForEach(product.sales) { sale in
                  BarMark(x: .value("Date", sale.date, unit: .day), y:
                     .value("Sales", sale.amount))
               }.foregroundStyle(by: .value("Products", product.name))
               .position(by: .value("Product", product.name))
            }
         }.frame(height: 300)
         .chartLegend(.hidden)
         .chartScrollableAxes(.horizontal)
         .chartXVisibleDomain(length: 3600 * 24 * 4)
         .padding()
         Spacer()
      }
   }
}
```

In this example, we implement the **chartScrollableAxes()** modifier to make the chart scrollable on the **x** axis, and then use the **chartXVisibleDomain()** modifier to tell the **Chart** view how many bars to display at a time. Since the **x** axis in our model is determined by **Date** values, we calculate the number of seconds in four days to display four days at a time (3600 * 24 * 4).

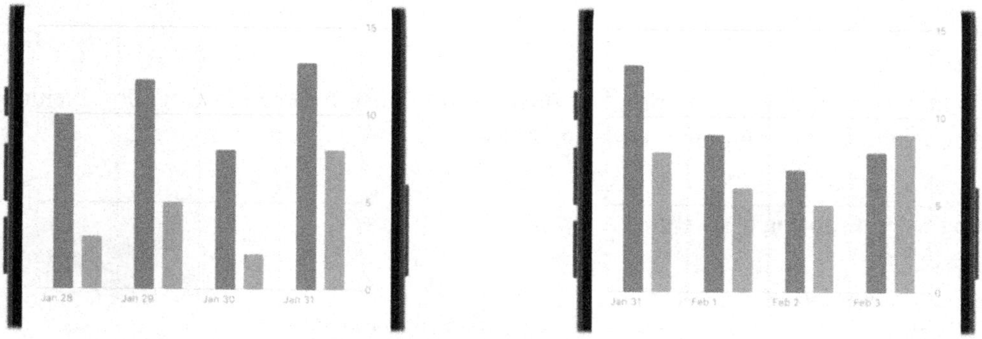

Figure 8-47: *Scrollable chart*

PRO

3D Charts

In addition to 2D charts, SwiftUI also supports 3D charts. To create them, the framework provides a dedicated view called **Chart3D**. The following is the view's initializer.

Chart3D(Data, content: Closure)

This initializer creates a view to display a three-dimensional chart. The first argument specifies the data to be represented, and the **content** argument is the closure that returns the views required to create the chart.

To create the views for a 3D chart, the framework provides initializers for the **PointMark**, **RuleMark**, and **RectangleMark** views that accept values for all three axes (**x**, **y**, and **z**). For instance, we can use the **PointMark** view to create a 3D chart with dots. The following is the data model required to provide the set of coordinates for this example.

Listing 8-55: Defining the coordinates values for a 3D chart

```
import SwiftUI

struct Sample3D: Identifiable {
    let id = UUID()
    let x: Double
    let y: Double
    let z: Double
}
@Observable class ApplicationData {
   var values: [Sample3D] = []

   static let shared: ApplicationData = ApplicationData()
   private init() {
      for x in 0..<15 {
         for y in 0..<15 {
            let xValue = Double(x)
            let yValue = Double(y)
            let zValue = (sin(xValue * 0.4) + cos(yValue * 0.4)) * 2
            values.append(Sample3D(x: xValue, y: yValue, z: zValue))
         }
      }
   }
}
```

The chart is created as before, but now we must use a **Chart3D** view and include the three coordinates for the mark, as shown below.

Listing 8-56: Creating a 3D chart

```
struct ContentView: View {
   @State private var appData = ApplicationData.shared
```

```
        var body: some View {
            VStack {
                Chart3D(appData.values) { value in
                    PointMark(x: .value("Elevation", value.x), y:
                        .value("Prominence", value.y), z: .value("Isolation",
                        value.z))
                }
                .frame(height: 300)
                .padding()
                Spacer()
            }
        }
    }
```

Like the **Chart** view, the **Chart3D** view iterates over the data and creates a **PointMark** view for each point. In this case, the values in our model form a set of three-dimensional coordinates that produce a rolling hills graphic. The result is shown below.

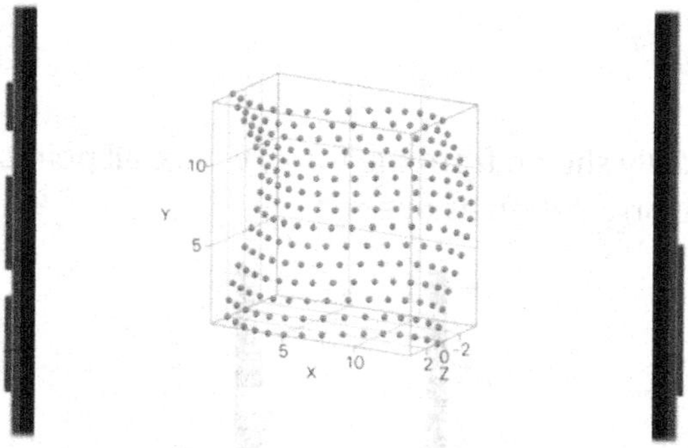

Figure 8-48: *3D Chart*

By default, the 3D chart is displayed using an orthographic perspective and in an orientation that exposes all axes, but the framework includes the following modifiers to configure the view and change this behavior.

chart3DPose(Binding)

This modifier controls the chart's orientation. The argument is a binding property of type **Chart3DPose**. This structure includes the initializer **Chart3DPose(azimuth: Angle2D, inclination: Angle2D)** to declare a specific orientation, as well as the properties **default**, **back**, **bottom**, **front**, **left**, **right**, and **top** to specify standard orientations.

chart3DCameraProjection(Chart3DCameraProjection)

This modifier determines the perspective of the chart. The argument is a structure with the properties **automatic**, **orthographic** and **perspective**.

The **chart3DPose()** modifier is used to set the initial orientation of the chart and to allow the user to manually change it. To apply this modifier, we need a binding property of type **Chart3DPose**. This property is used to define the initial orientation and to also store the orientation selected by the user, as shown in the following example.

Listing 8-57: Changing the orientation of a 3D chart

```
struct ContentView: View {
   @State private var appData = ApplicationData.shared
   @State private var orientation: Chart3DPose = .front

   var body: some View {
      VStack {
         Chart3D(appData.values) { value in
            PointMark(x: .value("Elevation", value.x), y:
               .value("Prominence", value.y), z: .value("Isolation",
               value.z))
         }
         .chart3DPose($orientation)
         .frame(height: 300)
         .padding()
         Spacer()
      }
   }
}
```

The chart is now initially shown from the front, where all points are visible, but the user can drag it to change the orientation as needed.

Figure 8-49: 3D Chart with custom orientation

In addition to the standard views used to create 3D charts, the framework also defines the **SurfacePlot** view to create 3D representations of mathematical functions. The following is the view's initializer.

SurfacePlot(x: String, **y:** String, **z:** String, **function:** Closure)

This initializer creates a plot view to visualize a mathematical function in three dimensions. The **x**, **y** and **z** arguments specify the labels for the axes, and the **function** argument provides the mathematical function to plot.

The closure assigned to the **function** argument receives two values representing the **x** and **y** coordinates and must return the corresponding **z** value, as shown in the following example.

Listing 8-58: Plotting a mathematical function in 3D

```
struct ContentView: View {
   @State private var orientation: Chart3DPose = .default

   var body: some View {
      VStack {
         Chart3D {
            SurfacePlot(x: "x", y: "y", z: "z", function: { x, y in
               sin(x) * cos(y)
            })
         }
         .chart3DPose($orientation)
         .frame(height: 300)
         .padding()
         Spacer()
      }
   }
}
```

In this example, we provide a function that creates a rolling hills graphic, similar to what we achieved before with our own dataset. The result is shown below.

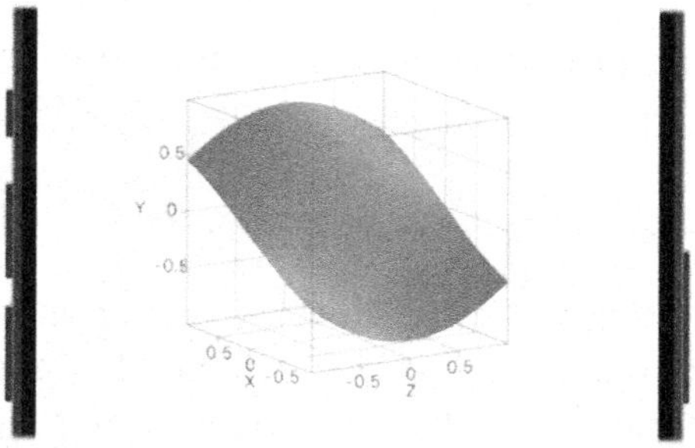

Figure 8-50: *3D representation of a mathematical function*

BASIC

8.7 - Animations

SwiftUI automatically animates views when they change or transition to a new view, but not always. To create our own animations, the framework includes the following functions.

withAnimation(Animation?, Closure)

This function performs an animation and returns the result. The first argument defines the type of animation to use, and the second argument specifies the closure that performs the changes we want to animate.

withAnimation(Animation?, **completionCriteria:** AnimationCompletionCriteria, Closure, **completion:** Closure)

This function performs an animation and executes a closure when finished. The first argument defines the type of animation to use. The **completionCriteria** argument determines when the animation is considered to be completed. It is a structure with the properties **logicallyComplete** (the animation is complete when the logical process is over) and **removed** (the animation is complete when the entire process is over). The third argument is the closure that performs the changes we want to animate, and the **completion** argument is the closure we want to execute after completion.

These functions apply the animation to the states, but the animation is determined by an instance of the **Animation** structure. The structure provides properties and methods to create and configure the animation, including the following type properties to define standard animations.

default

This type property returns the animation defined by the system by default.

easeIn

This type property returns an animation that is slow at the beginning and faster at the end.

easeInOut

This type property returns an animation that is slow at the beginning and the end.

easeOut

This type property returns an animation that is fast at the beginning and slow at the end.

linear

This type property returns an animation that is always performed at the same speed.

The animation returned by the value **default** is a spring animation with a specific configuration (a response of 0.55, a damping fraction of 1.0, and a blend duration of 0.0). The **Animation** structure includes the following properties to specify spring animations with different configurations.

bouncy

This type property returns a spring animation with a predefined duration and a high bounce effect.

smooth

This type property returns a spring animation with a predefined duration and no bounce effect.

snappy

This type property returns a spring animation with a predefined duration and a small bounce effect that feels more snappy.

The **withAnimation()** function asks the system to perform an animation if a state changes. The process is easy to implement. We set the new state, declare the type of animation we want, and SwiftUI takes care of producing the animation. For instance, if we change the scale of a **Rectangle** view from the closure of the **withAnimation()** function, the change is animated, as in the following example.

Listing 8-59: Animating a view

```
struct ContentView: View {
   @State private var boxScale: CGFloat = 1

   var body: some View {
      VStack {
         HStack {
            Rectangle()
               .fill(Color.blue)
               .frame(width: 50, height: 50)
               .scaleEffect(boxScale)
         }.frame(width: 250, height: 120)
         Button("Animate") {
            withAnimation(.default) {
               boxScale = 2
            }
         }.buttonStyle(.glassProminent)
      }.padding()
   }
}
```

This view defines a **@State** property of type **CGFloat** with the value **1**, uses this value to define the scale of a **Rectangle** view with the **scaleEffect()** modifier, and provides a button to change it. When the button is pressed, we assign the value **2** to the property, expanding the view, but because the assignment is done within an animation closure, the change is animated.

Figure 8-51: *Animation by default*

The animation in this example is of type **default**, which on most systems is set as an **easeInOut** animation, but we can specify a different type. The following example applies a **linear** animation instead.

Listing 8-60: Applying a linear animation

```
Button("Animate") {
   withAnimation(.linear) {
      boxScale = 2
   }
}.buttonStyle(.glassProminent)
```

Do It Yourself

Create a new App project. Update the `ContentView` structure with the code in Listing 8-59. Run the application on an iPhone simulator. Press the Animate button. You should see the blue square grow, as shown in Figure 8-51. Specify another type of animation as we did in Listing 8-60 to see the difference between one type and another.

The duration of a standard animation uses a default value, but the `Animation` structure provides methods to specify a custom duration.

`easeIn(duration:` `Double)`

This type method creates an **`easeIn`** animation with the duration determined by the argument.

`easeInOut(duration:` `Double)`

This type method creates an **`easeInOut`** animation with the duration determined by the argument.

`easeOut(duration:` `Double)`

This type method creates an **`easeOut`** animation with the duration determined by the argument.

`linear(duration:` `Double)`

This type method creates a **`linear`** animation with the duration determined by the argument.

There are also methods available to customize spring animations.

`bouncy(duration:` `TimeInterval,` **`extraBounce:`** `Double)`

This type method creates a **`bouncy`** animation with the duration specified by the **duration** argument and an additional bounce effect specified by the **extraBounce** argument.

`smooth(duration:` `TimeInterval,` **`extraBounce:`** `Double)`

This type method creates a **`smooth`** animation with the duration specified by the **duration** argument and an additional bounce effect specified by the **extraBounce** argument.

`snappy(duration:` `TimeInterval,` **`extraBounce:`** `Double)`

This type method creates a **`snappy`** animation with the duration specified by the **duration** argument and an additional bounce effect specified by the **extraBounce** argument.

For example, we can run the previous animation for 5 seconds.

Listing 8-61: Declaring a specific duration

```
Button("Animate") {
   withAnimation(.linear(duration: 5)) {
      boxScale = 2
   }
}.buttonStyle(.glassProminent)
```

The **Animation** structure also includes the following methods to set the animation's behavior.

delay(Double)

This method sets the seconds the animator waits before starting the animation.

repeatCount(Int, **autoreverses:** Bool)

This method sets the number of times the animator performs an animation. The first argument determines the number of animations to be performed, and the **autoreverses** argument determines if the process of going back to the initial state is going to be animated as well (**true** by default).

repeatForever(**autoreverses:** Bool)

This method determines if the animator is going to perform the animation indefinitely. The **autoreverses** argument determines if the process of going back to the initial state is going to be animated as well (**true** by default).

speed(Double)

This method sets the speed of the animation (1 by default).

These methods are applied to the **Animation** structure. We create the **Animation** structure, call the methods to configure the animation, and then apply it to the state with the **withAnimation()** method, as in the following example.

Listing 8-62: Configuring the animation

```
Button("Animate") {
   let animation = Animation.bouncy
      .delay(1)
      .speed(2)
      .repeatCount(3)
   withAnimation(animation) {
      boxScale = 2
   }
}.buttonStyle(.glassProminent)
```

This animation is delayed by one second, plays at twice the normal speed, and repeats three times. By default, the **repeatCount()** method sets the auto-reverse option to **true**, which means the view animates back to its initial state. Because we specified three cycles, the animation runs three times: forward, backward, and forward again.

Standard animations are enough for most applications, but the **Animation** structure also includes the possibility to set any parameter we need. The following are some of the methods available to create custom animations.

spring(duration: TimeInterval, **bounce:** Double, **blendDuration:** Double)

This type method creates a spring animation. The **duration** argument specifies the duration of the animation, the **bounce** argument specifies the bounce effect, and the **blendDuration** argument determines the time it takes for the animation to stop and the next animation to begin.

spring(response: Double, **dampingFraction:** Double, **blendDuration:** Double)

This type method creates a spring animation. The **response** argument determines the duration of one animation period, the **dampingFraction** argument determines the amount of oscillation, and the **blendDuration** argument determines the time it takes for the animation to stop and the next animation to begin.

interpolatingSpring(duration: TimeInterval, **bounce:** Double, **initialVelocity:** Double)

This type method creates a spring animation that combines the values with previous animations. The **duration** argument determines the duration of the animation, the **bounce** argument specifies the bounce effect, and the **initialVelocity** argument determines the initial velocity of the animation.

interpolatingSpring(mass: Double, **stiffness:** Double, **damping:** Double, **initialVelocity:** Double)

This type method creates a spring animation that combines the values with previous animations. The **mass** argument determines the mass we want to assign to the view, the **stiffness** argument determines the stiffness of the spring, the **damping** argument determines the amount of oscillation, and the **initialVelocity** determines the initial velocity of the animation.

interactiveSpring(response: Double, **dampingFraction:** Double, **blendDuration:** Double)

This type method creates a spring animation that can interact with the user. The **response** argument determines the duration of one animation period, the **dampingFraction** argument determines the amount of oscillation, and the **blendDuration** argument determines the time it takes for the animation to stop and the next animation to begin.

timingCurve(UnitCurve, **duration:** TimeInterval)

This type method creates an animation with a custom timing curve. The first argument specifies the characteristics of the curve. It is a structure with the type properties **linear**, **easeIn**, **easeOut**, **easeInOut**, **circularEaseIn**, **circularEaseOut**, and **circularEaseInOut**, and the type method **bezier(startControlPoint: UnitPoint, endControlPoint: UnitPoint)**. The **duration** argument determines the duration of the animation.

timingCurve(Double, Double, Double, Double, **duration:** Double**)**

This type method creates an animation with a custom timing curve. The four initial arguments determine the coordinates of the control points of a cubic Bezier curve, and the **duration** argument determines the duration of the animation.

These custom animations are created in the same way as standard animations, and they can even use the same methods for configuration. For example, we can create a custom spring animation with a specific speed and repetition cycle.

Listing 8-63: Defining a custom animation

```
Button("Animate") {
   let animation = Animation.interpolatingSpring(mass: 0.15,
      stiffness: 0.8, damping: 0.5, initialVelocity: 5)
      .speed(5)
      .repeatForever()
   withAnimation(animation) {
      boxScale = 2
   }
}.buttonStyle(.glassProminent)
```

Do It Yourself

Update the **`Button`** view in the **`ContentView`** structure with the code in Listing 8-63. Press the Animate button. You should see the square bouncing indefinitely. Try different values for the **`interpolatingSpring()`** animation and implement other types of animations to see how they work.

The **`withAnimation()`** function can animate multiple states at a time. The system takes care of combining the animations, as shown in the following example.

Listing 8-64: Animating multiple states at a time

```
struct ContentView: View {
   @State private var boxScale: CGFloat = 1
   @State private var roundCorners: Bool = false

   var body: some View {
      VStack {
         HStack {
            Rectangle()
               .fill(Color.blue)
               .frame(width: 50, height: 50)
               .clipShape(RoundedRectangle(cornerRadius: roundCorners ?
                  15 : 0))
               .scaleEffect(boxScale)
         }.frame(width: 250, height: 120)
```

```
            Button("Animate") {
                withAnimation(.easeInOut(duration: 2)) {
                    boxScale = 2
                    roundCorners = true
                }
            }.buttonStyle(.glassProminent)
        }.padding()
    }
}
```

This example defines two **@State** properties, one to control the scale of the box and another to change the radius of the corners. When the button is pressed, we change the values of these two properties, and both changes are animated.

Do It Yourself

Update the **ContentView** structure with the code in Listing 8-64. Run the application on an iPhone simulator. Press the Animate button. You should see the square grow and the corners become round, all happening at the same time.

PRO

Animating Custom Shapes

The system knows how to animate views because they conform to a SwiftUI protocol called **Animatable**. This protocol defines a computed property called **animatableData**, which provides the data required to generate the frames of an animation. Whenever a view is animated, the system reads this property, increases or decreases its value, redraws the view, and repeats the process until the value reaches the new target. Most SwiftUI views already implement **animatableData**, so the system can animate them automatically, but for custom **Shape** views, we must implement this behavior ourselves. To simplify this task, the framework provides the following macros.

@Animatable

This macro generates all the code necessary to animate the properties of a custom modifier or a **Shape** structure.

@AnimatableIgnored

This macro excludes a property from the animation.

Animatable shapes are defined in the same way as regular shapes. We declare a structure that conforms to the **Shape** protocol and implement the **path()** method to draw the shape. However, if we want the shape to be animatable, we must also define properties for the values to be animated and prefix the structure with the **@Animatable** macro, as shown below.

Listing 8-65: Defining an animatable shape

```
import SwiftUI

@Animatable
struct Face: Shape {
   var smile: CGFloat

   func path(in rect: CGRect) -> Path {
      let width = rect.width
      let smileClamp = min(max(smile, 0), 1)
      let section = rect.height / 5
      let smilePos = section + (section * 3 * smileClamp)

      var path = Path()
      path.addEllipse(in: CGRect(x: width/10*2 - 10, y: rect.minY + 10,
         width: 20, height: 20))
      path.addEllipse(in: CGRect(x: width/10*8 - 10, y: rect.minY + 10,
         width: 20, height: 20))

      path.move(to: CGPoint(x: width/10*2, y: rect.midY))
      path.addCurve(to: CGPoint(x: width/10*8, y: rect.midY),
         control1: CGPoint(x: width / 4, y: smilePos),
         control2: CGPoint(x: width / 4 * 3, y: smilePos))
      return path
   }
}
```

This shape draws a face and animates the mouth based on the value of the **smile** property. When the value is **1**, the mouth is drawn with a downward curvature that produces a smiling expression, and when the value is **0**, the curvature is inverted, producing a frowning expression. To draw the mouth, we first clamp the **smile** value to the valid range using the **min()** and **max()** functions, and then use that value to calculate the vertical position of the bottom of the mouth. When the value is close to **0**, the bottom of the mouth is positioned higher, and as the value approaches **1**, the bottom of the mouth moves downward. The continuous movement between these positions creates the animated transition between a sad and a happy face.

An animatable shape is drawn on the screen like any other shape, but we need to provide a binding property to store the current state, pass that value to the shape so it knows what to draw, and update the value from within a **withAnimation()** block so the transition is animated, as shown in the following example.

Listing 8-66: Animating a shape

```
struct ContentView: View {
   @State private var smiling: Bool = true

   var body: some View {
      VStack {
         Face(smile: smiling ? 1 : 0)
            .stroke(Color.blue, lineWidth: 5)
            .frame(width: 100, height: 120)
```

```
            Button("Change") {
                withAnimation(.default) {
                    smiling.toggle()
                }
            }.buttonStyle(.glassProminent)
        }
    }
}
```

In this example, we send a value to the shape depending on the value of a Boolean property. If the **smiling** property is **true**, we send the value 1, otherwise, we send the value 0. This means that the system can create an animation by instantiating the shape with values from 0 to 1. The result is shown below.

Figure 8-52: *Animated path*

Do It Yourself

Create a new Swift file called **Face.swift** for the structure in Listing 8-65. Update the **ContentView** structure with the code in Listing 8-66. Run the application on an iPhone simulator and press the Change button. You should see the shapes illustrated in Figure 8-52.

PRO

Canvas Animations

The content of a **Canvas** view can also be animated. This is especially useful when working with complex animations or highly interactive applications. To achieve this effect, the canvas must be redrawn over and over again. For this purpose, SwiftUI provides the following view.

TimelineView(Schedule, **content:** Closure**)**

This initializer creates a view that redraws its content according to a schedule. The first argument specifies the schedule the view must follow, and the **content** argument is a closure with the views we want to redraw at each point in time. The closure receives a **Context** structure, which includes the **date** property with the date that triggered the update, and the **cadence** property with the rate at which the views are updated.

The **TimelineView** view needs a schedule to know when to perform the task again. This schedule is defined by a structure that conforms to the **TimelineSchedule** protocol. SwiftUI defines several structures to create built-in schedules. These structures include the following type properties and methods.

explicit(Dates**)**

This type method creates a schedule from the **Date** values specified by the argument. The argument is an array of **Date** values with the dates and times to schedule the task.

periodic(from: Date, **by:** TimeInterval**)**

This type method creates a schedule from the dates specified by the arguments. The **from** argument determines when the process begins, and the **by** argument determines the intervals at which the task is performed.

everyMinute

This type property creates a schedule that performs the task every minute.

animation

This type property creates a schedule that performs the task over and over again to produce an animation.

animation(minimumInterval: Double?, **paused:** Bool**)**

This type method creates a schedule to produce an animation that can be paused. The **minimumInterval** argument specifies the interval at which the animation should be performed (the value **nil** sets the interval by default), and the **paused** argument determines if the animation should be running or paused.

The **TimelineView** view can be used for any task that requires updating the interface after a period of time. This may involve anything from single strings to complex graphics. When the interface needs simple updates, we can use a periodic or explicit schedule, as shown below.

Listing 8-67: Updating the interface

```
struct ContentView: View {
   var body: some View {
      TimelineView(.periodic(from: Date(), by: 2)) { time in
         let calendar = Calendar.current
         let components = calendar.dateComponents([.second], from: time.
date)
         HStack {
            Text("Time: \(components.second ?? 0)")
               .font(.largeTitle.bold())
         }
      }
   }
}
```

In this example, the **TimelineView** view begins drawing the views from the current date and does it again every two seconds. In the closure, we use the value produced by the view to get the date when the drawing is performed, extract the seconds, and show the number on the screen.

The **TimelineView** view works with any content, but it is particularly useful with the **Canvas** view. SwiftUI even defines a specific schedule structure to create animations with a canvas that can be obtained from the **animation** property or the **animation()** method. There is a caveat, though. The system doesn't know what we want to animate on the canvas, so we must take care of everything, including the frequency of the animation, the positions of the graphics, and more. The following example illustrates how to create a simple animation that repositions a circle on the screen after a few fractions of a second.

Listing 8-68: Animating the canvas

```
class ContentViewData {
   var posX: CGFloat = 0
   var posY: CGFloat = 0
   var lastTime: Double = 0
   var maxTime: Double = 0.2
}
struct ContentView: View {
   let contentData = ContentViewData()

   var body: some View {
      TimelineView(.animation) { time in
         let interval = time.date.timeIntervalSinceReferenceDate
         let delta = interval - contentData.lastTime

         Canvas { context, size in
            if delta > contentData.maxTime {
               contentData.posX = CGFloat.random(in: 0..<size.width - 20)
               contentData.posY = CGFloat.random(in: 0..<size.height - 20)
               contentData.lastTime = interval
            }
            let circleFrame = CGRect(x: contentData.posX,
               y: contentData.posY, width: 20, height: 20)
            context.fill(Circle().path(in: circleFrame),
               with: .color(.red))
         }.ignoresSafeArea()
      }
   }
}
```

For this example, we have defined a simple class called **ContentViewData** to be able to store and update the position of the circle and all the values required to control the frequency of the animation.

The timing is controlled from the date produced by the **TimelineView** view. From this value, we get the current date, extract the seconds with the **timeIntervalSince-ReferenceDate** property, check how many seconds have passed since the last iteration, and update the position of the circle if the difference is greater than the maximum time set by the **maxTime** property. Note that after the position of the circle is determined, we assign the current date in seconds to the **lastTime** property to know when the last iteration happened, so the graphics are only updated every 0.2 seconds.

Do It Yourself

Update the **ContentView.swift** file with the code in Listing 8-68. Run the application on an iPhone simulator. You should see a red circle appearing in different locations on the screen every 0.2 seconds.

The previous example shows how graphics are updated on the canvas, but it does not produce an animation. To animate a graphic, we must manually draw each frame. This means that the position of each graphic has to be calculated at every step of the animation. To illustrate this process, the following example animates a circle at the center of the screen. The animation is achieved by changing the radius of the circle.

Listing 8-69: Creating a real animation

```
class ContentViewData {
   var radius: CGFloat = 0
   var step: CGFloat = 5
   var lastTime: Double = 0
   var maxTime: Double = 0.02
}
struct ContentView: View {
   let contentData = ContentViewData()

   var body: some View {
      TimelineView(.animation) { time in
         let interval = time.date.timeIntervalSinceReferenceDate
         let delta = interval - contentData.lastTime

         Canvas { context, size in
            if delta > contentData.maxTime {
               calculateRadius()
               contentData.lastTime = interval
            }
            let rad = contentData.radius
            let circleFrame = CGRect(x: size.width/2 - rad,
               y: size.height/2 - rad, width: rad * 2, height: rad * 2)
            context.fill(Circle().path(in: circleFrame),
               with: .color(.red))
         }.ignoresSafeArea()
      }
   }
   func calculateRadius() {
      contentData.radius = contentData.radius + contentData.step
      if contentData.step < 0 && contentData.radius < 0 {
         contentData.radius = 0
         contentData.step = 5
      }
      if contentData.step > 0 && contentData.radius > 150 {
         contentData.radius = 150
         contentData.step = -5
      }
   }
}
```

The process of controlling the frequency of the animation is the same as before, but we have defined a function to calculate the radius. If the radius is small, we add 5 points to expand the circle, otherwise we start the opposite animation by reducing the radius by -5 points. To know whether the circle is expanding or contracting, we store the difference in an additional property called **`step`**. When the value of this property is negative, it means that the circle is contracting, otherwise it is expanding.

PRO

Transitions

As we have already seen, we can add or remove views from the interface based on a state by using a simple **`if else`** statement (see Chapter 3, Listing 3-12). The process by which a view appears or disappears on the screen is called *transition*. By default, the system does not apply a transition and simply displays or removes views, but we can assign a specific transition to a view using the following modifier.

`transition``(AnyTransition)`

This modifier assigns the transition specified by the argument to the view.

The following are the type properties provided by the **`AnyTransition`** structure to create standard transitions.

`opacity`

This type property returns a transition that inserts or removes a view by modifying its opacity.

`scale`

This type property returns a transition that inserts or removes a view by modifying its scale.

`slide`

This type property returns a transition that inserts or removes a view by sliding it to the sides.

`identity`

This type property returns a transition that inserts or removes a view without any effect. This is the transition by default.

The **`AnyTransition`** structure determines the type of transition, but in order for the transition to be applied, we must specify how it should be animated. For this purpose, the **`AnyTransition`** structure provides the following method.

`animation``(Animation)`

This method applies an animation to the transition.

The **animation()** method is called on the instance of the **AnyTransition** structure, so we have to define the transition and then call this method to determine the animation we are going to apply to it. In the following example, we show and hide a **Text** view with a transition of type **scale** and an animation of type **default**.

Listing 8-70: Adding and removing a view with a transition

```
struct ContentView: View {
   @State private var showInfo = false

   var body: some View {
      VStack {
         Button("Show Information") {
            showInfo.toggle()
         }.padding()
         .buttonStyle(.glassProminent)

         if showInfo {
            Text("This is the information")
               .transition(.scale.animation(.default))
         }
         Spacer()
      }
   }
}
```

The button in this view toggles the value of the **showInfo** property. When the value is **true**, a **Text** view is added to the interface, otherwise, the view is removed, but because of the **scale** transition, the view expands until it reaches its natural size when the value of the property is **true**, and contracts until it disappears from the screen when it is **false**.

Do It Yourself

Create a new App project. Update the **ContentView** structure with the code in Listing 8-70. Run the application on an iPhone simulator and press the Show Information button. You should see the **Text** view appear or disappear from the screen every time the button is pressed. Replace the **scale** transition by the **opacity** and **slide** types to see how they work.

The transition applied in the last example is symmetric, which means it behaves the same when the view is added to the interface and when it is removed. To create an asymmetric transition, the **AnyTransition** structure includes the following method.

asymmetric(insertion: AnyTransition, **removal:** AnyTransition**)**

This type method defines an asymmetric transition. The **insertion** argument specifies the transition to use when the view is inserted, and the **removal** argument specifies the transition to use when the view is removed.

For example, we can fade-in the view by modifying the opacity when it is added to the interface, and then remove it by reducing the scale.

Listing 8-71: Defining an asymmetric transition

```
if showInfo {
   Text("This is the information")
      .transition(AnyTransition.asymmetric(insertion: .opacity,
         removal: .scale).animation(.easeInOut(duration: 2)))
}
```

Do It Yourself

Update the **ContentView** structure with the code in Listing 8-71. Run the application on an iPhone simulator and press the Show Information button. You should see the text fade in, and then shrink when the button is pressed again.

In addition to defining one transition for the insertion and another for the removal, we can combine two transitions with the following method.

combined(with: AnyTransition)

This method combines the transition with the transition specified by the **with** argument.

The following example combines a **scale** transition with an **opacity** transition. The text fades in and out and also scales as it appears and disappears on the screen.

Listing 8-72: Combining transitions

```
if showInfo {
   Text("This is the information")
      .transition(AnyTransition.scale.combined(with: .opacity).animation(.
easeInOut(duration: 2)))
}
```

The **AnyTransition** structure also includes the following type methods to create custom transitions.

move(edge: Edge)

This type method defines a transition that moves the view in and out of the interface from the side defined by the argument. The **edge** argument is an enumeration of type **Edge** with the values **bottom**, **leading**, **top**, and **trailing**.

```
offset(x: CGFloat, y: CGFloat)
```

This type method defines a transition that moves the view in and out of the interface by the space determined by the arguments. The **x** and **y** arguments specify the offset of the view from the center of the frame.

```
scale(scale: CGFloat, anchor: UnitPoint)
```

This type method defines a transition that scales the view. The **scale** argument determines the initial scale for the transition, and the **anchor** argument determines the point from which the view is going to be scaled.

Custom transitions require an explicit animation. This means that instead of animating the transition itself, we must animate the change of the state with the **withAnimation()** function, as shown in the following example.

Listing 8-73: Customizing the transition

```
struct ContentView: View {
   @State private var showInfo = false

   var body: some View {
      VStack {
         Button("Show Information") {
            withAnimation {
               showInfo.toggle()
            }
         }.padding()
         .buttonStyle(.glassProminent)

         if showInfo {
            Text("This is the information")
               .transition(.offset(x: 400, y: 0))
         }
         Spacer()
      }
   }
}
```

This example creates a transition that moves the view in and out of the interface from the right side of the screen. Note that this transition reproduces the **slide** transition, but in this case the view always uses the same side of the screen.

Of course, multiple views can transition at the same time, and because the interface is updated all at once, the animations are coordinated. For instance, we can use the same **showInfo** property to show and hide two **Text** views.

Listing 8-74: Coordinating transitions

```
struct ContentView: View {
   @State private var showInfo = false
```

```swift
    var body: some View {
        VStack {
            Button("Show Information") {
                showInfo.toggle()
            }.padding()
            .buttonStyle(.glassProminent)

            HStack {
                if !showInfo {
                    Text("Left")
                        .transition(.scale.animation(.default))
                }
                Spacer()
                if showInfo {
                    Text("Right")
                        .transition(.scale.animation(.default))
                }
            }.padding()
            Spacer()
        }
    }
}
```

The **showInfo** property is initialized with the value **false**. This means that the first view we see is the **Text** view displaying the string "Left". However, when the button is pressed, the value of the **showInfo** property is toggled, so the **Text** view displaying the string "Right" is shown instead. Both transitions are animated with a scale effect, so the views shrink or expand as they appear or disappear from the screen.

The transitions in the last example look coordinated, but the strings are displayed by two different **Text** views and therefore each animation is independent. If we want to transition from one view to another with a single animation, we must declare both views to be the same. SwiftUI includes the following modifier for this purpose.

matchedGeometryEffect(id: Value, **in:** Namespace.ID, **properties:** MatchedGeometryProperties, **anchor:** UnitPoint, **isSource:** Bool)

This modifier adds views to an animation group for synchronization. The **id** argument is a hashable value that identifies the associated views. The **in** argument is the namespace that groups the animations together. The **properties** argument is a structure that indicates the types of properties we want to synchronize. The type properties available to create these structures are **frame** (default), **position**, and **size**. The **anchor** argument determines the position shared by the views (**center** by default). And the **isSource** argument determines if the view should be used as the source of the geometry for the rest of the views (**true** by default).

This modifier can be used to group and associate multiple views. To associate the views, we need to provide a common identifier, usually a string, but to create an animation group, we need to define a namespace (see Chapter 5, Listing 5-41). In the following example, we create a **@Namespace** property to define the namespace and then apply the **matchedGeometryEffect()** modifier to each view to tell the system that they are related.

Listing 8-75: Coordinating views

```
struct ContentView: View {
   @Namespace private var myAnimations
   @State private var showInfo = false

   var body: some View {
      VStack {
         Button("Show Information") {
            withAnimation(.easeInOut) {
               showInfo.toggle()
            }
         }.padding()
         .buttonStyle(.glassProminent)

         HStack {
            if !showInfo {
               Text("Left")
                  .matchedGeometryEffect(id: "TextAnimation",
                     in: myAnimations)
            }
            Spacer()
            if showInfo {
               Text("Right")
                  .matchedGeometryEffect(id: "TextAnimation",
                     in: myAnimations)
            }
         }.padding()
         Spacer()
      }
   }
}
```

This example includes the same views as before. There is a **Text** view that appears on the left and another on the right, but because we apply the **matchedGeometryEffect()** modifier to the views with the same identifier and assign them to the same namespace, they are animated as one view. In this case, when the value of the **showInfo** property changes, the views move from left to right and right to left, and also the text gradually changes from "Left" to "Right", and vice versa. Note that for the transition to be animated, we had to animate the state change with the **withAnimation()** function.

If what we want is to animate changes in the content of a view, we must apply the **contentTransition** modifier.

contentTransition(ContentTransition)—This modifier assigns the transition specified by the argument to the content of the view.

This modifier takes a structure of type **ContentTransition** to indicate the type of transition to perform. The structure includes properties and methods to specify the transition. The following are the most frequently used.

opacity

This transition fades the content in and out as old content is replaced by new one.

numericText(value: Double)

This transition is used to animate numbers. The value argument is the value that is being changed.

The most interesting effect is the one produced by the **numericText()** transition. This transition takes the number assigned to the view and animates the view's content depending on whether the value is increasing or decreasing, as shown in the following example.

Listing 8-76: Performing a content transition

```
struct ContentView: View {
   @State private var mynumber = 25

   var body: some View {
      VStack {
         HStack {
            Button("Increase") {
               withAnimation(.easeInOut) {
                  mynumber += 1
               }
            }.buttonStyle(.glassProminent)

            Button("Decrease") {
               withAnimation(.easeInOut) {
                  mynumber -= 1
               }
            }.buttonStyle(.glassProminent)
         }
         Text(String(mynumber))
            .font(.largeTitle)
            .padding()
            .contentTransition(.numericText(value: Double(mynumber)))
        Spacer()
      }
   }
}
```

This example defines a property called **mynumber** with the value **25**, two buttons to increase or decrease the property's value, and a **Text** view with a transition of type **numericText()** to animate the text. The transition uses the **mynumber** property to determine whether the number has been increased or decreased and animates the digits accordingly. If the number increases, it scrolls the digits up; if it decreases, it scrolls them down.

PRO

SF Symbols Animations

SF Symbols can also be animated. The **View** protocol defines the following modifiers to apply a transition to the changes in the content of a single view.

```
symbolEffect(SymbolEffect, options: SymbolEffectOptions,
isActive: Bool)
```

This modifier creates a content transition to animate a symbol. The first argument defines the effect to apply to the transition, the **options** argument defines the configuration of the effect, and the **isActive** argument is a Boolean binding property that determines whether the symbol is animated or not.

```
symbolEffect(SymbolEffect, options: SymbolEffectOptions, value:
Binding)
```

This modifier creates a content transition to animate a symbol. The first argument defines the effect to apply to the transition, the **options** argument defines the configuration of the effect, and the **value** argument is a binding property used to run the animation each time its value changes.

The effect applied by these modifiers is defined by a structure that conforms to the **SymbolEffect** protocol. Apple provides a framework called **Symbols** that defines a set of structures with predefined effects, as well as type properties to return instances of these structures. The properties currently available are **appear**, **automatic**, **bounce**, **breathe**, **disappear**, **pulse**, **replace**, **rotate**, **scale**, **variableColor**, **drawOff**, **drawOn**, and **wiggle**. The structures returned by these properties in turn contain their own properties for configuration. Some share the same properties, such as **up** and **down**, which can be used to specify whether the animation should be upwards or downwards, but others are more specific, as we will see later.

By default, the animation is not repeated and runs at a speed of 1.0, but we can change these values by specifying a **SymbolEffectOptions** structure. The structure includes the following properties and methods for configuration.

```
repeating
```

This property returns a set of options that repeat the effect indefinitely.

```
nonRepeating
```

This property returns a set of options that specify that the effect does not repeat.

```
repeat(Int)
```

This method creates a set of options that repeat the effect as many times as specified by the argument.

```
speed(Double)
```

This method creates a set of options that determine the speed of the effect according to the value specified by the argument.

Animating an SF Symbol that was designed for animation is easy. All we have to do is display the symbol with an **Image** view and apply the **symbolEffect()** modifier with the desired effect and configuration, as shown below.

Listing 8-77: Animating an SF Symbol

```
struct ContentView: View {
   @State private var isActive = false

   var body: some View {
      VStack(spacing: 10) {
         Image(systemName: "wifi")
            .font(.largeTitle)
            .symbolEffect(.variableColor.iterative, options: .repeating,
               isActive: isActive)
         Button("Animate") {
            isActive.toggle()
         }.buttonStyle(.glassProminent)
      }
   }
}
```

In this example, we use the **variableColor** effect. This property returns a **VariableColorSymbolEffect** structure that contains properties for configuring the effect. The most useful are **cumulative** and **iterative** to determine how the layers should be animated, and **dimInactiveLayers** and **hideInactiveLayers** to dim or hide the inactive layers. In this case, we use the **iterative** version of the effect to simulate the propagation of radio waves.

To start or stop the animation, we assign a Boolean **@State** property to the **isActive** argument. If the property is **true**, the symbol will be animated, otherwise it will be displayed as a static symbol. The **isActive** argument takes a Boolean value, but we can also use the **value** argument to control the animation with a different value. For example, the following modifier starts or stops a **bounce** animation when a value changes. In this case, we use the same **isActive** property as before, but the argument can take any type of value we want.

Listing 8-78: Animating an SF Symbol when a value changes

```
.symbolEffect(.bounce, value: isActive)
```

The structure returned by the **bounce** property includes the properties **up** and **down** to determine the direction of the effect (**bounce.up** or **bounce.down**), but each effect includes its own configuration properties. For example, the structure returned by the **wiggle** property includes properties to determine the angle of the effect. The properties available are **backward**, **byLayer**, **clockwise**, **counterClockwise**, **down**, **forward**, **left**, **right**, **up**, and **wholeSymbol**. The structure also includes the **custom(angle: Double)** method to specify a custom angle between 0 and 360 degrees, as shown below.

Listing 8-79: Configuring animations

```
.symbolEffect(.wiggle.custom(angle: 45), value: isActive)
```

The previous effects execute the animation and then show the symbol again in its initial state. However, some effects execute the animation and remain in that state until the animation is deactivated. For example, if we enlarge the symbol with the **scale** effect, it will remain in that state until we scale it down.

Listing 8-80: Scaling a symbol

```
.symbolEffect(.scale.up, isActive: isActive)
```

The same happens with other effects like **disappear**. In this case, the symbol appears or disappears from the screen and remains in that state until the animation is activated again.

Listing 8-81: Removing a symbol from the screen

```
.symbolEffect(.disappear, isActive: isActive)
```

This effect removes the symbol from the screen, but the layout remains unchanged. If we want the layout to adapt to the new space, we must apply the effect within a transition, as in the following example.

Listing 8-82: Adapting the layout to the effect

```
struct ContentView: View {
   @State private var isActive = true

   var body: some View {
      VStack(spacing: 10) {
         if isActive {
            Image(systemName: "wifi")
               .font(.largeTitle)
               .transition(.symbolEffect(.disappear))
         }
         Button("Animate") {
            isActive.toggle()
         }.buttonStyle(.glassProminent)
      }
   }
}
```

In this example, the **Image** view is displayed only when the value of the **isActive** property is **true**, but because we apply the **transition()** modifier, the symbol is added to or removed from the interface with an animation. In this case, we use the **disappear** animation again, so the symbol vanishes as it is removed from the screen.

In addition to removing a symbol, we can also replace it by using the **replace** effect. This effect is called Magic Replace because, when the symbols are related, the replacement can be animated. The only requirement is that it must be applied with the **contentTransition()** modifier so the effect is applied to the content of the view rather than to the view itself. In the following example, we replace the Wi-Fi symbol with the same symbol but with a slash, so the slash is animated.

Listing 8-83: Replacing a symbol

```
struct ContentView: View {
   @State private var isActive = false

   var body: some View {
      VStack(spacing: 10) {
         Image(systemName: isActive ? "wifi" : "wifi.slash")
            .font(.largeTitle)
            .contentTransition(.symbolEffect(.replace))
         Button("Animate") {
            isActive.toggle()
         }.buttonStyle(.glassProminent)
      }
   }
}
```

BASIC

8.8 - Liquid Glass

In previous chapters, we explored how to apply a liquid glass effect to buttons. For standard buttons, we used the **buttonStyle()** modifier with the **glass** or **glassProminent** values, while toolbar buttons receive the glass effect automatically from the system. However, the liquid glass effect is not limited to buttons. We can also apply it to any other view by using the following modifier.

glassEffect(Glass, **in:** Shape)

This modifier applies a liquid glass effect to a view. The first argument defines the configuration of the material. It is a structure with the properties **clear**, **identity**, and **regular**, and also the methods **interactive(Bool)** and **tint(Color)** to make the view interactive and apply a custom tint color. And the **in** argument defines the shape of the glass.

The **glassEffect()** modifier can be applied to any view. For example, we can use it with a **Text** view to give the view's background a glass appearance.

Listing 8-84: Applying the liquid glass effect to a view

```
struct ContentView: View {
```

```
    var body: some View {
        ZStack {
            Image("spot1")
                .resizable()
                .scaledToFit()
            Text("Glass Effect")
                .font(.largeTitle)
                .padding()
                .glassEffect()
        }
    }
}
```

In this example, we use a **ZStack** view to place an image in the background and highlight the visual effect. By default, the **glassEffect()** modifier renders the view using the **regular** configuration and a **Capsule** shape, as shown below.

Figure 8-53: *Regular Liquid Glass effect*

Do It Yourself

Create a new App project. Download the **spot1.jpg** image from our website and add it to an Asset Catalog. Update the **ContentView** structure with the code in Listing 8-84. Run the application on an iPhone simulator. You should see the **Text** view with a liquid glass effect on the screen, as shown in Figure 8-53. Use this project to test the rest of the examples in this section.

By default, the system applies the regular glass effect to the view. To achieve a more translucent appearance, we can assign the **clear** value.

Listing 8-85: Applying a clear liquid glass effect

```
Text("Glass Effect")
    .font(.largeTitle)
    .padding()
    .glassEffect(.clear)
```

Figure 8-54: *Clear Liquid Glass effect*

Another aspect of the liquid glass effect that is defined by default is the shape. The system uses a **`Capsule`** shape, but we can change it to any shape we want. In the following example, we apply the effect using a rectangle with rounded corners.

Listing 8-86: Applying a different shape to the liquid glass effect

```
Text("Glass Effect")
   .font(.largeTitle)
   .padding()
   .glassEffect(.regular, in: .rect(cornerRadius: 5))
```

Figure 8-55: *Rectangular Liquid Glass effect*

If the view is performing a task, we can make it interactive with the **`interactive()`** method. This method makes the view responsive, so it is animated every time the user taps or clicks it. In the following example, we add this effect to our **`Text`** view and apply the **`onTapGesture()`** modifier to perform a task. Now the view behaves like a button.

Listing 8-87: Making the view interactive

```
Text("Glass Effect")
   .font(.largeTitle)
   .padding()
   .glassEffect(.regular.interactive())
   .onTapGesture {
      print("Text pressed")
   }
```

So far, we have used a single view, but an interface can include multiple views with the liquid glass effect. When two or more of these views are placed close to each other, the effect may appear distorted. To inform the system that the views should be rendered as a single group, SwiftUI provides the **`GlassEffectContainer`** view. The following is the view's initializer.

GlassEffectContainer(spacing: CGFloat, **content:** Closure)

This initializer creates a container for views that use the liquid glass effect. The **spacing** argument defines the size of the region shared by the views, and the **content** argument is a closure that provides the views.

The `GlassEffectContainer` view defines the region shared by its child views, allowing the system to correctly render the glass effect. In the following example, we use this container to group two SF Symbols together.

Listing 8-88: Applying the liquid glass effect to a group of views

```
struct ContentView: View {
   var body: some View {
      ZStack {
         Image("spot1")
            .resizable()
            .scaledToFit()
         GlassEffectContainer(spacing: 40) {
            HStack {
               Image(systemName: "paperplane.circle")
                  .font(.largeTitle)
                  .padding()
                  .glassEffect(.regular.interactive())
               Image(systemName: "music.microphone")
                  .font(.largeTitle)
                  .padding()
                  .glassEffect(.regular.interactive())
            }
         }
      }
   }
}
```

In this example, we define a spacing of 40 points. This tells the system that the views share a region extending 40 points beyond their frames, causing the glass effect to merge across that area, as shown below.

Figure 8-56: *Extending the Liquid Glass effect*

On its own, the `GlassEffectContainer` view only defines the region shared by the views for rendering the liquid glass effect. If we also want to indicate that the views share similar functionality, we need to apply the following modifier.

```
glassEffectUnion(id: Value, namespace: Namespace)
```

This modifier unifies the liquid glass effect across all views that share the same identifier. The **id** argument is a value, typically a string or an integer, that identifies each participating view, and the **namespace** argument defines a shared namespace SwiftUI uses to keep track of the views.

To apply the **glassEffectUnion()** modifier, we need a namespace that SwiftUI uses to associate related views, along with an identifier that tells the system which views belong to the same group, as shown in the following example.

Listing 8-89: Joining views with the Liquid Glass effect

```
struct ContentView: View {
   @Namespace var glassSpace

   var body: some View {
      ZStack {
         Image("spot1")
            .resizable()
            .scaledToFit()
         GlassEffectContainer {
            HStack {
               Image(systemName: "arrow.left.circle")
                  .font(.largeTitle)
                  .padding()
                  .glassEffect(.regular.interactive())
                  .glassEffectUnion(id: 1, namespace: glassSpace)
               Image(systemName: "arrow.right.circle")
                  .font(.largeTitle)
                  .padding()
                  .glassEffect(.regular.interactive())
                  .glassEffectUnion(id: 1, namespace: glassSpace)
            }
         }
      }
   }
}
```

In this example, we assign the same identifier to both **Image** views, causing the liquid glass effect to merge into a single shape. The result is shown below.

Figure 8-57: *Joining views*

The **GlassEffectContainer** view can also be used to animate the views. When the views inside the container are animated, their liquid glass effect animates as well, producing a smooth transition. For views to participate in the animation, they must be identified. To provide this identifier, the framework defines the following modifier.

glassEffectID(Value, in: Namespace)

This modifier associates the view's liquid glass effect with an identifier. The first argument is a value, typically a string or an integer, that identifies the view, and the **namespace** argument defines a shared namespace SwiftUI uses to keep track of the views.

In the following example, we define three buttons. The first button controls the visibility of the others, so when it is pressed, the remaining two buttons appear on the screen. As always, we implement this behavior using an **if** statement and a **withAnimation()** function, but because the views are placed inside a **GlassEffectContainer** view, their liquid glass effect animates as well, creating a smooth transition between the two states.

Listing 8-90: Animating views with Liquid Glass effect

```
struct ContentView: View {
   @Namespace var glassSpace
   @State private var openButtons = false

   var body: some View {
      GlassEffectContainer {
         HStack {
            Button(action: {
               withAnimation {
                  openButtons.toggle()
               }
            }, label: {
               Image(systemName: openButtons ? "xmark.circle" :
                  "arrow.right.circle")
                  .font(.largeTitle)
            }).buttonStyle(.glassProminent)
            .glassEffectID("open", in: glassSpace)

            if openButtons {
               Button(action: {
                  print("Send Value")
               }, label: {
                  Image(systemName: "paperplane.circle")
                     .font(.largeTitle)
               }).buttonStyle(.glass)
               .glassEffectID("send", in: glassSpace)

               Button(action: {
                  print("Record")
               }, label: {
                  Image(systemName: "music.microphone")
                     .font(.largeTitle)
               }).buttonStyle(.glass)
```

```
                .glassEffectID("mic", in: glassSpace)
            }
            Spacer()
        }.padding()
      }
    }
  }
```

In this example, we also use two different SF Symbols for the main button, so when the button is pressed, the symbol changes to reflect the current state. The result is shown below.

Figure 8-58: *Animating the Liquid Glass effect*

Chapter 9
Gestures

BASIC

9.1 - Gesture Recognizers

Gestures are actions that users perform on the screen, such as tapping, swiping, or pinching. These actions are difficult to detect because the screen only reports the position and movement of the fingers. To bridge this gap, Apple provides gesture recognizers. A gesture recognizer performs the calculations required to identify a gesture, allowing us to respond to high-level events instead of manually processing low-level touch data.

BASIC

Gesture Modifiers

The most common gesture is a tap gesture, which is recognized when the user touches the screen with a finger. Since this gesture is used very frequently, SwiftUI defines two convenient modifiers to handle it.

onTapGesture(count: Int, **coordinateSpace:** CoordinateSpaceProtocol, **inputKinds:** GestureInputKinds, **perform:** Closure)

This modifier recognizes a single or multiple taps. The **count** argument determines how many taps are required for the gesture to be recognized (1 by default), the **coordinateSpace** argument determines the coordinate space to use to calculate the location of the finger. Some of the values available are **local** (default), **global** and **immersiveSpace**. The **inputKinds** argument determines the input to be recognize. The possible values are **all** (default), **directTouch**, **indirectTouch**, **pencil** and **pointer**. And the **perform** argument is the closure to be executed when the gesture is detected. The closure receives a **CGPoint** value with the location of the tap in the view's coordinates.

onLongPressGesture(minimumDuration: Double, **maximumDistance:** CGFloat, **inputKinds:** GestureInputKinds, **perform:** Closure, **onPressingChanged:** Closure)

This modifier recognizes a long press gesture (the user keeps pressing the screen with a finger). The **minimumDuration** argument is the time in seconds the user must press the screen with the finger until the gesture is recognized. The **maximumDistance** argument is the distance in points the user can move the finger from the original position before the gesture is no longer recognized. The **inputKinds** argument determines the input to be recognize. The possible values are **all** (default), **directTouch**, **indirectTouch**, **pencil** and **pointer**. The **perform** argument is the closure to be executed when the gesture is confirmed, and the **onPressingChanged** argument is the closure to be executed when the user begins and ends pressing the view. The closure receives a Boolean value to indicate whether the user is pressing or not.

We have used the **onTapGesture()** modifier in previous examples to detect a tap and perform an action. What we have not shown yet is how to determine the position of the finger when the tap occurs. This information is provided by the **CGPoint** value passed to the closure, which contains the **x** and **y** coordinates of the finger within the view. In the following example, we open a sheet when an image is tapped and demonstrate how to access this value.

Listing 9-1: Detecting a tap gesture on an image

```
struct ContentView: View {
   @State private var expand: Bool = false

   var body: some View {
      VStack {
         Image("spot1")
            .resizable()
            .scaledToFit()
            .frame(width: 160, height: 200)
            .onTapGesture { location in
               expand = true
               print("Location: \(location)")
            }
            .sheet(isPresented: $expand) {
               ShowImage()
            }
         Spacer()
      }.padding()
   }
}
```

This code defines an **Image** view of a size of 160 by 200 points. The **onTapGesture()** and **sheet()** modifiers are applied to the view to detect the tap and present a sheet. The following is the **ShowImage** view opened by the sheet.

Listing 9-2: Showing the image

```
import SwiftUI

struct ShowImage: View {
   var body: some View {
      Image("spot1")
         .resizable()
         .scaledToFill()
         .edgesIgnoringSafeArea(.all)
   }
}
```

This view creates an **Image** view and expands it to fill the sheet, including the safe area. As a result, the interface presents a small image on the screen, and when the user taps on it, a sheet is opened to show it in full size.

Figure 9-1: *Image responds to the tap gesture*

Do It Yourself

Create a new App project. Download the **spot1.jpg** image from our website and add it to an Asset Catalog. Update the **ContentView** structure with the code in Listing 9-1. Create a SwiftUI file called **ShowImage.swift** for the code in Listing 9-2. Run the application on an iPhone simulator. You should see the interface illustrated in Figure 9-1 (left). Tap the image to open the sheet and print the location of your finger on the console.

The long press gesture is similar to the tap gesture, but the system waits a moment before acknowledging the gesture and performing the task. With the **onLongPressGesture()** modifier, we can set the waiting time and also execute a task while the user presses and waits for the gesture to complete, as in the following example.

Listing 9-3: Detecting a long press gesture

```
struct ContentView: View {
   @State private var expand: Bool = false
   @State private var pressing: Bool = false

   var body: some View {
      VStack {
         Image("spot1")
            .resizable()
            .scaledToFit()
            .frame(width: 160, height: 200)
            .opacity(pressing ? 0 : 1)

            .onLongPressGesture(minimumDuration: 1, maximumDistance: 10,
               perform: {
               expand = true
            }, onPressingChanged: { value in
```

```
                withAnimation(.easeInOut(duration: 1.5)) {
                    pressing = value
                }
            })
            .sheet(isPresented: $expand) {
                ShowImage()
            }
        Spacer()
    }.padding()
  }
}
```

The closure assigned to the **onPressingChanged** argument is executed when the user starts touching the image, and again when the finger is lifted. In this closure, we change the value of a `@State` property called `pressing`, which we use to set the opacity of the view. When the gesture begins, the value received by the closure is `true`, so the opacity is set to 0, but when the user moves the finger away, lifts the finger, or ends the gesture, the closure receives the value `false`, so the opacity is set to 1. The change in opacity is animated with an `easeInOut` animation that lasts 1.5 seconds, so the sheet is opened before the image completely disappears, giving the user the necessary feedback to know they must wait until the process is complete.

Do It Yourself

Update the `ContentView` structure with the code in Listing 9-3. Run the application on an iPhone simulator. Press and hold the finger on the image (long click). You should see the image fading-out and the sheet opening after 1 second.

PRO

Hit Testing

Because views can overlap, the system must decide whether a view should process a gesture or pass it to the views behind it. The process of determining which view the user intends to interact with, and whether that view should respond to the gesture, is called *hit testing*. The `View` protocol defines the following modifiers to control this process.

`allowsHitTesting``(Bool)`

This modifier determines whether the detection of hits is enabled on the view or not.

`contentShape``(Shape, `**`eoFill:`**` Bool)`

This modifier defines the shape of the hitting area. The first argument is a shape view that determines the area the user can interact with, and the **eoFill** argument determines the algorithm to use to detect the hit.

The **allowsHitTesting()** modifier can be used to disable a gesture. For instance, we can enable or disable the tap gesture on the **Image** view of the previous example.

Listing 9-4: Disabling the tap gesture

```
struct ContentView: View {
   @State private var expand: Bool = false
   @State private var allowExpansion: Bool = false

   var body: some View {
      VStack(spacing: 20) {
         Image("spot1")
            .resizable()
            .scaledToFit()
            .frame(width: 160, height: 200)
            .onTapGesture {
               expand = true
            }
            .allowsHitTesting(allowExpansion)
            .sheet(isPresented: $expand) {
               ShowImage()
            }
            Toggle("", isOn: $allowExpansion)
               .labelsHidden()
            Spacer()
      }.padding()
   }
}
```

In this example, we add a **Toggle** view below the image to control the value of a **@State** property. This property determines whether hit testing is allowed for the **Image** view. The initial value of the property is set to **false** so that the user cannot tap the image to open the sheet, but when the switch is turned on, the value **true** is assigned to the property, and the gesture is therefore recognized by the **Image** view.

Do It Yourself

Update the **ContentView** structure with the code in Listing 9-4. Run the application on an iPhone simulator. Tap on the image. Nothing should happen. Turn on the switch. Now, the image should open the sheet when you tap on it.

The **contentShape()** modifier also plays an important role in gesture recognition. When we apply a gesture recognizer to an **Image** view or a **Text** view, the gesture is recognized when the user touches any part of the area occupied by the view. However, this is not always the case. Container views, such as **VStack** and **HStack**, recognize the gesture only when it is performed on the area occupied by their content. To ensure that every part of the view can recognize a gesture, we need to force the content to occupy the entire area. We have encountered this problem before (see Chapter 4, Listing 4-36). In those examples, we had to define a background with a **`Color`** view to create an area for the tap gesture to be recognized. This is enough to get the container to recognize the gesture, but it creates content that is not required by the interface. A better solution is to apply the **`contentShape()`** modifier. This modifier allows us to define the hitting area for the gesture without adding any real content to the view.

In the following example, we recreate the views used in previous projects to create the rows of a list, but this time we do not use a **`Color`** view to respond to the tap gesture, instead we define the content of the row with a **`Rectangle`** view and the **`contentShape()`** modifier. This allows the user to tap anywhere on the row to select it.

Listing 9-5: Defining the shape of the content

```
struct ContentView: View {
   @State private var selected: Bool = false

   var body: some View {
      VStack {
         HStack(alignment: .top) {
            Image("spot1")
               .resizable()
               .scaledToFit()
               .frame(width: 80, height: 100)
               .border(selected ? Color.yellow : Color.clear, width: 5)
            VStack(alignment: .leading, spacing: 2) {
               Text("Balmy Beach").bold()
               Text("Toronto")
               Text("2020").font(.caption)
               Spacer()
            }
            Spacer()
         }.frame(height: 100)
         .padding(5)
         .border(.gray, width: 1)
         .contentShape(Rectangle())
         .onTapGesture {
            selected.toggle()
         }
         Spacer()
      }
   }
}
```

This example displays a row with information about a location. If the user taps anywhere on the row, the gesture recognizer toggles the value of a **`@State`** property called **`selected`**, which is used to define the color of the image's border. A value of **`false`** makes the border transparent (deselected), while a value of **`true`** makes it yellow (selected).

Figure 9-2: *Responding to hits*

BASIC

9.2 - Gesture Structures

The gestures processed by the **onTapGesture()** and **onLongPressGesture()** modifiers are defined by structures that conform to the **Gesture** protocol. The following are the most frequently used.

```
TapGesture(count: Int, inputKinds: GestureInputKinds)
```

This initializer creates a gesture recognizer to detect a tap gesture. The **count** argument determines the number of taps required for the gesture to be recognized, and the **inputKinds** argument determines the input to be recognize. The possible values are **all** (default), **directTouch**, **indirectTouch**, **pencil** and **pointer**.

```
LongPressGesture(minimumDuration: Double, maximumDistance:
CGFloat, inputKinds: GestureInputKinds)
```

This initializer creates a gesture recognizer to detect a long-press gesture. The **minimumDuration** argument is the time in seconds the user must press the screen with the finger until the gesture is recognized. The **maximumDistance** argument is the distance in points the user can move the finger from the original position before the gesture is no longer recognized. And the **inputKinds** argument determines the input to be recognize. The possible values are **all** (default), **directTouch**, **indirectTouch**, **pencil** and **pointer**.

```
MagnifyGesture(minimumScaleDelta: CGFloat, inputKinds:
GestureInputKinds)
```

This initializer creates a gesture recognizer to detect a magnification gesture. The **minimumScaleDelta** argument is the minimum increment or decrement on the scale required for the gesture to be recognized, and the **inputKinds** argument determines the input to be recognize. The possible values are **all** (default), **directTouch**, **indirectTouch**, **pencil** and **pointer**.

```
RotateGesture(minimumAngleDelta: Angle, inputKinds:
GestureInputKinds)
```

This initializer creates a gesture recognizer to detect a rotation gesture. The **minimumAngleDelta** argument is the minimum increment or decrement on the angle of the view required for the gesture to be recognized, and the **inputKinds** argument determines the input to be recognize. The possible values are **all** (default), **directTouch**, **indirectTouch**, **pencil** and **pointer**.

These initializers configure the gestures recognizers, but to respond to the different states of the gesture, the structures implement the following methods.

onChanged(Closure)

This method executes a closure when the state of the gesture changes. The closure receives a value with information about the state of the gesture.

onEnded(Closure)

This method executes a closure when the gesture ends. The closure receives a value with information about the state of the gesture.

updating(GestureState, **body:** Closure)

This method executes a closure when the state of the gesture is updated, either because its value changed or the gesture was cancelled. The first argument is a binding property that stores the gesture's state values, and the **body** argument is the closure to be executed every time the state is updated. The closure receives a value with information about the state of the gesture, a reference to the binding property, and a value of type **Transaction** that contains information about the animation.

Because of the frequency with which the **updating()** method is called, we cannot use a normal **@State** property to track the state of a gesture. Any attempt to change a state within the updating closure will result in an error. Therefore, SwiftUI defines the following property wrapper to work with this method.

@GestureState

This property wrapper stores the state of a gesture and resets its value to its initial value when the gesture ends.

Once we have an instance of the gesture recognizer properly configured, we must apply it to the view. The **View** protocol defines the following modifiers for this purpose.

gesture(Gesture)

This modifier assigns a gesture recognizer to the view with a lower priority than the gesture recognizers already applied to the view.

highPriorityGesture(Gesture)

This modifier assigns a gesture recognizer to the view with a higher priority than the gesture recognizers already applied to the view.

simultaneousGesture(Gesture)

This modifier assigns a gesture recognizer to the view that is processed along with the gesture recognizers already applied to the view.

BASIC

Tap Gesture

Because of the simplicity of the tap gesture, there is not much difference between applying the **onTapGesture()** modifier and implementing the **TapGesture** structure. As well as the modifier, the structure can also define the number of taps required to detect the gesture, and since there are no changes to report over time, only the **onEnded()** method is useful. The following example reproduces the previous project, but this time we define the gesture recognizer with a **TapGesture** structure.

Listing 9-6: Defining a TapGesture recognizer

```
struct ContentView: View {
   @State private var expand: Bool = false

   var body: some View {
      VStack {
         Image("spot1")
            .resizable()
            .scaledToFit()
            .frame(width: 160, height: 200)
            .gesture(
               TapGesture(count: 1)
                  .onEnded {
                     expand = true
                  }
            )
            .sheet(isPresented: $expand) {
               ShowImage()
            }
         Spacer()
      }.padding()
   }
}
```

The **TapGesture** structure defines the gesture recognizer, but to associate it with a view we must apply the **gesture()** modifier. The result is the same as before. When the image is tapped, the closure assigned to the **onEnded()** method is executed, and the value **true** is assigned to the **expand** property to open the sheet. Note that the **onEnded()** method belongs to the **TapGesture** structure and therefore it is called on the instance of that structure, not the view.

BASIC

Long Press Gesture

Like the **TapGesture** structure, the **LongPressGesture** structure creates a simple gesture recognizer, but in this case there is some activity while the gesture is being performed, so in addition to the **onEnded()** method, we can also implement the **updating()** method if we want to perform a task while the view is being pressed.

When implementing the **updating()** method, we need to keep a few things in mind. First, as mentioned earlier, this method requires a **@GestureState** property instead of a **@State** property. A **@GestureState** property stores the current state, but also resets itself to the initial value when the gesture ends, so we should make sure that the initial value is what the property should have by default. Second, we need to update the state ourselves from the closure assigned to the method, but we must do it from the reference received by the method (usually called **state**). And third, because we are performing the changes inside the **updating()** method, the system cannot animate the process. For this purpose, we need to assign an **Animation** structure to the **animation** property of the **Transaction** structure created by the gesture, as shown below.

Listing 9-7: Defining a `LongPressGesture` **recognizer**

```
struct ContentView: View {
   @GestureState private var pressing: Bool = false
   @State private var expand: Bool = false

   var body: some View {
      VStack {
         Image("spot1")
            .resizable()
            .scaledToFit()
            .frame(width: 160, height: 200)
            .opacity(pressing ? 0 : 1)

            .gesture(LongPressGesture(minimumDuration: 1)
               .updating($pressing) { value, state, transaction in
                  state = value
                  transaction.animation = Animation.easeInOut
                     (duration: 1.5)
               }
               .onEnded { value in
                  expand = true
               }
            )
            .sheet(isPresented: $expand) {
               ShowImage()
            }
         Spacer()
      }.padding()
   }
}
```

This is the same application created with the **onLongPressGesture()** modifier (see Listing 9-3). When the user touches the image for a second, the opacity changes, and when the time is up, the sheet opens. The values are processed in the same way as before, but instead of working directly with the **@State** property, we assign the new value received by the closure to a reference of the **pressing** property. In this case, we identify the value and the reference with the names **value** and **state**, but these names are arbitrary. Once the new value is assigned to **state**, the value of the **pressing** property changes and the opacity is adjusted accordingly. After one second, the **onEnded()** method is executed, and the value **true** is assigned to the **expand** property to open the sheet.

Although we can work directly with the values generated by the **updating()** method, as we did in Listing 9-7, this method is designed to process the state through an enumeration. Instead of assigning the value received by the method directly to the **@GestureState** property, we assign an enumeration value to that property and then get the state from the enumeration, as in the following example.

Listing 9-8: Controlling the states of a gesture with an enumeration

```
enum PressingState {
   case active
   case inactive

   var isActive: Bool {
      switch self {
         case .active:
            return true
         case .inactive:
            return false
      }
   }
}
struct ContentView: View {
   @GestureState private var pressingState = PressingState.inactive
   @State private var expand: Bool = false

   var body: some View {
      VStack {
         Image("spot1")
            .resizable()
            .scaledToFit()
            .frame(width: 160, height: 200)
            .opacity(pressingState.isActive ? 0 : 1)

            .gesture(LongPressGesture(minimumDuration: 1)
               .updating($pressingState) { value, state, transaction in
                  state = value ? .active : .inactive
                  transaction.animation = Animation.easeInOut
                     (duration: 1.5)
               }
               .onEnded { value in
                  expand = true
               }
            )
            .sheet(isPresented: $expand) {
               ShowImage()
            }
         Spacer()
      }.padding()
   }
}
```

This example works as before, but now we use an enumeration to capture the state of the gesture. The enumeration is called **PressingState** and contains two cases, **active** and **inactive**, as well as a computed property that returns a Boolean value corresponding to the current value of the instance (**true** for active and **false** for inactive). Now, instead of defining a **@GestureState** property of type **Bool** to store the value received by the **updating()** method, we can define a property of type **PressingState** and store an enumeration value. We call this property **pressingState** and assign it to the **updating()** method. When the method is called, we assign this property the value **active** or **inactive**, depending on the value the method receives. When it is time to read the state in the **opacity()** modifier, we get the Boolean value from the **isActive** property instead of the **@GestureState** property. If the current value of the **pressingState** property is active, the **isActive** property returns **true** and the opacity is set to 0. Otherwise, the returned value is **false** and the opacity is set to 1. The result is the same as before, but the use of enumeration values becomes necessary when working with more complex gestures or when several gestures are combined.

BASIC

Magnify Gesture

The magnify gesture is often called the pinch gesture because it is recognized when the user spreads two fingers apart or pinches them together. This gesture is commonly used to allow the user to zoom in or out on an image. In this case, the value sent to the **updating()**, **onChanged()** and **onEnded()** methods is a **CGFloat** that represents a multiple of the scale that we must multiply by the current scale to get the final scale of the image, as shown in the following example.

Listing 9-9: Defining a MagnifyGesture recognizer

```
struct ContentView: View {
   @GestureState private var magnification: CGFloat = 1
   @State private var zoom: CGFloat = 1

   var body: some View {
      Image("spot1")
         .resizable()
         .scaledToFit()
         .frame(width: 160, height: 200)
         .scaleEffect(zoom * magnification)

         .gesture(MagnifyGesture()
            .updating($magnification) { value, state, transaction in
               state = value.magnification
            }
            .onEnded { value in
               zoom = zoom * value.magnification
            }
         )
   }
}
```

The code in Listing 9-9 defines two states: one to track the magnification and another to store the final value. The idea is to allow the user to zoom in and out multiple times. While the gesture is being performed, the magnification value is stored in the **magnification** property, but the value of the **zoom** property is not changed until the gesture is over, so the next time the user tries to zoom in or out, the new scale is calculated based on the last one.

To set the scale of the image to the one chosen by the user, we apply the **scaleEffect()** modifier to the **Image** view and calculate the new scale by multiplying the value of the **zoom** property (the last scale set by the user) by the value of the **magnification** property (the multiple produced by the gesture). The result is that the image is zoomed in and out according to the movement of the fingers.

Do It Yourself

Update the **ContentView.swift** file with the code in Listing 9-9. Run the application on an iPhone simulator. Press and hold the Option key on your keyboard to activate the gesture in the simulator, then pinch the view with two fingers to zoom in or out.

The example in Listing 9-9 allows users to zoom an image in and out as much as they want, but in most cases we need to limit the scale of the view to values that make sense for the interface and the purpose of our application. To set these limits, we need to control the scale in two places: when it is applied to the view with the **scaleEffect()** modifier, and when the gesture ends and the final scale is assigned to the **zoom** property, as shown below.

Listing 9-10: Determining a minimum and a maximum scale

```
struct ContentView: View {
   @GestureState private var magnification: CGFloat = 1
   @State private var zoom: CGFloat = 1

   var body: some View {
      Image("spot1")
         .resizable()
         .scaledToFit()
         .frame(width: 160, height: 200)
         .scaleEffect(getCurrentZoom(magnification: magnification))

         .gesture(MagnifyGesture()
            .updating($magnification) { value, state, transaction in
               state = value.magnification
            }
            .onEnded { value in
               zoom = getCurrentZoom(magnification: value.magnification)
            }
         )
   }
   func getCurrentZoom(magnification: CGFloat) -> CGFloat {
      let minZoom: CGFloat = 1
      let maxZoom: CGFloat = 2

      var current = zoom * magnification
      current = max(min(current, maxZoom), minZoom)
```

```
        return current
    }
}
```

In this example, the view scaling is limited to a minimum of 1 and a maximum of 2. Since we need to perform some operations to limit the scaling to these values, we move the process to a method called **`getCurrentZoom()`** and call it every time it is needed. The method defines two constants with the minimum and maximum values for the scale, then calculates the current scale by multiplying the values of the **`zoom`** property and the magnification, and finally limits the result to a minimum of 1 and a maximum of 2 using the **`min()`** and **`max()`** functions. The **`min()`** function compares the scale with the maximum scale allowed and returns the smallest value (if the value is greater than 2, it returns 2), and then the **`max()`** function compares the result with the minimum scale allowed and returns the largest value (if the value is less than 1, it returns 1). The **`getCurrentZoom()`** method is called by the **`scaleEffect()`** modifier to set the scale for the view, and by the **`onEnded()`** method to set the final scale. As a result, the user can zoom the image in and out, but up to a maximum of 2 and a minimum of 1.

BASIC

Rotate Gesture

The rotate gesture is recognized when the user touches the screen with two fingers and performs a circular motion, and it is commonly used to rotate an image. As with the previous gestures, if we want the user to perform the gesture multiple times, we need to store two states: one for the current rotation and another for the last rotation. The value generated by the gesture is an **`Angle`** structure, which includes the **`degrees(Double)`** method to create an instance with a value in degrees and the **`radians(Double)`** method to create one in radians. In this example, we rotate an image to follow the movement of the fingers, so we only need to add the current angle to the delta angle produced by the gesture.

Listing 9-11: Defining a `RotateGesture` recognizer

```
struct ContentView: View {
    @GestureState private var rotationAngle: Angle = Angle.zero
    @State private var rotation: Angle = Angle.zero

    var body: some View {
        Image("spot1")
            .resizable()
            .scaledToFit()
            .frame(width: 160, height: 200)
            .rotationEffect(rotation + rotationAngle)

            .gesture(RotateGesture()
                .updating($rotationAngle) { value, state, transaction in
                    state = value.rotation
                }
                .onEnded { value in
```

```
                rotation = rotation + value.rotation
            }
        )
    }
}
```

This example applies the **rotationEffect()** modifier to rotate the view. The angle is calculated by adding the values of the two state properties. We also add the current rotation to the previous one when the gesture ends to preserve the current state in case the user wants to rotate the image again from that angle.

Figure 9-3: *Image rotated by the user*

Do It Yourself

Update the **ContentView** structure with the code in Listing 9-11. Run the application on an iPhone simulator. You should be able to rotate the view with your fingers, as shown in Figure 9-3. Remember to press and hold the Option key on your keyboard to activate the gesture in the simulator.

BASIC

Drag and Drop Gesture

Drag and drop is an interaction that allows users to move an item from one app to another or between sections of the same app. This capability is especially useful on devices that support opening multiple windows on screen at the same time, such as iPads and Mac computers. To enable drag and drop in our application, we must indicate which views can be dragged and which ones can accept a drop. SwiftUI provides the following modifiers for this purpose.

draggable(Transferable, **preview:** Closure)

This modifier designates the view as the source of a drag and drop operation. The first argument is a value that conforms to the **Transferable** protocol and represents the data that will be transferred in the process. The **preview** argument provides the view to show to the user while the drag gesture is performed.

dropDestination(for: Type, action: Closure)

This modifier designates the view as the destination of a drag and drop operation. The **for** argument is a reference to the data type of the values we want the view to be able to receive, and the **action** argument provides a closure to process the data transferred by the gesture.

Drag and drop gestures are performed in the views, but the data to be transferred is determined by the code. This doesn't mean that we cannot send any value we want, but the data must be presented in such a way that applications can recognize it. For this purpose, the framework defines the **Transferable** protocol. This protocol prepares the data to be sent and processes the data received in an operation. Although our custom data types can conform to this protocol, some Swift data types and SwiftUI views do so by default. For example, if we want to let the user drag an image from our app to another app, we can use the **Image** view.

Listing 9-12: Allowing the user to drag an image

```
struct ContentView: View {
   var body: some View {
      VStack {
         Image("husky")
            .resizable()
            .scaledToFit()
            .frame(width: 300, height: 400)
            .draggable(Image("husky"))
         Spacer()
      }.padding()
   }
}
```

This is a simple application with an **Image** view to show the image of a husky, but since we applied the **draggable()** modifier, the user can drag the image to another application. To tell the system what data to share between applications, we provide the modifier another **Image** view with the same picture. The **Image** view conforms to the **Transferable** protocol, so the system knows how to pass the data, and the external applications know how to process it. Figure 9-4 below shows the app running on an iPad and sharing the screen with the Photo Library. When we drag the husky into an album on the right, the image is added to that album.

***Figure 9-4:** Drag and drop operation between apps*

Do It Yourself

Create a new App project. Download the **husky.png** image from our website and add it to an Asset Catalog. Update the **ContentView** structure with the code in Listing 9-12. Run the application on an iPad simulator. Drag the window from the bottom-right corner to reduce its size. Open the Photo Library and drag it to the right. You should see a layout similar to Figure 9-4. Open an album in the Photo Library and drag and drop the husky image into it. The image should be added to the album.

The system creates an image from the view being dragged and uses it to show a preview to the user, but we can assign an additional view to the **draggable()** modifier to create a custom preview. For instance, the following example shows an SF Symbol instead.

Listing 9-13: Providing a custom preview for the gesture

```
struct ContentView: View {
   var body: some View {
      VStack {
         Image("husky")
            .resizable()
            .scaledToFit()
            .frame(width: 300, height: 400)
            .draggable(Image("husky"), preview: {
               Image(systemName: "scope")
                  .font(.system(size: 50))
            })
         Spacer()
      }
   }
}
```

Figure 9-5: *Custom preview*

The **draggable()** modifier allows us to drag a view to another app. If we want to allow the user to drop items into our app, we need to provide a view that can receive the data and apply the **dropDestination()** modifier instead. This modifier takes a data type that determines the kind of data the view can receive and a closure to process it. As before, the type must conform to the **Transferable** protocol. For example, we can use an **Image** view.

Listing 9-14: Dropping images into an Image view

```
struct ContentView: View {
   @State private var picture: Image = Image("nopicture")

   var body: some View {
      VStack {
         picture
            .resizable()
            .scaledToFit()
            .frame(minWidth: 0, maxWidth: .infinity)
            .frame(height: 400)
            .dropDestination(for: Image.self, action: {
               elements, location in
               if let image = elements.first {
                  picture = image
                  return true
               }
               return false
            })
         Spacer()
      }
   }
}
```

The closure assigned to the **action** argument receives two values: an array containing a list of the items dropped by the user, and a **CGPoint** structure with the position in the view where the items were dropped. Since we are processing the data as **Image** structures, the user can only drop images and the values are automatically converted to **Image** views, so we can assign them directly to a **@State** property and show them on the screen. Note that the closure must return a Boolean value to indicate the result of the operation. If we are able to get and process the values, we must return **true**, otherwise **false**.

Figure 9-6: *Dropping an image into our app*

Do It Yourself

Update the **ContentView** structure with the code in Listing 9-14. Download the **nopicture.png** image from our website and add it to the Asset Catalog. Run the application on an iPad simulator and split the screen to share it with the Photo Library, as before. Drag an image from the Photo Library into the app. The **nopicture.png** image should be replaced by the new image.

The **dropDestination()** modifier can use a binding property to tell the application when the item dragged by the user enters or leaves the area occupied by the view. For example, we can add a **@State** property to our previous example to change the color of the view when the item enters or leaves the area.

Listing 9-15: Providing feedback to the user

```
struct ContentView: View {
   @State private var picture: Image = Image("nopicture")
   @State private var didEnter: Bool = false

   var body: some View {
      VStack {
         picture
            .resizable()
            .scaledToFit()
            .frame(minWidth: 0, maxWidth: .infinity)
            .frame(height: 400)
            .overlay(didEnter ? Color.green.opacity(0.2) : Color.clear)
            .dropDestination(for: Image.self, action: {
               elements, location in
               if let image = elements.first {
                  picture = image
                  return true
               }
```

```
                return false
            }, isTargeted: { value in
                didEnter = value
            })
        Spacer()
      }
   }
}
```

The **didEnter** property stores a Boolean value. If the item is inside the area of the view, the **dropDestination()** modifier assigns the value **true** to this property, so we can use it to provide feedback to the user. In this case, we have created an overlay for the **Image** view. If the value of the **didEnter** property is **true**, we show a green overlay, otherwise the color is clear.

Figure 9-7: *Feedback for the drag and drop operation*

Do It Yourself

Update the **ContentView** structure with the code in Listing 9-15. Run the application on an iPad simulator and split the screen as before. The drop area should turn green when you drag an image over it, as shown in Figure 9-7.

So far, we have used an **Image** view to transfer data. This type already conforms to the **Transferable** protocol, so it can be used to transfer data via drag and drop without any additional effort. However, if we want to transfer other kinds of data, such as custom structures or classes, we must explicitly make them conform to the **Transferable** protocol. The protocol's only requirement is the implementation of the following type property.

transferRepresentation

This type property returns a structure that represents the data to be transferred.

The property must return a structure that conforms to a protocol called **TransferRepresentation**. The framework defines several structures for creating these representations. The most frequently used are **CodableRepresentation** for sending and receiving encodable and decodable data, **DataRepresentation** for raw data, **FileRepresentation** for files, and **ProxyRepresentation** for using predefined representations. The following are some of the initializers available to create these structures.

CodableRepresentation(for: Type, **contentType:** UTType)

This initializer creates a structure that represents data that can be encoded and decoded. The **for** argument is a reference to the data type, and the **contentType** argument determines the type of values the user is allowed to drag and drop.

DataRepresentation(contentType: UTType, **exporting:** Closure, **importing:** Closure)

This initializer creates a structure that represents raw data. The **contentType** argument determines the type of values the user is allowed to drag and drop, the **exporting** argument provides the data to send when the view is dragged, and the **importing** argument creates an instance of the data type with the data dropped by the user.

FileRepresentation(contentType: UTType, **shouldAttemptToOpenInPlace:** Bool, **exporting:** Closure, **importing:** Closure)

This initializer creates a structure that represents files. The **contentType** argument determines the types of files the user is allowed to drag and drop, the **shouldAttemptToOpenInPlace** argument indicates if the receiver can access the original file, the **exporting** argument provides the file to be sent in a drag operation, and the **importing** argument creates the file from the information received from a drop operation.

ProxyRepresentation(exporting: Closure, **importing:** Closure)

This initializer creates a structure that uses an existent transfer representation that is suitable for the type. The **exporting** argument provides a reference to the transfer representation used when an element is dragged, and the **importing** argument provides a reference to the transfer representation used when an element is dropped.

The purpose of these structures is to prepare the data to be sent and to process the data received in a drag and drop interaction. But no matter what structure we use, the values are transferred as **Data** structures. In order for the applications to know how to process this data, we need to declare the content type with a **UTType** structure. We have already introduced this structure in Chapter 7 (see Listing 7-67). As we will see later, we can define our own types, but we can also use the standard types provided by the framework. In the following example, we use the type **png** to send a PNG image when the view is dragged to other applications.

Listing 9-16: Dragging custom values

```
import SwiftUI
import UniformTypeIdentifiers

struct ImageRepresentation: Transferable {
   let name: String
   let image: UIImage

   static var transferRepresentation: some TransferRepresentation {
      DataRepresentation(exportedContentType: .png, exporting: { value in
         return value.image.pngData()!
      })
   }
}
struct ContentView: View {
   @State private var picture: UIImage = UIImage(named: "nopicture")!

   var body: some View {
      VStack {
         Image(uiImage: picture)
            .resizable()
            .scaledToFit()
            .draggable(ImageRepresentation(name: "My Picture",
               image: picture))
            .dropDestination(for: Data.self, action: {
               elements, location in
               if let data = elements.first,
                  let image = UIImage(data: data) {
                  picture = image
                  return true
               }
               return false
            })
         Spacer()
      }.padding()
   }
}
```

For this application, we want to transfer only the image, so we define a structure called **ImageRepresentation**, get the structure to conform to the **Transferable** protocol, implement the **transferRepresentation** property, and define a **DataRepresentation** structure to get the data from the image and return it.

Although we are transferring data that represents an image, we are using our own custom data type to process it. When the user drags the view, the **draggable()** modifier creates an instance of the **ImageRepresentation** structure and the structure is sent to the closure assigned to the **DataRepresentation** structure so we can get the **UIImage** object in the **image** property, convert it to data using the **pngData()** method, and return it. The external application receives this data, recognizes it as a PNG image thanks to the **UTType** structure and processes it as such.

Note that to know which image the user is dragging, we have changed the data type of the **picture** property to a **UIImage** object, and therefore we need to display the image on the screen using the **Image(uiImage:)** initializer. And because we are processing the image with a **UIImage** object instead of an **Image** view, we have also updated the **dropDestination()** modifier to work with this value. The process is simple. We tell the **dropDestination()** modifier that the value received is a **Data** structure, and then convert that value to an image using the **UIImage(data:)** initializer (see **Images** in Chapter 7). Now the user can drag and drop images between this view and an external application, and everything is automatically converted from data to image and vice versa.

Do It Yourself

Update the **ContentView.swift** file with the code in Listing 9-16. Run the application on an iPad simulator. Split the screen as before. Open the Photo Library. You should be able to drag and drop images back and forward between the apps.

In the last example, we use a **DataRepresentation** structure to prepare the data to be sent in a drag operation (exporting), but use a **Data** type to receive an image dropped by the user. This is because we have no control over the data that other applications send to us. However, we can send and receive custom data types as long as the application knows how to process them. For example, when we allow the user to drag and drop items within our application, we have control over the entire process and can therefore transfer any custom data type we want. The only requirement is that the data be encoded. When data is sent, it must be encoded, and when data is received, it must be decoded. This is easily accomplished with the **Codable** protocol and the **CodableRepresentation** structure, but since we are using custom data types, we also need to define a custom **UTType**. The following is the structure's initializer.

```
UTType(exportedAs: String, conformingTo: UTType?)
```

This initializer creates a custom **UTType** identified by the string assigned to the **exportedAs** argument. The **conformingTo** argument is a predefined **UTType** that the custom type uses as reference.

The **UTType** structure requires an identifier, which we must create from settings. We need to go to the project's settings, open the **Info** panel, expand the Exported Type Identifiers section, press the + button, and insert the values, as shown below.

Figure 9-8: *Custom content type*

The values we need are the Description, the Identifier, and the Conforms To. The Description is just text describing the type, the Identifier must be unique, so it is recommended to declare it with an inverted domain, as we did in our example, and the Conforms To option is a predefined **UTType** that closely matches what our type will represent. In this case, we use the **public.data** type, so that the system knows we are transferring raw data.

Once we have the custom content type, we need to extend the **UTType** structure to include a type property that represents it. In the following example, we create a custom structure to manage the data (an image and an identifier), and extend the **UTType** structure with a property called **product** to store our custom type.

Listing 9-17: Using a custom content type

```
import SwiftUI
import UniformTypeIdentifiers

struct PictureRepresentation: Identifiable, Codable, Transferable {
   var id = UUID()
   var image: Data

   static var transferRepresentation: some TransferRepresentation {
      CodableRepresentation(for: PictureRepresentation.self,
         contentType: .product)
   }
}
extension UTType {
   nonisolated static let product = UTType(exportedAs:
      "com.formasterminds.pictures")
}

@Observable class ApplicationData {
   var listPictures: [PictureRepresentation]

   static let shared: ApplicationData = ApplicationData()
   private init() {
      listPictures = [
         PictureRepresentation(image:
            UIImage(named: "spot1")!.pngData()!),
         PictureRepresentation(image:
            UIImage(named: "spot2")!.pngData()!),
         PictureRepresentation(image: UIImage(named: "spot3")!.pngData()!)
      ]
   }
}
```

After defining the **PictureRepresentation** structure to contain the data and extending the **UTType** to include our content type, we initialize the model with three instances containing the images **spot1.jpg**, **spot2.jpg**, and **spot3.jpg**. The purpose of this application is to allow the user to drag these images from the top of the screen to a view at the bottom. Note that after dropping an image, we want that image to be deleted from the list, so we include a **UUID** value to identify it.

For the interface, we need a **ForEach** loop to list all the images available at the top and another **Image** view at the bottom where the user can drop them.

Listing 9-18: Dragging and dropping custom values

```
struct ContentView: View {
   @State private var appData = ApplicationData.shared
   @State private var currentPicture:
      UIImage = UIImage(named: "nopicture")!

   var body: some View {
      VStack {
         HStack(spacing: 10) {
            ForEach(appData.listPictures) { picture in
               Image(uiImage: UIImage(data: picture.image) ??
                  UIImage(named: "nopicture")!)
                  .resizable()
                  .frame(width: 80, height: 100)
                  .draggable(picture)
            }
         }.frame(height: 120)
         Image(uiImage: currentPicture)
            .resizable()
            .scaledToFit()
            .padding(10)
            .dropDestination(for: PictureRepresentation.self, action: {
               elements, location in
               if let picture = elements.first {
                  currentPicture = UIImage(data: picture.image) ??
                     UIImage(named: "nopicture")!
                  appData.listPictures.removeAll(where: {
                     $0.id == picture.id })
                  return true
               }
               return false
            })
      }
   }
}
```

The **draggable()** and **dropDestination()** modifiers work with the **PictureRepresentation** structure to transfer the data. When the user drags an image, the structure encodes the data, including the identifier and the image, and when the user drops the image into the target view, the data is decoded, an instance of the **PictureRepresentation** structure is created, and we can process the values. In this case, we assign the image to the **Image** view and then remove the original picture from the list. The result is shown below.

Figure 9-9: *Drag and drop custom data*

Do It Yourself

Create a Swift file called **ApplicationData.swift** for the code in Listing 9-17. Update the `ContentView` structure with the code in Listing 9-18. Download the **spot1.jpg**, **spot2.jpg** and **spot3.jpg** images from our website and add them to the Asset Catalog. Go to the project's settings, open the **Info** panel, expand the Exported Type Identifiers section, press the + button, and insert the values, as shown in Figure 9-8. Run the application on an iPhone simulator. Drag an image and drop it over the **nopicture.png** image. The original image should be removed from the list, as shown in Figure 9-9 (right).

IMPORTANT

SwiftUI also provides modifiers that allow multi-item drag-and-drop interactions, but they are currently available only on macOS. The topic is beyond the scope of this book. For more information, visit our website and follow the links for this chapter.

PRO

Clipboard

In Chapter 2, we learned how to enable text selection with the `textSelection()` modifier. When this modifier is applied to a view, the system automatically provides the standard tools for selecting its content. On iOS, users can tap and hold to open the contextual menu and choose Copy to copy the text, while on macOS they can drag the pointer to select the text and use the usual copy and paste commands. These system behaviors are often sufficient for most applications, but we can also use tools provided by SwiftUI and older frameworks to take direct control over clipboard interactions. For example, SwiftUI offers a view called `PasteButton` that lets the user paste the contents of the clipboard into a view.

```
PasteButton(payloadType: Type, onPaste: Closure)
```

This initializer creates a button that pastes the contents of the clipboard. The **payloadType** argument specifies the type of data the button accepts, and the **onPaste** argument is a closure that processes the pasted value.

When the user presses the `PasteButton`, the pasted value is passed to the closure assigned to the **onPaste** argument. This closure receives an array containing the contents of the clipboard, and we are responsible for processing or displaying those values. In the following example, we show how to extract the content when it is a string and assign it to a `Text` view to display it on the screen.

Listing 9-19: Pasting values from the clipboard

```
struct ContentView: View {
   @State private var pastedText = "Nothing pasted yet"

   var body: some View {
      VStack {
         Text("Always remember that you are absolutely unique. Just like
everyone else. - Margaret Mead")
            .padding()
            .background(.gray.opacity(0.5))
            .textSelection(.enabled)
         PasteButton(payloadType: String.self) { items in
            guard let firstItem = items.first else { return }
            pastedText = firstItem
         }.padding(.top, 30)

         Text(pastedText)
            .padding([.leading, .trailing])
      }.padding()
   }
}
```

This interface includes a `Text` view at the top containing text that can be copied to the clipboard, and a `PasteButton` that pastes the contents of the clipboard into a second `Text` view at the bottom. When the button is pressed, we retrieve the first item in the array and assign it to a binding property. As a result, the interface is updated and the text is displayed on the screen.

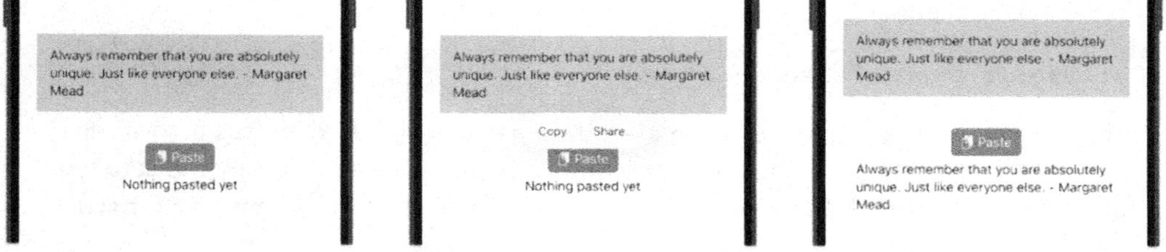

Figure 9-10: *Paste button*

Do It Yourself

Create a new App project. Update the **ContentView** structure with the code in Listing 9-19. Run the application on an iPhone simulator. Press and hold the **Text** view above the button until the contextual menu appears, as shown in Figure 9-10, center. Select Copy to copy the text, and press the Paste button to paste it. The copied text should appear below the button, as shown in Figure 9-10, right.

If we need more control over the process, we can use the **UIPasteboard** and **NSPasteboard** classes provided by the UIKit and AppKit frameworks. These two classes let us work with the clipboard, but they were designed to target different platforms. The **UIPasteboard** class is used on iOS, while **NSPasteboard** is used on macOS. The following are the most frequently used properties of the **UIPasteboard** class for writing to and retrieving values from the clipboard on iOS devices.

general

This type property returns the shared **UIPasteboard** instance that represents the system-wide clipboard.

string

This property sets or returns the first **String** value stored in the clipboard, or **nil** if no string is available. The class also provides the **strings** property to retrieve an array of string values currently stored in the clipboard.

image

This property sets or returns a **UIImage** value with the first image stored in the clipboard, or **nil** if no image is available. The class also provides the **images** property to retrieve an array of images currently stored in the clipboard.

The properties and methods defined by the **NSPasteboard** class are slightly different, but they serve the same purpose. The following are the most frequently used.

general

This type property returns the shared **NSPasteboard** instance that represents the system-wide clipboard.

string(forType: PasteboardType)

This method returns the first **String** value stored in the clipboard, or **nil** if no string is available. The **forType** argument is a structure with properties that specify the data type of the value to retrieve. Some of the properties available are **string**, **png**, **pdf**, **html** and **fileURL**.

data(forType: PasteboardType)

This method returns the first **Data** value stored in the clipboard, or **nil** if no data is available. The **forType** argument is a structure with properties that specify the data type of the value to retrieve. Some of the properties available are **string**, **png**, **pdf**, **html** and **fileURL**.

setString(String, forType: PasteboardType)

This method sends a string to the clipboard. The first argument is the string we want to copy, and the **forType** argument is a structure with properties that specify the data type of the value being copied. Some of the properties available are **string**, **png**, **pdf**, **html** and **fileURL**.

setData(Data, forType: PasteboardType)

This method sends data to the clipboard. The first argument is the data we want to copy, and the **forType** argument is a structure with properties that specify the data type of the value being copied. Some of the properties available are **string**, **png**, **pdf**, **html** and **fileURL**.

clearContents()

This method clears the clipboard to prepare it to receive new values.

The **UIPasteboard** class uses the same properties to write and read values from the clipboard, whereas the **NSPasteboard** class relies on specific methods to perform each operation. Although their APIs differ, the overall process is essentially the same. In the following example, we copy a piece of text and then paste it back to display it on the screen.

Listing 9-20: Copying and pasting values from the clipboard

```
struct ContentView: View {
   @State private var pastedText = ""

   var body: some View {
      VStack {
         HStack {
            Button("Copy") {
               #if os(macOS)
               let clip = NSPasteboard.general
               clip.clearContents()
               clip.setString("Hello, World!", forType: .string)
               #else
               let clip = UIPasteboard.general
               clip.string = "Hello, World!"
               #endif
            }.buttonStyle(.glass)
            Button("Paste") {
               #if os(macOS)
               let clip = NSPasteboard.general
               let text = clip.string(forType: .string)
               pastedText = text ?? "The clipboard is empty"
               #else
```

```
                let clip = UIPasteboard.general
                pastedText = clip.string ?? "The clipboard is empty"
                #endif
            }.buttonStyle(.glassProminent)
        }
        Text(pastedText)
            .padding()
    }.padding()
  }
}
```

This interface includes two buttons: one to copy text to the clipboard and another to retrieve it and display it on the screen. The code executed by each button depends on the platform. On macOS, we obtain a reference to the **NSPasteboard** instance that represents the system-wide clipboard and call its methods, on iOS, we access the shared **UIPasteboard** instance and read or write values through its properties, but the process is essentially the same. The result is shown below.

Figure 9-11: *Copy and paste buttons*

Do It Yourself

Update the **ContentView** structure with the code in Listing 9-20. Run the application on an iPhone simulator. Press the Paste button first. If there is no content on the clipboard, you should see the message "The clipboard is empty." Press the Copy button and then the Paste button again. This time, you should see the text copied to the clipboard displayed on the screen.

IMPORTANT

When the content of the clipboard originates from another application, the system may request the user's permission before allowing it to be pasted. This security feature was introduced in iOS to prevent apps from accessing clipboard data without the user's consent. To reduce how often this alert appears, use the **PasteButton** view instead.

Chapter 10

MapKit

BASIC

10.1 - Map View

Users usually need to visualize their current location or explore places they plan to visit on a map. To offer this feature, Apple provides the **MapKit** framework. This framework includes the tools required to create and configure maps, as well as the `Map` view, which allows us to display a map in our SwiftUI interface. The following are some of the view's initializers.

```
Map(initialPosition: MapCameraPosition, bounds: MapCameraBounds?,
interactionModes: MapInteractionModes, selection: Binding, scope:
Namespace.ID?, content: Closure)
```

This initializer creates a map with the configuration defined by the arguments. The **initialPosition** argument specifies the initial position of the camera. The **bounds** argument is a structure that defines the area of the map that the user is allowed to use. The **interactionModes** argument defines the user interaction allowed. It is a structure with the properties `all`, `pan`, `zoom`, `pitch`, and `rotate`. The **selection** argument is a binding property used to store the map item that was selected by the user. The **scope** argument is a value that can be used to identify the map and associate it with external controls. And the **content** argument specifies the additional content for the view.

```
Map(position: Binding, bounds: MapCameraBounds?,
interactionModes: MapInteractionModes, selection: Binding, scope:
Namespace.ID?, content: Closure)
```

This initializer creates a map with the configuration defined by the arguments. The **position** argument is a binding of type `MapCameraPosition` that sets and keeps track of the position of the camera. The **bounds** argument is a structure that defines the area of the map that the user is allowed to use. The **interactionModes** argument defines the user interaction allowed. It is a structure with the properties `all`, `pan`, `zoom`, `pitch`, and `rotate`. The **selection** argument is a binding property used to store the map item selected by the user. The **scope** argument is a value that can be used to identify the map and associate it with external controls. And the **content** argument specifies the additional content for the view.

If all we want is to display a map, we just need to insert the `Map` view without any parameters, as shown below.

Listing 10-1: Displaying a map

```
import SwiftUI
import MapKit

struct ContentView: View {
    var body: some View {
        Map()
            .ignoresSafeArea()
    }
}
```

The **Map** view takes up all available space, but considers the safe area before placing labels and tools, such as the Apple logo. If we want the view to ignore the safe area, we can apply the **ignoresSafeArea()** modifier, as we did in this example.

If we don't specify the position of the camera, the **Map** view shows the whole world, but the user can zoom in to find a location.

Figure 10-1: *Standard map*

By default, the view shows a representation of the map that includes the names of roads and locations, as well as icons to indicate points of interest, but it can also show a satellite image or a combination of both. To set the style, the framework includes the following modifier.

mapStyle(MapStyle**)**

This modifier sets the style of the map. The argument is a structure with properties and methods to define and configure the style.

The **MapStyle** structure includes the properties **hybrid**, **imagery**, and **standard** to represent the three possible styles, but also provides the following methods for configuration.

hybrid(elevation: Elevation, **pointsOfInterest:** PointOfInterestCategories, **showsTraffic:** Bool**)**

This method returns the style for rendering a hybrid map with the configuration specified by the arguments. The **elevation** argument specifies whether the map displays elevations. It is a structure with the properties **automatic** (standard 2D map), **flat** (2D map), and **realistic** (3D map). The **pointsOfInterest** argument is a structure with properties and methods for specifying the points of interest that the map should contain. And the **showsTraffic** argument determines whether the map should contain roads.

```
imagery(elevation: Elevation)
```

This method returns the style for rendering a satellite map with the configuration specified by the argument. The **elevation** argument specifies whether the map displays elevations. It is a structure with the properties **automatic** (standard 2D map), **flat** (2D map), and **realistic** (3D map).

```
standard(elevation: Elevation, emphasis: StandardEmphasis,
pointsOfInterest: PointOfInterestCategories, showsTraffic: Bool)
```

This method returns the style for rendering a standard map with the configuration specified by the arguments. The **elevation** argument specifies whether the map displays elevations. It is a structure with the properties **automatic** (standard 2D map), **flat** (2D map), and **realistic** (3D map). The **emphasis** argument determines whether map features are highlighted. It is a structure with the properties **automatic** and **muted**. The **pointsOfInterest** argument is a structure with properties and methods for specifying the points of interest that the map should contain. And the **showsTraffic** argument determines whether the map should contain roads.

If it is just a matter of displaying a particular map, we can apply the **mapStyle()** modifier with the property that represents the map we want to use.

Listing 10-2: Displaying a hybrid map

```
struct ContentView: View {
   var body: some View {
      Map()
         .mapStyle(.hybrid)
         .ignoresSafeArea()
   }
}
```

In this example, we use the **hybrid** property to get a map that shows satellite imagery along with roads, locations, and icons to represent points of interest.

Figure 10-2: *Hybrid map*

By default, the map displays all points of interest in the area, but we can select the ones we want by specifying an instance of the **PointOfInterestCategories** structure. The structure includes the following initializer.

PointOfInterestCategories(arrayLiteral: MKPointOfInterestCategory...**)**

This initializer creates a structure to represent points of interest. The **arrayLiteral** argument is a list of structures representing the points of interest to be included. The values are separated by commas.

The **PointOfInterestCategories** structure also defines the following type methods to include or exclude specific points of interest.

excluding([MKPointOfInterestCategory]**)**

This method returns a **PointOfInterestCategories** structure that excludes the points of interest specified by the argument.

including([MKPointOfInterestCategory]**)**

This method returns a **PointOfInterestCategories** structure that includes only the points of interest specified by the argument.

The points of interest are represented by an instance of the **MKPointOfInterestCategory** structure. The structure includes a long list of type properties to return structures that represent every category available. These properties are **airport**, **amusementPark**, **aquarium**, **atm**, **bakery**, **bank**, **beach**, **brewery**, **cafe**, **campground**, **carRental**, **evCharger**, **fireStation**, **fitnessCenter**, **foodMarket**, **gasStation**, **hospital**, **hotel**, **laundry**, **library**, **marina**, **movieTheater**, **museum**, **nationalPark**, **nightlife**, **parkparking**, **pharmacy**, **police**, **postOffice**, **publicTransport**, **restaurant**, **restroom**, **school**, **stadium**, **store**, **theater**, **university**, **winery**, and **zoo**.

With these properties, we can specify exactly what should be displayed on the map. For example, we can show only coffee shops.

Listing 10-3: Selecting points of interest

```
struct ContentView: View {
   var body: some View {
      Map()
         .mapStyle(.standard(pointsOfInterest: .including([.cafe])))
         .ignoresSafeArea()
   }
}
```

If we zoom in on the map enough to see a neighborhood, the **Map** view will automatically load and display icons representing the points of interest we have selected, as shown below.

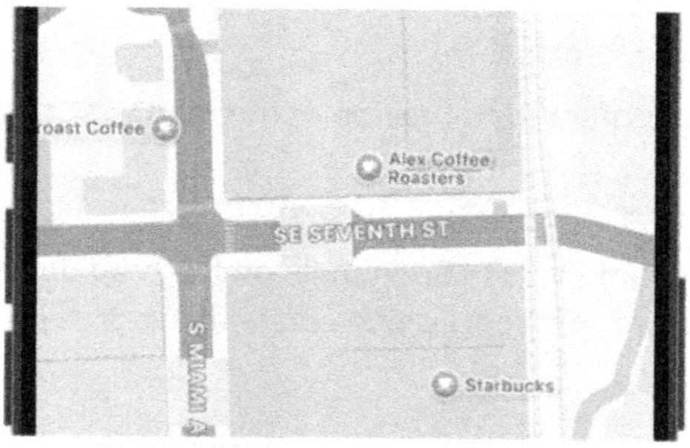

Figure 10-3: *Points of interest*

Do It Yourself

Create a new App project. Update the **`ContentView`** structure with the code in Listing 10-3. Run the application on an iPhone simulator. You should see a world map. Press and hold the Option key while dragging the mouse to zoom in until you see a neighborhood. You should see icons representing coffee shops, as shown in Figure 10-3.

BASIC

Camera

The area of the map that the user sees is determined by a camera. The **MapKit** framework includes the following structure to create it.

```
MapCamera(centerCoordinate: CLLocationCoordinate2D, distance: Double, heading: Double, pitch: Double)
```

This initializer creates a camera with the configuration defined by the arguments. The **centerCoordinate** argument specifies the coordinates at the center of the visible map, the **distance** argument specifies the distance in meters from the center of the visible map to the camera, the **heading** argument specifies the orientation of the camera in degrees relative to the true north, and the **pitch** argument specifies the viewing angle in degrees.

The **`Map`** view automatically creates a camera for us, so we don't have to provide our own, but it sets the camera's viewpoint to show the entire planet. To move the camera to a specific location, the framework includes the **`MapCameraPosition`** structure. This structure defines the **`automatic`** property to ask the system to determine the camera's position, as well as the following methods to set a specific position.

```
camera(MapCamera)
```

This method configures the camera based on the configuration of the camera specified by the argument.

```
region(MKCoordinateRegion)
```

This method directs the camera to the region of the map specified by the argument.

```
rect(MKMapRect)
```

This method directs the camera to the rectangle on the map defined by the argument. The argument is a structure that represents a rectangular area on a two-dimensional map.

```
item(MKMapItem, allowsAutomaticPitch: Bool)
```

This method directs the camera to the point of interest indicated by the first argument. The first argument is a structure representing a point of interest or the user's location, and the **allowsAutomaticPitch** argument determines whether the camera automatically selects a pitch.

```
userLocation(followsHeading: Bool, fallback: MapCameraPosition)
```

This method directs the camera to the user's location. The **followsHeading** argument determines whether the camera should follow the user, and the **fallback** argument specifies a position the camera should point to when the user's location cannot be determined.

The most frequently used method for setting the camera position is `region()`. This method requires the region to be specified with an `MKCoordinateRegion` structure. The structure includes the following initializer.

```
MKCoordinateRegion(center: CLLocationCoordinate2D,
latitudinalMeters: CLLocationDistance, longitudinalMeters:
CLLocationDistance)
```

This initializer creates an `MKCoordinateRegion` structure with the values specified by the arguments. The **center** argument specifies the region's coordinates, and the **latitudinalMeters** and **longitudinalMeters** arguments determine the vertical and horizontal size of the region in meters (`CLLocationDistance` is a typealias of `Double`).

The latitude and longitude of a location are determined by a `CLLocationCoordinate2D` structure. The structure includes the following initializer.

```
CLLocationCoordinate2D(latitude: CLLocationDegrees, longitude:
CLLocationDegrees)
```

This initializer creates a `CLLocationCoordinate2D` structure with the values specified by the arguments. The **latitude** argument is a typealias of `Double` that determines the location's latitude, and the **longitude** argument is a typealias of `Double` that determines the location's longitude.

With these values, we can move the camera and zoom in and out the map to show the area we want, but because they may change or more may be required later, it is better to manage the location from the data model, as we do in the following example.

Listing 10-4: Configuring the map from the data model

```
import SwiftUI
import MapKit

@Observable class ApplicationData {
   var cameraPos: MapCameraPosition

   static let shared: ApplicationData = ApplicationData()
   private init() {
      let coordinates = CLLocationCoordinate2D(latitude: 40.7637825011971,
         longitude: -73.9731328627541)
      let region = MKCoordinateRegion(center: coordinates,
         latitudinalMeters: 1000, longitudinalMeters: 1000)
      cameraPos = MapCameraPosition.region(region)
   }
}
```

In this model, we include a property to store the **MapCameraPosition** structure, and then initialize it with the coordinates of the Apple Store in New York City and a region of 1000 meters around that location. Now we can set the map to this location.

Listing 10-5: Zooming in on a region of the map

```
struct ContentView: View {
   @State private var appData = ApplicationData.shared

   var body: some View {
      Map(position: $appData.cameraPos)
   }
}
```

When we specify a location, the map is automatically zoomed to that region. In this case, that is the area around the Apple Store in New York City.

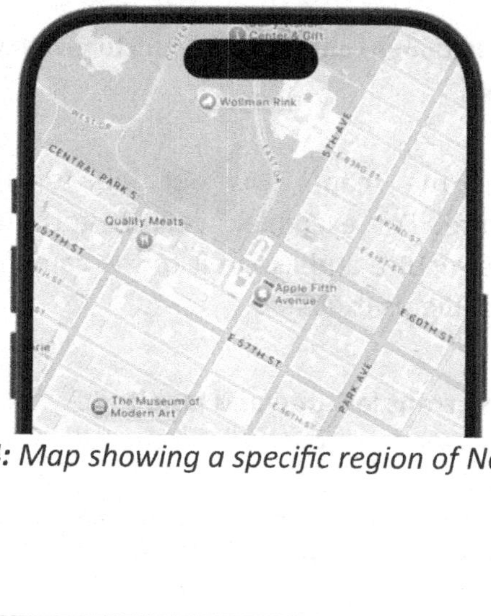

Figure 10-4: *Map showing a specific region of New York City*

Do It Yourself

Create a Swift file called **ApplicationData.swift** for the code in Listing 10-4. Update the **ContentView** structure with the code in Listing 10-5. Run the application on an iPhone simulator. You should see the map of New York City with the Apple Store at the center.

In the previous example, we specified the map's initial location, but when the user scrolls the map, the location of the camera is not updated. To respond to these changes, the framework includes the following modifier.

onMapCameraChange(frequency: MapCameraUpdateFrequency, Closure)

This modifier executes a closure when the location of the camera changes. The **frequency** argument determines how often the system should check for updates. It is a structure with the properties **continuous** (while the interaction is taking place) and **onEnd** (when the interaction is over).

The closure assigned to the **onMapCameraChange()** modifier receives a **MapCameraUpdateContext** structure with information about the camera. The structure includes the following properties.

camera

This property returns a reference to the **MapCamera** structure that represents the camera assigned to the map.

rect

This property returns an **MKMapRect** structure with a rectangle representing the visible area on the map.

region

This property returns an **MKCoordinateRegion** structure with values representing the visible region on the map.

When the user scrolls the map, it is our job to update the values in the **MapCameraPosition** structure. For example, we can get the region returned by the **MapCameraUpdateContext** structure and assign it to the camera every time the closure of the **onMapCameraChange** modifier is executed.

Listing 10-6: Showing the current latitude and longitude

```
struct ContentView: View {
   @State private var appData = ApplicationData.shared
```

```
    var body: some View {
        Map(position: $appData.cameraPos)
            .safeAreaInset(edge: .bottom) {
                HStack {
                    if let region = appData.cameraPos.region {
                        Text(String(region.center.latitude))
                        Text(String(region.center.longitude))
                    }
                }.padding([.top, .bottom])
                .frame(minWidth: 0, maxWidth: .infinity)
                .background(.white)
            }
            .onMapCameraChange { context in
                appData.cameraPos = .region(context.region)
            }
    }
}
```

Once the **`MapCameraPosition`** structure is updated, we can use this value to present information to the user. In this example, we display the current latitude and longitude at the bottom of the map. Note that we use the **`safeAreaInset()`** modifier so that the safe area is expanded and the view does not obscure the labels on the map.

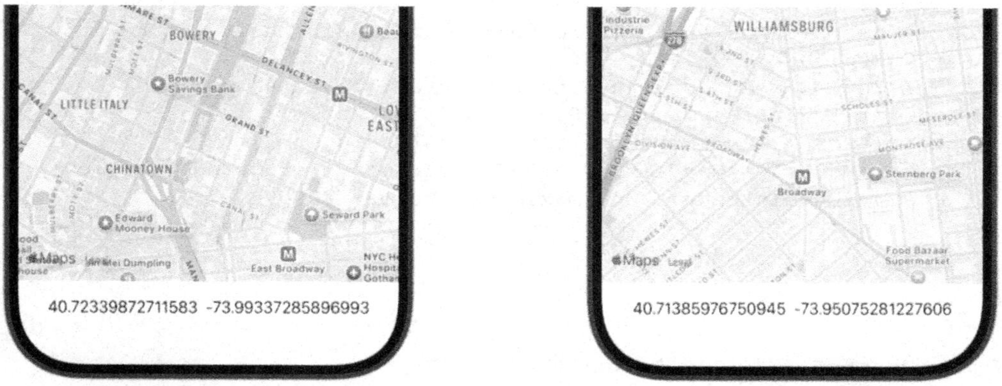

Figure 10-5: *Current latitude and longitude*

By default, the **`Map`** view allows the user to zoom and pan the map, but the view's initializer can include the **interactionModes** argument to restrict interaction. For example, we can enable only zooming to not allow the user to change the region.

Listing 10-7: Disabling panning

```
struct ContentView: View {
    @State private var appData = ApplicationData.shared

    var body: some View {
        Map(position: $appData.cameraPos, interactionModes: .zoom)
    }
}
```

Another option is to limit the area through which the user can navigate. The framework includes the following structure to determine the area available to the user.

```
MapCameraBounds(centerCoordinateBounds: MKCoordinateRegion,
minimumDistance: Double?, maximumDistance: Double?)
```

This initializer creates a **MapCameraBounds** structure to limit user interaction. The **centerCoordinateBounds** argument determines the center of the visible area, and the **minimumDistance** and **maximumDistance** arguments specify how large this area may be.

If we specify the **centerCoordinateBounds** argument, the structure limits how far the user can scroll the map, and if this argument is ignored, the structure limits how far the user can zoom in or out. For example, in the following application, the user cannot move further than 1000 meters from the center. As always, we define the values in the data model, but they could also be provided by the view or a method.

Listing 10-8: Defining the boundaries for the camera

```
@Observable class ApplicationData {
   var cameraPos: MapCameraPosition
   var cameraBounds: MapCameraBounds

   static let shared: ApplicationData = ApplicationData()
   private init() {
      let coordinates = CLLocationCoordinate2D(latitude: 40.7637825011971,
         longitude: -73.9731328627541)
      let region = MKCoordinateRegion(center: coordinates,
         latitudinalMeters: 1000, longitudinalMeters: 1000)
      cameraPos = MapCameraPosition.region(region)
      cameraBounds = MapCameraBounds(centerCoordinateBounds: region,
         minimumDistance: 200, maximumDistance: 1000)
   }
}
```

Applying this bounds to the camera is easy. All we need to do is to provide the **MapCameraBounds** structure to the **Map** view initializer.

Listing 10-9: Applying the boundaries to the map

```
struct ContentView: View {
   @State private var appData = ApplicationData.shared

   var body: some View {
      Map(position: $appData.cameraPos, bounds: appData.cameraBounds)
   }
}
```

Do It Yourself

Update the **ApplicationData** class with the code in Listing 10-8 and the **ContentView** structure with the code in Listing 10-9. Run the application on an iPhone simulator. You shouldn't be able to scroll the map more than 1000 meters.

Map Content

The previous examples set the visible area around the Apple Store. Since this is a relevant location, the **Map** view displays an icon with the name of the store, but this is not always the case. For most locations, no indication is shown at all, and the user has to guess where the location actually is. To mark locations, the framework includes the **Marker** structure. The following are some of the structure's initializers.

Marker(String, **coordinate:** CLLocationCoordinate2D**)**

This initializer creates a standard pin for a **Map** view with the title and at the location specified by the arguments. The first argument specifies the text that appears under the pin, and the **coordinate** argument specifies the location.

Marker(item: MKMapItem**)**

This initializer creates a standard pin for a **Map** view that represents the map item specified by the argument. The **item** argument is a structure used to represent a location.

The **Marker** structure adds a standard pin to the map. If we need more customization, we can create an annotation instead. For this purpose, the framework provides the **Annotation** structure.

Annotation(String, **coordinate:** CLLocationCoordinate2D**, anchor:** UnitPoint**, content:** Closure**)**

This initializer creates an annotation for a **Map** view. The first argument specifies the text that appears under the annotation, the **coordinate** argument specifies the location, the **anchor** argument determines where to position the annotation around that location, and the **content** argument defines the views that represent the annotation.

The **Marker** and **Annotation** structures display a title below the pin. The framework includes the following modifier to specify the visibility of this title.

annotationTitles(Visibility**)**

This modifier determines the visibility of the pin's title. The argument is an enumeration with the values **automatic**, **visible**, and **hidden**.

The framework also includes the following structures for using graphics to represent areas on the map.

MapCircle(center: CLLocationCoordinate2D**, radius:** CLLocationDistance**)**

This initializer creates a circular overlay to represent an area on the map. The **center** argument specifies the location, and the **radius** argument specifies the radius of the circle.

MapPolygon(coordinates: [CLLocationCoordinate2D])

This initializer creates a polygonal overlay to represent an area on the map. The **coordinates** argument is an array with the locations of each corner of the polygon.

MapPolyline(coordinates: [CLLocationCoordinate2D], **contourStyle:** ContourStyle)

This initializer creates an overlay with a single line. The **coordinates** argument is an array of locations for the line to follow, and the **contourStyle** argument specifies the style of the line. This is a structure with the properties **geodesic** (the line follows the contours of the earth) and **straight** (a straight line between points).

The overlays are displayed along with the rest of the content, including labels and icons. To determine which content should be displayed on top, the framework provides the following modifier.

mapOverlayLevel(level: MKOverlayLevel)

This modifier specifies the position of the overlay. The **level** argument is an enumeration with the values **aboveRoads** and **aboveLabels**.

The framework also includes a list of modifiers for styling overlays, pins and annotations.

tint(ShapeStyle)

This modifier applies a color or pattern to the view. The argument is a value that conforms to the **ShapeStyle** protocol, such as **Color**.

stroke(ShapeStyle, **lineWidth:** CGFloat)

This modifier applies a stroke with the style specified by the arguments. The first argument is a value that conforms to the **ShapeStyle** protocol, such as **Color**, and the **lineWidth** argument specifies the width of the stroke.

stroke(ShapeStyle, **style:** StrokeStyle)

This modifier applies a stroke with the style specified by the arguments. The first argument is a value that conforms to the **ShapeStyle** protocol, such as **Color**, and the **style** argument specifies the style.

foregroundStyle(ShapeStyle)

This modifier fills the view with the color or pattern specified by the argument. The argument is a value that conforms to the **ShapeStyle** protocol, such as **Color**.

The markers, annotations and graphics are added to the map from the closure assigned to the **Map** view's initializer. For example, we can add a marker at the location of the Apple Store in New York City.

Listing 10-10: Adding markers to the map

```
struct ContentView: View {
    @State private var appData = ApplicationData.shared
    let coordinatesApple = CLLocationCoordinate2D(latitude:
       40.7637825011971, longitude: -73.9731328627541)

    var body: some View {
       Map(position: $appData.cameraPos) {
          Marker("Apple Store", coordinate: coordinatesApple)
             .tint(.blue)
       }
    }
}
```

In this example, we store the location of the Apple Store in a property and use that value to add a marker to the map. The marker is represented by a red pin, but we change its color to blue with the **tint()** modifier. The result is shown below.

Figure 10-6: *Marker*

The **Marker** view creates a pin in the shape of a balloon. We can change the color, the title, and the symbol inside the balloon, but if we want more customization, we need to create an annotation. Annotations work like markers, but can be represented by any view we want. In the following example, we use an **Image** view with the picture of the Apple Store.

Listing 10-11: Displaying annotations

```
struct ContentView: View {
    @State private var appData = ApplicationData.shared
    let coordinatesApple = CLLocationCoordinate2D(latitude:
       40.7637825011971, longitude: -73.9731328627541)

    var body: some View {
       Map(position: $appData.cameraPos) {
          Annotation("Apple Store", coordinate: coordinatesApple,
             content: {
             Image("appstore")
          })
       }
```

```
    }
}
```

Figure 10-7: *Annotation*

Do It Yourself

Update the **ContentView** structure with the code in Listing 10-10. Run the application on an iPhone simulator. You should see a blue pin at the Apple Store location in New York City (Figure 10-6). Update the **Map** view with the code in Listing 10-11. Download the **appstore.png** image from our website and add it to the Asset Catalog. Run the application again. You should see a custom marker with the picture of the Apple Store, as shown in Figure 10-7.

If what we need is to highlight an area of the map, we can show graphics instead. In the following example, we display a circle at the Apple Store location.

Listing 10-12: Drawing a circle over the labels

```
struct ContentView: View {
   @State private var appData = ApplicationData.shared
   let coordinatesApple = CLLocationCoordinate2D(latitude:
      40.7637825011971, longitude: -73.9731328627541)

   var body: some View {
      Map(position: $appData.cameraPos) {
         MapCircle(center: coordinatesApple, radius: 100)
            .foregroundStyle(.blue)
            .mapOverlayLevel(level: .aboveLabels)
      }
   }
}
```

In this example, we apply the **mapOverlayLevel()** modifier to the **MapCircle** view to draw the circle over the labels. Figure 10-8, below, shows the difference when the modifier is applied or not.

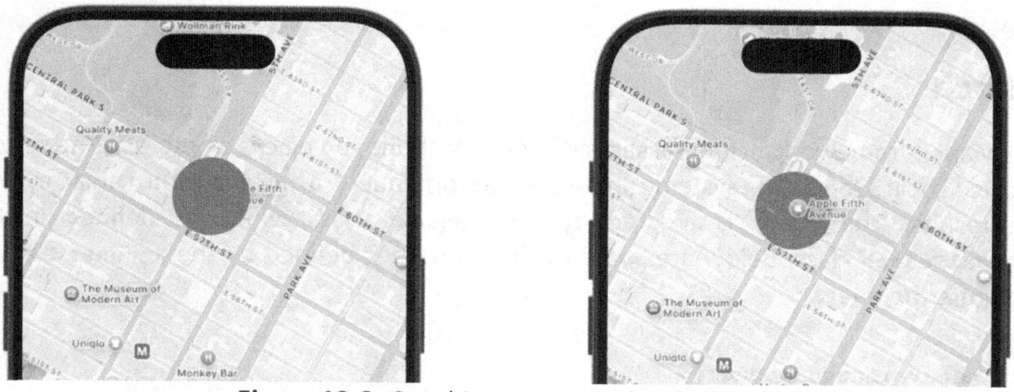

Figure 10-8: Graphics over or under the labels

In addition to circles, we can also draw rectangles and lines to represent areas on the map. In the following example, we show how to draw a line from the Apple Store to Trump Tower in New York City.

Listing 10-13: Drawing a line

```
struct ContentView: View {
   @State private var appData = ApplicationData.shared
   let coordinatesApple = CLLocationCoordinate2D(latitude:
      40.7637825011971, longitude: -73.9731328627541)
   let coordinatesTower = CLLocationCoordinate2D(latitude:
      40.76260429912616, longitude: -73.97378658614556)

   var body: some View {
      Map(position: $appData.cameraPos) {
         MapPolyline(coordinates: [coordinatesApple, coordinatesTower])
            .stroke(.red, lineWidth: 5)
      }
   }
}
```

The **MapPolyline** view draws a straight line between two or more points on the map, but it can also be used to trace routes, as we will see later. In this example, we use it to show the direct connection between two locations. Note that we use the **stroke()** modifier to draw the line in red and with a width of 5 points.

Figure 10-9: Straight lines between locations

BASIC

Search

The MapKit framework includes a service to find locations and places of interest. The service is called Local Search. The system can take a free-form query string and return an array with the results. The query is created by the **Request** class, which is defined in the **MKLocalSearch** class. Below are some of the properties defined by the **Request** class to configure the query.

naturalLanguageQuery

This property sets or returns a string with the term or address we want to search.

region

This property sets or returns an **MKCoordinateRegion** structure that specifies the region in which the search is performed.

To perform a search, the **MKLocalSearch** class includes the following initializer and method.

MKLocalSearch(request: MKLocalSearchRequest**)**

This initializer creates an **MKLocalSearch** object to perform a search request.

start()

This asynchronous method performs a search and returns an **MKLocalSearchResponse** object with the results.

The search returns an **MKLocalSearchResponse** object that contains the following properties.

mapItems

This property returns an array of **MKMapItem** objects that represent the results produced by the search.

boundingRegion

This property returns an **MKCoordinateRegion** structure that determines the region occupied by the results produced by the search.

The Local Search service is designed to find all the locations that match the query. The framework defines the **MKMapItem** class to represent a location. Below are some of the properties included in the class to return the data.

name

This property sets or returns a string with the name of the location.

phoneNumber

This property sets or returns a string with the location's phone number.

url

This property sets or returns a **URL** value with the URL of the location's website.

address

This property sets or returns an **MKAddress** structure with the location's address. The structure includes the properties **fullAddress** and **shortAddress** to return strings with the complete address or an abbreviated version.

addressRepresentations

This property sets or returns an **MKAddressRepresentations** object that describes the location's address. The structure provides the **cityName**, **cityWithContext**, **regionName**, and **region** properties to retrieve specific components of the address, and also the methods **fullAddress(includingRegion: Bool, singleLine: Bool)** and **cityWithContext(_:)**, which allow us to generate a formatted address using the desired options.

location

This property sets or returns a **CLLocation** structure to determine the coordinates of the location. The structure includes the **coordinate** property that we can use to retrieve the **CLLocationCoordinate2D** structure with the location's latitude and longitude.

There are several ways an app can perform a search and display the results. As an example, we can search for places related to the word "Pizza" every time the position of the camera changes. First, we need a property in the model to store the locations found by the system and a method to perform the search.

Listing 10-14: Finding places with Local Search

```
import SwiftUI
import MapKit

@Observable class ApplicationData {
   var cameraPos: MapCameraPosition
   var listLocations: [MKMapItem] = []

   static let shared: ApplicationData = ApplicationData()
   private init() {
      let coordinates = CLLocationCoordinate2D(latitude: 40.7637825011971,
longitude: -73.9731328627541)
      let region = MKCoordinateRegion(center: coordinates,
latitudinalMeters: 1000, longitudinalMeters: 1000)
      cameraPos = MapCameraPosition.region(region)
   }
   func findPlaces() async {
      if let region = cameraPos.region {
```

```
            let request = MKLocalSearch.Request()
            request.naturalLanguageQuery = "Pizza"
            request.region = region

            let search = MKLocalSearch(request: request)
            if let results = try? await search.start() {
               let items = results.mapItems
               listLocations = []
               for place in items {
                  listLocations.append(place)
               }
            }
         }
      }
   }
```

Now we can perform a search, store the results in the model, and display the locations on the map.

Listing 10-15: Searching for places

```
struct ContentView: View {
   @State private var appData = ApplicationData.shared

   var body: some View {
      Map(position: $appData.cameraPos) {
         ForEach(appData.listLocations, id: \.self) { place in
            Marker(item: place)
         }
      }
      .onMapCameraChange(frequency: .onEnd) { context in
         appData.cameraPos = .region(context.region)
         Task {
            await appData.findPlaces()
         }
      }
   }
}
```

This code defines the **findPlaces()** method to search for places associated with the term "Pizza" and adds each location found to the **listLocations** property. When the view is loaded, the **onMapCameraChange()** modifier calls this method asynchronously to start the process. The method creates a request with the query "Pizza" and the region the camera is pointed at. This query is used to create the **MKLocalSearch** object, and then the search is initiated by calling the **start()** method. This method is asynchronous, so we have to wait for the results. Once the results come back from Apple servers, we remove the current locations in the **listLocations** property and save the new ones found by the search. The **Map** view is updated and the **Marker** views are created to display the current locations.

Figure 10-10: *Places found by the Local Search system*

Do It Yourself

Update the **ApplicationData.swift** file with the code in Listing 10-14 and the **`ContentView`** structure with the code in Listing 10-15. Run the application on an iPhone simulator. You should see the pizzerias around the Apple Store in New York City. Scroll across the map. The app should search for and display the pizzerias around the new location.

BASIC

Selection

The **`Map`** view allows users to select locations on the map. To enable this feature, we just need to provide a binding property to store the value that identifies the selected item and initialize the **`Map`** view with that property. The framework includes the **`MapSelection`** structure to store the selected value.

`MapSelection``(SelectionValue)`

This initializer creates a structure to store the identifier of the item selected by the user. The argument is the value we use to identify the item.

The **`MapSelection`** structure includes the following properties to return the information about the selected item.

`value`

This property returns the value used to identify the item selected by the user.

`feature`

This property returns a **`MapFeature`** structure with information about the feature selected by the user.

The **MapSelection** structure is generic, so we can use any value we want to identify the markers. In the following example, we create a property to store the selected value and then use the **MKMapItem** value to identify the markers. When a marker is selected by the user, the **MapSelection** structure associated with that marker is assigned to the property so we know which one was selected.

Listing 10-16: Selecting markers

```
struct ContentView: View {
   @State private var appData = ApplicationData.shared
   @State private var selectedItem: MapSelection<MKMapItem>?

   var body: some View {
      Map(position: $appData.cameraPos, selection: $selectedItem) {
         ForEach(appData.listLocations, id: \.self) { place in
            Marker(item: place)
               .tag(MapSelection(place))
         }
      }
      .onMapCameraChange(frequency: .onEnd) { context in
         if selectedItem == nil {
            appData.cameraPos = .region(context.region)
            Task {
               await appData.findPlaces()
            }
         }
      }
      .onChange(of: selectedItem, { old, value in
         if let item = value?.value {
            print(item.name ?? "Undefined")
            print(item.phoneNumber ?? "Undefined")
            print(item.addressRepresentations?.cityName ?? "Undefined")
         }
      })
   }
}
```

When a marker is selected by the user, the **Map** view assigns the marker's identifier to the **selectedItem** property. It is now up to us to process the selected value and do something with it. In this example, we just print some of the values to the console, but we could also have saved them in the model or displayed them to the user. Displaying information to the user is actually quite common in this type of application. For this reason, the framework includes some modifiers to simplify our work.

> **mapItemDetailSelectionAccessory**(MapItemDetailSelectionAccessoryStyle)

This modifier specifies the type of accessory to be shown when an item on the map is selected. The argument is a structure with the properties **automatic**, **callout**, **caption** and **sheet**, and also the **callout(CalloutStyle)** method to select a specific callout style (**automatic**, **compact** or **full**).

mapFeatureSelectionAccessory(MapItemDetailSelection AccessoryStyle)

This modifier specifies the type of accessory to be shown when a feature on the map is selected. The argument is a structure with the properties **automatic**, **callout**, **caption** and **sheet**, and also the **callout(CalloutStyle)** method to select a specific callout style (**automatic**, **compact** or **full**).

The **mapItemDetailSelectionAccessory()** modifier is applied to the markers. For example, we can use it to show a small callout window with additional information for the location selected by the user.

Listing 10-17: Showing a callout with additional information

```
Map(position: $appData.cameraPos, selection: $selectedItem) {
    ForEach(appData.listLocations, id: \.self) { place in
        Marker(item: place)
            .tag(MapSelection(place))
    }
    .mapItemDetailSelectionAccessory(.callout)
}
```

Figure 10-11: *Map callouts*

There are different styles for the callout. We can show only a link to Apple Maps, a small callout (Figure 10-11), or open a popover or a sheet. Showing the information in a popover or a sheet is useful because it allows us to include more valuable data about a location. Since we may need to open this sheets outside the **Map** view, the framework includes the following modifiers.

mapItemDetailSheet(isPresented: Binding, **item:** MKMapItem, **displaysMap:** Bool)

This modifier opens a view in a sheet with information about a location. The **isPresented** argument is a Boolean binding property that determines if the sheet is open or not, the **item** argument specifies the location we want to show, and the **displaysMap** argument determines whether the sheet is going to include a small map showing the location.

```
mapItemDetailPopover(isPresented: Binding, item: MKMapItem,
displaysMap: Bool, attachmentAnchor: PopoverAttachmentAnchor,
arrowEdge: Edge)
```

This modifier opens a view in a popover with information about a location. The **isPresented** argument is a Boolean binding property that determines if the popover is open or not, the **item** argument specifies the location we want to show, the **displaysMap** argument determines whether the sheet is going to include a small map showing the location, the **attachmentAnchor** argument is an enumeration with two cases, `point()` and `rect()`, to specify a point or a rectangle inside the view where the popover is going to be anchored, and the **arrowEdge** argument is an enumeration that determines the direction of the arrow (`top`, `bottom`, `leading` and `trailing`).

These modifiers can be applied to any view. All we need is a binding property that stores a Boolean value to control the sheet or popover, and an action to change the value of this property when we want the view to be opened. In the following example, we use the `onChange()` modifier for this purpose. Every time a new marker is selected by the user, a sheet opens to display additional information.

Listing 10-18: Opening a sheet with additional information

```
struct ContentView: View {
   @State private var appData = ApplicationData.shared
   @State private var selectedItem: MapSelection<MKMapItem>?
   @State private var showCallout = false

   var body: some View {
      Map(position: $appData.cameraPos, selection: $selectedItem) {
         ForEach(appData.listLocations, id: \.self) { place in
            Marker(item: place)
               .tag(MapSelection(place))
         }
      }
      .onMapCameraChange(frequency: .onEnd) { context in
         appData.cameraPos = .region(context.region)
         Task {
            await appData.findPlaces()
         }
      }
      .onChange(of: selectedItem, { old, value in
         if value != nil {
            showCallout = true
         }
      })
      .mapItemDetailSheet(isPresented: $showCallout, item: selectedItem?.
value, displaysMap: true)
   }
}
```

In this example, we use the same map and locations as before to show how to open a sheet, but sheet and popovers can be opened from anywhere in the app as long as we have the `MKMapItem` structure that represents the location we want to show.

Figure 10-12: Map sheets

PRO

Controls

A map can display controls on the screen to change the map orientation, check the zoom level, find the user's location, and more. The framework includes the following modifiers to add these controls to the map.

mapControls(Closure)

This modifier adds controls to the map. The argument is a closure that provides the views to create the controls to be included.

mapControlVisibility(Visibility)

This modifier determines the visibility of the controls. The argument is an enumeration with the values **automatic**, **visible** and **hidden**.

mapScope(Namespace.ID)

This modifier creates a space to connect external controls to the map.

Each control is represented by a view and added to the map from the closure assigned to the **mapControls()** modifier. The following are the views available to create controls for iOS applications (the framework also defines views to present controls that are exclusive to Mac computers).

MapCompass(scope: Namespace.ID?)

This initializer creates a view that displays the current orientation of the map. The **scope** argument specifies the space used to connect the control with a map.

MapPitchToggle(scope: Namespace.ID?)

This initializer creates a view that displays a button to toggle the map between 2D and 3D representations. The **scope** argument specifies the space used to connect the control with a map.

MapScaleView(anchorEdge: HorizontalEdge, scope: Namespace.ID?)

This initializer creates a view that displays the zoom level of the map. The **anchorEdge** argument determines the side from which the scale grows. It is an enumeration with the values **leading** and **trailing**. And the **scope** argument specifies the space used to connect the control with a map.

MapUserLocationButton(scope: Namespace.ID?)

This initializer creates a view that displays a button to show the user's location. The **scope** argument specifies the space used to connect the control with a map.

Adding controls is simple. We need to apply the **mapControls()** modifier to the **Map** view and provide all the views we want to include. In the following example, we add a compass, a scale view, and a pitch toggle.

Listing 10-19: Displaying map controls

```
struct ContentView: View {
   @State private var appData = ApplicationData.shared

   var body: some View {
      Map(position: $appData.cameraPos)
         .mapControls {
            MapCompass()
            MapScaleView()
            MapPitchToggle()
         }
         .mapControlVisibility(.visible)
   }
}
```

In this example, we also included the **mapControlVisibility()** modifier to keep the controls visible, but some controls are still hidden until the user performs an action. For example, the compass is only shown on the screen when the map is rotated.

***Figure 10-13:** Map controls*

The position of the controls on the screen is automatically determined by the **Map** view. If we want to customize the interface, we need to define the controls as independent views and associate them to the map using a namespace. A namespace is declared with the

@Namespace property wrapper and is used to provide a name that objects and structures can use to identify themselves. To connect the **Map** view to the control views, we need to declare a property with the namespace we want to use and then assign it to all the views involved, including the **Map** view and the control views. In addition, we must implement the **mapScope()** modifier to create a scope that the views can use to connect to each other, as shown below.

Listing 10-20: Creating custom controls

```
struct ContentView: View {
   @State private var appData = ApplicationData.shared
   @Namespace var mapSpace

   var body: some View {
      Map(position: $appData.cameraPos, scope: mapSpace)
         .mapControlVisibility(.hidden)
         .safeAreaInset(edge: .top) {
            HStack {
               MapPitchToggle(scope: mapSpace)
                  .padding(5)
                  .background {
                     Circle()
                        .fill(.thinMaterial)
                        .stroke(.red, lineWidth: 3)
                  }
            }.padding()
            .frame(minWidth: 0, maxWidth: .infinity)
         }
         .mapScope(mapSpace)
   }
}
```

For this example, we create a namespace called **mapSpace** and define a scope for the map using the **mapScope()** modifier. After establishing this scope, we assign it to each relevant view so the **Map** view and the control view remain connected. In the interface, we place a pitch toggle at the center of the screen to let the user switch between a 2D and a 3D map. The result is shown below.

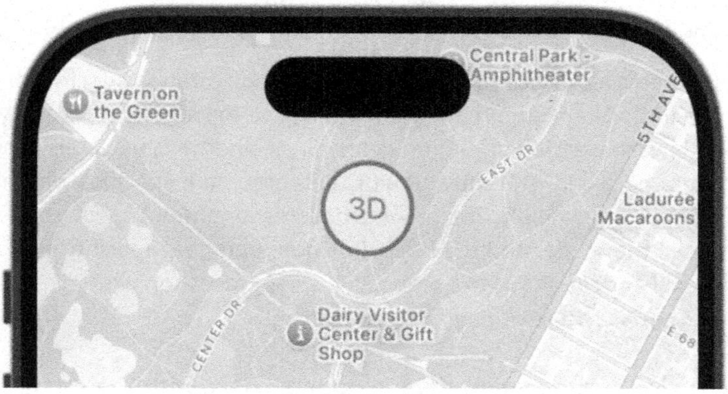

Figure 10-14: *Custom control*

PRO

Look Around

The **Map** view includes a feature called *Look Around*, which provides interactive street-level panoramas, similar to the Street View service provided by Google Map. To enable this feature, we need to perform a request to Apple servers with the location we want to show to the user. The MapKit framework includes the **MKLookAroundSceneRequest** class for this purpose. The following are the initializers.

MKLookAroundSceneRequest(coordinate: CLLocationCoordinate2D)

This initializer creates a Look Around request for the location specified by the argument.

MKLookAroundSceneRequest(mapItem: MKMapItem)

This initializer creates a Look Around request for the location of the item specified by the argument.

The scenes returned by Apple servers are represented by an **MKLookAroundScene** object. This is a utility class that encapsulates all the information needed to render the scene for the user. To get this object, the **MKLookAroundSceneRequest** structure includes the following property.

scene

This property returns the **MKLookAroundScene** object produced by the request or **nil** in case of failure.

There are two ways to present this scene to the user. We can create a preview that the user can tap to open the scene, or present the scene directly with a modifier. To create the preview, the framework defines the **LookAroundPreview** structure. The following is the most frequently used initializer.

LookAroundPreview(initialScene: MKLookAroundScene?, **allowsNavigation:** Bool, **showsRoadLabels:** Bool, **pointsOfInterest:** PointOfInterestCategories, **badgePosition:** MKLookAroundBadgePosition)

This initializer creates a preview of a scene with the configuration specified by the arguments. The **initialScene** argument is a reference to the scene returned by the request. The **allowsNavigation** argument determines whether the user is allowed to navigate through the scene. The **showsRoadLabels** argument specifies whether the scene should display road labels. The **pointsOfInterest** argument specifies the items we want to include in the scene. And the **badgePosition** argument specifies the position of the labels that will appear above the scene. It is an enumeration with the values **bottomTrailing**, **topLeading** and **topTrailing**.

The framework also includes modifiers to open a sheet with the scene and all the tools for the user to navigate. The following is the most frequently used.

```
lookAroundViewer(isPresented: Binding, initialScene:
MKLookAroundScene?, allowsNavigation: Bool, showsRoadLabels:
Bool, pointsOfInterest: PointOfInterestCategories, onDismiss:
Closure)
```

This initializer opens a sheet with a scene configured with the values specified in the arguments. The **isPresented** argument is a Boolean binding property that determines whether the sheet is open or not. The **initialScene** argument is a reference to the scene returned by the request. The **allowsNavigation** argument determines whether the user is allowed to navigate through the scene. The **showsRoadLabels** argument specifies whether the scene should display road labels. The **pointsOfInterest** argument specifies the items we want to include in the scene. And the **onDismiss** argument is the closure that should be executed when the sheet is closed.

The following example shows how to perform a request for a scene and how to present a preview to the user. As we did in previous examples, we are going to manage the process from the data model.

Listing 10-21: Creating a Look Around preview

```
@Observable class ApplicationData {
   var cameraPos: MapCameraPosition
   var openView: Bool = false
   var lookScene: MKLookAroundScene?

   static let shared: ApplicationData = ApplicationData()
   private init() {
      let coordinates = CLLocationCoordinate2D(latitude: 40.7637825011971,
         longitude: -73.9731328627541)
      let region = MKCoordinateRegion(center: coordinates,
         latitudinalMeters: 1000, longitudinalMeters: 1000)
      cameraPos = MapCameraPosition.region(region)
   }
   func lookAround() {
      if let region = cameraPos.region {
         Task {
            let request = MKLookAroundSceneRequest(coordinate:
               region.center)
            if let scene = try? await request.scene {
               lookScene = scene
               openView = true
            }
         }
      }
   }
}
```

This model includes two properties, one to control the view and another to store the `MKLookAroundScene` object, as well as a method to create it. After the object is initialized, we request the scene of the camera's location from Apple servers and assign the information to the properties when the values are received.

In the view, we need to present the preview with the `LookAroundPreview` structure and provide the buttons for the user to start and finish the process.

Listing 10-22: Creating a Look Around preview

```
struct ContentView: View {
   @State private var appData = ApplicationData.shared

   var body: some View {
      Map(position: $appData.cameraPos)
         .safeAreaInset(edge: .bottom) {
            if appData.openView {
               VStack {
                  LookAroundPreview(initialScene: appData.lookScene)
                     .frame(height: 200)
                     .padding()
                  Button("Hide Street") {
                     appData.openView = false
                  }.buttonStyle(.borderedProminent)
               }
            } else {
               Button("Show Street") {
                  appData.lookAround()
               }.buttonStyle(.borderedProminent)
            }
         }
   }
}
```

In this example, we use the **safeAreaInset()** modifier to present views at the bottom of the screen without obscuring the map's labels. The modifier displays different views depending on the value of the **openView** property. If the property is **false**, we show a button to perform a request, and when the values are received, the modifier displays the preview with the **LookAroundPreview** structure and a button to close it.

The view created by the **LookAroundPreview** structure adapts to the space available. In our example, we set the height of the view to 200 and give it a standard padding. The result is shown below.

***Figure 10-15:** Look Around preview*

When the Show Street button is pressed, the application shows a Look Around preview, and when the user taps on this preview, a sheet opens showing the scene (Figure 10-15, right). However, we can also open this sheet directly with the **lookAroundViewer()** modifier, as shown below.

Listing 10-23: Presenting the Look Around sheet

```
struct ContentView: View {
   @State private var appData = ApplicationData.shared

   var body: some View {
      Map(position: $appData.cameraPos)
         .safeAreaInset(edge: .bottom) {
            Button("Show Street") {
               appData.lookAround()
            }.buttonStyle(.borderedProminent)
         }
         .lookAroundViewer(isPresented: $appData.openView, initialScene:
            appData.lookScene)
   }
}
```

The request is created as before, but instead of showing a preview, we use the **openView** property to display the scene with the **lookAroundViewer()** modifier. When the **openView** property is assigned the value **true**, the modifier opens a sheet to display the scene.

PRO

Directions

Maps are not only used to find places, but also to find routes that indicate how to get from one place to another. The **MapKit** framework includes a number of classes to calculate a route and draw it on the map. The first class we need to implement is called **Request** and is defined inside the **MKDirections** class. The **Request** class generates a request for a route between two locations. The following are the properties available in this class to configure the request.

source

This property sets or returns the route's starting point. It is of type **MKMapItem**.

destination

This property sets or returns the route's destination. It is of type **MKMapItem**.

requestsAlternateRoutes

This property sets or returns a Boolean value that determines whether multiple routes will be returned when available.

transportType

This property sets or returns a value that determines the type of transportation used to travel the route. It is an **MKDirectionsTransportType** structure with the properties **automobile**, **walking**, **transit**, and **any**.

departureDate

This property sets or returns a **Date** structure that determines the date of departure to help the system estimate the better route.

arrivalDate

This property sets or returns a **Date** structure that determines the date of arrival to help the system estimate the better route.

The request is sent to Apple servers for processing. The framework defines the **MKDirections** class to perform the request and process the results. The class includes the following initializer and method.

MKDirections(request: Request)

This initializer creates an **MKDirections** object with the request specified by the **request** argument.

calculate()

This asynchronous method performs the request and returns an **MKDirectionsResponse** object with the routes found.

The routes are returned as objects of the **MKRoute** class. The class includes the following properties to get the route's information.

polyline

This property sets or returns the route's geometry that we can use to draw the route on the map. It is an **MKPolyline** object.

steps

This property sets or returns an array of **MKRouteStep** objects that describe every step the user needs to take to reach the destination.

advisoryNotices

This property sets or returns an array of strings with additional information that the user may need to travel the route, such as traffic jams or interruptions.

distance

This property sets or returns a **CLLocationDistance** value (a typealias of **Double**) with the route distance in meters.

expectedTravelTime

This property sets or returns a **TimeInterval** value with the expected travel time in seconds.

After the server has returned the **MKRoute** object with the description of the route, we need to present it to the user. The **MapPolyline** structure introduced earlier defines the following initializer for this purpose.

MapPolyline(MKRoute)

This initializer draws a route on the map.

The values assigned to the **origin** and **destination** properties of the request define the origin and destination of the route. These are objects of a class we have introduced before called **MKMapItem**. Objects of this class are usually returned by methods, but we can also create our own with the following initializer.

MKMapItem(location: CLLocation, **address:** MKAddress?)

This initializer creates an **MKMapItem** object that represents the map item at the location specified by the arguments. The location argument specifies the coordinates and the address argument describes the physical address.

The following example shows how to display a route between two places. We first update the model to include a property to store the route and a method to perform the request.

Listing 10-24: Calculating a route

```
import SwiftUI
import MapKit

@Observable class ApplicationData {
   var cameraPos: MapCameraPosition = .automatic
   var route: MKRoute?

   static let shared: ApplicationData = ApplicationData()
   private init() {}

   func calculateRoute() {
      let coordOrigin = CLLocation(latitude: 40.7637825011971,
         longitude: -73.9731328627541)
      let origin = MKMapItem(location: coordOrigin, address: nil)
      let coordDestination = CLLocation(latitude: 40.7523809365088,
         longitude: -73.9778321046893)
      let destination = MKMapItem(location: coordDestination,
         address: nil)

      let request = MKDirections.Request()
      request.source = origin
      request.destination = destination
      request.requestsAlternateRoutes = false

      Task {
         let directions = MKDirections(request: request)
         if let results = try? await directions.calculate() {
            let routes = results.routes
            route = routes.first!
         }
      }
   }
}
```

The **calculateRoute()** method creates a request, assigns the locations to the **origin** and **destination** constants, and then runs an asynchronous task to perform the request. The task creates the **MKDirections** object to process the request and then calls the **calculate()** method to determine the route. This method returns the results in an

MKDirectionsResponse object, which contains the **routes** property. This property returns an array of **MKRoute** objects representing all the routes found by the system. However, since we have set the **requestsAlternateRoutes** property to **false**, the array contains only one object. Once we get this object, we assign it to the **route** property, and show the route on the map.

Listing 10-25: Displaying a route

```
struct ContentView: View {
   @State private var appData = ApplicationData.shared

   var body: some View {
      Map(position: $appData.cameraPos) {
         if let route = appData.route {
            MapPolyline(route)
               .stroke(.red, lineWidth: 5)
         }
      }.onAppear {
         appData.calculateRoute()
      }
   }
}
```

The **MapPolyline** structure creates the path, but we need to specify how it should be drawn. In this example, we use the **stroke()** modifier to display a red line with a width of 5 points.

Figure 10-16: *Route*

PRO

Map Reader

Up to this point, we have only allowed users to select predefined locations, but we can also access arbitrary locations anywhere on the map. To accomplish this, SwiftUI provides the **MapReader** view. This view acts as a container for the **Map** view, so it is aware of the map's position within the interface, which allows it to convert screen coordinates into geographic coordinates, and vice versa. The following is the view's initializer.

MapReader(content: Closure)

This initializer creates a **MapReader** view that allows us to detect geographic coordinates on a map. The **content** argument is a closure used to define the **Map** view displayed inside the container.

The closure assigned to the **MapReader** view receives a **MapProxy** structure that acts as a bridge between the interface and the **Map** view. This structure defines the following methods to convert coordinates from one coordinate space to another.

convert(CGPoint, from: CoordinateSpaceProtocol)

This method converts a point from a specified coordinate space on the screen into geographic coordinates on the map. The first argument is the **CGPoint** value to convert, and the **from** argument defines the coordinate space the system should use for the conversion. It is a structure with the properties **global** and **local**.

convert(CLLocationCoordinate2D, to: CoordinateSpaceProtocol)

This method converts geographic coordinates on the map into a point on the screen. The first argument specifies the coordinates on the map to convert, and the **to** argument defines the coordinate space in which the resulting **CGPoint** should be expressed. It is a structure with the properties **global** and **local**.

With the **MapReader** view, we can detect where the user taps on the screen and obtain the exact geographic coordinates on the map. To accomplish this, we must embed the **Map** view inside a **MapReader**, apply the **onTapGesture()** modifier, and call the appropriate method on the proxy to convert the values, as shown below.

Listing 10-26: Determining a location on a map

```
struct ContentView: View {
   @State private var appData = ApplicationData.shared
   @State private var location: CLLocationCoordinate2D?

   var body: some View {
      MapReader { reader in
         Map(position: $appData.cameraPos)
            .onTapGesture { coordinates in
               if let mapCoordinates = reader.convert(coordinates,
                  from: .local) {
                  location = mapCoordinates
               }
            }
      }
      .safeAreaInset(edge: .bottom) {
         if let location {
            Text("\(location.latitude) | \(location.longitude)")
               .padding()
               .glassEffect(.regular)
         } else {
            Text("Tap to select location")
               .padding()
               .glassEffect(.regular)
```

```
            }
        }
    }
}
```

In this example, we determine the selected location and assign it to a binding property to display the latitude and longitude on the screen. The result is shown below.

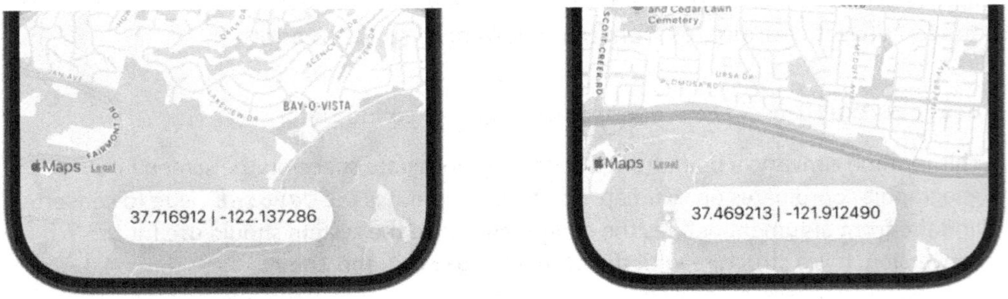

Figure 10-17: *Coordinates selected by the user*

PRO

Geocoding

Geographic coordinates identify a precise location on the map, but latitude and longitude values are not easy for users to interpret. To present meaningful information, we must convert those coordinates into a readable street address. For this purpose, MapKit includes the **`MKGeocodingRequest`** and **`MKReverseGeocodingRequest`** classes. These classes can convert addresses into map coordinates and map coordinates into addresses. The following are the initializers.

`MKGeocodingRequest(addressString:` `String)`

This initializer creates a structure to convert a street address into map coordinates. The **addressString** argument specifies the address to convert.

`MKReverseGeocodingRequest(location:` `CLLocation)`

This initializer creates a structure to convert map coordinates into a street address. The **location** argument specifies the coordinates we want to convert.

Both classes implement the following properties and methods to retrieve information from the servers and control the process.

`mapItems`

This asynchronous property returns an array of **`MKMapItem`** objects containing information about each detected location.

`isLoading`

This property returns a Boolean value indicating whether the system is currently retrieving information from the servers.

```
isCancelled
```

This property returns a Boolean value indicating whether the request has been cancelled.

```
cancel()
```

This method cancels the process.

The **MKGeocodingRequest** and **MKReverseGeocodingRequest** classes can convert addresses into map coordinates and map coordinates into addresses, so we can use them to obtain exactly the information we need. For example, we can implement the **MKReverseGeocodingRequest** class together with a **MapReader** view to determine the street address at the latitude and longitude selected by the user. The following data model implements a function that we can call from the views to obtain this value.

Listing 10-27: Finding the street address from map coordinates

```
@Observable class ApplicationData {
   var cameraPos = MapCameraPosition.automatic

   static let shared: ApplicationData = ApplicationData()
   private init() { }

   func findLocation(location: CLLocation) async -> String {
      if let request = MKReverseGeocodingRequest(location: location) {
         let mapitems = try? await request.mapItems
         if let address = mapitems?.first?.address {
            return address.fullAddress
         }
      }
      return "Address not found"
   }
}
```

The **MKReverseGeocodingRequest** class receives a map coordinate, contacts Apple's servers, and returns the matching addresses. The values are returned asynchronously, so we must wait until they become available. The results are delivered as an array of **MKMapItem** objects containing the possible addresses for the location. In this case, we only need one result, so we access the first item, retrieve the address from the **fullAddress** property of the **MKAddress** object, and return it.

From the view, we need to embed the map inside a **MapReader**, obtain the coordinates selected by the user, call the **findLocation()** method on the model with these values, and display the address returned by that method on the screen. The following is our implementation.

Listing 10-28: Allowing the user to select a location to find an address

```
struct ContentView: View {
   @State private var appData = ApplicationData.shared
   @State private var address = "No address found"
```

```
   var body: some View {
      ZStack {
         MapReader { reader in
            Map(position: $appData.cameraPos)
               .onTapGesture { coordinates in
                  if let mapCoordinates = reader.convert(coordinates,
                     from: .local) {
                     Task {
                        let location = CLLocation(latitude:
                           mapCoordinates.latitude, longitude:
                           mapCoordinates.longitude)
                        address = await appData.findLocation(location:
                           location)
                     }
                  }
               }
         }
         VStack {
            Spacer()
            Text(address)
               .padding()
               .glassEffect(.regular)
         }.padding()
      }
   }
}
```

This interface includes a **Map** view and a **Text** view on top to display the address of the selected location. Each time the user taps on the map, the **MapReader** view determines the corresponding coordinates and, if available, the street address is displayed on the screen, as shown below.

Figure 10-18: *Street address of a location selected by the user*

We can also perform the reverse process. If we have an address, we can determine its coordinates on the map. In the following example, we replace the **MKReverseGeocodingRequest** class in our model with the **MKGeocodingRequest** class to obtain the location of the street address provided by the user.

Listing 10-29: Finding the map coordinates of an address

```
@Observable class ApplicationData {
   var cameraPos: MapCameraPosition = .automatic
   static let shared: ApplicationData = ApplicationData()
   private init() {}
```

```
    func findLocation(address: String) async {
        if let request = MKGeocodingRequest(addressString: address) {
            do {
                let mapitems = try await request.mapItems
                if let mapitem = mapitems.first {
                    let coordinates = CLLocationCoordinate2D(latitude: mapitem.
                        location.coordinate.latitude, longitude:
                        mapitem.location.coordinate.longitude)
                    let region = MKCoordinateRegion(center: coordinates,
                        latitudinalMeters: 1000, longitudinalMeters: 1000)
                    cameraPos = MapCameraPosition.region(region)
                }
            } catch {
                print("Address not found \(error)")
            }
        }
    }
}
```

In this example, the **findLocation()** method receives a string containing the address entered by the user, implements the **MKGeocodingRequest** class to obtain the coordinates of that address on the map, and then moves the camera to display that area on the screen.

The view required for this example is similar to the previous one, but it must include a text field where the user can enter an address. The following is our implementation.

Listing 10-30: Allowing the user to find an address on the map

```
struct ContentView: View {
    @State private var appData = ApplicationData.shared
    @State private var address = ""

    var body: some View {
        ZStack {
            Map(position: $appData.cameraPos)
            VStack {
                HStack {
                    TextField("Enter an address", text: $address)
                        .textFieldStyle(.roundedBorder)
                    Button("Find") {
                        Task {
                            await appData.findLocation(address: address)
                        }
                    }.buttonStyle(.glassProminent)
                }.padding()
                .glassEffect(.regular)
                Spacer()
            }.padding()
        }
    }
}
```

This interface is very simple. We display the **Map** view as before and place a text field and a button on top to allow the user to enter an address and send it to the model to obtain the coordinates and scroll the map to that area. The result is shown below.

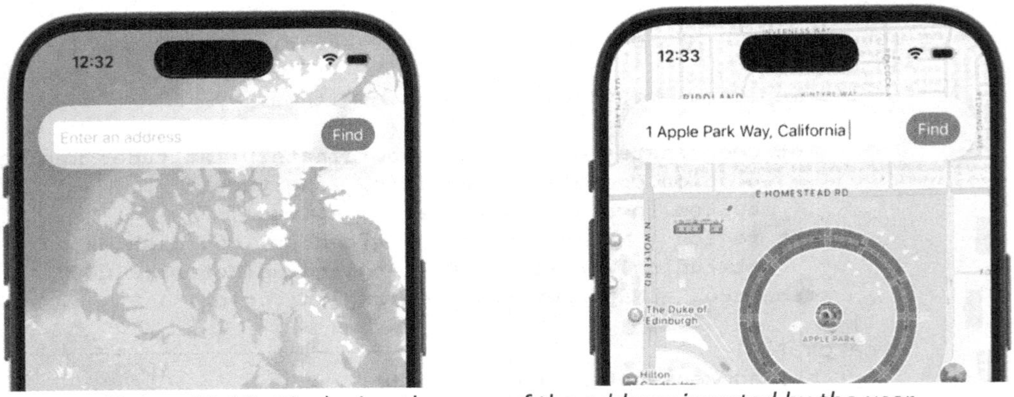

Figure 10-19: Displaying the area of the address inserted by the user

PRO

User Location

A **Map** view can show the user's location. The **MapKit** framework includes the **MapUserLocationButton** structure to add a button to the map that, when pressed, moves the camera to the user's location, and also the **UserAnnotation** structure to show an icon at that location. The following is the initializer for this structure.

UserAnnotation(anchor: UnitPoint, **content:** Closure)

This initializer creates an annotation that is displayed at the user's location. The **anchor** argument determines the position of the icon around the user's location, and the **content** argument is the closure that provides the views to be displayed on the map.

Before we display the user's location, we must ask for permission. The Core Location framework defines the **CLServiceSession** structure for this purpose. An instance of this structure is automatically created for our app, so all we need to do is to check for updates. To manage updates, the framework includes the **CLLocationUpdate** structure which in turn defines the following type method.

liveUpdates(LiveConfiguration)

This type method returns an instance of the **CLLocationUpdate** structure with information about the current location. The argument is an enumeration that determines the types of updates the framework is going to deliver. The available values are **default**, **airborne**, **automotiveNavigation**, **fitness** and **otherNavigation**.

IMPORTANT

The system requires the app to inform users why it needs access to their location. This option is configured in the project's settings. You must select the project in the Navigator panel, open the **Info** panel, and add the key "Privacy - Location When In Use Usage Description" with the message you want to display to the user (see Chapter 2, Figure 2-16). This can also be set from the **Signing & Capabilities** panel by enabling the **Location (When in Use)** service.

The **liveUpdates()** method returns **CLLocationUpdate** structures representing the current location. The **CLLocationUpdate** structure includes properties to report for errors, including **accuracyLimited**, **authorizationDenied**, **authorizationDeniedGlobally**, **authorizationRequestInProgress**, **authorizationRestricted**, **insufficientlyInUse**, **locationUnavailable**, **serviceSessionRequired** and **stationary**, and also the **location** property to report the user's current location. This property returns a **CLLocation** object with properties that contain information about the location, including the **coordinate** property, which returns a **CLLocationCoordinate2D** structure with the latitude and longitude.

The **liveUpdates()** method returns an asynchronous sequence and throw errors, so we need to check the values with a **for in** loop and the **try await** keywords, but the rest of the implementation depends on what we want for our app. The following is a basic example that checks for updates in the user's location and respond to errors.

Listing 10-31: Asking permission and responding to errors

```
@Observable class ApplicationData {
   var cameraPos: MapCameraPosition = .automatic
   var lastLocation = CLLocation()
   var isAuthorized: Bool = false
   static let shared: ApplicationData = ApplicationData()
   private init() {}

   func requestAuthorization() {
      Task {
         do {
            let updates = CLLocationUpdate.liveUpdates()
            for try await update in updates {
               if let loc = update.location {
                  lastLocation = loc

                  if !isAuthorized {
                     let coordinates = CLLocationCoordinate2D(latitude:
                        loc.coordinate.latitude, longitude:
                        loc.coordinate.longitude)
                     let region = MKCoordinateRegion(center: coordinates,
                        latitudinalMeters: 1000, longitudinalMeters: 1000)
                     cameraPos = MapCameraPosition.region(region)
                     isAuthorized = true
                  }
               } else {
                  checkErrors(update: update)
               }
            }
         } catch {
            print("Error: \(error)")
         }
      }
   }
   func checkErrors(update: CLLocationUpdate) {
      if update.authorizationDeniedGlobally {
```

```
print("Error: Authorization denied globally")
         isAuthorized = false
      } else if update.authorizationDenied {
         print("Error: Authorization denied")
         isAuthorized = false
      } else if update.authorizationRestricted {
         print("Error: Authorization restricted")
         isAuthorized = false
      } else if update.accuracyLimited {
         print("Error: Accuracy limited")
         isAuthorized = false
      } else if update.insufficientlyInUse {
         print("Error: Insufficientrly in use")
         isAuthorized = false
      }
   }
}
```

This model includes a method called **requestAuthorization()** that we are going to call from the view to start the process. The method starts an asynchronous task to call the **liveUpdates()** method on the **CLLocationUpdate** structure. Every time this method returns a value, we read the **location** property. If this property contains a value, it means that the user authorized the device to access his or her location and a location was found so we use the value to change the position of the camera, otherwise we call a method to check for errors.

In the view, we need to call the **requestAuthorization()** method to start the process when the view appears on the screen, and then add the **UserAnnotation** view to the map to show the location.

Listing 10-32: Requesting authorization and showing the user's location

```
struct ContentView: View {
   @State private var appData = ApplicationData.shared

   var body: some View {
      Map(position: $appData.cameraPos) {
         if appData.isAuthorized {
            UserAnnotation()
         }
      }
      .mapControls {
         if appData.isAuthorized {
            MapUserLocationButton()
         }
      }
      .onAppear {
         appData.requestAuthorization()
      }
   }
}
```

This example also includes the **MapUserLocationButton** control, so the user can tap the button to scroll to his or her location on the map. The result is shown below.

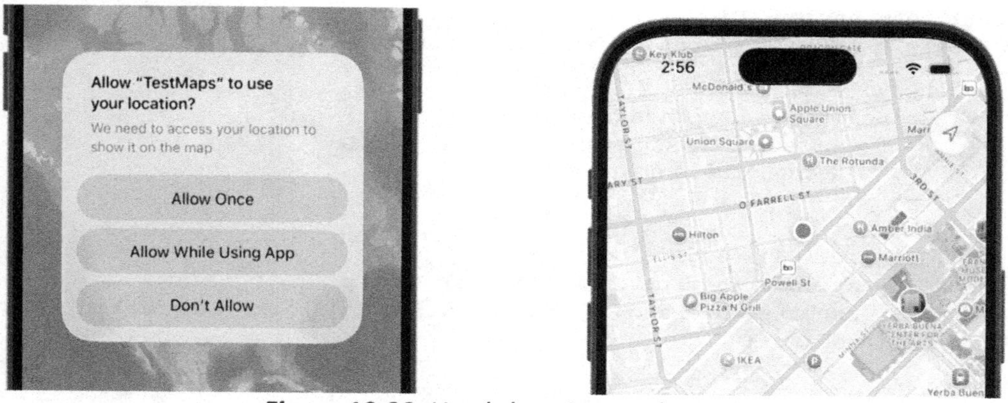

Figure 10-20: *User's location on the map*

Do It Yourself

Update the **ApplicationData.swift** file with the code in Listing 10-31 and the **`ContentView`** structure with the code in Listing 10-32. Add the "Privacy - Location When In Use Usage Description" option to the project's configuration with the message you want to show to the user (see Chapter 2, Figure 2-16). Run the application on an iPhone simulator. If you want to see your current location, you must run it on a real device. Allow the application to access your location. You should see a blue circle over your location on the map.

Sometimes all we need is to have quick access to the user's location. For this purpose, SwiftUI includes the **`LocationButton`** view.

```
LocationButton(Title, action: Closure)
```

This view creates a button to prompt the user for a one-time access to his or her location. The first argument is a predefined title determined by a **`Title`** structure. To define these values, the structure includes the type properties **`currentLocation`** ("Current Location"), **`sendCurrentLocation`** ("Send Current Location"), **`sendMyCurrentLocation`** ("Send My Current Location"), **`shareCurrentLocation`** ("Share Current Location"), and **`shareMyCurrentLocation`** ("Share My Current Location"). The **action** argument is a closure that is executed after the user grants or denies access.

When we implement the **`LocationButton`** view, we no longer need to ask permission from the model, but the process works the same way. The button opens a view that requests one-time access to the user's location, and when access is granted, it shows the location on the map.

Listing 10-33: Implementing the user location button

```
import SwiftUI
import MapKit
import CoreLocationUI
```

```swift
struct ContentView: View {
   @State private var appData = ApplicationData.shared

   var body: some View {
      Map(position: $appData.cameraPos) {
         if appData.isAuthorized {
            UserAnnotation()
         }
      }
      .safeAreaInset(edge: .bottom) {
         LocationButton(.currentLocation) {
            appData.cameraPos = .userLocation(fallback: .automatic)
         }.padding()
      }
   }
}
```

Note that the **LocationButton** structure is defined in the **CoreLocationUI** framework, so we need to import that framework for the view to become available. When the button is pressed, the system displays a simplified Alert View with two buttons to grant or deny access. If the user grants access, the **LocationButton** view changes the position of the camera and the user's location is displayed on the screen.

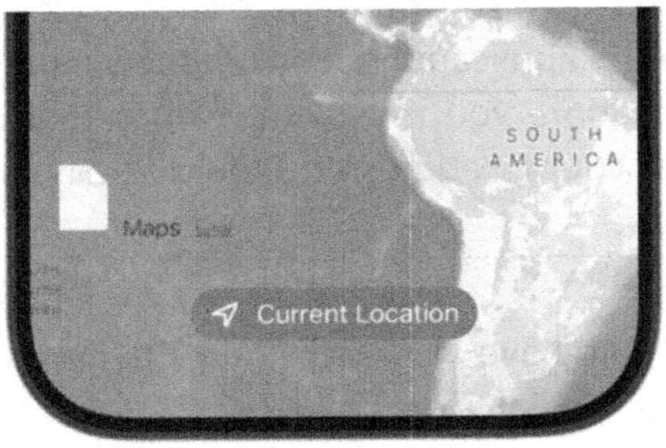

Figure 10-21: *User location button*

Do It Yourself

Update the **ContentView.swift** file with the code in Listing 10-33. Run the application on an iPhone simulator. If you want to see your current location, you must run it on a real device. Press the Location button. You should see a window asking for authorization. Authorize the app. You should see a circle over your location on the map.

IMPORTANT

Apple Maps are available for the web and Apple offers a service to configure maps, find locations, create unique identifiers to share locations, and more. The topic is beyond the scope of this book. For more information visit **https://developer.apple.com/maps/resources/**.

Chapter 11

Web

BASIC

11.1 - Web

Web access is essential for many modern applications, but the way we implement it depends on the experience we want to deliver. We can add links that open content in the system browser, embed a browser directly within the app's interface to keep users inside our environment, or even fetch and process online data in the background without presenting a webpage at all.

BASIC

Links

A link is a text or image associated with a URL that indicates the location of a document. When the user clicks or taps on the link, the document opens. Links were designed for the web, but we can also insert them into our applications and let the system decide where to open the document (in a browser or another application). SwiftUI includes the **Link** view to create them. The following is the view's initializer.

```
Link(String, destination: URL)
```

This initializer creates a button to open a link. The first argument specifies the button's title, and the **destination** argument is a **URL** structure with the location of the document we want to open.

The following example opens the **www.formasterminds.com** website when a button is pressed. The code defines a binding property to store the website's URL and then use this value to create the **URL** structure for the **Link** view. When the button is pressed, the system reads the URL, recognizes that it is a web address, and opens the browser to load the website.

Listing 11-1: Opening a website

```
struct ContentView: View {
   @State private var searchURL = "https://www.formasterminds.com"
```

```
    var body: some View {
        VStack {
            Link("Open Web", destination: URL(string: searchURL)!)
                .buttonStyle(.borderedProminent)
            Spacer()
        }.padding()
    }
}
```

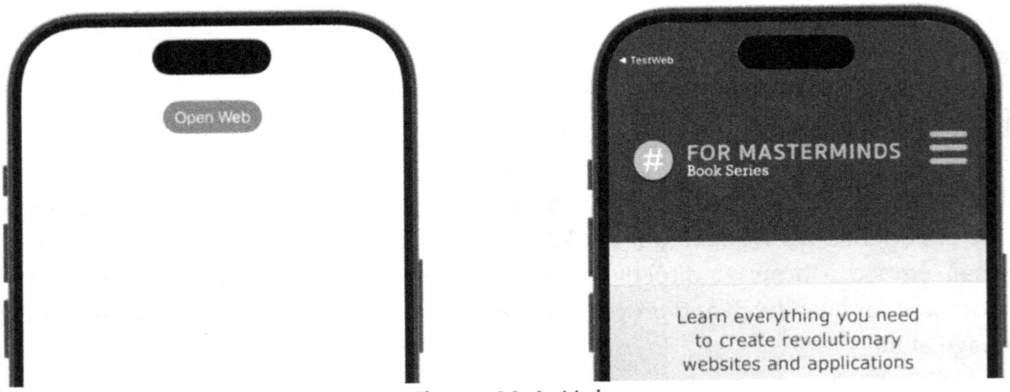

Figure 11-1: *Link*

Do It Yourself

Create a new App project. Update the **ContentView** structure with the code in Listing 11-1. Run the application on an iPhone simulator and press the button. The system should open an external browser and load the website.

To give us more control over how links are handled, the environment provides a property called **openURL** that we can use to open a URL. All we need to do is to declare an **@Environment** property to retrieve this value and then call it with the URL we want to open, as shown in the following example.

Listing 11-2: Opening URLs from code

```
struct ContentView: View {
    @Environment(\.openURL) var openURL
    @State private var searchURL = "https://www.formasterminds.com"

    var body: some View {
        VStack {
            Button("Open Web") {
                if let url = URL(string: searchURL) {
                    openURL(url)
                }
            }.buttonStyle(.borderedProminent)
            Spacer()
        }.padding()
```

```
    }
}
```

In this example, we are processing a URL that we know works, but that is not always the case. Usually, URLs come from external sources or are provided by the user. In such cases, we must verify that all the components of the URL are present. For example, if the user only provides the domain (**www.formasterminds.com**) without the protocol (**https**), we need to create the full URL before attempting to open it. To read, create, or modify URL components, the **Foundation** framework defines the **`URLComponents`** structure. The structure includes the following initializer.

`URLComponents(string: String)`

This initializer creates a **`URLComponents`** structure with the components from the URL specified by the **string** argument.

The **`URLComponents`** structure includes several properties to read and modify the components. The following are the most frequently used.

`scheme`

This property sets or returns the URL's protocol (e.g., "https").

`host`

This property sets or returns the URL's domain (e.g., "www.google.com").

`path`

This property sets or returns the URL's components after the domain (e.g., "/index.php").

`query`

This property sets or returns the URL's parameters (e.g., "id=22").

`queryItems`

This property sets or returns an array of **`URLQueryItem`** structures containing each of the parameters included in the URL.

The **`URLComponents`** structure also includes the following property to return the URL created from the components.

`url`

This property returns the URL built from the values of the components.

In the following example, we allow the user to insert a URL, but we make sure that the https protocol is always included.

Listing 11-3: Processing the user's URLs

```
struct ContentView: View {
   @Environment(\.openURL) var openURL
   @State private var searchURL = ""

   var body: some View {
      VStack {
         HStack {
            TextField("Insert URL", text: $searchURL)
               .textFieldStyle(.roundedBorder)
               .autocapitalization(.none)
               .autocorrectionDisabled(true)
            Button("Open") {
               let search = searchURL.trimmingCharacters(in: .whitespaces)
               if !search.isEmpty {
                  var components = URLComponents(string: search)
                  components?.scheme = "https"
                  if let newURL = components?.url {
                     openURL(newURL)
                  }
               }
            }.buttonStyle(.borderedProminent)
         }.padding()
         .glassEffect(.regular)
         Spacer()
      }.padding()
   }
}
```

The **`URLComponents`** structure takes a string with the URL, extracts the components, and assigns them to the properties of the structure so that we can read or modify them. In this example, we assign the string "https" to the **`scheme`** property to ensure that the URL is valid and can be processed by the system. Once the components are ready, we get the full URL from the **`url`** property and open it. The result is shown below.

Figure 11-2: *Opening user URL*

BASIC

WebKit Framework

Links allow us to direct users to any website we want, but they open the content in an external browser. If we want to maintain full control over the experience, we must open the website within our app. For this purpose, Apple provides the **WebKit** framework. This framework includes all the tools we need to render web content directly within our interface and control navigation.

To present web content, the framework defines the **WebView** structure. The following are the structure's initializers.

WebView(url: URL)

This initializer creates a view that renders web content. The **url** argument specifies the address of the website to load.

WebView(WebPage)

This initializer creates a view that renders web content. The argument is an object that manages the content, controls navigation, and interacts with dynamic page elements.

If all we want is to load a website, we can initialize a **WebView** with a URL, as shown in the following example.

Listing 11-4: Loading a website with a WebView view

```
import SwiftUI
import WebKit

struct ContentView: View {
   @State private var searchURL = URL(string: "https://www.formasterminds.
com")!

   var body: some View {
      WebView(url: searchURL)
   }
}
```

In this example, we define a **URL** structure that points to the **www.formasterminds.com** website and then initialize a **WebView** view with this value. By default, the view expands to fill the available space, so the website occupies the entire screen, as shown below.

Figure 11-3: *Web view*

If we need more control over the content, we must initialize the **WebView** view with a **WebPage** object. This object is responsible for loading the web page, but it can also manage navigation, so we can provide tools for the user to return to previous pages, reload the current page, stop a page from loading, configure how pages are rendered, and more. The following is the structure's initializer.

```
WebPage(configuration: Configuration, navigationDecider: NavigationDeciding)
```

This initializer creates a **WebPage** object to manage interactive web content. The **configuration** argument defines the object's initial setup, and the **navigationDecider** argument determines how navigation behaves.

The **WebPage** initializer creates an object that loads web content and manages navigation, but we still need to specify the content it should load. To control the loading process, the class defines the following properties and methods.

```
isLoading
```

This property returns a Boolean value indicating whether the page is currently loading.

```
estimatedProgress
```

This property returns a **Double** value between 0.0 and 1.0 indicating the level of progress in downloading the resource.

```
load(Item)
```

This method loads the content specified by the argument. The argument can be an **Item** structure representing a resource from the navigation history, a **URLRequest** structure representing a resource to load, or a **URL** structure containing the website's address.

```
reload(fromOrigin: Bool)
```

This method reloads the current content. The **fromOrigin** argument specifies whether the content should be reloaded from its original source or validated using cached data.

```
stopLoading()
```

This method stops loading the resources on the current page.

Each time a new page is loaded, the **WebPage** object retrieves information about it, such as the page's title, URL, media type, and other metadata. The following are some of the properties defined by the class to provide access to this information.

```
title
```

This property returns a string with the page's title.

```
url
```

This property returns a **URL** structure with the page's URL.

hasOnlySecureContent

This property returns a Boolean value indicating whether the content of the page was loaded through secure channels.

With a **WebPage** object, we can load any website, including those specified by the user. We just need to provide a way for the user to enter a URL, as we did in the previous examples, and then execute the **load()** method to load it. In the following example, we create a simple model to demonstrate how to initialize a **WebPage** object with a standard configuration and use it to load the website entered by the user.

Listing 11-5: Initializing a `WebPage` object for navigation

```
import SwiftUI
import WebKit

@Observable class ApplicationData {
   var page = WebPage()

   static let shared: ApplicationData = ApplicationData()
   private init() {}

   func loadPage(domain: String) {
      let search = domain.trimmingCharacters(in: .whitespaces)
      if !search.isEmpty {
         var components = URLComponents(string: domain)
         components?.scheme = "https"
         if let newURL = components?.url {
            page.load(newURL)
         }
      }
   }
}
```

In this example, we initialize a **WebPage** object and define a method called **loadPage()** that calls the **load()** method on that object to load the domain entered by the user. Because all the logic resides in the model, the view only needs to provide a text field for the user to type the domain and then call the **loadPage()** method on the model to load it, as shown below.

Listing 11-6: Allowing the user to load a website

```
struct ContentView: View {
   @State private var appData = ApplicationData.shared
   @State private var searchURL = ""

   var body: some View {
      VStack {
         TextField("Insert Domain", text: $searchURL)
            .textFieldStyle(.roundedBorder)
            .autocapitalization(.none)
```

```
            .autocorrectionDisabled(true)
            .onSubmit {
               appData.loadPage(domain: searchURL)
            }
            .padding()
            .glassEffect(.regular)
         WebView(appData.page)
      }
   }
}
```

This view includes a **TextField** view at the top to let the user enter a domain and a **WebView** below it to load and display the page. In this case, instead of using a button, we apply the **onSubmit()** modifier to the text field so that the user can start the process by just pressing the Done or Return key on the keyboard. The result is shown below.

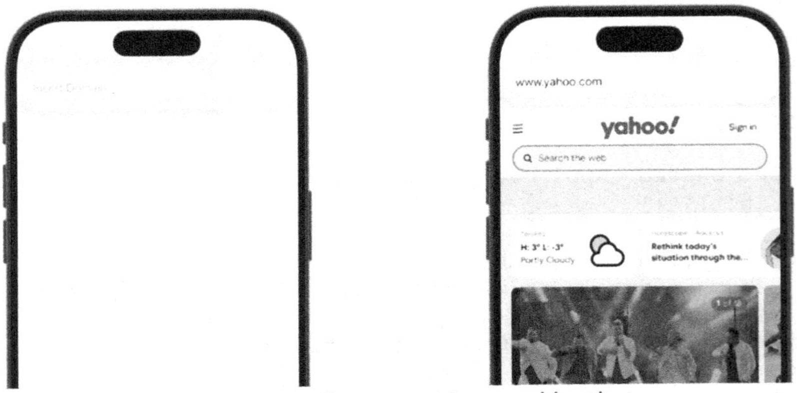

Figure 11-4: *Loading pages inserted by the user*

Do It Yourself

Create a new App project. Create a Swift file called **ApplicationData.swift** for the code in Listing 11-5. Update the **ContentView** structure with the code in Listing 11-6. Run the application on an iPhone simulator. Type a domain and press Return. The page should load, as shown in Figure 11-4.

Although the previous example works, it does not provide any navigation controls. For instance, if the user selects a link to navigate to a different page, the value displayed in the text field does not reflect the new location. To keep this value updated, we can monitor changes to the **url** property of the **WebPage** object, as shown below.

Listing 11-7: Updating the URL in the text field

```
.onChange(of: appData.page.url) {
   if let newURL = appData.page.url?.absoluteString {
      searchURL = newURL
   }
}
```

In this example, the **onChange()** modifier monitors the value of the **url** property. When the value changes, we read the **absoluteString** property of the **URL** structure to obtain the address as a string and assign it to the **searchURL** property. As a result, each time the user navigates to a new page, the closure attached to this modifier is executed and the updated URL is displayed in the text field.

Do It Yourself

Apply the **onChange()** modifier in Listing 11-7 to the **VStack** in the **ContentView** view. Run the application on an iPhone simulator, type a domain, and press Return. The domain in the text field should update to reflect the page's full URL. Select a link to navigate to a new page. The text field should display the URL of the new page.

The **WebPage** object stores the navigation history, allowing us to return to URLs the user has previously visited. To provide access to this information, the class defines the following property.

backForwardList

This property returns a structure of type **BackForwardList** that contains the resources accessed by the user during the current session. To return these values, the structure includes the properties **backList**, **currentItem**, and **forwardList**.

The resources in the navigation history are represented by a structure called **Item**. The following are some of the properties provided by the structure to return information about each item.

title

This property returns the page's title.

url

This property returns the page's URL.

The **backList** property returns an array of **Item** structures representing the resources that precede the current page, while the **forwardList** property returns an array of **Item** structures representing the resources that follow the current page. Using these values, we can allow the user to navigate backward and forward, as shown below.

Listing 11-8: Moving through the navigation history

```
struct ContentView: View {
   @State private var appData = ApplicationData.shared
   @State private var searchURL = ""
```

```
    var body: some View {
      VStack {
        TextField("Insert Domain", text: $searchURL)
          .textFieldStyle(.roundedBorder)
          .autocapitalization(.none)
          .autocorrectionDisabled(true)
          .onSubmit {
            appData.loadPage(domain: searchURL)
          }
          .padding()
          .glassEffect(.regular)
          .disabled(appData.page.isLoading)
        WebView(appData.page)
      }
      .onChange(of: appData.page.url) {
        if let newURL = appData.page.url?.absoluteString {
          searchURL = newURL
        }
      }
      .toolbar {
        ToolbarItem(placement: .bottomBar) {
          Button("Refresh", systemImage: "arrow.clockwise", action: {
            appData.page.reload()
          })
          .disabled(appData.page.url == nil)
        }
        ToolbarSpacer(.flexible, placement: .bottomBar)
        ToolbarItemGroup(placement: .bottomBar) {
          Button("Back", systemImage: "arrow.left", action: {
            if let previous = appData.page.backForwardList.backList.
              last {
              appData.page.load(previous)
            }
          })
          .disabled(appData.page.backForwardList.backList.isEmpty)
          Button("Forward", systemImage: "arrow.right", action: {
            if let next = appData.page.backForwardList.forwardList.
              first {
              appData.page.load(next)
            }
          })
          .disabled(appData.page.backForwardList.forwardList.isEmpty)
        }
      }
    }
  }
```

In this example, we add a toolbar at the bottom of the screen with three buttons. The first button calls the **reload()** method on the **WebPage** object to refresh the page, and the other two buttons load the resource that precedes and the one that follows the current page. To retrieve the previous resource, we read the last element in the array returned by the **backList** property, and to retrieve the next resource, we read the first element in the array returned by the **forwardList** property, allowing the user to move one item at a time. Because a resource is not always available, we disable the buttons when these arrays are empty. The result is shown below.

Figure 11-5: *Navigation buttons*

Do It Yourself

Update the **ContentView** structure with the code in Listing 11-8. Run the application on an iPhone simulator. The navigation buttons should appear at the bottom of the screen, as shown in Figure 11-5. Enter a domain and select a link. You should then be able to tap the Back button to return to the previous page.

IMPORTANT

In this example, we also disable the text field while the page is loading by checking the **isLoading** property. This step is not really necessary, but we do it because changes to the **backList** and **forwardList** properties are not currently reported to the view. By also observing the value of **isLoading**, we ensure that the view refreshes and reflects the state of the navigation history.

PRO

Web Content

Instead of loading and displaying the full content of a website, as we have done so far, we may sometimes need to retrieve only specific information. In these situations, we can load the document in the background and parse it to extract only the data we want. For this purpose, the **Foundation** framework includes the **URLSession** class. This class creates and manages an HTTP session used to retrieve data from a server and download or upload files. The following are some of the properties and initializers provided by the class to create and configure a session.

shared

This type property returns a standard session with a configuration by default that is suitable to perform basic requests.

URLSession(configuration: URLSessionConfiguration)

This initializer creates a new session with the configuration set by the argument. The **configuration** argument is an object that specifies the session's behavior.

URLSession(configuration: URLSessionConfiguration, **delegate:** URLSessionDelegate?, **delegateQueue:** OperationQueue?)

This initializer creates a new session with the configuration set by the arguments. The **configuration** argument is an object that specifies the session's behavior, the **delegate** argument is a reference to the delegate object we want to assign to the session, and the **delegateQueue** argument is the queue in which the delegate methods are going to be executed.

The session sets up the connection, but it does not perform any tasks. To download or upload data we must implement the following methods.

data(from: URL, **delegate:** URLSessionTaskDelegate?)

This asynchronous method adds a task to the session to download the data at the URL indicated by the **from** argument. The **delegate** argument is the delegate object used by the task to report updates during the process. The method returns a tuple with two values: a **Data** structure with the data returned by the server and a **URLResponse** object with the status of the request.

download(from: URL, **delegate:** URLSessionTaskDelegate?)

This asynchronous method adds a task to the session to download the file at the URL indicated by the **from** argument. The **delegate** argument is the delegate object used by the task to report updates during the process. The method returns a tuple with two values: a **URL** structure that indicates the location of the downloaded file and a **URLResponse** object with the status of the request.

The following are the methods defined by the class to upload data and files.

upload(for: URLRequest, **from:** Data, **delegate:** URLSessionTaskDelegate?)

This asynchronous method adds a task to the session to upload the data indicated by the **from** argument. The **delegate** argument is the delegate object used by the task to report updates during the process. The method returns a tuple with two values: a **Data** structure with the data returned by the server and a **URLResponse** object with the status of the request.

upload(for: URLRequest, **fromFile:** URL, **delegate:** URLSessionTaskDelegate?)

This asynchronous method adds a task to the session to upload the file in the URL indicated by the **fromFile** argument. The **delegate** argument is the delegate object used by the task to report updates during the process. The method returns a tuple with two values: a **Data** structure with the data returned by the server and a **URLResponse** object with the status of the request.

These methods are asynchronous, meaning they return the result after the data has been downloaded or uploaded. The types of values returned depends on the method. For example, the **data()** method returns a value with the data and an object of type **URLResponse** with the status of the request. When we access a URL over the HTTP protocol, the response is represented by an object of type **HTTPURLResponse** (a subclass of **URLResponse**). This class includes the **statusCode** property to return a code that determines the status of the request. Several codes are available, such as the value 200, which reports the success of the request, or the value 301, which reports that the website has moved to a different address. If we just want to make sure that the data was downloaded correctly, we can check if the value of the **statusCode** property is equal to 200 before processing anything. The following example shows how to perform a simple request.

Listing 11-9: Loading a remote document from the model

```
import SwiftUI

@Observable class ApplicationData {
   var webContent: String = ""
   var buttonDisabled: Bool = false

   static let shared: ApplicationData = ApplicationData()
   private init() { }
   func loadWeb() async {
      buttonDisabled = true

      let session = URLSession.shared
      let webURL = URL(string: "https://www.yahoo.com")
      do {
         let (data, response) = try await session.data(from: webURL!)
         if let resp = response as? HTTPURLResponse {
            let status = resp.statusCode
            if status == 200 {
               if let content = String(data: data,
                  encoding: String.Encoding.utf8) {
                  await MainActor.run {
                     webContent = content
                     buttonDisabled = false
                  }
                  print(content)
               }
            } else {
               print("Error: \(status)")
            }
         }
      } catch {
         print("Error: \(error)")
      }
   }
}
```

This model loads the content of the website at **www.yahoo.com** and assigns it to the **webContent** property. The operation is performed by the **loadWeb()** method. The method defines the request with the URL **https://www.yahoo.com** and then calls the session's **data()** method to download the page. The method downloads the content at that address, checks if the operation was successful (200), takes a string from the data, and updates the **webContent** property with that value to make it available for the view. The following is a simple view for processing this data.

Listing 11-10: Displaying the document's content

```
struct ContentView: View {
   @State private var appData = ApplicationData.shared

   var body: some View {
      VStack {
         Button("Load Web") {
            Task {
               await appData.loadWeb()
            }
         }.disabled(appData.buttonDisabled)
         Text("Total Characters: \(appData.webContent.count)")
            .padding()
         Spacer()
      }.padding()
   }
}
```

The content returned by **www.yahoo.com** is extensive. For didactic purposes, we print the entire content on the console and show the number of characters on the screen, but a professional application usually processes the value to extract information, as we will see next.

Do It Yourself

Create a new App project. Create a Swift file called **ApplicationData.swift** for the code in Listing 11-9. Update the **ContentView** structure with the code in Listing 11-10. Run the application on an iPhone simulator. Press the Load Web button. After a few seconds, you should see the content of the document printed on the console and the number of characters on the screen.

Web documents, such as those returned by **www.yahoo.com**, are written in HTML. This language is used by websites to structure and present information on the screen. Extracting specific data from these documents can be tedious and error prone. For this reason, many websites provide additional services that deliver data in JSON format. These JSON documents are generated dynamically and contain only the information requested by the application, ensuring that each time we download them, we receive exactly the data we need.

To illustrate how to access and process documents generated by these services, we can retrieve posts from a website called JSONPlaceholder at **jsonplaceholder.typicode.com**. This site generates sample JSON documents that allow us to practice accessing and processing this type of information. The process does not introduce any new concepts. We create a

URLSession to download the document, as we did before, and then decode it using a **JSONDecoder** object, as shown below.

Listing 11-11: Loading a JSON document

```
import SwiftUI

struct Post: Codable, Identifiable {
   var id: Int
   var userId: Int
   var title: String
   var body: String
}
@Observable class ApplicationData {
   var listOfPosts: [Post] = []

   static let shared: ApplicationData = ApplicationData()
   private init() {
      Task {
         await loadJSON()
      }
   }
   func loadJSON() async {
      let session = URLSession.shared
      let webURL = URL(string: "https://jsonplaceholder.typicode.com/
         posts")

      do {
         let (data, response) = try await session.data(from: webURL!)
         if let resp = response as? HTTPURLResponse {
            let status = resp.statusCode
            if status == 200 {
               let decoder = JSONDecoder()
               if let posts = try? decoder.decode([Post].self,
                  from: data) {
                  await MainActor.run {
                     listOfPosts = posts
                  }
               }
            } else {
               print("Error: \(status)")
            }
         }
      } catch {
         print("Error: \(error)")
      }
   }
}
```

As we learned in Chapter 7, to decode a JSON document, we need to define a structure that matches the JSON values. The URL **https://jsonplaceholder.typicode.com/posts** returns a list of posts, each with four values: an integer containing the user's identifier, another integer containing the post's identifier, a string containing the title, and a string containing the message. To store these values, the model in Listing 11-11 defines the **Post** structure. This structure conforms to the **Codable** protocol to be able to decode the values, and the **Identifiable** protocol to be able to list the instances with a **List** view.

The process to download the document is the same as before. We get the session, call the **data()** method, decode the data into an array of **Post** structures using a **JSONDecoder** object, and store the values in the **listOfPosts** property to update the view. Since the document is downloaded when the model is initialized, all we need to do in the view is to list the values.

Listing 11-12: Listing the values from the document

```
struct ContentView: View {
   @State private var appData = ApplicationData.shared

   var body: some View {
      VStack {
         List {
            ForEach(appData.listOfPosts) { post in
               VStack(alignment: .leading) {
                  Text(post.title).bold()
                  Text(post.body)
               }.padding(5)
            }
         }.listStyle(.plain)
      }.padding()
   }
}
```

Because a JSON document returns a predictable set of values defined by the service, we know exactly what to expect when we access it. In this case, the response includes the title and body of the post, so we can reliably extract those values and present them to the user.

***Figure 11-6:** JSON document*

Do It Yourself

Update the **ApplicationData.swift** file with the code in Listing 11-11 and the **ContentView** structure with the code in Listing 11-12. Run the application on an iPhone simulator. You should see 100 messages on the screen, as shown in Figure 11-6. To see the structure of the JSON file returned from the URL **https://jsonplaceholder.typicode.com/posts**, access the URL from your browser.

Chapter 12
Notifications

BASIC

12.1 - Notification Center

In addition to the techniques we have seen so far to pass data between different parts of an application, such as sending values from one view to another or providing a common model from which each view can get the information it needs, we can also send notifications across the application to report changes. Foundation includes the **`NotificationCenter`** class to create an object that serves as a notification center for the entire application. We send notifications (messages) to this object and then listen to these notifications from anywhere in the code. The class includes the following type property to get a reference to this object.

`default`

This type property returns the **`NotificationCenter`** object assigned to the application by default.

The Notification Center is like a bulletin board; we can post a notification and then read it from anywhere in the code. The **`NotificationCenter`** class defines the following methods to post and read notifications.

`post(name:` `Name,` **`object:`** `Any?,` **`userInfo:`** `Dictionary)`

This method posts a notification to the Notification Center. The **name** argument determines the name of the notification, the **object** argument is a reference to the object that sent the notification, and the **userInfo** argument is a dictionary with the information we want to send with the notification.

`notifications(named:` `Name,` **`object:`** `AnyObject?)`

This method returns a **`Notifications`** object with an asynchronous sequence that contains all the notifications posted to the Notification Center. The **named** argument is the name of the notification we want to read, and the **object** argument is a reference to the object that sent the notification (set to **`nil`** if we want to read notifications posted by any object).

Notifications are created by the **`Notification`** class. The **`post()`** method automatically creates a **`Notification`** object to represent the notification to be sent, but we can also create these objects ourselves using the **`Notification`** class initializer.

Notification(name: Name, **object:** Any?, **userInfo:** Dictionary)

This initializer creates a **Notification** object with the information provided by the arguments. The **name** argument determines the name of the notification, the **object** argument is a reference to the object that is sending the notification, and the **userInfo** argument is a dictionary with the information we want to send with the notification.

The class includes the following properties to read the values of the notification.

name

This property returns the name of the notification.

object

This property returns a reference to the object that posted the notification.

userInfo

This property returns the dictionary attached to the notification.

The name of the notification is created from a structure included in the **Notification** class called **Name**. The structure provides the following initializer to define custom names.

Name(String)

This initializer creates a structure that represents the notification's name. The argument is a string with the name we want to assign to the notification.

Notifications are used for multiple purposes. We can send a notification after a long process is complete to tell the system that it is time to update the interface, we can communicate views with each other, or we can keep a view up to date by sending notifications from the model with the information we receive from the Internet, to name a few. In the following example, a notification is sent every time a new value is entered by the user. For didactic purposes, we use a simple interface with two views, one that allows the user to enter the title of a book and another that shows the number of books already stored in the model.

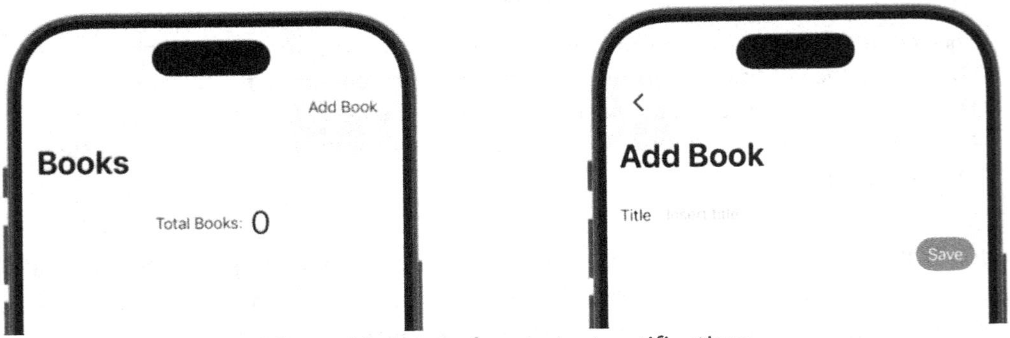

Figure 12-1: *Interface to test notifications*

The model must store the values inserted by the user, as always, but also read the notifications to update the main view.

Listing 12-1: Listening to notifications from the model

```
import SwiftUI

@Observable class ApplicationData {
   var total: Int = 0
   @ObservationIgnored var titles: [String] = []

   static let shared: ApplicationData = ApplicationData()
   private init() {
      Task {
         await readNotifications()
      }
   }
   func readNotifications() async {
      let center = NotificationCenter.default
      let name = Notification.Name("Update Data")

      for await _ in center.notifications(named: name, object: nil) {
         await MainActor.run {
            total = titles.count
         }
      }
   }
}
```

The Notification Center creates an asynchronous sequence with all the notifications. The sequence is managed by a **Notifications** object, which we get from the **notifications()** method. To read this sequence, we create an asynchronous **for in** loop with this object. Each time a notification arrives, the loop performs one cycle, we get the total number of titles stored in the **titles** array and assign it to the label.

The initial view needs to show the value of the **total** property on the screen and include a button in the navigation bar to open a second view where the user can insert new values.

Listing 12-2: Listening to notifications

```
struct ContentView: View {
   @State private var appData = ApplicationData.shared

   var body: some View {
      NavigationStack {
         VStack {
            HStack {
               Text("Total Books:")
               Text("\(appData.total)")
                  .font(.largeTitle)
            }
            Spacer()
         }.padding()
         .navigationTitle("Books")
```

```
            .toolbar {
                ToolbarItem(placement: .topBarTrailing) {
                    NavigationLink("Add Book", destination: {
                        AddBook()
                    })
                }
            }
        }
    }
}
```

The values in the model for this example are added from the **AddBook** view, which is opened by the button in the navigation bar. This view must contain a **TextField** view where the user can enter a new value and a button to save it. When the button is pressed, we save the value in the model and send a notification.

Listing 12-3: Sending notifications

```
import SwiftUI

struct AddBook: View {
    @State private var appData = ApplicationData.shared
    @Environment(\.dismiss) var dismiss
    @State private var titleInput: String = ""

    var body: some View {
        VStack {
            HStack {
                Text("Title")
                TextField("Insert title", text: $titleInput)
                    .textFieldStyle(.roundedBorder)
            }
            HStack {
                Spacer()
                Button("Save") {
                    let title = titleInput.trimmingCharacters(in: .whitespaces)
                    if !title.isEmpty {
                        addValue(title: title)
                        dismiss()
                    }
                }.buttonStyle(.borderedProminent)
            }
            Spacer()
        }.padding()
        .navigationBarTitle("Add Book")
    }
    func addValue(title: String) {
        appData.titles.append(title)

        let center = NotificationCenter.default
        let name = Notification.Name("Update Data")
        center.post(name: name, object: nil, userInfo: nil)
    }
}
```

When a name is inserted into the **TextField** view and the Save button is pressed, we call a method to store the value and post the notification. To post the notification, we get a reference to the **NotificationCenter** object assigned to the app, define a custom name for the notification ("Update Data"), and post it using the **post()** method. In the model, the asynchronous **for in** loop defined in the **readNotifications()** method detects that there is a new notification, performs a new cycle, the number of titles stored in the **titles** property is assigned to the **total** property, and the initial view is updated with the new value.

Do It Yourself

Create a new App project. Create a Swift file called **ApplicationData.swift** for the code in Listing 12-1. Update the **ContentView** structure with the code in Listing 12-2. Create a SwiftUI file called **AddBook.swift** for the code in Listing 12-3. Run the application on an iPhone simulator. Press the Add Book button. Insert a title and press the Save button. The view should be closed and the interface should show the total number of titles inserted so far.

The **Notification** object includes the **userInfo** property, which allows us to attach additional information to the notification. The values that can be included in the dictionary assigned to this property are Property List values (**NSNumber**, **NSString**, **NSDate**, **NSArray**, **NSDictionary**, **NSData**, and the equivalents in Swift), but beyond that there are no other restrictions on what we can assign to this property. For example, we could modify our code to pass the string inserted by the user and perform an additional task if the value matches a specific title. The following are the changes we need to make to the **addValue()** method in the **AddBook** view to attach the title to the notification.

Listing 12-4: Adding information to the notification

```
func addValue(title: String) {
   appData.titles.append(title)

   let center = NotificationCenter.default
   let name = Notification.Name("Update Data")
   let info = ["type": title]
   center.post(name: name, object: nil, userInfo: info)
}
```

This code declares a dictionary with the key "type" and the value entered by the user, and assigns it to the **userInfo** argument of the **post()** method. Now we can check this value in our model every time a notification is received.

Listing 12-5: Reading the value in the notification

```
func readNotifications() async {
   let center = NotificationCenter.default
   let name = Notification.Name("Update Data")

   for await notification in center.notifications(named: name,
      object: nil) {
      if let info = notification.userInfo {
         let type = info["type"] as? String
         if type == "Miracle" {
            print("Miracle was inserted")
         }
      }
      await MainActor.run {
         total = titles.count
      }
   }
}
```

The values from the dictionary are returned as values of type **`Any`**, so we need to cast them to the correct type. In the **`for in`** loop in Listing 12-5, we read the value of the "type" key, cast it as a **`String`**, and then compare it to the string "Miracle". If the values match, a message is printed on the console.

Do It Yourself

Update the **`addValue()`** method in the **`AddBook`** view with the code in Listing 12-4, and the **`readNotifications()`** method in the **`ApplicationData`** class with the code in Listing 12-5. Run the application on an iPhone simulator. A message should be printed on the console every time you insert the title "Miracle".

If we do not want to post any more notifications, we can stop the process in the **`AddBook`** view, but if we want to stop processing the notifications from a receiver, we must cancel the task by calling the **`cancel()`** method. In the following example, we create a timer in the initializer of the **`ApplicationData`** class to cancel the task after 20 seconds, so that the initial view is no longer updated with the values entered by the user after the time expires.

Listing 12-6: Cancelling the task

```
private init() {
   let myTask = Task {
      await readNotifications()
   }
   Timer.scheduledTimer(withTimeInterval: 20, repeats: false) { timer in
      myTask.cancel()
   }
}
```

Do It Yourself

Update the **`init()`** method in the **`ApplicationData`** class with the code in Listing 12-6. Run the application on an iPhone simulator. Press the Add Book button to insert a title. The initial view should stop counting new values after 20 seconds.

BASIC

System Notifications

In addition to the notifications sent by our app, the system also sends notifications to the Notification Center to report changes to the interface or the device. There are dozens of notifications available. They work just like the custom notifications introduced before but are predefined as type properties of UIKit classes. We will probably never need most of them, but some are very useful. For example, the UIKit framework defines a class called **`UIWindow`**, which is used to create the app's windows and send notifications about the state of the keyboard. The following are the most frequently used.

`keyboardDidShowNotification`

This notification is posted after the keyboard was shown.

`keyboardDidHideNotification`

This notification is posted after the keyboard was hidden.

SwiftUI automatically adjusts the interface when the keyboard appears, so in most cases we do not need to observe keyboard notifications. For example, the following interface displays an image and a text field where the user can enter a caption. When the user taps the text field, the keyboard appears and the image automatically resizes to fit the remaining space on the screen.

Listing 12-7: Interface to test the keyboard

```
struct ContentView: View {
   @FocusState var focusTitle: Bool
   @State private var inputTitle: String = ""

   var body: some View {
      VStack {
         Image("spot1")
            .resizable()
            .scaledToFit()
         HStack {
            TextField("Insert Title", text: $inputTitle)
               .textFieldStyle(.roundedBorder)
               .focused($focusTitle)
```

```
            Button("Save") {
               focusTitle = false
            }.buttonStyle(.borderedProminent)
         }
         Spacer()
      }.padding()
   }
}
```

In this example, we include a **@FocusState** property to be able to remove focus from the **TextField** view and close the keyboard when the Save button is pressed (see Chapter 3). When the keyboard opens, the **Image** view adapts to the space available, and when it closes, the **Image** view expands back to its initial state.

Figure 12-2: *Interface adapting to the keyboard*

If we don't want the interface to adapt to the space available, we can embed it in a **ScrollView** view, as shown below.

Listing 12-8: Scrolling the interface to make room for the keyboard

```
struct ContentView: View {
   @FocusState var focusTitle: Bool
   @State private var inputTitle: String = ""

   var body: some View {
      ScrollView {
         VStack {
            Image("spot1")
               .resizable()
               .scaledToFit()
            HStack {
               TextField("Insert Title", text: $inputTitle)
                  .textFieldStyle(.roundedBorder)
                  .focused($focusTitle)
               Button("Save") {
                  focusTitle = false
               }.buttonStyle(.borderedProminent)
            }
```

```
            Spacer()
         }.padding()
      }
   }
}
```

The only difference from the previous example is that we now have the views embedded in a **ScrollView** view. so instead of adapting the interface, the system scrolls the views to keep the **TextField** view visible when the keyboard is opened.

Figure 12-3: *The interface scrolls to adapt to the keyboard*

This is the automatic behavior provided by SwiftUI, but we can customize the process by listening to keyboard notifications. For example, if the interface is embedded in a **ScrollView** view, the **TextField** view scrolls up enough to be visible, but there is no space between that view and the keyboard (see Figure 12-3, right). If we want to improve the design, we can apply some modifiers to the views and change the styles when the state of the keyboard changes.

Although we can make these changes in the views, it is better to do so in the model. For example, the following model listens to keyboard notifications and changes the value of an observable property to apply a -20 point offset to the **ScrollView** view when the keyboard is opened.

Listing 12-9: Listening to keyboard notifications

```
import SwiftUI

@Observable class ApplicationData {
   @ObservationIgnored let center = NotificationCenter.default
   var scrollOffset: CGFloat = 0

   static let shared: ApplicationData = ApplicationData()
   private init() {
      Task {
         await receiveNotificationOpen()
      }
```

```
        Task {
            await receiveNotificationClose()
        }
    }
    func receiveNotificationOpen() async {
        let name = UIWindow.keyboardDidShowNotification
        for await _ in center.notifications(named: name, object: nil) {
            await MainActor.run {
                scrollOffset = -20
            }
        }
    }
    func receiveNotificationClose() async {
        let name = UIWindow.keyboardDidHideNotification
        for await _ in center.notifications(named: name, object: nil) {
            await MainActor.run {
                scrollOffset = 0
            }
        }
    }
}
```

The asynchronous **for in** loop waits for new values to arrive. This means that we cannot declare one loop after the other, since the second loop will never be executed. For this reason, we created two tasks, one that waits for a **keyboardDidShowNotification** notification and another that waits for a **keyboardDidHideNotification** notification. When a **keyboardDidShowNotification** notification is received, we assign the value -20 to the **scrollOffset** property, and when a **keyboardDidHideNotification** notification is received, we assign the value 0.

In the view, we can use the value of the **scrollOffset** property to set the offset of the **ScrollView**, as shown below.

Listing 12-10: Modifying the interface when the keyboard state changes

```
struct ContentView: View {
    @State private var appData = ApplicationData.shared
    @FocusState var focusTitle: Bool
    @State private var inputTitle: String = ""

    var body: some View {
        ScrollView {
            VStack {
                Image("spot1")
                    .resizable()
                    .scaledToFit()
                HStack {
                    TextField("Insert Title", text: $inputTitle)
                        .textFieldStyle(.roundedBorder)
                        .focused($focusTitle)
                    Button("Save") {
                        focusTitle = false
                    }.buttonStyle(.borderedProminent)
                }
                Spacer()
```

```
            }.padding()
        }
        .offset(CGSize(width: 0, height: appData.scrollOffset))
    }
}
```

The **ScrollView** view now moves up 20 points when the keyboard is opened, and returns to its original position when it is closed, creating padding between the views and the keyboard.

Do It Yourself

Create a new App project. Create a Swift file called **ApplicationData.swift** for the code in Listing 12-9. Update the **ContentView** structure with the code in Listing 12-10. Download the **spot1.jpg** image from our website and add it to an Asset Catalog. Run the application on an iPhone simulator. Tap on the text field to activate the keyboard. You should see the interface scrolling up, creating a padding between the views and the keyboard.

BASIC

12.2 - User Notifications

Another type of notifications are User Notifications. These are notifications that the system displays to the user when the app has an event to report, such as the completion of a task or real-life events that the user wants to be reminded of. There are three different types of User Notifications: Alert, Badge, and Sound. A Badge notification displays a badge with a number over the app's icon, a Sound notification plays a sound, and an Alert notification can be displayed as a banner, as an Alert View, or as a message on the lock screen, depending on the current state of the device and the configuration set by the user. They can be scheduled all at once or independently. For example, one notification can be scheduled to display an alert and play a sound, another to display an alert and show a badge, or another to only play a sound.

IMPORTANT

User Notifications are divided into Local Notifications and Remote Notifications (also known as Push Notifications). Local Notifications are notifications generated by the application running on the device, while Remote Notifications are generated by remote servers and received by the system through the network. In this chapter, we are going to study Local Notifications. For more information on Remote Notifications, visit our website and follow the links for this chapter.

User Notifications Framework

User Notifications are created and managed by classes of the User Notifications framework. The framework includes the **UNUserNotificationCenter** class to create a Notification Center that we can use to schedule and manage user notifications. This is like the Notification Center we have worked with earlier, but specifically designed for User Notifications. The class includes the following type method to get the **UNUserNotificationCenter** object assigned to the app.

current()

This type method returns a reference to the **UNUserNotificationCenter** object assigned to the app.

The first step to send notifications is to request authorization from the user. For this purpose, the class includes the following methods.

requestAuthorization(options: UNAuthorizationOptions)

This asynchronous method requests authorization from the user to show notifications and returns a Boolean value to report the result. The **options** argument is a set of properties that determine the type of notifications we want to show. The properties available are **badge**, **sound**, **alert**, **carPlay**, **criticalAlert**, **provisional**, and **announcement**.

notificationSettings()

This asynchronous method returns a **UNNotificationSettings** object with the current settings. The most useful property is **authorizationStatus**, which returns an enumeration value with the authorization status. (The user may change the status of the authorization anytime from the Settings app.) The possible values are **notDetermined**, **denied**, **authorized**, **provisional**, and **ephemeral**.

For the notifications to be sent, they must be added to the User Notification Center. The **UNUserNotificationCenter** class includes the following methods to add and remove them.

add(UNNotificationRequest)

This asynchronous method schedules a new notification in the User Notification Center. The argument is the request for the notification.

removePendingNotificationRequests(withIdentifiers: [String])

This method removes the pending notifications with the identifiers specified by the argument.

The framework includes the **UNMutableNotificationContent** class to store the content of a notification. The following are the properties included in this class to set the values.

title

This property sets or returns the notification's title.

subtitle

This property sets or returns the notification's subtitle.

body

This property sets or returns the notification's message.

badge

This property sets or returns a number to show over the app's icon.

sound

This property sets or returns the sound we want to play when the notification is delivered to the user. It is an object of type **UNNotificationSound**.

userInfo

This property sets or returns a dictionary with the information we want to send with the notification.

Some of these properties store strings, except for the **badge** property, which takes an **NSNumber** object, and the **sound** property, which takes an object of the **UNNotificationSound** class. This class includes the following initializer and property to get the object.

UNNotificationSound(named: UNNotificationSoundName)

This initializer creates a **UNNotificationSound** object with the sound specified by the **named** argument.

default

This type property returns a **UNNotificationSound** object with the sound defined by the system.

The names of the sounds are defined by a structure of type **UNNotificationSoundName**. The structure includes the following initializer.

UNNotificationSoundName(rawValue: String)

This initializer creates a **UNNotificationSoundName** object with the name of the file that contains the sound we want to play with the notification.

The **UNMutableNotificationContent** class also allows us to specify the level of interruption. By default, notifications are active, which means they turn on the screen and play a sound, but they can also be set to passive (they do not turn on the screen), time sensitive (they are displayed immediately but take user settings into account), and critical (they bypass user settings). The class includes the following property to define the interruption level.

interruptionLevel

This property sets or returns a value that determines the importance and delivery timing of the notification. It is a **UNNotificationInterruptionLevel** enumeration with the values **active** (default), **critical**, **passive**, and **timeSensitive**.

User Notifications are posted to the User Notification Center and then displayed by the system when a certain condition is met. These conditions are set by objects called *triggers*. There are three types of triggers for local notifications: Time Interval (the notification is delivered after a specified period of time), Calendar (the notification is delivered on a specified date), and Location (the notification is delivered at a specified location). The framework defines three classes to create these triggers: **UNTimeIntervalNotificationTrigger**, **UNCalendarNotificationTrigger** and **UNLocationNotificationTrigger**.

UNTimeIntervalNotificationTrigger(timeInterval: TimeInterval, **repeats:** Bool)

This initializer creates a Time Interval trigger that will deliver the notification after the period of time determined by the **timeInterval** argument (in seconds). The **repeats** argument determines if the notification will be delivered once or infinite times.

UNCalendarNotificationTrigger(dateMatching: DateComponents, **repeats:** Bool)

This initializer creates a Calendar trigger that delivers the notification at the date determined by the **dateMatching** argument. The **repeats** argument determines if the notification will be delivered once or infinite times.

UNLocationNotificationTrigger(region: CLCircularRegion, **repeats:** Bool)

This initializer creates a Location trigger that delivers the notification when the device is inside a region in the real world determined by the **region** argument. The **repeats** argument determines if the notification will be delivered once or infinite times.

To deliver a notification, we must create a request that contains the notification, an identifier, and a trigger. For this purpose, the framework defines the **UNNotification-Request** class.

UNNotificationRequest(identifier: String, **content:** UNNotificationContent, **trigger:** UNNotificationTrigger?)

This initializer creates a request to deliver the notification specified by the **content** argument and at the time or place specified by the **trigger** argument. The **identifier** argument is a string that we can use later to identify and manage the request.

As we mentioned earlier, before sending user notifications, we need to ask the user for permission. Apple recommends that we do this only when it is really necessary. For example, if our application includes a view with a switch that allows the user to enable notifications, or a button to send notifications, we should ask the user for permission in that view and not right after the application is launched. The following example shows how the process works.

Listing 12-11: Sending notifications

```
import SwiftUI
import UserNotifications

@Observable class ApplicationData {
   @ObservationIgnored let center = UNUserNotificationCenter.current()

   static let shared: ApplicationData = ApplicationData()
   private init() { }

   func askAuthorization() async -> Bool {
      do {
         let authorized = try await center.requestAuthorization(options:
            [.alert, .sound])
         return authorized
      } catch {
         print("Error: \(error)")
         return false
      }
   }
   func postNotification(message: String) async {
      let authorization = await center.notificationSettings()
      if authorization.authorizationStatus == .authorized {
         let content = UNMutableNotificationContent()
         content.title = "Reminder"
         content.body = message

         let trigger = UNTimeIntervalNotificationTrigger(timeInterval: 10,
            repeats: false)
         let id = "reminder-\(UUID())"
         let request = UNNotificationRequest(identifier: id,
            content: content, trigger: trigger)

         do {
            try await center.add(request)
         } catch {
            print("Error: \(error)")
         }
      }
   }
}
```

This model gets a reference to the **UNUserNotificationCenter** object assigned to our app and then defines two asynchronous methods: The **askAuthorization()** method to ask the user permission to post notifications and the **postNotification()** method to create a notification and send it to the Notification Center.

The **askAuthorization()** method calls the **requestAuthorization()** method to ask the user for authorization to post notifications of type **alert** and **sound**, and then returns a Boolean value to report the decision to the view. The **postNotification()** method, on the other hand, takes care of posting the notification. When the user presses the button to post a notification, we check if the app is still allowed to send notifications with the **notificationSettings()** method (This is a recommended practice), and if the value of the **authorizationStatus** property is equal to **authorized**, we schedule the notification.

The procedure to schedule the notification is simple, we need to create an instance of the **UNMutableNotificationContent** class with the values we want to include in the notification, create a trigger (in this case, we use a time interval trigger), create an instance of the **UNNotificationRequest** class with those values to request the delivery of the notification, and finally add the request to the User Notification Center with the **add()** method. Note that the identifier of the request must be unique. In our example, we define it with the word "reminder" followed by a random value generated with the **UUID()** function.

Since everything is processed by the model, all we need to do in the view is to allow the user to send the notification and call the methods. For this example, we include a **TextField** view where users can insert the message they want to send with the notification, and a button to post it.

Listing 12-12: Scheduling a notification

```
struct ContentView: View {
   @State private var appData = ApplicationData.shared
   @State private var inputMessage: String = ""
   @State private var isButtonDisabled: Bool = false

   var body: some View {
      VStack(spacing: 12) {
         HStack {
            Text("Message:")
            TextField("Insert Message", text: $inputMessage)
               .textFieldStyle(.roundedBorder)
         }
         HStack {
            Spacer()
            Button("Post Notification") {
               Task {
                  let message = inputMessage.trimmingCharacters(in:
                     .whitespaces)
                  if !message.isEmpty {
                     inputMessage = ""
                     await appData.postNotification(message: message)
                  }
               }
            }.buttonStyle(.borderedProminent)
            .disabled(isButtonDisabled)
         }
         Spacer()
      }.padding()
      .task {
         let authorization = await appData.askAuthorization()
         isButtonDisabled = !authorization
      }
   }
}
```

To ask for authorization, we initiate a task as soon as the view is loaded with the **task()** modifier. Once the user inserts a text and presses the button, the notification is scheduled and we can see it appear later in the home screen.

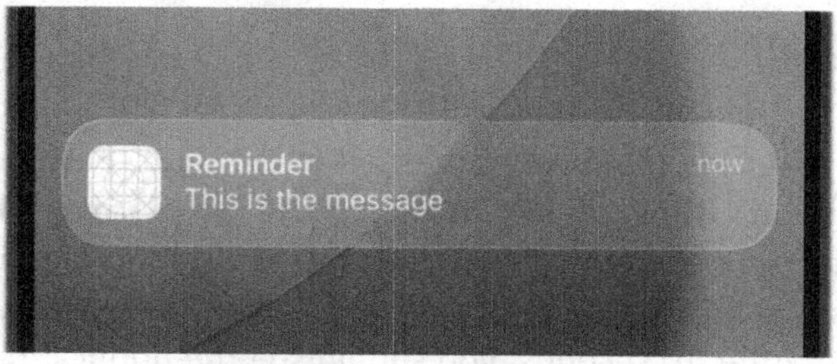

Figure 12-4: User notification

Do It Yourself

Create a new App project. Create a file called **ApplicationData.swift** for the code in Listing 12-11. Update the `ContentView` structure with the code in Listing 12-12. Run the application on an iPhone simulator. The first time you run the application the system will ask you to allow the app to deliver notifications. Press the Allow button. Type a message and press the Post Notification button to post the notification. Press the Home button to close the app (**Controls > Home**). You should see the notification popping up on the screen after 10 seconds.

Notifications can also play a sound. All we need to do is to add the sound file to the project, create the `UNNotificationSound` object with it, and assign it to the `sound` property.

Listing 12-13: Playing a sound

```
func postNotification(message: String) async {
   let authorization = await center.notificationSettings()
   if authorization.authorizationStatus == .authorized {
      let content = UNMutableNotificationContent()
      content.title = "Reminder"
      content.body = message
      content.sound = UNNotificationSound(named:
         UNNotificationSoundName(rawValue: "alarm.mp3"))

      let trigger = UNTimeIntervalNotificationTrigger(timeInterval: 10,
         repeats: false)
      let id = "reminder-\(UUID())"
      let request = UNNotificationRequest(identifier: id,
         content: content, trigger: trigger)

      do {
         try await center.add(request)
      } catch {
         print("Error: \(error)")
      }
   }
}
```

Do It Yourself

Update the **`postNotification()`** method in the **`ApplicationData`** class with the code in Listing 12-13. Download the file **alarm.mp3** from our website and drag it to your project. Run the application on your iPhone. Insert a message and press the button to post the notification. Go to the Home screen. After 10 seconds, you should see the notification and hear the alert sound.

PRO

Media Attachments

In addition to sound, notifications can also contain other media types such as images and videos. The **`UNMutableNotificationContent`** class includes the following property to attach media files to the notification.

`attachments`

This property sets or returns an array of **`UNNotificationAttachment`** objects with the media files we want to show in the notification.

The attachments are loaded by an object of the **`UNNotificationAttachment`** class. The class includes the following initializer.

`UNNotificationAttachment(identifier:` `String`, **`url:`** `URL`, **`options:`** `Dictionary?)`

This initializer creates an attachment with the media loaded from the URL specified by the **url** argument. The **identifier** argument is the attachment's unique identifier, and the **options** argument is a dictionary with predefined values to configure the media. The most useful are **`UNNotificationAttachmentOptionsThumbnailClippingRectKey`** to use only a portion of an image, and **`UNNotificationAttachmentOptionsThumbnailTimeKey`** to select a frame from a video.

To attach an image or a video to the notification, we must create the **`UNNotificationAttachment`** object and assign it to the content's **`attachments`** property. This object takes a unique identifier and the URL of the file that contains the media we want to add to the notification. This means that we need the media to be in a file or to create the file ourselves. The following example illustrates how to take an image from the Asset Catalog, store it in a file, and assign it to the notification.

Listing 12-14: Attaching an image to a notification

```
func postNotification(message: String) async {
   let content = UNMutableNotificationContent()
   content.title = "Reminder"
   content.body = message

   let idImage = "attach-\(UUID())"
   if let urlImage = await getThumbnail(id: idImage) {
      if let attachment = try? UNNotificationAttachment(identifier:
         idImage, url: urlImage, options: nil) {
         content.attachments = [attachment]
      }
   }
   let trigger = UNTimeIntervalNotificationTrigger(timeInterval: 10,
      repeats: false)

   let id = "reminder-\(UUID())"
   let request = UNNotificationRequest(identifier: id, content: content,
      trigger: trigger)
   do {
      let center = UNUserNotificationCenter.current()
      try await center.add(request)
   } catch {
      print("Error: \(error)")
   }
}
func getThumbnail(id: String) async -> URL? {
   let manager = FileManager.default
   if let docURL = manager.urls(for: .documentDirectory,
      in: .userDomainMask).first {
      let fileURL = docURL.appendingPathComponent("\(id).png")
      if let image = UIImage(named: "husky") {
         if let thumbnail = await image.byPreparingThumbnail(ofSize:
            CGSize(width: 100, height: 100)) {
            if let imageData = thumbnail.pngData() {
               if let _ = try? imageData.write(to: fileURL) {
                  return fileURL
               }
            }
         }
      }
   }
   return nil
}
```

Because we need to load the image, process it, and save it to a file, we moved the code to a new method called **getThumbnail()**. In this method, we get the URL of the Documents directory, append the name of the file, then load the image from the Asset Catalog, convert it to data, resize it using the **byPreparingThumbnail()** method, and store it. The URL of the file is returned by the method and used by the code to attach the image to the notification. The result can be seen below. The image is displayed inside the banner and expands when the user taps and holds over the notification or drags the notification down, depending on the state of the application.

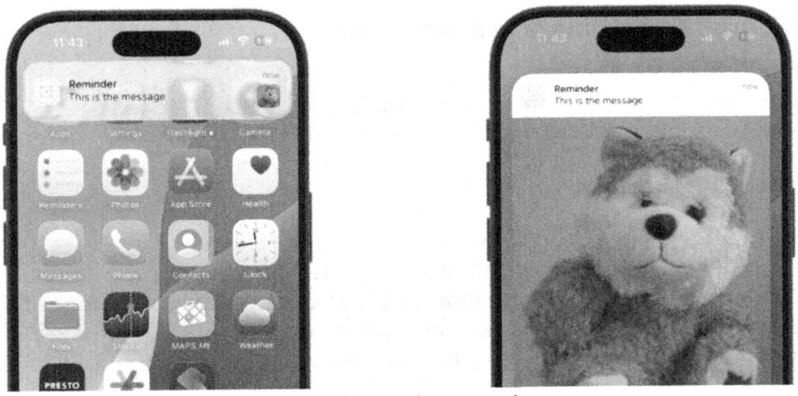

Figure 12-5: Media Attachment

Do It Yourself

Update the **`postNotification()`** method with the code in Listing 12-14 and add the **`getThumbnail()`** method below. Download the **husky.png** image from our website and add it to an Asset Catalog. Run the application on your iPhone. Insert a message and press the button to post the notification. Go to the Home screen. You should see a notification with the image of the husky. Drag the notification down to expand the image.

PRO

Notifications Delegate

If the user is working with the app at the time a notification is delivered, the notification will not be displayed on the screen. To change this behavior, we can assign a delegate to the User Notification Center. For this purpose, the framework includes the **`UNUserNotification-CenterDelegate`** protocol. To determine when the notification should be shown, the protocol defines the following method.

`userNotificationCenter(``UNUserNotificationCenter,` **`willPresent:`** `UNNotification)`

This asynchronous method is called by the User Notification Center on the delegate when the application is active and a notification has to be delivered. The method must return a structure of type **`UNNotificationPresentationOptions`** to indicate how we want to alert the user. The structure includes the type properties **`badge`**, **`banner`**, **`list`**, and **`sound`**.

When a notification is triggered and the application is running, the User Notification Center calls the protocol method on its delegate to ask the application what to do. In this method, we can perform any task we want and then return a **`UNNotification-PresentationOptions`** value to specify the type of notification to display. As always, we can declare any object as the delegate. For this example, we decided to create a separate class called **`CenterDelegate`**, as shown below.

Listing 12-15: Defining a delegate for the User Notification Center

```
import SwiftUI
import UserNotifications

class CenterDelegate: NSObject, UNUserNotificationCenterDelegate {
   func userNotificationCenter(_ center: UNUserNotificationCenter,
      willPresent notification: UNNotification) async ->
         UNNotificationPresentationOptions {
      return [.banner]
   }
}
```

This class conforms to the **UNUserNotificationCenterDelegate** protocol and implements the **userNotificationCenter(UNUserNotificationCenter, willPresent:)** method to show the notification in a banner while the app is running. Note that the **UNUserNotificationCenterDelegate** protocol was defined in Objective-C and therefore it needs the class to inherit the functionality provided by the **NSObject** class to work properly.

Once the delegate class is defined, we need to create an instance from the model and assign it as the delegate, as shown below.

Listing 12-16: Showing notifications while the app is running

```
@Observable class ApplicationData {
   @ObservationIgnored let center = UNUserNotificationCenter.current()
   @ObservationIgnored let centerDelegate: CenterDelegate =
      CenterDelegate()

   static let shared: ApplicationData = ApplicationData()
   private init() {
      center.delegate = centerDelegate
   }
   func askAuthorization() async -> Bool {
      do {
         let authorized = try await center.requestAuthorization(options:
            [.alert, .sound])
         return authorized
      } catch {
         print("Error: \(error)")
         return false
      }
   }
   func postNotification(message: String) async {
      let content = UNMutableNotificationContent()
      content.title = "Reminder"
      content.body = message

      let trigger = UNTimeIntervalNotificationTrigger(timeInterval: 10,
         repeats: false)
      let id = "reminder-\(UUID())"
      let request = UNNotificationRequest(identifier: id,
         content: content, trigger: trigger)
      do {
         let center = UNUserNotificationCenter.current()
```

```
            try await center.add(request)
         } catch {
            print("Error: \(error)")
         }
      }
   }
```

When a notification is received, the system calls the delegate method and the notification is shown on the screen.

Figure 12-6: *Notifications in an active application*

Do It Yourself

Create a new file called **CenterDelegate.swift** for the code in Listing 12-15 and update the **ApplicationData** class with the code in Listing 12-16. Run the application on your iPhone and post a notification. After a few seconds, the notification should appear over the app at the top of the screen, as shown in Figure 12-6.

PRO

12.3 - Key/Value Observing

KVO (Key/Value Observing) is a system we can use to perform a task when the value of a property is modified. This is similar to what the **didSet()** method does for the properties of our own structures and classes, except that we can use it with properties contained in classes defined by frameworks provided by Apple. To perform a task when the property's value changes, we need to add an observer to the object to which the property belongs. Swift includes the following method for this purpose.

observe(KeyPath, **options:** NSKeyValueObservingOptions, **changeHandler:** Closure)

This method adds an observer to the object. The first argument is the key path to the property we want to observe, the **options** argument is a Set with enumeration values that determine the values returned by the observer (possible values are **new**, **old**, **initial**, and **prior**), and the **changeHandler** argument is the closure we want to execute when the value of the property changes. The closure receives two values, one with a reference to the object and another that represents the value required by the options.

As we will see later, KVO is typically used to observe properties of classes defined in frameworks provided by Apple, but we can also observe properties in our own objects. The only requirement is that the properties must be defined as Objective-C properties. This is because KVO is a system designed for the Objective-C programming language. To define properties in Swift that behave like Objective-C properties, we need to use the **@objc** and **dynamic** keywords. The **@objc** keyword makes the property available to Objective-C systems, while the **dynamic** keyword is required for the property to work with a system called Dynamic Dispatch, which is designed to perform operations in the background (in this case, reporting when the property has been updated). The following example illustrates how to define these properties.

Listing 12-17: Defining an observable property for KVO

```
import SwiftUI

class MyObject: NSObject {
   @objc dynamic var testValue: Int = 0
}
```

Our class contains only one property called **testValue**, but since it has been modified with the **@objc** and **dynamic** keywords, we can add an observer to keep track of its value. Note that all the classes defined in Objective-C require the basic functionality of the **NSObject** class, so our class inherits from that class to be able to include observable properties.

Once there is a property that we can observe, we must add the observer to the object. In the following model, we define a property to provide a value for the view, but also two other properties to control the process. The **myObject** property contains an instance of our Objective-C class, and the **myObserver** property stores a reference to the observer so we can disable it later from the view.

Listing 12-18: Observing a property

```
import SwiftUI

@Observable class ApplicationData {
   var showValue: String = ""
   @ObservationIgnored var myObject = MyObject()
   @ObservationIgnored var myObserver: NSKeyValueObservation?

   static let shared: ApplicationData = ApplicationData()
   private init() {
      myObserver = myObject.observe(\.testValue, options: [.new],
         changeHandler: { obj, value in
         if let newValue = value.newValue {
            Task { @MainActor in
               self.showValue = "Value: \(newValue)"
            }
         }
      })
   }
}
```

The observer is defined in the initializer by calling the **observe()** method on the **MyObject** object. The arguments specify that we want to observe the **testValue** property, that we only want to check the new value assigned to the property, and what to do with it. In this case, we use the value of the property to create a string and assign it to the **showValue** property, so it can be displayed by the view.

The property's new value is received by the closure in a generic structure called **NSKeyValueObservedChange**. The structure includes the properties **oldValue** and **newValue**, so we read the value from the **newValue** property and create the string.

Now we have to show the string from the view, allow the user to update the value of the observable property, and disable the observer when the view disappears, as shown below.

Listing 12-19: Working with a KVO property

```
struct ContentView: View {
   @State private var appData = ApplicationData.shared

   var body: some View {
      VStack {
         Text(appData.showValue)
         Button("Add Value") {
            appData.myObject.testValue += 100
         }.buttonStyle(.borderedProminent)
         Spacer()
      }.padding()
      .onDisappear {
         appData.myObserver = nil
      }
   }
}
```

This view includes a **Text** view to show the string created by the observer and a **Button** view to add 100 to the current value of the **testValue** property. When the user presses the button, the value of this property is modified, the observer recognizes the change, and the closure creates the new string that is displayed on the screen.

The **observe()** method returns an object that conforms to the **NSKeyValueObservation** protocol. When the observer is created, we assign it to the **myObserver** property so that we can disable the observer by assigning **nil** to this property, as we do in the **onDisappear()** modifier. This destroys the **NSKeyValueObservation** object and therefore the observer no longer responds to changes in the property.

Do It Yourself

Create a new App project. Create a Swift file called **MyObject.swift** for the class in Listing 12-17. Create a Swift file called **ApplicationData.swift** for the model in Listing 12-18. Update the **ContentView** structure with the code in Listing 12-19. Run the application on an iPhone simulator. You should see the value increase by 100 every time the button is pressed. We will apply observers in more practical scenarios in later chapters.

PRO

12.4 - App States

An application can be in three different states: active, inactive, or in the background. The app is active when it is visible and the user can interact with it, inactive when it is visible but not in focus, and in the background when it is still open but no longer visible. The states are reported by an environment property called **scenePhase**. This property returns an enumeration value of type **ScenePhase**. The available values are **active**, **inactive**, and **background**. To detect changes in the state of the app, we can track this property with the **onChange()** modifier from the **App** structure, as shown below.

Listing 12-20: Detecting changes in the app's state

```
@main struct MyApp: App {
   @Environment(\.scenePhase) var scenePhase

   var body: some Scene {
      WindowGroup {
         ContentView()
            .onChange(of: scenePhase, initial: false) { old, phase in
               if phase == .active {
                  print("The app is active")
               } else if phase == .background {
                  print("The app is in the background")
               }
            }
      }
   }
}
```

In this example, we compare the value returned by the **scenePhase** property with the values **active** and **background**, so we can print a message to the console when the state changes between these two. If the app becomes active, the message "The app is active" is printed on the console, and when the app moves to the background, the message "The app is in the background" is printed instead.

Do It Yourself

Create a new App project. Update the **App** structure with the code in Listing 12-20. Run the application on an iPhone simulator. You should see the message "The app is active" when the **ContentView** view appears on the screen. Press the Home button to close the app (**Controls > Home**). This time, you should see on the console the message "The app is in the background".

Chapter 13
Framework Integration

PRO

13.1 - Integration with UIKit

Although SwiftUI has been around for years, not everything we need to build a professional application is available in this framework. As a result, we sometimes have to rely on tools provided by older frameworks such as **UIKit** or **AppKit**. We have already used some of these features in previous chapters, but there are many more that we can integrate into our code to further expand the capabilities of our applications.

On iOS in particular, it is often necessary to work directly with views and view controllers defined in the **UIKit** framework. These components, created from the `UIView` and `UIViewController` classes, either extend the capabilities of standard SwiftUI views or offer features that are not available in SwiftUI at all. To bridge this gap, SwiftUI introduces two protocols that allow us to wrap and integrate these UIKit components into a SwiftUI interface: `UIViewRepresentable` and `UIViewControllerRepresentable`.

IMPORTANT

In this chapter, we use simple examples to demonstrate how to integrate UIKit views and view controllers into SwiftUI interfaces. We will see more practical examples in later chapters.

PRO

Representable View

The `UIViewRepresentable` protocol defines a structure that serves as a wrapper for objects created from the `UIView` class or its subclasses. A structure that conforms to this protocol can present a UIKit view within a SwiftUI interface. To create and manage the UIKit view, the structure must implement the following methods.

`makeUIView(context: Context)`

This method creates the UIKit view and returns it. The **context** argument is a reference to a structure of type `UIViewRepresentableContext` that provides information about the state of the view.

updateUIView(UIViewType, **context:** Context)

This method updates the UIKit view with information provided by the SwiftUI interface through a binding property. The first argument is a reference to the UIKit view, and the **context** argument is a reference to a structure of type **UIViewRepresentableContext** that provides information about the state of the view.

dismantleUIView(UIViewType, **coordinator:** Coordinator)

This type method prepares the view to be dismissed. The first argument is a reference to the UIKit view, and the **coordinator** argument is the object that sends values back to the SwiftUI interface.

makeCoordinator()

This method creates the object that communicates information from the UIKit view back to the SwiftUI interface.

To include a **UIView** object in a SwiftUI interface (or an object created from one of its subclasses), we need to define a structure that conforms to the **UIViewRepresentable** protocol and implement the methods listed above. The **makeUIView()** and **updateUIView()** methods are mandatory. In the **makeUIView()** method we must create and return the instance of the UIKit view, and the **updateUIView()** method is used to update the view with values coming from the SwiftUI interface.

The following example creates a UIKit view with a blue background and includes it in a SwiftUI interface. In this case, we only need the **makeUIView()** method to create the UIKit view, but we also have to implement the **updateUIView()** method because it is required by the protocol.

Listing 13-1: Preparing a UIKit view to work with SwiftUI

```
import SwiftUI

struct MyCustomView: UIViewRepresentable {
   func makeUIView(context: Context) -> some UIView {
      let view = UIView()
      view.backgroundColor = UIColor(.blue)
      return view
   }
   func updateUIView(_ uiView: UIViewType, context: Context) { }
}
```

The **makeUIView()** method is called every time a new instance of the **MyCustomView** structure is created. In this method, we create the **UIView** view, give it a blue background, and return it. Therefore, every time we create an instance of the **MyCustomView** structure, a **UIView** is created and included in our SwiftUI interface, as in the following example.

Listing 13-2: Showing a UIKit view within a SwiftUI view

```
struct ContentView: View {
   var body: some View {
      VStack {
         MyCustomView()
            .frame(width: 200, height: 150)
            .padding()
         Spacer()
      }
   }
}
```

A representable view has a flexible size by default, but we can use SwiftUI modifiers to change it. In this example, we use the **`frame()`** modifier to assign a fixed width and height. The result is shown below.

Figure 13-1: *UIKit view in a SwiftUI interface*

A **`UIView`** object creates an empty view, but we can also implement views that take input from the user, such as text fields, switches, and more. To pass values from the SwiftUI view to the UIKit view, we use the **`updateUIView()`** method. However, if we want to send values from the UIKit view back to the SwiftUI interface, we need to implement the **`makeCoordinator()`** method. From this method, we must create an instance of a coordinator object and return it. A coordinator is an object that can send information back from the UIKit view to the SwiftUI interface, usually by modifying binding properties. How to process these values depends on the type of UIKit view we are working with. For example, a **`UITextView`** view creates an input field where the user can enter multiple lines of text, like the **`TextEditor`** view in SwiftUI. This view reports changes by calling delegate methods. Therefore, to get the text inserted by the user in a **`UITextView`** view and process it in SwiftUI, we need to create a coordinator class that conforms to the **`UITextViewDelegate`** protocol and implements its methods. The following example illustrates how to create a **`UIViewRepresentable`** structure to work with this class.

Listing 13-3: Sending and receiving values from the SwiftUI view

```
import SwiftUI

struct TextView: UIViewRepresentable {
   @Binding var input: String
```

```
    func makeUIView(context: Context) -> UITextView {
        let view = UITextView()
        view.backgroundColor = UIColor.yellow
        view.font = UIFont.systemFont(ofSize: 17)
        view.delegate = context.coordinator
        return view
    }
    func updateUIView(_ uiView: UITextView, context: Context) {
        uiView.text = input
    }
    func makeCoordinator() -> CoordinatorTextView {
        return CoordinatorTextView(input: $input)
    }
}
class CoordinatorTextView: NSObject, UITextViewDelegate {
    @Binding var inputCoordinator: String

    init(input: Binding<String>) {
        self._inputCoordinator = input
    }
    func textViewDidChange(_ textView: UITextView) {
        inputCoordinator = textView.text
    }
}
```

This example creates a **UIViewRepresentable** structure called **TextView**. The structure includes a **@Binding** property called **input** to receive the values and pass them to the SwiftUI view. Below the definition of the **TextView** structure, we define a class called **CoordinatorTextView**. This is our view coordinator whose job is to send values back to the SwiftUI view. For this purpose, we initialize it with a **@Binding** property that is linked to the **input** property defined by the **TextView** structure, and then implement a delegate method that is executed when a character is inserted or removed by the user. The method gets the current text in the input field, so we assign it to the **@Binding** property to send it back to the SwiftUI view.

The view is added to the SwiftUI interface as before, but now we need a **@State** property to store and pass the value to the **input** property.

Listing 13-4: Receiving and sending values to a UIKit view

```
struct ContentView: View {
    @State private var inputText: String = "Initial text"

    var body: some View {
        VStack {
            HStack {
                Text(inputText)
                Spacer()
                Button("Clear") {
                    inputText = ""
                }.buttonStyle(.glass)
            }
            TextView(input: $inputText)
        }.padding()
```

```
    }
}
```

This view defines a **@State** property called **inputText**, a **Text** view to display its value, a button to replace the current value with an empty string, and an instance of our **TextInput** view. The **TextInput** view gets a reference to the **inputText** property so that the property is connected to the **input** property in the representable view and we can pass values back and forth.

When the user enters or removes a character in the editor, the representable view calls the **textViewDidChange()** method in the coordinator and the method assigns the current value in the text view to the **inputCoordinator** property. This means that the value is now available in the **@State** property and the **Text** view can show it on the screen. On the other hand, when the user presses the Clear button, we assign an empty string to the **@State** property, the system executes the **updateUIView()** method in the representable view, and the value of the **@Binding** property connected to the **@State** property is assigned to the view, so the text view is cleared.

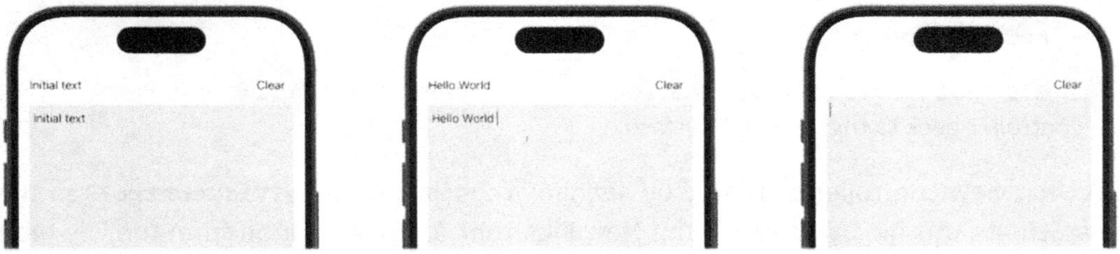

Figure 13-2: *`UITextView` view in a SwiftUI interface*

Do It Yourself

Create a new App project. Create a Swift file called **TextView.swift** for the code in Listing 13-3. Update the **ContentView** structure with the code in Listing 13-4. Run the application on an iPhone simulator. Insert a text. You should see the text changing at the top. Press the Clear button. You should see the text removed from the text view and also from the view at the top.

PRO

Representable View Controller

The **UIViewControllerRepresentable** protocol defines a structure that serves as a wrapper for objects created from the **UIViewController** class or its subclasses. This class presents a view that can include other views to define the interface for a window or the entire screen, like the views defined by SwiftUI files. A structure that conforms to the **UIViewControllerRepresentable** protocol can present these view controllers within a SwiftUI interface. To create and manage the view controller, the structure must implement the following methods.

makeUIViewController(context: Context)

This method creates the UIKit view controller and returns it. The **context** argument is a reference to a structure of type **UIViewControllerRepresentableContext** that provides information about the state of the view controller.

updateUIViewController(UIViewControllerType, **context:** Context)

This method updates the UIKit view controller with information provided by the SwiftUI interface. The first argument is a reference to the UIKit view controller, and the **context** argument is a reference to a structure of type **UIViewControllerRepresentableContext** that provides information about the state of the view controller.

dismantleUIViewController(UIViewControllerType, **coordinator:** Coordinator)

This type method prepares the view controller to be dismissed. The first argument is a reference to the UIKit view controller, and the **coordinator** argument is the object that sends values back to the SwiftUI interface.

makeCoordinator()

This method creates the object that communicates information from the UIKit view controller back to the SwiftUI interface.

A UIKit view controller is created by defining a subclass of the **UIViewController** class. We can create this file by choosing the New File from Template option from the File menu, just as we do when creating new SwiftUI views. In this case, however, the template we must select is called Cocoa Touch Class. After selecting this option, Xcode presents a dialog where we can specify the file name and the class from which the new subclass will inherit. For this example, we created a class called **DetailViewController** that inherits from **UIViewController**, as shown below.

Listing 13-5: Creating a UIKit view controller

```
import UIKit

class DetailViewController: UIViewController {
   override func viewDidLoad() {
      super.viewDidLoad()
      let label = UILabel()
      label.frame = CGRect(x: 20, y: 16, width: 250, height: 30)
      label.font = UIFont.systemFont(ofSize: 30)
      label.text = "Hello World!"
      view.addSubview(label)
   }
}
```

When the view controller class is instantiated, it creates a view to represent the interface, assigns it to the **view** property, and calls the **viewDidLoad()** method to tell our code that the view is ready. In this method, we can perform all the necessary tasks to initialize the view. In our example, we create a **UILabel** object to display a text on the screen. This object works like the SwiftUI **Text** view, but requires some configuration. In this case, we give it a position and a size by assigning a **CGRect** value to the **frame** property, define a font with a size of 30 points, give it the text to display, and then add it to the view controller's view with the **addSubview()** method.

Now that we have the view controller, we need to create a representable view to turn it into a SwiftUI view, as in the following example.

Listing 13-6: Creating the representable view for a UIKit view controller

```
import SwiftUI

struct MyViewController: UIViewControllerRepresentable {
   func makeUIViewController(context: Context) -> DetailViewController {
      let controller = DetailViewController()
      return controller
   }
   func updateUIViewController(_ uiViewController: UIViewControllerType,
      context: Context) {
   }
}
```

The **UIViewControllerRepresentable** protocol works like the **UIViewRepresentable** protocol. We must define a structure that conforms to this protocol, and then add the methods we need to create and update the view. In our example, we only define the **makeUIViewController()** method because we only need to create an instance of our view controller to present it on the screen. The following SwiftUI view loads this view controller inside a **NavigationStack** view when the user presses a button.

Listing 13-7: Loading a UIKit view controller from a SwiftUI view

```
struct ContentView: View {
   var body: some View {
      NavigationStack {
         VStack {
            NavigationLink("Open UIKit View", destination: {
               MyViewController()
            }).buttonStyle(.borderedProminent)
            Spacer()
         }.padding()
      }
   }
}
```

This view includes a **NavigationLink** view that loads an instance of the **MyViewController** structure, so we can navigate from the initial view to the view controller created by this structure, as we do with normal SwiftUI views.

Figure 13-3: *UIKit view controller in a SwiftUI interface*

Do It Yourself

Select the **File from Template** option from the File menu at the top of the screen to create a new file. Click on the Cocoa Touch Class icon in the iOS section to create a UIKit file. Select the `UIViewController` class from the Subclass option. Insert the name DetailViewController and press Next to save it. Update the `DetailViewController` class with the code in Listing 13-5. Create a Swift file called **MyViewController.swift** for the code in Listing 13-6. Update the `ContentView` structure with the code in Listing 13-7. Run the application on an iPhone simulator. Press the button to open the UIKit view controller. You should see the label created by the controller on the screen, as shown in Figure 13-3, right.

Chapter 14

Media

BASIC

14.1 - Pictures

Today, personal devices are used primarily to capture, edit, and share visual content. As a result, access to the camera, the Photos library, and image processing capabilities has become essential for modern applications. In this chapter, we will explore the SwiftUI features and Apple frameworks that allow us to add these capabilities to our apps.

BASIC

Photos Picker

One of the tools SwiftUI provides for working with images is the **PhotosPicker** structure. This structure creates a view that allows the user to select one or more images from the Photo library. The following is the view's initializer.

```
PhotosPicker(selection: Binding, maxSelectionCount: Int?,
selectionBehavior: PhotosPickerSelectionBehavior, matching:
PHPickerFilter?, preferredItemEncoding:
EncodingDisambiguationPolicy, photoLibrary: PHPhotoLibrary,
label: Closure)
```

This initializer creates a **PhotosPicker** view with the configuration specified by the arguments. The **selection** argument is the binding property that stores the references to the selected items. The **maxSelectionCount** argument is the maximum number of items we want to user to be able to select. The **selectionBehavior** argument specifies how the selection is performed. It is a structure with the type properties **default** (checkmark selection), **ordered** (number selection), **continuous** (live selection) and **continuousAndOrdered** (live number selection). The **matching** argument determines the type of items the view should include. It is a structure with the type properties **bursts**, **cinematicVideos**, **depthEffectPhotos**, **images**, **livePhotos**, **panoramas**, **screenRecordings**, **screenshots**, **slomoVideos**, **timelapseVideos**, and **videos**. The **preferredItemEncoding** argument determines the encoding to use to process the items. It is a structure with the type properties **automatic** (default), **current**, and **compatible**. The **photoLibrary** argument provides access to the library. It is a structure with the type method **shared()**. And the **label** argument is a closure that provides the label for the button generated by the view.

Since retrieving the items can take time, the picker does not return the images or videos directly, but a reference to the items that we can use to retrieve them later. The framework defines the **PhotosPickerItem** structure for this purpose. The structure includes the following property and method for accessing the media.

itemIdentifier

This property returns a string with the item's identifier.

loadTransferable(type: Type)

This asynchronous method loads the item and assigns it to an instance of the data type specified by the **type** argument. The data type assigned to this argument must conform to the **Transferable** protocol.

To get access to the **PhotosPicker** structure, we must import the **PhotosUI** framework. In addition, the view needs a **@State** property to store the selected items. To enable multiple selection, this property must store an array of **PhotosPickerItem** structures, but for single selection, the property only needs to store an optional **PhotosPickerItem** value, as shown below.

Listing 14-1: Creating a Photo picker

```
import SwiftUI
import PhotosUI

struct ContentView: View {
   @State private var selected: PhotosPickerItem?
   @State private var picture: UIImage?

   var body: some View {
      VStack {
         PhotosPicker(selection: $selected, matching: .images,
            photoLibrary: .shared()) { Text("Select a photo") }
            .buttonStyle(.borderedProminent)
         Image(uiImage: picture ?? UIImage(named: "nopicture")!)
            .resizable()
            .scaledToFit()
         Spacer()
      }.padding()
      .onChange(of: selected, initial: false) { old, item in
         Task {
            if let data = try? await item?.loadTransferable(type:
               Data.self) {
               picture = UIImage(data: data)
            }
         }
      }
   }
}
```

Most of the arguments in the **PhotosPicker** initializer are optional. In this example, we only need to tell the picker where to store the references of the selected items, what kind of items we want to show the user (images), and where to get them from (the shared library).

With this information, the **PhotosPicker** structure creates a button that opens a view to select the items when pressed. When an item is selected in this view, a reference is stored in the **@State** property. This means that we can monitor this property for changes with the **onChange()** modifier. When a new image is selected, we start an asynchronous task to call the **loadTransferable()** method for the selected item. This method loads the image, converts it to a **Data** structure, and returns it. If the process is successful, we use the data to initialize a **UIImage** object and assign it to the **picture** property to display it on the screen. The result is shown below.

Figure 14-1: *Photo Library's interface (center)*

Do It Yourself

Create a new App project. Update the **ContentView** structure with the code in Listing 14-1. Download the image **nopicture.png** from our website and add it to an Asset Catalog. Run the application on an iPhone simulator. Press the button. Tap on a picture to select it. The image should be assigned to the **Image** view and displayed on the screen, as shown in Figure 14-1 (right).

IMPORTANT

In this example, we have used the **Data** structure to transfer the value with the **loadTransferable()** method. We could have used an **Image** view instead, but this data type can only receive PNG images. For more information on the **Transferable** protocol, read the Drag and Drop Gesture section in Chapter 9.

By default, the **PhotosPicker** view creates a button that opens a view on top of our app, but we can also embed the view in our interface with the following modifier.

photosPickerStyle(PhotosPickerStyle)

This modifier specifies the presentation style for the view. The argument is a structure with the properties **compact**, **inline** and **presentation** (default).

The **presentation** style presents the view in a sheet, as was the case in the previous example. If we want to embed the view in our interface, we can use the **compact** or **inline** styles. These styles are very similar, but the **inline** style provides more options and easy access to the content, as shown by the following example.

Listing 14-2: Embedding the Photos Picker in our interface

```
struct ContentView: View {
    @State private var selected: PhotosPickerItem?
    @State private var picture: UIImage?
    @State private var showPicker = true

    var body: some View {
        VStack {
            Image(uiImage: picture ?? UIImage(named: "nopicture")!)
                .resizable()
                .scaledToFit()
                .onTapGesture {
                    withAnimation {
                        showPicker.toggle()
                    }
                }
            Spacer()
            if showPicker {
                PhotosPicker(selection: $selected, matching: .images,
                    photoLibrary: .shared()) { Text("Select a photo") }
                    .buttonStyle(.borderedProminent)
                    .photosPickerStyle(.inline)
                    .frame(height: 300)
            }
        }.padding()
        .onChange(of: selected, initial: false) { old, item in
            Task {
                if let data = try? await item?.loadTransferable(type:
                    Data.self) {
                    picture = UIImage(data: data)
                }
            }
            withAnimation {
                showPicker.toggle()
            }
        }
    }
}
```

The size of a **compact** or **inline** photos picker is determined by the available space, so it automatically adapts when the interface changes. However, we can assign a fixed size using the **frame()** modifier. In this example, we set the picker's height to 300 points and define a Boolean property called **showPicker** to control when it appears on the screen. This allows us to dismiss it after the user selects an image. The result is shown below.

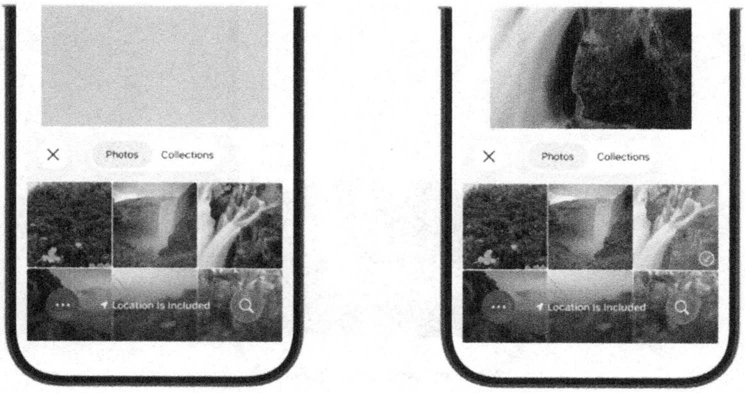

Figure 14-2: *Inline Photos Picker*

In addition to the **frame()** modifier, we can also use the following modifiers provided by the framework to configure the view.

photosPickerDisabledCapabilities(PHPickerCapabilities)

This modifier specifies which capabilities are to be excluded from the view. The argument is a structure (or a set of structures) designed to represent a capability. The structure includes the properties **collectionNavigation**, **selectionActions**, **search**, **sensitivityAnalysisIntervention**, and **stagingArea**.

photosPickerAccessoryVisibility(Visibility, **edges:** Edge)

This modifier specifies whether the controls should be visible or not. The first argument specifies the visibility. It is an enumeration with the values **automatic**, **visible** and **hidden**. And the **edges** argument is a set of **Edge** values that specify the side of the Photos Picker from which the controls should be removed. The **Edge** enumeration includes the values **top**, **bottom**, **leading** and **trailing**.

These modifiers allow us to select the controls we want to include or hide. For example, the interface of a Photo Picker includes a button to close the view. This button was designed for a sheet presentation, but we can remove it with the photosPickerDisabledCapabilities() modifier when the view is embedded in our interface, as in the following example.

Listing 14-3: Hiding controls

```
PhotosPicker(selection: $selected, matching: .images, photoLibrary:
.shared()) { Text("Select a photo") }
    .buttonStyle(.borderedProminent)
    .photosPickerStyle(.inline)
    .photosPickerDisabledCapabilities([.selectionActions])
    .frame(height: 300)
```

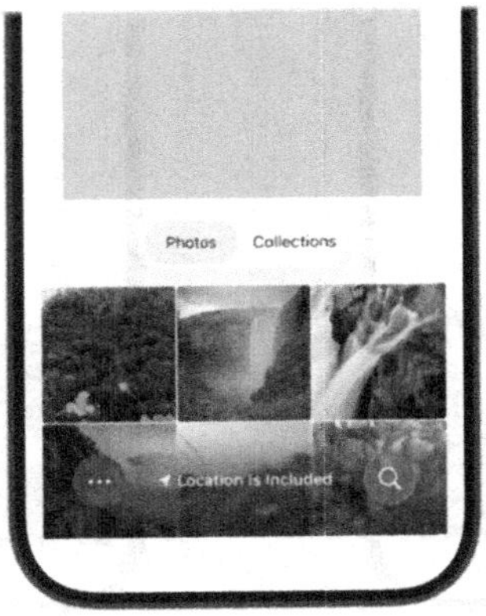

Figure 14-3: *Photos Picker with custom controls*

In the previous example, the user has only been able to select one item at a time. By assigning an array of **PhotosPickerItem** structures to the **@State** property, we can allow the user to select multiple items. Although this is all we need to enable multiple selection, we must consider how the items will be removed from the list when they are deselected by the user. We could clear the array and reload each element, but some of the items may take a while to load. Another option is to store the items in a separate array and compare the values, so we can remove only the deselected elements, but keep the rest. This is the approach we take in the following example. For this purpose, we need a model with a structure to store the images and their identifiers, as shown below.

Listing 14-4: Defining the model for multiple selection

```
import SwiftUI
import PhotosUI

struct ItemsData: Identifiable {
   var id: String
   var image: UIImage
}
@Observable class ApplicationData {
   var listPictures: [ItemsData] = []
   var selected: [PhotosPickerItem] = []

   static let shared: ApplicationData = ApplicationData()
   private init() { }

   func removeDeselectedItems() {
      listPictures = listPictures.filter { value in
         if selected.contains(where: { $0.itemIdentifier == value.id }) {
            return true
         } else {
            return false
         }
      }
   }
   func addSelectedItems() {
      for item in selected {
         Task {
            if let data = try? await item.loadTransferable(type:
               Data.self) {
```

```
            if let id = item.itemIdentifier, let image = UIImage(data:
                data) {
                if !listPictures.contains(where: { $0.id == id }) {
                    let newPicture = ItemsData(id: id, image: image)
                    await MainActor.run {
                        listPictures.append(newPicture)
                    }
                }
            }
        }
    }
  }
}
```

This model includes two properties: one to store an array of **ItemsData** structures to deliver the currently selected images to the views, and another with an array of **PhotosPickerItem** structures for the **PhotosPicker** view to store the references of the items selected by the user. There are also two methods in the model: **removeDeselectedItems()** and **addSelectedItems()**. Both are executed by the view every time the user modifies the selection (every time the value of the **selected** property changes). The **removeDeselectedItems()** method iterates through the items in the **listPictures** array to check which ones are still selected by the user, so any item that has been deselected is no longer on the list. On the other hand, the **addSelectedItems()** method adds to the **listPictures** array the items that the user added to the selection. The view can now use the **listPictures** array to display the selected images on the screen and call these methods each time the selection is modified.

Listing 14-5: Allowing the user to perform multiple selections

```
struct ContentView: View {
   @State private var appData = ApplicationData.shared

   let guides = [
      GridItem(.flexible()),
      GridItem(.flexible()),
      GridItem(.flexible())
   ]
   var body: some View {
      VStack {
         ScrollView {
            LazyVGrid(columns: guides) {
               ForEach(appData.listPictures) { item in
                  Image(uiImage: item.image)
                     .resizable()
                     .scaledToFit()
               }
            }
         }.padding()
         Spacer()
         PhotosPicker(selection: $appData.selected, maxSelectionCount: 4,
            selectionBehavior: .continuous, matching: .images,
            photoLibrary: .shared()) { Text("Select Photos") }
         .photosPickerStyle(.inline)
```

```
            .photosPickerDisabledCapabilities(.selectionActions)
      }
      .onChange(of: appData.selected, initial: false) { old, items in
         appData.removeDeselectedItems()
         appData.addSelectedItems()
      }
   }
}
```

In this example, we have configured the picker to select a maximum of 4 items, but this is not necessary. If no limit is specified, users can select all the items they want. Note that because the Photos Picker is embedded in our interface, the selection buttons are not required, and the selection behavior is set to **continuous**, so the selection is updated live (the user doesn't need to press the Add button).

Figure 14-4: *Multiple selection*

Do It Yourself

Create a Swift file called **ApplicationData.swift** for the model in Listing 14-4. Update the **ContentView** structure with the code in Listing 14-5. Run the application on an iPhone simulator. Select multiple pictures. You should see the selected pictures on the list, as shown in Figure 14-4 (right).

BASIC

Camera

Mobile devices are widely used to capture and store photos, so a built-in camera is now a standard feature on every device. Because many applications need direct access to the camera and must manage the images or videos captured by the user, the system provides ready-to-use tools to handle this task. For iOS devices, the **UIKit** framework defines the **UIImagePickerController** class. This class presents an interface that allows users to take photos or record videos without requiring us to build the camera interface from scratch. The following are the most frequently used properties to configure this controller.

sourceType

This property sets or returns a value that determines the type of source we want to use to get the pictures. It is an enumeration called **SourceType** included in the **UIImagePickerController** class. At this moment, only the value **camera** is available.

mediaTypes

This property sets or returns a value that determines the type of media we want to work with. It takes an array of strings with values that represent every media we want to use. The most common are **public.image** for pictures and **public.movie** for videos. (These values can be represented by the constants **kUTTypeImage** and **kUTTypeMovie**.)

cameraCaptureMode

This property sets or returns a value that determines the capture mode used by the camera. It is an enumeration called **CameraCaptureMode** included in the **UIImagePickerController** class. The values available are **photo** and **video**.

cameraFlashMode

This property sets or returns a value that determines the flash mode used by the camera. It is an enumeration called **CameraFlashMode** included in the **UIImagePickerController** class. The values available are **on**, **off**, and **auto**.

allowsEditing

This property sets or returns a Boolean value that determines if the user is allowed to edit the image.

videoQuality

This property sets or returns a value that determines the quality of the recorded video. It is an enumeration called **QualityType** included in the **UIImagePickerController** class. The values available are **typeHigh**, **typeMedium**, **typeLow**, **type640x480**, **typeIFrame960x540**, and **typeIFrame1280x720**.

The **UIImagePickerController** class also offers the following type methods to detect the source available and the type of media it can manage.

isSourceTypeAvailable(SourceType**)**

This type method returns a Boolean value that indicates if the source specified by the argument is supported by the device. The argument is an enumeration called **SourceType** included in the **UIImagePickerController** class. At this moment, only the value **camera** is available.

availableMediaTypes(for: SourceType**)**

This type method returns an array with strings that represent the media types available for the source specified by the argument. The argument is an enumeration called **SourceType** included in the **UIImagePickerController** class. At this moment, only the value **camera** is available.

isCameraDeviceAvailable(CameraDevice)

This type method returns a Boolean value that indicates if the camera specified by the argument is available on the device. The argument is an enumeration called **CameraDevice** included in the **UIImagePickerController** class. The values available are **rear** and **front**.

The **UIImagePickerController** class creates a new view where the user can take pictures or record videos. After the image or the video is created, the view must be dismissed, and the media processed. The way our code gets access to the media and knows when to dismiss the view is through a delegate that conforms to the **UIImagePickerControllerDelegate** protocol. The protocol includes the following methods.

imagePickerController(UIImagePickerController, **didFinishPickingMediaWithInfo:** Dictionary)

This method is called on the delegate when the user finishes taking the image or recording the video. The second argument contains a dictionary with the information about the media. The values in the dictionary are identified with properties of the **InfoKey** structure included in the **UIImagePickerController** class. The properties available are **cropRect**, **editedImage**, **imageURL**, **livePhoto**, **mediaMetadata**, **mediaType**, **mediaURL**, and **originalImage**.

imagePickerControllerDidCancel(UIImagePickerController)

This method is called on the delegate when the user cancels the process.

An image picker can be presented with a sheet or a popover, but if we want the view to take up the entire screen, we can embed it in a **NavigationStack** view and open it with a **NavigationLink**. This is the approach we take in the following example. The interface includes a button to open the image picker and an **Image** view to display the photo taken by the user.

Figure 14-5: *Interface to work with the camera*

IMPORTANT

To access the camera, you must request authorization from the user. The process is automatic, but you must add the "Privacy - Camera Usage Description" key to the **Info** panel in the app's settings, along with the message you want to display to the user (see Chapter 2, Figure 2-16). You can also add the camera as a capability from the Signing & Capabilities panel in the project's settings.

The image picker controller is a UIKit view controller, so we must integrate it into the SwiftUI interface using a representable view controller (see Chapter 13). To handle the image captured by the camera, we also need to define a coordinator and implement the corresponding delegate methods. This coordinator must conform to two protocols: **`UINavigationControllerDelegate`** and **`UIImagePickerControllerDelegate`**, as shown in the following example.

Listing 14-6: Creating the Image Picker Controller to take pictures

```
import SwiftUI

struct ImagePicker: UIViewControllerRepresentable {
   let sendPicture: (UIImage?) -> Void

   func makeUIViewController(context: Context) ->
      UIImagePickerController {
      let mediaPicker = UIImagePickerController()
      mediaPicker.delegate = context.coordinator
      if UIImagePickerController.isSourceTypeAvailable(.camera) {
         mediaPicker.sourceType = .camera
         mediaPicker.mediaTypes = ["public.image"]
         mediaPicker.allowsEditing = false
         mediaPicker.cameraCaptureMode = .photo
      } else {
         print("The media is not available")
      }
      return mediaPicker
   }
   func updateUIViewController(_ uiViewController:
UIImagePickerController, context: Context) {}

   func makeCoordinator() -> ImagePickerCoordinator {
      ImagePickerCoordinator(sendPicture: sendPicture)
   }
}
class ImagePickerCoordinator: NSObject, UINavigationControllerDelegate,
   UIImagePickerControllerDelegate {
   let sendPicture: (UIImage?) -> Void

   init(sendPicture: @escaping (UIImage?) -> Void) {
      self.sendPicture = sendPicture
   }
```

```
    func imagePickerController(_ picker: UIImagePickerController,
       didFinishPickingMediaWithInfo info:
          [UIImagePickerController.InfoKey : Any]) {
       if let newpicture = info[.originalImage] as? UIImage {
          sendPicture(newpicture)
       } else {
          sendPicture(nil)
       }
    }
    func imagePickerControllerDidCancel(_ picker:
       UIImagePickerController) {
       sendPicture(nil)
    }
}
```

This representable view controller creates an instance of the **UIImagePickerController** class and assigns the **ImagePickerCoordinator** object as its delegate. After this, we check if the camera is available with the **isSourceTypeAvailable()** method and configure the controller if successful or display a message on the console otherwise. The value **camera** is assigned to the **sourceType** property to tell the controller to retrieve the image from the camera, an array with the value **public.image** is assigned to the **mediaTypes** property to specify images as the media to retrieve, the **allowEditing** property is set to **false** to prevent the user from editing the image, and the value **photo** is assigned to the **cameraCaptureMode** property to allow the user to capture images only.

The camera's interface includes buttons for controlling the camera and capturing the image. After the user takes a picture, a new set of buttons appears, allowing the user to select the image or capture another one. If the user decides to use the current image, the controller calls the **imagePickerController(didFinishPickingMediaWithInfo:)** method on its delegate to report the action. This method receives a parameter called **info**, which we can read to get the media returned by the controller and process it (save it to a file, a database, or display it on the screen). In this example, we decided to use a closure to send the picture back to the view. The view sends a closure to the controller that receives a **UIImage** view. The controller then stores this closure in a property called **sendPicture**, and when the picture is ready, it calls this closure with it. Note that this closure is also responsible for dismissing the picker, so we also call it from the **imagePickerControllerDidCancel()** method with a **nil** value to dismiss the controller when the user presses the Cancel button.

The view must include a navigation link to open the Image Picker Controller and an **Image** view to show the picture taken by the user, as in the following example.

Listing 14-7: Defining the interface to take pictures

```
struct ContentView: View {
   @State private var path = NavigationPath()
   @State private var picture: UIImage?

   var body: some View {
      NavigationStack(path: $path) {
         VStack {
            HStack {
```

```
                Spacer()
                NavigationLink(value: "Open Picker", label: {
                   Text("Get Picture")
                })
                .buttonStyle(.glassProminent)
                .padding()
                .navigationDestination(for: String.self) { _ in
                   ImagePicker { newpicture in
                      picture = newpicture
                      path.removeLast()
                   }
                   .ignoresSafeArea()
                }
             }
             Image(uiImage: picture ?? UIImage(named: "nopicture")!)
                .resizable()
                .scaledToFit()
             Spacer()
          }.padding()
       }.statusBarHidden()
    }
}
```

This view creates an instance of the **ImagePicker** structure and sets it as the destination of a **NavigationLink** button. When the button is pressed, the picker view is presented. If the user captures an image, the closure provided to the **ImagePicker** view is executed. Inside this closure, we assign the captured image to a **@State** property, the interface is updated, and the new picture is displayed on the screen, as shown in Figure 14-5, right.

Do It Yourself

Create a new App project. Create a Swift file called **ImagePicker.swift** for the code in Listing 14-6. Update the **ContentView.swift** file with the code in Listing 14-7. Download the **nopicture.png** image from our website and add it to an Asset Catalog. Add the "Privacy - Camera Usage Description" option to the **Info** panel in the app's settings with the text you want to show to the user (see Chapter 2, Figure 2-16), or add the **Camera** capability from the **Signing & Capabilities** panel. Run the application on your iPhone and press the button. Take a picture and press the button to use it. You should see the photo on the screen, as shown in Figure 14-5, right.

PRO

Storing Pictures

In the previous example, we show the image on the screen, but we can also store it in a file or a database. An alternative, which is sometimes useful when working with the camera, is to store the image in the device's Photo library so that other applications can access it. The UIKit framework offers the following functions for saving images and videos.

```
UIImageWriteToSavedPhotosAlbum(UIImage, Any?, Selector?,
UnsafeMutableRawPointer?)
```

This function adds the image specified by the first argument to the camera roll album. The second argument is a reference to the object that contains the method we want to execute when the process is over, the third argument is a selector that represents that method, and the last argument is an object with data to pass to the method.

```
UISaveVideoAtPathToSavedPhotosAlbum(String, Any?, Selector?,
UnsafeMutableRawPointer?)
```

This function adds the video to the camera roll at the path indicated by the first argument. The second argument is a reference to the object that contains the method we want to execute when the process is over, the third argument is a selector that represents that method, and the last argument is an object with additional data for the method.

IMPORTANT

To store pictures or videos in the device, the app must ask permission to the user. As always, this is done from the **Info** panel in the app's settings (see Chapter 2, Figure 2-16). In this case, you must add the "Privacy - Photo Library Additions Usage Description" option with the message you want to show to the user when authorization is requested. You can also add the Photo library as a capability from the Signing & Capabilities panel in the project's settings.

The functions to store pictures are defined in Objective-C, so they require some parameters that are not common in SwiftUI applications, but if all we want is to save the image, we can specify the first argument and define the rest as **nil**, as shown in the following example.

Listing 14-8: Saving the picture in the Photo Library

```
struct ContentView: View {
   @State private var path = NavigationPath()
   @State private var picture: UIImage?
   @State private var showAlert: Bool = false

   var body: some View {
      NavigationStack(path: $path) {
         VStack {
            HStack {
               Button("Share Picture") {
                  showAlert = true
               }.buttonStyle(.glass)
               .disabled(picture == nil ? true : false)

               Spacer()
               NavigationLink(value: "Open Picker", label: {
```

```
                Text("Get Picture")
            })
            .buttonStyle(.glassProminent)
            .padding()
            .navigationDestination(for: String.self) { _ in
                ImagePicker { newpicture in
                    picture = newpicture
                    path.removeLast()
                }
                .ignoresSafeArea()
            }
            .alert("Save Picture", isPresented: $showAlert, actions: {
                Button("Cancel", role: .cancel, action: {
                    showAlert = false
                })
                Button("YES", role: .none, action: {
                    if let picture {
                        UIImageWriteToSavedPhotosAlbum(picture, nil, nil,
                            nil)
                    }
                })
            }, message: { Text("Do you want to store the picture in the
                Photo Library?") })
        }
        Image(uiImage: picture ?? UIImage(named: "nopicture")!)
            .resizable()
            .scaledToFit()
        Spacer()
    }.padding()
  }.statusBarHidden()
 }
}
```

The process is the same as before. The image picker controller opens a view for the user to take a picture and then calls the delegate method to process it. The image is assigned to the **picture** property to display it on the screen, but now we have an additional button to present an alert view that allows the user to save the image to the Photo Library.

Do It Yourself

Update the **ContentView.swift file** with the code in Listing 14-8. Add the "Privacy - Photo Library Additions Usage Description" and the "Privacy - Camera Usage Description" options to the **Info** panel in the app's settings to get access to the Photo Library and the Camera. (Remember that you can also set these values by adding the capabilities from the **Signing and Capabilities** panel.) Run the application on your iPhone and take a picture. You should see the image on the screen. Press the Share Picture button. You should see an alert view asking for permission to save the picture. Press YES. The picture should be available in your Photo Library.

PRO

Share Link

Another way to share pictures with other applications is a share sheet. This is a sheet provided by the system that includes icons to open applications with which we can share content. SwiftUI provides the following view to open the sheet.

```
ShareLink(String, item: Item, subject: Text?, message: Text?,
preview: SharePreview)
```

This initializer creates a button that presents a share sheet, allowing the user to choose the application with which to share the data. The first argument is the button's label. The **item** argument is the value we want to share (it must conform to the `Transferable` protocol). The **subject** argument is the item's title. The **message** argument is the item's description. And the **preview** argument is a structure that provides a representation of the item.

If we want to share an image, we must provide a preview. SwiftUI includes the `SharePreview` structure for this purpose.

```
SharePreview(String, image: Image)
```

This initializer creates a representation of the item to share. The first argument is the description of the item, and the **image** argument is an `Image` view to represent the item.

Share links are frequently used to share text, but they can share any type of values we want as long as they conform to the `Transferable` protocol. For instance, we can share the picture taken by the camera.

Listing 14-9: Sharing the image with other applications

```
struct ContentView: View {
   @State private var path = NavigationPath()
   @State private var picture: UIImage?

   var body: some View {
      NavigationStack(path: $path) {
         VStack {
            HStack {
               if let picture {
                  let photo = Image(uiImage: picture)
                  ShareLink("Share Picture", item: photo, preview:
                     SharePreview("Photo", image: photo))
                     .buttonStyle(.glass)
               }
               Spacer()
               NavigationLink(value: "Open Picker", label: {
                  Text("Get Picture")
               })
               .buttonStyle(.glassProminent)
```

```
                .padding()
                .navigationDestination(for: String.self) { _ in
                    ImagePicker { newpicture in
                        if let newpicture {
                            let width = newpicture.size.width / 3
                            let height = newpicture.size.height / 3
                            picture = newpicture.preparingThumbnail(of:
                                CGSize(width: width, height: height))
                        }
                        path.removeLast()
                    }
                    .ignoresSafeArea()
                }
            }
            Image(uiImage: picture ?? UIImage(named: "nopicture")!)
                .resizable()
                .scaledToFit()
            Spacer()
        }.padding()
    }.statusBarHidden()
  }
}
```

Each time we share an image with other applications or online services, we must consider its size and quality. Modern device cameras capture high-resolution photos, so it is often advisable to reduce their size before processing or sharing them. In this case, the purpose of the application is to let the user post the image on social media, so we call the **preparingThumbnail()** method to scale the image down to one third of its original size before assigning it to the binding property.

The **ShareLink** view creates a button with a predefined label that includes an SF Symbol on the left. In this example, we place it in the upper left corner, but only display it if there is an image to share (if the user has already taken a picture with the camera). When the button is pressed, the system opens a small sheet with icons representing the apps with which we can share information, and when we scroll up the sheet, options are revealed to perform additional actions such as copying and printing the data. For example, if we have the Facebook app installed, we can post a message with our picture, as shown below.

Figure 14-6: *Share sheet*

Do It Yourself

Update the **ContentView** structure with the code in Listing 14-9. Run the application on your iPhone. Press the Get Picture button and take a picture. Press the Share Picture button. You should see the share sheet at the bottom of the screen. Select an app to share the image.

PRO

Custom Camera

The **UIImagePickerController** controller is built using classes defined in the **AVFoundation** framework. This framework provides the tools required to process media and control input devices such as the camera and microphone, so we can use its classes directly to build a custom controller and tailor both the process and the interface.

Creating a custom controller that accesses the camera and retrieves data from input devices requires coordinating multiple components. We must configure the inputs from the camera and microphone, process the data received from those inputs, present a preview to the user, and generate the final output in the form of an image, video, or audio file. Figure 14-7 shows the elements involved.

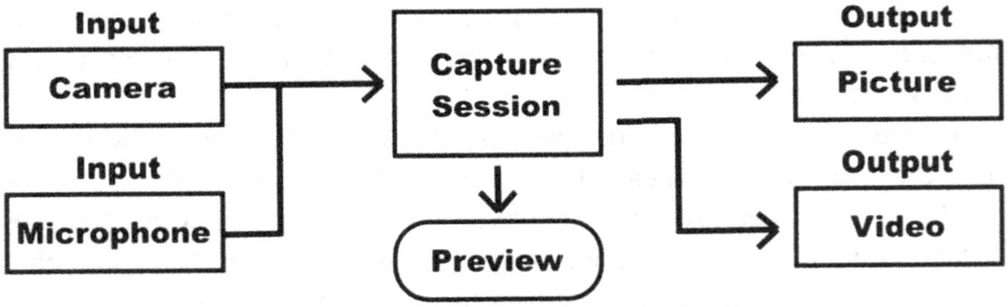

Figure 14-7: *System to capture media*

The first thing we need to do to build this structure is to determine the input devices. The **AVFoundation** framework defines the **AVCaptureDevice** class for this purpose. An instance of this class can represent any type of input device, including cameras and microphones. The following are some of the methods included in the class to access and manage a device.

default(for: AVMediaType)

This type method returns an **AVCaptureDevice** object that represents the default capture device for the media specified by the argument. The **for** argument is a structure of type **AVMediaType** with properties to define the type of media. The properties available to work with the cameras and microphones are **video** and **audio**.

requestAccess(for: AVMediaType)

This asynchronous type method asks the user for permission to access the device. The **for** argument is a structure of type **AVMediaType** with properties to define the type of media. The properties available to work with the cameras and microphones are **video** and **audio**.

authorizationStatus(for: AVMediaType)

This type method returns a value that determines the status of the authorization to use the device. The **for** argument is a structure of type **AVMediaType** with properties to define the type of media. The properties available to work with the cameras and microphones are **video** and **audio**. The method returns an enumeration of type **AVAuthorizationStatus** with the values **notDetermined**, **restricted**, **denied**, and **authorized**.

An instance of the **AVCaptureDevice** class represents a capture device, such as the camera or the microphone. The class includes properties and methods for configuring and managing a device. The following are the most frequently used.

isSubjectAreaChangeMonitoringEnabled

This property sets or returns a Boolean value that determines whether the device monitors the area for changes, such as lighting and orientation.

formats

This property returns an array of **Format** objects that represent the formats the device supports.

activeFormat

This property returns a Format object representing the format in use by the device.

lockForConfiguration()

This method requests exclusive access to configure the device.

unlockForConfiguration()

This method releases the device for configuration.

To define the capture device as an input device, we must create an object that controls the ports and connections. The framework defines the **AVCaptureDeviceInput** class for this purpose. The class includes the following initializer to create the input object for the device.

AVCaptureDeviceInput(device: AVCaptureDevice)

This initializer creates an input for the device specified by the **device** argument.

In addition to inputs, we also need outputs to capture and process the data received from the device. The framework defines subclasses of a base class called **AVCaptureOutput** to describe the outputs. Several subclasses are available, such as **AVCaptureVideoDataOutput** to process the frames of a video and **AVCaptureAudioDataOutput** to get the audio data, but the most useful is the **AVCapturePhotoOutput** class, used to capture a single video frame (take a picture). This class includes many properties and methods to configure the output. Below you can find the property to set the maximum dimensions of the image and the method to capture a photo.

maxPhotoDimensions

This property sets or returns the dimensions of the image to be captured. It is a structure of type **CMVideoDimensions** with the properties **width** and **height**.

capturePhoto(with: AVCapturePhotoSettings, **delegate:** AVCapturePhotoCaptureDelegate**)**

This method initiates a photo capture with the settings specified by the **with** argument. The **delegate** argument is a reference to the object that implements the methods of the **AVCapturePhotoCaptureDelegate** protocol to receive the data generated by the output.

The **AVCapturePhotoOutput** class works with a delegate that conforms to the **AVCapturePhotoCaptureDelegate** protocol, which among other methods defines the following to return a still image.

photoOutput(AVCapturePhotoOutput, **didFinishProcessingPhoto:** AVCapturePhoto, **error:** Error?**)**

This method is called on the delegate after the image is captured. The **didFinishProcessingPhoto** argument is a container with information about the image, and the **error** argument is used to report errors.

To control the flow of data from input to output, the framework defines the **AVCaptureSession** class. From an instance of this class, we can control the inputs and outputs and determine when the process begins and ends by calling the following methods.

addInput(AVCaptureInput**)**

This method adds an input to the capture session. The argument represents the input device we want to add.

addOutput(AVCaptureOutput**)**

This method adds an output to the capture session. The argument represents the output we want to generate from the capture session.

startRunning()

This method starts the capture session.

stopRunning()

This method stops the capture session.

The framework also defines the **AVCaptureVideoPreviewLayer** class to show a preview to the user. This class creates a layer to display the video captured by the input device. The class includes the following initializer and properties to create and manage the preview layer.

AVCaptureVideoPreviewLayer(session: AVCaptureSession**)**

This initializer creates an **AVCaptureVideoPreviewLayer** object with a preview layer connected to the capture session defined by the **session** argument.

connection

This property returns an object of type **AVCaptureConnection** that defines the connection between the capture session and the preview layer.

session

This property sets or returns an **AVCaptureSession** object representing the session assigned to the preview layer.

The input, output, and preview layer are connected to the capture session by objects of the **AVCaptureConnection** class. The class manages the information for the connection, including ports, data, and orientation. The following are the property and method used to set the orientation of the preview layer.

videoRotationAngle

This property sets or returns a **CGFloat** value that represents the rotation angle the connection applies to the preview (the angles are 0.0, 90.0, 180.0 and 270.0).

isVideoRotationAngleSupported(CGFloat**)**

This method returns a Boolean value to indicate whether the rotation to the angle specified by the argument is supported.

Rotation angles are determined by a rotation coordinator. To create it, the framework includes a class called **RotationCoordinator**. The class includes the following initializer.

AVCaptureDevice.RotationCoordinator(device: AVCaptureDevice, **previewLayer:** CALayer?**)**

This initializer creates a rotation coordinator for the device and the preview layer specified by the arguments.

The **RotationCoordinator** class includes the following two properties that we can read to get the current angle of rotation.

videoRotationAngleForHorizonLevelPreview

This property returns the angle of rotation we need to apply to the preview layer to match the device's orientation.

videoRotationAngleForHorizonLevelCapture

This property returns the angle of rotation we need to apply to the image captured by the camera to match the device's orientation.

Now that we understand all the components involved, we can build our own custom interface to take pictures. The interface for this example needs a button to open the view that allows the user to take a picture with the camera, and an **Image** view to show it on the screen.

Figure 14-8: *Interface for a custom camera*

The process for activating the camera and retrieving the picture taken by the user is independent of the interface, but if we want the user to see the image coming from the camera, we need to create a preview layer. Layers are the way views display graphics on the screen. Views define the area and provide functionality, but the graphics are presented by a layer created from a class called **`CALayer`**. Each view created from the **`UIView`** class contains a layer that can be used to display a video, but the layer must be casted as an **`AVCaptureVideoPreviewLayer`**. To do this, we need to create a subclass of **`UIView`**, override a type property called **`layerClass`** to turn the view's layer into a preview layer, and then create a **`UIViewRepresentable`** structure to be able to display the view in our SwiftUI interface, as in the following example.

Listing 14-10: Defining a `UIView` subclass to show the camera's preview video

```
import SwiftUI
import AVFoundation

class CustomPreviewView: UIView {
   override class var layerClass: AnyClass {
      return AVCaptureVideoPreviewLayer.self
   }
}
struct CustomPreview: UIViewRepresentable {
   let view = CustomPreviewView()

   func makeUIView(context: Context) -> UIView {
      return view
   }
   func updateUIView(_ uiView: UIView, context: Context) { }
}
```

The **`layerClass`** property is a type property that the system reads to determine the data type of the layer. In this example, we override this property to return a reference to the **`AVCaptureVideoPreviewLayer`** class so that the system knows that we will use the view layer to display video. The rest of the code for the representable view is created as before.

For this example, we are going to manage all the logic for the camera in a data model. The following are the basic elements we need to set up the system.

Listing 14-11: Defining the properties we need to manage the camera

```
import SwiftUI
@preconcurrency import AVFoundation

class ViewData {
   var captureDevice: AVCaptureDevice?
   var captureSession: AVCaptureSession?
   var stillImage: AVCapturePhotoOutput?
   var rotationCoordinator: AVCaptureDevice.RotationCoordinator?
   var previewObservation: NSKeyValueObservation?
}
@Observable class ApplicationData: NSObject,
   AVCapturePhotoCaptureDelegate {
   var path = NavigationPath()
   var picture: UIImage?
   @ObservationIgnored var cameraView: CustomPreview!
   @ObservationIgnored var viewData: ViewData!

   static let shared: ApplicationData = ApplicationData()
   private override init() {
      cameraView = CustomPreview()
      viewData = ViewData()
   }
}
```

This code is only the first part of our data model, but it provides the properties required to store references to every element of the system. Since these properties are required by several methods, we declare them in a separate class called **ViewData**. When the model is initialized, we create an instance of this class and the representable view (**CustomPreview**) and store them in non-observable properties to make them accessible to the rest of the code.

The next step is to define a method to get permission from the user to access the camera. This is done automatically if we use a **UIImagePickerController** controller, but we need to do it ourselves in a custom controller using the type methods provided by the **AVCaptureDevice** class. The following is the method we must add to our model for this purpose.

Listing 14-12: Asking for permission to use the camera

```
func getAuthorization() async {
   let granted = await AVCaptureDevice.requestAccess(for: .video)
   await MainActor.run {
      if granted {
         self.prepareCamera()
      } else {
         print("Not Authorized")
      }
   }
}
```

The **requestAccess()** method is asynchronous; it waits for the user to respond and returns a value of type **Bool** to report the result. If the user grants access, we execute a method called **prepareCamera()**. Here we begin to build the network of objects introduced in Figure 14-7. The **prepareCamera()** method must get a reference to the current capture device for video and create the inputs and outputs we need to capture a still image (to take a picture).

Listing 14-13: Initializing the camera

```
func prepareCamera() {
   viewData.captureSession = AVCaptureSession()
   viewData.captureDevice = AVCaptureDevice.default(for:
      AVMediaType.video)

   if let _ = try? viewData.captureDevice?.lockForConfiguration() {
      viewData.captureDevice?.isSubjectAreaChangeMonitoringEnabled = true
      viewData.captureDevice?.unlockForConfiguration()
   }
   if let device = viewData.captureDevice {
      if let input = try? AVCaptureDeviceInput(device: device) {
         viewData.captureSession?.addInput(input)
         viewData.stillImage = AVCapturePhotoOutput()
         if viewData.stillImage != nil {
            viewData.captureSession?.addOutput(viewData.stillImage!)
            if let max = viewData.captureDevice?.activeFormat.
               supportedMaxPhotoDimensions.last {
               viewData.stillImage?.maxPhotoDimensions = max
            }
         }
         showCamera()
      } else {
         print("Not Authorized")
      }
   } else {
      print("Not Authorized")
   }
}
```

This method starts by creating a new session and requesting access to the camera. If the **default()** method returns a value, we assign **true** to the **isSubjectAreaChange-MonitoringEnabled** property to start monitoring changes in the orientation of the device.

Once we have created the session and obtained access to the device, we can configure the inputs and outputs required for the capture process. There is no strict order for doing this, but because the **AVCaptureDeviceInput()** initializer can throw an error, we typically create the input first. This initializer returns an object that manages data coming from the capture device. If the initialization succeeds, we add the input to the capture session using the **addInput()** method, and then configure the corresponding output. In this example, we want to use the session to capture a still image. Therefore, we use the **AVCapturePhoto-Output** class to create the output, add it to the session, and then configure it to return images of the maximum size allowed. Note that the maximum size is determined by the **maxPhotoDimensions** property, but we cannot assign an arbitrary value; we need to retrieve the list of possible dimensions that the camera can produce and use the highest one. To do this, we read the **activeFormat** property to get the **Format** object that represents the format currently used by the camera, and read its **supportedMaxPhotoDimensions** property. This property returns an array of **CMVideoDimensions** structures with the dimensions supported by the device, so we get the last one and assign it to the output to get an image of the maximum possible size.

After adding the inputs and outputs to the capture session, the **prepareCamera()** method executes an additional method called **showCamera()** to define the preview layer and display the video coming from the camera on the screen. The following is our implementation of that method.

Listing 14-14: Showing the video from the camera on the screen

```
func showCamera() {
   let previewLayer = cameraView.view.layer as? AVCaptureVideoPreviewLayer
   previewLayer?.session = viewData.captureSession

   if let device = viewData.captureDevice, let preview = previewLayer {
      viewData.rotationCoordinator = AVCaptureDevice.
         RotationCoordinator(device: device, previewLayer: preview)
      preview.connection?.videoRotationAngle = viewData.
         rotationCoordinator!.videoRotationAngleForHorizonLevelPreview

      nonisolated(unsafe) let preview = preview
      viewData.previewObservation = viewData.rotationCoordinator!.
         observe(\.videoRotationAngleForHorizonLevelPreview,
         changeHandler: { old, value in
         Task{ @MainActor in
            preview.connection?.videoRotationAngle = self.viewData.
            rotationCoordinator!.videoRotationAngleForHorizonLevelPreview
         }
      })
   }
   Task.detached {
      await self.viewData.captureSession?.startRunning()
   }
}
```

As mentioned earlier, the layer included with the view created by the **UIView** class is defined by an object of type **CALayer**. This is a basic class that can display graphics and perform animations. However, to display the video from the camera, we need to cast it as an **AVCaptureVideoPreviewLayer** object.

After converting the layer to a preview layer, we can create the rotation coordinator to set the orientation of the video. The coordinator checks the device and the preview layer and stores the current rotation angle in the **videoRotationAngleForHorizonLevel-Preview** property, so we assign the value of this property to the **videoRotationAngle** property of the **AVCaptureConnection** object to set the current orientation. To keep this value up to date, we add an observer for the **videoRotationAngleForHorizonLevel-Preview** property and set the orientation of the video each time the value of this property changes.

Once the preview layer and the rotation coordinator are ready, the capture session is initiated with the **startRunning()** method. (The system requires this method to be executed in a background thread.) At this point, the video is playing on the screen and the system is ready to capture an image. The process of capturing the image is initiated with the **capturePhoto()** method provided by the **AVCapturePhotoOutput** object, and the type of photo captured by the output is determined by an **AVCapturePhotoSettings** object. This class includes multiple initializers. The following is the most frequently used.

AVCapturePhotoSettings()

This initializer creates an **AVCapturePhotoSettings** object with the format by default.

The following are some of the properties available in this class to configure the image and the preview.

maxPhotoDimensions

This property sets or returns the dimensions of the captured image. It is a structure of type **CMVideoDimensions** with the properties **width** and **height**.

previewPhotoFormat

This property sets or returns a dictionary with keys and values that determine the characteristics of the preview image. The keys available are **kCVPixelBufferPixelFormatTypeKey** (uncompressed format), **kCVPixelBufferWidthKey** (width) and **kCVPixelBufferHeightKey** (height).

flashMode

This property sets or returns the flash mode used when the image is captured. It is an enumeration of type **FlashMode** with the values **on**, **off**, and **auto**.

To capture an image, we have to define the settings with an **AVCapturePhotoSettings** object, call the **capturePhoto()** method of the **AVCapturePhotoOutput** object, and define the delegate method that is going to receive the image. The following is the method we need to add to the model to take the picture.

Listing 14-15: Taking a picture

```
func takePicture() {
   let settings = AVCapturePhotoSettings()
   if let max = viewData.captureDevice?.activeFormat.
      supportedMaxPhotoDimensions.last {
      settings.maxPhotoDimensions = max
   }
   viewData.stillImage?.capturePhoto(with: settings, delegate: self)
}
```

When the user presses the button to take a picture, the **takePicture()** method is executed and the **capturePhoto()** method is called to ask the output object to capture an image. After the image is captured, this object sends the result to a delegate method. Note that we have declared the **ApplicationData** class as the delegate object (see Listing 14-11), so we can implement the delegate method in the model. The following is our implementation of this method.

Listing 14-16: Processing the image

```
func photoOutput(_ output: AVCapturePhotoOutput, didFinishProcessingPhoto
photo: AVCapturePhoto, error: Error?) {
   Task { @MainActor in
      let scene = UIApplication.shared.connectedScenes.first as?
         UIWindowScene
      let scale = scene?.screen.scale ?? 1
      let orientationAngle = viewData.rotationCoordinator!.
         videoRotationAngleForHorizonLevelCapture
      var imageOrientation: UIImage.Orientation!
      switch orientationAngle {
         case 90.0:
            imageOrientation = .right
         case 270.0:
            imageOrientation = .left
         case 0.0:
            imageOrientation = .up
         case 180.0:
            imageOrientation = .down
         default:
            imageOrientation = .right
      }
      if let imageData = photo.cgImageRepresentation() {
         picture = UIImage(cgImage: imageData, scale: scale,
            orientation: imageOrientation)
         path = NavigationPath()
      }
   }
}
```

The **photoOutput(AVCapturePhotoOutput, didFinishProcessingPhoto:)** method receives the picture produced by the camera. The value received by this method is an object of type **AVCapturePhoto**, which is a container with information about the image. The class includes two convenient methods to get the data representing the image.

fileDataRepresentation()

This method returns a data representation of the image that we can use to create a **UIImage** object.

cgImageRepresentation()

This method returns the image as a **CGImage** object (Core Graphics).

In our example, we implemented the **cgImageRepresentation()** method because the **UIImage** class defines a convenient initializer to create an image from a **CGImage** object that includes the scale and orientation. We get the orientation from the **videoRotationAngle-ForHorizonLevelCapture** property of the rotation coordinator. This property returns a **CGFloat** value with the rotation angle, which we can convert to **Orientation** values to set the orientation of the image.

To set the scale, we need to access the screen. The screen is managed by an object of the **UIScreen** class, which is automatically created for the device and assigned to a property of the scene. Therefore, to access the screen and get the scale, we need to read the

UIWindowScene object that controls the current scene from the **connectedScenes** property of the **UIApplication** object. We introduced this object in Chapter 12. It is created by the system to control the application. The object is returned by a type property provided by the class called **shared**. To access the scenes opened by the application, we read the **connectedScenes** property from this object. In this example, we are developing an application for mobile devices, so we only need to access the first available scene. The **UIWindowScene** object includes the **screen** property to return a reference to the **UIScreen** object that represents the screen, and the **UIScreen** object contains, among other things, the **scale** property to return the current scale and the **bounds** property to return the size of the screen. With these values, we create the **UIImage** object and assign it to the **picture** property to update the view and display the image, as shown below.

Listing 14-17: Showing the image

```
struct ContentView: View {
   @Environment(ApplicationData.self) private var appData

   var body: some View {
      @Bindable var appData = appData

      NavigationStack(path: $appData.path) {
         VStack {
            HStack {
               Spacer()
               NavigationLink("Take Picture", value: "Open Camera")
                  .buttonStyle(.glassProminent)
                  .padding()
            }
            .navigationDestination(for: String.self, destination: { _ in
               CustomCameraView()
            })
            Image(uiImage: appData.picture ?? UIImage(named:
               "nopicture")!)
               .resizable()
               .scaledToFit()
            Spacer()
         }.padding()
         .toolbarVisibility(.hidden, for: .navigationBar)
      }.statusBarHidden()
   }
}
```

There is nothing new in the view in Listing 14-17, with the exception that now instead of opening a **UIImagePickerController** with a standard interface, we open a view that has to provide the buttons and custom controls required for the user to take a picture. The following is our implementation of that view.

Listing 14-18: Taking a picture

```
import SwiftUI

struct CustomCameraView: View {
   @Environment(ApplicationData.self) private var appData
```

```
    var body: some View {
        ZStack {
            appData.cameraView
            VStack {
                Spacer()
                HStack {
                    Button("Cancel") {
                        appData.path = NavigationPath()
                    }.buttonStyle(.glass)
                    Spacer()
                    Button("Take Picture") {
                        appData.takePicture()
                    }.buttonStyle(.glassProminent)
                }.padding()
                .frame(height: 80)
                .background(Color(red: 0.9, green: 0.9, blue: 0.9,
                    opacity: 0.8))
            }
        }
        .edgesIgnoringSafeArea(.all)
        .frame(minWidth: 0, maxWidth: .infinity, minHeight: 0,
            maxHeight: .infinity)
        .toolbarVisibility(.hidden, for: .navigationBar)
        .task {
            await appData.getAuthorization()
        }
        .onDisappear {
            appData.viewData.previewObservation = nil
        }
    }
}
```

As shown in Figure 14-8 (right), this view contains our **`UIView`**, which displays the video coming from the camera, and another view at the bottom, which provides two buttons, one to cancel the process and dismiss the view, and another to take a picture. When the view appears on the screen, we call the **`getAuthorization()`** method to start the process. If the user presses the Take Picture button, we call the **`takePicture()`** method to capture the image. Once the image is processed, the delegate method dismisses the view and displays the image on the screen. Note that we apply the **`onDisappear()`** modifier to remove the observer. This is necessary to ensure that no observers are active after they are no longer needed.

Do It Yourself

Create a new App project. Download the **nopicture.png** image from our website and add it to an Asset Catalog. Create a Swift file called **CustomPreview.swift** for the code in Listing 14-10, and another called **ApplicationData.swift** for the code in Listing 14-11. Add to the model the methods in Listings 14-12, 14-13, 14-14, 14-15, and 14-16. Update the **`ContentView`** structure with the code in Listing 14-17. Create a SwiftUI file called **CustomCameraView.swift** for the code in Listing 14-18. Remember to add the option "Privacy - Camera Usage Description" to the **Info** panel in the app's settings and to inject the **ApplicationData** object into the environment for the app and the previews (Chapter 4, Listing 4-4). Run the application on a device and take a picture.

BASIC

14.2 - Video

Recording and playing videos is just as important to users as capturing and displaying photos. As with images, Apple frameworks provide the tools we need to play videos and even build a fully customized video player.

BASIC

Video Player

SwiftUI defines the **VideoPlayer** view to play videos. This view provides all the controls required to play, stop, and move the video back and forth. The view includes the following initializer.

VideoPlayer(player: AVPlayer?, **videoOverlay:** Closure)

This initializer creates a video player to play the video provided by the argument. The **player** argument is the object in charge of playing the media, and the **videoOverlay** argument provides the views we want to show on top of the video.

The **VideoPlayer** view presents the interface for the user to control the video, but the video is played by an object of the **AVPlayer** class. The class includes the following initializer.

AVPlayer(url: URL)

This initializer creates an **AVPlayer** object to play the media in the URL indicated by the **url** argument.

The **AVPlayer** class also includes properties and methods to control the video programatically.

volume

This property sets or returns a value that determines the player's volume. It is a value of type **Float** between 0.0 and 1.0.

isMuted

This property is a Boolean value that determines whether the player's audio is muted or not.

rate

This property sets or returns a **Float** value that determines the rate at which the media is being played. A value of 0.0 pauses the video and 1.0 sets the normal rate.

```
play()
```

This method begins playback.

```
pause()
```

This method pauses playback.

```
addPeriodicTimeObserver(forInterval: CMTime, queue:
DispatchQueue?, using: Closure)
```

This method adds an observer that executes a closure every certain period of time. The **forInterval** argument determines the time between executions, the **queue** argument is the queue in which the closure should be executed (the main thread is recommended), and the **using** argument is the closure we want to execute. The closure receives a value of type **CMTime** with the time at which the closure was called.

The **VideoPlayer** view requires an **AVPlayer** object to play the video, and that object loads the video from a URL. If we want to play a video available online, we only need the URL, but if the video is provided by the app, we need to get it from the bundle (see **Bundle** in Chapter 7). In the following model, we add a video called **videotrees.mp4** to the project, get the URL that points to the file from the **Bundle** object, and create an **AVPlayer** object with that value.

Listing 14-19: Preparing the video to be played

```
import SwiftUI
import AVKit

@Observable class ApplicationData {
   var player: AVPlayer!

   static let shared: ApplicationData = ApplicationData()
   private init() {
      let bundle = Bundle.main
      if let videoURL = bundle.url(forResource: "videotrees",
         withExtension: "mp4") {
         player = AVPlayer(url: videoURL)
      }
   }
}
```

The **VideoPlayer** view and the **AVPlayer** class are defined in the **AVKit** framework. After importing this framework, we get the URL for the video **videotrees.mp4**, create the **AVPlayer** object and store it in an observable property to make it available to the view. In the view, we need to check this property and display the **VideoPlayer** view when a video is ready to play.

Listing 14-20: Playing a video

```
import SwiftUI
import AVKit
```

```
struct ContentView: View {
   @State private var appData = ApplicationData.shared

   var body: some View {
      if appData.player != nil {
         VideoPlayer(player: appData.player)
            .ignoresSafeArea()
      } else {
         Text("Video not available")
      }
   }
}
```

Figure 14-9: *Standard video player*

Do It Yourself

Create a new App project. Download the file **videotrees.mp4** from our website and add it to your project. Create a Swift file called **ApplicationData.swift** for the code in Listing 14-19. Update the **`ContentView`** structure with the code in Listing 14-20. Run the application on an iPhone simulator. Press play to play the video.

In the previous example, the video doesn't play until the user presses the play button, but we can implement **`AVPlayer`** properties and methods to control the video programatically. For instance, the following example starts the video as soon as the view is loaded.

Listing 14-21: Automatically playing a video

```
struct ContentView: View {
   @State private var appData = ApplicationData.shared

   var body: some View {
      if appData.player != nil {
         VideoPlayer(player: appData.player)
            .onAppear {
               appData.player.play()
            }
            .ignoresSafeArea()
```

```
        } else {
            Text("Video not available")
        }
    }
}
```

The **VideoPlayer** view initializer can also include an argument that takes a closure to add a layer of views over the video. In the following example, this initializer is implemented to add a caption with the title of the video at the top.

Listing 14-22: Presenting views over the video

```
struct ContentView: View {
    @State private var appData = ApplicationData.shared

    var body: some View {
        if appData.player != nil {
            VideoPlayer(player: appData.player, videoOverlay: {
                VStack {
                    Text("Title: Trees at the park")
                        .font(.title)
                        .padding([.top, .bottom], 8)
                        .padding([.leading, .trailing], 16)
                        .foregroundStyle(.black)
                        .background(.ultraThinMaterial)
                        .clipShape(RoundedRectangle(cornerRadius: 10))
                        .padding(.top, 8)
                    Spacer()
                }
            })
            .ignoresSafeArea()
        } else {
            Text("Video not available")
        }
    }
}
```

The views returned from the closure are displayed on top of the video but below the controls, so they cannot take input from the user, but we can use them to provide additional information, as in this case. The result is shown below.

Figure 14-10: *Overlay views*

Custom Video Player

In addition to the **AVKit** framework, Apple provides the **AVFoundation** framework, which includes the classes required to build a video player from the ground up. The framework includes a class to represent the asset, such as a video or audio file, another to handle the delivery of that media to the player, a separate class to manage playback, and another responsible for rendering the media on the screen. Figure 14-11, below, shows how these components interact to form the complete playback structure.

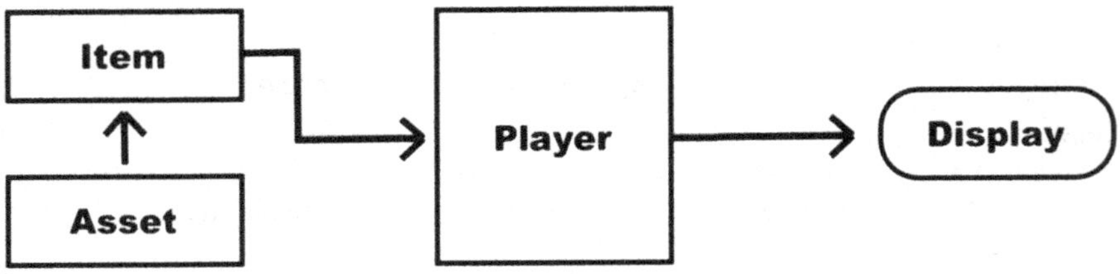

Figure 14-11: *System to play media*

The media to be played is provided as an asset. An asset consists of one or more tracks of media, including video, audio, and subtitles. The **AVFoundation** framework defines a class called **`AVAsset`** to represent an asset, and the following subclass to load it.

> **`AVURLAsset(url:`** `URL)`
>
> This initializer creates an **`AVURLAsset`** object with the media in the location indicated by the **url** argument. The argument is a **`URL`** structure with the location of a local or remote resource.

An asset contains static information and cannot manage its state when it is played. To control the asset, the framework defines the **`AVPlayerItem`** class. With this class we can reference an asset and manage its timeline. The class includes several initializers. The following is the most frequently used.

> **`AVPlayerItem(asset:`** `AVAsset)`
>
> This initializer creates an **`AVPlayerItem`** object to represent the asset defined by the **asset** argument.

The **`AVPlayerItem`** class also includes properties and methods to control the status of the asset. The following are the most frequently used.

> **`status`**
>
> This property returns a value that indicates the status of the player item. It is an enumeration called **`Status`** included in the **`AVPlayerItem`** class. The values available are **`unknown`**, **`readyToPlay`**, and **`failed`**.

duration

This property returns a value that indicates the duration of the player item. It is a structure of type **CMTime**.

currentTime()

This method returns a **CMTime** value with the current time of the player item.

seek(to: CMTime)

This asynchronous method moves the playback cursor to the time specified by the **to** argument and returns a Boolean value that determines whether the seek operation is finished or not.

The **AVPlayerItem** object manages the information needed for playback, but does not play the media; this is handled by an instance of the **AVPlayer** class. This is the same class we used earlier to load a video for the **VideoPlayer** view. The class includes the following initializer to create a player from an **AVPlayerItem** object.

AVPlayer(playerItem: AVPlayerItem?)

This initializer creates an **AVPlayer** object to play the media represented by the **playerItem** argument.

The last object required by the system is the one responsible for displaying the media. It is a subclass of the **CALayer** class called **AVPlayerLayer**, which provides the code necessary to draw the frames on the screen. The class includes the following initializer and property to create and configure the layer.

AVPlayerLayer(player: AVPlayer)

This initializer creates an **AVPlayerLayer** object associated with the player specified by the **player** argument.

videoGravity

This property defines how the video adjusts its size to the size of the preview layer. It is a **AVLayerVideoGravity** structure with the type properties **resize**, **resizeAspect**, and **resizeAspectFill**.

All these classes define the system we need to play media, but we also need a way to control time. Since the precision of floating-point values is not suitable for media playback, the framework implements, among other things, the **CMTime** structure from an old framework called Core Media. This structure contains several values to represent time as a fraction. The most important are the value and timescale, which represent the numerator and denominator, respectively. For example, if we want to create a **CMTime** structure to represent 0.5 seconds, we can specify 1 as the numerator and 2 as the denominator (1 divided by 2 equals 0.5). The class includes initializers and type properties to create these values. The following are the most frequently used.

CMTime(value: CMTimeValue, **timescale:** CMTimeScale)

This initializer creates a **CMTime** structure with the values specified by the **value** and **timescale** arguments. The arguments are integers of type **Int64** and **Int32**, respectively.

CMTime(seconds: Double, **preferredTimescale:** CMTimeScale)

This initializer creates a **CMTime** structure from a floating-point value that represents the time in seconds. The **seconds** argument determines the seconds we want to assign to the structure, and the **preferredTimescale** argument determines the scale we want to use. A value of 1 preserves the value in seconds assigned to the first argument.

zero

This type property returns a **CMTime** structure with the value 0.

The **CMTime** structure also includes several properties for setting and retrieving values. The following are the most frequently used.

seconds

This property returns the time of a **CMTime** structure in seconds. It is of type **Double**.

value

This property returns the value of a **CMTime** structure.

timescale

This property returns the time scale of a **CMTime** structure.

To create a custom video player, we must load the asset (**AVURLAsset**), create the item to manage the asset (**AVPlayerItem**), add the item to the player (**AVPlayer**), and associate the player to a layer to display the media on the screen (**AVPlayerLayer**).

As with the preview layer we previously used to display video from the camera, we must convert the layer provided by the **UIView** object into a player layer. In this case, the **CALayer** instance must be cast to an **AVPlayerLayer**. The following shows the implementation of the representable view required for this example.

Listing 14-23: Building a custom video player

```
import SwiftUI
import AVFoundation

class CustomPlayerView: UIView {
   override class var layerClass: AnyClass {
      return AVPlayerLayer.self
   }
}
struct PlayerView: UIViewRepresentable {
   var view = CustomPlayerView()
   func makeUIView(context: Context) -> UIView {
      return view
   }
```

```
    func updateUIView(_ uiView: UIView, context: Context) { }
}
```

Now that we have the representable view, the next step is to build the video player and then call the **play()** method to start playing the video as soon as it is ready.

Listing 14-24: Building a custom video player

```
import SwiftUI
import AVFoundation

class ViewData: NSObject {
    var playerItem: AVPlayerItem?
    var player: AVPlayer?
    var playerLayer: AVPlayerLayer?
    var playerObservation: NSKeyValueObservation?

    func setObserver() {
        playerObservation = playerItem?.observe(\.status, options: .new,
            changeHandler: { item, value in
            if item.status == .readyToPlay {
                Task { @MainActor in
                    self.player?.play()
                }
            }
        })
    }
}
@Observable class ApplicationData {
    @ObservationIgnored var customVideoView: PlayerView!
    @ObservationIgnored var viewData: ViewData

    static let shared: ApplicationData = ApplicationData()
    private init() {
        customVideoView = PlayerView()
        viewData = ViewData()

        let bundle = Bundle.main
        let videoURL = bundle.url(forResource: "videotrees",
            withExtension: "mp4")
        let asset = AVURLAsset(url: videoURL!)
        viewData.playerItem = AVPlayerItem(asset: asset)
        viewData.player = AVPlayer(playerItem: viewData.playerItem)

        Task { @MainActor in
            viewData.playerLayer = customVideoView.view.layer as?
                AVPlayerLayer
            viewData.playerLayer?.player = viewData.player
            viewData.setObserver()
        }
    }
}
```

The media is not immediately available, it has to be loaded and prepared for playback, so we cannot play it right away, we have to wait until it is ready. The status of the media is reported by the **status** property of the **AVPlayerItem** object. This means that we must observe the value of this property to start playing the media only when its value is equal to

readyToPlay. Therefore, after defining the basic properties we need for the player, we define a method to add an observer to the **AVPlayerItem** object to keep track of the **status** property. When the current status is **readyToPlay**, we play the video.

To set up the video player, we load the video from the bundle, create the player structure, cast the **UIView** layer as an **AVPlayerLayer** layer, and assign it to the player. Since everything is prepared in the model, all the interface needs to do is to display the representable view. The video fills the screen, adapts to the screen orientation, and plays as soon as the view is loaded.

Listing 14-25: Showing a video

```
struct ContentView: View {
   @State private var appData = ApplicationData.shared

   var body: some View {
      appData.customVideoView
         .ignoresSafeArea()
   }
}
```

Do It Yourself

Create a new App project. Download the file **videotrees.mp4** from our website and add it to your project. Create a Swift file called **CustomPlayerView.swift** for the code in Listing 14-23 and another called **ApplicationData.swift** for the code in Listing 14-24. Update the **ContentView** structure with the code in Listing 14-25. Run the application. The video should start playing as soon as the application is launched.

The previous example plays the video, but does not provide the user with any tools to control it. The **AVPlayer** class includes methods for playing, pausing, and checking the status of the media, but we are responsible for creating the interface. For the following example, we will create an interface that provides a button and a progress bar so that the user can play, pause, and see the progress.

Figure 14-12: *Video player with custom controls*

How we control the process and respond to the interface depends on the requirements of our application. For this example, we decided to define two states, one that indicates whether the video is playing or not, and another that determines the size of the progress bar. Below are the changes we need to make to our model to allow the user to play and pause the video and update the progress bar.

Listing 14-26: Preparing the video player

```
import SwiftUI
import AVFoundation

class ViewData: NSObject {
   var playerItem: AVPlayerItem?
   var player: AVPlayer?
   var playerLayer: AVPlayerLayer?
}
@Observable class ApplicationData {
   var playing: Bool = false
   var progress: CGFloat = 0
   @ObservationIgnored var customVideoView: PlayerView!
   @ObservationIgnored var viewData: ViewData

   static let shared: ApplicationData = ApplicationData()
   private init() {
      customVideoView = PlayerView()
      viewData = ViewData()

      let bundle = Bundle.main
      let videoURL = bundle.url(forResource: "videotrees",
         withExtension: "mp4")
      let asset = AVURLAsset(url: videoURL!)
      viewData.playerItem = AVPlayerItem(asset: asset)
      viewData.player = AVPlayer(playerItem: viewData.playerItem)

      Task {
         await MainActor.run {
            viewData.playerLayer = customVideoView.view.layer as?
               AVPlayerLayer
            viewData.playerLayer?.player = viewData.player
         }
         let interval = CMTime(value: 1, timescale: 2)
         viewData.player?.addPeriodicTimeObserver(forInterval: interval,
            queue: DispatchQueue.main, using: { time in
            Task { @MainActor in
               if let duration = self.viewData.playerItem?.duration {
                  let position = time.seconds / duration.seconds
                  self.progress = CGFloat(position)
               }
            }
         })
      }
   }
   func playVideo() {
      if viewData.playerItem?.status == .readyToPlay {
         if playing {
            viewData.player?.pause()
```

```
                playing = false
            } else {
                viewData.player?.play()
                playing = true
            }
        }
    }
}
```

In this example, we include a method called **playVideo()** that is executed when the user presses the Play button. The method checks whether the media can be played or not, and then performs an action according to the value of the **playing** property. If the video is playing, we pause it, and if it is paused, we play it. In either case, the value of the **playing** property is updated to reflect the new state.

To calculate the size of the progress bar, we must implement an observer. However, this is not a KVO observer like the one implemented before. Normal observers are not fast enough, so the **AVFoundation** framework includes the **addPeriodicTimeObserver()** method to create an observer that provides a more accurate response. The method requires a **CMTime** value to specify the frequency with which the task should be performed, a reference to the main queue, and a closure with the code to be executed each time the observer is triggered. In this example, we create a **CMTime** value representing a time of 0.5 seconds, and then use it in the call to the **addPeriodicTimeObserver()** method to register the observer. After that, the closure passed to the observer is executed every 0.5 seconds during playback. In this closure, we get the current time and duration of the video in seconds and calculate the progression by converting the seconds to a value between 0.0 and 1.0, which we can later convert to points to display the progress bar on the screen.

IMPORTANT

The **addPeriodicTimeObserver()** method doesn't work with Swift concurrency. Instead, it requires the thread to be defined by a **DispatchQueue** object. This is an old class defined by the **Dispatch** framework to create asynchronous tasks. The class includes a type property called **main** to define a task for the main queue (the Main Actor), and this is how we make sure that the closure assigned to this method runs in the main thread. Note that because Xcode doesn't recognize the dispatch queue, we still had to embed the code in a task that performs in the Main Actor to avoid data race warnings.

The player is ready. It is time to define the interface. In this occasion, we need to present the representable view inside a **ZStack** so we can display the progress bar on top.

Listing 14-27: Playing and pausing the video

```
struct ContentView: View {
   @State private var appData = ApplicationData.shared
```

```
    var body: some View {
        ZStack {
            appData.customVideoView
                .ignoresSafeArea()
            VStack {
                Spacer()
                HStack {
                    Button(appData.playing ? "Pause" : "Play") {
                        appData.playVideo()
                    }.frame(width: 90)
                    .buttonStyle(.glass)
                    GeometryReader { geometry in
                        HStack {
                            Rectangle()
                                .fill(Color(red: 0, green: 0.4, blue: 0.8,
                                   opacity: 0.8))
                                .frame(width: geometry.size.width *
                                   appData.progress, height: 20)
                            Spacer()
                        }
                    }.padding(.top, 15)
                }
                .padding([.leading, .trailing])
                .frame(height: 50)
                .background(Color(red: 0.9, green: 0.9, blue: 0.9,
                   opacity: 0.8))
            }
        }.background(.black)
    }
}
```

The toolbar contains a button and a **Rectangle** view representing the progress bar. The button's label depends on the value of the **playing** property. When the video is playing, the text "Pause" is displayed, and when it is paused, the text "Play" is shown instead. To calculate the size of the **Rectangle** view that represents the progress bar, we embed the view in a **GeometryReader** and then multiply its width by the value of the **progress** property. Since this property contains a value between 0.0 and 1.0, the operation returns the value we need to set the width of the bar and display the progress on the screen.

Do It Yourself

Update the **ApplicationData** class with the code in Listing 14-26 and the **ContentView** structure with the code in Listing 14-27. Run the application on an iPhone simulator in landscape mode. You should see the video player illustrated in Figure 14-12.

The observer added with the **addPeriodicTimeObserver()** method is not the only way to get information from the player. The **AVPlayerItem** class also defines several notifications to report events that occur during media playback. For example, we can listen to the **AVPlayerItem.didPlayToEndTimeNotification** notification to know when the video has finished playing. For this purpose, we need to define a method in the model that listens and responds to that notification, and a task that calls this method once the representable view is created. The following are the changes we need to introduce to the **ApplicationData** class.

Listing 14-28: Executing an asynchronous method to detect the end of the video

```
@Observable class ApplicationData {
   var playing: Bool = false
   var progress: CGFloat = 0
   @ObservationIgnored var customVideoView: PlayerView!
   @ObservationIgnored var viewData: ViewData

   static let shared: ApplicationData = ApplicationData()
   private init() {
      customVideoView = PlayerView()
      viewData = ViewData()

      let bundle = Bundle.main
      let videoURL = bundle.url(forResource: "videotrees",
         withExtension: "mp4")
      let asset = AVURLAsset(url: videoURL!)
      viewData.playerItem = AVPlayerItem(asset: asset)
      viewData.player = AVPlayer(playerItem: viewData.playerItem)

      Task {
         await MainActor.run {
            viewData.playerLayer = customVideoView.view.layer as?
               AVPlayerLayer
            viewData.playerLayer?.player = viewData.player
         }
         let interval = CMTime(value: 1, timescale: 2)
         viewData.player?.addPeriodicTimeObserver(forInterval: interval,
            queue: DispatchQueue.main, using: { time in
            Task { @MainActor in
               if let duration = self.viewData.playerItem?.duration {
                  let position = time.seconds / duration.seconds
                  self.progress = CGFloat(position)
               }
            }
         })
         await rewindVideo()
      }
   }
   func rewindVideo() async {
      let center = NotificationCenter.default
      let name = AVPlayerItem.didPlayToEndTimeNotification
      for await _ in center.notifications(named: name, object: nil) {
         if let finished = await viewData.playerItem?.seek(to:
           CMTime.zero), finished {
            await MainActor.run {
               playing = false
               progress = 0
            }
         }
      }
   }
}
```

```
    func playVideo() {
        if viewData.playerItem?.status == .readyToPlay {
            if playing {
                viewData.player?.pause()
                playing = false
            } else {
                viewData.player?.play()
                playing = true
            }
        }
    }
}
```

In the **rewindVideo()** method, we must listen to the **AVPlayerItem.didPlayToEndTimeNotification** notification and prepare the video to be played again. For this purpose, the **AVPlayerItem** class provides the **seek()** method. This method moves the playback to the time specified by the argument and executes a closure after the process is complete. In this case, we use a **CMTime** value of 0 to move the player to the beginning of the video and then reset the **playing** and **progress** properties to allow the user to replay the video.

Do It Yourself

Update the **ApplicationData** class with the code in Listing 14-28. Run the application on an iPhone simulator. Press play and wait until the video is over. The player should reset itself and you should be able to play the video again.

If we want to play multiple videos in sequence, we could use the **AVPlayerItem.didPlayToEndTimeNotification** notification to assign a new asset to the **AVPlayer** object, but the framework offers a subclass of the **AVPlayer** class called **AVQueuePlayer** designed specifically to manage a list of videos. The class creates a playlist from an array of **AVPlayerItem** objects. The following are the initializer and some of its methods.

AVQueuePlayer(items: [AVPlayerItem])

This initializer creates a play list with the items specified by the **items** argument.

advanceToNextItem()

This method advances the playback to the next item on the list.

insert(AVPlayerItem, **after:** AVPlayerItem?)

This method inserts a new item on the list.

remove(AVPlayerItem)

This method removes an item from the list.

An **AVQueuePlayer** object replaces the **AVPlayer** object used to represent the media. All we have to do to play a sequence of videos is to create the **AVPlayerItem** object for each video and an **AVQueuePlayer** object to replace the **AVPlayer** object we have used so far, as in the following example.

Listing 14-29: Playing a list of videos

```
import SwiftUI
import AVFoundation

class ViewData: NSObject {
   var playerItem1: AVPlayerItem!
   var playerItem2: AVPlayerItem!
   var player: AVQueuePlayer!
   var playerLayer: AVPlayerLayer?
   var playerObservation: NSKeyValueObservation?

   func setObserver() {
      playerObservation = playerItem1?.observe(\.status, options: .new,
         changeHandler: { item, value in
         if item.status == .readyToPlay {
            Task { @MainActor in
               self.player?.play()
            }
         }
      })
   }
}
@Observable class ApplicationData {
   var playing: Bool = false
   var progress: CGFloat = 0
   @ObservationIgnored var customVideoView: PlayerView!
   @ObservationIgnored var viewData: ViewData

   static let shared: ApplicationData = ApplicationData()
   private init() {
      customVideoView = PlayerView()
      viewData = ViewData()

      let bundle = Bundle.main
      let videoURL1 = bundle.url(forResource: "videotrees",
         withExtension: "mp4")
      let videoURL2 = bundle.url(forResource: "videobeaches",
         withExtension: "mp4")

      let asset1 = AVURLAsset(url: videoURL1!)
      let asset2 = AVURLAsset(url: videoURL2!)
      viewData.playerItem1 = AVPlayerItem(asset: asset1)
      viewData.playerItem2 = AVPlayerItem(asset: asset2)
      viewData.player = AVQueuePlayer(items: [viewData.playerItem1,
         viewData.playerItem2])

      Task {
         await MainActor.run {
            viewData.playerLayer = customVideoView.view.layer as?
               AVPlayerLayer
```

```
            viewData.playerLayer?.player = viewData.player
            viewData.setObserver()
         }
      }
   }
}
```

In this example, we assume that we are using the **ContentView** view defined in Listing 14-25. The code loads two videos, **videotrees.mp4** and **videobeaches.mp4**, and then creates two **AVURLAsset** objects and two **AVPlayerItem** objects to represent them. The **AVQueuePlayer** object is defined next to play both videos in sequence. Note that because the interface we are using for this example does not include a button to play the videos, we add an observer to the first video and call the **play()** method when it is ready.

Do It Yourself

Update the **ApplicationData.swift** file with the code in Listing 14-29. This example is designed to work with the **ContentView** view defined in Listing 14-25. Download the **videobeaches.mp4** and **videotrees.mp4** videos from our website and add them to your project. Run the application on an iPhone simulator. The videos should be played one after another.

BASIC

14.3 - Color Picker

SwiftUI includes the **ColorPicker** view to allow the user to pick a color. The view creates a button that opens a predefined interface with tools to select and configure a color. The following is the view's initializer.

ColorPicker(String, **selection:** Binding, **supportsOpacity:** Bool**)**—This initializer creates a color picker. The first argument provides the label to show next to the button, the **selection** argument is a binding property that stores a **Color** view with the color selected by the user, and the **supportsOpacity** argument determines whether the user will be allowed to set the color's opacity. The value by default is **true**.

The implementation of the color picker is simple. We define a binding property with a **Color** view and then use it to initialize the **ColorPicker** view so that each time the user selects a color, it is stored in that property and we can use it to modify other views. In the following example, we use the value of the property to change the background color of the interface.

Listing 14-30: Showing a color picker

```
struct ContentView: View {
   @State private var selectedColor: Color = .white

   var body: some View {
      VStack {
         ColorPicker("Select a Color", selection: $selectedColor)
            .padding()
         Spacer()
      }.background(selectedColor)
   }
}
```

The **ColorPicker** view shows a button that opens an interface for the user to select a color. Once the user makes the selection, the color is automatically assigned to the **@State** property. This means that the user can change the selection as many times as he or she wants, but only the last color selected will be preserved in the property.

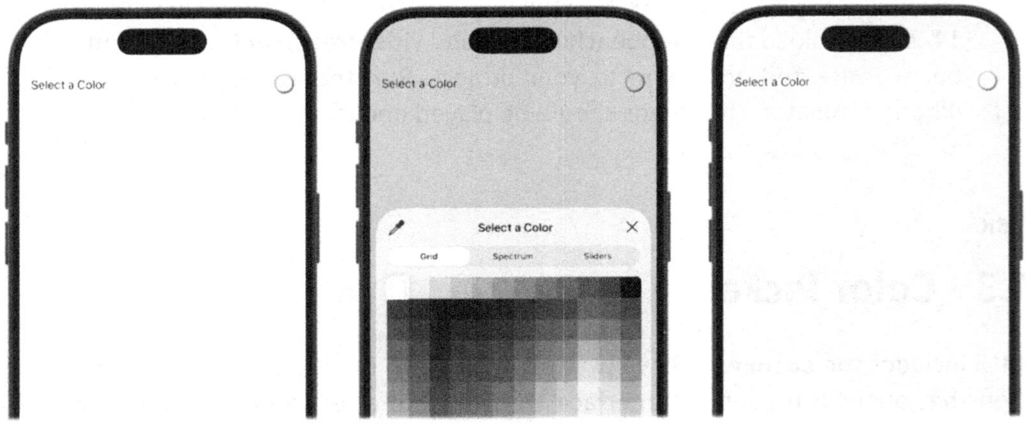

Figure 14-13: *Color picker*

Do It Yourself

Create a new App project. Update the **ContentView** structure with the code in Listing 14-30. Run the application on an iPhone simulator and press the color picker button. Select a color. You should see the color of the interface change, as shown in Figure 14-13, right.

Chapter 15
iCloud

BASIC

15.1 - iCloud Services

iCloud is Apple's cloud storage and synchronization service that allows users to keep their data consistent and available across all their devices. With iCloud, we can automatically store content such as documents, photos, preferences, and app data in the cloud and keep it up to date everywhere the user runs our app.

The first step to enable iCloud is to add it as a capability for our app. This option is available from the **Signing & Capabilities** panel in the project's settings, as shown in Figure 15-1, below. We must open the project settings (number 1), select the **Signing & Capabilities** panel (number 2), click the **+ Capability** button (number 3), and double-click the **iCloud** option (number 4).

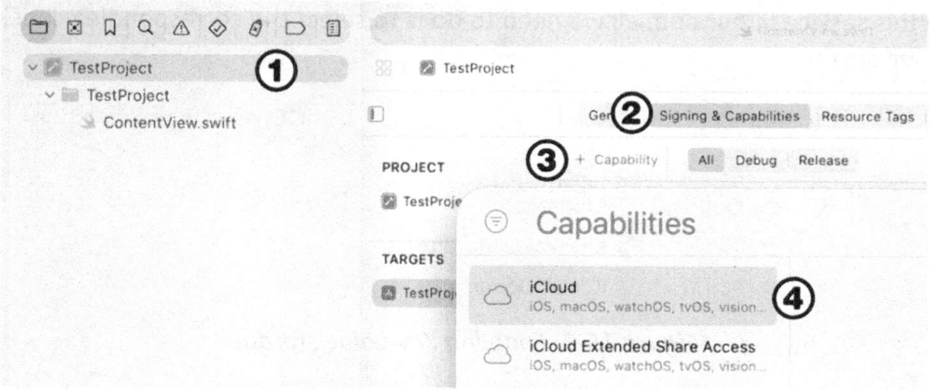

***Figure 15-1:** Enabling iCloud for our app*

After iCloud is added to the app, it appears in the **Signing & Capabilities** panel. From there, we can choose the iCloud services we want to enable. Three services are available: **Key-Value Storage** for storing small pieces of data, **iCloud Documents** for storing documents, and **CloudKit** for storing complete databases in the cloud.

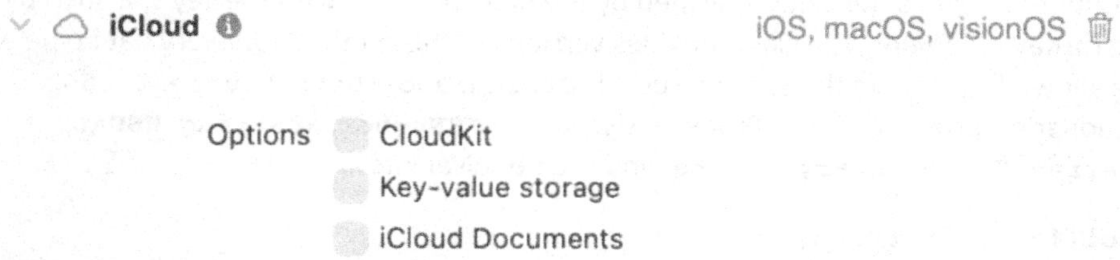

***Figure 15-2:** Enabling iCloud services*

IMPORTANT

There are two requirements for iCloud to work in our application. First, we must specify the app's bundle identifier. This is a unique string Apple uses to identify our app. When we create a new project, Xcode generates a random identifier used as a placeholder. To access iCloud services, we must specify our own from the Signing & Capabilities panel in Settings (to learn more about the bundle identifier and how to specify your own, read Bundle Identifier in Chapter 17). Second, iCloud services are available only to developers enrolled in the Apple Developer Program, so we must join the program to test these applications. At the time of writing, membership costs 99 US dollars per year. You can find more information at **developer.apple.com**.

BASIC

15.2 - Key-Value Storage

The Key-Value storage system works the same way as User Defaults, but all the data is stored on iCloud servers instead of the device. We can use it to store the app's preferences, states, or any other value that we need to automatically set on each device owned by the user. To enable this service in our app, all we need to do is to select the corresponding checkbox in the iCloud section.

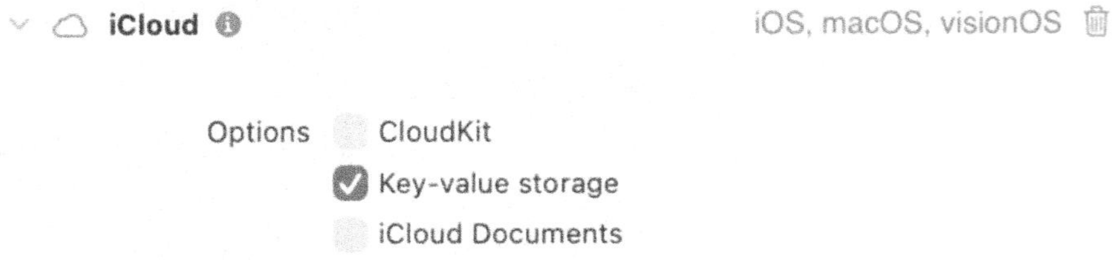

Figure 15-3: *Enabling Key-value storage*

To provide access to this service, the **Foundation** framework defines the **NSUbiquitousKeyValueStore** class. The class includes the following methods to store and retrieve values.

```
set(Value, forKey: String)
```

This method stores the value specified by the first argument with the key specified by the **forKey** argument. The class provides versions of this method for every data type we are allowed to store in the system, such as **String**, **Bool**, **Data**, **Double**, **Int64**, dictionaries, arrays, and also Property List values (**NSNumber**, **NSString**, **NSDate**, **NSArray**, **NSDictionary**, **NSData**, and their equivalents in Swift).

```
bool(forKey: String)
```

This method retrieves a value of type **Bool**.

```
double(forKey: String)
```

This method retrieves a value of type **Double**.

```
longLong(forKey: String)
```

This method retrieves a value of type **Int64**.

```
string(forKey: String)
```

This method retrieves a value of type **String**.

```
array(forKey: String)
```

This method retrieves an array.

```
dictionary(forKey: String)
```

This method retrieves a dictionary.

```
data(forKey: String)
```

This method retrieves a value of type **Data**.

```
object(forKey: String)
```

This method retrieves an object.

To store or access a value, we must initialize an **NSUbiquitousKeyValueStore** object and then call one of the methods above. The object takes care of connecting to iCloud and downloading or uploading the values, but it doesn't keep the values up to date. When a value is changed on one device, that change needs to be reflected in real time on the other devices. For this purpose, the **NSUbiquitousKeyValueStore** class defines the following notification.

```
didChangeExternallyNotification
```

This notification is posted by the system when a change in the values on the Key-Value storage is detected.

The Key-Value Storage service is designed to store discrete values that represent the user's preferences or the app's current state. For example, we might include a stepper that lets the user define a limit on the number of items the app can manage and make that value available on every device where the app runs. To keep the value synchronized, the app must load the current value from iCloud when the interface is initialized, save any new value set by the user, and update the local value when it changes on another device. The most effective way to handle this process is from a data model. We need to define an observable property to store the local value and include methods to send and retrieve the value from iCloud, as shown below.

Listing 15-1: Storing a value in iCloud

```
import SwiftUI

@Observable class ApplicationData {
   var control: Double = 0
   @ObservationIgnored let storage: NSUbiquitousKeyValueStore

   static let shared: ApplicationData = ApplicationData()
   private init() {
      storage = NSUbiquitousKeyValueStore()
      control = storage.double(forKey: "control")
   }
   func valueChanged(value: Double) {
      if control != storage.double(forKey: "control") {
         storage.set(value, forKey: "control")
         storage.synchronize()
      }
   }
   func valueReceived() async {
      let center = NotificationCenter.default
      let name = NSUbiquitousKeyValueStore.didChangeExternallyNotification
      for await notification in center.notifications(named: name,
         object: nil) {
         if notification.name == name {
            await MainActor.run {
               control = storage.double(forKey: "control")
            }
         }
      }
   }
}
```

This model defines an observable property called **control** that we use to keep track of the value set by the stepper, and a non-observable property to store the **NSUbiquitousKeyValueStore** object, which we need to access the values in iCloud. When the observable object is initialized, we create the **NSUbiquitousKeyValueStore** object and load a value stored with the key "control". (If the value is not available, the value 0 is returned.)

After the **NSUbiquitousKeyValueStore** object is initialized, we define two methods. The **valueChanged()** method is executed each time the value of the **control** property is modified. This method sends the new value to iCloud using the **set()** method and then calls the **synchronize()** method to ensure that the system sends it immediately. Note that we only want to send the value when it is modified by the user, so we do it when the new value is different from the current value. The second method is called **valueReceived()**. This method initializes an asynchronous **for in** loop that waits for the **didChangeExternallyNotification** notification. When the value is modified from another device, the notification is posted by the system so that we can read the new value from iCloud and update the **control** property.

All the work is done by the model, so the view only needs to include a **Stepper** and a **Text** view to show the current value.

Listing 15-2: Defining the interface to store and read values from iCloud

```
struct ContentView: View {
   @State private var appData = ApplicationData.shared

   var body: some View {
      VStack {
         HStack {
            Stepper("", value: $appData.control)
               .labelsHidden()
            Text("\(appData.control.formatted(.number.precision(.
               fractionLength(0))))")
               .font(.title)
            Spacer()
         }
         Spacer()
      }.padding()
      .onChange(of: appData.control, initial: false) { old, value in
         appData.valueChanged(value: value)
      }
      .task {
         await appData.valueReceived()
      }
   }
}
```

To begin the synchronization process, we apply the **`onChange()`** and **`task()`** modifiers. The **`onChange()`** modifier monitors the value of the **`control`** property, so when the user selects a new value, we call the **`valueChanged()`** method in the model to store it in iCloud. The **`task()`** modifier, in contrast, executes the **`valueReceived()`** method when the app is launched to start listening for updates from iCloud, so we know when the value is changed from another device.

Do It Yourself

Create a new App project. Click on the app's settings option at the top of the Navigator and open the **Signing & Capabilities** panel (Figure 15-1). Click on the **+ Capability** button at the top-left corner to add a capability. Select the **iCloud** option and check **Key-value** storage (Figure 15-3). Create a Swift file called **ApplicationData.swift** for the code in Listing 15-1. Update the **`ContentView`** structure with the code in Listing 15-2. Run the application on two different devices. Press the stepper's buttons to change the value to 5 on one device. You should see the value changing on the other device. Stop the application from Xcode and run it again. You should see the value 5 on the screen.

Just as we can store one value, we can store several. The Key-Value Storage service can manage multiple values using different keys, but if we want to simplify our work, we can use a structure to store all the values, encode that structure into data using JSON, and then store only one value with that data in iCloud (see JSON in Chapter 7). Our next example follows this approach. We define a structure to store the user's name, address, and city, and then encode and decode an instance of that structure to store the values in iCloud.

Listing 15-3: Storing multiple values in iCloud

```
import SwiftUI

struct PersonalInfo: Codable {
   var name: String
   var address: String
   var city: String
}
@Observable class ApplicationData {
   var userInfo: PersonalInfo
   @ObservationIgnored let storage: NSUbiquitousKeyValueStore

   static let shared: ApplicationData = ApplicationData()
   private init() {
      storage = NSUbiquitousKeyValueStore()

      userInfo = PersonalInfo(name: "", address: "", city: "")
      if let dataInfo = storage.data(forKey: "info") {
         let decoder = JSONDecoder()
         if let info = try? decoder.decode(PersonalInfo.self,
            from: dataInfo) {
            userInfo = info
         }
      }
   }
   func setInfo() {
      let encoder = JSONEncoder()
      if let data = try? encoder.encode(userInfo) {
         storage.set(data, forKey: "info")
      }
   }
   func valueReceived() async {
      let center = NotificationCenter.default
      let name = NSUbiquitousKeyValueStore.didChangeExternallyNotification
      for await notification in center.notifications(named: name,
         object: nil) {
         if notification.name == name {
            await MainActor.run {
               if let dataInfo = storage.data(forKey: "info") {
                  let decoder = JSONDecoder()
                  if let info = try? decoder.decode(PersonalInfo.self,
                     from: dataInfo) {
                     userInfo = info
                  }
               }
            }
         }
      }
   }
}
```

The process is the same as before. We read the value from iCloud when the observable object is initialized, and then implement two methods, one to send the `PersonalInfo` structure to iCloud when the user inserts new values, and another to listen for the **didChangeExternallyNotification** notification and update the structure when new values are inserted from another device. The only difference is how the value is processed. This time we are dealing with a structure that is encoded as a JSON value. Therefore, we need to use a **JSONDecoder** object when a value is received and a **JSONEncoder** object to send the value to iCloud.

For this example, we need two views: one that shows the current values, and another where the user can insert new ones. The initial view is simple. All it needs to do is get the values from the model, display them on the screen, and initialize a task to update them each time they are modified from another device.

Listing 15-4: Reading multiple values from iCloud

```
struct ContentView: View {
    @State private var appData = ApplicationData.shared
    @State private var openSheet: Bool = false

    var body: some View {
        NavigationStack {
            VStack {
                HStack {
                    Text("Name:")
                    Text(appData.userInfo.name)
                    Spacer()
                }
                HStack {
                    Text("Address:")
                    Text(appData.userInfo.address)
                    Spacer()
                }
                HStack {
                    Text("City:")
                    Text(appData.userInfo.city)
                    Spacer()
                }
                Spacer()
            }.padding()
            .navigationBarTitle("Personal Info")
            .toolbar {
                ToolbarItem(placement: .topBarTrailing) {
                    Button("Change") {
                        openSheet = true
                    }
                }
            }
            .sheet(isPresented: $openSheet) {
                InsertInfoView()
            }
            .task {
                await appData.valueReceived()
            }
        }
    }
}
```

This view includes a button in the navigation bar to open a view called **InsertInfoView** in a sheet. The following is our implementation of this view.

Listing 15-5: Saving multiple values in iCloud

```
import SwiftUI

struct InsertInfoView: View {
   @State private var appData = ApplicationData.shared
   @Environment(\.dismiss) var dismiss

   @State private var inputName: String = ""
   @State private var inputAddress: String = ""
   @State private var inputCity: String = ""

   var body: some View {
      VStack(spacing: 10) {
         TextField("Insert Name", text: $inputName)
            .textFieldStyle(.roundedBorder)
         TextField("Insert Address", text: $inputAddress)
            .textFieldStyle(.roundedBorder)
         TextField("Insert City", text: $inputCity)
            .textFieldStyle(.roundedBorder)
         HStack {
            Spacer()
            Button("Save") {
               appData.userInfo = PersonalInfo(name: inputName,
                  address: inputAddress, city: inputCity)
               appData.setInfo()
               dismiss()
            }.buttonStyle(.borderedProminent)
         }
         Spacer()
      }.padding()
      .onAppear {
         inputName = appData.userInfo.name
         inputAddress = appData.userInfo.address
         inputCity = appData.userInfo.city
      }
   }
}
```

This view includes three **TextField** views that allow the user to insert and modify the values. Since values may already be stored in iCloud, we assign them to the **@State** properties so that they are displayed to the user when the view appears. When the user presses the button to save the values, we create a new **PersonalInfo** structure and call the **setInfo()** method in the model to encode it and send it to iCloud.

The application is ready. When the user enters new values, they are sent to iCloud, and when the app is launched or a notification is received, the values are downloaded from iCloud and displayed on the screen.

Figure 15-4: *Multiple values stored in the Key/Value storage*

Do It Yourself

Update the **ApplicationData.swift** file with the code in Listing 15-3. Update the `ContentView` structure with the code in Listing 15-4. Create a SwiftUI file called **InsertInfoView.swift** for the code in Listing 15-5. Run the application on two devices. Press the Change button. Insert new values and press Save. The values should appear on the second device.

PRO

15.3 - iCloud Documents

The Key-Value Storage system is designed to store small values. The purpose of that system is to allow users to set preferences or configuration parameters across devices. Although useful, it has some limitations, especially in the amount of data we can store. An alternative is to enable the **iCloud Documents** option in the **Signing & Capabilities** panel and upload files.

Figure 15-5: *Enabling iCloud Documents service*

The operating system uses a container to store iCloud files. This container is a folder within the app's storage space where iCloud files are created. Whenever a file is added, modified, or removed from this container, the system automatically reports the changes to iCloud so that copies of the app running on other devices can update their own containers and remain in sync. Although synchronization is automatic, we must create the container ourselves. To do this, we need to click the + button at the bottom of the container list (Figure 15-5, number 1) and enter the name we want to assign to the container. This name must be unique, and the best way to ensure this is to use the app's bundle identifier, as shown in Figure 15-5.

Do It Yourself

Create a new App project. Click on the app's settings option at the top of the Navigator area and open the **Signing & Capabilities** panel (Figure 15-1). Click on the **+ Capability** button at the upper-left corner to add a capability. Select the **iCloud** option, press return, and check the option **iCloud Documents** (Figure 15-5). Press the + button to add a container (Figure 15-5, number 1). In the containers window, press the Create button to create a new container. Apple recommends to define the name with the iCloud prefix, an inverted domain, and the name of the app, as in **iCloud.com.formasterminds.TestProject**. To learn more about bundle identifiers and how to define them, read Bundle Identifier in Chapter 17.

An iCloud container is called *Ubiquitous Container* because its content is shared with other devices and therefore available everywhere. The **`FileManager`** class includes properties and methods to work with an ubiquitous container. The following are the most frequently used.

`url(forUbiquityContainerIdentifier:` `String?)`

This method returns the URL pointing to the app's iCloud container. The **forUbiquityContainerIdentifier** argument is the name of the container we want to access. The value **`nil`** returns the container assigned by default.

`evictUbiquitousItem(at:` `URL)`

This method removes the local copy of the document at the URL specified by the **at** argument.

Although the files are stored in a container on the device and are automatically synchronized by the system, working with iCloud presents some challenges that the **`FileManager`** class cannot handle. The most important of these is coordination. Due to the unreliability of network connections, iCloud can find different versions of the same file at any given time. Changes made to the file by one device may not have reached iCloud yet and may therefore later conflict with updates made by another device. In situations like that, the application must decide which version of the file to keep or which data is more valuable. These problems are not easy to solve and can turn the development of these applications into a nightmare. Considering all these issues, Apple has introduced a class called **`UIDocument`**, which was specifically designed to manage files for iCloud. The class can coordinate and synchronize files of any size and provides tools that simplify editing documents on mobile devices, such as progression reports, automatic thumbnail generation, undo manager, and others.

The **UIDocument** class is not meant to be implemented directly in our code; it is like an interface between the app's data and the files we use to store it. To take advantage of this class, we must create a subclass and override some of its methods. Once we have defined the subclass, we can create the object with the following initializer.

```
UIDocument(fileURL: URL)
```

This initializer creates a new **UIDocument** object. The **fileURL** argument is a **URL** structure with the location of the file in the container.

The following are the methods we must override in the subclass of **UIDocument** to provide the data for the file and to retrieve it later.

```
contents(forType: String)
```

This method is called when the **UIDocument** object needs to store the content of the document on the file. The method must return an object with the document's data (usually a **Data** structure). The **forType** argument identifies the type of the file (by default, it is determined from the file's extension).

```
load(fromContents: Any, ofType: String?)
```

This method is called when the **UIDocument** object loads the content of the document from the file. The **fromContents** argument is an object with the file's content (usually a **Data** structure), and the **ofType** argument is a string that identifies the file's type (by default, it is determined from the file's extension).

Once an object is created from our **UIDocument** subclass, we can manage the file from the asynchronous methods provided by the class. The following are the most frequently used.

```
open()
```

This asynchronous method asks the **UIDocument** object to open the file and load its content. The method returns a Boolean value to indicate if the operation was successful.

```
save(to: URL, for: SaveOperation)
```

This asynchronous method asks the **UIDocument** object to save the content of the document on file. The **for** argument is an enumeration value that indicates the type of operation to perform. The values available are **forCreating** (to save the file for the first time) and **forOverwriting** (to overwrite the file's current version). The method returns a Boolean value to indicate if the operation was successful.

```
close()
```

This asynchronous method saves any pending changes and closes the document. The method returns a Boolean value to indicate if the operation was successful.

The first thing we have to do to work with documents in iCloud is to define a subclass of **UIDocument**. The following is the one we are going to use for the examples in this chapter.

Listing 15-6: Creating the document

```
import SwiftUI

class MyDocument: UIDocument {
   var fileContent: Data?

   override func contents(forType typeName: String) throws -> Any {
      return fileContent ?? Data()
   }
   override func load(fromContents contents: Any, ofType
      typeName: String?) throws {
      if let data = contents as? Data, !data.isEmpty {
         fileContent = data
      }
   }
}
```

The **`UIDocument`** subclass requires at least three elements: a property to store the contents of the file (**`fileContent`**), the **`contents()`** method to provide the data to be stored in the file, and the **`load()`** method to retrieve the data from the file. When the **`UIDocument`** object is asked to save or load the data in the file, it calls these methods and uses the **`fileContent`** property as a proxy to move the data. Therefore, every time we want to access the contents of the file, we need to open the document and read this property.

PRO

Metadata Query

Accessing the files managed by iCloud is also complicated. We cannot simply request a list of files because some of them may not have been downloaded to the device yet. Instead, we need to retrieve the information associated with each file, known as metadata. A file's metadata includes details such as its name, extension, creation date, and other attributes. To obtain this metadata, the **Foundation** framework provides the **`NSMetadataQuery`** class, which defines the properties and methods required to search for files and monitor changes.

`predicate`

This property sets or returns the predicate for the query. It is an optional of type **`NSPredicate`**.

`sortDescriptors`

This property sets or returns the sort descriptors for the query. It is an array of **`NSSortDescriptor`** objects.

`searchScopes`

This property sets or returns a value that indicates the scope of the query. It is an array with constants that represent a predefined scope. The constants available for mobile devices are **`NSMetadataQueryUbiquitousDocumentsScope`** (searches for all the files in the Documents directory of the iCloud's container) and

NSMetadataQueryUbiquitousDataScope (searches for all the files that are not in the Documents directory of the iCloud's container).

results

This property returns an array with the query's results. By default, the array contains **NSMetadataItem** objects with the metadata of every file found.

resultCount

This property returns an **Int** with the number of results produced by the query.

result(at: Int)

This method returns the **NSMetadataItem** object from the query's results array at the index specified by the **at** argument.

start()

This method initiates the query.

stop()

This method stops the query.

enableUpdates()

This method enables query updates.

disableUpdates()

This method disables query updates.

The **NSMetadataQuery** class also includes some notifications to report when new data is available. The following are the most frequently used.

NSMetadataQueryDidUpdate

This notification is posted when the results of the query change.

NSMetadataQueryDidFinishGathering

This notification is posted when the query finishes getting all the information.

The predicate used to filter files in a query is similar to the one we used earlier with SwiftData, but it is created from a Foundation class called **NSPredicate**. This class takes in a string with a format that specifies the conditions and comparisons we want to use to filter the values.

NSPredicate(format: String, **argumentArray:** [Any]?)

This initializer creates an **NSPredicate** object with the conditions set by the **format** argument. The **argumentArray** argument is an optional array of values that replace placeholders in the string assigned to the **format** argument. The **argumentArray** argument may be ignored or replaced by a list of values separated by commas.

The results of a query are returned by the **results** property in the form of an array of **NSMetadataItem** objects. This is a simple class defined to contain the attributes of a file. The class provides the following method to retrieve the values.

value(forAttribute: String)

This method returns the value of the file's attribute determined by the **forAtttribute** argument. The **NSMetadataItem** class defines a list of constants to represent the attributes. The constants available are **NSMetadataItemFSNameKey** (file's name), **NSMetadataItemDisplayNameKey** (document's name), **NSMetadataItemURLKey** (file's URL), **NSMetadataItemPathKey** (file's path), **NSMetadataItemFSSizeKey** (file's size), **NSMetadataItemFSCreationDateKey** (date of creation), and **NSMetadataItemFSContentChangeDateKey** (date the file was last modified).

PRO

Single Document

The interface of an application that can process documents must allow the user to select the document and provide the tools to process its contents. In the following example, we work with only one document to show how the process works. The initial view includes a button that opens a sheet with a **TextEditor** view where the user can edit the content of the document.

Figure 15-6: *Interface to edit a document*

The codes listed below make up the model of our application. The first part, next, initializes the **NSMetadataQuery** object and starts listening to the **NSMetadataQueryDidFinishGathering** notification to update the document when new information is received.

Listing 15-7: Initializing the model required to store a document in iCloud

```
import SwiftUI

@Observable class ApplicationData {
   var metaData: NSMetadataQuery!

   static let shared: ApplicationData = ApplicationData()
   private init() {
```

```
        metaData = NSMetadataQuery()
        metaData.predicate = NSPredicate(format: "%K == %@",
           NSMetadataItemFSNameKey, "myfile.dat")
        metaData.searchScopes = [NSMetadataQueryUbiquitousDocumentsScope]

        Task {
           let center = NotificationCenter.default
           let name = NSNotification.Name.NSMetadataQueryDidFinishGathering
           for await notification in center.notifications(named: name,
              object: nil) {
              if notification.name == name {
                 await createFile()
              }
           }
        }
        metaData.start()
     }
  }
```

When the model is initialized, we create the **NSMetadataQuery** object, configure the query to search for documents inside the iCloud container (**NSMetadataQueryUbiquitous-DocumentsScope**), listen for the **NSMetadataQueryDidFinishGathering** notification, and initiate the process with the **start()** method. Since we are working with only one document, we make sure that the query returns the correct file with a predicate (myfile.dat). The format of the predicate for a query requires comparing the value of a file attribute to the string we are looking for. The attribute is represented by the constants defined in the **NSMetadataItem** class. In this case, we use the **NSMetadataItemFSNameKey** constant to filter the files by name. (Note that the value of the constant is inserted in the string with the placeholder **%K**. This placeholder is called *Dynamic Key* and is used to insert the value without quotes.)

The query gets the document and then posts a **NSMetadataQueryDidFinishGathering** notification. When the notification is received, we can get the list of documents in the container and use them. In this example, we execute a method called **createFile()** to perform that task.

Listing 15-8: Processing query results

```
func createFile() async {
   if metaData.resultCount <= 0 {
      let manager = FileManager.default
      if let fileURL = manager.url(forUbiquityContainerIdentifier: nil) {
         let documentURL = fileURL.appendingPathComponent(
            "Documents/myfile.dat")

         let newDocument = MyDocument(fileURL: documentURL)
         newDocument.fileContent = Data()
         if manager.fileExists(atPath: documentURL.path) {
            let _ = await newDocument.save(to: documentURL,
               for: .forOverwriting)
         } else {
            let _ = await newDocument.save(to: documentURL,
               for: .forCreating)
         }
```

```
            await newDocument.close()
        }
    }
}
```

Since this application works with a single document, the **createFile()** method only needs to verify whether the file already exists and create it if none is found. To determine whether the query returned a document, we check the value of the **resultCount** property of the **NSMetadataQuery** object. This property indicates the number of available documents. If the value is less than or equal to 0, no document has been created yet. In that case, we obtain the URL of the app's iCloud container using the **url(forUbiquityContainer-Identifier:)** method of the **FileManager** object, and append the Documents directory and the file name (Documents/myfile.dat). With the URL prepared, we create a **MyDocument** object, assign an empty **Data** value to its **fileContent** property to define the initial contents of the document, and call the **save()** method to save it in the container. If a document already exists at that URL, we call this method with the **forOverwriting** argument to update it; otherwise, we use the **forCreating** argument to create a new file. Internally, the **MyDocument** instance calls the **contents()** method to retrieve the document's data and writes the file into the container.

From the views, we must open the document, save the changes, and close it. The following are the methods we need to include in the model for this purpose.

Listing 15-9: Updating the document

```
func openDocument() async -> String {
    let manager = FileManager.default
    if let fileURL = manager.url(forUbiquityContainerIdentifier: nil) {
        let documentURL = fileURL.appendingPathComponent(
            "Documents/myfile.dat")
        let newDocument = MyDocument(fileURL: documentURL)
        let success = await newDocument.open()
        if success {
            if let data = newDocument.fileContent {
                let content = String(data: data, encoding: .utf8) ?? ""
                await newDocument.close()
                return content
            }
        }
    }
    return ""
}
func saveDocument(text: String) async {
    let manager = FileManager.default
    if let fileURL = manager.url(forUbiquityContainerIdentifier: nil) {
        let documentURL = fileURL.appendingPathComponent(
            "Documents/myfile.dat")

        let newDocument = MyDocument(fileURL: documentURL)
        if let data = text.data(using: .utf8) {
            newDocument.fileContent = data
            let _ = await newDocument.save(to: documentURL,
                for: .forOverwriting)
        }
```

```
      await newDocument.close()
   }
}
```

The `openDocument()` method is called every time the user opens the view to edit the document. In this method, we build the URL, create an instance of `MyDocument` again, open the document with the `open()` method, read the contents, and return a string so that the view can display it on the screen. The `saveDocument()` method performs the opposite process; it takes the text inserted by the user, converts it to a `Data` structure with the `data()` method, assigns it to the document, and saves the document in the container.

With these methods, the model is ready. The next step is to provide the views. As always, they are very simple. The initial view only needs a button to open the editor.

Listing 15-10: Defining the main interface

```
struct ContentView: View {
   @State private var editDocument: Bool = false

   var body: some View {
      VStack {
         Text("My Document")
            .padding()
         Button("Open Document") {
            editDocument = true
         }.buttonStyle(.borderedProminent)
         .padding()
         Spacer()
      }
      .sheet(isPresented: $editDocument) {
         EditDocumentView()
      }
   }
}
```

The button opens a sheet with a view to edit the document. We call it `EditDocumentView`.

Listing 15-11: Editing the document

```
import SwiftUI

struct EditDocumentView: View {
   @State private var appData = ApplicationData.shared
   @Environment(\.dismiss) var dismiss
   @State private var inputText: String = ""

   var body: some View {
      VStack {
         HStack {
            Button("Close") {
               dismiss()
            }.buttonStyle(.glass)
            .padding()
            Spacer()
```

```
            Button("Save") {
               Task {
                  await appData.saveDocument(text: inputText)
                  dismiss()
               }
            }.buttonStyle(.glassProminent)
            .padding()
         }
         GroupBox {
            TextEditor(text: $inputText)
         }
      }
      .task {
         inputText = await appData.openDocument()
      }
   }
}
```

This view includes a **TextEditor** view to edit the contents of the document and a button to save it. The editor's content is stored in a **@State** property called **inputText**. When the view is loaded, we initiate a task that calls the **openDocument()** method in the model and assigns the value returned by the method to this property, so that the **TextEditor** view is initialized with the document's content, and when the user taps the Save button to save the changes, we call the **saveDocument()** method in the model to store the new value and dismiss the view.

Do It Yourself

In the project you have created before to work with iCloud documents, create a Swift file called **MyDocument.swift** for the **UIDocument** subclass defined in Listing 15-6 and another called **ApplicationData.swift** for the code in Listing 15-7. Add the methods in Listings 15-8 and 15-9 to the **ApplicationData** class. Update the **ContentView** structure with the code in Listing 15-10. Create a SwiftUI file called **EditDocumentView.swift** for the view in Listing 15-11. Run the application on two devices. On the first device, press the Open Document button, insert some text and press the Save button. Wait a few seconds and press the Open Document button on the second device. You should see on the screen the same text you inserted on the first device.

PRO

Multiple Documents

In the previous example, we worked with only one document, but most applications allow users to create and manage all the documents they need. The requirements for working with a single document or many are the same. We must define a query and listen to the notifications to update the data in our model and the interface. But this time we also need to store information about each document in the model, so the views can show the list of available documents and users can select the one they want to work with. The following model includes a structure called **FileInfo** for this purpose.

Listing 15-12: Data model to work with multiple documents

```
import SwiftUI

struct NotificationWrapper {
   let value: Notification
}
struct FileInfo: Identifiable {
   let id: UUID = UUID()
   var name: String
   var url: URL
}
@Observable class ApplicationData {
   var listOfFiles: [FileInfo] = []
   var metaData: NSMetadataQuery!

   static let shared: ApplicationData = ApplicationData()
   private init() {
      metaData = NSMetadataQuery()
      metaData.searchScopes = [NSMetadataQueryUbiquitousDocumentsScope]

      Task {
         let center = NotificationCenter.default
         let name = NSNotification.Name.NSMetadataQueryDidFinishGathering
         for await notification in center.notifications(named: name,
            object: nil) {
            if notification.name == name {
               getFiles()
            }
         }
      }
      Task {
         let center = NotificationCenter.default
         let name = NSNotification.Name.NSMetadataQueryDidUpdate
         for await notification in center.notifications(named: name,
            object: nil) {
            if notification.name == name {
               let wrapper = NotificationWrapper(value: notification)
               updateFiles(notification: wrapper)
            }
         }
      }
      metaData.start()
   }
}
```

This model includes a new structure called **FileInfo** and an observable property called **listOfFiles** to store the instances that represent the documents in the container. In addition to the **NSMetadataQueryDidFinishGathering** notification, we now listen to the **NSMetadataQueryDidUpdate** notification to keep the files up to date. When this notification is received, we execute a method called **updateFiles()**. This method receives the **Notification** object created by the **notifications()** method to know what changes need to be made in the model. Note that the **Notification** object comes from an asynchronous thread. This means that the object is not safe (a data race may occur). To be able to pass this value to the method without receiving warnings and errors from the compiler, we wrap it in a structure called **NotificationWrapper**.

The rest of the code in the observable object is the same as before, only the methods change. For example, when the **NSMetadataQueryDidFinishGathering** notification is posted by the **NSMetadataQuery** object, we execute a method called **getFiles()** to process the list of files available in the container.

Listing 15-13: Processing the list of files in the container

```
func getFiles() {
   if metaData.resultCount > 0 {
      let files = metaData.results as! [NSMetadataItem]
      for item in files {
         let fileName = item.value(forAttribute: NSMetadataItemFSNameKey)
            as! String
         if !listOfFiles.contains(where: { $0.name == fileName }) {
            let documentURL = item.value(forAttribute:
               NSMetadataItemURLKey) as! URL
            listOfFiles.append(FileInfo(name: fileName, url: documentURL))
         }
      }
      listOfFiles.sort(by: { $0.name < $1.name })
   }
}
```

The **getFiles()** method includes a **for in** loop to go through the list of documents retrieved by the query, get the name of each file, check whether the **listOfFiles** array already contains a file with that name, and add it to the list if necessary.

As mentioned earlier, another method we need to add to the model is the one that is called when an **NSMetadataQueryDidUpdate** notification is received. This notification is sent every time the **NSMetadataQuery** object detects an update in the container (local or remote). In this case, we need to respond when a document is added or removed. To detect the type of change, the **NSMetadataQuery** class defines the following constants.

NSMetadataQueryUpdateAddedItemsKey

This constant retrieves an array of **NSMetadataItem** objects that represent the documents added to the container.

NSMetadataQueryUpdateChangedItemsKey

This constant retrieves an array of **NSMetadataItem** objects that represent the documents that were modified.

NSMetadataQueryUpdateRemovedItemsKey

This constant retrieves an array of **NSMetadataItem** objects that represent the documents that were removed from the container.

This information is returned by the **userInfo** property of the **Notification** object produced by the **NSMetadataQueryDidUpdate** notification and passed to the **updateFiles()** method, so we can process the changes accordingly, as shown below.

Listing 15-14: Updating the container

```
func updateFiles(notification: NotificationWrapper) {
   metaData.disableUpdates()

   let manager = FileManager.default
   if let modifications = notification.value.userInfo {
      if let removed = modifications[NSMetadataQueryUpdateRemovedItemsKey]
         as? [NSMetadataItem] {
         for item in removed {
            let name = item.value(forAttribute: NSMetadataItemFSNameKey)
               as! String
            if let index = listOfFiles.firstIndex(where: {
               $0.name == name }) {
               listOfFiles.remove(at: index)
            }
         }
      }
      if let added = modifications[NSMetadataQueryUpdateAddedItemsKey]
         as? [NSMetadataItem] {
         for item in added {
            let name = item.value(forAttribute: NSMetadataItemFSNameKey)
               as! String
            if !listOfFiles.contains(where: { $0.name == name }) {
               if let fileURL = manager
                  .url(forUbiquityContainerIdentifier: nil) {
                  let documentURL = fileURL
                     .appendingPathComponent("Documents/\(name)")
                  listOfFiles.append(FileInfo(name: name,
                     url: documentURL))
               }
            }
         }
         listOfFiles.sort(by: { $0.name < $1.name })
      }
   }
   metaData.enableUpdates()
}
```

This method receives the wrapper with the **Notification** object, so we can read the notification's **userInfo** property and determine the type of updates performed by the user. If the value is of type **NSMetadataQueryUpdateRemovedItemsKey**, we remove the deleted documents from the **listOfFiles** array, but if the value is of type **NSMetadataQueryUpdateAddedItemsKey**, we create a **FileInfo** structure to represent the file and add it to the **listOfFiles** array as before.

Note that to avoid concurrent updates, we temporarily disable the **NSMetadataQuery** object with the **disableUpdates()** method and re-enable it with the **enableUpdates()** method when the updates are complete.

The remaining methods are those required by the views to process the documents. For example, we need the following two methods to create and remove files from the container.

Listing 15-15: Adding and removing documents from the container

```
func createFile(name: String) async {
   let manager = FileManager.default
   if let fileURL = manager.url(forUbiquityContainerIdentifier: nil) {
      let documentURL = fileURL.appendingPathComponent(
         "Documents/\(name)")
      let document = MyDocument(fileURL: documentURL)
      document.fileContent = Data()
      let _ = await document.save(to: documentURL, for: .forCreating)
      await document.close()
   }
}
func removeFiles(indexes: IndexSet) async {
   let manager = FileManager.default
   for index in indexes {
      let fileURL = listOfFiles[index].url
      do {
         try manager.removeItem(atPath: fileURL.path)
         await MainActor.run {
            let _ = listOfFiles.remove(at: index)
         }
      } catch {
         print("Error deleting file: \(error)")
      }
   }
}
```

The **createFile()** method defines a URL with the name of the file, creates an empty document, and stores it in the container. The **removeFiles()** method, on the other hand, removes the user-selected files from the container and the corresponding **FileInfo** structures from the array. This last method receives an **IndexSet** value with the indexes of the documents to be removed. This is the value generated by the **onDelete()** modifier. We iterate through these values with a **for in** loop, get the URL of the file from the **url** property, and remove it from the container with the **removeItem()** method and from the **listOfFiles** array with the **remove()** method.

As before, the model also needs a few more methods to open and save the documents.

Listing 15-16: Opening, saving, and closing a document

```
func openDocument(url: URL) async -> String {
   let newDocument = MyDocument(fileURL: url)
   let success = await newDocument.open()
   if success {
      if let data = newDocument.fileContent {
         let content = String(data: data, encoding: .utf8) ?? ""
         await newDocument.close()
         return content
      }
   }
   return ""
}
```

```
func saveDocument(url: URL, content: String) async {
   let newDocument = MyDocument(fileURL: url)

   if let data = content.data(using: .utf8) {
      newDocument.fileContent = data
      let _ = await newDocument.save(to: url, for: .forOverwriting)
      await newDocument.close()
   }
}
```

The model is ready, now we must prepare the views. For this example, we need three views: one to list the available documents, one to allow the user to add new documents, and another to edit them. The following are the changes we need for the `ContentView` view.

Listing 15-17: Listing the documents available in the container

```
struct ContentView: View {
   @State private var appData = ApplicationData.shared
   @State private var openSheet: Bool = false

   var body: some View {
      NavigationStack {
         List {
            ForEach(appData.listOfFiles) { file in
               NavigationLink(destination:
                  EditDocumentView(selectedFile: file)) {
                  Text(file.name)
               }
            }
            .onDelete { indexes in
               Task {
                  await appData.removeFiles(indexes: indexes)
               }
            }
         }
         .navigationBarTitle("List of Files")
         .toolbarTitleDisplayMode(.inline)
         .toolbar {
            ToolbarItem(placement: .topBarTrailing) {
               Button("Add File", systemImage: "plus", action: {
                  openSheet = true
               })
            }
         }
         .sheet(isPresented: $openSheet) {
            CreateFileView()
         }
      }
   }
}
```

This view creates a list with the values in the `listOfFiles` property, applies the `onDelete()` modifier to the `ForEach` view to allow the user to delete a document, and includes a button in the navigation bar to open a sheet to add new documents. The view opened by the `sheet()` modifier is called `CreateFileView`.

Listing 15-18: Creating new documents

```
import SwiftUI

struct CreateFileView: View {
   @State private var appData = ApplicationData.shared
   @Environment(\.dismiss) var dismiss
   @State private var inputFileName: String = ""
   @State private var buttonDisabled: Bool = false

   var body: some View {
      VStack {
         HStack {
            Button("Close") {
               dismiss()
            }.buttonStyle(.glass)
            Spacer()
            Button("Create") {
               let fileName = inputFileName.trimmingCharacters(in:
                  .whitespaces)
               if !fileName.isEmpty && !appData.listOfFiles
                  .contains(where: { $0.name == fileName }) {
                  buttonDisabled = true
                  Task {
                     await appData.createFile(name: fileName)
                     dismiss()
                  }
               }
            }.buttonStyle(.glassProminent)
            .disabled(buttonDisabled)
         }.padding()
         TextField("Insert name and extension", text: $inputFileName)
            .textFieldStyle(.roundedBorder)
            .autocapitalization(.none)
            .autocorrectionDisabled(true)
            .padding()
         Spacer()
      }
   }
}
```

This view includes a **TextField** view where the user can type the name of the document and a button to save it. When the user presses the Save button, the code checks to see if a file with that name already exists in the **listOfFiles** array, disables the button to show the user that the action is being processed, and calls the **createFile()** method to add it to the container.

The **ForEach** loop in the **ContentView** view includes a **NavigationLink** view for the rows. This navigation link opens the **EditDocumentView** view so the user can edit the selected document. The following are the changes we need to make to this view.

Listing 15-19: Displaying the document's content

```
struct EditDocumentView: View {
   @State private var appData = ApplicationData.shared
   @Environment(\.dismiss) var dismiss
   @State private var inputText: String = ""
   let selectedFile: FileInfo

   var body: some View {
      GroupBox {
         TextEditor(text: $inputText)
      }
      .navigationBarTitle(selectedFile.name)
      .toolbarTitleDisplayMode(.inline)
      .toolbar {
         ToolbarItem(placement: .topBarTrailing) {
            Button("Save") {
               Task {
                  await appData.saveDocument(url: selectedFile.url,
                     content: inputText)
                  dismiss()
               }
            }
         }
      }
      .task {
         inputText = await appData.openDocument(url: selectedFile.url)
      }
   }
}
#Preview {
   NavigationStack {
      EditDocumentView(selectedFile: FileInfo(name: "",
         url: URL(fileURLWithPath: "")))
   }
}
```

This view receives a value of type **FileInfo** with the information about the file selected by the user. Once the view is loaded, we start an asynchronous task to open the document for that file and assign the contents to the **TextEditor** view so the user can see and modify it.

Figure 15-7: *Interface to read and save multiple documents*

Do It Yourself

Update the **ApplicationData.swift** file with the code in Listing 15-12 and the methods in Listings 15-13, 15-14, 15-15, and 15-16. Update the `ContentView` structure with the code in Listing 15-17. Create a SwiftUI file called **CreateFileView.swift** for the code in Listing 15-18, and update the `EditDocumentView` view with the code in Listing 15-19. Run the application simultaneously on two devices. Press the Create File button to add a document. The document should appear on both devices. Move the row to the left to delete it. The document should be removed on both devices.

BASIC

15.4 - CloudKit

CloudKit is Apple's cloud-based database service built on iCloud. It allows us to store structured data online with different levels of access, so users can retrieve and manage their information from any device where the app runs. CloudKit provides three types of databases to control access: **private**, **public**, and **shared**. The **private** database stores data that belongs to a specific user and is synchronized across that user's devices, the **public** database stores data that is accessible to all users of the app, and the **shared** database allows users to share specific records with selected users.

Enabling CloudKit

The **private** database is the one we use to synchronize data across the user's devices. SwiftData can automatically create this CloudKit database, but we must first enable the service. As we did with the previous iCloud services, we select the corresponding option in the **iCloud** section of the **Signing & Capabilities** panel, as shown below.

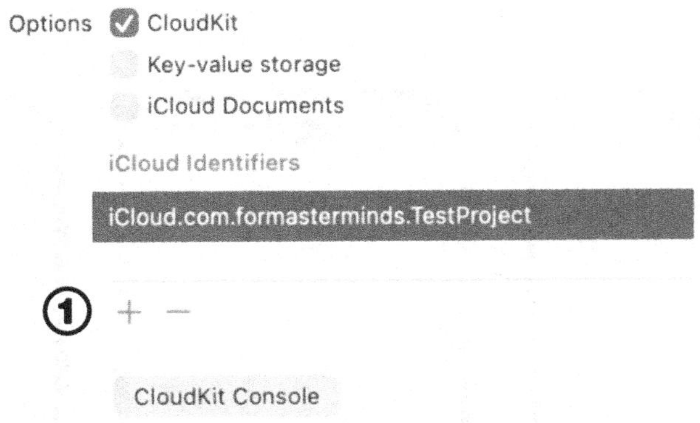

Figure 15-8: *Enabling CloudKit service*

CloudKit requires a container on Apple servers to store and manage the database. To create a new container, we must press the + button (Figure 15-8, number 1). This opens a window where we can select a container or create a new one. The name must be unique, and, as always, the best way to ensure this is to use the app's bundle identifier (see Bundle Identifier in Chapter 17).

Because CloudKit uses Remote Notifications to report changes in the database, when we activate CloudKit, Xcode automatically includes an additional service called *Push Notifications*. Push Notifications (also known as Remote Notifications) are messages sent from a server to inform our app that something has changed or needs attention. Remote Notifications posted by CloudKit are sent from Apple servers when something changes in the database. Since this can happen not only when the user is working with the app, but also when the app is running in the background, we need to add the Background Mode capability and enable a service called *Remote Notifications* to receive these notifications at any time.

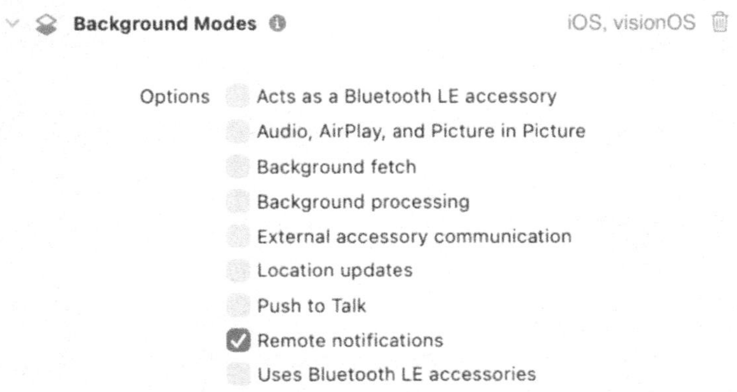

Figure 15-9: *Background Mode*

Do It Yourself

Create a new App project. Click on the app's settings option at the top of the Navigator, and open the **Signing & Capabilities** panel. Click on the **+ Capability** button at the top-left corner to add a capability. Select the **iCloud** option, press return, and check the option **CloudKit** (Figure 15-8). Press the + button to add a container (Figure 15-8, number 1). In the containers window, press the Create button to create a new container. Apple recommends to define the name with the iCloud prefix, an inverted domain, and the name of the app, as in **iCloud.com.formasterminds.TestProject** (see Bundle Identifier in Chapter 17). Click on the **+ Capability** button again to add another capability. Select the **Background Modes** capability and check the option **Remote Notifications** (Figure 15-9). We will use this project next.

In theory, this is all we need for the system to start uploading and downloading data from CloudKit, but in practice CloudKit has some additional requirements. First, all properties of the model must have a value by default or be optional. This includes the properties used to create relationships, which must be optional for the connections to work in the CloudKit database. And second, CloudKit cannot work with the **unique** attribute, so we must remove this attribute from all our models.

The following example reproduces the application created in Chapter 7 to store data with SwiftData, but adapted to work with CloudKit. Below is the model used to store books.

Listing 15-20: Preparing the models for CloudKit

```
import SwiftUI
import SwiftData

@Model
class Book: Identifiable {
    var id: UUID = UUID()
    var title: String = ""
    var author: String = ""
    var cover: String = ""
    var year: Int = 0

    init(title: String, author: String, cover: String, year: Int) {
        self.title = title
        self.author = author
        self.cover = cover
        self.year = year
    }
    var displayYear: String {
        get {
            let value = year > 0 ? String(year) : "Undefined"
            return value
        }
    }
}
```

Once we have the model, we need to create the container from the **App** structure, as shown below.

Listing 15-21: Creating the container

```
import SwiftUI
import SwiftData

@main struct MyApp: App {
    var body: some Scene {
        WindowGroup {
            ContentView()
                .modelContainer(for: [Book.self])
        }
    }
}
```

The next step is to list the books stored in the database from the main view. The following is our implementation of this view.

Listing 15-22: Showing the list of books

```
struct ContentView: View {
   @Query var listBooks: [Book]

   var body: some View {
      NavigationStack {
         List(listBooks) { book in
            CellBook(book: book)
         }
         .navigationTitle("Books")
         .toolbar {
            ToolbarItem(placement: .topBarTrailing) {
               NavigationLink(destination: AddBook(), label: {
                  Image(systemName: "plus")
               })
            }
         }
      }
   }
}
struct CellBook: View {
   let book: Book

   var body: some View {
      HStack(alignment: .top) {
         Image(book.cover)
            .resizable()
            .scaledToFit()
            .frame(width: 80, height: 100)
         VStack(alignment: .leading, spacing: 2) {
            Text(book.title).bold()
            Text(book.author)
            Text(book.displayYear).font(.caption)
            Spacer()
         }
         Spacer()
      }.padding([.top], 10)
   }
}
#Preview {
   ContentView()
      .modelContainer(for: [Book.self], inMemory: true)
}
```

There is nothing new in this view. We define a **@Query** property to retrieve the list of books and implement a **List** view to display them on the screen. The view also includes a button that presents the **AddBook** view to add new books. The following is our implementation of that view.

Listing 15-23: Adding books

```
import SwiftUI
import SwiftData
```

```
struct AddBook: View {
   @Environment(\.modelContext) var dbContext
   @Environment(\.dismiss) var dismiss

   @State private var titleInput: String = ""
   @State private var authorInput: String = ""
   @State private var yearInput: String = ""

   var body: some View {
      VStack(alignment: .trailing, spacing: 10) {
         TextField("Insert Title", text: $titleInput)
            .textFieldStyle(.roundedBorder)
         TextField("Insert Author", text: $authorInput)
            .textFieldStyle(.roundedBorder)
         TextField("Insert Year", text: $yearInput)
            .textFieldStyle(.roundedBorder)
            .keyboardType(.numbersAndPunctuation)
         Button("Save") {
            storeBook()
         }.buttonStyle(.glassProminent)
         Spacer()
      }.padding()
   }
   func storeBook() {
      let title = titleInput.trimmingCharacters(in: .whitespaces)
      let author = authorInput.trimmingCharacters(in: .whitespaces)
      if let year = Int(yearInput), !title.isEmpty && !author.isEmpty {
         let newBook = Book(title: title, author: author,
            cover: "nocover", year: year)
         dbContext.insert(newBook)
         try? dbContext.save()
         dismiss()
      }
   }
}
#Preview {
   AddBook()
      .modelContainer(for: [Book.self], inMemory: true)
}
```

The app is now ready. We can store books, and the data is automatically synchronized with iCloud and saved in a CloudKit database. This example defines a simple model that stores the book's cover, title, author, and year of publication, but we can apply the same approach to the more advanced applications developed in Chapter 7. As long as we enable CloudKit and adjust the models to meet its requirements, as described above, the data will be uploaded automatically and available on every device.

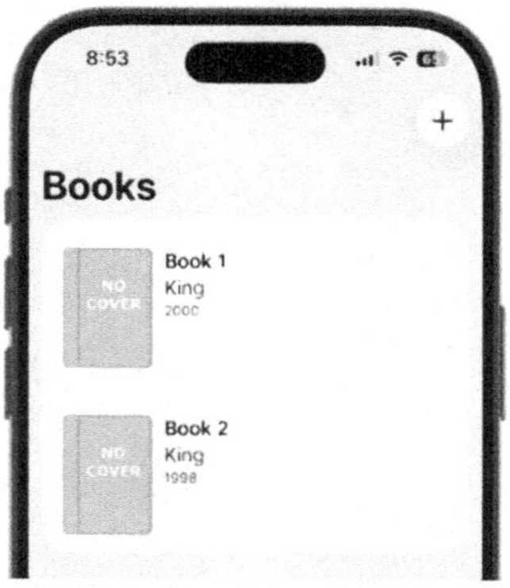

***Figure 15-10:** Books stored in CloudKit*

Do It Yourself

Create a Swift file called **BookModel.swift** for the code in Listing 15-20. Update the **`App`** structure with the code in Listing 15-21. Update the **`ContentView`** structure with the code in Listing 15-22. Create a SwiftUI file called **AddBook.swift** for the code in Listing 15-23. Download the **nocover.png** file from our website and add it to an Assets Catalog. Run the application on two devices. Press the + button to add a book. After a few seconds, the book should appear on the second device.

BASIC

CloudKit Dashboard

Objects created from SwiftData models are stored on CloudKit servers as records. In order to know what type of records the database may contain, CloudKit creates a model on its servers every time a new object is added to the local database. For example, if we create an object of type **`Book`**, CloudKit adds a record type called "CD_Book" to the model and creates fields representing each of the object's properties. In this way, the system sets up the structure of the database based on the data we store during development, saving us the trouble of configuring the database beforehand. The process is automatic, but if we want to check or change this structure, we can access it through the CloudKit dashboard.

The CloudKit dashboard is a control panel that allows us to manage CloudKit databases, add, update or remove records and configure the model (also called schema). The panel is available at **icloud.developer.apple.com/dashboard/** or by clicking the **CloudKit Console** button at the bottom of the iCloud section in the **Signing & Capabilities** panel (see Figure 15-8). The Dashboard's home page contains several buttons for accessing tools and documentation. We can configure the database, check its performance, control user activity, and manage our account.

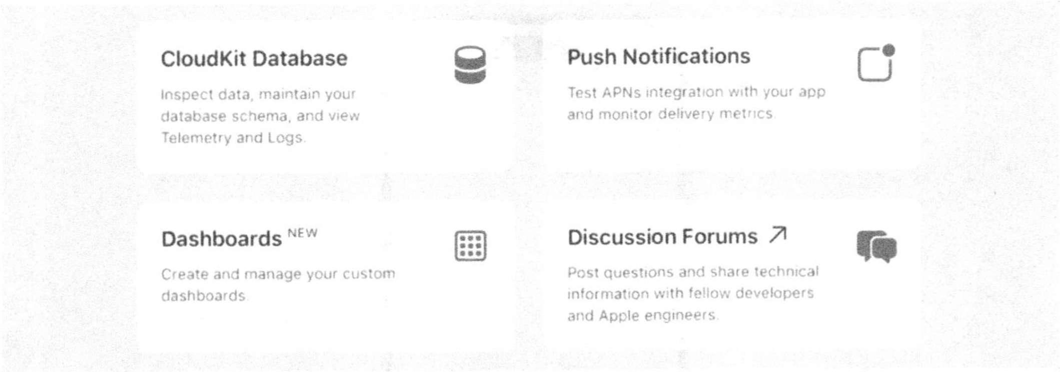

***Figure 15-11:** Dashboard's home page*

If we click on the **CloudKit Database** button, a panel appears to edit the database. The panel includes an option at the top to select the container (Figure 15-12, number 1), a panel on the left to edit the data and the schema, and another on the right to show and edit the values, as shown below.

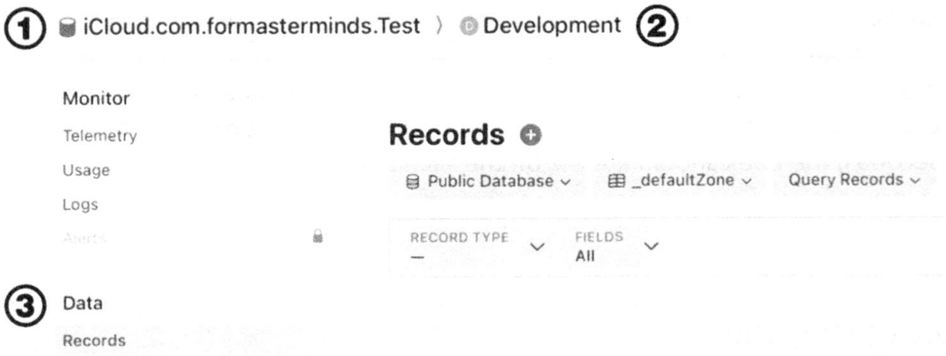

***Figure 15-12:** CloudKit Database*

Once we have selected the container, we can see the database structure and records. Next to the container, there is an option to choose between two configurations: Development and Production (Figure 15-12, number 2). The Development option shows the configuration of the database that is used during development. This is the database that is created for us as we test the application. The Production option shows the configuration of the database that we will ship with our application (the one that will be available to our users). Below these buttons is the Data section (Figure 15-12, number 3), where we can select the data we want to edit, including records, zones, and subscriptions.

CloudKit automatically creates records, zones and subscriptions for us. Records are the data structures that represent the objects created by SwiftData, zones are containers in the database where those records are stored, and subscriptions are messages that CloudKit sends to notify each device of changes in the database, so the devices stay in sync. When we enable CloudKit for our application and start adding objects to the database, the system creates a zone in the private database called com.apple.coredata.cloudkit.zone to store the records and a subscription called com.apple.coredata.cloudkit.private.subscription to send notifications when changes are introduced to the database.

To represent the SwiftData models, CloudKit creates record types. These record types are like classes that describe how the data is structured. CloudKit defines a record type for each SwiftData model in our application and creates fields to represent their properties. Record types are managed from the Schema section in the left panel. When we select the Record Types option, we get a list of record types created by our application on the right. Note that the names of the record types and the fields are defined by prefixing the SwiftData model name with the string "CD_". In our example, we get the record type CD_Book.

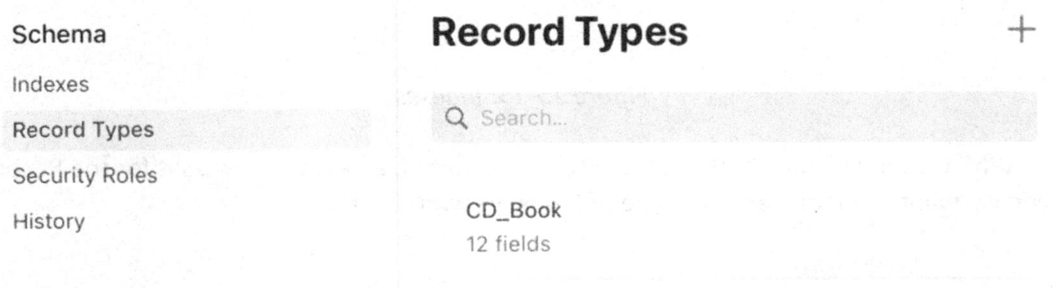

Figure 15-13: *Database schema*

The SwiftData objects added to the database by our app during testing are uploaded to CloudKit servers and stored as records. If we add a **Book** object, CloudKit creates a CD_Book record with those values. From CloudKit's dashboard, we can list these records and create more. The option is available when we click on the Records item in the Data section, as shown in Figure 15-12 (number 3). As mentioned earlier, the records for SwiftData are stored in the private database and a zone called com.apple.coredata.cloudkit.zone, so we must select these values to be able to list the records created by our app, as shown below.

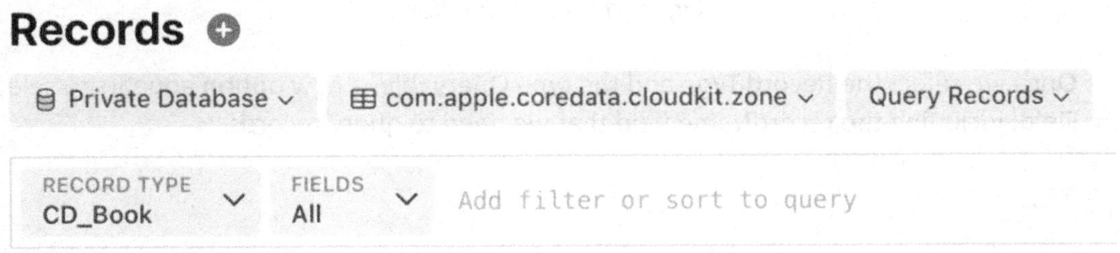

Figure 15-14: *Listing records*

To list the records, we must select the Record Type, as shown in Figure 15-14, and then click the Query Records button. However, when we do this with the default configuration, we get the error message "Field 'recordName' is not marked queryable." This is because the CloudKit dashboard is trying to sort the objects by the recordName field. This is a field that CloudKit adds to a record type to identify the records. The problem is that there is no index associated with the recordName field. Indexes are values that are added to the database to improve performance. To search for a value, the fields must be associated with a Queryable index. All the fields created to represent the properties of SwiftData objects are associated with a Queryable index, but not the recordName field. To add a Queryable index to the recordName field, we must select the Indexes option in the Schema section. This option lists the available record types in the right panel and shows a button on the top-right corner to add more, as shown below.

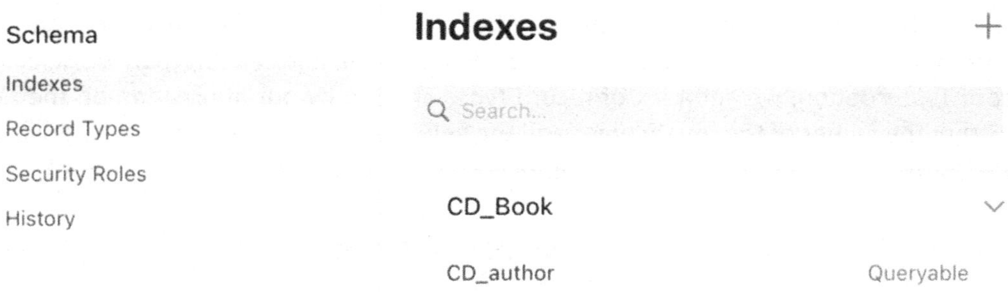

Figure 15-15: *Indexes*

When we press the + button on the top-right corner, a new window asks for the Record Type we want to modify and the type of Index we want to create.

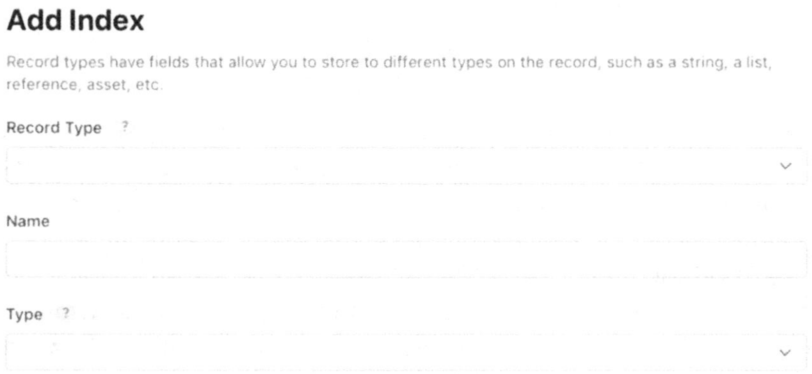

Figure 15-16: *Add Index*

Once we select the Record Type and the type Queryable, a new option appears to select the Field, including the recordName field that we need to query records.

Figure 15-17: *Queryable index for the recordName field*

After the Queryable index for the recordName field is added to the list, we can query records. All we need to do is to select the Private Database, the zone com.apple.coredata.cloudkit.zone, the Record Type we want to search (CD_Book in our case), and press the Query Records button. The result is shown below.

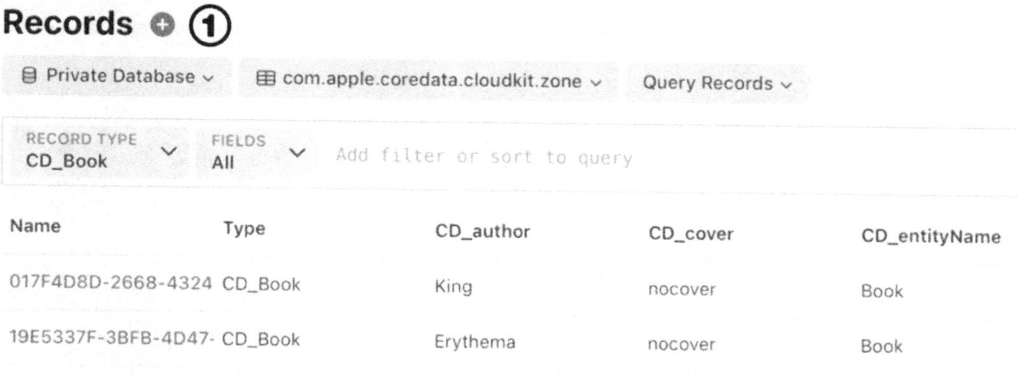

Figure 15-18: *List of CD_Book records*

The records in this list are those added to the database during testing. From this panel, we can check that the records were uploaded correctly to the CloudKit server and also add new records. This is useful when we only have one device. We can add a record from the CloudKit dashboard and see if it appears on the device. The option to add a new record is at the top of the list (Figure 15-18, number 1). When we press this button, a third panel opens on the right with text fields to provide all the information for the record.

BASIC

Deploy to Production

In the CloudKit's dashboard, at the bottom of the left panel, there is a list of options for working with the database schema. We can export the schema, import a schema from our computer, reset the schema to start from scratch, and deploy the schema to production. This last option is the one we have to choose if we want to prepare our app for distribution (to sell it in the App Store).

The option called Deploy Schema Changes opens a window that displays the features that are to be transferred to the Production environment. These include record types and indexes, but not the records added during testing. If we agree, we need to click the Deploy button to complete the process, and our database in CloudKit is ready for distribution.

IMPORTANT

The Production environment is used by apps that are submitted to Apple for distribution. This step is required for your application to be published in the App Store. If you don't deploy the changes to production, the database is not going to be available to your users. We will learn how to submit an app to the App Store in Chapter 17.

Chapter 16
Internationalization

BASIC

16.1 - Localization

Apple platforms reach users in more than a hundred countries, and apps are delivered in dozens of languages and regional variations. Even though we build a single codebase, that app must adapt to each market. This adaptation goes beyond translating words. It also involves adjusting the layout of the interface, formatting dates and numbers correctly, handling measurement units, and respecting language direction. This entire process is known as localization.

SwiftUI automates much of this work. Views are aligned using leading and trailing constraints, which automatically map to the appropriate side of the screen depending on whether the language reads left to right or right to left, and system types such as dates, numbers, and measurements are formatted according to the current locale. However, the app's text still needs to be translated. To manage translations efficiently, Xcode provides String Catalogs.

BASIC

String Catalogs

String Catalogs provide a centralized way to manage the text that appears in our app. Instead of storing translations in multiple files, we define all strings in a single catalog and assign translations for each supported language. Xcode automatically extracts localizable text from our project and organizes it within this catalog, making the localization process more efficient and easier to maintain. String Catalogs also support variations, pluralization rules, and device-specific adaptations, helping us deliver accurate and natural translations across different regions and platforms.

Xcode includes a dedicated template for creating a String Catalog file. To add one to the project, we must open the **File** menu, choose **New > File from Template**, and then scroll through the list until we find the String Catalog template, as shown below.

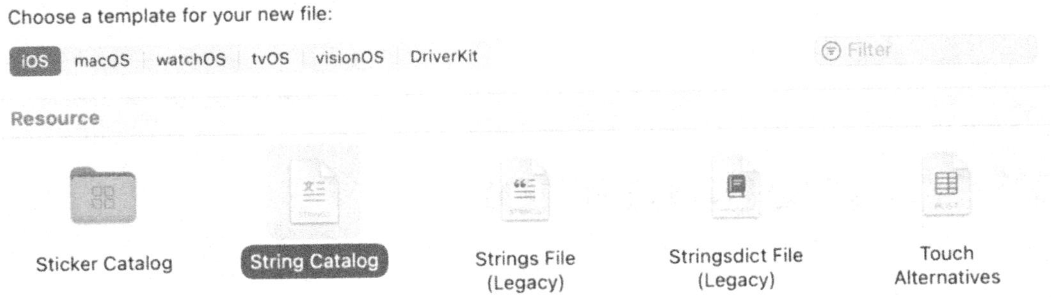

***Figure 16-1:** String Catalog file*

We can give the file any name we want, and it will be added to the project as always.

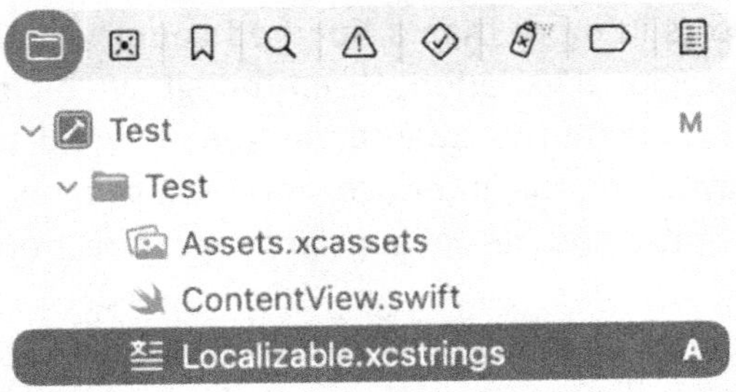

***Figure 16-2:** String Catalog file added to the project*

Every time the application is run or built, the system tracks the views and updates the contents of this file with strings that can be localized. The following example shows how this process works.

Listing 16-1: Testing String Catalogs

```
struct ContentView: View {
   var body: some View {
      VStack {
         Text("Hello World!")
            .padding()
         Spacer()
      }
   }
}
```

This view contains only a **Text** view with the text "Hello World!". When we run or build the application (Command + B), this text is included in the String Catalog file, as shown below.

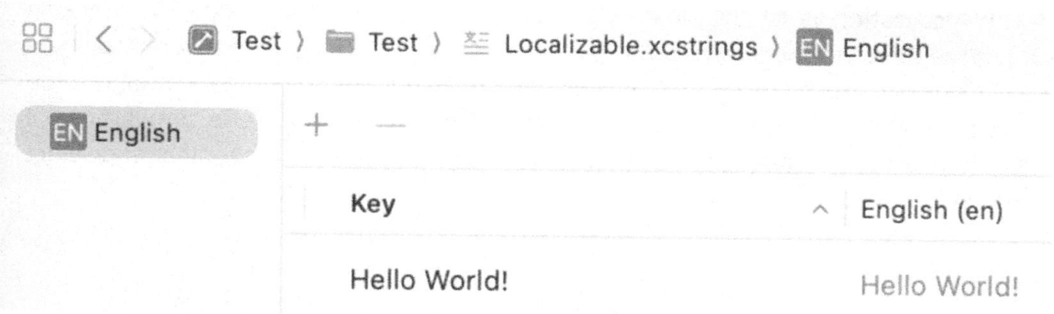

Figure 16-3: *String Catalog file updated*

The editor that Xcode provides for a String Catalog file displays a panel on the left with the available languages and a panel on the right where we enter translations and language-specific adaptations. When the file is first created, it includes only the default language, which in our example is English. To add another language, we use the + button located in the lower left corner of the panel. Clicking this button opens a pop-up menu with the list of languages available to add.

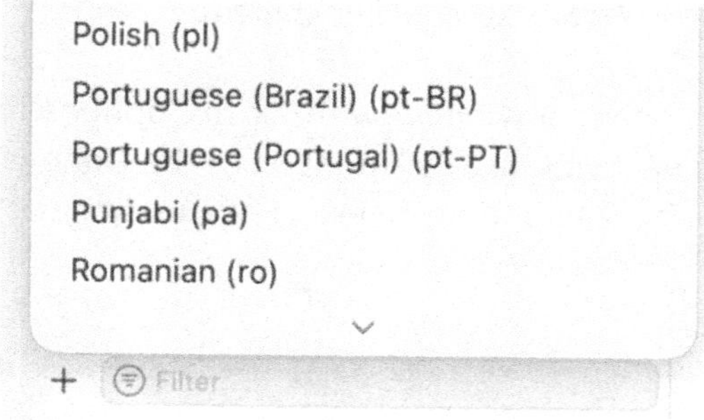

Figure 16-4: *Languages*

Once a language is added, we can click on it and enter the translation for each text. In the following example, we add Spanish and translate the text.

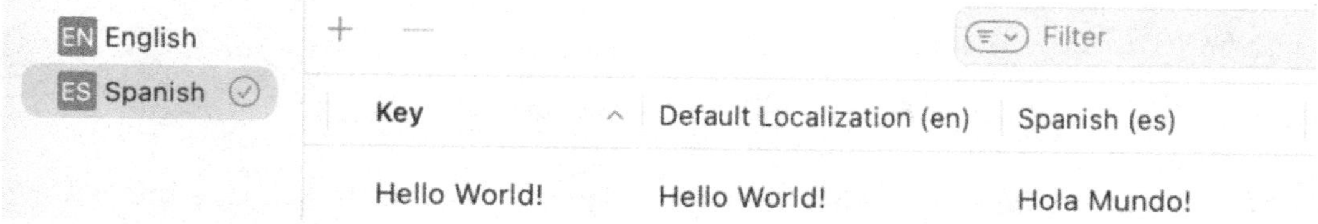

Figure 16-5: *Translation to Spanish*

Do It Yourself

Create a new App project. Update the `ContentView` structure with the code in Listing 16-1. Open the File menu, select the options **New > File from Template**, and create a **String Catalog** file (Figure 16-1). Run the application on an iPhone simulator or press Command + B to build it. Open the String Catalog file. You should see the text "Hello World!" in the list. Add the Spanish language, as shown in Figure 16-4. Use this project to test the rest of the examples in this chapter.

The localization is ready. Now, when our app is opened in a Spanish-speaking country, the **Text** view will display the text "Hola Mundo!". This works automatically on the user's device, but to test it in Xcode we need to change the scheme or configure the previews. By changing the scheme, we can test the localization in the simulator or a device. To edit the scheme, we must click on the scheme in the Xcode toolbar and select the Edit Scheme option.

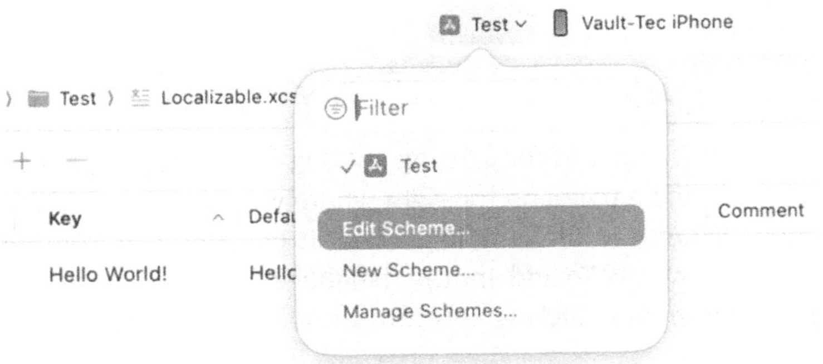

***Figure 16-6:** Scheme menu*

The Edit Scheme option opens a window with all the options for configuring the project. To change the language, we must click Run, open the Options panel, and select the language from the App Language option (Figure 16-7, number 1).

***Figure 16-7:** App Language option*

After we configure the scheme with the language we want to see, the previews, simulators and devices will run the app with that configuration. If we only want to test the localization in the previews, we can implement the following Environment properties instead.

layoutDirection

This property determines the direction of the text. It is a **LayoutDirection** enumeration with the values **leftToRight** and **rightToLeft**.

locale

This property determines the locale the views should use. It is a **Locale** structure.

To modify these properties, we must apply the **environment()** modifier to the preview, as we did in Chapter 2 (see Listing 2-80). For example, we can create two previews, one for the default language and another for Spanish.

Listing 16-2: Selecting the language for the previews

```
#Preview {
   ContentView()
}
#Preview {
   ContentView()
      .environment(\.locale, Locale(identifier: "es"))
}
```

Now we have two previews on the canvas, one with the text in English ("Hello World!") and another in Spanish ("Hola Mundo!").

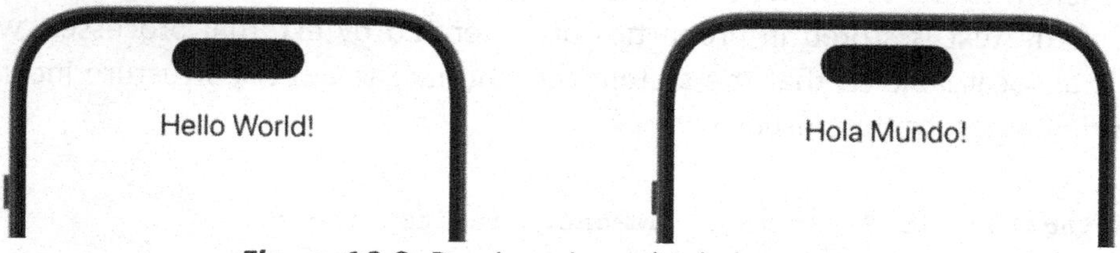

Figure 16-8: *Previews in multiple languages*

The interface provided by Xcode for editing String Catalogs is only available to developers. If we are working with third-party translators, we can export the files and then import them when we get them back from the translator. The options are available in the Product menu (Figure 16-9, number 1).

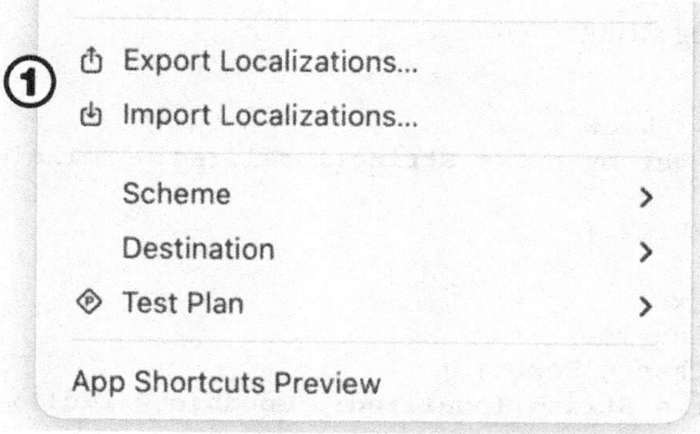

Figure 16-9: *Export/Import options*

When we send the localization files to a translator, it is recommended to include comments that can help the translator to achieve the most accurate result. For this purpose, the **Text** view includes the following initializer.

Text(String, **comment:** StaticString?)—This initializer creates a **Text** view with the text specified by the first argument and the comment specified by the **comment** argument. The **StaticString** structure is designed to represent text that will not change after the application is compiled.

We can use this initializer to create all the **Text** views in our interface. In the following example, we add a comment to our **Text** view so that the translator knows what the purpose of the text is.

Listing 16-3: Including comments for the translator

```
struct ContentView: View {
   var body: some View {
      VStack {
         Text("Hello World!", comment: "This is a welcome message")
            .padding()
         Spacer()
      }
   }
}
```

The system tracks the views to find localizable text that can be included in the String Catalog. If the text is stored in properties or generated by external processes, we must declare it as localizable so that the system can find it. The **String** structure includes the following initializer for this purpose.

String(localized: String, **comment:** StaticString?)

This initializer creates a **String** structure with a localized string.

With this initializer, we can localize any text that our interface needs to display to the user. For example, we can add a button to our view that changes the text of a **Text** view when pressed, and localize both the original text and the new one assigned by the button.

Listing 16-4: Localizing strings

```
struct ContentView: View {
   @State private var mytext = String(localized: "Hello World!")

   var body: some View {
      VStack {
         Text(mytext)
            .padding()
         Button("Change Text") {
            mytext = String(localized: "Goodbye World!")
         }
         Spacer()
      }
   }
}
```

When the application is built, the system tracks the views, finds the text in the **Button** view, and then checks the code to find more localizable text. In this example, we declare two localizable **String** structures, one to set the initial text for the **Text** view, and another to be assigned to that view later when the button is pressed. The String Catalog now includes three texts for translation.

Key	Default Localization (en)	Spanish (es)
Change Text	Change Text	Cambiar Texto
Goodbye World!	Goodbye World!	Adios Mundo!
Hello World!	Hello World!	Hola Mundo!

Figure 16-10: *Localizable texts to be translated*

If we receive normal strings from a process, we can tell the system that the strings are localizable by defining properties of type **`LocalizedStringResource`**. This structure includes the following initializer to specify a string and a comment.

`LocalizedStringResource``(String, `**`comment:`**` StaticString?)`

This initializer creates a structure to represent a localizable string that is received from another process.

We can use this structure, for example, when we know that the view will receive normal strings, but we want those strings to be localized.

Listing 16-5: Localizing values

```
struct ContentView: View {
   var body: some View {
      VStack {
         MyView(mytext: "Hello World!")
         Spacer()
      }
   }
}
struct MyView: View {
   let mytext: LocalizedStringResource

   var body: some View {
      Text(mytext)
         .padding()
   }
}
```

In addition to translations, String Catalogs also allow us to specify the singular and plural versions of a text. If the text contains a value, the system automatically selects the correct text to display to the user. For example, the following view includes a **`@State`** property to store an integer and a **`Text`** view to display it on the screen. Each time a button is pressed, the value is incremented by one.

Listing 16-6: Specifying singular and plural versions of the text

```
struct ContentView: View {
   @State private var counter = 1
```

```
    var body: some View {
        VStack {
            Text("\(counter) Item")
                .padding()
            Button("Add Unit") {
                counter += 1
            }.buttonStyle(.glass)
            Spacer()
        }
    }
}
```

Along with the value of the **counter** property, the **Text** view also displays the word "Item". The problem is that the text should read "Items" if the value is greater than 1. To set the two versions of this text, we can open the String Catalog, hold down the Control key and click on the word. This opens a menu with options to set versions for specific devices and also for singular and plural text.

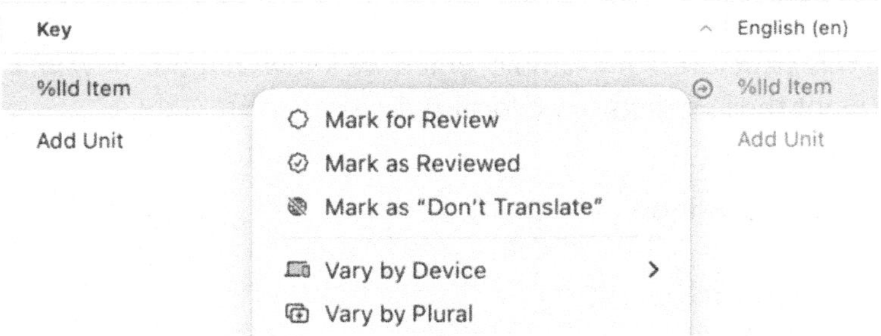

Figure 16-11: *Version menu*

If we select the option Vary by Plural, the system creates two new fields for each case.

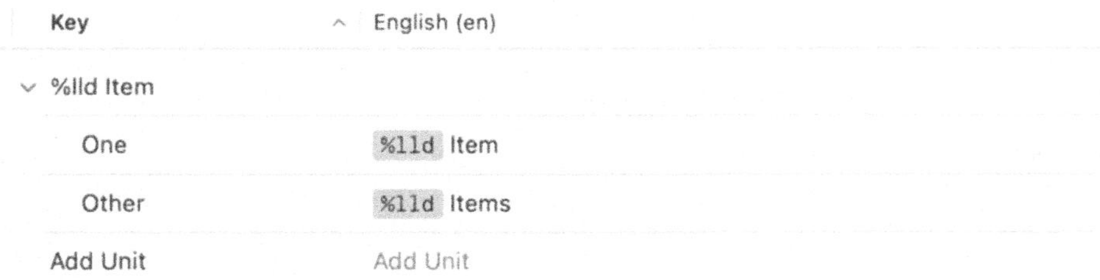

Figure 16-12: *Singular and plural versions*

In our example, we specify the word "Item" for the singular and "Items" for the plural version. Now the text that is displayed to the user depends on the value of the **counter** property.

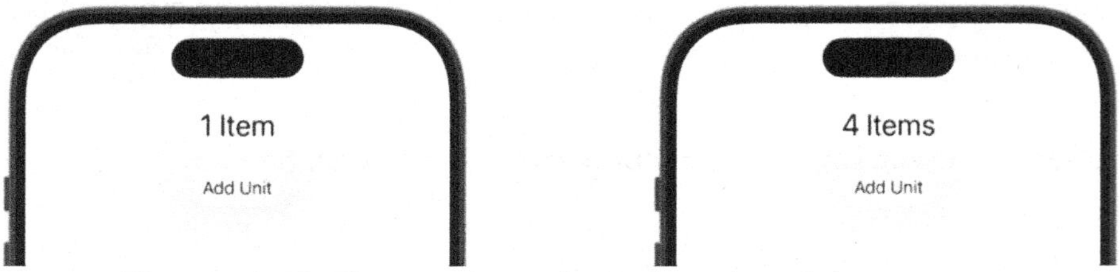

Figure 16-13: *The text depends on the value of the property*

Xcode also provides additional options for each entry. We can define device-specific variations with the Vary by Device option or mark a string as not requiring translation. One of the most useful features, however, is the ability to generate a descriptive comment automatically using Apple Intelligence. The system analyzes where the text appears in the app, infers its purpose, and creates an appropriate comment. To use this feature, we must open the contextual menu and select Generate Comment, as shown below.

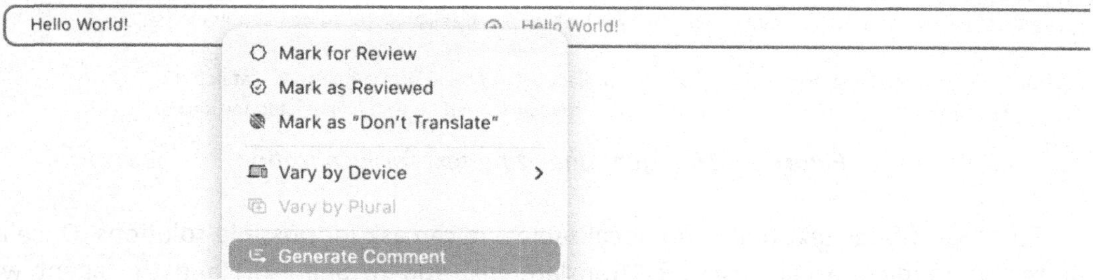

Figure 16-14: *Comment generator for String Catalogs*

In this example, we use the simple application from Listing 16-1, which contains a single `Text` view displaying the string "Hello World." After opening the contextual menu and choosing Generate Comment, the system analyzes the text, determines its role in the interface, and automatically creates a descriptive comment, as shown below.

Figure 16-15: *Comment generated by Xcode*

Do It Yourself

Update the `ContentView` structure in your project with the example in Listing 16-1. Press Command + B to compile the project. Click on the String Catalog file to open it in the editor. Press the Control key and click on the "Hello World!" entry. Select the option Generate Comment. After a few seconds, you should see a new comment added by Xcode for that entry (Figure 16-15).

Xcode can do much more than generate comments for our text. Using an AI agent, we can ask Xcode to do all the work for us, including preparing the texts in our app for localization, creating the String Catalog files, and translating everything to any language we want.

The first step is to make sure that all the text we display in our app is localizable. We must open a new conversation and ask something like "Check that all the texts in this app are localizable." The AI agent will check the whole code and provide a summary of what it finds. For example, the following is what we may see if we send this request in the project created by the Xcode's template.

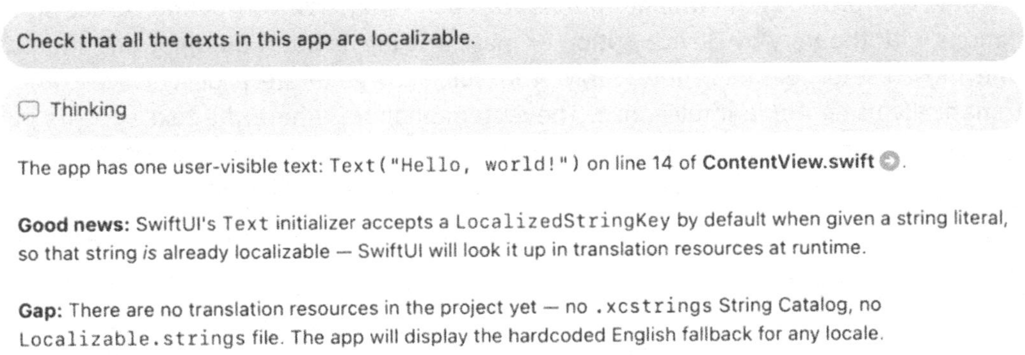

Figure 16-16: *Agent analyzing text for localization*

If the agent finds text that is not localizable, we can ask for possible solutions. Once all our text is ready, we can just ask "Translate this app to Spanish," and the agent will automatically create the String Catalog files for us and all the entries necessary to translate the app to the language we requested.

> **IMPORTANT**
>
> The translation is performed by the AI agent. This means that the quality of the translation will depend on the agent you are using. It is recommended to translate one language at a time, and always check the results and make any adjustments if necessary. For more information on AI translation, visit our website and follow the links for this chapter.

Chapter 17
App Store

BASIC

17.1 Publishing

Xcode allows us to run our applications on personal devices, but making them available to the public requires submitting them to the App Store. Although Xcode provides all the tools we need to archive and upload our apps, publishing involves far more than generating a build. Apple imposes a range of technical, legal, and administrative requirements that every application must meet before it can be reviewed, approved, and distributed to users. The following steps outline this process.

- We must enroll in the Apple Developer Program.
- We must create a distribution certificate.
- We must generate a provisioning profile configured for distribution.
- We must define an App ID to uniquely identify the application.
- We must register the app in App Store Connect.
- We must create an archive of the app for each target platform.
- We must upload the archive to App Store Connect and submit it for review.

BASIC

Apple Developer Program

Developing and testing can be done with a free Apple Developer account, but distributing an app on the App Store requires enrollment in the Apple Developer Program. To enroll, we must visit **developer.apple.com/programs/**, scroll to the bottom of the page, and select the option **Enroll Now**. At the time of writing, the membership fee is USD 99 per year.

BASIC

Bundle Identifier

The first step to prepare our app for distribution is to set the bundle identifier. This is a value that uniquely identifies the app to Apple's operating systems, App Store Connect, and other services. When we create a new project, Xcode assigns a provisional value created from a random key and the project's name, but we must specify our own. The option is available from the **Signing & Capabilities** panel in the project's settings, as shown below.

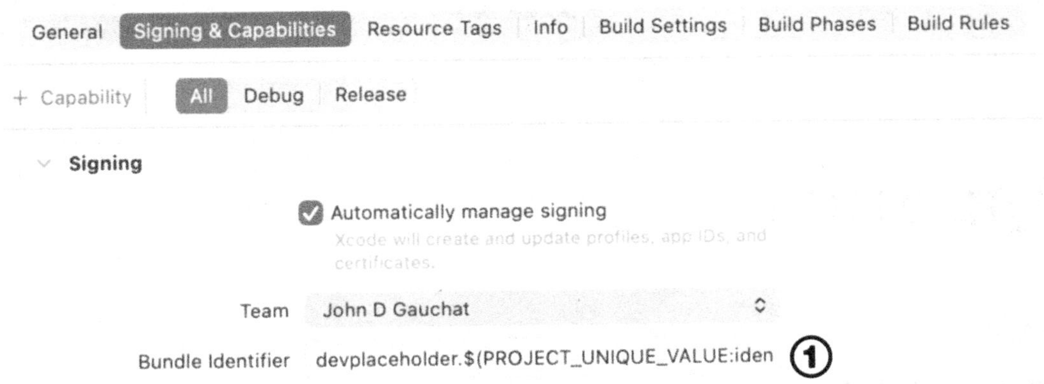

***Figure 17-1:** Specifying the bundle identifier*

As shown in Figure 17-1 (number 1), Xcode creates a bundle identifier using the string devplaceholder and the values of system variables. Before submitting our app, we must replace this whole string with a value that uniquely identifies it. Apple's recommendation is to use an inverted domain. For example, if we have a website with the domain **www.mywebsite.com** and create an app with the name **My App**, we can set the bundle identifier as **com.mywebsite.My_App** (spaces must be replaced with an underscore). But how we declare this identifier is up to us. We can use any values we want as long as they don't collide with those used by other developers.

> **IMPORTANT**
>
> Although it is not mandatory, you should get your own domain and website. Apple not only recommends using an inverted domain to generate the bundle identifier, but also requires you to provide a promotional website and a support page when submitting your app to the App Store.

BASIC

Certificates, Provisioning Profiles, and Identifiers

Apple ensures that only trusted software runs on its devices by requiring every app to be digitally signed. To distribute an app, three elements are involved: certificates, provisioning profiles, and identifiers. A **certificate** identifies the developer or organization that signs the app, a **provisioning profile** defines how the app can be distributed and which devices are allowed to run it, and an **app identifier**, known as the App ID, uniquely identifies the application within Apple's ecosystem. These elements are embedded in the app bundle so the system can verify who signed the app, what app it is, and whether it is authorized to run.

After we sign in on Xcode with our developer account (see Chapter 1, Figure 1-7) and specify the bundle identifier, Xcode takes care of creating everything for us, so we rarely need to define these values ourselves. However, Apple provides a management section in our developer account for cases that require manual configuration. This option is available only to paid members of the Apple Developer Program. Figure 17-2, below, shows the menu that appears on **developer.apple.com** after selecting **Account** and then **Certificates** under the **Certificates, IDs & Profiles** section.

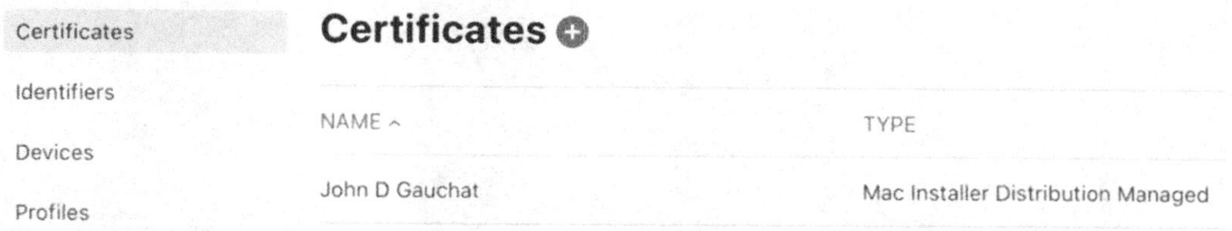

Figure 17-2: *Managing certificates, provisioning profiles, and identifiers*

On this page, we can create, edit or remove certificates, provisioning profiles and identifiers. The page contains two sections. The left panel provides a list of options to select the type of values we want to work with, and the right panel shows the list of available values and buttons to create new ones. When a value is selected, a new window opens with tools for editing the value.

BASIC

Icon Composer

The next step we must take before submitting the app is to provide the app's icon. Icons are the small images that users tap or click on to launch the app. To create these icons, Apple provides a tool called **Icon Composer**. This tool generates app icons for all supported platforms and automatically adapts them to system appearances such as Light, Dark, Tinted, and other variations. We can access **Icon Composer** from Xcode by opening the Xcode menu and selecting Open Developer Tool, as shown below.

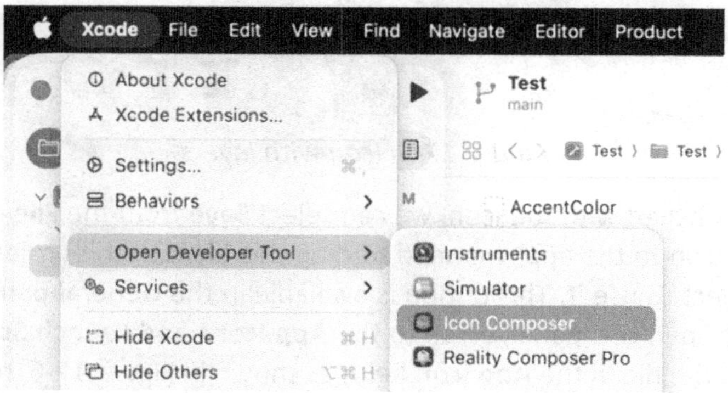

Figure 17-3: *Opening Icon Composer*

The Icon Composer's interface includes a central editor area and two side panels. The panel on the left displays the list of layers that make up the icon, while the panel on the right provides editing and configuration options. When we create a new document, the editor presents a template that serves as the starting point for designing the icon, as shown below.

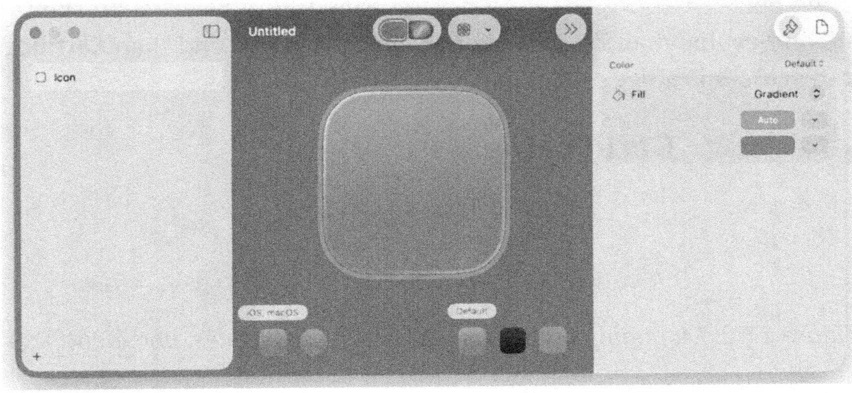

Figure 17-4: *Template*

The template initially displays a plain blue icon, but we can modify the background from the panel on the right and add graphics from the panel on the left. These graphics can be imported as SVG or PNG files. The SVG format defines artwork as vector data, which makes it easy to scale and adapt to different sizes and styles without losing quality. PNG files, on the other hand, are useful when we need to include detailed or photographic images. For the following example, we imported an SVG image of a palette and changed its color to yellow and the background to a pink gradient.

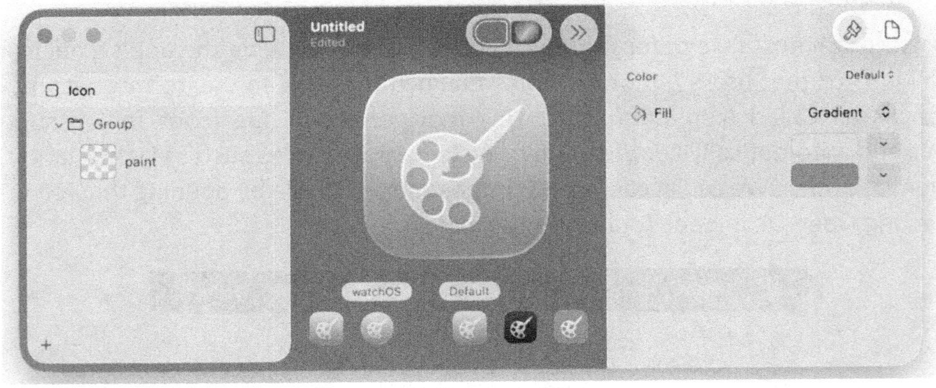

Figure 17-5: *Icon with layers*

Once we are satisfied with the icon, we can select **Save** from the **File** menu to store the file. To assign the icon to the app, we need to drag this file into the project (Navigator) and configure the project to use it. This option is available in the **General** panel of the project's settings. We must open this panel, scroll to the **App Icons and Launch Screen** section, and enter the name of the file in the **App Icon** field, as shown in Figure 17-6, number 1.

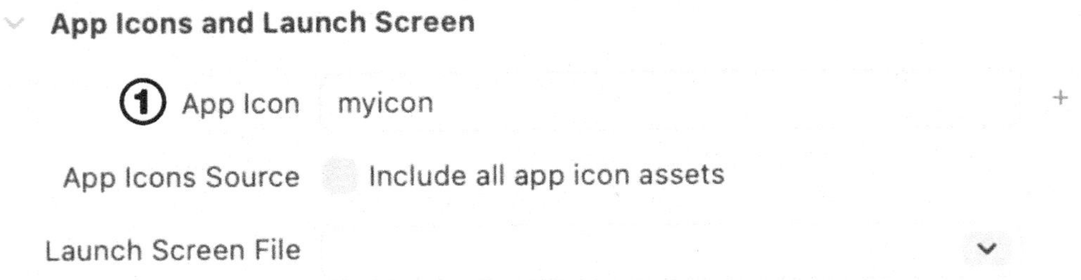

Figure 17-6: *Assigning our icon to the app*

Do It Yourself

Create a new App project. From the Xcode menu, choose Open Developer Tool and select **Icon Composer** (Figure 17-3). The interface should look similar to Figure 17-4. Select the Icon item in the left panel and modify the background colors from the right panel. Download the **paint.png** or **paint.svg** files from our website and drag it into the left panel. The graphic will appear in the layer list and inside the icon preview, as shown in Figure 17-5. Select the graphic in the left panel and adjust its attributes from the right panel. Use the options at the bottom of the window to preview the icon in different configurations. When you are satisfied with the result, select **Save** from the **File** menu, drag the saved file into your project, open the project settings, select the **General** panel, and assign the file name to the **App Icon** field, as shown in Figure 17-6.

IMPORTANT

Icon Composer includes a wide range of tools to customize the background, edit graphics, apply effects, and organize layers. The topic is beyond the scope of this book. For additional information, visit our website and follow the links for this chapter.

BASIC

Launch Screen

The launch screen is the first interface the user sees when the application is launched. No matter how small or optimized an app is, it still requires a brief moment to load. The launch screen helps create the impression of responsiveness during this short transition.

The option to configure the launch screen is available in the **Info** panel of the project's settings. We must add the "Launch Screen" key and then select the values we want to assign, as shown below.

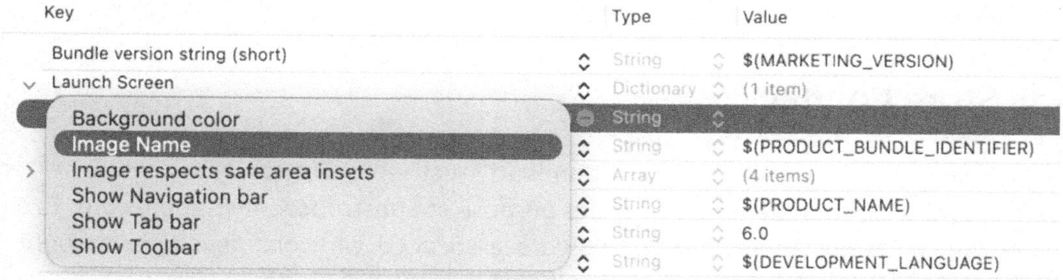

Figure 17-7: *Launch Screen options*

Two options are available to specify the content and four to configure the screen. The Background color option specifies the name of the Color Set in the Asset Catalog that will be used to define the background color of the screen, and the Image Name option specifies the name of the Image Set that contains the image to be displayed. For configuration, there is the Image respects safe area insets option to specify the behavior of the image with respect to the safe area, and the Show Navigation bar, Show Tab bar, and Show Toolbar options to specify whether these bars should be displayed when the app is launched.

The following example shows what happens when we add a background color and an image. In this case, we use an Image Set called **launchLogo** and a Color Set called **launchColor**.

Figure 17-8: *Launch Screen configuration*

Apple's guidelines recommend creating a launch screen that closely resembles the app's first screen. For example, if the background of the user interface is yellow, we should assign a yellow background to the launch screen as well. In our example, we define two sets in the Asset Catalog. The launchLogo set contains a PNG image with a logo, and the launchColor set defines a yellow color for the light and dark appearance. The result is shown below.

Figure 17-9: *Launch screen*

BASIC

App Store Connect

The first step in submitting our application is to create a record for it on Apple's servers. Apple provides a dedicated website for this purpose at **appstoreconnect.apple.com**. To sign in, we use the same Apple ID and password associated with our developer account at **developer.apple.com**. Figure 17-10 shows the options available after we log in.

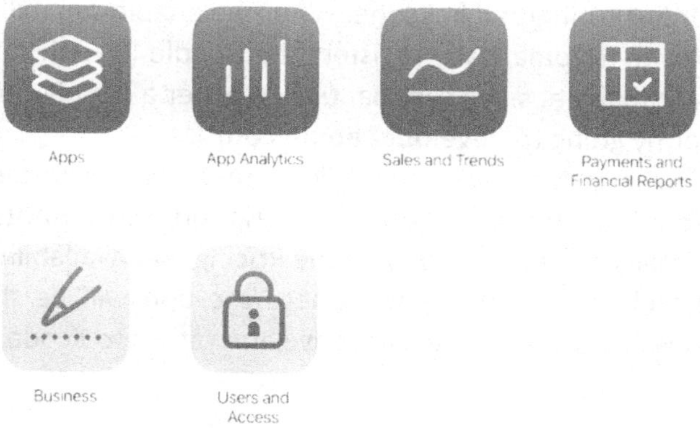

Figure 17-10: *App Store Connect menu*

In this section we can enter our financial information (Business), publish our apps (Apps), and see how the business is doing (Sales and Trends). The first step is to create a record for the app we want to publish in Apps. When we click on this icon, a new window will open with a list of our apps and a + button at the top to add more.

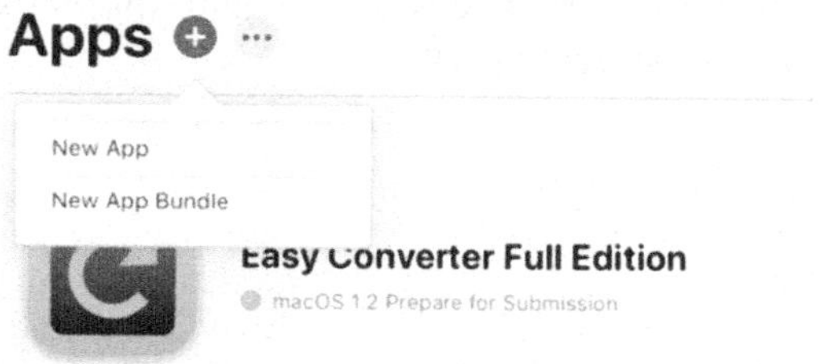

Figure 17-11: *Menu to add apps to our account*

To add a new app, we must select the New App option and enter the app's information. The first window asks for the platform for which we developed the app (in our case iOS and macOS), the name of the app, the main language, the bundle ID, and a custom ID (SKU) that we can use later to identify the app.

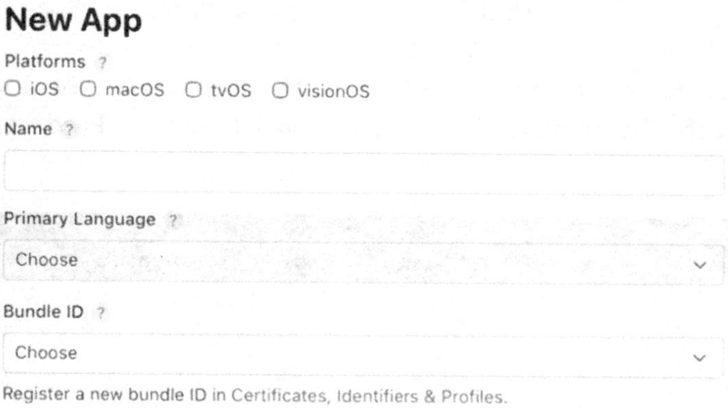

Figure 17-12: *New app*

The name and primary language are values we already defined for the project, and the SKU is a custom string that we create for internal identification. The Bundle ID, however, must match the identifier configured in Xcode. When we enable capabilities in the Signing & Capabilities panel, Xcode automatically registers the Bundle ID with Apple's servers. If the app does not use any capabilities, we can manually register a new Bundle ID by clicking the link below the field or by going to **developer.apple.com**.

After entering these values, we must click Create and proceed to complete the remaining information. This includes the app description, screenshots, and the required contact and review details. We must also open the Pricing and Availability section on the left to define the price and select the regions where the app will be distributed. Once all required information is provided, we can click Save and return to Xcode to upload the build.

BASIC

Submitting the Application

The application and its resources must be compiled into a single archive for each target platform before being submitted to App Store Connect. The first step is to choose the platform for which we want to build the app. We can do this by selecting a specific device from the destination list or by choosing one of the generic platform options provided by Xcode (Any iOS or Any Mac), as shown below.

Figure 17-13: *Selecting a platform*

In this example, we selected the Any Mac destination to build the app for macOS. The next step is to create the archive. This option is available in the Product menu, as shown below.

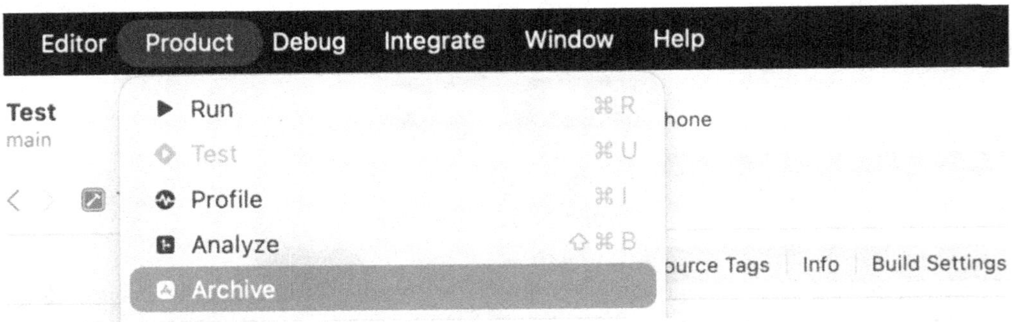

Figure 17-14: *Archive option*

After we click the Archive option, Xcode compiles the application and creates the archive. The next window displays the archive and offers buttons to validate and submit the application.

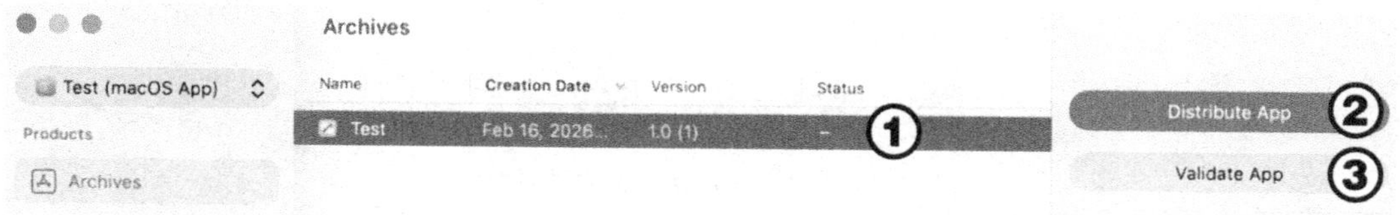

Figure 17-15: *List of archives created for our app*

Figure 17-15 shows an archive created for an application called Test (number 1). The item representing the archive includes the date it was created, the app's version, and the number of the build. (We can send multiple builds to App Store Connect and later decide which one we want Apple to review.)

IMPORTANT

The app's version and the number of the build (archive) are determined from the app's settings (by default, both values are set to 1.0). If we want to specify a different version, we must declare the numbers separated by one or two periods (e.g., 1.0 or 1.2.5). The values represent different revisions of our app, with the order of relevance from left to right. The values are arbitrary, but we are required to change them every time an update is published to the App Store to reflect how big the update is.

Although it is not required, we should always validate the archive before submitting the app. This process allows Xcode to detect errors and make suggestions on how to fix them. To start the validation process, we can click the Validate App button (Figure 17-15, number 3). The first window displays icons for selecting the validation method. There is an option for automatic validation called Validate and another one to customize the process.

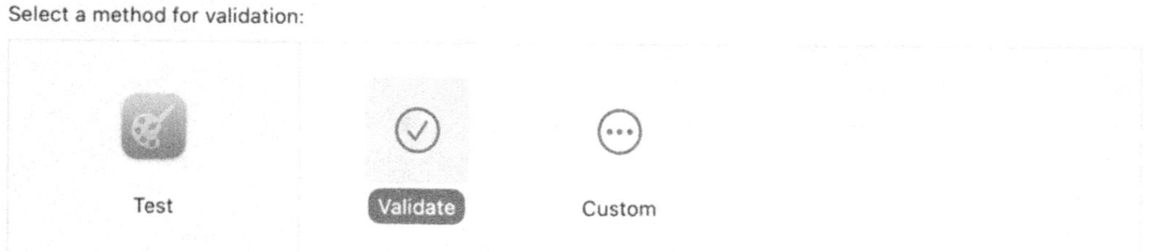

Figure 17-16: *Options for validation*

When this process is complete and no errors are found, we can finally submit our app to Apple by clicking the Distribute App button (Figure 17-15, number 2). The first window displays icons for selecting the distribution method. We can use TestFlight to submit the app for testing to other users or team members, distribute it internally, or submit it to the App Store. The latter is the option we need to choose to make the app available to the public.

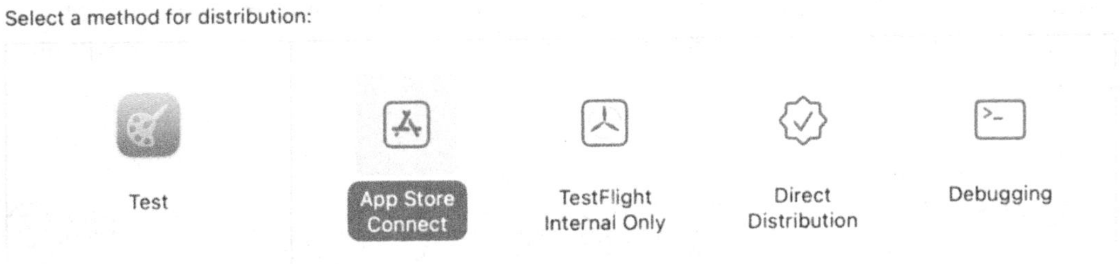

Figure 17-17: *Options for distribution*

As mentioned earlier, we can submit multiple archives to the server (builds). For this reason, we need to return to the App Store Connect website, open the description of our application, and select the archive we just uploaded (it may take a few minutes for it to become available). Figure 17-18 below shows what we see in the Build section.

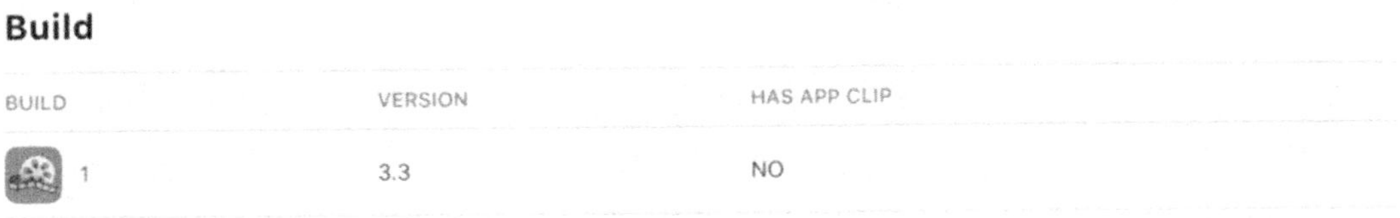

Figure 17-18: *Selecting the build to send to the App Store*

After the build is selected, we can click on the Save button to save the description of the app. If all the required information has been provided, we can click on the Submit for Review button at the top of the page to submit the application. The system will ask some questions and then the application will be sent to Apple for review (the message Waiting for Review will be displayed under the app's title).

The process takes a few days. If the app is approved, Apple sends us an email to let us know that the app is available in the App Store.

Where To Go From Here

The world of app development is evolving at an extraordinary pace. With the rise of artificial intelligence assistants and autonomous agents, building applications for Apple platforms demands not only a solid understanding of the underlying technologies, but also the ability to collaborate effectively with AI systems to accelerate development, optimize workflows, and create truly innovative applications. Developers who know how to combine their technical expertise with intelligent tools can prototype faster, solve complex problems with greater efficiency, and deliver richer, more immersive user experiences than ever before.

From this book, you have acquired all the knowledge required to embrace these new tools with confidence and elevate your applications beyond traditional boundaries. If you are ready to deepen your understanding of artificial intelligence, explore how intelligent models work, and harness their full potential to transform your applications, continue your journey with *Apple Intelligence for Masterminds*.

Apple Intelligence for Masterminds

How to create intelligent applications for iPhones, iPads and Macs

How to take advantage of Apple Intelligence to create intelligent applications for iPhones, iPads, and Macs. After reading this book, you will know how to integrate artificial intelligence into your applications, how to use Apple Intelligence and Siri effectively, and how to train your own models to build innovative and revolutionary applications.

www.formasterminds.com

Index

Made in the USA
Monee, IL
08 November 2026

68028676R00450